Time Out

Las Vegas

Penguin Books

PENGUIN BOOKS

Published by the Penguin Group
Penguin Books Ltd, 27 Wrights Lane, London W8 5TZ, England
Penguin Books USA Inc., 375 Hudson Street, New York, New York 10014, USA
Penguin Books Australia Ltd, Ringwood, Victoria, Australia
Penguin Books Canada Ltd, 10 Alcorn Avenue, Toronto, Ontario, Canada M4V 3B2
Penguin Books (NZ) Ltd, 182-190 Wairau Road, Auckland 10, New Zealand

Penguin Books Ltd, Registered Offices: Harmondsworth, Middlesex, England

First published 1998
Second edition 2000
10 9 8 7 6 5 4 3 2 1

Copyright © Time Out Group Ltd, 1998, 2000
All rights reserved

Colour reprographics by Westside Digital Media, 9 Bridle Lane, London W1
and Precise Litho, 34-35 Great Sutton Street, London EC1
Printed and bound by Cayfosa-Quebecor, Ctra. de Caldes, Km 3 08 130 Sta, Perpètua de Mogoda,
Barcelona, Spain

Edited and designed by

Time Out Guides Limited
Universal House
251 Tottenham Court Road
London W1P 0AB
Tel + 44 (0)20 7813 3000
Fax+ 44 (0)20 7813 6001
Email guides@timeout.com
http://www.timeout.com

Editorial

Editor Cath Phillips
Consultant Editor James P Reza
Deputy Editor Sophie Blacksell
Researcher & Listings Editor Anne Kellogg
Casino Consultant Deke Castleman
Proofreader Tamsin Shelton
Indexer Jackie Brind

Editorial Director Peter Fiennes
Series Editor Caroline Taverne

Design

Art Director John Oakey
Art Editor Mandy Martin
Senior Designer Scott Moore
Designers Benjamin de Lotz, Lucy Grant
Scanning/Imaging Chris Quinn
Picture Editor Kerri Miles
Deputy Picture Editor Olivia Duncan-Jones
Picture Admin Kit Burnet

Advertising

Group Advertisement Director Lesley Gill
Sales Director Mark Phillips
Advertisement Directory North American Guides
Liz Howell (1-808 732 4661)
Advertising co-ordinated in the US by
Alison Tocci (Publisher), Andy Gersten (Advertising
Production Manager),
Tom Oesau (Advertising Production Co-ordinator), Claudia
Pedala (Assistant to the Publisher)

Administration

Publisher Tony Elliott
Managing Director Mike Hardwick
Financial Director Kevin Ellis
Marketing Director Gillian Auld
General Manager Nichola Coulthard
Production Manager Mark Lamond
Production Controller Samantha Furniss
Accountant Bridget Carter

Features in this guide were written and researched by:

Introduction James P Reza. **History** Deke Castleman. **Las Vegas Today** James P Reza. **Gambling** Deke Castleman, Richard J
Grula. **Architecture** Frances Anderton. **Weddings** Jonathan Cox, Scott Dickensheets. **Casinos** David Hofstede, David Stratton.
Attractions David Stratton. **Las Vegas by Area** James P Reza. **Las Vegas by Season** Renée LiButti. **Children** Renée LiButti.
Accommodation David Stratton. **Restaurants & Buffets** John Curtas, James P Reza, David Stratton (Restaurants), David Stratton
(Buffets). **Bars & Cafés** Geoff Carter. **Shops & Services** Dianne Cauzillo, Stephanie Reidy (*Only in Vegas* James P Reza).
Las Vegas on the Cheap David Stratton. **Culture** Gregory Crosby. **Casino Entertainment** David Stratton. **Nightlife** James P Reza
(Adult, Dance clubs), Anne Davis Mulford (Gay & lesbian), Geoff Carter (Music: rock, folk & jazz). **Sport & Fitness** David Hofstede.
Trips Out of Town Cath Phillips, Deke Castleman (Reno, *Home on the range*), Frances Anderton (Los Angeles), Jonathan Cox
(Laughlin). **Getting Around** David Hofstede, James P Reza. **Resources** Ruth Jarvis, James P Reza, David Hofstede (Business,
Media), Geoff Carter (*Websites*).

The Editor would like to thank:

Continental Airlines, Wayne Bernath of Lance Burton, Davey Boy, Charlie Germack of the Yucca Mountain Project, Judy Gibbons of
Alamo, Mike Harrison, Linda Hines, Ruth Jarvis, Lori Kennedy of the Four Seasons, Lesley McCave, Beki Morris, Kurt Ouchida of
the Venetian, Paula Pettit of Mandalay Bay, Colleen M Reid of Budget Suites, Caro Taverne, Lance Taylor of Cirque du Soleil,
Donna Thomas of the Las Vegas News Bureau, Michael Toole.

Maps by JS Graphics, 17 Beadles Lane, Old Oxted, Surrey RH8 9JG.

Photography by Amanda Edwards except: pages 5, 6, 7, 8, 9, 10, 17 (bottom), 25, 35, 37, 88, 209, 255 and 256
Las Vegas News Bureau/LVCVA; page 14 **Associated Press**; page 197 **Bellagio Gallery of Fine Art**; page 217 **Joan
Marcus**; page 228 **Strutt Hurley/Blue Neon Productions**; page 242 **Glyn Kirk/Action Plus**; page 243 **Mary Nichols**;
pages 245, 249, 254, 257, 261, 262, 265, 275, 276 and 281 **Cath Phillips**; page 258 **Ruth Jarvis**; page 266 **Corbis**;
page 271 **Richard Price/Telegraph Colour Library**; pages 272 and 283 **Chris Coe/Axiom**; page 279 **Laurence Cottrell**;
page 280 **S Francis/Esto/J Paul Getty Trust**. The following photographs were supplied by the featured establishments:
pages 103, 104, 115, 116, 127, 136, 204 and 238.

Time Out staff flew to Las Vegas with Virgin Atlantic (reservations: UK 01293 747747; US 1-800 862 8621).
Car rental was through Alamo (reservations: UK 0990 994000; US 1-800 327 9633).

Contents

About the Guide

This is the second edition of the *Time Out Las Vegas Guide*, part of our ever-expanding series of city guides. It has been thoroughly revised and updated by a team of resident experts to bring you the best that Vegas has to offer, and to bring the guide bang up to date with the city's notoriously fast-evolving scene. Since Las Vegas is defined by its casino-hotels, our **Casinos** chapter (starting on *page 40*) reviews all the major properties, with an overview and an assessment of their gambling facilities. For details of their hotel facilities, see **Accommodation** (*page 113*). Most casinos also contain all manner of other attractions, from restaurants to games arcades. Those worthy of a visit in their own right have also been reviewed in the appropriate chapter.

Too late for inclusion in this guide is the name change announced by the brand-new Resort at Summerlin: it is now called the Regent Las Vegas.

DETAILED DESCRIPTION

We have tried to make this book as useful as possible. Addresses, telephone numbers, transport details, opening times, admission prices and credit card details are all included in our listings, as well as websites and fax numbers where we think you'll find them useful. To help those not familiar with the city locate the places we've listed, we've included an area name in each address, even if the postal address is technically just 'Las Vegas'. Similarly, the full postal address and zip code is included for anywhere you might want to write to. The area names we have used – The Strip, Stratosphere Area, East of Strip, West of Strip, University District, Downtown, North Las Vegas, East Las Vegas, North-west Las Vegas and South-west Las Vegas – are in common use, but not all are official appellations. A **map** on *page 311* shows how we have divided up the city. The Strip **maps** on *pages 42* and *43* mark the casinos and other sights of interest.

TALKING TELEPHONE NUMBERS

Since the last edition of this guide, telephone area codes in Nevada have changed. There are now two area codes: **702** for Clark County (including Las Vegas) and **775** for the rest of the state. Within the Las Vegas area, from Mount Charleston in the north to Boulder City in the south, calls are local and there is no need to use the area code (just dial the seven-figure number). If you're calling from outside the area, however, you need to prefix the seven-figure number with 1-702. Similarly if you are calling an out-of-city Nevada number from Las Vegas, you will need to dial the 1-775 prefix, then the number. To call Nevada from abroad, dial your country's exit code, then 1 for the USA, followed by 702 or 775 and the number.

Note that you can now dial almost all 1-800 numbers from outside the US. Calls will be charged at the usual international rates.

CREDIT CARDS

The following abbreviations have been used for credit cards: **AmEx**: American Express; **DC**: Diners' Club; **Disc**: Discovery; **JCB**: Japanese credit cards; **MC**: Mastercard; **V**: Visa. Virtually all shops, restaurants, attractions and gas stations will accept US dollar travellers cheques issued by a major financial outfit such as American Express.

PRICES

The prices we've given should be treated as guidelines, not gospel. Seasonal variations and inflation can cause them to change rapidly, especially in the case of accommodation. Note that prices marked on goods in shops do not include sales tax, which is currently 7.25 per cent.

CHECKED & CORRECT

All listings information and other factual details have been thoroughly checked. However, inevitably businesses open and close, change their hours, relocate or alter their service in some other way. We strongly recommend that you phone ahead before setting out anywhere other than the casino floor. While every effort and care has been made to ensure the accuracy of the information contained in this guide, the publishers cannot accept responsibility for any errors it may contain.

RIGHT TO REPLY

It should be stressed that all the information we give is impartial. No organisation has been included in this guide because it has advertised in any of *Time Out*'s publications, and all the opinions given are wholly independent. We hope you enjoy the *Time Out Las Vegas Guide*, but we'd also like to know if you don't. There's a reader's reply card for your comments at the back of the book.

There is an online version of this guide, as well as weekly events listings for more than 30 international cities, at http://www.timeout.com

Introduction

Buzz, bang! Snippets of the aural landscape, field recordings sampled from the desert surrounding Las Vegas as it is slowly enveloped by vast farms of stucco. Slap, slam! The incessant sounds of a hundred architects' work being assembled by squads of journeymen labouring under the harsh Mojave sun. Whack, wham! Yet another faux-Southwestern subdivision of mere mud and sticks rapidly takes form, desperately trying to keep pace with an influx of humanity that is collectively and individually chasing a dream of independence that only the American West can impart.

Life in the desert is not easy, and the Mojave is an environmental poster child of extreme extremes. Las Vegas – ensconced in a Mojave valley and steeped in that legendary dry heat – is a product of this harsh environment in every way. This is where summer temperatures poke arrogantly at 120°F (49°C) and then, only four months later, struggle to make company with the 60°F (15°C) mark. Where more than 50 per cent of the annual 4¼ inches of rain can fall in 20 minutes in July. And where a millionaire' millionaire can drop the annual salary of his baccarat dealer on a single wager.

This extremist environment infects Las Vegas existence to its very core. Without a hint of irony, a Smithsonian-quality library/museum building juts boldly above a sea of bland strip malls and suburbs, never-closed casino doors blast mid-afternoon sidewalkers with a rush of enticing air-conditioned comfort, and lush golf courses battle back the natural drought with sprinkled water piped from the Colorado River.

Travellers to Vegas have long recognised its conflicted nature; a modern Sin City founded by the Mormons, raised by the Mob and popularised by Marriot. More than that, they have embraced it, as did the city's early settlers, as an escape from the retrogressive realities and hyperbolic hypocrisy that taint so many of the world's cities today. Why be burdened with the pressures of foreseeing the future and preserving the past when what is important in Las Vegas is the right here, right now? Such freedom can be addictive.

To call Las Vegas an adult Disneyland is both an inspiring insight and a tired cliché. Heavily-themed attractions aside, where the Strip truly intersects with Disneyland's Main Street is in the way it permits adults to act not like children, but like hormone-drunk, carefree adolescents. Visitors and new residents alike arrive in Las Vegas en masse, ready to absolve themselves of past deals with the devil and to forge new ones, to cast off obligations and indulge in fierce individualism. Sometimes that pursuit results in success and happiness; at other times, failure and despair. Not every deal is worth a million, but many end with someone winning a fortune and someone else painfully losing one.

And therein lies the relentless, twisted appeal of the place – the potential that the next move you make could turn you into a prince or a pauper. Travellers, attracted by the city's undeniable allure, are so dedicated to this experience that every gas station has become a mini-casino and every shop sells at least one item emblazoned with the words 'Las Vegas'. Still, at odds with all the glamour and hype, one can never forget the reality that tugs at the conscience: Las Vegas is a city of monumental success built on the gambling drop of 35 million visitors a year and the thousands of pioneers who, tired of its winner-take-all psyche, abandon the town each month in search of another rainbow.

It is important to remember, however, that this city is not selling Disneyland or Wolfgang Puck or even gambling, but mythology, and it is here that reality and perception diverge. While Las Vegas may seem like the ultimate place for adults to forego responsibility, in reality it may be the last city in the States where personal responsibility is paramount. Temptations are everywhere, but safety nets are not. If you want to drink like a fish at 8am, gamble away your rent money or find yourself hungover and broke two days into a week's stay, go ahead, no one will stop you, In a society increasingly bent on passing responsibility on to the next guy, such an attitude can be refreshing; people in Las Vegas have all the freedoms an adult could possibly want – the freedom to win or lose, succeed or fail, stand or fall – and no one telling them they cannot.

With so much temptation at hand and limited energy remaining after you have lived the 24/7 life to the edge of your existence, take care to respect Las Vegas. This is is not a quaint garden to be tended or a meandering river to be dammed; it is a surging, powerful wave that can be ridden but not controlled. Understand this and Vegas can be your most exhilarating travel experience to date; failure to do so means you risk returning home bitter and frustrated. But you'll return, and it is better to do so wearing a smile rather than a frown. Remember, Vegas hates losers.

James P Reza
● *James P Reza is a Las Vegas native who has spent almost his entire life studying and chronicling the city. He can be reached at jpreza@lvcm.com*

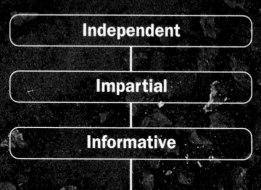

Independent

Impartial

Informative

Time Out
THE GREATEST
LONDON AUTHORITY

Las Vegas in Context

History

From cow town to casino town, via Mormons and mobsters, Las Vegas's history has been one of unparalleled expansion.

Around 25,000 years ago, the large valley that Las Vegas inhabits – and which is quickly filling up with casinos, amusement parks and suburbs – was partially underwater. It was the tail end of the last ice age. Glaciers were retreating from the mountains that surround the Las Vegas Valley and the glacial run-off fed a great lake, 20 miles (32 kilometres) across and thousands of feet deep. Lake Las Vegas's outlet was a river, known now as the Las Vegas Wash: larger than anything that remains in the western United States today, even though it flowed for only 40 miles (64 kilometres). At its mouth, the Wash was swallowed, with barely a ripple, by a monster waterway, the same waterway that had been carving the Grand Canyon for a couple of hundred million years, on and off. Where Downtown and the Strip now shine was the deepest and darkest part of the lake.

According to archeological evidence, Paleo-Indians lived in caves near the shoreline of the lake, which was shrinking as the climate changed gradually from cold and wet to warm and dry. History tells us that prehistoric horses, giant ground sloths, American camels and massive condors all congregated around the tule marsh at the edge of the lake, which they shared with the first 'Las Vegans'; these humans hunted other big Pleistocene mammals, such as woolly mammoth, bison, mastodon and caribou, as early as 13,000 BC. Paleontologists have uncovered prehistoric hearths, fluted arrowheads and spear points, primitive stone tools and charred animal bones. Little is known, beyond these finds, about Las Vegas's earliest inhabitants, but from around 5,000 years ago, a clearer picture of the local prehistoric people starts to emerge.

Known as Archaic Indians, these hunter-foragers introduced an Indian culture that evolved for 4,000 years. The Archaics occupied what was by then desert, even though plentiful spring water bubbled up to the surface and flowed down Las Vegas Wash (now a creek) to the canyon-carving Colorado River. They lived and travelled in small bands, used the atlatl (an arrow launcher), hunted bighorn sheep and desert tortoise, harvested screw-bean mesquite and cholla fruit, and built rock shelters.

But it wasn't until the beginning of the common era that signs of civilisation began to show themselves in the area in and around Nevada's southern desert. The Anasazi were the natives of the area, residing in pit houses (holes in the ground, topped with brush roofs) and living very basically. Still, by around AD 500, the Anasazi had evolved into an organised people: they were hunting with bows and arrows, learning how to make pottery and mining salt. In addition, they had started to trade with their neighbours and had refined their building techniques (for example, their dwellings now had adobe walls). Three hundred years later, the Anasazi cultivated beans and corn in irrigated fields, lived in huge 100-room pueblos, fashioned artistic pots and baskets and mined turquoise. An Anasazi village in Las Vegas Valley is the first known prehistoric architecture in Nevada.

Mysteriously, however, the Anasazi people disappeared from the area around 1150. No one is sure exactly why; theories have included disease, drought, overpopulation and warring with neighbours. A large Anasazi village was discovered in 1924, parts of which are now preserved and commemorated at the Lost City Museum in Overton, 45 miles (72 kilometres) north-east of Las Vegas.

Southern Paiutes, a tribe of hunter-foragers more like the Archaic than the Anasazi, claimed the abandoned territory, but they never regained the advanced elements of their predecessors' society. For the next 700 years, the Paiute remained semi-nomadic: they established base camps of movable wickiups (similar to teepees), cultivated squash and corn at the springs and creeks, and travelled seasonally to hunt and harvest wild foods, such as pine nuts, screw beans, tules, rabbit, deer and sheep. A frequent stopover on their travels was at the Big Spring, the centre of a lush riparian habitat.

MEXICANS & MORMONS

These were the folks who greeted the earliest European explorers and settlers in the mid-nineteenth century. The first white men to enter what is now Las Vegas were Mexican traders, travelling along the Old Spanish Trail blazed by Franciscan friars to connect Spanish-Catholic missions scattered between New Mexico and the California coast. Then in 1830, a mere three decades before the American Civil War, one Antonio Armijo set out from Santa Fe to trade goods along the trail. An experienced scout in his party, Rafael Rivera, discovered a short cut, by

*The **Hoover Dam** under construction.*

way of Las Vegas's Big Springs, and became the first non-Indian to set foot on the land that only 75 years later would become the beginnings of the city we know today. He named the area Las Vegas, meaning 'the Meadows'.

By the time John C Fremont, legendary surveyor and cartographer for the Army Topographical Corps (whose name lives on, attached to the main street in Downtown Las Vegas) passed through Las Vegas Valley in 1845, the Old Spanish Trail had become the most travelled route through the Southwest. Las Vegas by then was a popular camping spot, thanks to Big Springs, the only fresh water within a day's march. Latter-day Saints, who had settled at the shore of Great Salt Lake a few hundred miles north-east, passed through Las Vegas regularly on their way to Los Angeles. By the early 1850s, Mormon pioneer parties, wagon trains and mail carriers travelling between central Utah and southern California overnighted at Big Springs so frequently that Church elders decided to colonise the area.

In 1855, a party of Mormon missionaries was dispatched from Salt Lake City to establish a community at Las Vegas that would serve the travellers on the trail and convert the Paiute. The missionaries erected a fort, dug irrigation ditches, cultivated crops and managed to befriend some Indians. But the rigours of domesticating a vast desert took their toll on the settlers. The climate proved unbearably inhospitable. Crops failed and rations were meagre. Timber had to be hauled from high on the nearest mountainsides, 20 miles (32 kilometres) away. And the isolation further sapped morale.

Still, the mission might have succeeded had the colonists not located deposits of lead nearby. This discovery attracted miners from Salt Lake City, whose needs for food, lumber and shelter taxed the colonists' already inadequate supplies to breaking point. Despite the miners' vociferous objections, the colonists petitioned Salt Lake City to be recalled, and the mission was finally abandoned in 1858. A small remnant of the Mormon fort survives and is the oldest standing structure in Las Vegas today, 50 years older than any other.

OD GASS & HELEN STEWART

Soon after the Mormons abandoned Las Vegas, prospectors picked up where the lead miners left off and discovered that the ore averaged a rich $650 per ton in silver. A small mining boomtown mushroomed from the desert around Big Springs. Miners who arrived too late to get in on the excitement fanned out from Las Vegas and discovered gold along the Colorado River, about 50 miles (80 kilometres) south-west of the Meadows.

One of the gold seekers, Octavius Decatur Gass, saw a better opportunity in homesteading the well-watered valley. In 1865, he and his family appropriated the Mormon fort, using the lumber to build a ranch house and utility shop. Gass dug irrigation canals, planted grains, vegetables and fruit trees, and ran cattle on a ranch that was known as Las Vegas Ranch. Over the next ten years, Gass expanded his land and water holdings, assumed civil duties such as justice of the peace and territorial legislator, and helped other homesteaders get established in Las Vegas.

But in the mid-1870s, Gass was in financial trouble and took a loan from Archibald Stewart, a wealthy rancher from Pioche, another mining boomtown 100 miles (160 kilometres) north. When Gass couldn't repay the loan, Stewart foreclosed and took Las Vegas Ranch. An enterprising Scotsman, Stewart worked and expanded his property. But in 1884, he got into an argument with a ranch hand from a neighbouring spread and was shot dead. Stewart's wife, Helen, managed the ranch for another 20 years, buying up more acreage, making a tidy living in the livestock business and running a resort for nearby ranchers and a campground for travellers on the Mormon Trail.

In 1903, the San Pedro, Los Angeles and Salt Lake Railroad arrived, planning a right-of-way that would run through the heart of the ranch. Thanks to its strategic location and plentiful water, Las Vegas had already been designated as a division point for crew changes, a service stop for through trains and an eventual site for maintenance shops. Ready to retire, Mrs Stewart sold all but ten acres of her 2,000-acre (810-hectare) shootin' match for $55,000, and deeded the other ten acres to the Las Vegas Paiute, who'd been reduced to living on the edge of town, dependent on government largesse. For this and other civic-minded deeds, Helen Stewart is considered the First Lady of Las Vegas to this day.

LONG TRAIN COMING

In preparation for the sale of her land to the railroad, Helen Stewart hired JT McWilliams to survey her property. McWilliams discovered and immediately claimed 80 untitled acres (32 hectares) just west of the big ranch. McWilliams planned a town site and began selling lots to a steadfast group of Las Vegas 'sooners' (the earliest speculators on the scene). In late 1904, two railroad construction crews, one coming from the north-east and the other from the south-west, converged on Las Vegas Valley, and in January 1905, the golden spike was driven into a tie near Jean, Nevada, 23 miles (37 kilometres) to the south of Las Vegas.

On the day that the first train travelled through Big Springs on its inaugural run between Salt Lake City and Los Angeles, McWilliams's settlement, known as Ragtown, was one of a long line of boom-towns that had been erupting from the desert floor all across the state of Nevada for the past 50 years. Its saloons, banks, newspaper office and tent hotels teemed with boomtowners – settlers, speculators, merchants, tradesmen, itinerants. But the San Pedro, Los Angeles and Salt Lake Railroad had other plans. It organised a subsidiary, Las Vegas Land and Water, to build its own town of Las Vegas. Officials laid out the town site, scraped the desert scrub from 40 square blocks, and staked 1,200 lots. The new railroad town received enough national publicity to create an immediate demand for the land; prospective buyers came by train from Los Angeles ($16 return) and Salt Lake City ($20).

The competition for the prime locations proved so overwhelming that in order to handle the hordes of hopefuls, the railroad scheduled an auction to sell the remaining lots, thereby pitting eager settlers, hoping for jobs with the railroad, against Los Angeles real estate speculators and East Coast investors: all were gambling on the initial prosperity of yet another western railroad boomtown. It's fitting that Las Vegas was founded on the principles that would sustain it to the present.

The auction was held at the corner of Main and Fremont Streets, on the site of today's Plaza Hotel in the heart of Downtown, on 15 May 1905. The bidding quickly inflated the value of the choice lots to more than double their listed values. The locals, who lived across the tracks in JT McWilliams's Ragtown, grumbled about the railroad tactic of encouraging out-of-town investors to heat up the prices; as one participant observed, 'The auction was a nice clever scheme – the simplest way of giving everyone a fair shake (down).' When it was over, nearly 1,000 lots had been sold for the grand total of $265,000 dollars, $195,000 more than the railroad had paid for the entire Las Vegas Ranch only three years earlier.

DOWNTOWN DOWNTURN

Immediately, the proud new property owners searched out the stakes sticking out from the desert sand that marked lot boundaries and erected makeshift shelters. Ragtown residents rolled their possessions over to the new Las Vegas on horse- and oxen-drawn wagons; what remained of the first town site burned to the ground four months later. Las Vegas's first building boom followed. The saloons and honky-tonks and cribs were the first to go up on Block 16, between Ogden and Stewart and First and Second Streets (where a Binion's Horseshoe parking lot stands today); Block 16 was the designated nightlife and red-light district. Hotels, restaurants, banks and shops were quickly erected along Fremont Street. Railroad and town administrative offices, a school, the post office and two churches surrounded the Downtown core. The company installed the infrastructure: gravel streets and plank sidewalks, water service and electricity. Houses went up on the residential streets of the eight-block long and five-block wide town, with all the building supplies arriving daily on the through trains. On New Year's Day 1906, 1,500 pioneers called Las Vegas home.

But the initial boom was shortlived. Barely a year had passed before the railroad-town managers showed their true colours, concerned first with operating the main line and last with servicing the town. Their refusal to extend water pipes beyond the town site stunted growth and forced the rural dwellers to dig wells and tap into the aquifer. The usual fires, political conflicts and growing pains of a young and remote settlement slowed the influx of new residents, reduced property values and dampened local optimism; the heat, dust and isolation also contributed to the consensus of discomfort.

*Night-time neon on **Fremont Street**, 1954.*

Las Vegas's oldest hotel-casino, the **El Cortez**, as it looked in 1953.

A rare bit of good news arrived in 1909, when the Nevada Legislature created Clark, a new county in the south of the state named after William Clark, the chairman of the San Pedro, Los Angeles and Salt Lake Railroad; Las Vegas was installed as its seat. Soon after, the railroad gave the new county seat a boost by building a shop for maintaining the steam locomotives, passenger coaches and freight cars along the line. When the facility opened in 1911, it created hundreds of jobs and by the time the shop was fully staffed, the population of Las Vegas had doubled to 3,000. Telephone service arrived when the first phone – boasting the number '1', of course – was installed at the cigar counter in the lobby of the Hotel Nevada (now the Golden Gate, and the oldest hotel in Las Vegas) at the corner of Main and Fremont Streets. And in 1915, the big town generators began supplying electricity to the residents 24 hours a day.

But it was all downhill for the next 15 years. The railroad found itself losing more and more business to car and truck traffic, with the result that workers were laid off. A nationwide railroad, Union Pacific, bought up the San Pedro, Los Angeles and Salt Lake, relegating it to the status of a small siding on its vast network. The UP shut down the maintenance shops, eliminating more jobs and driving out residents. They also implemented policies, in particular one concerning water delivery, that severely inhibited growth. Las Vegas would have dried up and blown away by the late 1920s if it hadn't been for a monumental federal dam-building project gearing up nearby.

HOOVER DAM

The 1,450-mile (2,333-kilometre) long Colorado River, the principal waterway of the arid Southwest,

had been gouging great canyons and watering lush valleys for eons, until the US government became determined to harness the flow in the service of irrigation, electricity, flood control and recreation. In 1907, the federal Bureau of Reclamation began to consider damming the Colorado, and by 1924, the Bureau had narrowed the location for the dam to two canyons east of Las Vegas. In 1930, Congress appropriated the $165 million to build it.

Anticipation of the dam project began to fuel noticeable growth in the railroad town. By 1931, when construction began, long-distance phone service, a federal highway from Salt Lake City to Los Angeles and regularly scheduled airmail and air-passenger service arrived in Las Vegas. The population soared to 5,000, with thousands more passing through Las Vegas en route to the Colorado River, which was about to be tamed.

The building of Hoover Dam, even today, is mind-boggling in its immensity. The nearest power plant was 200 miles (322 kilometres) away in southern California, from where wires had to be strung to supply the necessary electricity. Five thousand workers had to be hired and an entire town (Boulder City) built to house them and their families. And, most daunting of all, the mighty Colorado River had to be diverted. It took 16 months to hack four diversion tunnels through the canyon walls before the river could be routed around the construction site. Finally, the great dam itself, one of the man-made wonders of the world, had to be put into place.

Five million buckets of concrete were poured into the dam over a two-year period. When it was completed in 1935, Hoover Dam stood 656 feet (200 metres) wide at its base, 49 feet (15 metres) thick

*The changing face of the **Strip**: from desert beginnings in 1960, era of the Dunes and the*

at its crest, 1,358 feet (414 metres) across and 794 feet (242 metres) tall. The diversion tunnels were closed and it took three years to fill Lake Mead, the largest man-made lake in North America: 109 miles (175 kilometres) long, 545 feet (166 metres) at its deepest, impounding 37.4 billion gallons (170 billion litres) of water. The dam's legacy has been monumental, endowing Las Vegas with all the power and water it would need to fulfil its promise.

THE NEW BOOM

Another event occurred in the early 1930s that had long-lasting implications for Las Vegas: the statewide legalisation of wide-open casino gambling. Backroom illegal gambling had long been the norm for a libertine frontier state such as Nevada, but when the legislators gave it their official blessing (along with easy divorces, no-wait marriages, legal prostitution and championship boxing matches), it began the process of transforming Las Vegas from a railroad company town into a casino company town.

Casino operators migrated in droves to the only state in the Union where they could ply their trade without risking arrest and jail, and vice-starved visitors streamed into town to partake in the naughtiness. The bars and casinos moved a block, from the shadows of Ogden Street to the cachet of Fremont Street, and though the ladies of the night remained behind at Block 16, neon lights began brightening the gambling joints along Las Vegas's main street, which would soon come to be known to the world as Glitter Gulch.

In addition, Las Vegas enjoyed widespread publicity from the building of the dam; in 1935, 20,000 people (Las Vegas's first real crowd) attended the Hoover Dam dedication ceremony, presided over by popular President Franklin Delano Roosevelt. Word got around that this little town by the dam site was a slice of authentic Wild West, with its legal casinos, legal prostitution and legal everything else to boot; that and the attractions of Hoover Dam and Lake Mead, filling up behind it, flooded the town with visitors. The prosperity of the early 1940s ushered in a new luxury casino, the El Cortez in Downtown, and the casino-resorts El Rancho Vegas and the Last Frontier on the Los Angeles Highway, soon to be known as the Las Vegas Strip. Finally, with the nation preparing for World War II, the federal government took over a million acres just north of Las Vegas for use as a training school for military pilots and gunners.

Between 1940 and 1945, the Las Vegas Aerial Gunnery School trained thousands of pilots, navigators, bombers, gunners and other warriors, then shipped them to the front in Europe and the Pacific. The school eventually expanded to three million acres (1.2 million hectares). In 1942, Basic Magnesium, one of the largest metal-processing factories in the country, was built halfway between Las Vegas and Boulder City; at the peak of production, 10,000 workers processed millions of tons of magnesium, a newly developed metal used in the manufacture of flares, bomb casings and airplane components. To house them, other workers built an entire town, Henderson, Las Vegas's first next-door neighbour. During the war years, the local population doubled, from 8,500 in 1940 to 17,000 in 1945.

Fabulous Flamingo, to world-famous symbol of Las Vegas today.

BUGSY

As much as the war benefited Las Vegas, it also benefited organised crime throughout the US, which profited handsomely from the vast black market in scarce consumer goods. And to the masters of the underworld, Las Vegas, where everything was legal, looked like the Promised Land. Gangsters from all over the country, flush with cash from bootlegging during Prohibition and the black market during the war, stood poised to invade Nevada with their particular brand of gambling money, management and muscle. All they needed was an advance man to raise a torch and show them the way. Enter Benjamin 'Bugsy' Siegel, tall, handsome, fearless and partnered by the most powerful underworld bosses.

In the early 1940s, Bugsy arrived on Fremont Street and set up shop at the El Cortez hotel-casino, one of Las Vegas's classiest joints at the time and today the oldest original casino wing in the whole country. Over the next few years, he elbowed into and bowed out of several casinos, both right in the heart of Downtown and out on the Los Angeles Highway. In the process, Bugsy raised a million dollars, which he intended to sink into his vision of an opulent casino-resort in the desert, the Fabulous Flamingo.

Construction, which began in 1946, was beset with disasters from the start. Bugsy, whose reputation as a dangerous hothead preceded him, had limited patience for the details of managing a construction site, and it's long been rumoured that the contractors stole the building materials at night and sold them back to him the next day. The

Flamingo, which was budgeted at a healthy $2 million, eventually cost $6 million to build. Worse still for Bugsy, the extra cash had come from the big East Coast bosses, who tacked their usual usurious interest rates on to the loan. Worst of all, the bosses believed that Bugsy was skimming from the cash flow, an infraction punishable, in the laws of the violent mob, by death.

The hotel opened the day after Christmas 1946; movie stars attended and big acts performed at the opening night. But Bugsy's notorious ruthlessness notwithstanding, the dealers, in cahoots with the customers and even some of the supervisors, robbed the joint blind, and less than three weeks later, the Flamingo closed. It reopened in March and started showing a profit in May, but Siegel's fate had been sealed. In his girlfriend's Beverly Hills mansion in June 1947, Benny Siegel took three high-powered slugs in the face. Fifty years later, most people still believe that the hit was ordered by Bugsy's boyhood buddy, Meyer Lansky. But according to some historians, Siegel was killed by his local Las Vegas associates, who were afraid the infamous madman might endanger Nevada's role as the gamblers' promised land.

THE DIATRIBE

And so began 20 years of the Italian-Jewish crime-syndicate's presence in Las Vegas, and ten years of the biggest hotel-building boom that the country had ever seen. Black money from the top bosses of the mob, along with their fronts, pawns, soldiers and workers, poured in from the underworld power centres of New York, New England, Cleveland, Chicago, Kansas City, New Orleans,

The infamous **'Bugsy' Siegel**.

Miami and Havana. Between 1951 and 1958, 11 major hotel-casinos opened in Las Vegas, nine on the Strip and two Downtown: all but one were financed by underworld cash. Finally, a full 25 years after gambling was legalised in Nevada, the state and federal governments began to wake up to the questionable histories of the people – considered criminals in every other state in the country – who were in charge of the largest industry in Las Vegas. The war between the police and the gangsters had begun.

Then something else happened that cast Las Vegas in a strange light. The federal government, which had split the atom and ended the war, needed a vast uninhabited tract of land to perfect its nuclear-weapons technology, and it found the optimal site at the Las Vegas Aerial Gunnery School. A mere 70 miles (113 kilometres) north-west of the city, the Nuclear Test Site was the scene of approximately 120 above-ground nuclear test explosions, roughly one a month for ten years (*see opposite* **Nevada Test Site**). The first Nuclear Test Ban treaty drove the explosions underground; 600 underground tests have taken place since then, the last in 1992. Thousands of guinea-pig soldiers were deployed near Ground Zero of the explosions, purposefully exposed to the shockwaves in order that medical teams might measure the effects of the radiation. A few locals worried which way the wind blew, but most of the 65,000 Las Vegans seemed to revel in the notoriety radiating outward from the test explosions. The Las Vegas boosters had a field day, marketing everything from atom burgers to tacky frames of Miss Atomic Blast; in fact, the grand openings of several hotel-casinos were scheduled to coincide with nuclear blasts. People had picnics atop the tallest buildings in town, which afforded a bird's-eye view of the mushroom clouds.

The mob, the bombs, the gambling and the general Sin Cityness of Las Vegas attracted a lot

of heat from the rest of the country, most of it magnified by the media. A steamroller of criticism levelled Las Vegas's reputation as Wild West Central; the media, article by article and book by book, turned the whole town into a scandal. Known as the Diatribe, it remains the greatest public castigation of an American city in history. It was so damning that it coloured Las Vegas's image for another 30 years.

At the same time, however, people were flocking to Las Vegas, proving the rule that even bad publicity is good publicity. And these pilgrims found that a strange thing happened at the Nevada state line: criminals who crossed it suddenly were accorded the status of legitimate businessmen, while the good citizens of the rest of the country suddenly became naughty boys and girls. These were the glamour years, when you didn't go out in Las Vegas after dark if you weren't wearing a cocktail dress or suit and tie. Crap shooters rolled the bones elbow to elbow with hit men. Mafia pit bosses had the 'power of the pencil' (to hand out free rooms, food and beverages at their discretion), and the comps flowed as easily as the champagne.

It was during this time that Frank Sinatra's Rat Pack – which consisted of Dean Martin, Sammy Davis Jr and Lena Horne, among others – performed in the famous Copa Room at the Sands, then invaded lounges around town where Shecky Greene, Buddy Hackett or Louis Prima and Keely Smith were appearing, and treated the audiences to a night they would never forget. The majority of the locals and visitors who were around from the early 1950s through to the mid-1960s still pine for those lost years.

HOWARD HUGHES

Enter an elusive billionaire, transferred in the middle of the night on a stretcher from a private train to an ambulance, which delivered him to his floor of suites at the Desert Inn. In 1966, when the Howard Hughes roadshow stopped off in Vegas for a three-year engagement, Hughes was already sickly (it's now believed he suffered from untreated syphilis, strange and heavily screened from the rest of the world. He immediately converted the Desert Inn's entire ninth floor into an airtight, light-proof, armed command centre: the story goes that when the hotel managers needed the suites to accommodate its high-rollers, Hughes plunked down $13 million cash to buy the joint, fired the hotel managers – and didn't have to move.

Holed up securely in his high-rise bunker, Hughes got down to business. He'd just sold his interest in TWA for a half-billion dollars, and either had to spend some or give it up in taxes. So he decided to see how much a medium-sized American city might cost. As well as this, he also had a plan to build an airport of the future, big enough to handle the supersonic aircraft Hughes

Nevada Test Site

An hour's drive outside Las Vegas to the northwest is a vast tract of uninhabited desert, covering nearly 5,500 square miles (14,250 square kilometres). A reminder of the stark grandeur of nature on the doorstep of one of the world's most artificial cities? Yes, but also one of the largest secured areas of government-owned land in the United States, and since 1951 the home of more than 1,200 nuclear blasts. Welcome to the Nevada Test Site.

In 1940, the US Army Air Corps was gearing up for possible participation in World War II. Searching for a practice range for fighter pilots and gunners, the Army selected Western Air Field, the small airport on the edge of tiny Las Vegas and to the south of a huge area of unpopulated desert. When the US entered the war in late 1941, the air field, now called the Las Vegas Bombing & Gunnery Range, went into full operation. At the height of the war build-up, classes of 4,000 bombers and gunners were graduating every six weeks and the practice range had grown to cover 3.3 million acres (1.34 million hectares) of south-central Nevada.

After the war, the base and range shut down – but not for long. In the late 1940s, after blowing off a few A-bombs over the Marshall Islands in the South Pacific, the Atomic Energy Commission needed a more convenient location to conduct its tests. The federal government still 'owned' the old bombing range, and the military and AEC deemed the Rhode Island-sized plot of desert at its heart perfect for its nuclear purposes.

The first test, in January 1951, was a relatively small one-kiloton bomb dropped from an airplane roughly 90 miles (145 kilometres) north of Vegas on what is now known as Frenchman Flat. Over the next 11 years, 126 atomic weapons were detonated above ground, until the first Limited Nuclear Test Ban Treaty prohibited atmospheric explosions. For 30 years after that, another 1,100 warheads, including the so-called hydrogen or fusion bomb, were detonated deep underground in the same area. By the early 1990s, the tests had slowed to one or two a year, and in 1996, President Clinton signed the Comprehensive Test Ban Treaty, which ended all nuclear testing in the US.

But the feds weren't through with the Nevada Test Site. Not by a long shot. An area near the centre of the site, known as Yucca Mountain, is earmarked to become the only permanent repository for nearly 70,000 metric tons of high-level radioactive waste. A 'study' of the area has been going on for years; its cost runs into billions of dollars, as opposing factions (the feds versus the state, the nuclear power industry versus environmentalists) battle it out in Congress, the courts, scientific journals and the mainstream media.

You can visit the Department of Energy-sponsored Yucca Mountain Science Center or sign up for one of the following tours.

Nevada Test Site Tour

US Department of Energy, Nevada Operations Office, Office of Public Affairs & Information, Visit Coordination Staff, PO Box 98518, Las Vegas NV 89193 (295 0944/fax 295 0943/ carter@nv.doe.gov). **Tours** *once a month.*

The Test Site Tour, though very informative, is also more than a little sinister. The site is massive – miles and miles of uninhabited desert, pockmarked by vast subsidence craters formed by the underground nuclear explosions. An atmosphere of Big Brother surveillance and secrecy pervades the whole experience: from the initial bus search to the bizarre, 1950s-style printed propaganda. Tour buses are sometimes surrounded by workers in protective suits toting Geiger-counters, and woe betide any hapless tourist found with binoculars or a camera – both are forbidden. The tour visits Mercury, the operations centre of the Test Site, then Frenchman Flat, site of the first tests – where visitors used to be allowed to gather glass, formed as the heat of the nuclear blasts melted the exposed sand. Other points of interest include News Nob, where journalists would gather to watch the mushroom clouds.

Due to the popularity of the tour, six weeks' advance booking is required. There are 270 places on each tour, which are allocated on a first come, first served basis.
Website: www.nv.doe.gov

Yucca Mountain Science Center

4101B Meadows Lane, at Valley View Boulevard, North-west Las Vegas (1-800 225 6972/Science Center 295 1312/tours 295 5555). Bus 104.
Open *10am-6pm Tue-Fri; 10am-4pm Sat.*
Tours *Sept-Nov, Mar-May once a month.*
The centre has interactive exhibits on the geology, culture, volcanics and storage technology of the Yucca Mountain project. The free monthly tour to the mountain itself gives visitors a chance to walk into the underground repository, talk to experts at the site and see the huge drilling equipment used to bore the storage tunnels. To join a tour, contact the centre well in advance – applications by non-nationals can take up to 70 days to be processed. All visitors require photo ID, and both cameras and recording equipment are forbidden.
Website: www.ymp.gov

envisaged converging on Vegas. He bought six casinos, vacant lots up and down the Strip, an airport, an airline, a television station, huge tracts of surrounding desert and mines and claims all over Southern Nevada. By the time his shopping spree was over, he'd parted with a cool $300 million.

The publicity generated by Hughes's spending spree turned Las Vegas's reputation around. The billionaire financier, according to the media, had singlehandedly returned the town to some semblance of respectability. If a headline had been written about it, it would have read 'Hughes buys out the Mob'. Although he ultimately contributed nothing new to the Las Vegas skyline or its industrial sector during his three-year stint in town, Hughes's presence added an enormous amount of long-needed legitimacy to Las Vegas's tarnished image. And the $300 million stimulated an unprecedented building boom; between 1968 and 1973, another dozen hotel-casinos opened and tens of thousands more people moved to the city.

In addition, Hughes paved the way for publicly traded corporations to see the city as a strong long-term investment. For the first time since gambling was legalised in Nevada, bankers and lenders from outside Las Vegas began to finance the building of hotels and casinos. Furthermore, when respected companies such as Hilton and Holiday Inn entered the legal gambling business, it marked the end of the Diatribe and the beginning of Las Vegas's coverage on the business pages.

Of course, as anyone who's seen Martin Scorsese's movie *Casino* knows, in reality it took another 15 years for the various government taskforces to hound the old gangsters into oblivion. Scandals erupted at the so-called 1950s casinos one after another, where the mob was still entrenched. But finally, by the mid-1980s, experts agreed that Las Vegas was as free of mob involvement as could be detected.

THE NEW LAS VEGAS

In November 1989, a 47-year-old casino chairman called Steve Wynn opened a 3,000-room, $650-million pleasure palace called Mirage in the heart of the Strip. Its size, elegance and price tag stunned the old guard of the gambling business in Las Vegas, where a new major casino-resort hadn't been built for 16 years. But the phenomenal enthusiasm, not to mention the $1-million-a-day profits, with which the public greeted the Mirage galvanised the industry into action. Excalibur, a medieval casino-resort, opened in June 1990, while the great pyramid Luxor, the pirate-technic Treasure Island and the MGM Grand, with 5,005 rooms the world's largest hotel, opened in 1993. The 1,257-foot (383-metre) tall Stratosphere Tower, the opulent Monte Carlo and the pop-art New York-New York all opened within a nine-month period from April 1996 to January 1997.

Yet another wave of casino construction crested in October 1998 with the grand opening of the $1.8-billion Bellagio, the most expensive hotel ever built, in a sort of Mob-contemporary style. The billion-dollar Mandalay Bay followed close on Bellagio's heels, opening in March 1999, with a New Age hipness and whimsy. A mere two months later, the $1.5-billion Venetian opened (though it took till the end of the year for the behemoth complex to be fully finished). Finally, in September, the $760-million Paris debuted, the most highly themed mega-resort of them all.

And that's just on the Strip. Counting all the smaller neighbourhood joints, including the upscale Resort at Summerlin (opened July 1999) and the ultra-posh Hyatt Regency at Lake Las Vegas (opened December 1999), a total of 30 major hotel-casinos have come on the scene in Las Vegas since the Mirage ten years ago.

Today, Las Vegas is the only city in the world that's home to more than 100,000 hotel rooms: it's up to nearly 125,000 and counting. Eighteen of the 21 largest hotels in the world are here. And this isn't the last of the building boom: the 3,000-room Aladdin is scheduled to open in summer 2000, the 800-room Sundance (next door to the Resort at Summerlin) is slated for a December 2000 opening, and rumours of new local casinos and even a new mega-resort or two constantly circulate around town. The latest word? A possible James Bond-themed property on the site of the Mirage-owned Holiday Inn & Casino on the Strip.

Upwards of 33 million visitors a year lose more than $6 billion in Las Vegas casinos. They leave another $6 billion from non-gambling expenses. Many of them check out Sin City once just to see what all the excitement is about, but millions more become regular returnees, attracted by the agreeable climate, the new mega-resorts, the latest thrill rides and high-tech attractions, the good deals on rooms, food and entertainment and, of course, the chance of instant riches.

In fact, many have relocated to the greatest boomtown in the history of the world. Upwards of 4,000 people move to Southern Nevada every month (though another 2,000 leave). Las Vegas, the largest American city founded in the twentieth century, has been the fastest growing major city in the US for more than a decade (though technically its neighbour Henderson now holds that honour), and Mesquite, the border boomtown 90 miles (144 kilometres) north-east, is the country's fastest growing small town. Las Vegas is growing so fast that it's the only city in the country to need two new phone books a year, one in January and one in July, and a new street map every year. It has gone from a dusty and desolate railroad town to the glitter capital of the world in a mere nine decades. And there's no end in sight.

Las Vegas Today

To infinity and beyond? There's everything to play for as America's adult playground grows up.

Nothing characterises the whole of Las Vegas's brief, flashy history more than the singular defining ethos of its present: explosive and nearly unmitigated growth. From that moment atop a railroad platform at the first land auction in 1905, to the continuing Bureau of Land Management auctions of today, Las Vegas has both suffered and celebrated an astonishing thousandfold increase in population, quickly unfolding into a flatland metropolis of 1.2 million.

Most of these settlers have come in waves, separated by very brief troughs. The search for gold, the missions of Mormons, the settling of the western United States, the building of the Hoover Dam, the legalisation of gambling, the war effort, the opening of the Nevada Test Site and more – each contributed to the economic and population growth of what was, less than a century ago, a diminutive and dusty railroad stop of a mere 1,500 plucky pioneers.

Is Las Vegas running out of space?

GROWING PAINS

Las Vegas's current growth wave, motivated by casino mogul Steve Wynn's dramatic repainting of the city with a Mirage-shaped stroke in 1989, has only just begun to exhibit preliminary signs of slowing. In the 1990s, Clark County (in which Las Vegas sits) grew by an amazing 89 per cent in population – a rate 800 per cent greater than the US average. During that period, Las Vegas as a whole rapidly doubled itself like fresh dough in a Mojave desert oven: the county built more schools than had previously existed, visitor counts nearly doubled, gambling drops more than doubled. The city is the only one in the US that prints two phone books a year to keep pace with the turnover.

Acting in concert with its defining explosive growth is Las Vegas's continued existence under the sociological microscope, a society endlessly examined by pundits and prognosticators everywhere. Is Las Vegas the quintessential American city, the model for American cities in the twenty-first century, as many are excitedly exclaiming? It would hardly seem so, given the manner in which it has suffered at the hands of public opinion.

Throughout its boomtown history, Las Vegas has been forced into a defensive position with regards to its morality and place in American society. In its most basic manifestation, Las Vegas is a heady combination of the Bible's Gomorrah and Caligula's Rome, where the basest instincts of humanity – desire and greed – are not merely indulged but puckishly encouraged.

As such, Las Vegas has long been the train wreck of American cities, a place from which neither the professional nor casual observer can avert their voyeuristic glances. Throughout the assault, the city has defiantly stood tall while suffering the taunts, emerging into 2000 as the fresh new face of American society. Interest in Las Vegas has not abated in recent years; it has, rather, increased tenfold. It seems everyone wants to read about Las Vegas, form an opinion about it, decide its fate.

And why not? In an America where nearly every state offers some form of legalised gambling, and 'adult entertainment' (pornography, strip clubs and the like) is an $8-billion-a-year industry, the country as a whole may be shyly emerging from the closet and, to some degree, emulating Sin City. So how does the mother of metropolitan reinvention respond? Just as America begins to stage a naughty little G-string show, Las Vegas turns the tables, pulls up its pants and starts acting a little more like the rest of big-city America. How else could one explain the incredible success of Wolfgang Puck, *Chicago* and day spas? Those 35 million visitors want it all – sex and gambling one night, Broadway and Beluga caviar the next. And no other city is as well equipped as Las Vegas to give it to them.

That said, consider this: what would it be like to live in a city where every second resident did not live there ten years ago, where every third person moved into town less than three years ago, where only six in 100 are natives? For that matter, imagine life in a city where the growing population can rise by 50 per cent in 24 short hours during a busy convention or holiday like New Year's Eve; where 400 inbound airline flights per day – an amazing number in itself – carry but 47 per cent of visitors, the rest arriving by road.

Imagine living in one city – the residential suburbs of Las Vegas – and depending upon another – the tourist city of the Strip and Downtown – for your existence; a city where two-thirds of every dollar spent originates in the tourist industry; where in order to merely maintain survival let alone sustain growth, you must court and encourage precisely that kind of tourism lest the city dry up and blow away. These are at once the challenges and successes of modern Las Vegas, the quintessential vacation city in which the past means nothing unless it somehow advances the tourism brigade.

BEST & WORST

All that humanity bearing down on what was, just a few decades before, a small desert town, is bound to foster trouble – especially when what accompanies it are powerful, demanding expectations of what Las Vegas is and what it should be. New residents and tourists are similar in this respect; it is said that new residents are merely tourists on a month-to-month lease. Those who arrive and immediately start complaining about the city unsettle long-time locals, though valid points have recently been made.

For evidence, one need look no further than the recent top ten lists of many publications. Las Vegas fares poorly when it comes to health issues, education, suicide, teen pregnancy and other social concerns. It is named among the worst cities in the US for cyclists and, until recently, public transport meant a bus system that moved tourists from the Strip to Downtown and back again. Conversely, Las Vegas is a great place for launching businesses, finding employment and retiring.

However, companies requiring skilled workers (such as the high-tech industry) often bypass the city due to a shallow workforce. Skilled workers who come seeking satisfaction often leave quickly or end up droning in the service industry. Sure, there's plenty of work here – provided that you're satisfied with tip-jobs in the casinos or labouring on construction sites. To many who arrive seeking dream fulfilment, Las Vegas looks like a good plan gone wrong, and therein lies another of its defining characteristics: transiency.

For every 4,000 who arrive, brimming with hope as wide as the American West, 2,000 abandon the place, still running from whatever ills they thought Las Vegas would cure. Long the colourful epitome

The voice of Vegas: mayor Oscar Goodman.

of the American Dream – fame, fortune, escape, freedom, individuality – Las Vegas attracts far more dreamers than doers. The local landscape is littered with the fruits and failures of each person's wins and losses, proving that such an atmosphere comes paired with a darker side. While some families move into sparkling new homes in wealthy Summerlin, others find themselves living four deep in a one-room weekly rental apartment, struggling to survive. When someone shouts 'I've won!' at a slot machine, they do so at the expense of thousands of others who have paid into that singular jackpot.

There is no escaping it; this kind of yin and yang is built into the psyche of Las Vegas and, for many, constitutes its allure. Escapees from other states where social engineering and safety netting are at a peak move to Las Vegas specifically for its supposedly hands-off, live-and-let-die attitude. And this creates yet another of modern Las Vegas's paradoxes: the conservative Sin City.

Like much of America, Las Vegas struggles with the country's Puritan roots. This is further compounded by the distinctly conservative religious background of the city itself; there is no denying the Mormon influence on Vegas's past development or its current political and social make-up, and many believe this has irreversibly determined the city's current conflicts. But any such dissonance in the city's character is more likely to have arisen from the varied backgrounds of newcomers who emerge from all religious and social environments. They come to Las Vegas seeking success, but lacking the understanding that success in Sin City is built on the failures of others – most notably the failure to control passions for money, food, alcohol and sex.

How else could one explain the grass-roots efforts to ban showgirl advertising from taxis, to limit the number of adult entertainment licences, to control the spread of gambling? Why else would a city that honours Liberace as one of its historical figures move to ban the recognition of same-sex marriages? It would seem that many new residents of twenty-first-century Vegas have forgotten why they are here, even why the city is here, rising from the desert as it does. Las Vegas's existence as a deeply conflicted city is at a slow roll right now; give it a few years and it will surely boil over.

THE FUTURE?

Las Vegas – which entered 2000 softly on the weakness of a poorly planned, poorly executed Strip-wide New Year's Eve street party – has quite a challenge before it: should it exchange its historical role as a brash, winner-take-all frontier town of fierce individuality and freedom for an adapted model of the traditional, liberalised American city? Or should it pursue the path that has brought it so far and shun the semi-successful attempts of other large US cities to mix a cocktail of capitalism and socialism?

Enter the quirky and outspoken Oscar Goodman. The mayor – a long-time Las Vegas resident, former Mafioso defence attorney and near-perfect personification of Las Vegas – stepped into his new role rather aggressively, loudly setting his agenda for the future of the city. Though many newcomers to town are rather embarrassed by the election of the so-called 'Mob Mouthpiece', old-timers revel in its obvious propriety, and see him as the ideal figurehead for this singularly idiosyncratic city.

Since taking office in June 1999, Goodman has appeared on numerous national news shows touting the city while deftly deflecting the obvious questions arising from its past. To Goodman, the future is part old-school gambling, part new-century resort city, and all Las Vegas. Art galleries and cafés will rise from the dusty acreage directly behind Glitter Gulch. Young professionals will rent skyrise apartments there, walking to work in creative and high-tech environments, surrounded by upscale retail shops, outdoor restaurants and public art. Feeding into this Downtown rebirth will be a performing arts centre. Or a sports arena. Or a high-tech monorail system from the Strip. Or, perhaps, all three. Goodman isn't picky, but he is

pushy, and the revitalisation of Downtown (or lack thereof) will be the yardstick by which his success is measured.

While the mayor plans Las Vegas's future, the city – unlike many of its new residents – must not forget why it exists. Las Vegas must faithfully continue to plant the seeds of economic vitality as legalised gambling continues to spread. It must examine itself and adapt, as it always has, to the ever-changing needs, desires and whims of the travellers' marketplace. It must continue to service its 35 million annual visitors and service them well, while at the same time seriously considering the well-being of its citizens. If it can accomplish these goals, if it can successfully blend a service economy with livability, if it can rise to the challenge of an overburdened infrastructure and correct the problems facing so many of America's older metropolises, then it will truly have earned the title 'America's Twenty-First-Century City'.

Las Vegas by numbers

Population of Las Vegas in 1940 **8,422**

Population of Las Vegas in 1999 **1.25 million**

Population of Clark County in 1989 **708,750**

Population of Clark County in 1999 **1,337,400**

Clark County growth in 1990s **89 per cent**

US growth in 1990s **11 per cent**

Proportion of new residents from California **one-third**

Number of babies born each month **475**

Increase in home sales (1998-9) **6 per cent**

Total home sales in November 1999 **4,010** (2,265 resales, 1,745 new) – double the monthly Las Vegas average

Total number of visitors in 1989 **18.1 million**

Total number of visitors in 2000 **35 million** (projected)

Clark County gross gaming revenue in 1989 **$3.4 billion**

Clark County gross gaming revenue in 1999 **$6.7 billion**

Total number of vehicles in 1999 **800,000**

Total number of vehicles in 2020 **1.6 million** (projected)

Ranking in US for new job creation (1999) **first**

Ranking in US for professionals/technicians **last**

Ranking in US for new business start-ups **first**

Ranking in US for business failures **first**

Gambling

We can't turn you into an expert gambler, but we can point you in the right direction.

There should be a sign hanging over the luggage carousels at McCarran Airport reading: 'Welcome to Las Vegas. Now give us your money.' Yes, friends, taking your dollars via the currency exchange known as legalised gambling is the whole purpose of this town. Don't buy into the 'Disneyland of Nevada' pitch being tossed about. Las Vegas has just one industry – gambling (or 'gaming' as its proponents euphemistically call it). Everything else runs a distant second. Luckily, gambling is scads of fun if you learn a bit about the process and bet within your limits. You'll pay for the pleasure, but you might also win a few dollars... maybe a few million dollars. And if you're clever, your losses won't hurt too much.

HOW CASINOS MAKE MONEY

Before learning the games, it's smart to know the casinos' angle. There are four ways of generating gaming revenue: the house edge, favourable rules, commissions and dumb players.

● Every casino game (and bet within that game) has a house edge. It's the difference between the true odds of an event occurring and the odds used for actual payouts. For example, in double-zero roulette, there are 38 possible winning numbers. If the casino paid true odds, it would pay off a winning number at 37 to 1 (for a total of $38, which includes your $1 stake). Instead, the casino pays off a winning number at 35 to 1. To calculate the house edge, imagine placing a $1 bet on every spot in roulette – a total wager of $38. Whatever number wins, you'll be given $36 ($35 plus your $1 stake). That's $2 less than the true odds payout – that $2 went directly into the house's pocket. Now divide the money kept by the house by the total it would have paid on true odds (two divided by 38), and you get a house edge of 5.26 per cent. So the house expects to retain 5.26¢ of every dollar bet. The house edge varies from game to game and within each game. Casinos love it when gamblers play for hours and hours because the house edge grinds away at every dollar wagered.

● Rules for casino games are structured to favour the house. The best example is blackjack, where the dealer gets to play his hand last. Should a player bust, the dealer wins by default immediately. Even if the dealer ends up busting himself a few seconds later, the player loses and the house wins.

● Commissions are collected by the house in a few table games. In poker, the house serves as dealer, but doesn't play a hand. So to make money from poker, the house takes a percentage of every pot, called the 'rake', or charges players a flat fee of $5 to $7 per half hour of play. In baccarat, the house takes 5 per cent of all winnings from bank bets.

● Finally, be they drunk, careless, superstitious or ill-informed, dumb gamblers are a boundless source of funds for casinos. That's why they provide free drinks. Alcohol is wonderful for loosening inhibitions (namely the inhibition against losing next month's rent). Thus, although the house edge in blackjack has been calculated at an average of only 2 per cent, casinos expect a win (or 'hold') of 15-20 per cent of the total amount of money brought to the table (the 'drop').

BETTING LIMITS & TABLE MINIMUMS

At every table game, there's a sign detailing the minimum (and often maximum) allowable bet. At blackjack, it might be $5-$500. Casinos expect players to bet towards the low end of the limit. This separates players by class, so a guy seeking a speedy $500-a-hand game doesn't have to endure poky play from a tourist betting $5. High-rollers can bet at higher than posted limits if the house is willing to 'fade' (cover) them. In roulette, the minimum means the sum total of all bets you place in one round. Hence, if the table has a $5 minimum, five $1 bets satisfies it. But in blackjack, if you play two hands simultaneously, you must bet the minimum (usually twice the minimum) on each.

ETIQUETTE

Before you lay your money down on a table, take note of the minimum-bet requirement posted on a sign, usually in the far left corner. Don't toss out a red ($5) chip on a $100-minimum table, unless you want to look like a goob. Likewise, don't put a quarter into a dollar slot or video poker machine; the coin will pass through the machine and clank, embarrassingly, into the hopper.

Table games have strict rules about when players can touch chips or cards – these exist to discourage cheaters. Many blackjack games are dealt face up and players never touch the cards. As for chips, once you make a bet, never touch them. If you're splitting or doubling down in blackjack, push out a separate pile of new chips but don't touch the original ones. This rule is to discourage 'past posting', a scam by which cheats sneak more chips into their bet after peeking at their cards.

Similarly, you should only handle dice with one hand. Everyone, from the players to the dealers and the bosses, will get very nervous if you touch them with two hands, or even make a fist around them with one hand so they can't be seen. Blow on them, shake them and turn them so your favourite numbers are up, but don't hide them, not for the briefest moment. That's how dice cheats use sleight of hand to get loaded dice into a craps game. And if you must kiss them, instead of touching them to your lips, just pantomime the kiss; no one likes shooters to slobber on dice.

You must be 21 to gamble. There are no exceptions to this rule. If you're under 21 and you start winning (or hit a jackpot that requires you to sign federal tax forms), not only will your chips or jackpot be confiscated, you'll be tossed out of the casino faster than you can say, 'But…'.

Most casinos subscribe to the old tradition that cameras are unwelcome. Leave your SLRs and videocams in your room, car or backpack. On the other hand, wherever you go in a casino (except the toilets), you'll be watched by 'eye in the sky' cameras and taped by video recorders in a central surveillance room. Nowhere on earth are civilians under more surveillance than in a casino; make sure you behave accordingly.

MONEY, MONEY, MONEY
To play table games, you'll need chips, though you can usually throw down a bill for your first plays (rules vary from casino to casino). In blackjack, cash can always play, though any winnings will be paid as chips. You can purchase chips at the table in a process called a 'buy in' or at the 'cage' (the casino cashier, who works at the 'teller window' of the casino's in-house bank). Redemption of chips occurs only at the cage.

Chips are like currency within the casino from which they're issued. But due to counterfeiting and other problems, casinos no longer honour each others' chips for gambling (unless, like Treasure Island and the Mirage, they're under the same ownership). However, you can sometimes exchange sub-$100 denominations from other casinos for house chips at the cage.

Most modern slot machines have bill acceptors that change your greenbacks into credits on the machine's credit meter. If you don't want to use the bill acceptor, or if you have a bill that's larger than what's accepted by the machine, press the 'Change' button on the machine. That activates a light on top, which summons a roving change person.

LEARNING TO GAMBLE
If you want to practise before arriving in Las Vegas, study the games further. There are hundreds of books on gambling, covering everything from baccarat to video poker; for our recommendations, *see page 301* **Further Reading**. Some of

Casino, chips, dice: get gambling!

the best are available by mail order from Huntington Press, 3687 S Procyon Avenue, Las Vegas, NV 89103 (1-800 244 2224 enquiries and credit card orders) and in specialist bookshops, such as the Gamblers Book Club. If you prefer computers to books, in the past decade numerous software programs have been developed to teach you how to play most games, from blackjack to craps, video poker, even roulette and slots. Send for catalogues from the Gamblers Book Club and Gambler's General Store (for both, *see chapter* **Shops & Services: Only in Vegas**) and Huntington Press.

Almost all the large casinos offer free hands-on lessons for most table games, taught by personable, informative and experienced instructors. They take you step by step through the playing procedures and etiquette (but don't expect them to warn you about sucker games and bets; they're paid by the casino, after all). Lessons are usually held in the late morning, when the casino is least busy; some open low-minimum 'live' games right afterwards for people who want to celebrate their new-found skills under actual casino conditions. One of the best places to learn is Caesars Palace, where the instructor, Barney Vinson, is a local gambling author and celebrity. *See chapter* **Casinos** for details of which casinos offer lessons.

When you're ready to join a game in progress, first stand back, watch the action for a while and pick up the rhythms and routines (don't stand too long behind a blackjack table before you sit down, however; most bosses will suspect you of 'back counting' the deck in order to slip in a bet at the most advantageous time). Choose a table with the lowest minimum possible, so you're not risking $100, $25 or even $10 a hand at a game you're playing for the first time. The locals and Downtown casinos tend to have lower minimums than those on the Strip – *see chapter* **Casinos** for more details. For an explanation of some of the common gambling terms, *see page 29* **Gambling jargon**.

TIP TALK

From bellmen to doormen, Las Vegas is a town that runs on tips. Limo drivers ($10-$25 per ride), valet parking attendants ($1-$2), cocktail waitresses (50¢ to $1), housekeepers ($1 a night), even front desk clerks ($10-$20 if you're looking for a better room): all ride the tip gravy train.

It's the same for casino dealers, who are officially paid little more than the minimum wage. Every shift of dealers combines and divides their tips and this makes up a majority of their pay. Giving tips (or 'tokes', as dealers call them) is smart because a happy dealer is your friend. Dealers can assist players in a number of ways: they can slow down the pace of the game (this is extremely useful when you're playing for comps), create a more sociable atmosphere, and even deal a little deeper in the deck.

You can toke the dealer as you leave the table; this will certainly be appreciated, but it won't gain you any help while you're playing. The second method is to toke after a big win – better, because the dealer knows you're thinking of him and could start to help you. But the best way is to place a bet for the dealer alongside your wager. If you win, the toke is paid off at regular odds and the dealer takes it. If you lose, the house wins the toke, but the dealer will still appreciate the thought.

In blackjack, there are two ways to bet for the dealer. You can place a chip outside the line surrounding your wager circle, but if this toke bet wins, it has to be scooped up by the dealer right away. Instead, if you're riding a hot streak, place the dealer's toke next to your bet within your wager circle. That way, if you win you can let the toke ride (continue to the next deal), because it's actually yours until you give it to the dealer. Just tell the dealer that the extra bet is a toke.

Don't bother toking if the dealer is rude, creepy or unco-operative. There is no reason to reward this type of behaviour. In fact, don't even play with such a dealer; instead, get up and move to another table, fast.

The games

Baccarat

Long viewed as an obscure, weirdly ritualised game for high-rollers, baccarat (pronounced 'bah-cah-rah') is a table game with a small house edge that's especially popular with Asians. Up to 15 players sit around the layout and bet on BANK, PLAYER or TIE. Tuxedo-clad dealers lay out two hands of two cards each, titled PLAYER and BANK. The object is for each hand to total as close to nine as possible. Face cards and tens count as zero and any total over nine is reduced by eliminating the first digit (for instance, a 15 is valued as a five). Players have no control over whether to 'draw' or 'stand'. Dealers follow a strict set of rules to determine if they must 'hit' either hand with a third card.

If PLAYER or BANK bets win, the house pays off at even money. Since the rules determine that BANK wins slightly more often, the house retains a 5 per cent commission on all BANK winnings. Even with the commission, the house holds only a 1.17 per cent edge on BANK bets and 1.36 per cent on PLAYER bets. (The TIE bet should be avoided. It pays off at 8 to 1, giving the house a 14 per cent edge since the true odds are about 9.5 to 1.)

The rhythm of baccarat is leisurely and the mood subdued. In fact, it's rarely necessary for players to speak (which might be why the game is so popular with Far Eastern gamblers). Baccarat pits are usually secluded behind velvet ropes to lend an air of exclusivity, but if you can handle the minimum – often $100 – you're welcome to join the action. Casinos catering to low-end gamblers tend to ignore baccarat but high-end casinos hold it dear for good reason – it's very profitable. The Mirage estimates that about 10 per cent of its annual revenue comes from baccarat.

Mini baccarat

Mini baccarat is a low-stakes version of baccarat played in the main pit, usually near the blackjack tables. It's a good introduction to the game, since the rules are the same, the bets lower and the pace faster because there are fewer players.

Novice gamblers should head for low-limit table games at casinos such as **Excalibur.**

Blackjack (21)

Blackjack is by far the most popular table game in the casinos. The reasons are obvious – it's a snap to play, there's a basic strategy that slims the house edge to nearly zero, and dozens of books on the market claim the house can be easily beaten with a skill known as card counting. At least the first two things are true.

You'll hear a lot about card counting. It's a technique whereby a player visually tracks exposed cards and mentally keeps a running total to determine if the deck is positive or negative. In the simplest count, the ten-value cards and aces are valued at –1 and small cards (two to seven) at +1. The eights and nines have no value. If the running total is positive, players have an advantage and should raise their bets. Does it work? Yes, but only if you devote hours and days and weeks of practice to it, develop good camouflage skills so that the house doesn't know you're counting – you'll be 'backed off' or 'barred' if they think you are – and are very cool under the distractions and pressures of real-time casino play. Counting cards is a gruelling discipline at which most fail, but successful card counters, especially high-stakes players, are the legendary gamblers who beat the casinos at their own game.

The rest of us pikers should stick to basic strategy. This involves memorising a few tables that explain how to play your hand. Alternatively, you can usually bring the charts to the table and check them as you play, as long as you don't slow down the game.

In blackjack, everyone at the table is dealt two cards after putting up their bets. Single- and double-deck blackjack is dealt from the dealer's hand, while multiple decks are combined and placed in a 'shoe', from which the dealer pulls cards. All face (picture) cards count as ten and aces can count as one or 11 (a hand that includes an ace is known as a 'soft' hand). Each player competes against the dealer's hand in trying to get as close as possible to a total of 21 without exceeding it (that's called 'busting'). After checking your cards, indicate a 'hit' for each extra card you want. When satisfied with your total, you 'stand'. After all players 'stand' or 'bust', the dealer reveals and plays his hand, according to fixed rules: he must 'hit' totals of 16 or less, and must 'stand' on 17 or above (the rules can vary if the hand contains an ace; *see page 20*). Once he 'stands' or 'busts', hands are compared and players who beat the dealer are paid off at even money. Ties between the house and player are a 'push' and no money changes hands (dealers indicate a 'push' by knocking gently on the layout just beyond your wager). If a player is dealt an ace and a ten-value card, it's considered a 'natural' blackjack and they're paid off at 3 to 2 immediately (unless the dealer shows an ace or ten, indicating a possible blackjack).

Almost all multi-deck games are dealt face up (except the dealer's second card). In these games, players never touch the cards, but instead indicate hit or stand with hand motions. This reduces the potential for misunderstandings when the casino is noisy – which it is most of the time – and makes it easier for disputed plays to be reviewed on security videos filmed by an overhead camera. For a 'hit', players hold one hand palm down just above the felt and brush their fingers toward themselves. For 'stand', hold the hand the same way, but with fingers straight outward, and move it right and left. Single- and double-deck games are almost always dealt face down, and players hold their own cards. 'Hitting' is indicated by scratching the cards towards you on the layout. 'Standing' is indicated by sliding the cards face down under the chips.

There are four ways players can alter their bets once the cards are dealt: 'doubling down', 'splitting', 'insurance' and 'surrender'. Aggressively 'splitting' and 'doubling down' is the secret to winning at basic strategy blackjack, giving players the chance to press bets when holding strong hands.

When a player 'doubles down', he wagers another bet equal to the original and receives one (and only one) more card. It's the choice move when you've got a total of nine, ten or 11 and the dealer shows a weak card such as a six. You can 'double down' only if you haven't already taken a hit. 'Splitting' is an option when players are dealt two cards of the same value. An additional bet equal to the original bet is put out and the cards are split with each played as a separate hand. It's to the player's advantage to be able to 'double down' or 'split' each of the post-split hands, though some casinos limit what you can do. Check the chart opposite to see when you should 'double down' or 'split' a hand.

'Insurance' is a side bet offered when the dealer has a possible blackjack (ie is showing an ace or ten-value card). An 'insurance' bet is limited to 50 per cent of the original bet and is lost immediately if the dealer doesn't have blackjack. If he does, insurance pays off at 2 to 1. Despite the warm connotations of the word 'insurance', this is a sucker bet. There's no reason to take 'insurance', even if you're holding a natural blackjack.

'Surrender' is an obscure but useful rule that's not in effect everywhere. When it's on, 'surrender' permits players to fold and sacrifice half their bet as long as they haven't played their hand. It's an excellent way to drop out and minimise losses when dealt weak cards. If used correctly, 'surrender' increases the player's edge by 0.2 per cent.

Here's another easy rule to help players. Some casinos require dealers to hit a 'soft 17' (an ace plus a six or cards totalling six), while others require them to stand. If possible, play at places that require the dealers to stand on a soft 17 – it shifts the edge about 0.2 per cent to the players' favour.

One final note. Though blackjack sets each player's hand against the dealer's, most players view the game as everyone against the dealer. Their goal is to make the dealer bust, which means pay-offs for all the players still in the game. These folks don't take kindly to people who play stupidly and split tens or hit a 14 against a dealer's six, especially if the offending party sits in the last seat on the left (known as 'third base'), since they feel those cards should have gone to the dealer. We suggest you don't sit at third base unless you have a good grasp of the game.

Blackjack strategy

Dealer's up card

	2	3	4	5	6	7	8	9	10	A
If you have										
8 or below hit										
9	H	D	D	D	D	H	H	H	H	H
10	D	D	D	D	D	D	D	D	H	H
11	D	D	D	D	D	D	D	D	D	D
12	H	H	S	S	S	H	H	H	H	H
13-16	S	S	S	S	S	H	H	H	H	H
17 or above stand										

Dealer's up card

	2	3	4	5	6	7	8	9	10	A
If you have an ace										
Ace, 2	H	H	D	D	D	H	H	H	H	H
Ace, 3	H	H	D	D	D	H	H	H	H	H
Ace, 4	H	H	D	D	D	H	H	H	H	H
Ace, 5	H	H	D	D	D	H	H	H	H	H
Ace, 6	D	D	D	D	D	H	H	H	H	H
Ace, 7	S	D	D	D	D	S	S	H	H	S
Ace, 8	S	S	S	S	S	S	S	S	S	S
Ace, 9	S	S	S	S	S	S	S	S	S	S

Dealer's up card

	2	3	4	5	6	7	8	9	10	A
If you have a pair of										
2s	SP	SP	SP	SP	SP	SP	H	H	H	H
3s	SP	SP	SP	SP	SP	SP	H	H	H	H
4s	H	H	H	H	H	H	H	H	H	H
5s	D	D	D	D	D	D	D	H	H	H
6s	SP	SP	SP	SP	SP	H	H	H	H	H
7s	SP	SP	SP	SP	SP	SP	H	H	H	H
8s	SP	SP	SP	SP	SP	SP	SP	SP	SP	SP
9s	SP	SP	SP	SP	SP	S	SP	SP	S	S
10s	S	S	S	S	S	S	S	S	S	S
Aces	SP	SP	SP	SP	SP	SP	SP	SP	SP	SP

H=hit; **S**=stand; **D**=double down; **SP**=split

Players should consider surrender with:
All hard totals of 13-16 against a dealer's ace
All hard totals of 14-16 against a dealer's ten
All hard totals of 15-16 against a dealer's nine

Slot and video poker machines account for up to 70 per cent of total casino revenues.

Gambling tips for beginners

Everyone in the casino is playing a different game, even if they're sitting at the same table. It might appear as if the five players at a blackjack table, for example, are simply trying to get closer to 21 than the dealer without busting. But look closer.

In the first seat is a basic strategy player, playing every hand exactly by the book. In the second seat is a card counter, eyeing the cards like a hawk, doing mental gymnastics to calculate the correlation between the edge and his bet, and trying to spread his chips from minimum to maximum without attracting attention. In the third is a front-end loader, using a variety of strategies to spot the dealer's hole card, which gives him a huge advantage on the hand. In the fourth is a comp hustler, slowing down the game by engaging the dealer in small talk and taking time to play a hand. And in the fifth is a casino novice, who barely knows how to hold his cards, let alone recognise all the games that are being played under his very nose.

Here are a few tips to help you avoid sitting in that last seat.

● If you don't have the inclination to memorise the whole blackjack basic strategy chart (*see p20*), at least learn the following five golden rules:

– stand on 17 to 21, but always hit soft 17;
– stand on 12 to 16 against the dealer's 2 to 6, but hit on 12 to 16 against the dealer's 7, 8, 9, 10 and ace;
– always split 8s and aces, but never split 4s and 10s;
– double down on 10s and 11s against the dealer's 2s to 9s;
– never take insurance.

● Never play a slot or video poker machine without belonging to the casino's slot club. It costs nothing to join, you accrue slot club points as you play, and you can redeem those points for rooms, food, shows, even cash.

● Always ask for comps when you play table games. As soon as you sit down and make a bet, call over a floorman and ask: 'How long do I have to play to get a comp to the buffet?' He'll look at your bet and tell you. Play for as long as he indicates, then collect your free buffet.

● Especially if you're angling for comps, but even if you're not, it's best to play slow. You're better off exposing your bankroll to the house edge for 50 hands an hour (at a busy table) than 100 hands an hour (playing one-on-one against the dealer). Similarly, it's better to go for 400 spins an hour (by feeding coins into a slot machine and pulling

Bingo

It might not be posh, but bingo is a gambling stalwart in Vegas, especially in the neighbourhood casinos. The game is the same as found in church basements all over the world. The house edge is slightly better than the similar keno, though it's hard to pin down since so much depends on the variety of game and the number of cards being played. The one advantage bingo has over keno is that bingo numbers are called until somebody wins. By contrast, a million keno games can go by without anyone hitting the big jackpot.

Craps

Fast, furious and enormously confusing, craps is an action-filled dice game that terrifies most novices. Players curse and scream, chips fly across the table and everybody roots for different winning numbers. Fortunes can be won and lost in minutes, which is exactly why craps is worshipped by a subculture of dice players. It's confounding, but by sticking to a few smart bets, players can enjoy a boisterously fun game with a house edge as low as 1 per cent or less.

The basics

Craps is played on a large table surrounded by a low, padded wall (don't put your glass on it). The game is staffed by four casino employees and there's room for 12 to 14 players to belly up. The layout is divided into three sections. The two at each end are identical; in the centre is an area reserved for special wagers known as 'proposition bets'. A game of craps starts with dice being offered to a new 'shooter' by the 'stickman' (the dealer located mid-table who's holding the stick). Each player will be offered the shooter job at some point, though it's common to refuse the dice. The shooter must throw two dice so that they bounce off the far wall of the table.

Basically, crap players bet on which numbers the shooters will throw and in what order. The shooter must lay a bet before his first throw, and traditionally chooses PASS. Those betting with the shooter are called 'right' bettors, while those betting against the shoot are called 'wrong' bettors.

How to bet

There are four basic wagers known as 'line bets' marked on the layout – PASS, DON'T PASS,

the handle) than 800 spins an hour (by hitting the spin button like a madman).

● Most 'money management' advice is mathematically unsound. (Quick quiz: when does the size of your bet affect the outcome of a play? Answer: never.) However, some of it is emotionally supportive. For example, to ensure gambling funds for your whole trip, divide your money into session portions. If you drop one entire session portion quickly, end of session. Don't dig into your remaining bankroll until it's time for the next session.

● Look for coupons everywhere – in funbooks, the free magazines and handed out by hawkers in front of the casinos. Two-for-one, three-for-two and seven-for-five coupons on even-money bets give you a huge edge over the house at blackjack, craps and the like. A first-card-is-an-ace coupon at blackjack is like money in the bank.

● Keep an eagle eye on your coins, cash and chips. Always make sure back-to-back slot machines have a plastic or metal guard between them to prevent 'reach through' thievery of coin buckets or purses. Watch for 'rail thieves' at the crap table and sneak thieves everywhere.

COME and DON'T COME (the DON'T bets are for wrong bettors). The shooter's initial throw is called a 'come out roll'. Players bet on the PASS or DON'T PASS lines. If the shooter throws a seven (statistically the most likely roll) or 11 on the come out roll, PASS bettors win at even odds and DON'T PASS bettors lose. If the shooter throws a two or three, DON'T PASS wins and PASS loses. If a 12 is tossed, PASS bettors lose and it's a 'push' (or tie) for DON'T PASS bettors. Rolling a two, three or 12 is known as 'crapping out'. If any other number is thrown (four, five, six, eight, nine, ten), that becomes the 'point'.

Once a point is established, the shooter keeps rolling, attempting to repeat the point before rolling a seven (known as 'sevening out'). Other numbers tossed don't count in this context. PASS and DON'T PASS bets ride until the 'point' is hit or the shooter 'sevens out'. If the shooter hits the 'point', PASS bettors win and DON'T PASS bettors lose. If the shooter tosses a seven, DON'T PASS bettors win, PASS bettors lose and the shooter relinquishes control of the dice. The shortest roll a shooter can have is two throws – by hitting a point on the come out roll followed by a seven (that's when wrong bettors rake in the

chips). But if he avoids 'sevening out', the shooter can roll forever (that's when right bettors rack up big bucks). Every time the 'point' is hit, the game is reset and the next throw is a fresh 'come out roll'.

COME and DON'T COME bets represent an optional second layer of betting that runs concurrently. They are similar to PASS and DON'T PASS bets, with exactly the same set of outcomes – an immediate win, lose or 'push' or the establishment of a 'point' – but can only be made on throws subsequent to the 'come out roll'. For instance, the shooter establishes a point of four; on the next roll you make a COME bet. The next roll is nine, so nine becomes your 'point'. Should that throw have yielded a seven or 11, you would have won immediately. If a shooter hits their number, the COME bets ride, awaiting a seven or a repeat of their 'point'.

Taking the odds

If a player sticks to the four 'line' bets outlined above, the house edge is only about 1.4 per cent. But even that tiny amount can be reduced with the use of the 'odds' bet. The odds bet is a remarkable wager where the house holds an edge of zero. That's right, these bets are paid off at exactly true odds. They're the only such wagers in the casino, which is probably why the craps layout doesn't mention them at all.

Once a point is established, any player with a 'line' bet can 'back up' that wager with an 'odds' bet. This allows players to increase their bet midstream. In a craps game with single odds, the maximum 'odds' bet equals the 'line' bet. That alone slashes the house edge from about 1.4 per cent to 0.85 per cent. Some casinos offer double, triple, 10× or even 100× odds, all of which reduce the house edge even further. A few offer different odds on specified points. Anyone making line bets in craps should take at least single odds on every bet made. Since laying down 'odds' bets can be complicated for novices, check with the dealer or, better still, attend a lesson and ask questions.

The rest of the table

Smart players stick to line and odds bets, but action junkies need more. For them, crap tables offer another world of wagers, none of which is worthwhile to any right-thinking human. Granted, some 'place bets' offer an edge only slightly worse than 'line' bets. But most of the one-roll proposition bets are simply horrific. For instance, the ANY 7 proposition bet has a stunning house edge of 16.67 per cent, the worst edge of any table game wager apart from the Money Wheel. Don't waste chips on these bogus bets. Stick to the meat and potatoes of right and wrong betting with line bets pressed with odds and you'll get more than enough action. A straightforward odds-effective play is to bet the minimum stake on PASS, the same amount on two COME bets and take odds on both (double or triple, if they're offered and you can afford it).

Keno

Keno ranks as the worst bet in the casino. This lottery offshoot gives the house an intolerable edge of 25-40 per cent. You might as well climb to the top of the Stratosphere and throw your money into the wind. At least you'll have a nice view.

Like a lottery, keno involves a ticket (or 'blank') containing 80 numbers. Players circle up to 15 or 20 numbers on their blank. When the game starts, 20 numbers are selected at random (ping-pong balls are blown from a 'goose' into a pair of 'arms') and displayed on screens at the casino. If your numbers are picked, you win. If not, you lose (get used to the second option). The greater the proportion of your numbers picked, the higher the payback. If you win, you must claim your prize money before the next game begins or you forfeit your winnings.

There are many variations for betting keno, but none makes the edge even remotely acceptable. Worst of all, payouts in no way reflect the true odds of your bet, since they're capped at an arbitrary figure. For instance, your chances of selecting nine numbers and hitting all of them are about 1.38 million to 1. Your payout for such a feat? Usually no more than $250,000 on a $2 bet. Here's another fun fact: if by some bizarre chance two players hit the big jackpot, they have to split it. Amazingly, there are books published that claim to offer a strategy to beat the odds in keno. Ha! The only way to beat the odds in keno is to ignore it.

Money Wheel or Big Six

You have to worry when a casino game is imported from the morally challenged universe of carnivals. That's the case with Money Wheel, aka Big Six, the grandchild of spin-the-wheel games loved by carnies everywhere. The game is simple. A large, ornate wheel is mounted vertically a few feet above the floor. On it are 54 evenly spaced slots. Two show joker or house symbols; the other 52 are divided into $1, $2, $5, $10 and $20 denominations. There are usually 24 $1 slots and only two $20 slots. A layout in front of the wheel has squares matching those denominations. Players put cash or chips on the squares of their choice, the wheel spins, and when it stops bettors who selected the correct denomination win, with the payoff determined by the dollar value of the winning slot. A $20 symbol pays off at 20 to 1; a $1 symbol pays off at even money. House or joker symbols pay off at 40 to 1. As you might guess, the casino holds a serious edge, ranging from 11 per cent on a bet on the $1 symbol to 25.9 per cent on the joker.

This should be called the Clint Eastwood Wheel. Every time you lay down a bet, the dealer could sneer, 'Are you feeling lucky, punk?' If not, keep your money in your pocket.

Poker

In poker, gamblers bet against each other, not the house. A casino employee only deals and acts as a cashier. The house's income is limited to a percentage taken from each pot, or a seat rental of $5 or $7 per half hour. You'd think the casinos would have figured out a way to grab more of the action by now. Oh wait, that's what slot machines are for, right?

To join a game, just sit in an empty seat and buy in (which usually costs ten times the minimum or maximum bet, depending on the game) with chips or cash. If there's no space, you can put your name on a waiting list.

The traditional rules everyone knows are in effect for Vegas poker. The most popular games are Texas Hold 'Em and seven-card stud. In Hold 'Em, each player is given two cards face down, while five common cards are dealt for the table. Players assemble the best five-card hand possible from the seven cards available to them. In seven-card stud, players get two cards face down and one face up, followed by three cards face up and a final card face down. Again, they put together the best possible hand from their own seven cards.

Both of the above games have numerous rounds of betting and raising, so a hefty bankroll is essential. For games with betting limits, posted signs indicate the smallest and largest bet allowable (usually written in the form '$5/$10'). In a limit game, you'll need a bankroll equal to 20 times the maximum bet. There are also pot-limit games, which means raises can go as high as the pot, and no-limit games, in which raises can go as high as the largest bankroll on the table. In all games, no matter what the stakes, players are not allowed to bring more money to the table once a hand is dealt. If a player is 'all in' (meaning all their money is bet) and they can't match a raise, a side pot is formed for those who wish to continue betting. The player who is all in is now limited to playing for the main pot.

Explaining poker strategy here is impossible. Besides the complexities of the game, much of poker is psychological. Reading other players and bluffing is a huge part of the process, which, if you don't know so already, you'll learn the first time you sit down in a card room. If you're not a seasoned poker player, be especially careful of high-stakes games, which can be populated by sharks (sometimes operating in teams). They've learned the primary casino secret – it's easy to take money from amateur gamblers. As the old saying goes, 'If you don't know who the fish is, it's you.' If you're a novice, stick to low-stakes games, which are straightforward and friendly.

Roulette

Despite its popularity in Europe, roulette doesn't have much of a fan club in the US. That's partly due to the calm nature of the game. Americans want action and speed when they gamble. Roulette gives them neither. Another reason is a subtle but crucial change in the US version. In Europe, roulette wheels typically have 36 numbered slots and one zero slot. On most American wheels, there are two zero slots (marked as zero and double zero). That change alone nearly doubles the house edge to 5.26 per cent, as compared to 2.7 per cent on single-zero wheels.

Roulette is simple to play. The wheel is mounted horizontally and a matching table layout serves as the betting area. All the numbers are coloured red or black, except the zero and double zero, which are green. Players make their bets on the table, the wheel is spun and a little white ball is launched. Betting is halted, the ball comes to rest in a slot, then winners are paid off. To minimise confusion about who made which bet, each player receives specially coloured 'wheel' chips when they buy in (these chips can only be used at the roulette table).

The easiest wager is a straight-up bet, where the player drops a chip on a single number (17 is the most popular, supposedly due to its central location and the fact that James Bond bets it in the movies). If the number is the winner, it's paid off at 35 to 1. You can also make bets on groups of numbers; for example, on lines separating numbers, rows of numbers or in special areas denoting odd or even, red or black and so on. In this way, a single bet covers anywhere from two to 18 numbers. Needless to say, the

more numbers the wager covers, the lower the payoff. For instance, betting odd or even pays even money.

The variety of wagers makes roulette an interesting game, especially if you like the languid pace. But bear in mind, the odds are tough. Your best bet is to find a casino with a single-zero wheel – such as the MGM Grand, Monte Carlo and Stratosphere – and try to look elegant while losing.

Pai Gow, Let It Ride & Caribbean stud

Since almost everyone knows how to play poker, casinos are eagerly experimenting with variations that can be played outside the poker room.

Pai Gow poker is played with a 53-card deck (a standard deck plus a joker, which is wild). Players get seven cards, which they assemble into a five-card hand and a two-card hand. The five-card hand must score higher than the two-card hand. The object is to beat both the banker's hands. The banker wins all hands that tie. If a player wins only one hand, it's a push. The house or any player can be the banker. Winning hands are paid at even money, minus a 5 per cent commission.

Let It Ride offers the unusual feature of allowing players to take back two-thirds of their wager.

Players bet three equal amounts and are dealt three cards face down. Two common cards are dealt, also face down. At this point, players can pull back one of their bets (don't touch your chips, that's the dealer's job). When the first common card is turned over, players can withdraw their second bet. The final common card is then shown and payouts made according to a fixed schedule, ranging from even money for a pair of tens or better to 1,000 to 1 for a royal flush. As you might guess, that's way below true odds. For instance, the odds against drawing a flush are 508 to 1 but the payout is 8 to 1. Overall, the house holds about a 4 per cent edge, if players make all the right decisions.

The biggest lure of Let It Ride is that players compete against the cards, not each other, making it more appealing to amateurs. Also, there's that ability to withdraw two-thirds of the bet, which gives the illusion that your money is lasting longer than in other games. But don't be fooled. The house edge grinds down almost everyone eventually, and since this game is basically five-card stud, it's often a long time between winning hands.

Caribbean stud is a rather dumb game with a house edge of 5.27 per cent, just a hair worse than double-zero roulette. Sitting around a table similar to a blackjack layout, players put out a single ante bet and receive five cards face down. The dealer also gets five cards, though one is dealt face up. At this point, players either fold (and lose their ante) or 'call' by adding a bet that's twice their ante. Everyone then reveals their cards. If the dealer doesn't 'qualify' with at least an ace and king in his hand, all players win even money for their ante and the call bets are returned. Should the dealer's hand qualify, each player's hand is compared against the dealer's. If the player wins, the ante is paid off at even money and the call bet qualifies for a 'bonus' payout based on the hand. Bonus payouts range from even money for a pair to 100 to 1 for a royal flush (most of these payouts are even lower than those found in Let It Ride).

The maximum bonus payout is usually capped somewhere between $5,000 and $60,000, so make sure your bet is no higher than it needs to be to win that amount. For example, if the bonus payout is capped at $5,000, your ante should never be above $25 (this would make your call bet $50 and thus your 100-to-1 payout would hit the $5,000 ceiling exactly). The simple maths? Divide the maximum bonus payout by 200. Your ante should never exceed that amount.

For a side bet of another dollar per hand, Caribbean stud poker also offers players the chance to hit a progressive jackpot with payoffs based on the quality of their hand. A royal flush wins 100 per cent of the jackpot while a flush gets a mere $50. The fact that jackpots have been known to go up to $5 million will tell you something about how often a royal flush occurs.

Slot machines

Slot machines were once shunned, patronised only by the bored wives and girlfriends of gamblers. These days, they're the most popular and profitable part of Las Vegas, so much so that some casinos offer nothing but slots and video poker. Novice gamblers prefer slots because there's little to learn and no pressure from dealers or other players. Put in money, pull the handle and in a few seconds, you're either a winner or a loser. Simple. Plus, jackpots can reach millions of dollars. But there is a downside – slots give the house an edge from 2 to 25 per cent, often making them one of the worst bets in the house. And your chance of hitting a million-dollar jackpot is well, gee, what's the tiniest unit of measurement you can imagine? Your chances are smaller than that. Way smaller.

The basic slot machine accepts a maximum of either two or three coins (some take four or five, some just one, and a new breed of slots now takes up to hundreds of coins, including pennies). Each coin beyond the minimum increases the payout proportionally (twice as much for two coins, triple for three) should a winning combination appear. Sometimes the winnings on the final coin are exponentially higher: always check the pay tables at the top of the machine. Many machines have multiple pay lines (up to five). On these machines, an added pay line is activated each time another coin is wagered.

Modern slots usually have a coin counter that displays your credits. Instead of coins crashing into the steel bin, wins are registered as credits. Often, there's a bill changer attached, so players can simply slide in a $20, and $20 of credits appear on the counter. Bets are made by pulling a handle or pressing a button. When finished, players hit the 'Cash out' button, and coins for all unused credits drop into the bin. The casino provides plastic cups to carry coins to other machine or the cashier.

All slots fall into two categories: non-progressive (or stand-alone) and progressive. Stand-alone slots have fixed payouts, which are posted on the front of the machine. Progressive slots offer a fixed and posted payout schedule, too, as well as the chance to hit a huge jackpot. This jackpot (funded by a percentage of every coin wagered) grows continuously until somebody wins it. A meter above the machines displays a running total of the current jackpot. Many progressive slots are linked to form a system that feeds the jackpot. These machines might be from one carousel in a single casino (with a $1,000 jackpot), or spread across casinos throughout the state (with multi-million dollar jackpots). With hundreds of machines in the system, the jackpot can reach astronomical levels. A Megabucks machine at the Desert Inn paid almost $35 million in January 2000. Though rare, these payouts are well publicised and make excellent bait for more players.

New slots

Slot machines are getting increasingly flashy. A few years ago, video machines, such as Odyssey, with oversized screens, multiple games and all sorts of other gimmicks were all the rage. But at the 1999 World Gaming Congress & Expo, the premier gambling trade show that takes place in Las Vegas every October, a whole new generation of slots (and table games, such as a Monopoly Poker and Yahtzee) was on display. For the first time, the distinctions between slot machines and video poker machines are beginning to blur. Slot machines are becoming much more interactive and look a lot like video poker: when these skill-based

You'll soon learn to slot into Vegas life.

machines hit the casino floor, you'll be able to make choices about which symbols to hold or discard, based on a certain internal and intuitive logic.

Other new slots unveiled at the Gaming Expo were decidedly gimmicky. A Three Stooges machine has video clips (similar to the year-old Elvis slot) of the comedy trio and 'nyuk nyuk nyuk' sound effects. Others try to capitalise on nostalgia for 1960s American television series, such as *I Dream of Jeannie* and *The Addams Family*, as well as the popularity of contemporary programmes such as *South Park*. Slot reels display cigars, the Titanic and 'little green men'. There was even an Asian-themed machine with firecrackers, fortune cookies and MSG symbols. Though some observers predict that these new machines will have a maximum lifespan of 12 months (until the next crop of slots is rolled out), others project that 90,000 (of the total 450,000 slot machines in US casinos) will be replaced with these new machines.

Slot (and video poker) machines now account for upwards of 65 and even 70 per cent of total casino revenues, which means that gambling machines take in nearly twice as much revenue or more as all other casino games combined. Of the $8.5 billion won by Nevada casinos in fiscal 1999, $5.5 billion – nearly 65 per cent – was from slots and video poker.

Slots are much more fun to play today than they were even ten years ago, when they were still primarily 'one-armed bandits' (derisively referred to by table-game players as the 'idiot pull'). But they still won't line your pockets.

How slots work

Modern slots are controlled by a computer chip called a random number generator, which continually churns out strings of numbers whether the game is being played or not. Pulling the handle of a machine (or pressing the spin button) releases the reels and selects one of these randomly generated numbers. Each number corresponds to a certain set of symbols on the reels. That's how the outcome is determined. The force of the pull has nothing to do with where the reels stop.

Since this is computer technology, regulating the payout is a science. By adjusting the random number generator, a slot technician can make a machine 'tighter' (pays out less often) or 'looser' (pays out more often). In the old days, slots often had a built-in edge of 20 to 30 per cent or more. But players flocked to machines with the higher returns. Casinos did the maths and realised it was better to get 5 per cent of a lot than 30 per cent of nothing, hence, most Vegas slots now return about 95 per cent of the drop (slightly less on nickel machines), leaving the house with a 5 per cent edge.

Certain casinos boldly advertise 98 or 99 per cent payouts, but read the small print. It's usually 'up to 99 per cent'. That means one machine on the floor might be set at 98 or 99 per cent, if that. There's no way to find out which slots are set tight or loose. Payout percentages are supposedly verified by the state Gaming Control Board, but they rarely check unless a casino advertises something absurd.

The real advantage for the house comes with the constant repetition of slot plays. For instance, a player with $50 starts betting $1 per pull on a quarter machine (via four 25¢ bets per pull). Sometimes they win and those winnings are reinvested: the drop might only be $50, but they're giving the casino $240, say, of action every hour. With that tiny 5 per cent edge, a slot machine will retain about $12 an hour (5 per cent of $240). That's a hold equal to nearly a quarter of the original bankroll. With a little less luck, that money could vanish even quicker. Over time, even a 5 per cent edge grinds down players, which is why so many stumble away from machines empty-handed. That and the fact that most of the payouts go towards the big (and seldom won) jackpots.

Slot tips

Slot jockeys say non-progressive machines are looser than progressive machines, though payouts are smaller. And non-progressive machines with smaller top payouts are reportedly looser than those with large top payouts. Similarly, among progressive machines, those with smaller jackpots hit more often. Interestingly, the amount of your wager going to the progressive jackpot is an indication of payout frequency. According to one casino executive, if it's less than 1 per cent, that progressive machine is likely to have more non-jackpot winners. If 3 to 5 per cent of every bet goes toward the progressive jackpot, that game is seriously weighted toward fewer, large payouts. Of course, this percentage isn't posted, so you're flying mostly blind.

One oft-repeated belief states that slots placed near doorways and aisles are looser than others. The constant sound of coins dropping is supposed to lure folks into betting a few bucks. One casino exec said house machines (those with the casino's name and logo) are set looser than non-house brand slots. We know one tipster who's convinced that slots near waitress stations are looser because that yields more tips for the waitresses. Is any of this true? Who knows? Frankly, we think casinos start these rumours to generate more play.

The only recommendation that makes sense is that if you're going to play slots for big money, bet the maximum number of coins on each pull. This way, if lightning strikes and you're a winner, you'll get the biggest payout possible. If you want to lay out a dollar per pull, play four coins in a quarter machine (although $1 and higher machines tend to have higher percentage payouts). Avoid slots in non-casino locations such as the airport and convenience stores. They have a house edge one step below outright thievery.

Slot machines can only pay out so many coins at a time, so if you hit a monster jackpot, stay put and wait for an attendant. If you walk away, someone else might claim your prize. The attendant will inform you of your tax obligations (US citizens need to fill out IRS paperwork on slot wins of more than $1,200; the tax situation varies for non-nationals).

Video poker

This electronic cousin of live poker enjoys a huge following in Vegas, much of it from hardcore local gamblers. Although a video poker machine resembles a slot machine and is typically located in the slot pit, it is an entirely different beast. Make no mistake: video poker is a game not of chance but of skill. If played perfectly, the house edge can often be flattened to zero or even pushed into the negative, meaning a legitimate return to players of over 100 per cent. Casinos can afford to do this because perfect play is the province of only a handful of experts and pros, who use powerful computer programs to work out strategies that are accurate within ten-thousandths of a percentage point.

Instead of a slot machine's spinning reels, a video poker screen displays a five-card hand of draw poker. Every deal comes from a freshly shuffled 52-card deck. Buttons allow the player to hold or replace the dealt cards. After the draw, the game pays off according to a payout schedule listed on the screen. A pair of aces might pay at 1 for 1 while a royal flush might pay at 1,000 for 1. Most basic poker rules are in effect as far as hand rankings go, but the whole psychological angle is jettisoned. You're playing against a machine that doesn't respond to bluffing, so your hand is all.

There's no way to summarise basic strategy for video poker, partly because it's extremely complex and partly because the game comes in so many varieties. Each has unique characteristics, such as wild cards and bonus options, and consequently different pay tables and different strategies for optimum play.

The basic variation is 'Jacks or Better', which plays most like five-card stud (no wild cards) and pays on pairs of jacks or (you guessed it) better. The strategies for Jacks or Better are mostly intuitive for anyone who knows how to play poker, but some rules have to be learned: for example, you never hold a 'kicker' (unpaired or unsuited high card); you never draw to a four-card straight (for example, you hold 3, 4, 6, 7 and you're looking for a 5); and you always go for the royal flush if you hold four of the cards, even if it means sacrificing a flush or straight in the process.

As with slots, you should play the maximum number of coins, as this greatly increases the top payout for a royal flush. Another tip: be sure to play full-payout games as opposed to their partial-payout brethren. Since casino staff can adjust the payouts, the same style of game might pay the same hand differently in different casinos. For instance, in Jacks or Better, the full-payout version pays 9 for 1 on a full house and 6 for 1 on a flush (that's called a '9/6 machine'). On the partial-payout version, it's sliced to 8/5 or even as low as 6/5. The only reason to play a partial-payout version of Jacks or Better is if it's connected to a progressive jackpot or (as a rare few do) pays off on a pair of tens or better.

However, 8/5 Bonus, with extra payouts for four-of-a-kind, is a different animal. So are Double Bonus, Double Double Bonus and Triple Bonus variations. Then there are Joker Poker and several different varieties of Deuces Wild. Video poker players should consult the books and reports on the market that detail proper play for sample video poker hands. Excellent computer programs also tutor players in video poker strategies. Casinos don't mind if you refer to strategy charts while playing, but draw the line at laptop computers. Since it's impossible to absorb the tactics for all the variations at once, we recommend that you study and master strategy for Jacks or Better, then, as you feel more comfortable, move on to the more complex – and financially rewarding – games such as full-pay Deuces Wild and Double Bonus varieties.

The latest rage in video poker, introduced at the 1998 Gaming Expo and taking casino floors by storm almost immediately, are multi-play machines, such as Triple Play, Five Play and Ten Play. Here, three, five and ten hands of video poker

Gambling jargon

Black Book a list, kept by the State Gaming Control Board, of people legally excluded from any Nevada casino due to a history of cheating or connection to organised crime.

boxman casino executive who acts as the umpire in a game of craps.

buy in exchange cash for casino chips.

cage the main casino cashier, where chips and tokens are converted into cash, credit is established and, usually, foreign currency can be exchanged.

carousel group of slot machines often connected to a joint 'progressive jackpot'.

change colour swap chips for ones of a higher or lower denomination.

check another word for chip.

chip token issued by casinos and used, instead of cash, for table games.

comps short for 'complimentaries'. Comps range from free cocktails to 'RFB' – room, food and beverage. Their value is calculated by the gambler's average bet multiplied by the time spent playing multiplied by the house edge. To qualify for comps, you must be a rated player or belong to a slot club.

credit line amount of credit a gambler is allowed to play with.

drop the total amount of money, including chips, cash and markers, brought to the gaming table.

European wheel a roulette wheel with a single '0' position (which gives players better odds). Most wheels in Las Vegas have '0' and '00' positions.

eye in the sky the casino's in-house surveillance system.

grind joint a casino with low table minimums and low-denomination slot machines.

high-roller big-money gambler who bets a minimum of $100 per hand on a table game, and plays $5 slot machines or $1 multi-play machines.

house advantage, **house edge** *or* **vigorish** the percentage difference (retained by the casino) between the true odds and the actual payout.

juice the ultimate Las Vegas power and influence; who you know.

layout diagram on the playing table that marks the area of the game.

loose used to describe a slot machine that pays out frequently. Casinos compete in claiming that their slots are the loosest in town.

low-roller a gambler who bets almost exclusively at low-minimum slot machines, usually in grind joints.

marker IOUs signed by rated players to obtain extra chips. Markers are paid off with chips or cash.

pit area between the gaming tables reserved for casino employees.

pit boss *or* **pit bull** casino executive who oversees the gambling action from inside the pit.

progressive jackpot the potential payout on a slot or video poker machine (or group of machines) that increases as each coin is played.

rated player a player whose gambling habits are assessed by the casino and is thus eligible for comps.

shill casino employee who plays at empty tables (with house money) to encourage dithering visitors to get down to business.

shoe container for decks of cards from which card games are often dealt.

shooter the player who throws the dice in a game of craps.

slot clubs clubs for slot machine players. Members accrue points as they play, which can be redeemed against meals, gifts, cash and other perks.

toke a tip for a casino employee, often given in the form of a bet on their behalf.

true odds the real chances of winning on any game as opposed to the money actually paid out by the casino.

whale big-money gambler who is prepared to wager huge amounts (at least $5,000 per hand) at high-stake games.

---

are dealt at the same time from the same number of decks, requiring three, five and ten times the maximum bet. Only the bottom-hand cards are displayed, however; the upper hands are face down. When you hold cards from the bottom hand, the held cards appear in the upper hands and when you draw, all the hands' cards are filled in around the held cards.

At the 1999 Gaming Expo, a Fifty Play video poker machine was unveiled. With 50 hands of video poker jammed on to a screen, the cards are so small and go by so fast that you can only watch the credit tally to see if you're winning and losing. They look very similar to slot machines. In Spin Poker, another new video poker game that looked like a slot machine, when you discard cards, the open spots spin like slot reels. Heads Up Poker, also unveiled at the show, combines live poker with video poker. You're dealt five cards and you bet the hand. The machine responds by calling, raising or folding (the machine sometimes bluffs!). Then you play out the video poker hand, but you still have the live hand to be resolved. We predict that this one's going to be hot.

Architecture

Gaudy and dazzling, monumental and kitsch, architecturally, Las Vegas is like nowhere else on earth.

In the post-World War II era, Las Vegas developed its own distinctive style, a dazzlingly vulgar cocktail of expressionist modern architectecture and monumental neon signs, illuminating stretches of empty desert on the town's Las Vegas Boulevard. The old Vegas was Mafia-controlled, a world where men still dressed in coat and tie to gamble, and ballgown-clad women watched. Slot machines were for neophytes and children were not welcome.

Those were the days when gambling was illegal in much of the US. Now that you can gamble in 47 of 50 states and now that corporations control the industry, Vegas has had to reinvent itself. The new Vegas offers a greater range of attractions appealing to the whole family. It has upped the scale and the pseudo-sophistication of its hotels and casinos, fusing the two with shops and amusements in mega, themed, hotel-casino-shopping-complexes that replicate the walk-through fantasy experiences popularised by Disneyland. Sex and sin are now just part of the package of entertainments offered by a Las Vegas that has been so sanitised that city boosters now refer to the 'Strip' as the 'Boulevard'.

If the architecture of the old Las Vegas was about vivid abstraction, the architecture of the new Las Vegas is all about replication, and hyper-replication. It is quite all right for a casino to be themed in the style of any period or any place – just so long as it has nothing to do with Las Vegas. The Luxor has a sphinx and a glass pyramid; New York-New York features a skyline to rival Manhattan; Excalibur is a riot of candy-coloured turrets to put King Arthur to shame. Popular in the recent spate of casinos have been attempts to ape European cultural sophistication. The new Paris casino-hotel crashes the Eiffel Tower into the Paris Opera House, while the Venetian links the Rialto bridge to the Doges' Palace and the Piazza of St Mark's. Bellagio tries to evoke its namesake by Lake Como.

The main attraction in Vegas buildings used to be the magnificent neon signs, such as the sizzling maracas pylon at the off-Strip Rio casino. Reliant on electric light for effect, the Strip was a queen of the night, and a shoddy backdrop by day. Now the emphasis is on three-dimensional form, overly elaborate detailing and crowd-drawing atttractions such as the dancing water fountains cavorting to the tune of *Hey, Big Spender* at the vast lagoon of Bellagio, and pirates fighting British sailors on an almost full-size frigate in front of Treasure Island.

Where neon-sign designers used to be crucial to the cityscape, now the artistry lies in the styrofoam statuary, precast mouldings, fake frescoes and aged walls, and real and faux marble and ironwork of the pastiche Renaissance detailing. In the competition for verisimilitude in the increasingly literally themed casinos, owners have become, bizarrely, leading patrons of a new kind of arts and crafts. They are plunging millions of dollars into decorative effects, and Las Vegas has become a mecca for set designers and artists from all over the world.

Las Vegas used to be seen, if anything, as anti-architecture and exurban – a linear amusement park of buildings as disposable as last year's Christmas cards plunked down in the Nevada desert for the enjoyment of weekend trippers, who were oblivious to the surrounding community. Now it consists of a cacophony of cheek-by-jowl complexes that are small cities in their own right. The newly urbanised Strip has evolved into a pedestrian environment where crowds ogle the sidewalk attractions. So successful are the new casinos that they have fuelled a building and population boom, making Las Vegas one of the fastest growing cities in the US. In 20 years, off-Strip Las Vegas has grown in tandem with the resort district from 200,000 to over a million people, spawning infrastructure, housing, schools, civic architecture and all the urban problems of 'real' cities.

ENTERTAINMENT ARCHITECTURE

The architecture that most visitors experience is the resort or entertainment architecture, most of which is located on Las Vegas Boulevard South between Tropicana Avenue and the Stratosphere tower.

Prior to the arrival of the infamous Benjamin 'Bugsy' Siegel in the mid-1940s, gambling joints had a hokey Western flavour. Then Siegel arrived from the East Coast via Los Angeles and created the Flamingo, an LA-style Moderne tropical paradise. (The Flamingo still exists but none of the original building remains.) Chic Miami/LA Moderne reigned throughout the glamorous, adults-only-in-casinos, postwar years until 1966, when the irrepressible Jay Sarno opened his instantly sensational, cheeky, pseudo-Roman Caesars Palace. A year later he opened Circus Circus. With its big fuchsia tent, overhead acrobats and kid-friendly theming, this was the first family-oriented casino to hit the Strip.

New York-New York: *Las Vegas theming at its most extreme.*

THE THEME TEAM

The stakes in the theming game escalated in the mid-1980s with the arrival on the scene of colourful Las Vegas mogul Steve Wynn. Wynn first made his mark in the early 1970s when he bought and remodelled the Golden Nugget on Fremont Street, the original gambling heart of the city. He stripped off its neon (which to him represents 'Old Las Vegas'), replacing it with a white and gold façade, thereby creating the first neon-free casino on Fremont Street. Then, in 1989, he opened the Mirage, a full-on South Seas extravaganza complete with tropical forest, exploding volcano and Polynesian-themed interiors. The Mirage melded the upscale styling of Bugsy Siegel, the fantasy of Caesars Palace and the mass-appeal of Circus Circus.

In 1993, Wynn opened the Caribbean-inspired Treasure Island, next door to the Mirage, luring people in with a streetside spectacle – buccaneering pirates fighting and defeating the British navy on an artificial lagoon in front of a make-believe cliff town. Wynn's two casinos accomplished several things – they reversed the downward spiral of Las Vegas during the late 1970s and early 1980s; they reinvented the casino as a total 'family destination resort' (although initially under-18s were banned from the Mirage); they established a trend for free spectacles and attractions in front of privately owned casinos (which are now transforming parts of the Strip into a pedestrianised – albeit privately owned – domain); they helped make the Strip more popular than Fremont Street; and they set in motion a styling contest that shows no sign of abating.

In a bid to outdo Wynn, casino operators have gone for more and more extravagant theming, with standards raised to the quality and consistency of Disneyland. Furthermore, some new resorts, such as New York-New York and, further south on the Strip, the 1993 Luxor – a vast, black glass pyramid complete with squatting sphinx – have integrated hotel, casino and sign in one structure so that the building itself is the sign.

The most southerly themed complexes are the 1993 Luxor and the newly opened Mandalay Bay, a homage to the South Seas featuring a bronze tower like an upright gilt-wrapped candy bar, a gigantic artificial beach and lagoons (the current trend in arid Vegas is for extravagant water attractions), and genuinely stylish restaurants – particularly noteworthy are the sassy Border Grill by LA architect Josh Scheweitzer (a lighter, fresher variant of the Border Grill in Los Angeles), and sleek Aureole by New York restaurant designer Adam Tihany (which features a 40-foot/12-metre high steel tower of wine bottles, which waiters have to ascend on harnesses).

But the full-on themed 'Boulevard' really starts at the intersection of the Strip and Tropicana Avenue, where you find the cartoonish Excalibur; the outdated Tropicana; the humungous, sea-green MGM Grand with its bronze lion at the entrance and giant Coke bottle marking the adjacent Showcase Mall; and New York-New York. With fire boats on a waterway, a mini Grand Central station, a 150-foot (46-metre) high Statue of Liberty and 12 jaunty, one-third real size skyscrapers,

Ceiling frescoes adorn the **Venetian**.

New York-New York represented theming at its most fully realised when it opened in early 1997.

But it was swiftly upstaged by the Euro-styled competition that followed: in late 1998, Steve Wynn unveiled his 'romantic' fantasy, the $1.4-billion Bellagio, an Italianate theme park for high-rolling grown-ups. It's got nineteenth century-style Italian villas on an eight-acre (3.25-hectare) 'Lake Como', a gallery of real, classic paintings (Picassos and Monets included) and lashings of real marble, but the basic trefoil design is hardly innovative. The most imaginative moments are the crop of glass anenomes by glass sculptor Dale Chihuly on the ceiling of the lobby, and the dancing fountains display in the middle of the 'lake', which play to hotel guests and pedestrians on the tree-lined promenade created by Wynn on his section of the Strip.

Opposite is the new Paris; it's more tongue-in-cheek than super-tasteful Bellagio, with a half-size Eiffel Tower wedged into its casino, but is no less obsessive in its attention to detail. A few blocks further north is the Venetian, whose best features are the astonishing, fake-High Renaissance frescoes on the ceilings of the entrance hall and the fact that, unlike most other Las Vegas casinos, you do not enter directly into the gaming room.

Having pretty much squeezed all the theming potential out of Europe (could a London-themed casino be next?), casino owners are looking further east; next year will see the opening of the makeover of Aladdin (3667 Las Vegas Boulevard South), to replace the 1970s remodel of the 1960s casino, notable before its demise for its *porte-cochère* and ogee-arched tower. By all accounts this will claim the title for most OTTT (over-the-top theming).

On the other side of the street sits Caesars Palace, remodelled and expanded so many times it is now a gigantic hodgepodge whose worst additions are brutish towers with twee pedimented tops. The charms of Caesars Palace are inside, and include the Forum Shops, in its heyday (1993) one of Las Vegas's most stunning themed environments. With Paris and the Venetian creating the same effects, it is hard now to imagine the initial impact of this 'Roman' shopping street complete with *trompe l'oeil* sky and lighting simulating the transition from dawn to dusk. But it was considered a ground-breaker, because it not only showed casino owners that shopping malls could be money-spinners in casino complexes, but also introduced seriously convincing aged walls and styrofoam sculptures to a city that had been quite happy with cheerfully silly evocation.

For a whiff of the 1950s and 1960s, there's very little left – though the Stardust (on the Strip, at Stardust Road) and the Riviera opposite it are worth seeing for their classic neon signs (*see page 34*, **Light fantastic**). The one building on the Strip that does give an idea of how postwar Vegas might have been is now rather dowdy but still fab – La Concha motel (next door to the Riviera), a zinging, freeform concrete structure built in 1961 by noted black Los Angeles architect Paul Williams. This era is also now starting to be recaptured, albeit less dynamically, in new buildings such as the Hard Rock Hotel, located east of the Strip at 4455 Paradise Road.

For Old Las Vegas in a new package, visit Downtown's Fremont Street, once a breathtaking street of cascading neon signs, a Glitter Gulch that included the famed Vegas Vic and Vegas Vickie (both still there). But as the fortunes of the Strip ascended, so Fremont Street fell into decline. In a bid to stop the rot, the city fathers and Fremont Street casino owners formed an unprecedented partnership and created the Fremont Street Experience, designed by the Jerde Partnership. This involved covering an entire four blocks with a high space-frame vault and pedestrianising the street. The Fremont Street Experience is a must, mainly because of the incredible 'Light Spectacular' that plays on the hour every hour in the vault. This is architecture at its most kinetic.

NON-RESORT ARCHITECTURE

Times are changing off-Strip as well. Construction in Las Vegas used to be utterly utilitarian – unadorned metal frame and concrete block tract houses and industrial buildings – catering to a low-income community: wartime military personnel stationed at the nearby Nellis Air Force Base and, now, workers servicing the casino industry and retirees. Even the housing for the wealthy was pretty boring – with the exception of a few landmarks that can be peeked at from outside walls and fences, such as brain surgeon Lonny Hammargren's self-made palace of *objets trouvés*

(4318 Ridgecrest Drive); Luxor architect Veldon Simpson's cartoonish Frank Lloyd Wright-style house (6824 Tomiyasu Lane); and Siegfried and Roy's eccentric white mansion (1639 Valley Drive).

But, recently, things have changed. With the current boom, Vegas has begun to make faltering steps towards creating a public domain. The city first drew attention to itself architecturally in the mid-1980s when it launched an ambitious library building programme. The programme was abruptly halted, however, in the early 1990s, when the library board forced director Charles Hunsberger to resign for spending tax payers' money on a building project that some considered frivolous. But nine were completed.

The most interesting are Santa Fe architect Antoine Predock's 1989 Las Vegas Library/Lied Discovery Children's Museum at 833 Las Vegas Boulevard North, a striking combo of stark, sculptural volumes (more effective from outside than in), and the pompous but curious neo-classical Clark County Library and Performing Arts Center (1401 E Flamingo Road), built in 1994 by New York post-modernist Michael Graves. The Sahara West Library and Museum (9600 W Sahara Avenue) by local architects Meyer, Scherer & Rockcastle is a lively cocktail of trendy architectural styles, while the West Charleston Library (6301 W Charleston Boulevard) displays monolithic Stonehenge-style influences. S*ee also page 199* **Culture**.

The libraries reflect an attempt by architects to create, without precedent, a Las Vegas 'high' architecture style, which seems to be characterised by earthen forms, variegated concrete block and sandy stone, pyramids, cones and dry desert landscaping. These tendencies can be seen at their most extreme in the 1985 red sandstone Clark County Government Center (500 S Central Parkway) by

CW Fentress, JH Bradburn and Associates, and in the architecturally busy Department of Motor Vehicles office (8250 W Flamingo Avenue) by Holmes Sabatini Associates Architects. A new private house, the Court House, by Eric Strain Architect on Edgemont Drive, off Eastern Avenue and Lake Mead Drive, reflects desert architecture in its soft colours and the fact that the rooms are configured around courtyards.

Among lively new buildings are two by local architects Carpenter Sellars: one a fire station that makes a feature of its flagpole (on the Strip, just south of the Luxor), and the other a dental facility on the West Campus of the Community College of Southern Nevada (on Torrey Pines Drive and Charleston Boulevard), which features a sloping tin roof and Louis Barragan-esque brightly coloured, bare walls. Also of note is a new public swimming pool (between Las Vegas Boulevard and Veterans Memorial Drive on Bonanza Road), which goes for the industrial aesthetic with large roll-up glass garage doors opening on to the sunning area.

Despite growing aspirations, the above are still only a few bright points in what remains largely an architectural desert. Non-resort Las Vegas is defined by its endless estates of one- and two-storey, single-family tract housing, laid out on mile-long blocks and much of it behind high concrete walls. As new residents keep on coming, the construction industry has gone into overdrive, building endless identikit compounds to house them. There is little evidence of planning, just an ugly chequerboard of 'leapfrog' development spreading out in all directions. Las Vegas has less than twice the population of San Francisco but sprawls over 20 times the area. Being close to the centre of town – or anything else – is seen as undesirable in a city whose roads have not yet become permanently gridlocked.

The **La Concha** motel, next to the Riviera, is a rare relic from postwar Vegas.

Affluent families are moving out in droves to the fringes of the city into residential complexes built around golf courses and artificial lakes.

However, in recent years there has been a movement to create liveable, downtown dwellings, as well as low-income housing, of which there is very little in fervently free-market Las Vegas. Eric Strain Architect is working on an affordable housing complex in Downtown – a 12-plex (six gallery spaces, six living spaces above) in the arts district at Charleston Boulevard and Main Street.

As well as simply 'gated' communities (walled housing compounds), Las Vegas, as usual, goes one step further with 'masterplanned' communities. These are town-sized swathes of privately owned land on which the management company creates an entire society, complete with housing in several price brackets, gated communities, business and commercial districts, retirement complexes, schools, hospitals and arts centres. Residents contract in to the community's rules (no cars parked in the yard,

no non-standard paintwork) and – theoretically – settle back to enjoy their suburban utopia. It's too early to evaluate the success of such large-scale socio-architectural engineering; nevertheless, people are queuing to buy in to what has become the New American Dream, sterile though it may sound. The major examples of the genre are Summerlin, out to the far west, and Green Valley, near Henderson in the south-east.

There is one structure – not a building, not in Las Vegas, not designed by an architect – that you cannot miss: the Hoover Dam. Designed by engineer John Savage, built by the Bureau of Reclamation as part of Franklin D Roosevelt's public works programme and completed in 1935, this monumental dam is a marvel of human ingenuity (and has some fine art deco touches). Though utterly utilitarian in purpose, it has all the grandeur and permanence missing from most buildings in Las Vegas, particularly the absurd, if entertaining, confections parading up and down the Strip.

Light fantastic

Even though casino mogul Steve Wynn considers it part of 'Old Las Vegas', even though new digital light technology is fast taking its place (the latest trend in signage is large pylons with digital screens televising attractions now and future) and even though some new casinos are tending to forgo spectacular signs in favour of themed buildings and streetside spectacle, neon is still synonymous with Las Vegas. Think of any Vegas image and what you see are the signs, pylons, fascias, entrance ways and *porte-cochères* so caked in neon you can't help but wonder at the statistics – Lucky the Clown outside Circus Circus, for example, has 1,232 fluorescent lamps, 14,498 incandescent bulbs and three-quarters of a mile of neon tubing, connected by 100,000 feet (30,500 metres) of electrical wiring. Lucky is still mostly neon, but has been updated with a centre screen of digital and fibre optics.

Neon has been around for a long time. The gas – neon for reds and warm colours, argon for blues and cool colours – was first discovered in England in the nineteenth century and used to light up a sign in Paris in 1910, at about which time it also appeared on the West Coast of the US. Since the 1931 legalisation of gambling, it was raised to an artform in Las Vegas.

Six sign-making companies, of which the oldest and largest is the Mormon-owned YESCO (Young Electric Sign Company), dominate a very competitive field. Sign companies compete for commissions and sometimes end up with the

job of fabrication rather than the design: YESCO, for example, constructed the Fremont Street Experience Light Spectacular, which was designed by Jeremy Railton & Associates.

Even though sign-makers work largely in teams, there are star designers – the 'sculptor-artists-geniuses of Las Vegas' referred to by Tom Wolfe in *The Kandy Kolored Tangerine Flake Streamline Baby* – who deserve public credit. Luminaries among them include YESCO's Charles Barnard, who designed Vegas Vickie; Federal Sign's Marge Williams, who conceived the extraordinary wall of stars and swirls on the Riviera; Lucky the Clown's creator, YESCO's Dan Edwards; Rudy Crisostomo, also of YESCO and designer of the Rio pylon; and Ad-Art's Paul Miller, responsible for the eternal Stardust sign.

Sign companies are developing their technology to move with the times but many insist that neon is special; not only is its light richer and brighter than the new electronic signs, but the fabrication of a neon sign is considered a time-honoured craft that no computer can replace.

Weddings

How to get hitched without a hitch in the wedding capital of the world.

When most of your state is desert, you have to make more than ordinary efforts to pull in the visitors. Since the silver ran out, Nevada's come up with a string of winning ideas – legalised prostitution, legalised gambling and quickie weddings and divorces.

Between the wars, out-of-staters (Californians, in particular) drove into the Nevadan wilderness to take advantage of the state's liberal marriage and divorce laws. The marriage industry came of age in the early 1940s, when large numbers of the GIs stationed around Las Vegas wanted speedy, no-fuss weddings before being sent abroad – and the idea of the dedicated wedding chapel was born. For the next 40 years, the Las Vegas marriage business grew steadily until the mid-1980s, when the number of marriage licences issued in Clark County started to climb dramatically. In 1986, 63,874 licences were issued; a decade later the figure had risen to 104,920. Over 110,000 weddings now take place in the county each year. In the 1970s, there were around a dozen wedding chapels in Vegas; today, there are more than 50. What happened?

Much of the marriage boom is tied in with the city's general growth. As more people than ever before come to Vegas to gamble, more than ever before come to wed. The wedding business has learned to market itself as aggressively as any other industry. Look in a phone book in Pigswill, Iowa, and most of the wedding chapels listed will be in Las Vegas; scour the Internet and you'll find most chapels have their own websites (one offering a live Internet broadcast of your ceremony so even those who cannot make it, can); visit an international travel fair and you'll see the bigger chapels touting their services to the world market.

YOU'VE GAMBLED ONCE...

Another boost was provided by the big casinos jumping on the (already fast-moving) wedding bandwagon. Initially, casinos were rather sniffy about the marriage game (where's the sense in taking out 50 slots to make room for a chapel?), but, since the late 1980s, they got wise. What's the most popular post-nuptial activity in Vegas? You've guessed it – gambling. And if you marry in a casino, you'll probably gamble away your honeymoon in the same casino. So in came the chapels, often more elaborate than the little stand-alones, but rarely more tasteful (and always more expensive).

Welcome to fabulous married life...

The Tropicana hotel's 'tropical island' chapel comes complete with waterfalls, palm trees and swans; the Stratosphere built its chapels 800 feet (244 metres) above the Strip (although these have now ceased operating – money can't always buy you into the love business). Many casinos also provide elaborate honeymoon suites – such as the capacious Buccaneer Bay suite at Treasure Island – offering a taste of the sort of luxury that usually only serious high-rollers enjoy (except that honeymooners have to pay, of course).

TRAD OR TRASH?

Anything goes in Vegas – if you've got the money to pay for it. Irreverence and kitsch have always played a big part in the marriage business here. Want Elvis to serenade you in the chapel? Fancy dressing like an ancient Roman to get spliced? Want to bungee jump to your destiny? You got it. For $300 including a video and minister's fees, you can say your vows at the top of a bungee tower

Celebrity splicings

- Paul Newman and Joanne Woodward (El Rancho, 1958)
- Errol Flynn and Beverley Adland (Silver Bell Chapel, 1962)
- Jane Fonda and Roger Vadim (Dunes, 1965)
- Elvis Presley and Priscilla Beaulieu (Aladdin, 1967)
- Joan Collins and Peter Holm (Little White Chapel, 1985)
- Bruce Willis and Demi Moore (Little White Chapel, 1987)
- Richard Gere and Cindy Crawford (Little Chapel of the West, 1992)
- Noel Gallagher and Meg Matthews (Little Chapel of the West, 1997)
- Dennis Rodman and Carmen Elektra (Little Chapel of Flowers, 1999)

and then take the plunge, quite literally, courtesy of **AJ Hackett Bungy** (385 4321). Or, to really start your married life on a high, **Las Vegas Helicopters** (736 0013; www.lvhelicopters.com) charges $249 to $449 plus $50 minister's fees for an aerial wedding above the Strip.

Yet here is one of Vegas's many paradoxes. More and more couples are rejecting the wacky and tacky, and wearing white wedding dresses rather than purple togas; walking down the aisle to Pachelbel rather than Billy Idol. Most brides and grooms want to buy into the Vegas dream only up to a point; to get a whiff of the glitz without losing all touch with middle-American reality. As one wedding co-ordinator notes, the words 'Las Vegas' alone are often enough to impart the needed nuptial pizzazz.

And here's a second paradox: easy, cheap and fast as a Nevadan marriage is, relatively few Las Vegas weddings are what-the-hell, on-a-whim affairs (the union of basketball star Dennis Rodman and model-actress Carmen Elektra notwithstanding). The great majority of couples are from other states or abroad; they plan their weddings in advance and shell out considerable sums for airfares and accommodation. Few of their weddings end up being either cheap or quick. Again, it's that vicarious Vegas vibe that pulls them in – the thrill of following in the train of famous couples such as Priscilla and Elvis, Demi and Bruce, Cindy and Richard (*see above* **Celebrity splicings**); the feeling of getting married in Disneyland.

REQUIREMENTS

The straightforward, liberal marriage laws in Nevada are the main reason for the popularity of Las Vegan weddings. The requirements are the same for US and non-US citizens. No blood tests are needed and there's no waiting period between obtaining the licence and exchanging vows. All that is necessary is for both parties to present themselves at the **Clark County Marriage License Bureau** at first floor, 200 S Third Street (455 3156/outside office hours 455 4415; open 8am-midnight Mon-Thur, 8am Fri-midnight Sun) with some form of picture ID (a passport, for instance) and $35 in cash for the marriage licence. No appointment is necessary; the process shouldn't take longer than ten minutes. If you want to think it over first, the licence is good for a wedding in Nevada for up to one year.

From here, it's a one-block walk to the office of the **Commissioner of Civil Marriages** at 309 S Third Street (same hours as above) for an instant $35 civil ceremony. Or head for a wedding chapel.

WHAT WILL IT COST?

Getting married in Las Vegas is not only easy and fast, but relatively cheap. If a quick service at the Commissioner of Civil Marriages suffices, $70 is all you need fork out. Chapel services cost more – the most basic ten-minute, in-and-out ceremony will cost upwards of $125 including licence. Legally, all weddings must be witnessed; chapels will normally supply a witness without charge.

Most chapels offer various levels of package (subject to a number of extra costs), including arranging the licence if necessary. At the most basic end, expect to pay $50-$60 for use of the chapel, pre-recorded music (you can usually bring your own if you object to Mendelssohn) and, perhaps, a wedding scroll. Add in photographs (typically, six to 12 prints), a bouquet and a buttonhole, and the cost rises to $100-$200; a video recording and a limo will bump it up to at least $250. It pays to shop around at the pricier end of the scale – there's a lot of variation between chapels. Extras are also available à la carte – expect to pay a minimum of $99 for gown hire, $55 for tuxedo hire, $25 for a bouquet, $5 for a buttonhole. Be warned: most chapels reserve the right to provide all professional services themselves (including photos, flowers and video recording).

HIDDEN EXTRAS

Only qualified ministers can officiate at wedding chapel services and, because they are rarely employees of the chapel, a 'donation' of at least $40 will be expected (to be handed over discreetly after the service) on top of the chapel fee. If you want the minister to come to you, then expect to pay more. If you splash out on a limo, it's usual to tip the driver upwards of $25. Read between the lines when comparing the deals offered by chapels. For instance, all will provide a professional photographer on request, but few will let you take the negatives away; the idea being that you come back to the chapel (and pay extra) for further prints. All chapel packages are also subject to sales tax.

BREAKING UP IS EASY TO DO

And if it does all turn out to have been a horrible mistake, the flip side is that divorce couldn't be easier. A six-week residency requirement, minimal costs – easy come, easy go. Nevada has always drawn plenty of prospective divorcees from other states (especially California, where you have to wait six months) and continues to do so. An uncontested divorce can cost as little as $147 – good job, too, since you've got six weeks to gamble away the rest of the divorce settlement.

The rest of the US, while getting a guilty kick out of Nevadan naughtiness, has never been comfortable with such basically un-American values. Many states are considering legislation to introduce 'covenant marriages' whereby couples agree to have pre-marital counselling to assess whether they really are doing the right thing. Could Nevada follow suit? The land of immediate gratification and to hell with the consequences? The state that draws a hefty chunk of its tourist revenue from marriage business? What do you think?

The ever-popular **Little White Chapel** *(p38).*

Las Vegas is the wedding chapel capital of the world. It's not the only place in the US where you'll find these nuptial equivalents of fast-food joints (seems like a great idea beforehand, leaves you feeling queasy afterwards), but nowhere has spawned chapels in such number and nowhere has that special glitzy Vegas cachet. Yet, while a few, like the Little Church of the West (built in 1942 and the oldest building on the Strip), are picturesque, most are disappointingly small, tacky and decidedly unromantic, with all the atmosphere of a tarted-up garden shed.

The experience is perforce impersonal, with the minister – who has already officiated at a dozen hitchings before yours – pausing to glance at his script every time the service requires he mention your name. And most chapels are located in the less than salubrious section of the Strip between Circus Circus and Fremont Street, amid pawn and porn shops. Admittedly this adds a certain kitsch value, but if you want a bit more class, think about getting spliced in a casino chapel. The newer mega-resorts, in fact, are getting into weddings in a big way, capitalising on their meticulously detailed theme elements to make the ceremonies special (it's a uniquely Las Vegas mix of the classy and the offbeat to be married in a gondola on the Venetian's faux Grand Canal). We list six of the more interesting chapels below.

Bellagio Wedding Chapel

3600 Las Vegas Boulevard South, at W Flamingo Road, NV 89177 (1-888 987 3344/693 7700). Bus 202, 301, 302. **Open** 8am-6pm daily. **Credit** AmEx, DC, Disc, MC, V.

In keeping with this mega-resort's feeling of understated elegance, the goal of its chapel is the opposite of the stereotypical 'Vegas wedding'. No Elvis impersonators, no glitz. The atmosphere is posh and unhurried. Bellagio promises a wedding as lavish as one you'd pay $30,000 for at home, at a fraction of the price (although at $1,500 and $2,500, it's still among the priciest in the chapel business). The wedding area is decorated in an American version of European styling, heavy on peach and antique hues, draperies and chandeliers. The co-ordinator can supply all the flowers, photography and special touches you need. Throughout 2000, Bellagio is offering a 'Millennium' wedding package for $4,580. *Website: www.bellagiolasvegas.com*

The Chapel at Monte Carlo

3770 Las Vegas Boulevard South, at Rue de Monte Carlo, between W Flamingo Road & Tropicana Avenue, NV 89109 (1-800 822 8651/730 7575). Bus 201, 301, 302. **Open** 10.30am-7.30pm Mon-Fri, or call for appointment. **Credit** AmEx, Disc.

Among the more reasonably priced of the mega-resort chapels, the Monte Carlo has four packages that range from $220 to $995. For this you get a pleasant ceremony with all the trimmings, in the French-Victorian

chapel, complete with hand-painted murals. Let's be honest – this isn't Bellagio, with its $1.6 billion in appointments, but for those without Bellagio-style dollars, it's a fine substitute.
Website: www.monte-carlo.com

Divine Madness Fantasy Wedding Chapel

111 Las Vegas Boulevard South, at Fremont Street & Bridger Avenue, Downtown, NV 89101 (1-800 717 4734/384 5660). Bus 107, 301, 302. **Open** 10am-7.30pm Mon-Thur, Sun; 10am-10pm Fri, Sat. **Credit** DC, Disc, MC, V.
What this chapel lacks in tradition, it makes up for in outrageous cheek. Choose your wedding outfit from a huge wardrobe of costumes that range from virginal white lace to raunchy black leather. Fancy yourself as Cleopatra? Captain Kirk? Lorenzo de' Medici? Step this way. Themed rooms provide a suitably flamboyant backdrop. Weddings cost $175 or $275 including costumes for the bridal couple.
Website: www.fantasychapel.com

Graceland Wedding Chapel

619 Las Vegas Boulevard South, between Charleston Boulevard & Bonneville Avenue, Downtown, NV 89101 (1-800 824 5732/382 0091). Bus 206, 301, 302. **Open** 9am-9pm Mon-Thur, Sun; 9am-midnight Fri, Sat. **Credit** AmEx, DC, Disc, MC, V.
A favourite with rockers (such as Jon Bon Jovi) and their chicks. Should you so wish, Elvis will walk the bride down the aisle, strum a little light background music during the ceremony and then have everyone crying in the chapel with a moving mini-concert afterwards. Prices are $50-$200 plus minister's fees.
Website: www.gracelandchapel.com

Little White Chapel

PO Box 15229, 1301 Las Vegas Boulevard South, at Charleston Boulevard, Downtown, NV 89114 (1-800 545 8111/382 6134/iwedu@littlewhitechapel.com). Bus 206, 301, 302. **Open** 24 hours daily. **Credit** AmEx, Disc, MC, V.
The flagship of Charolette Richards' three-strong chapel chain (plus one hot-air balloon – 'my little white chapel in the sky', from $650) is famed for its friendliness and unique drive-by wedding window, the 'Tunnel of Love' ($60-$100). In close to 40 years, Charolette has married more than 300,000 couples and has become something of a cult figure. She swears she is still touched by each pairing – and the strange thing is, we believe her.
Website: www.littlewhitechapel.com

Venetian Wedding Services

3355 Las Vegas Boulevard South, just south of Sands Avenue, NV 89109 (1-877 883 6423/414 4242). Bus 301, 302. **Open** call for appointment.
This is the only wedding service in Vegas that offers singing gondoliers (so far, at least). The replica of Venice's famed Grand Canal inside the Venetian, including a painted skyscape on the ceiling, makes a lovely backdrop for a marriage ceremony. Depending on your package ($499-$1,450), you can be married on one of the canal's sides or in a gondola.
Website: www.venetian.com

Dress hire

Not surprisingly, the chapels try to keep control of related services – you won't be allowed to arrange your own flowers, photographer, Elvis, etc. But no one can stop you turning up in a frock or frock coat that you've rented elsewhere.

I&M Formalwear

3345 S Decatur Boulevard, between W Desert Inn & Spring Mountain Roads, South-west Las Vegas (1-800 249 5075/364 4696). Bus 103. **Open** 9am-7pm Mon-Fri; 9am-5pm Sat; 11-3pm Sun. **Credit** MC, V.
This outfit claims to have the biggest selection of famous-name wedding gowns and dresses in town. Prices range from $135 to $375, including any alterations and cleaning, for a three-day rental.

Tuxedo Palace

Renaissance Center West, 4001 S Decatur Boulevard, suite 21, at W Flamingo Road, South-west Las Vegas (1-800 777 1884/367 4433). Bus 103, 104, 202. **Open** 9am-6pm Mon-Thur; 9am-7pm Fri; 9am-5pm Sat; 11am-4pm Sun. **Credit** AmEx, Disc, MC, V.
You'll find a huge selection of tuxes here (all black, give or take some lapel detail). They cost from $50 to $109.95 for a two-day rental, including trousers, waistcoat and all accessories except shoes ($10-$15). The Bridal Salon within the store has bridesmaids' dresses from $65 and wedding dresses ranging from $99 to $450.

Williams Costume Company

1226 S Third Street, between Colorado Avenue & Charleston Boulevard, Downtown (384 1384). Bus 206, 301, 302. **Open** 10am-5pm Mon-Sat. **Credit** AmEx, Disc, MC, V.
Williams Costume Co, with more than 10,000 frocks in stock, is the only place in town that carries enough ancient Egyptians, Elvises and Pioneers (the latest trend) to dress the bride, groom and guests, too, for that matter. Rental costs run between $50 and $100 per night with a hefty deposit (from $50).

Wedding consultants

Aird & Associates

454 0646/daird@gte.net **Open** 8am-5pm Mon-Fri; by appointment Sat, Sun.
This nuptial consultant specialises in customised and themed ceremonies, particularly ethnic-specific marriages, but also covers the entire spectrum of offbeat, wacky weddings, from bungee jumping to elaborate costumes.

Andrea's Wedding Consultants

367 7799. **Open** 9am-5pm Mon-Fri; hours may vary. **Rates** wedding packages from $189. **Credit** MC, V.
This outfit has arranged ceremonies with celebrity impersonators, as well as in the spectacular outdoor settings surrounding Las Vegas, such as Red Rock Canyon and the Valley of Fire.

Sightseeing

Casinos

A complete overview of all Las Vegas's major casinos.

Nothing defines Las Vegas like its casinos. Ever since mobster Bugsy Siegel built his 'Fabulous Flamingo' in 1946, Las Vegas has been recognised, if not characterised, by its casino resorts. Mention Las Vegas and you evoke quicksilver images of Circus Circus's big top, the Luxor's pyramid, the Mirage's volcano, MGM's lion and, more recently, Paris's Eiffel Tower, the Venetian's canals and Bellagio's fountains.

As the city has grown, so have the size and scope of its casinos. The circus acts and midway games at Circus Circus pale in comparison with the Mirage's volcano or the Venetian's canals. Resorts like the Excalibur, Luxor and New York-New York were among the first to build their themes into their architecture. A pyramid, medieval castle and the Manhattan skyline plus the Statue of Liberty were a quantum leap from the simplistic pioneers such as the now-departed Dunes, Sands and Hacienda hotels.

Casino amenities have also evolved, especially over the past half-decade. The pirate battle at Treasure Island, for instance, has all the elements of a staged production – actors, music, pyrotechnics and, most of all, drama. Most recently, resorts have endeavoured to recreate exciting destinations in a Las Vegas setting. Bellagio, for instance, uses Tuscan architecture and a huge Strip-side lake to evoke the classic imagery of Italy. And Paris sprouted a half-sized Eiffel Tower to mimic France's capital. Why travel the world when you can visit Vegas, where the world will come to you?

The modern casino typically towers 30 storeys high and contains 3,000 rooms, as well as a mind-boggling array of amenities and attractions, ranging from adventure parks, bungee jumps and roller-coasters to water parks and convention centres. Construction costs routinely top $1 billion, and the roster of employees reads like the white pages of a small suburban community. Each of the larger hotels has a staff of between 4,000 and 7,500, who each day cater to guests' every hedonistic need.

Casinos offer all the amenities and services a visitor could want: accommodation, gambling, restaurants, nightlife, cocktail lounges and at least one production show or celebrity showroom. Recently, hoteliers have discovered tourists spend money outside the gambling hall, so the trend is to add shops to the mix of hotel amenities. In addition, spas and health clubs have become popular for a variety of services – massage, tanning booths

and other creature comforts – to go along with the aerobics classes and weights room.

Whatever gingerbread surrounds it, the heart of a resort is still the casino floor. Depending on the time of day or night, the action can be hot and furious as slot players shovel coins into machines and crap players whoop it up in the dice pit, all set to the distinctive soundtrack of clinking glasses, rattling chips, tinkling coins and the electronic arpeggios of slot machines. Once inside a casino, it can be difficult to get out again. There are no windows, few information desks and no clocks. Exits are poorly signed and direct access to them is blocked by slot machines arranged in maze-like patterns. The casino owners want to keep you there – and keep you gambling.

After all, it's the casino that makes the money – on the Strip, gambling accounts for 50 per cent of resort revenues, while hotel rooms bring in 20 per cent. And we're talking a lot of money. In the fiscal year 1999 (ending 30 June 1999 – the last for which figures are available), gambling revenues for Clark County totalled $6.7 billion. The casinos on the Strip alone won $366 million, of which slots and video poker machines amassed a staggering $243 million – no wonder they dominate every casino floor.

ADVICE & ETIQUETTE

There is little casino etiquette to worry about. Whatever you wear will be fine, from shorts to a dinner jacket (though you may want to carry a sweater – it may be 110°F (43°C) outside but the air-con will be deliberately chilly to dissuade you from leaving). All casinos are open 24 hours, have ATMs and multilingual dealers. For information on casino accommodation and other facilities such as health spas, *see chapter* **Accommodation**. For gambling etiquette and information on the various games, *see chapter* **Gambling**.

This chapter is divided into three main casino categories. **The Strip** is ruled by Disney-esque mega-resorts. **Downtown** is more of a jamboree where carny-like casino hawkers virtually snatch in passers-by and the gambling is down and dirty (low-budget beginners start here). More subdued in design and atmosphere are the **locals casinos**, which are targeted mainly at residents, but friendly atmosphere, budget rates and unique amenities make them attractive to visitors, too.

Las Vegas's casino scene is highly volatile, with resorts frequently opening, closing, expanding and

Best for...

Learning to gamble
Caesars Palace, home to Barney Vinson, author of several books on gambling and reputedly the city's best gaming instructor.

Playing roulette
Wherever they offer a single-zero wheel as standard, such as the **Stratosphere** or the **Monte Carlo** (although minimum bets will be higher). And head for the **Gold Spike** (400 E Ogden Avenue, Downtown) if you're really hard-up: the minimum is only 10¢.

Playing craps
The **Stratosphere** offers 100× odds while **Binion's Horseshoe** is known far and wide for its lively and raucous craps action.

Watching poker
Binion's Horseshoe, especially when the world's best players gather for the annual World Series of Poker tournament in spring.

Watching high-rollers
Wherever the high-limits room is not shielded from public gaze and you can just stand and gawk. Try the **Golden Nugget** and the **Rio**, the baccarat rooms at **Caesars Palace** and **Desert Inn** or the centre tables, by the cage, at **Binion's Horseshoe**.

Sexiest staff uniforms
Female: the cocktail waitresses at the Rio – widely acknowledged as the most revealing, sorry, appealing.
Male: the Roman gladiator-types with short leather tunics at Caesars Palace.

Becoming an instant millionaire
The 'Million Dollar Baby' slot machines at **Caesars Palace**. Unlike most progressive jackpots, which pay off in installments over ten or 20 years, these machines pay the million and change to the winner in one lump sum, right on the spot.

Best toilets
Women will find perfumes, hairspray, mints and an attendant at Drai's restaurant in the **Barbary Coast** (next door to the Flamingo Hilton), while men can pee in front of a futuristic light display in the toilets at the **Las Vegas Hilton**'s Space Quest Casino.

Worst carpets
Let's face it, most casino carpets are garish and tasteless but the **MGM Grand**'s are particularly stomach-churning – don't walk through here with a hangover.

Best video poker
The **Stratosphere** probably has the most machines returning over 100 per cent, while the **Gold Spike** has penny machines you can use as training aids.

All seven deadly sins
Caesars Palace, without a doubt. Avarice and gluttony in the casino and restaurants, of course; sloth in the Garden of the Gods pool area; pride and wrath follows winning and losing; envy of the high-roller guests; and lust for the toga-clad waitresses (and waiters). And if the eighth sin is poor grammar, Caesars gets that, too.

---

changing hands. The latest news is that the New Frontier on the northern end of the Strip is to be imploded in summer 2000, to make way for a San Francisco-themed casino called City by the Bay – but there may be others yet to be announced.

LISTINGS INFORMATION
The address we've given for each casino is also its main entrance: this is where to head whether you're on foot or driving, and where you'll find valet parking and directions to the self-parking garages, which are usually around the back. In some cases, the casino also has another entrance at the side or back, which is particularly useful if you're in a car and don't want to be always driving up and down the often traffic-choked Strip: for example, you can reach the parking areas at Caesars Palace from Industrial Road. To make it clear, we've listed which streets to take for valet parking and self-parking.

We've indicated which attractions – bars, restaurants, shows and so forth – are reviewed in more detail elsewhere in the guide, and we've also provided specific gambling information at the end of each casino review. This indicates which table games the casino offers, including more unusual games such as Pai Gow Tiles and Spanish 21; the minimum and maximum betting limits for baccarat, mini baccarat and blackjack; and the principal odds for craps (with variations where they are known to us). Remember that limits do fluctuate and minimum bets tend to be higher on the Strip, and in the evening, at weekends and during special events. For roulette, we've said if a casino offers only double-zero wheels (which have both a single-zero and a double-zero slot – the more common type) or if it also has a wheel with only a single-zero slot (which offers better odds for the gambler). Note that nearly all casinos offer keno and a sports book.

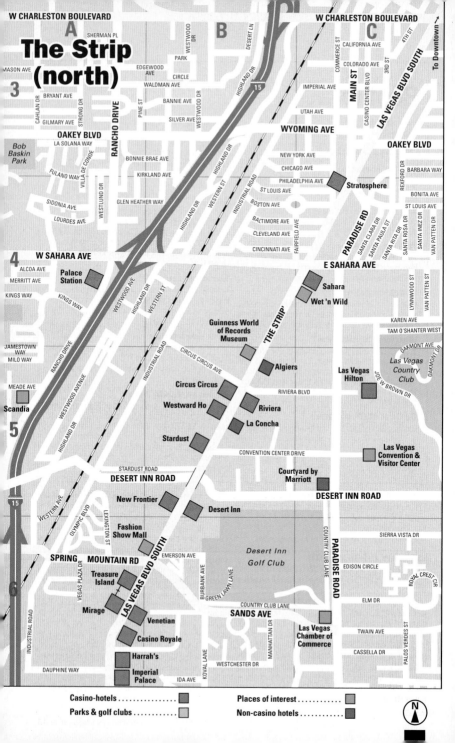

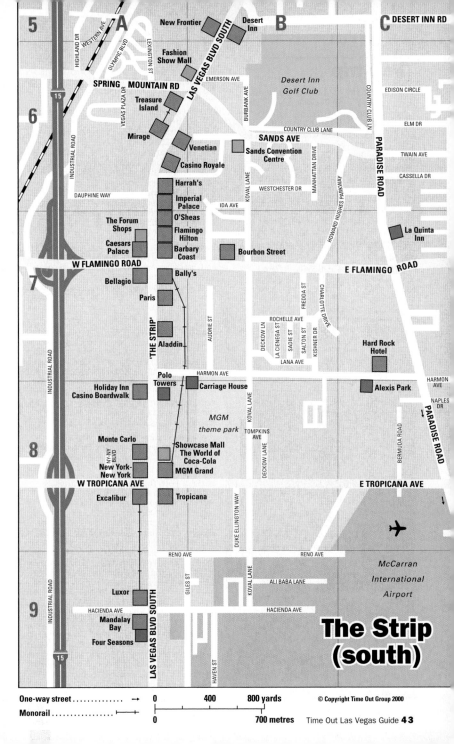

The Strip (south)

The Strip

The vast majority of casinos in Las Vegas are on the three-and-a-half-mile (5.6-kilometre) stretch of Las Vegas Boulevard South – aka the Strip – between **Mandalay Bay** casino at the south end and the **Sahara** at the north. The **Stratosphere**, although on Las Vegas Boulevard South, is not officially on the Strip and sits in a no-man's land (known, prosaically enough, as the Stratosphere Area and also as Naked City) between the top of the Strip and Downtown. There are also a few casinos that are 'Strip-like' in terms of size, décor and theming, but actually lie a few blocks off the Strip – these are the **Rio**, **Gold Coast** and the **Orleans** (to the west) and the **Hard Rock** and **Las Vegas Hilton** (to the east).

Aladdin

3667 Las Vegas Boulevard South, at Harmon Avenue, Las Vegas, NV 89109 (736 0111). Bus 301, 302.

Due to open in summer 2000, the new $1.3-billion Aladdin rises from the rubble where the original hotel stood before it was demolished in 1998. In keeping with the original hotel's Arabian Nights theme, the Aladdin will be punctuated with design features such as the phoenix from one of Sinbad the Sailor's tales, giant winged horses guarding the

Looking south down the Strip.

sports book, a two-storey replica of Scheherazade's Palace and the signature Aladdin's lamp. The centrepiece of hotel amenities will be the Desert Passage complex, a meandering collection of 130 shops and 21 restaurants, nightclubs and lounges set against backdrops ranging from Tangiers marketplaces to a North African harbour front.

The 100,000sq ft (9,300sq m) casino will have 87 table games, 2,800 slot machines, a live keno lounge and a race and sports book. Well-heeled players will like the London Club, a luxurious European-style casino within a casino developed by London Clubs International, featuring 30 high-limit tables including blackjack, roulette and baccarat and 100 high-denomination slot machines. The second phase of construction (timetable not yet announced) will include the Aladdin Music Project, with a second 1,000-room hotel and casino.

Entertainment

The Aladdin will stage a nightly production show, and headliner entertainment in the renovated 7,000-seat Theater for the Performing Arts, which was left over from the casino's previous incarnation and spared the blasters' caps. The New York-based Blue Note Jazz Club will present jazz and blues artists from around the world.

Eating & drinking

Expect innovative Southwest specialities at the Santa Fe-based Anasazi restaurant, and country Italian cuisine at Bice. The world's finest caviar can be savoured in its namesake, Beluga, which will feature a turn-of-the-century wharf bar motif. At the Macanudo Steakhouse & Club, diners will be able to indulge themselves with aged steaks, vintage wines and premium cigars.

Website: www.aladdincasino.com

Highlights reviewed in other chapters
Nightlife Aladdin Theater for the Performing Arts (p232).

Bally's

3645 Las Vegas Boulevard South, at E Flamingo Road (739 4111). Bus 202, 301, 302.
Self-parking & valet parking Las Vegas Boulevard South; E Flamingo Road.

Bally's was originally built as the MGM Grand in 1973 by multi-billionaire Kirk Kerkorian. In its original incarnation, the movie-themed resort offered an enticing combination of old Hollywood class and new Vegas flash. Bally's bought the place in 1985 and attempted to carve out its own identity, but the process seemed gradual to the point of reluctance. As late as 1996, the hotel ballrooms still carried their MGM names of Garland and Gable. That year, the Hilton Hotel Corporation bought Bally's for $3 billion – it remains a resort without a theme, but it's a class act, as understated in its charms as Las Vegas gets. Following the recent Las Vegas resort trend of building properties out to the street, Bally's installed a moving sidewalk, surrounded by a series of futuristic, colour-changing neon hoops and columns, palm trees and cascading fountains (cost: $14 million).

Inside, the casino is one large, rectangular space, a luxurious and inviting atmosphere of soft lighting and art deco accents. Not surprisingly, the machine selection includes all the latest creations from leading gaming-machine maker Bally Manufacturing, including laserdisc versions of craps, roulette and blackjack – these are excellent practice tools for getting comfortable with the games before heading to the actual tables. The buy-ins at the tables are lower than you might expect, though most of Bally's players wager far more than the minimum. The sports book, located on the lower level, is as classy and technically advanced as those in Caesars and the Las Vegas Hilton, but it's rarely crowded. At the back of the casino (so a bit of a trek) is a free monorail to the MGM Grand (open 9am-1am daily; departs every five minutes). An indoor walkway leads to the Paris resort next door.

Entertainment
A salute to classic Hollywood spectacle, *Jubilee!* is the ultimate old-time Las Vegas production show, and the only holdover from the property's days as the MGM Grand – where else can you watch the *Titanic* sink twice nightly, and not have to hear Celine Dion sing about it? The Celebrity Showroom shut down in 1999, to make room for the shop- and restaurant-laden promenade leading to the Paris resort next door. Headliners of an earlier Vegas era, such as Paul Anka, George Carlin and Englebert Humperdinck, alternate with *Jubilee!* in the remaining showroom.

Eating & drinking
Dining highlights include the Sterling Sunday Brunch and the Big Kitchen Buffet. Chang's, a terrific Chinese restaurant that was evicted from Caesars Palace for a Planet Hollywood, re-emerged at Bally's with quality and atmosphere intact. The Italian specialities at Al Dente have been winning rave reviews among a strong local clientele.
Website: www.ballyslv.com

Gambling
Gambling lessons.
Baccarat ($100-$5,000); mini baccarat ($5-$5,000); blackjack ($5-$5,000); Caribbean Stud; Casino War; craps (3× on 4 & 10, 4× on 5 & 9, 5× on 6 & 8); Let It Ride; Pai Gow Poker; roulette (single & double zero); Spanish 21.

Highlights reviewed in other chapters
Casino Entertainment *Jubilee!* (p217).
Restaurants & Buffets Bally's Big Kitchen (p157), Bally's Sterling Brunch (p158), Chang of Las Vegas (p136).

Bellagio
3600 Las Vegas Boulevard South, at W Flamingo Road (1-888 488 7111/693 7111). Bus 202, 301, 302.
Self-parking Las Vegas Boulevard South.
Valet parking Las Vegas Boulevard South; Flamingo Road.

Steve Wynn's latest creation is his most inspired. Set on the site of the old Dunes hotel and golf course, Bellagio opened in 1998 to rave reviews for its

Bellagio's *Italian lake and conservatory.*

Tuscan-style architecture, high-end art gallery, upscale shopping promenade and designer restaurants. Most of the hotel's shops and restaurants overlook an eight-acre (3.25ha) lake that faces the Strip. At night the lake comes alive with a dazzling fountain ballet that sends streams of water hundreds of feet into the air, choreographed to music as diverse as Strauss and Copland. The tree-lined sidewalk assures plenty of vantage points; other good viewpoints are from the lakefront restaurants or the top of the Eiffel Tower (at Paris casino) across the street. Enhancing Bellagio's charm is its conservatory, behind the hotel lobby, a huge, glass-roofed greenhouse of exotic flowers and plants. And its Gallery of Fine Art is a first in Las Vegas, bringing the works of Cézanne, Degas, Picasso, Gauguin, Matisse and other masters to visitors more used to Disney-like spectacles than high culture.

Bellagio is geared to well-heeled adult guests; in fact, it's downright child-unfriendly – under-18s and strollers are turned away, unless they're accompanied by adults who are guests of the hotel. The rooms are among the most expensive on the Strip and most of the dining facilities are high-end. Shops along the Via Bellagio, a walking version of Rodeo Drive, are a veritable A to Z of designer names, from Armani through Chanel to Tiffany.

The casino is luxurious if rather vulgar; the uphol-stery, carpets and striped canopies above the tables are a clash of colour and patterns. Still, it offers all the usual games including 21, roulette, craps, keno and baccarat. There is also a separate poker room and Pai Gow Poker. Celebs such as Drew Barrymore (playing $5 blackjack) and Dennis Rodman have been known to play here. As you might expect, table limits are higher than at most Strip properties: it's difficult to find a $5 blackjack game (maybe they opened one just for Drew) – minimums are often $25-$50. The race and sports book is one of the most comfortable in town: the low-slung seats have special headrests to help relax your spine.

Entertainment

An international cast of synchronised swimmers, divers, acrobats, aerialists and characters charm audiences in Cirque du Soleil's *O*, a new production from the famed Canadian circus, which also stages *Mystère*, at another Mirage resort, Treasure Island. Like its cousin down the street, the show is highly visual and often borders on the surreal.

Eating & drinking

Along with Mandalay Bay, Bellagio helped pioneer the influx of so-called celebrity chef restaurants. For fine French cuisine, check out Le Cirque (chef Sirio Maccioni) or sample regional cuisine of France and Spain at Julian Serrano's Picasso restaurant. Olives, a casual Mediterranean restaurant, traces its roots to Boston, where chef/owner Todd English has generated a loyal following of gourmands. Other choices include Prime (a steakhouse), Jasmine (a gourmet Chinese restaurant), Shintaro (a sushi bar) and Noodles (a traditional Asian noodle kitchen). If your tastes run to the exotic, try the Petrossian Bar, for caviar, champagne and smoked salmon.
Website: www.bellagioresort.com

Gambling

Baccarat ($100-$15,000); mini baccarat ($25-$15,000); blackjack ($5-$10,000); Caribbean Stud; Casino War; craps (2×); Let It Ride; poker; Pai Gow Poker; Pai Gow Tiles; roulette (single & double zero).

Highlights reviewed in other chapters

Attractions Casino freebies (p82).
Casino Entertainment *O* (p217).
Restaurants & Buffets Aqua (p152), Bellagio Buffet (p158), Le Cirque (p140), Noodles (p154), Olives (p141), Osteria del Circo (p147), Picasso (p141), Prime (p153).
Shops & Services Via Bellagio (p171).

*Bring your toga to the Garden of the Gods pool complex at **Caesars Palace**.*

Caesars Palace

3570 Las Vegas Boulevard South, at W Flamingo Road, Las Vegas, NV 89109 (731 7110). Bus 202, 301, 302.
Self-parking & valet parking Las Vegas Boulevard South; Industrial Road.

This opulent, Roman-themed fantasy palace epitomises the uniquely Las Vegan vision of luxury for the masses in a kitsch, no-holds-barred rendition untrammelled by any sense of irony. 'All that Caesar could, you have and can do,' wrote Ralph Waldo Emerson, and this feeling of unbounded potential embraces you from the moment you approach the signature entrance fountains. They've been the backdrop for countless films, the site of the infamous near-fatal motorcycle jump by Evel Knievel in 1969 (three years after the hotel opened), and witnessed a successful jump by Evel's son Robbie in 1989. Other corporations have developed bigger and more expensive properties since, but there is a timeless glamour to Caesars that is unmatched in Las Vegas or anywhere else, OTT though it may be.

Painstakingly crafted Italian marble abounds, in statuary, temples, heroic arches and ornate pediments. The Italian cypresses that line the property's rolling driveways are perfectly manicured, as are the buffed gladiators and centurions who greet guests as they arrive. And speaking of buffed, check out the rather tough-looking cocktail waitresses in togas. Empires must expand or fall: the Forum Shops, with their artificial sky and statues that come to life, have doubled in size, and a 29-storey Palace Tower has brought the total number of rooms to 2,500. There's also a new health spa and fitness facility, new restaurants and the football field-sized Palace Ballroom.

For gambling, few casinos offer the limits or the atmosphere of Caesars. On the main floor, the limits are generally as high as the Roman columns and when there's a big boxing match in town, they can go sky-high. The sports book is one of the highest-energy spots to watch live competition on big-screen TVs and accepts some of the highest bets. You get a good view of the baccarat pit, an intimate nook where wagers of $100,000 per hand are not uncommon. And for the boldest of slot players, the $500 machine – with a $1-million jackpot – uses gold-plated tokens. The machine itself only pays a jackpot of two $500 coins, so if the $1-million jackpot is won, the machine locks and an attendant pays the gambler. The high-limit slots are in the Palace Casino, near the main entrance. For the more plebeian, the blackjack pits and slots in the Forum Casino offer lower limits.

Entertainment

When the big names in Vegas-style entertainment come to town – recent among them Natalie Cole, Patti LaBelle and Huey Lewis & the News – Caesars' Circus Maximus Showroom is where they play. The casino also has three of the better lounges in the city, including the famed floating Cleopatra's Barge. An outdoor arena hosts world championship boxing, tennis and ice hockey, while the Omnimax cinema boasts a screen that sweeps 180° over and around the viewer. Techno buffs should try the Race for

Atlantis ride: it's the world's first IMAX 3-D motion simulator, situated in the Forum Shops – and it's pretty good. Avoid the Magical Empire, billed as an underground labyrinth where soothsayers and conjurers perform while patrons dine – it's really just an overpriced dinner accompanied by below-average trickery from amateur magicians.

Eating & drinking

Caesars' restaurant list is one of Las Vegas's most diverse and contemporary. At the high end, try the Bacchanal, famous for six-course feasts, Middle Eastern-style dancers and a soothing massage for the bill payer (who'll need it), or the haute cuisine French cuisine of the Palace Court. The Empress Court and Hyakumi Japanese Restaurant & Sushi Bar carve up the Orient between them. The La Piazza foodcourt and the Palatium Buffet – one of the best buffts in town – take care of the lower end. The Forum Shops mall is also good for dining, with outposts of big-brand restaurants including the upscale Spago, the Palm, Chinois and Caviarteria, and the Cheesecake Factory.
Website: www.caesars.com

Gambling

Gambling lessons. Games designed for sight- & hearing-impaired players.
Baccarat ($100-$15,000); mini baccarat ($20-$10,000); blackjack ($5-$3,000); Caribbean Stud; Casino War; craps (3× 4 & 10, 4× 5 & 9, 5× 6 & 8); Let It Ride; Pai Gow Poker; Pai Gow Tiles; roulette (single zero & double zero); Spanish 21.

Highlights reviewed in other chapters

Attractions Casino freebies (p82), Cinema Ride (p79), Omnimax Theater (p80).
Casino Entertainment Caesars Magical Empire (p215), Circus Maximus Showroom (p218), Cleopatra's Barge (p210).
Restaurants & Buffets Bertolini's (p145), Caviarteria (p152), Cheesecake Factory (p134), Chinois (p142), Palace Court (p141), Palatium Buffet (p161), Palm (p153), Spago (p144), Stage Deli (p138), Terrazza (p147).
Shops & Services The Forum Shops (p170).

Circus Circus

2880 Las Vegas Boulevard South, at Circus Circus Drive, between Desert Inn Road & W Sahara Avenue (734 0410). Bus 301, 302.
Self-parking Industrial Road. **Valet parking** Las Vegas Boulevard South; Industrial Road.

In the Las Vegas of the 1970s and 1980s, Circus Circus was the only family entertainment in town. Parents dropped off their kids under the big top, and then dashed away to lose their inheritance in the casino. Today's Las Vegas offers many more options for visitors with children, but Circus Circus is still the first stop on the family tour. The circus theme pervades every aspect of the place, though recent changes and additions have cut back on the glaring pinks and yellows. Traditionalists need not fear, however – the place is still a noisy carnival of cotton candy colours, as surreal as a Fellini movie in its medley of clowns, carousers and crass commercialism.

Circus Circus: *heaven for low-rollers...*

There are three full-sized casinos dispersed throughout the resort, connected by walkways and a monorail; a total of 107,000sq ft (9,950sq m), each offering the same gaming options (and some rather long walks). The circus acts are visible from the main casino; the race book is located near the back of the resort, in the Skyways Tower area. Wherever you play, it may take all day to find someone risking more than $10: Circus Circus is low-roller heaven, and a dollar or two will start you off at most tables. The mezzanine features a video arcade, free circus entertainment and sugary sweets.

'Classy' was never an adjective that came to mind when describing Circus Circus – Howard Hughes complained that it brought 'the poor, dirty, shoddy side of circus life' to the Strip – but the lobby, bedecked in royal purples and golds, draws its inspiration from nineteenth-century European circuses rather than American big-top extravaganzas and is unexpectedly beautiful. Of course, a place where you can stand on a revolving platform pumping dollar tokens into a clown-face slot machine while trapeze artists fly over your head can only be so refined. After building the upscale Mandalay Bay resort, Circus Circus Enterprises changed its name in 1999 to Mandalay Resort Group to reflect its changed and more upmarket image.

Entertainment

Adventuredome, an indoor amusement park under a giant pink dome, houses rollercoasters, a re-creation of a Pueblo Indian cliff dwelling and several mechanical dinosaurs. It almost makes sense when you actually see it. Inside the casino, there is seating for the free (though rather less-than-spectacular) circus acts on the mezzanine. Acrobats, trapeze artists, high-wire daredevils and magicians perform every 30 minutes from 11am to midnight.

Eating & drinking

The Steak House is the only quiet sanctuary under the big top. The mesquite-grilled steaks, aged for 21 days, live up to their billing. The Circus Circus Buffet serves over 10,000 people a day, and at times it seems as if they're all in line in front of you. A $9.5-million renovation, finished in 1999, has spruced up the setting, but the food's still mediocre at best. The Pink Pony coffeeshop is classic Vegas kitsch.
Website: www.circuscircus-lasvegas.com

Gambling

Gambling lessons.
Mini baccarat ($5-$5,000); blackjack ($2-$5,000); Caribbean Stud; Casino War; craps (10×); Let It Ride; Pai Gow Poker; poker; roulette (double zero).

Highlights reviewed in other chapters

Attractions Adventuredome (p78), AJ Hackett Bungy (p87), Casino freebies (p82).
Bars & Cafés Carousel Bar (p162).
Restaurants & Buffets Circus Circus Buffet (p159); The Steak House (p154).

Desert Inn

3145 Las Vegas Boulevard South, at E Desert Inn Road (733 4444). Bus 301, 302.
Self-parking & valet parking Las Vegas Boulevard South; Sands Avenue; Fashion Show Drive.
Too small to be considered a mega-resort and too historical to be converted into a futuristic hotel, the Desert Inn is in a class by itself. The half-century old resort, once owned and occupied by reclusive billionaire Howard Hughes, served for years as a plush-carpeted playground for wealthy high-rollers. In more recent times, it suffered something of an identity crisis as some of the polish wore off and newer themed resorts sprang up around it. But, after a $200-million face-lift completed in late 1997, the Desert Inn has emerged as a full-service, five-star-style hotel with 700-odd rooms – sizeable enough, but also small enough to retain its old-time exclusivity. Its public areas are adorned by gold-leafed

*...and the **Desert Inn**, home of high-rollers.*

*The fairytale castle of **Excalibur** looms above the Tropicana/Strip intersection.*

domed ceilings, crystal chandeliers and columns; the five-storey high Grand Lobby, which is designed to block out all casino sounds, is especially impressive, with a panoramic view of the Strip through the expansive glass wall.

The casino, while relatively small, offers a full complement of table and slot games. But the action here is not for the faint of heart: limits are high, especially at weekends, and all the blackjack action is dealt from six-deck shoes. Figure on $25 minimums, and that's in the main casino. In the casino's high-limit 21 and baccarat room, $500 minimum stakes are not uncommon, and the casino has taken bets as high as $200,000. If you don't want to risk a lot of cash, you're better off walking across the Strip to the Frontier. On the other hand, if you do play at the Desert Inn, and get lucky, you could end up with a small fortune (or a large one – a Monte Carlo cocktail waitress won a world record $34.95 million on a Megabucks slot machine in January 2000). The smiling floor supervisor will then offer to comp your room (so that you don't leave the property) – settle for nothing less than an opulently furnished poolside casa in the Villa Del Lago. Hughes himself never had it so good.

Entertainment

Just behind the hotel, the Desert Inn's 18-hole, palm-studded championship golf course is the only one on the Strip. Indoors, the 530-seat Crystal Showroom, where the likes of Frank Sinatra, Liza Minnelli, Shirley MacLaine and Juliet Prowse have held court in years past, still offers top-name celebrity entertainment, with the smaller Starlight Lounge a more intimate choice.

Eating & drinking

Excellent food is served in the hotel's three gourmet restaurants: the Monte Carlo (French), Portofino (Mediterranean) and Ho Wan (Mandarin, Cantonese and Sichuan). Snack-hunters should head for the Terrace Point, a pretty 180-seat coffeeshop serving buffet meals and sandwiches.
Website: www.desertinn.com

Gambling

Baccarat ($100-$10,000); mini baccarat ($25-$10,000); blackjack ($5-$5,000); Caribbean Stud; craps (5×); Let It Ride; Pai Gow Poker; Pai Gow Tiles; roulette (double zero).

Highlights reviewed in other chapters

Restaurants & Buffets Monte Carlo Room (p140), Portofino (p147).

Excalibur

3850 Las Vegas Boulevard South, at W Tropicana Avenue (597 7777). Bus 201, 301, 302.
Self-parking & valet parking W Tropicana Avenue.

The Excalibur resort is a perfect illustration of the accelerated evolutionary curve in Las Vegas. Built all the way back in the Year of Our Lord 1990, the property already seems like a throwback to yesterday's Las Vegas. The towering spires of its Bavarian castle façade now seem almost quaint, especially when compared to the more inventive and detailed architecture of New York-New York, its neighbour to the north. By any other standard, the resort is still quite charming. The bright red, blue and gold spires of the castle are beautifully illuminated at night, though they look a little prefabricated by day. Make sure you use the main entrance, on the moving

*Low-limits table games at **Excalibur**.*

sidewalk that leads from the Strip through the always-open drawbridge. The paths on each side wind though trees as thick as Sherwood Forest, and you could get lost in there for days.

Inside, the casino and common areas are often crowded but never uncomfortably so. The medieval theme is well developed through special slots, tournaments and promotions. It's especially fun to visit around Christmas, when light displays and a visit from Santa Claus enliven the Medieval Village Shoppes. For adults travelling with children, the resort is as family-friendly as Circus Circus, and not quite as noisy. Neon knights slay neon dragons in the 100,000sq ft (9,300sq m) casino, one of the few in town in which photography is allowed. Visitors are surrounded by images of playing-card kings and queens, but the table games are affordable for any commoner. Ten-cent slot and video poker machines – hard to find in Las Vegas – join the more common 5¢, 25¢ and $1 varieties. When you're done throwing coins in machines, toss a few in the moat for good luck – they'll be donated to local charities.

Entertainment

Tournament of Kings, with armour-clad knights on horseback squaring off against the forces of evil, is one of the few dinner shows left in Las Vegas (be prepared – you eat with your fingers). Wandering minstrels and other period acts perform throughout the day outside the Medieval Village Shoppes, and on the Fantasy Faire Midway, carnival games offering stuffed animal prizes pitch for those last few quarters that escaped the slots. If you play 'guess your weight' with the friendly barker, be warned that you have to step on a giant set of scales that will display your weight across the midway.

Eating & drinking

There are five restaurants in Excalibur, the best of which is Sir Galahad's Prime Rib House, where huge portions of beef are cooked to order and served with the best Yorkshire pudding in town; before going in, check out the replica of the resort, built to scale in chocolate. The Nitro Grill, a wrestling-themed restaurant owned by the World Championship Wrestling federation, serves 'broken' chicken fingers and 'Choke-hold Chili'. Fans view live events on giant screens and WCW stars visit almost weekly

for autograph sessions. For dessert, the American doughnut delicacy Krispy Kreme is served on the promenade – they're best while still warm.
Website: www.excalibur-casino.com

Gambling
Gambling lessons.
Mini baccarat ($5-$100); blackjack ($3-$2,000); Caribbean Stud; Casino War; craps (2×); Let It Ride; poker; Pai Gow Poker; roulette (single & double zero).

Highlights reviewed in other chapters
Attractions Casino freebies (p82).
Casino Entertainment Tournament of Kings (p215).

Flamingo Hilton

3555 Las Vegas Boulevard South, at E Flamingo Road (733 3333). Bus 202, 301, 302.
Self-parking & valet parking Las Vegas Boulevard South; Audrie Street.

A half-century ago, when Benjamin 'Bugsy' Siegel opened the 'Fabulous Flamingo' in the middle of nowhere, every employee including the janitors wore tuxedos. Today, the Strip site of the Flamingo Hilton is one of the busiest intersections in the world, and the hotel has evolved into a lavish resort with a 15-acre (6ha) tropical water playground. Although the dress code has been greatly relaxed – only the penguins in the resort's outdoor wildlife sanctuary wear black tie – the hotel is still very stylish. And it has one of the most memorable neon creations in the city: pulsing pink and orange flowers and flamingos along the entire front of the building. After a series of 'seamless' expansions, the resort now has 3,642 rooms. In the original, Siegel incorporated a maze of underground tunnels in which to seek refuge from surprise visitors in pin-striped suits. Today, he could pick his hiding spots among lavish tower suites and lush gardens and meandering streams that provide a haven for ducks, swans, penguins and flamingos. Amenities include five pools, four tennis courts, a health club and lots of upscale shops. The interior is filled with white marble walkways and mirrored glass and decorated with ersatz flora; check out the three banyans at the buffet entrance.

The casino area, accented by bright pinks, yellows and tangerines, offers you a real chance to survive: craps and blackjack minimums are a reasonable $3, and there are several new games with simple rules, such as Casino War. It's tougher to come out ahead in the slot area, which contains 2,100 machines, none considered especially loose. Hey, the last renovation cost $130 million! The casino conducts numerous slot tournaments, but they're not for the squeamish – entry fees average $2,000. There's also a lively card room, keno parlour and a sports book linked to the one at the Las Vegas Hilton.

Entertainment
The long-legged Rockettes in the long-running *Great Radio City Spectacular* (a homage to New York's Radio City Music Hall) in the 740-seat main showroom is better than you would think. *Forever Plaid*, in the smaller Bugsy Celebrity Theater, is an off-Broadway tribute to the 1950s and 1960s.

*The Egyptian-themed **Luxor**, at the south end of the Strip. See page 52.*

Eating & drinking

The Flamingo has a clutch of top-end international restaurants, with top-end international prices to match. Chinese cuisine is served against a background of carved teakwood at the Peking Market; you'll find succulent steaks and sushi at Hamada of Japan; and Alta Villa serves posh Italian. For a quick, low-cost bite, try Bugsy's Deli – and avoid the buffet and coffeeshop if possible.
Website: www.hilton.com/hotels

Gambling

Mini baccarat ($5-$3,000); blackjack ($3-$3,000); Caribbean Stud; craps (3× 4 & 10, 4× 5 & 9, 5× 6 & 8); Let It Ride; Pai Gow Poker; roulette (double zero).

Highlights reviewed in other chapters

Attractions Casino freebies (p82).
Casino Entertainment *Forever Plaid* (p216), *The Great Radio City Spectacular* (p216).

Harrah's

3475 Las Vegas Boulevard South, between Sands Avenue & E Flamingo Road (369 5000). Bus 301, 302.
Self-parking & valet parking Koval Road.

Just across the Strip from the Roman splendour of Caesars Palace and the South Sea-styled Mirage is Harrah's. Opened in 1973, and once called the Holiday Casino, Harrah's has seen many changes over the years. Its most recent incarnation was as a huge paddlewheeler but after the latest change – a $200-million upgrade completed in October 1997 – it has emerged with a worldwide carnival motif. In other words, insipid murals of festivals, bright colours, mirrors and a dark glass façade that fronts the Strip – one can't help but long for a few

deckchairs on the fan tail. Entertainers and musicians wander through the Carnaval Court, a festive patio area at the front entrance punctuated by shops, fountains, foliage and a diaphanous canvas cover supported by a maypole.

There's a wide selection of table games, including Caribbean Stud, Let It Ride and Casino War. Most blackjack games are dealt from the shoe, but higher limits – at least $25 minimum – are dealt from hand-held decks. Occasionally the gracious pit bosses will bring in the European single-zero roulette wheel for high-rollers. For lively action, take a seat in the compact poker room, while the race and sports book offers booths and table seating, with tableside food and drink service contributing to a sports-pub atmosphere. The casino area has been expanded by a third, but the 'Party Pit', once located at the north Strip entrance, has been removed. This was a mistake. The loose festive feel of the place, accentuated by low limits and dealers who jazzed it up like carnival barkers, can never be replaced.

Entertainment

Contemporary singer Clint Holmes performs live in Takin' It Up Town, in the main showroom. Top comics play the Improv, the hotel's comedy club, and owner Budd Friedman sometimes drops by. For more spontaneous fun, catch a band at La Playa, the city's first indoor-outdoor bar.

Eating & drinking

The Range Steak House is impressive, with towering mahogany pillars, copper accents and a panoramic view of the Strip through floor-to-ceiling windows. There are also Asian and Italian restaurants. For cheaper eats, the Fresh Market Square Buffet is good,

but be selective if you visit the 24-hour Garden Café coffeeshop. For a quick snack, you'll do better at walk-up coffee bar Club Cappuccino.
Website: www.harrahslv.com

Gambling
Gambling lessons.
Baccarat ($20-$10,000); mini baccarat ($20-$5,000); blackjack ($5-$5,000); Caribbean Stud; craps (2×); Let It Ride; poker; Pai Gow Poker; Pai Gow Tiles; roulette (double zero).

Highlights reviewed in other chapters
Casino Entertainment The Improv (p210), La Playa (p211), *Takin' It Up Town* (p216).
Restaurants & Buffets Fresh Market Square Buffet (p160).

Luxor
3900 Las Vegas Boulevard South, between W Tropicana Avenue & Russell Road (262 4400). Bus 301, 302.
Self-parking & valet parking Reno Avenue.
The stark shape of the Luxor's black glass pyramid, identifiable from planes cruising at 30,000ft; the laser beam shooting skywards from its apex, supposedly visible from 200 miles (350km) away (smog levels permitting); and, of course, the ten-storey replica of the Sphinx that squats at its entrance are all designed as giant billboards to lure the crowds. Some are disappointed – the Luxor is generally regarded as a 'warehouse' casino with little atmosphere to back up its impressive exterior. However, there's no denying that the $650-million resort is perfectly suited to its desert setting and to the modern vision of Las Vegas.

Like most properties on the Strip, the Luxor undergoes frequent (and expensive) changes. During the most recent $300-million renovation, nearly 2,000 rooms were added. The latest addition is an exterior lighting system: the black pyramid used to disappear against the night sky – not a good idea if the outside of your building is its main selling point. However, the changes won't satisfy superstitious Asian gamblers, who reputedly dislike the Luxor for being, basically, a tomb. Inside, the pyramid shape remains evident – a relief for those who prefer the interior of a building to bear some relation to its exterior, a rare commodity in this town. 'Inclinators', high-gradient escalators, take guests to their rooms, accessed from internal balconies (from where at least one bankrupted gambler has launched a suicide dive). The casino area takes up pretty much the entire ground floor; the buffet is down below, and shopping and entertainment are on an attractive, albeit un-Egyptian mezzanine.

The massive casino area, decorated with hieroglyphics and ancient artefacts, is filled with the latest high-tech slot and video poker machines. $5 minimums are the norm at the blackjack and crap tables. For poker players, the card room on weekend nights offers lively action that Cleopatra herself would appreciate.

Entertainment
Luxor has gone all out for the family and adolescent market with a gambling-free mezzanine stuffed with state-of-the-art attractions: there's a 3-D IMAX cinema and one of the best games arcades in the city. The full-scale reproduction of King Tutankhamen's Tomb contains a glittering inventory of handcrafted Egyptian artefacts. Adult entertainment in the form of a new topless revue, *Midnight Fantasy*, takes the stage in the evening. Alternatively, Bill Acosta's *Lasting Impressions* show is a tribute to former Vegas celebrities. There's also a very popular nightclub called Ra.

Eating & drinking
The Pharaoh's Pheast Buffet offers made-to-order cooking stations, and the taste is above average. You'll find a healthy selection of California cuisine at the Millennium Café, and if you're successful in the casino, consider Isis, the Luxor Steakhouse or the five-star Sacred Sea, three gourmet restaurants serving steak and seafood.
Website: www.luxor.com

Gambling
Gambling lessons.
Baccarat ($100-$15,000); mini baccarat ($5-$3,000); blackjack ($5-$5,000); Caribbean Stud; Casino War; craps (2×); poker; Pai Gow Poker; Pai Gow Tiles; roulette (single & double zero).

Highlights reviewed in other chapters
Attractions IMAX Theater (p80), King Tut's Tomb & Museum (p85).
Casino Entertainment *Lasting Impressions* (p215), *Midnight Fantasy* (p214).
Nightlife Ra (p226).
Restaurants & Buffets Isis (p136).

Mandalay Bay
3950 Las Vegas Boulevard South, between W Tropicana Avenue & Russell Road (632 7777). Bus 301, 302.
Self-parking & valet parking Hacienda Avenue (off Las Vegas Boulevard South).
Surf's up and it's always high tide at Mandalay Bay. At the heart of the resort, opened in March 1999, is an 11-acre (4.5ha) tropical water park that features a sandy beach with its own wave-making machine. If you're timid with the white water, there are two other pools, a lazy river ride and a jogging track set among lush green foliage and fountains. Occupying the old Hacienda site and now the southernmost casino-hotel on the Strip, the hotel's gold Y-shaped tower is a striking addition to the Vegas skyline, visible from practically everywhere – it looks particularly resplendent in the afternoon sun. The interior is pretty impressive, too: the South Seas theme (despite the resort's name) has resulted in island-style architecture, a spacious lobby, plenty of fake foliage and water features, and a generally classy air. A corridor off the lobby leads to the very upscale Four Seasons hotel, which shares the same site but is a separate concern. The resort also boasts two wedding chapels and a large health spa open to non-guests (for a fee). The only disappointment are the shops – but never fear, a huge mall between the Luxor and Mandalay Bay, anchored by the city's first Nordstrom's, is due to open in early 2001.

*The **MGM Grand** and its signature lion.*

The 135,000sq ft (12,500sq m) casino is airier and more spacious than many. It has 2,400 machines, including the new nickel slots that take up to 45 and 90 coins, such as Chairman of the Board and Reel 'Em In. You have to hunt for the better video poker machines. Table games (122 of 'em) include blackjack, roulette, craps, Let It Ride, Caribbean Stud, Pai Gow Poker and mini baccarat. You'll also find a poker room – fast becoming a rarity on the Strip – where you can play seven card stud, Texas Hold 'Em and Omaha Hold 'Em. The race and sports book has 17 large screens and nearly 300 seats .

Entertainment

What Mandalay lacks in visitor attractions, it makes up for in dining and entertainment choices. Bob Fosse's hit Broadway musical *Chicago* is a good choice if you've seen enough cleavage and G-strings, while the House of Blues has become a popular hangout for late-night jazz and R&B buffs. The 12,000-seat Events Center hosts superstar rock concerts (Bette Midler, the Eagles, ZZ Top and Ricky Martin were recent performers) as well as major sporting events, such as the second Evander

Holyfield-Lennox Lewis heavyweight title bout. The Rumjungle nightclub is crammed practically every night, and in the milder months, concerts are often held at the outdoor island stage on the beach.

Eating & drinking

Mandalay Bay is unusual in placing its restaurants all together in a separate area away from the casino – so you can drop in for a meal and not even see a slot machine (the self-parking garage leads straight to the restaurant area). It was also among the first to lure celebrity chefs from places like New York and San Francisco. Among them, Charlie Palmer set up shop in a designer version of his New York bistro, Aureole, which boasts one of the premier wine lists in the city (and a four-storey wine tower, to boot). Chefs Suzan Feniger and Mary Sue Milliken – from TV show *Too Hot Tamales* – present modish Southwest dishes at the pleasantly funky Border Grill (located next to the convention centre). Another pop icon of the dining business, Wolfgang Puck, opened Trattoria del Lupo for traditional Italian favourites with a California-chic twist. Other options include China Grill (Asian), Shanghai Lilly's (Chinese) and Red Square, a Moscow-inspired joint offering caviar, vodka and whispers of the pending revolution. You can't miss it – it's the one with the headless statue of Lenin outside.
Website: www.mandalaybay.com

Gambling
Baccarat ($100-$15,000); mini baccarat ($25-$15,000); blackjack ($5-$15,000); Caribbean Stud; craps (2×); Let It Ride; poker; Pai Gow Poker; Pai Gow Tiles; roulette (single & double zero).

Highlights reviewed in other chapters
Bars & Cafés Red Square (p163), Rumjungle (p163).
Casino Entertainment *Chicago* (p216), Coral Reef Lounge (p210).
Nightlife House of Blues (p233), Red Dragon Lounge (p226), Rumjungle (p226).
Restaurants Aureole (p136), Border Grill (p148), Red Square (p151), Trattoria del Lupo (p147).

MGM Grand
3799 Las Vegas Boulevard South, at E Tropicana Avenue (891 1111). Bus 201, 301, 302.
Self-parking Las Vegas Boulevard South; Koval Avenue. **Valet parking** E Tropicana Avenue.
Kirk Kerkorian's MGM Grand, the world's largest resort hotel with over 5,000 rooms (at least, until the second phase of the Venetian is complete), made something of a business blunder when in 1993 it set out to appeal to the family market. Since then it has scrapped its *Wizard of Oz* theme, dismantled its animatronic Oz attraction, removed the cartoony lion's-mouth entrance (largely because it was a big turn-off for superstitious Asian gamblers) and torn down part of its outdoor, family-oriented Grand Adventures theme park to build more hotel rooms and a convention centre. A 70ft (21m) high bronze sculpture of a lion now presides over the intersection of Tropicana and the Strip, and there are real lions on view in the small but popular Lion Habitat. The MGM is spread out over 114 acres (46ha): pay

close attention to the overhead signs or you will get lost. Looking for an elevator? There are 93 on the property. The casino area alone is the size of four football fields, while the valet parking area is wider than the San Diego Freeway.

Now billed as 'The City of Entertainment', the MGM has four gaming areas – Entertainment, Hollywood, Monte Carlo and Sports – where you'll find all the games, including Spanish 21, a version of blackjack with more strategy options but fewer ten-value cards. Table minimums can go down to $5 on weekdays but most are higher; in the Monte Carlo pit you'll find $25 minimums, $10,000 maximums – and single-zero roulette. The décor throughout is glittery and glitzy, with rainbow-patterned carpets, mirrored emblems and metallic stars: sort of Busby Berkeley on valium. There's also a large race and sports book with floor-to-ceiling screens and a very lively poker room, one of the best in town. As for slots, there are 3,700 of them, ranging from a nickel to $500. A monorail connects the MGM to Bally's.

Entertainment

Tommy Tune puts on a surprisingly good performance in *EFX*, the hotel's $45-million music and special effects theatrical production in the EFX Theatre. Barbra Streisand opened the hotel in its Grand Garden Arena and returned to usher in 2000; other stars to play the 16,300-seat venue have included the Beach Boys, Rolling Stones, Elton John and 'N Sync. There's also championship boxing (Mike Tyson et al) and other sporting events. The more intimate Hollywood Theater presents regular concerts with Penn & Teller, Randy Travis and Carrot Top. Nightclub Studio 54, modelled on the famous 1970s New York disco, is a big success.

Eating & drinking

The MGM lays on some of the best eating in town, with great pizzas at the Wolfgang Puck Café, excellent Southwest cuisine at Mark Miller's Coyote Café and nationally acclaimed seafood at Emeril Lagasse's New Orleans Fish House. The Brown Derby, a re-creation of the popular 1920s Hollywood eaterie, offers a good steak and even the signature Cobb salad and grapefruit cake from the original menu, and for Continental and French cuisine, Gatsby's is second to none. Kids will enjoy the Rainforest Café, complete with fake jungle and real parrots.

Website: www.mgmgrand.com

Gambling

Gambling lessons.
Baccarat ($100-$15,000); mini baccarat ($25-$15,000); blackjack ($5-$10,000); Caribbean Stud; Casino War; craps (2×; 3× 6 & 8); Let It Ride; Pai Gow Poker; Pai Gow Tiles; roulette (single zero & double zero); Spanish 21.

Highlights reviewed in other chapters

Attractions Lion Habitat (p78), Grand Adventures Theme Park (p79), Sky Screamer (p88).
Casino Entertainment *EFX* (p216), Hollywood Theatre (p218).
Nightlife MGM Grand Garden (p233), Studio 54 (p226).

Restaurants & Buffets Brown Derby (p152), Coyote Café (p148), Emeril's (p135), TreVisi & La Scala (p148).

Mirage

3400 Las Vegas Boulevard South, between Spring Mountain & W Flamingo Roads (791 7111).
Bus 301, 302.
Self-parking Spring Mountain Road. **Valet parking** Las Vegas Boulevard South.

Steve Wynn's tropical-themed hotel set the industry standard for modern mega-resorts when it opened in 1989. The Mirage has become a haven for high-rollers and a major draw for those of us without a private jet. Even if you never drop a quarter into a slot, there's plenty to do. And many of the resort's attractions are free, among them the famed erupting volcano on the Strip; the tropical atrium just inside the front entrance filled with 60ft (18m) high palm trees, waterfalls and lush foliage; and the huge fish tank behind the hotel reservation desk. Avoid, however, the Dolphin Habitat – not worth the money – and the not-so-secret Secret Garden – you can see Siegfried & Roy's white tigers for free in a glass-encased habitat in the casino.

Despite its huge size, the $730-million resort is surprisingly easy to find your way around, partly because the gaming areas are broken up into a conglomeration of Polynesian-styled villages, each with its own thatched roof – though note that it can get ridiculously busy, especially at weekends. There are nearly 100 blackjack tables, most dealt from six-deck shoes. As you would expect, minimums are high: $5 for 21 and roulette, $25 for mini baccarat, $100 for baccarat. Unless you have deep pockets, it's probably better to consider the pit area as visual rather than interactive entertainment. You can find a good game of poker at any hour of the day, and since many players are tourists, the action (both low- and high-limit) is good. You'll also find a variety of alternative table games, such as Let It Ride and Casino War.

For a break, check out the high-limit slots. If you're polite, and it's not too busy, an attendant will show you around, and perhaps offer you some fresh, sliced fruit, normally reserved for players who insert $100 tokens, five at a time. The Red, White & Blue slot offers a $1-million jackpot – though, like the machine at Caesars Palace, only the first $1,000 is paid out in gold coins. Two of them.

Entertainment

Unless you have an overpowering urge to have a tiny red heart pasted to your face and to pay an exorbitant amount to be able to tell your friends that you saw *Siegfried & Roy*, you might want to pass on the city's best-known illusion act. What the show boasts in pyrotechnics and costume, it lacks in spontaneity – and let's face it, Siegfried's not getting any younger. Acclaimed impersonator Danny Gans has recently moved to the Mirage, to his own purpose-built theatre, after a long stint at the Rio (and a short one at the Stratosphere). You can hear light jazz and reggae in the Lagoon Saloon or classic melodies and torch songs by a lone pianist in the Baccarat Bar (which, along with the Sports Bar, is the best place to play 'Can that really be his wife?'). There's no cover at either.

Eating & drinking

Top-class (and top-priced) restaurants include Melange, where you'll find French American cuisine and walls decorated with Picassos. The menu at Ristorante Riva offers regional Italian cooking; chef Tom Jannarone also teaches culinary arts at the Community College of Southern Nevada. For more reasonable family dining, try California Pizza Kitchen. And the Mirage Buffet is one of the best in town; we recommend the bread pudding.
Website: www.themirage.com

Gambling

Baccarat ($100-$15,000); mini baccarat ($25-$15,000); blackjack ($5-$10,000); Caribbean Stud; Casino War; craps (3× 6 & 8); Let It Ride; poker; Pai Gow Poker; Pai Gow Tiles; roulette (single zero & double zero); Spanish 21.

Highlights reviewed in other chapters

Attractions Casino freebies (p82), Dolphin Habitat & Secret Garden (p77).
Casino Entertainment *Danny Gans: The Ultimate Variety Performer* (p214), Lagoon Saloon (p211), *Siegfried & Roy* (p215).
Restaurants & Buffets California Pizza Kitchen (p151), Mirage Buffet (p160).

Monte Carlo

3770 Las Vegas Boulevard South, at Rue de Monte Carlo, between W Flamingo Road & Tropicana Avenue (730 7777). Bus 201, 301, 302.
Self-parking & valet parking Rue de Monte Carlo.

This $344-million joint venture between Mirage Resorts and Circus Circus Enterprises (as it was then known) went from conception to completion in just 15 months, and has proven one of the most appealing entries in the mid- to high-end resort market. The twin archway entrances, adorned by classical statuary and majestic fountains, have had flash-bulbs popping since the hotel first opened in 1996. This being Las Vegas, one half-expects the statues to break into song, but such theatrics would not be appropriate for a resort modelled on the Place du Casino in Monaco.

The resort's continental *Lifestyles of the Rich and Famous* theme is perfectly captured in the resplendent lobby area, so authentically European that Americans may expect to be asked for a passport. A magnificent crystal chandelier hangs from a dome in the centre of the casino, surrounded by imported marble and tiny white lights tracing geometric patterns in the ceiling. Perfume is subtly pumped in to offset the more colourful scent of tourists who walked over from the MGM Grand in soaring summer temperatures.

*And you thought the **Mirage**'s volcano was real?*

The bright lights of **New York-New York***: so good they named it twice.*

There's an abundant selection of $5 blackjack tables, plenty of 5¢ opportunities among the 2,200 slot machines and the atmosphere is bright and casual. But it's the smaller touches that players may appreciate most, such as chairs with backs at every machine instead of stools, wider walkways through the casino and the European-style single-zero roulette wheel. The Monte Carlo attracts brisk traffic from neighbouring casinos, but the tables never seem crowded. Players stand a better chance of landing a one-on-one blackjack game with the dealer here than at most Strip mega-resorts. Despite its austere posture, the Monte Carlo is actually one of the more kid-friendly hotels in Vegas; there's a huge video arcade, a wave pool and a lazy river, and a fast-food court with burgers, hot dogs and ice-cream. However, the monorail to Bellagio will not allow riders aged under 18 unless they are Bellagio registered guests.

Entertainment
Magician Lance Burton – actually one of the more innovative magicians in town – disappears six nights a week in the appropriately named Lance Burton Theatre. The Victorian-style showroom was designed specifically for its headliner, and its plush seating will delight Las Vegas show veterans who are used to being packed like sardines at long tables arranged perpendicular to the stage.

Eating & drinking
André Rochat, the man who in 1979 opened Las Vegas's first laudable French restaurant, brings his culinary act to the Strip at André's, the Monte Carlo's

marquee eaterie. Besides the de rigueur buffet and coffeeshop, there are other dining options: the Market City Caffe is a quaint trattoria; the Dragon Noodle Company features a speciality tea bar and four types of Asian cuisine; and there's also Blackstone's Steak House and the Monte Carlo Pub & Brewery, both good, though not outstanding.
Website: www.monte-carlo.com

Gambling
Gambling lessons (poker).
Baccarat ($25-$15,000); mini baccarat ($10-$5,000); blackjack ($5-$5,000); Caribbean Stud; craps (2×); poker (8 tables); Pai Gow Poker; Pai Gow Tiles; roulette (single & double zero).

Highlights reviewed in other chapters
Casino Entertainment *Lance Burton:*
Master Magician (p215); Monte Carlo Pub & Brewery (p212).
Restaurants & Buffets: André's (p138).

New York-New York
3790 Las Vegas Boulevard South, at W Tropicana Avenue (740 6969). Bus 201, 301, 302.
Self-parking Las Vegas Boulevard South;
W Tropicana Avenue. **Valet parking** W Tropicana Avenue.
How fitting. 'The city that never sleeps' comes to the city that really never sleeps. Built for $460 million by MGM Grand and Primadonna Resorts and opened in January 1997, New York-New York is Las Vegas-style theming at its most extreme – there isn't a more colourful, eye-catching building in the city. It's been called the 'largest piece of pop art in the

world', and its dozen towers, one-third real-size copies of the Empire State building, Chrysler building et al, are magnificently rendered. A 150ft (46m) replica of the Statue of Liberty looms over the intersection of Tropicana and the Strip, and a mini-Brooklyn Bridge serves as a walkway to the Strip entrance. Above them all the Manhattan Express rollercoaster twists, turns and rolls, with a 144ft (44m) dive past the hotel's valet entrance.

Inside, you'll find every New York cliché, from a fake subway station to graffitied mail boxes. The steaming manhole covers in the Village Eateries area are a particularly clever touch. The slot club is cheekily named the New York-New York Slot Exchange and the cashiers cages are in (where else?) the Financial District. The attention to detail is amazing, although the layout is rather chaotic: it may be yet another homage to the Big Apple, but the real Manhattan is far easier to navigate.

The 84,000sq ft (7,800sq m) casino area is modelled on Central Park, with street lamps, a footbridge over a winding stream and fake trees in autumnal colours. It's pleasant and picturesque, and you don't have to worry about muggers (though a hot dealer will take your money just as fast). But everything's more expensive in NYC, and the tuxedo-backed chairs at the gaming tables set the right tone. Minimums for blackjack (practically all six-deck shoes) are $5 and $10, $5 for craps and $1 for roulette. There's a terrific variety of slot machines – one of the best on the Strip – in all the usual denominations.

Upstairs, the Coney Island Emporium mixes Daytona-style interactive driving simulators with low-tech carnival games. It's one of the only arcades in town with real personality: ghoulish kids will love the 'electric' chair. Carny hawkers wear straw hats, garters, vests and striped shirts, and you can hear the screams from the riders starting their journey on the Manhattan Express.

Trivia point: note the old-fashioned Pepsi and Pete sign at the front of the property on the Strip, opposite the World of Coca-Cola and the MGM Grand (where only Coca-Cola is served). Only Pepsi is served at New York-New York. Las Vegas has become the latest battleground in the cola wars, and the stakes are enormous. Coke reportedly pays the MGM $1 million each year for sponsorship rights and exclusivity at the Strip hotel, and Pepsi has a similar arrangement at New York-New York.

Entertainment
Michael Flatley's Lord of the Dance is performed five nights a week, without Michael Flatley, which is either good or bad depending on your point of view. It's a scaled-down production from the one on the videotape release; there have been rumours that its thunderous toe-tapping is electronically augmented. Two duelling pianists entertain lively crowds at the Bar at Times Square, while more romantic melodies are played at the Empire Bar.

Eating & drinking
Contemporary Italian dining is offered at Il Fornaio, a chic and popular restaurant and bakery next to the Central Park bridge, and there's also

Gallagher's Steakhouse and Chinese restaurant Chin-Chin. Pop into America if only to gawp at the huge, 3-D map of the States hanging from the ceiling. The food at the Village Eateries, ranging from New York deli sandwiches to pizza and Mexican, isn't bad, but what's really delicious is the Greenwich Village setting, a jumble of brownstone façades, fire escapes and street signs. You'll have to dress up for Hamilton's cigar bar, which has the feel of an old-time club car. It's elegant, moody and a bit smoky. It's also pricey. Wall humidors rent for $1,800 a year.

Website: www.nynyhotelcasino.com

Gambling
Gambling lessons.
Mini baccarat ($10-$5,000); blackjack ($5-$5,000); Caribbean Stud; Casino War; craps (2×); Let It Ride; Pai Gow Poker; roulette (double zero).

Highlights reviewed in other chapters
Attractions Manhattan Express (p87).
Bars & Cafés Hamilton's (p163).
Casino Entertainment Hamilton's (p211); *Michael Flatley's Lord of the Dance* (p217).
Restaurants & Buffets America (p134); Gallagher's (p152); Motown Café (p155).

Paris
3655 Las Vegas Boulevard South, between Harmon Avenue & E Flamingo Road (946 7000). Bus 202, 301, 302.
Self-parking & valet parking Las Vegas Boulevard South; Audrie Street.

Ooh la la, Las Vegas imports a mega dose of savoir faire. Opened in September 1999, Paris Las Vegas welcomes guests into a shrunken version of 'Gay Paris', which, bizarrely, was fully endorsed by French government officials. Casino giant Park Place Entertainment (owner of Bally's, Hilton and Caesars Palace) has created an exact, half-sized replica of the Eiffel Tower, an Arc de Triomphe with the same statues as the original, and copies of famous buildings, including the Opéra, the Louvre and Hôtel de Ville. The authenticity even extends to parking valets yelling 'allez allez' to one another and casino employees muttering 'bonjour' to guests.

Three of the four Eiffel Tower's legs plunge into the casino itself, which is smaller, noisier and more crowded than most. The 100 table games and more than 2,000 slot machines are budget-friendly, meaning you'll find a $5 blackjack and craps tables and 25¢ slot machines. Hot slots include Monopoly, Wheel of Fortune, Let's Make a Deal and Reel 'Em In. The race and sports book has large-screen TVs and pari-mutuel betting on horse racing from throughout the country. As you might expect, the theming is rampant, from the Monet-style floral carpet and Metro-like wrought-iron canopies above the table games to the security guards in gendarme uniforms. Check out the original LeRoy Neiman paintings on the walls. The bartender at Gaston's will tell the tale of Gaston Eiffel, the tower's designer, and the French capital's history. The restaurants and shops are clustered at the back of the casino among a Parisian streetscape

Paris's Eiffel Tower, inside and out.

with cobblestone pathways and old-fashioned streetlamps. Bicycle-riding bakers deliver fresh bread to the resort's restaurants. There's also a walkway to Bally's next door.

Entertainment

Opened in January 2000, *Notre Dame De Paris* is an English-speaking pop-rock adaptation of Victor Hugo's classic, *The Hunchback of Notre Dame*. In the Le Cabaret Lounge you can rock to 'Euro Bands' under a huge tree draped with hundreds of sparkling lights and surrounded by a Left Bank street scene. For a more intimate encounter, try Napoleon's, a clubby cigar and pipe lounge with good French wine.

Eating & drinking

When Paris opened, the city nearly doubled the number of its French restaurants. Two of the better options are Mon Ami Gabi (with a Strip-side open-air terrace) and La Rotisserie des Artistes. The casino's signature restaurant, the Eiffel Tower Restaurant, is perched 11 storeys above the Strip – a great view to go with classic French cuisine. In keeping with the French theme, the 24-hour fast-food restaurant is a boulangerie, selling bread baked on site, while the steakhouse is a French rotisserie. The buffet, while one of the most expensive in town, is worth it: where else will you find duck, venison, coq au vin and bouillabaisse?

Website: www.paris-lv.com

Gambling

Baccarat ($100-$15,000); mini baccarat ($25-$5,000); blackjack ($5-$10,000); Caribbean Stud; Casino War; craps (3×, 4×, 5×); Let It Ride; Pai Gow Poker; Pai Gow Tiles; roulette (single & double zero); Spanish 21.

Highlights reviewed in other chapters

Attractions Eiffel Tower (p79).
Casino entertainment *Notre Dame De Paris* (p217).
Restaurants Mon Ami Gabi (p140); Eiffel Tower Restaurant (p139).

Riviera

2901 Las Vegas Boulevard South, at Riviera Boulevard (734 5110). Bus 301, 302.
Self-parking Riviera Boulevard; Paradise Road.
Valet parking Las Vegas Boulevard South.
Conjuring up images of the upscale South of France, the Riviera name implies affluence and class. When the hotel opened in 1955, its nine-storey tower was Las Vegas's first high-rise. Orson Welles and Marlene Dietrich appeared in the show-room and tuxedoed patrons passed the shoe at the baccarat tables like James Bond in *Dr No*. Today, as pitchmen hand out leaflets to lure low-rollers inside with the promise of a free T-shirt, the name no longer seems appropriate. The beachfront-style architecture always suggested Florida more than St Tropez, but now the side of the building is covered with a multi-coloured neon collage that sparkles and pops like a fireworks display – impressive, yes, but hardly sophisticated. Like the now-defunct Dunes and Sands hotel-casinos, the Riviera's glory days belong to the past. Several expansions to the casino area over a ten-year period have resulted in

a lack of cohesion, while guests need a map to find the right elevator to their room.

The underwater theme of the Riv's acclaimed *Splash!* show (which has been updated for 2000) is carried into the area outside the showroom, which is awash in blue-green hues, mermaid statues and seashell-patterned carpeting. The rest of the gaming area is an L-shaped expanse of red and gold with an elevated lounge and bar in the centre (your best bet for a meeting place that everyone can find). Minimum wagers at the tables are not as low as the surroundings would suggest: $5 blackjack in a $2 setting. The lowest limits and nickel slots are found in a part of the casino dubbed Nickel Town, which these days is actually a better name for the whole resort. Outside, near the underground valet entrance off the Strip, is a rear-view sculpture of the hotel's *Crazy Girls* cast, their exposed derrières immortalised in bronze. Passers-by like to rub the sculpture's bums for good luck.

Entertainment
More than any other resort in town, the Riviera depends on live entertainment to drum up business. Two shows a night are performed in each of the four showrooms: *Splash!* is the headliner. By combining the elaborate sets and costumes of traditional production shows with high-energy choreography and rock 'n' roll music, the show was a revelation when it opened in 1985. Fifteen years on and it's still playing to packed houses. *Crazy Girls* bills itself as the most risqué show on the Strip – actually, you won't see any more skin here than at other showgirl extravaganzas, but the presentation is more overt. *An Evening at La Cage* is probably the best of the female impersonator shows in town, while the Riviera Comedy Club presents stand-up comics and speciality performers such as comic magicians and ventriloquists.

Eating & drinking
Seafood is a speciality at both Ristorante Italiano and Kristofer's Steak House – maybe it's the *Splash!* influence. Rik'Shaw serves Cantonese favourites and the World's Fare Buffet offers a fine selection of international cuisine: watch for special deals combining the buffet and one of the Riviera's shows. For quick and cheap, the Mardi Gras food-court houses seven fast-food joints. But the best bargains are to be found in Nickel Town, which has the cheapest snack bar on the Strip: 25¢ for lemonade, 50¢ for draft beer, 99¢ for foot-long hot dogs and $1.50 for hamburgers.
Website:www.theriviera.com

Gambling
Gambling lessons.
Mini baccarat ($5-$2,000); blackjack ($5-$2,000); Caribbean Stud; craps (2×); Let It Ride; poker; Pai Gow Poker; roulette (single & double zero); Spanish 21.

Highlights reviewed in other chapters
Casino Entertainment *An Evening at La Cage* (p215); *Crazy Girls* (p213); Le Bistro Lounge (p211); Riviera Comedy Club (p210); *Splash! 2000* (p218).

Sahara
2535 Las Vegas Boulevard South, at E Sahara Avenue (737 2111). Bus 204, 301, 302.
Self-parking & valet parking Las Vegas Boulevard South; Paradise Road.
For those looking for the biggest bang for the buck, the newly renovated Sahara is a must-see. Owner Bill Bennett spent $100 million between 1995 and 1997 in an attempt to bring back lustre to the hotel once known as the 'jewel of the desert'. Built in 1952, the Sahara thrived in the early days of Las Vegas, but has faced difficult times trying to compete with the growth of the mega-resorts at the south end of the Strip. But, while its North Strip location is a bit removed, the revamped Sahara comes across as both passably lavish and affordable to locals and middle-income tourists. The main entrance has been relocated on to Las Vegas Boulevard to give the Sahara more of a Strip presence – and a commanding presence it is. The long-famous camel statues have gone the way of the hotel's original 35¢ hot fudge sundaes, replaced by a new $4.6-million *porte-cochère* topped by a Moroccan-style dome. The camels have been recaptured on a video display in the hotel's 190ft (58m) high minaret-topped electric marquee, where they watch over an expanded Moroccan-themed casino.

There are single-deck, double-deck and shoe blackjack games with $1 minimum limits – the

Find bounty at **Treasure Island***: page 60.*

The **Venetian** brings the buildings, gondolas and even the canals of Venice to Vegas.

With the possible exception of the desolate New Frontier Hotel (which will be imploded in spring 2000 to make way for a $700-million San Francisco-themed mega-resort), the Tropicana earns the dubious distinction of being the Strip property most in need of a top-to-bottom face-lift – or a just-start-over implosion. The resort once dubbed 'The Tiffany of the Strip' has abandoned its original Polynesian theme, but forgot to replace it with anything else. Most areas of the casino are generic, and not particularly attractive.

The first sight to greet visitors passing through the front door of the Tropicana is a huge canopy ceiling made of leaded stained glass and mirrors. It's a work of art worthy of a symphony hall or an opera house, but blends with absolutely nothing else on the property. And don't think you'll be able to see the dealer's hole card in one of the mirrored panels: the casino is wise to such tricks.

Between the twin hotel towers are five acres of gardens, waterfalls and lagoons in the pool area, and one of only two swim-up blackjack games in town. Players sit half-submerged in the pool, hitting and splitting waterproof cards. Don't worry about getting your cash wet: when you reach the table, the dealer will insert the bills into a money dryer. The Wildlife Walk, an enclosed bridge that connects the casino to the Island Tower, is home to tufted-eared marmosets, African tortoises and enough exotic macaws and cockatoos to stock a tropical zoo.

The swim-up blackjack is really the one unique gaming aspect at the property. Otherwise, there's the usual variety of games, though not quite as many video poker machines as at other places, and some of the slots are showing their age. In short, not as high-roller as it used to be. A tiny, dingy sports book is located at the back of the casino, at the bottom of a stairway, apparently hidden as if the hotel were embarrassed by it. It should be.

Entertainment

The *Folies Bergère*, the longest-running production show in America, has been a mainstay at the Tropicana's Tiffany Theatre for three decades and celebrated its 25,000th show in August 1999. This popular musical tribute to the Parisian cabaret, featuring can-can dancers, showgirls and speciality acts, hasn't changed much down the years, but its consistency is part of its charm. In the afternoons, the theatre hosts the *Illusionary Magic of Rick Thomas*, a fun, moderately priced show. The Casino Legends Hall of Fame, featuring artefacts from Las Vegas's gambling history, is worth a look: admission is $4, but coupons to get in free are in all the casino giveaway publications. The Comedy Stop features a rotating bill of comics; the early show is no-smoking.

Eating & drinking

Mizuno's, a Japanese steakhouse, is the most acclaimed of the Tropicana's seven restaurants. Steaks, Gulf shrimp and Australian lobster are served tableside, teppan-yaki style. Other dining options include Golden Dynasty (Chinese), Ristorante de Martino (Italian) and exotic specialities (including ostrich) at Savanna.

Website: www.tropicana.lasvegas.com

Gambling

Gambling lessons.
Baccarat ($100-$15,000); mini baccarat ($25-$5,000); blackjack ($5-$3,000); Caribbean Stud; craps (3×); Let It Ride; Pai Gow Poker; Pai Gow Tiles; roulette (double zero).

Highlights reviewed in other chapters

Attractions Casino Legends Hall of Fame (p84).
Casino Entertainment Comedy Stop (p210);
Folies Bergère (p216).

Venetian

3355 Las Vegas Boulevard South, just south of Sands Avenue; also accessible from Sands Avenue (414 1000). Bus 203, 301, 302.
Self-parking Las Vegas Boulevard South; Harmon Avenue. **Valet parking** Las Vegas Boulevard South.
Built on the former site of the Sands Hotel, the first phase of the Venetian opened in May 1999, when much of the construction was still incomplete. The so-called 'soft opening' left guests (the ones who weren't sent to other hotels) without room service or other guest services. Thankfully, things have improved since. Amazingly, this reproduction of Venice in the middle of the desert is quite convincing. Unlike the tongue-in-cheek pastiche of, say, New York-New York, owner Sheldon Adelson has tried to recreate the real Venice, with accurate duplicates of the Doge's Palace, Rialto bridge, Campanile and other landmarks. The wooden gondolas are authentic – as are the black and white swans swimming around them. The exterior is certainly a showstopper, and the interior's not bad, either. You enter a grand lobby and hall with a ceiling covered in gilt and hand-painted frescoes. Lavishly decorated with marble floors, plush furniture and glimmering lamps that create the feeling of afternoon sunlight, the Venetian is perhaps the most ornate of the new casinos.

The Grand Canal Shoppes – a themed shopping complex with flowing canals, arched bridges, fake house fronts and a simulated sky – lies one floor above the casino. Head for St Mark's Square if you want a gondola ride, steered by singing gondoliers. The strolling minstrels in carnival costumes, who lapse into Verdi at the slightest prodding, are fun, but the retail selection compares poorly with the Forum Shops. The smart Canyon Ranch Spa, the largest health and fitness facility in Nevada, offers massage, movement therapy, Pilates studios, a beauty salon, healthfood café and a climbing wall. The resort also connects to the recently expanded Sands Expo & Convention Centre, which Adelson, creator of the Comdex computer show, also owns; the Venetian is banking on pulling in a lot of business from Vegas's growing convention market.

In the casino itself, the 122 table games include blackjack, craps, Caribbean Stud, Let It Ride and Pai Gow, as well as a James Bond-friendly, single-zero roulette wheel, of which there are only a handful in all Nevada. The casino's 2,500 slot machines are weighted toward reel games, with a large mix of $1 machines. For the player with pull, there are some high denomination machines – $5, $25 and $100 – in the casino's high-limit salon, which also includes a baccarat pit and 12 table games where you can play blackjack for $50,000 a hand.

This is only the first phase of the Venetian. The owners' ambitious (some would say overambitious) plan is to create a second resort, with more casino space and another 3,000 hotel rooms. Construction has yet to start.

Entertainment

Madame Tussaud's wax museum has more than 100 reproductions of celebs in various settings. In the Hollywood VIP party, you'll see perky versions of Whoopi Goldberg, Brad Pitt, Jerry Springer and Oprah Winfrey. November 1999 saw the opening of C2K, an entertainment complex that has four levels and several auditoriums, with seating for 1,400 people; at night, it turns into a storming dance club.

Eating & drinking

Following the trend of importing tried-and-tested restaurants from other cities, the Venetian features an eclectic group of upscale restaurants including Joachim Splichal's Pinot Brasserie (French), Emeril Lagasse's Delmonico Steakhouse, Wolfgang Puck's Postrio, Stephen Pyle's Star Canyon (new Texas cuisine) and Canaletto, the 'quintessential' Venetian ristorante by the creators of Il Fornaio.
Website: www.venetian.com

Gambling

Baccarat ($50-$15,000); mini baccarat ($25-$10,000); blackjack ($10-$10,000); Caribbean Stud; Casino War; craps (2×, 3× 6 & 8); Let It Ride; poker; Pai Gow Poker; Pai Gow Tiles; roulette (single & double zero).

Highlights reviewed in other chapters

Attractions Gondola rides (p79), Madame Tussaud's Celebrity Encounter (p85).
Nightlife C2K (p224).

Restaurants Delmonico's (p152), Il Canaletto (p146), Pinot Brasserie (p141), Postrio (144), Star Canyon (p150), WB Stage 16 (p156), Zeffirino (p148).
Shops & Services The Grand Canal Shoppes (p170).

Stratosphere Area

Stratosphere

2000 Las Vegas Boulevard South, at St Louis Avenue, between Charleston Boulevard & Sahara Avenue (380 7777). Bus 301, 302.
Self-parking & valet parking Las Vegas Boulevard South.

Las Vegans still recall, with a mix of fascination and horror, the legendary Vegas World. From its inexplicable outer space theme, featuring a giant plastic astronaut crawling along the building, to its grammatically incorrect sign reading 'Gambling At It's Best', Vegas World topped local polls every year as the tackiest hotel-casino ever conceived. When flamboyant owner Bob Stupak ran short of money trying to build the city's tallest tower, he sold the property to Grand Casinos of Minnesota and Mississippi. In 1996, the tower was completed and Vegas World was incorporated into the Stratosphere. The 1,149ft (350m) tower, topped with a revolving restaurant and thrill rides, has become every bit the tourist attraction that Stupak intended, but the attached resort seems like an afterthought.

The casino area is spacious and comfortable, if somewhat generic – a World's Fair theme was toyed with and then abandoned altogether. The layout approximates a series of attached circles, which looks good but complicates an attempt to plot a straight course from one end to the other. The emphasis is on liberal machines and table game gimmicks to improve the player's odds. The Stratosphere advertises a 98 per cent return on more than 150 dollar slots, a 100 per cent return on some of its video poker machines and 100x odds on craps as well as single-zero roulette and double-exposure blackjack (in which both the dealer's cards are dealt face up).

Long beset by financial problems, the property's economic status has finally stabilised (Carl Icahn, a renowned corporate bargain hunter, now owns it, along with locals casino Arizona Charlie's), but its North Strip location remains a liability. The Stratosphere borders one of the more dangerous areas of Las Vegas, and can be inconvenient for tourists to reach without a car – hence the free shuttle bus to and from the Strip.

Entertainment

You can perch on the observation decks (indoor and outdoor) near the top of the Stratosphere's 12-storey pod. The brave (or foolhardy) can ride the world's highest rollercoaster, High Roller, which makes three clockwise rotations around the top of the tower, banking at an angle of 32°. A second ride, Big Shot, propels passengers straight up 160ft (49m) and then drops them back to the launching pad. *American Superstars*, a celebrity impersonation show plays in the Broadway Showroom. It's the only

place where you can still see Ginger performing with the Spice Girls.

Eating & drinking

The revolving Top of the World restaurant, 832ft (253m) up the tower, is the ultimate room with a view in Las Vegas, and the food – the speciality is an ice-cream and chocolate dessert in the shape of the Stratosphere Tower – isn't bad. Those with a fear of heights can stay on terra firma and opt for the barbecue specialities at the Big Sky Feast, a fine Italian dinner at the Tower of Pasta, or a burger and milkshake at Roxy's, a 1950s-themed diner.
Website: www.stratlv.com

Gambling

Gambling lessons (craps, poker).
Mini baccarat ($5-$2,000); blackjack ($5-$3,000); Caribbean Stud; craps (10×); Let It Ride; Pai Gow Poker; roulette (single & double zero).

Highlights reviewed in other chapters

Attractions High Roller & Big Shot (p87).
Bars & Cafés Top of the World Lounge (p164).
Casino Entertainment *American Superstars* (p214).
Restaurants & Buffets Top of the World (p136).

East of Strip

Hard Rock

4455 Paradise Road, at Harmon Avenue (693 5000). Bus 108.
Self-parking Paradise Road. **Valet parking** Harmon Avenue.

'This is not your father's Vegas any more,' proclaimed a cocky newcomer called the Hard Rock Hotel, and when Sheryl Crow opened the showroom in 1994, nobody disagreed. London entrepreneur Peter Morton's first resort venture is an unqualified winner. The town's only rock 'n' roll-themed casino sports Grateful Dead lyrics on the crap tables, Sex Pistols lyrics on the blackjack tables and roulette tables in the shape of pianos. Players bet with $5 Red Hot Chili Peppers 'Give it Away' chips, $25 Jimi Hendrix chips and $100 Tom Petty chips. Punk rocker Sid Vicious urges you to line up three Anarchy bars on his slot machine, while the Hendrix 'Purple Haze' machines have handles shaped like Fender guitar necks. Instead of a neon sign, a 90ft (27m) high Fender Stratocaster, on its own by the side of the street, beckons to visitors outside. Changing displays of rock memorabilia – from one of Elvis's jumpsuits to Elton John's jewel-encrusted piano – are dispersed throughout, and classic and modern rock is piped at loud, though not ear-splitting, volume.

A 1990s beast it may be, but the Hard Rock is fundamentally a return to a more intimate, glamorous Las Vegas. Design standards are high both outside – the 11-storey hotel curves gently around a sand-beached pool – and in. A 1998 expansion doubled the room capacity and added a number of restaurants and a spa, but no space to the casino, which remains small by Vegas standards – only 800 slot and video poker machines and 76 tables. The main floor is one

*Rock 'n' roll memorabilia abounds at the funky **Hard Rock**, just east of the Strip.*

big circle, with an outer hardwood walkway around the gaming area and an elevated bar in the centre. The layout is aesthetically perfect, but choosing to forego casino expansion might come back to haunt the place in the face of ever-growing crowds. Quiet as a church in the day, the Hard Rock starts warming up at 10pm and is packed by midnight. This is the best place in town for celeb-spotting; after any big Vegas event, this is where the beautiful people come.

Morton got in big trouble for using an authentic Catholic altarpiece for a bar decoration – somehow that seems in character with the rebellious nature of the place (it was eventually removed). Dealers are encouraged to be friendly and enthusiastic; some will even give you a high-five if you hit a natural blackjack, a stunt that would give the pit boss a heart attack at another casino. There's no keno room.

Entertainment

The Hard Rock's 1,400-seat theatre, the Joint, has busted any Vegas showroom stigma by drawing artists from all musical disciplines: Blur, the Rolling Stones, Danzig, Bob Dylan and Seal have all played here. It provides a rare chance to see big-name bands in a venue this small, but you'll pay for the privilege (from $20 up to a whopping $250 for Steely Dan). The acoustics are great, the folding chairs aren't. After hours, the crowd pours into Baby's, a trendy undergound nightclub co-owned by Morton and Los Angeles hipster impresario Sean MacPherson.

Eating & drinking

Mortoni's serves northern Italian specialities, and turns the volume down on the music for the sake of atmosphere. New restaurants include AJ's

Steakhouse, a retro-style meat and potatoes place; Nobu, an outpost of the Tracy Nieporent/Robert De Niro celebrity sushi hotspot in New York; and the Pink Taco, a funky Mexican cantina. Mr Lucky's 24/7 coffeeshop has an innovative selection of pizzas and sandwiches – if you want to feel like an insider, order the steak and shrimp special for $5.95 that isn't on the menu, and save room for the scrumptious blueberry cobbler dessert. The Hard Rock Café, located in a separate building across the parking lot from the hotel – and indeed a separate concern – is nothing to write home about.

Website: www.hardrockhotel.com

Gambling

Baccarat ($100-$5,000); mini baccarat ($5-$2,000); blackjack ($5-$2,000); Caribbean Stud; craps (2×); Let It Ride; Pai Gow Poker; roulette (double zero).

Highlights reviewed in other chapters

Attractions Casino freebies (p82).
Bars & Cafés Viva Las Vegas Lounge (p165).
Nightlife Baby's (p224); The Joint (p233).
Restaurants & Buffets AJ's Steakhouse (p151), Mr Lucky's 24/7 Café (p135); Mortoni's (p146); Nobu (p142), Pink Taco (p149).

Las Vegas Hilton

3000 Paradise Road, between Karen Avenue & E Desert Inn Road (732 5111). Bus 108, 112.
Self-parking Paradise Road; Joe W Brown Drive.
Valet parking Paradise Road.
The Las Vegas Hilton was the first resort to reach the size of a small city. The objective was to have everything – gaming, food, shopping, activities – under one roof, so guests would never have to leave. There's a feeling of tremendous space, as one might expect, but it's well distributed, so that it never seems overwhelming or unmanageable. On entering, you're greeted by a statue of Elvis Presley, commemorating his 837 consecutive sold-out performances in the showroom from 1969 to 1977. This was also the place where James Bond battled Blofeld in *Diamonds Are Forever* and Demi Moore blew on Robert Redford's dice in the film *Indecent Proposal*. Redford's $100,000 bets would not be uncommon in this high-roller haven, where class divisions are more conspicuous than at most casinos. The baccarat pit and high-limit tables are detached from the main gaming area, and the Platinum Plus slot machines, $5 and up per pull, also have their own space. High limits dominate the main floor as well: $5 is the minimum at any table, and the $100 tables are jumping year-round. They'll bring out a single-zero roulette wheel if you agree to bet $25-plus per spin.

There's also the Space Quest Casino, a starship-like chamber located west of the lobby. It has $5 tables, roulette and sci-fi slot machines that offer the singular experience of starting the game by passing your hand though a laser beam. This is also the area where the Star Trek: The Experience themed entertainment complex is housed, which has led to some problems for the Hilton – the Nevada Gaming Commission fined the Hilton for the number of children who were in the casino, either coming or going from the twenty-third century.

Access to the attraction has been rerouted, but the hotel is still hypersensitive about under-21s. A visit is a must for families, but walk the kids briskly out or risk the wrath of Khan-like security personnel. Sports bettors flock to the Hilton's 400-seat Super Book, where they can follow the action from different racetracks and stadiums on 30 giant screens. Posted explanations on how to bet on various sports are helpful to novices.

Entertainment

The Hilton Showroom features an eclectic mix of celebrity headliners, from Johnny Mathis to Pat Benatar. A successful run of *Starlight Express* has prompted more Broadway offerings, including *Rent*. The Nightclub, so billed to avoid the negative connotation of 'lounge' (that is, a place full of middle-aged has-beens nodding to grandiose ballads), features high-energy shows that draw high-energy crowds, but the $10 cover charge is a bit steep.

Eating & drinking

The very French Bistro Le Montrachet serves six impeccably presented entrées that change with the season and are accompanied by offerings from its extensive wine cellar. Benihana, of the famous flying knives (diners sit around on large hibachis while chefs perform rapid knife tricks as they slice and dice), and the more upscale Garden of the Dragon share the same Japanese Village setting. There are several other restaurants as well, none more fun than the futuristic Quark's Bar & Restaurant, located in Star Trek: The Experience.

Gambling

Baccarat ($100-$15,000); mini baccarat ($10-$5,000); blackjack ($5-$10,000); Caribbean Stud; Casino War; craps (3×, 4× & 5×); Let it Ride; Pai Gow Poker; Pai Gow Tiles; roulette (double zero; single zero on request).

Highlights reviewed in other chapters

Attractions Star Trek: The Experience (p80).
Casino Entertainment Las Vegas Hilton Nightclub (p211).
Nightlife Las Vegas Hilton Nightclub (p231).
Restaurants & Buffets Benihana Village (p142), Le Montrachet (p140).

West of Strip

Rio

3700 W Flamingo Road, at Valley View Boulevard (252 7777). Bus 202.
Self-parking & valet parking W Flamingo Road; Valley View Boulevard; Viking Street.
The Rio has the unique distinction of being the only Vegas resort to appeal to both tourists and locals in equal measure. Close to extinction in its early days, the pink and blue Brazilian-themed hotel has been in perpetual growth mode for a decade, adding another tower of rooms or more space to the casino every year. The Rio changed most recently – and dramatically – in 1997 with the opening of Masquerade Village, a $200-million tower capped by the VooDoo Lounge and anchored by two floors

Head west from the Strip for a party atmosphere at the Brazilian-themed **Rio**.

of fashion-oriented shops. This is where the Masquerade Show in the Sky, the Rio's much touted attraction, takes place: guests don costumes and masks and join dancers, musicians and aerialists on floats suspended from a ceiling track.

The casino pit is huge, and the predominant colours in betting circles are green and black – for $25 and $100 chips. At weekends, it's hard to find even a $5-minimum blackjack table. Smaller-stakes gamblers should aim for the lower-limit tables in the outlying areas of the casino, or better yet, walk across the street to the Gold Coast. Poker is offered, but it's a tough room filled with locals, joined, on occasion, by *Hustler* publisher Larry Flynt in his gold wheelchair. A shuttle bus runs between the Rio and the Strip from 9am to 1am daily.

Entertainment
Acclaimed impersonator Danny Gans departed the Rio after a public relations fiasco: the hotel repeatedly raised the tab to see his show (it topped out at $95), despite protestations by both Gans and his fans. David Cassidy and Sheena Easton took over the room in January 2000. Club Rio has become one of the hottest dance clubs in the city, and the only Vegas nightspot to rival the Hard Rock in its 'cool' factor. The Rio also hosts visiting acts during the summer, with recent visitors including Richard Marx and Art Garfunkel.

Eating & drinking
The Rio's eating options are up there with the best – and include what many say is the best restaurant

in town, Napa. There are two other gourmet rooms, eight less formal spots and two buffets: the state-of-the-art Carnival World Buffet and Las Vegas's only dedicated seafood buffet, served nightly. Another seafood favourite, especially among locals, is Buzio's. For chutzpah, the VooDoo Lounge is the place to go. Forty floors up in a glass elevator (the floor is numbered 50 but this is because numbers 40-49 aren't used, in deference to the Asian superstition about the number four), it has to work hard not to be upstaged by its own view – there are animal-skin patterned booths, live music, lurid cocktails, bottle-juggling bartenders and Creole-Cajun food.
Website: www.playrio.com

Gambling
Baccarat ($100-$10,000); mini baccarat ($100-$10,000); blackjack ($5-$10,000); Caribbean Stud; Casino War; craps (2× on 4 & 10; 3× on 5 & 9; 5× on 6 & 8); Let It Ride; Pai Gow Poker; Pai Gow Tiles; roulette (single & double zero).

Highlights reviewed in other chapters
Attractions Casino freebies (p82); *Titanic* Exhibit (p86).
Bars & Cafés VooDoo Lounge (p165).
Casino Entertainment Copacabana Showroom (p218), Mambo's Lounge (p210); VooDoo Lounge (p210).
Nightlife Club Rio (p225).
Restaurants & Buffets Carnival World Buffet (p158); Napa (p141); Village Seafood Buffet (p161); VooDoo Café & Lounge (p135).

Downtown

Those in search of the historic Las Vegas won't find much of it left standing. This is a city that cares little about its past, and thinks nothing of imploding legendary resorts in favour of bigger and better pleasure palaces. But a few vintage buildings have survived against the odds, and almost all of them are located in the Fremont Street area of Downtown.

Before the volcano, before the Rat Pack, even before Bugsy Siegel, there were casinos in Downtown Las Vegas. In 1906, just one year after the land auction that gave birth to the city, railroad workers, ranchers and frontier tradesmen were gathering in rustic gambling halls to try their luck at games of chance. By the 1930s, the area was bustling with activity, much of it centred on Fremont Street. The Apache hotel (now the site of Binion's Horseshoe), which opened in 1932, was the first major hotel in Las Vegas, with 100 rooms on three storeys. At the Meadows Casino, 13-year-old Frances Gumm performed with her sisters, three years before changing her name to Judy Garland.

The Downtown resort corridor prospered throughout the next three decades, but could not match the booming activity a few miles south on the Strip. The availability of land on Las Vegas Boulevard made possible the construction of huge resorts, while Fremont Street, surrounded on all sides by the city it had helped to create, had no room to grow. Still, the street could lay claim to some of the city's most photographed sights, including Vegas Vic, the neon cowboy, who has beckoned players into the Pioneer Club (sadly, now converted into a junky gift shop) since 1951. Vic's girlfriend, Vegas Vickie, sits atop the Girls of Glitter Gulch gentlemen's club; unlike the women inside, she was not required to remove her top.

The concentrated assemblage of lights on Fremont Street between Fourth Street and Main Street remains without peer in the world: someone once counted 50 miles of neon tubing within five blocks. Visitors have called it 'Glitter Gulch' since the 1940s, though the area also goes by its official, and less imaginative name of 'Casino Center'.

In 1995, the Fremont Street casinos clubbed together and helped finance the pedestrian-only **Fremont Street Experience** (*see page 86* **Attractions**), a colour, sound and light show that brought a splash of futuristic dazzle – with two million lightbulbs – to the city's heart. The move has succeeded in keeping the tourist numbers up but, even without its drawing power, the area still has its own particular appeal. While the rest of Las Vegas becomes increasingly upmarket or Disney-like, the Downtown area has tried to preserve the spirit of what Las Vegas used to be: Sin City, a playground for adults. In other words, keep your pirate-ship battles and pass the dice.

The house rules at Downtown casinos are often more flexible than on the Strip, permitting very high or (at Binion's Horseshoe) no limits on some tables and offering more esoteric variations of certain games. For example, when playing black-jack at the Las Vegas Club, it's legal to double down on any of the first two or three cards, split and re-split aces and split any pair any time you choose. If you draw six cards without busting, the hand is an automatic winner. Minimum bets in Downtown casinos also tend to be lower than on the Strip, making it a good place for beginners or low-rollers to polish their skills.

Below we've listed the most interesting casinos in Downtown Las Vegas; others worth visiting include the **Four Queens** (next door to Fitzgeralds) and the **Las Vegas Club** (at Fremont and Main Streets).

GETTING THERE

To reach Downtown from the Strip, catch bus 301 or the evening express 302. If you're driving, head north on either the I-15 then east on US 93/95 and take the Casino Center Exit (which is faster) or simply drive north on the Strip (which is more interesting). The public and hotel parking garages are safe, and free with validation (you must stamp your parking ticket in a machine inside the casino, usually located near the cage – there is no need to gamble). After sunset, however, it is not advisable to wander too far beyond the safety of the Fremont Street pedestrian mall.

Binion's Horseshoe

128 Fremont Street, at Casino Center Boulevard (382 1600). Bus 107, 403.
Self-parking Ogden Avenue; Casino Center Boulevard; Stewart Avenue. **Valet parking** Ogden Avenue; Casino Center Boulevard.
No rollercoasters or costumed cartoon characters here. Instead, you will find savvy, renegade dealers – the best anywhere with a deck or a crap stick in their hands. Founded by famed gambling pioneer Benny Binion, everything about the Horseshoe, from the whorehouse-velvet wallpaper to the dark mahogany furnishings, tells you this is a gambling joint. In the 21 pit, there are 50 or so single-deck games, most with $5 minimums, and another 14 crap tables, with 50¢ or $1 minimums. The standard maximum bet is $25,000 (though it's not posted anywhere; there are only minimum-bet signs at the tables), which is higher than in any other casino in Las Vegas – but the house will play for more. The only restriction: your first bet is your highest bet. In the late 1980s, a gambler tested Binion's standing offer by betting $1 million on the pass line – and won.

Since 1988, when Binion's acquired the Mint Casino next door, the property has been divided unofficially into the East and West sections. The East is the original Binion's; the West is lighter,

Neon still rules in Downtown.

more modern and more comfortable, though it doesn't have as much personality. There are 1,200 slots, with denominations ranging from a nickel to $100. Binion's Bonanza $1 progressive, offering up to a $15,000 jackpot on a two-coin bet, is very popular. Monthly slot tournaments each offer a $50,000 grand prize. The large race book occupies a former lounge in the West Horseshoe; the sports book is located in a separate part of the casino.

The Horseshoe is most famous for hosting the world's biggest poker tournament, the annual World Series of Poker, which rewards the champion with a $1-million prize. There's a gallery area where 'railbirds' can watch the action: most interesting are the side games where the players use real dollars, not chips, often risking tens of thousands on one hand. If you wish to join in the poker action in a low-limit game, beware: some of the best and most ornery players in the world make Binion's poker room their home.

Entertainment
Sadly, Binion's main entertainment – its display of a million dollars in cash, which had been on show for 50 years – was sold to a private collector in January 2000.

Eating & drinking
Gee Joon offers some of the best Chinese food in Downtown and Binion's Ranch Steak House on the 24th floor provides a good cut and a great view. If you get killed at the tables, don't worry – you can still fill your palate with an excellent breakfast for a mere $2.75. The lunch counter in the East Horseshoe is a Las Vegas institution, serving a legendary ham and bean soup with cornbread and a real roast turkey sandwich. The $2 late-night steak special in the 24-hour coffeeshop is an amazing bargain.

Gambling
Mini baccarat ($5-$10,000); blackjack ($2-$25,000); craps (10×); Let It Ride; roulette (single zero and double zero); Spanish 21.

Highlights reviewed in other chapters
Las Vegas by Season World Series of Poker (p104).

El Cortez
600 Fremont Street, between Sixth & Seventh Streets (385 5200). Bus 107, 113.
Self-parking Ogden Avenue. **Valet parking** Sixth Street.

Built in 1941, the El Cortez is the oldest unchanged hotel-casino in town (the Golden Gate may be the oldest hotel building, but it didn't open as a casino until 1955). It was once owned by Benjamin 'Bugsy' Siegel, who sold it to raise cash to build the Flamingo, and is now owned by gambling pioneer Jackie Gaughan. The air is redolent with stale perspiration and smoke, and the carpet is so worn by the Runyonesque characters constantly shuffling along it that it's generally assumed that Gaughan has never changed it. In fact, he does so every five or six years, and once announced it in a full-page ad in the local newspaper.

Situated in a somewhat squalid section of town, the El Cortez is a bit of a walk from the safety of the Fremont Street Experience, so you might want to take a taxi. But once you're there, the glass doors will open to a safely patrolled den of low-limit action. The Cortez is the place to go if you're short on cash and high on hope. There are plenty of penny and nickel video poker and keno machines, and lots of $2 single-deck blackjack games in the pit. Craps and roulette also offer cheap entertainment: the minimums (among the lowest in town) are 25¢ for both, and tapped-out gamblers can also try to win big in the keno lounge on 40¢ tickets. Twice a year, in the spring and autumn, the casino hosts a social security number lottery: if they draw your number (nine digits, in order), you win $50,000.

Entertainment
Aside from the occasional sight of owner Jackie Gaughan ambling through the casino with his poodle, Charlie, there is none. Rumour has it that Charlie knows how to push the elevator button for

The Midas touch: Steve Wynn's neon-free **Golden Nugget**.

the penthouse where he and Jackie reside. One floor above the casino, the barber and beauty shop is a good place to get to know the colourful regulars – which should qualify as entertainment.

Eating & drinking
The filling stations here may be functional but they do have a downbeat charm. There's Roberta's restaurant, whose circular booths and kelly-green and hot-pink décor – which matches the cocktail waitresses' retro uniforms – scream Tarantino; the Emerald Room coffeeshop, unrivalled for local colour and its myriad late-night specials; and a snack bar.
Website: www.elcortez.net

Gambling
Blackjack ($2-$500); craps (10×); Let It Ride; roulette (double zero).

Fitzgeralds
301 Fremont Street, at Third Street (388 2400).
Bus 107, 403.
Self-parking Third Street; Carson Avenue.
Valet parking Third Street.
Formerly known as the Sundance and formerly the tallest building in the entire state, the casino was bought by the Fitzgeralds Group in the 1980s. Hotel rooms are managed by Holiday Inn. A giant statue of Lucky the leprechaun welcomes visitors and bids good luck to all who enter. The interior of the Fitz (as it's known among locals) used to be a festival of green, where St Patrick's Day was celebrated year round. The Irish theming was downplayed in recent years, but of late the property has re-embraced its

Emerald Isle heritage. Shamrocks and other Irish symbols are back in abundance, including a chunk of the real Blarney Stone, located opposite the Limerick Steakhouse.

The casino action is strictly of the low-roller variety, appropriate to the Fitz's clientele of retirees on package deals and junket tourists chasing funbook giveaways. Some of the $5 blackjack tables deal single-deck – good for those trying to master basic strategy. The three-card poker table game usually draws a crowd (same rules as poker: the object is to make your best three-card hand and beat the dealer), while the $1 crap and 50¢ roulette tables bustle with beginners learning the games without losing a bundle. A good variety of slot machines offer players the prospect of 'Dublin' their jackpot (that's their pun, not ours).

Restaurants and additional casino space occupy the floor above. This used to be a no-smoking zone, but now the only place in the Fitz still off-limits to cigarettes is the McDonald's on the main floor. The spacious booths in the keno lounge are a comfortable place to relax and risk a few dollars.

Entertainment
The First Floor Stage at ground level is a small embarrassment of a lounge, amounting to little more than a raised platform in a dormant corner of the casino.

Eating & drinking
The Shamrock Café serves breakfast, lunch and dinner around the clock. Molly's Buffet is located

right next door. The Limerick Steak House offers the usual steakhouse menu at moderate prices.
Website: www.fitzgeralds.com

Gambling
Blackjack ($5-$1,000); craps (2×), Let It Ride; poker; roulette (double zero).

Golden Nugget
129 Fremont Street, at Casino Center Boulevard (385 7111). Bus 107, 403.
Self-parking First Street. **Valet parking** Casino Center Boulevard.

There's the rest of Downtown, and there's the Golden Nugget. A fixture on the flashiest street in the world since 1946, the Nugget was made over from top to bottom by Steve Wynn, reopened in 1987, and now draws attention away from the surrounding neon landscape with its refreshing lack of ostentation. The huge neon sign is gone and the exterior is now lined with a series of tastefully understated white-gold awnings. The motif is carried inside, with awnings outlined in tiny lights over the gaming areas, and white latticework and gold everywhere. Even the elevators and payphones look gold-plated. Near the elevators inside a glass case sits a collection of Alaskan gold nuggets, as well as the world's largest gold nugget, known as the 'Hand of Faith', discovered in Australia in 1980; it is valued at $1 million.

The Nugget's doorman and elegant marble lobby may seem out of place on Fremont Street, but the low table minimums are appropriate. You'll find $3 craps and a selection of nickel machines. Check out the 25¢ zodiac slots – there's one machine for each astrological sign – a cheap but irresistible ploy that plays on the gambler's superstitious nature.

As in most casinos, there's a segregated baccarat pit for players with larger bankrolls, but you'll also find $10-minimum blackjack tables, which make the Golden Nugget the mid-level player's best chance to experience life inside a high-roller haven. The sports book is more of a sports boutique: small but plush and comfortable.

Entertainment
A lounge next to the sports book offers the only live entertainment in the hotel. The main showroom (currently closed) has hosted a series of failed shows, including the provocatively titled *History of Sex*. It is unclear what will be on the programme when the showroom reopens.

Eating & drinking
The Golden Nugget's buffet is among the best in town at any price, even though it is priced lower than its closest competitors at the Mirage, Bellagio and the Resort at Summerlin. The seating area is small, however, so be prepared to take a ticket and wait for at least half an hour for your foody fix. Other good dining options include northern Italian specialities at Stefano's, great Cantonese cuisine and mesquite-grilled steaks at Lillie Langtry's, and tasty pizzas at the California Pizza Kitchen, a popular West Coast chain.
Website: www.goldennugget.com

Gambling
Mini baccarat ($10-$5,000); blackjack ($5-$5,000); Caribbean Stud; Casino War; craps (2×); Let It Ride; Pai Gow Poker; roulette (double-zero).

Highlights reviewed in other chapters
Restaurants & Buffets The Buffet (p158).

Jackie Gaughan's Plaza
1 Main Street, at Fremont Street (386 2110). Bus 108, 207.
Self-parking & valet parking Main Street.

Ignored by most guidebooks, Jackie Gaughan's Plaza is a marvellous, old-styled caravanserai anchored by a bus station and the train depot (trains to Los Angeles start running again in 2000). On the corner of Main and Fremont Streets at the heart of the Fremont Street Experience, it's a bit grimy and smoky, but has a lot to offer in the way of colourful atmosphere and value, 1970s style.

The ground-level casino area teems with 1,600 slot machines, including 40 penny machines next to the snack bar. For longtime Vegas visitors, several old-style poker machines (the kind without paper money acceptors and coin credits) provide an opportunity for nostalgic gaming. In the pit, cautious gamblers can play $1 craps or $5 blackjack. Seven-card stud, Texas Hold 'Em and Omaha Hold 'Em poker are played daily in the card room, where limits are low and the players more gentlemanly than some of the sharks in the higher-action games on the Strip. There is also a pan game (a variation of gin rummy) – the only one in Downtown. But if you really want to gamble on the cheap, the keno lounge is your best bet. The Plaza is the only place in the US that offers double keno – simultaneous action on two boards – with games starting at 40¢ – a bargain, despite the ridiculous odds against the player.

Entertainment
The Kenny Kerr Show features Vegas's best-known female impersonator, who was a fixture for years at the now-defunct Silver Slipper (where the Mirage now stands). The Sunspots at the Omaha Lounge have a sizable local following. Dressed like a bridegroom's attendants at a 1970s Vegas wedding and crooning like half-drunk revellers at a karaoke bar in a bad section of Manila, they're well worth the no-drink minimum.

Eating & drinking
For a quick meal or late-night special, sink into a red leatherette booth at the casino-level Plaza Diner. For a classier menu and a better view, dine one floor up at the Center Stage restaurant. And don't leave without trying a Vienna beef hot dog or a 50¢ shrimp cocktail at the snack bar.
Website: www.plazahotelcasino.com

Gambling
Mini baccarat ($5-$2,000); blackjack ($5-$2,000); craps (10×); Let It Ride; poker; Pai Gow Poker; roulette (double zero).

Highlights reviewed in other chapters
Casino Entertainment The Kenny Kerr Show (p215).

Main Street Station

*200 N Main Street, at Stewart Avenue (387 1896).
Bus 107, 403.*
Self-parking & valet parking Main Street.
From the moment construction began on Main
Street Station in 1990, the hotel-casino (not to be
confused with the other Station casinos in town,
which are under different ownership) suffered the
most tumultuous history of any Downtown property.
There were signs of financial difficulty within
months of the August 1991 grand opening, and
bankruptcy was imminent by December. It closed
in June 1992, less than ten months after opening. In
1996, new owner Boyd Gaming and a prominent
advertising campaign started to bring in customers,
and today the resort has finally left its troubles
behind. It is now celebrated as the Golden Nugget's
only Downtown rival in understated elegance (or
elegance of any kind, for that matter).

The location remains a liability – Main Street
Station is not even visible from the Fremont Street
Experience mall (head to Main Street, at the western
end of Fremont Street, and walk north two blocks)
– but those who find it are in for a treat, as this is
one of the most attractive places to play in
Downtown. The Victorian design is accentuated by
genuine antiques, stained glass, bronze, marble, bas
reliefs and one-of-a-kind artefacts, including a
carved oak fireplace from Scotland's Preswick
Castle and a set of doors from an old London bank.
A piece of the Berlin Wall is on display in one of the
men's restrooms, though no one is quite sure why.

There's a good selection of slot and video poker
machines, three-card poker and low limits at the
tables; $3 blackjack dominates and the craps tables
offer 20x odds. An illuminated sign over the roulette
area depicts a single-zero wheel, which is wrong
since the actual wheel contains both the single zero
and the double zero. On the first level above ground
there's an indoor walkway to Main Street's sister
property, the California Club, another attractive and
often overlooked Downtown resort.

Entertainment
A jazz/swing trio billed as Rhythm and Brews
performs inside the Triple 7 Brew Pub.

Eating & drinking
The Triple 7 Brew Pub earned 'Best of Las Vegas'
honours in the *Las Vegas Review-Journal*'s 1997 poll.
The buffet, featuring a wood-fired pizza oven, is
absolutely marvellous. Even without the food, the
room itself, a sort of antique conservatory with brass
and illuminated accents, is nearly worth the price of
admission on its own.

Website: www.mainstreetcasino.com

Gambling
*Blackjack ($3-$1,000); craps (20×); Let It Ride; Pai
Gow Poker; roulette (double zero); Spanish 21 (at the
California Club).*

Highlights reviewed in other chapters
Bars & Cafés Triple 7 Brew Pub (p164).
Restaurants & Buffets Garden Court Buffet
(p160).

Locals casinos

Most people who live in Las Vegas gamble,
whether they'll admit to it or not. Ask them where
the machines are paying, and they'll probably steer
you to one of the so-called locals casinos – those
located away from the Strip and Downtown areas.
This isn't another gambler's superstition. The
locals casinos really do deliver better payouts on
video poker, and probably on slots, too. Of course,
you've still got to find the right machine at the right
time – that's why they call it gambling.

The divide between tourist and local hangouts
seems to widen every year, since Las Vegans are less
inclined to fight the traffic in the resort corridors.
There used to be resistance to building casinos near
residential areas, but gambling has lost so much of
its sinister reputation that casinos are now welcomed
into most neighbourhoods (some are still resistant)
like any other commercial venture. Residents use
them as convenient places to meet for lunch or on
social occasions. Some casinos have movie theatres
(the **Station** chain, **Orleans**) and bowling alleys
(**Showboat, Sam's Town, Gold Coast, Orleans,
Fiesta**) that also draw a strong local following;
some even have dedicated childcare facilities where
parents can stash the kids in safety while they play,
eat, drink or catch a flick (*see page 107* **Children**
for more information).

The **Gold Coast** and its sister casino, the
Orleans, the four **Station** casinos, **Arizona
Charlie's** and the **Fiesta** are the busiest gambling
dens in town. Most of the locals casinos are
scattered around the city, but the **Showboat,
Boulder Station** and **Sam's Town** are relatively
near one another, in what is known locally as the
Boulder Strip. The **Fiesta, Texas Station** and
Santa Fe all lie along North Rancho Drive, in what
is called the Rancho Strip.

If you're in town to see the fabulous Las Vegas
of the tourist brochures, you won't find it in the
neighbourhood casinos, which are attractive, clean
and marginally themed but hardly as lavish as the
mega-resorts that have made the city world-
famous. The popularity of these casinos derives
from other attributes: there's plenty of parking,
both valet and self; it's easier to get in and out,
without dealing with the gridlock of the Strip; the
food, especially buffets, is generally good and
inexpensive; the video poker is positive and there's
plenty of hand-held blackjack; they offer easy
comps through the liberal slot clubs and rating
systems; and they promote extensively to the
surrounding zip codes with coupons, drawings,
two-for-ones and assorted freebies.

Arizona Charlie's

*740 S Decatur Boulevard, at Alta Drive, South-west
Las Vegas (258 5200). Bus 103, 207.*
Self-parking & valet parking S Decatur Boulevard.

A no-frills bunkhouse for serious players, Arizona Charlie's is long on action and short on atmosphere. The theme is the Yukon gold rush, though you won't notice much of it – the interior design here consists of little more than a floor and a ceiling and row after row of machines. There's $2 double-deck blackjack, $1 roulette, poker (seven-card stud and Hold 'Em), bingo and a plain but spacious sports book. Play a table game for an hour and the house will buy you a meal. For those who don't want to spend much time away from the casino, burgers and pizzas are available at a good snack bar adjacent to the gaming floor. China Charlie's has replaced the more popular Chin's for Chinese food; the Yukon Grille is a good steak and chop house. The Sourdough Café's steak-and-eggs special will set you back just $2.49.

Website: www.azcharlies.com

Highlights reviewed in other chapters
Casino Entertainment Naughty Ladies Saloon (p211).

Fiesta

2400 N Rancho Drive, between Lake Mead Boulevard & Carey Avenue, North Las Vegas (631 7000). Bus 106, 211.
Self-parking Rancho Drive; Lake Mead Boulevard; Carey Avenue. **Valet parking** Lake Mead Boulevard.
The 'ultimate' locals joint – so called because Las Vegans travel from all over the city to play and eat here. The Fiesta bills itself as 'the Royal Flush Capital of the World' and for good reason: it offers some of the best video poker on the planet, and the slots are considered extremely loose, too. The slot club is known for once-a-week triple-point days and no-hassle food comps, even to the buffet, which has been named Las Vegas's best by numerous judges. The Fiesta also has a 'drive-up sports-betting window', where you don't even have to get out of your car to place a bet on an upcoming game. There are only 100 rooms and few guest amenities, but along with the buffet, there's Garduno's Mexican restaurant and the San Francisco Steakhouse.

In November 1999, the Fiesta unveiled a stunning $26-million casino annexe called Spin City, which added a fast-food court and Garduno's Margarita Factory and Blue Agave Oyster Bar, with 300 types of margarita and the most extensive selection of tequilas in town. But the centrepiece is Roxy's Pipe Organ Pizzeria, serving Regina's Pizza (famous in Boston since the 1920s) and featuring a 1927 Kimball organ, which consists of 3,000 pipes, horns and fluted tubes, occupies a three-storey back wall of Roxy's and fills the big pizzeria with every sound known to man. Don't miss the Fiesta.

Website: www.fiestacasinohotel.com

Highlights reviewed in other chapters
Restaurants & Buffets Garduno's (p149), Festival Buffet (p160).

Gold Coast

4000 W Flamingo Road, at Valley View Boulevard, West of Strip (367 7111). Bus 202.
Self-parking & valet parking Valley View Boulevard; Flamingo Road; Wynn Road.

In 1984, the Barbary Coast took its act off the Strip and begat the Gold Coast. Like most sequels, it is bigger – 100,000sq ft (9,300sq m) of casino space, compared with 30,000sq ft (2,790sq m) at the Barbary – and relies on the same formula for success. The Barbary's Victorian trappings and San Francisco ambience have been maintained, though not with the same attention to detail. Locals love the machine selection and the slot club, both of which always take top honours in the *Las Vegas Review-Journal*'s 'Best of Vegas' survey. Banks of non-smoking machines were a good idea – putting them next to the smoking machines was not. There's $2 blackjack and $1 roulette for low-rollers, one of the city's bigger bingo rooms and a large bowling alley. Two lounges and an intimate showroom churn out country, jazz and swing music. The Gold Coast is next to the Rio, and there are shuttle buses to both from the Strip.

Website: www.goldcoastcasino.com

Highlights reviewed in other chapters
Culture Gold Coast Twin cinema (p199).

Orleans

4500 W Tropicana Avenue, at Arville Street, South-west Las Vegas (365 7111). Bus 201.
Self-parking & valet parking W Tropicana Avenue; Cameron Street; Arville Street.
This trim, bright casino off the main drag is a big hit with locals, and worth a visit for its easy parking, easy navigation, good gaming returns and some great lounge acts. However, despite painstaking attention to detail – French Quarter-style latticework, hand-carved door frames and ceiling trim – the overall feel is closer to an aircraft hangar than the jazz-soused intimacy of Bourbon Street. Still, the high ceilings do make an airy (and less smoky) change from the oppressive, chandeliered norm.

The casino offers lively, low-limit action: the poker room is one of the best in town with 'bad-beat jackpots' (awarded to the player who loses with a very big hand) that sometimes top $40,000, and tournaments daily, at noon and 7pm. The Orleans has a local reputation for loose slots, although it has moved out some of the best video poker machines. Even louder than the slot machines are the sports fans in the casino book – especially on weekends and Monday nights during football season.

You might hope to find some great jazz in the 999-seat Orleans Showroom but in fact country and classic rock are the usual fare. Prices are reasonable and the intimate feel and good acoustics give ageing performers such as Jerry Lewis and the Everly Brothers a perfect setting to recapture a bit of their lost magic. For a more Dixieland sound, try Bourbon Street Cabaret. You'll also hear some great zydeco at the small stage next to the Piano Bar. The cinema has 12 huge screens, great sound and stadium-style seating. Six different restaurants prepare everything from beef to Las Vegas-style jambalaya. However, for good food and a quiet atmosphere, your only choices are Vito's (Italian delicacies) and the Canal Street Grille. Don't forget to try a grilled frankfurter at Terrible's (it's a locals' favourite).

Website: www.orleanscasino.com

Highlights reviewed in other chapters
Casino Entertainment Bourbon Street Cabaret (p210).
Culture Century Orleans 12 cinema (p198).

Santa Fe
4949 N Rancho Drive, at US 95 (junction 90A), North-west Las Vegas (658 4900). Bus 106.
Self-parking & valet parking N Rancho Drive; Lone Mountain Road.
The Santa Fe opened in 1991, one of the earliest, and still the furthest out, of the locals casinos. It has 200 rooms and a smallish casino, with low-limit table games, low-hold video poker and slot machines, and a big bingo barn. There's also a 60-lane bowling alley and a professional ice-skating arena. Its five restaurants include three upper-end dining choices – the Kodiak steakhouse, Ti Amo Italian restaurant (which has a good bargain Sunday brunch), and Suzette's, a fancy French room – along with a coffeeshop and popular buffet (the rear seats overlook the ice-skating rink). The Santa Fe has had some financial trouble in the past few years; it could become the next Station Casinos property.
Website: www.santafecasino.com

Highlights reviewed in other chapters
Restaurants & Buffets Suzette's (p142).
Sport & Fitness Santa Fe Ice Arena (p241).

Sam's Town
5111 Boulder Highway, at Flamingo Road, East Las Vegas (456 7777). Bus 107, 201, 202.
Self-parking & valet parking Boulder Highway; Flamingo Road; Nellis Boulevard.
Opened in 1979, Sam's Town remained a low-key, Western-themed gambling hall for 15 years until the 1990s, when several expansions and makeovers transformed the property into a cowboy theme park. The casino has the same selection of low-limit tables and machines as before, but now it's big enough to drive cattle through. Take the escalator downstairs for 24-hour bowling or head upstairs for a free Texas two-step lesson in the dance hall. The lounge features country music from up-and-coming bands.
An enclosed atrium, with real trees and a rock waterfall, houses shops, restaurants and the Sunset Stampede water and laser show, complete with animatronic animals and a booming Western soundtrack; it's presented four times daily. In December, the holiday light display in the courtyard is the most beautiful in Las Vegas, and definitely worth a visit.
Website: www.samstownlv.com

Showboat
2800 Fremont Street, between E Charleston Boulevard & Sahara Avenue, East Las Vegas (385 9123). Bus 107, 206.
Self-parking Fremont Street; Atlantic Street.
Valet parking Fremont Street.
The granddaddy of all locals casinos, the Showboat opened for business in 1954; to bestow good fortune on the riverboat-shaped resort, ten gallons of real Mississippi River water were poured into the resort's swimming pool. A steady local clientele has sailed on the Boat ever since, even after its lustre had

begun to fade. In 1996 a $50-million facelift brought new life to the resort and added Southern plantation trappings with a dash of New Orleans style. The property was acquired by Harrah's in 1998, though no significant changes resulted from the purchase.
The bright, festive casino has 25¢ table-top video poker machines with a clear view of the lounge, and blackjack tables that do not allow mid-deck entry by new players – a counter-measure against card counting. The 24-hour, 106-lane bowling centre is the largest in the US, and plays host to several professional tournaments.
Website: www.showboat-LV.com

Highlights reviewed in other chapters
Restaurants & Buffets Captain's Buffet (p158).

Station chain
The suburban Station Casinos chain (website: www.stationcasinos.com) is the proud owner of four hyper-popular casinos, and it's looking for more – it recently bought an option on the money-troubled Santa Fe. The phenomenal success of the railroad station-themed Palace Station led to the opening of three sister properties, all of which are bigger and slightly fancier (the Las Vegas version of Monopoly features all four of them as the railroad properties). In the past decade, the Station chain has picked up a total of 118 'Best of Las Vegas' awards from the *Las Vegas Review-Journal*. It's also beloved by Las Vegans for its four-in-one slot club. You can earn points in one of the casinos and redeem them in any of the other three; no other locals chain can claim that perk.

Boulder Station
4111 Boulder Highway, at E Desert Inn Road, East Las Vegas (432 7777). Bus 107, 112.
Self-parking & valet parking Boulder Highway.
Families with small children flock to Boulder Station for its 11-screen cinema and for Kids Quest, a huge indoor play area that can entertain toddlers through to 12-year-olds. The play area for adults is pretty big, too – there's plenty of elbow room in the casino, one of the largest in town, and it features all the usual games plus a few of the more cutting-edge machines. Dark wood and stained glass provide a posher-than-usual setting for locals. The lounge is practically a mini-showroom; the sights and sounds inside are usually open to the casino, but a black curtain drops for shows featuring more prominent performers. The soup and salad bar in Boulder's steakhouse, the Broiler, is one of the best in town.

Highlights reviewed in other chapters
Casino Entertainment The Railhead (p212).
Children Kids Quest (p107).
Culture Regal Cinema (p198).

Palace Station
2411 W Sahara Avenue, at Rancho Drive, West of Strip (367 2411). Bus 204, 401.
Self-parking & valet parking W Sahara Avenue; Rancho Drive; Teddy Drive.

Barcelona comes to Vegas: the gaudy Gaudi bar at **Sunset Station**.

Once known as the Bingo Palace, this is the flagship property of the Station chain. Local Las Vegans love it, despite the too-smoky, no-frills atmosphere. However, customer service has plummeted of late; long, slow-moving lines at the cashier's cages and a shortage of casino floormen and change girls have even the most loyal Station patrons grumbling. The tables offer $1 blackjack and 50¢ roulette. Amid the 2,200 gaming machines are six restaurants of varying quality – the buffet is overrated but the Pasta Palace serves delicious Italian fare at very reasonable prices. The Trax Nightclub – a converted lounge – features a variety of high-energy music, plus the occasional jazz band.

Highlights reviewed in other chapters
Casino Entertainment Loading Dock Lounge (p212).
Restaurants & Buffets The Feast (p159).

Sunset Station

1301 W Sunset Road, at Stephanie Street, Henderson (547 7777). Bus 212, 217, 402.
Self-parking & valet parking Stephanie Street; W Sunset Road; Marks Street; Warm Springs Road.
Opened in 1997, Sunset Station is now the most satisfying and successful manifestation of the Station chain's winning formula. It's big, colourful, friendly, fancy but not too fancy, and features an excellent assortment of table and electronic games. It is also one of the first casinos in town to debut new slot machines, such as the Betty Boop and Three Stooges progressive games. The sloping, cavern-like walls and coloured glass that surround the gaming tables are fairly garish, but the Spanish-style architecture of the exterior, the lobby and the shopping and restaurant areas is rendered in surprisingly fine detail. Finding landmarks inside the low-ceilinged, labyrinthine gaming area can be a challenge, and as a result, it's easy to get lost. Don't miss the gaudy Gaudi Bar in the centre, or the buffet – the queues start early for lunch and dinner, but the food is worth it. The Sonoma Steakhouse has earned honours in national publications for its beefy choices, but if your food budget is limited there's also Fatburger,

a fine fast-food joint. As at Boulder Station, the Sunset's enclosed lounge occasionally draws big-name performers, and there's a great 13-screen cinema and a Kids Quest childcare centre. Sunset Station can also be a convenient stop on the way back into town after a visit to Boulder City or the unmissable Hoover Dam.

Highlights reviewed in other chapters
Bars & Cafés Gaudi Bar (p166).
Children Kids Quest (p107).
Culture Regal Cinema (p198).

Texas Station

2101 Texas Star Lane, at N Rancho Drive, between Lake Mead Boulevard & Vegas Drive, North Las Vegas (631 1000). Bus 106, 208.
Self-parking N Rancho Drive. **Valet parking** Lake Mead Boulevard; N Rancho Drive.
Everything's bigger in Texas, or so they say, and you'll believe it after walking the length of this 90,000sq ft casino (8,370sq m), past the impressive variety of machines for which all Station casinos are renowned. The Lone Star theme is picked up in the miniature oil wells that rhythmically pump over the slot carousels; the red-fringed dance hall-girl attire of the cocktail waitresses; and in the poker room, where the game of choice is, of course, Texas Hold 'Em. Country music plays in the Armadillo Lounge, and visitors are invited to take to the stage every Thursday evening for karaoke. The 3,000-seat South Padre Amphitheater presents nationally known country stars. There's an 18-screen cinema on the north side of the casino and a full complement of restaurants, from Italian and Chinese to steaks and seafood, and a Texas-sized buffet with a unique Texas chilli serving station. As you enter from either side of the building, note the historical plaque next to the doors: 'On this site in 1897, nothing happened'.

Highlights reviewed in other chapters
Casino Entertainment Texas Station lounges (p212).
Children Kids Quest (p107).
Culture Regal Cinema (p198).

Attractions

Exploding volcanoes and dancing fountains, exotic animals, theme parks and rollercoasters: there's no shortage of eye-popping spectacles and amusements.

For years Las Vegas was known as an adult amusement park – a fantasy world of gambling halls, stage shows, topless revues and cocktail lounges – where visitors were free to pursue the decadence of their choice, 24 hours a day. But times change and so has Sin City. In an effort to legitimise itself as a tourist destination, Las Vegas evolved, mainly in the past ten years, into an oversized fairground with an orgy of sights and sounds that vary from the sublime to the exotic, from the outrageous to the bewildering.

No longer confined to smoke-filled casinos, visitors can pass the time watching pirate battles, volcanic eruptions, laser light shows or cigars being made by hand. They can ride a rollercoaster or a Venetian gondola, bungee jump or leave offerings at a Brahma shrine. They can marvel at soaring replicas of New York skyscrapers, enjoy the view from the top of a half-sized Eiffel Tower or take batting practice in a regulation-sized baseball cage. They can even spend hours pondering a Picasso, poring over rock 'n' roll memorabilia or examining artefacts from the ill-fated *Titanic*.

Most of the new generation of attractions are either part of, or built into, the city's hotel-casinos. And while the casinos are detailed in the **Casinos** chapter, we have included here those casino attractions worthy of a visit in their own right. We've also included batches of spectacles, sights and diversions outside the casinos. Exploring these attractions can be a good way to detox from a busy convention or a marathon gambling session. In any case, take the time to explore.

Animal attractions

Dolphin Habitat & Secret Garden

Mirage, 3400 Las Vegas Boulevard South, between W Spring Mountain & Flamingo Roads (791 7111). Bus 203, 301, 302. **Open** 11am-3.30pm Mon-Thur; 10am-5.30pm Fri-Sun. *Secret Garden closed Wed.* **Admission** $10 Mon, Tue, Thur-Sun; $5 Wed; free under-10s. **Credit** AmEx, DC, Disc, JCB, MC, V.
Flipper in the desert? Anything's possible in Las Vegas. Casino mogul Steve Wynn believes dolphins are better off here than in tuna cans: he has seven bottlenosed dolphins swimming in a special habitat behind his Mirage hotel. You can watch these playful mammals from above and below water level. You

The climbing wall at **GameWorks** *(page 79).*

Tasteful, restrained costume displays at the **Liberace Museum**. *See page 85.*

can also ask the staff to toss beach balls into the water; the dolphins will knock them out with their noses – it's your job to catch the ball and toss it back. It might be your best memory of Sin City: playing catch with a dolphin.

You can see Siegfried & Roy's white tigers for free inside the hotel, but for a closer look at the illusionists' exotic pets visit the Secret Garden adjacent to the Dolphin Habitat. It's really just a small, glorified zoo, but the setting is attractive, with plenty of vegetation and Asian-themed architecture. The best part is getting close to the big-ticket animals: white tigers, white lions, Bengal tigers, an Indian elephant, a panther and a snow leopard.

Lion Habitat
MGM Grand, 3799 Las Vegas Boulevard South, at E Tropicana Avenue (891 7777). Bus 201, 301, 302. **Open** 24hrs daily. **Admission** free.
Not to be outdone by the Mirage's white tigers, the MGM is proud of its own pride of lions on display. The habitat is disappointingly small but the glass walls that surround it mean you can get a close-up view of the cubs and adult lions – up to five at any one time may be lurking among the foliage. Admission is free, but if you want your photo taken with Simba, it will cost twenty bucks.

Southern Nevada Zoological Park
1775 N Rancho Drive, between Vegas Drive & Lake Mead Boulevard, North Las Vegas (648 5955). Bus 106, 208, 209. **Open** 9am-4pm daily.
Admission $5.95; $3.95 seniors, 2-12s; free under-2s. **Credit** AmEx, MC, V.
This will never be confused with the Bronx or San Diego zoos, but it contains an interesting collection

of reptiles and birds indigenous to the state of Nevada, as well as a variety of endangered cats and the last family of Barbary apes in the US. The park also has a coati exhibit (a racoon-like animal), botanical displays of endangered palms and rare bamboos, and a children's petting zoo. Staff are friendly and informative.

Arcades, theme parks & rides

Adventuredome
Circus Circus, 2880 Las Vegas Boulevard South, at Circus Circus Drive, between Desert Inn Road & W Sahara Avenue (794 3912). Bus 301, 302. **Open** 10am-6pm Mon-Thur; 10am-midnight Fri, Sat; 10am-8pm Sun. **Admission** *park* free; *unlimited rides* $16.95 visitors over 4ft (1.22m) tall; $12.95 visitors under 4ft (1.22m) tall; *individual rides* $2-$5. **Credit** AmEx, DC, Disc, MC, V.
This is one of the most popular kids' spots in town, especially with teens. The five-acre (2ha) park, climate-controlled under a pink plastic dome, is a scene Fred Flintstone would love: waterfalls, faux mountains and animated spitting dinosaurs stuck in fake tar pits. The rides are pretty good, though hardly of the white-knuckle variety; the best is the double-loop, double-corkscrew rollercoaster ($5), but it lasts only a minute and a half. The Rim Runner is a tame but fun log-flume ride that will get you soaked. Also popular is laser tag ($5) in the Lazer Blast Arena, played with non-injury laser guns in a black-lit room. Tots will like the bumper cars, Ferris wheel and other small rides, as well as new attractions such as a wall for climbing and mini obstacle course for crawling.

All-American SportPark

*121 E Sunset Road, at Las Vegas Boulevard South,
East of Strip (798 7777). Bus 212, 301, 302.* **Open**
2-9pm Mon-Thur; 2pm-midnight Fri; noon-midnight
Sat; noon-8pm Sun. **Admission** $24.95; $19.95
children under 4ft 9in (1.43m), seniors. **Credit**
AmEx, Disc, MC, V.

This sports complex, owned in part by Andre
Agassi, has everything imaginable for the wannabe
jock: baseball batting cages, indoor rock climbing,
putting green, go-kart race track, rollerskating and
plenty of room to jog on the 23-acre (9ha) facility. If
this place can't raise your testosterone level, check
for a pulse. Opening times can vary considerably;
phone ahead for details.

Cinema Ride

*The Forum Shops, Caesars Palace, 3500 Las Vegas
Boulevard South, between W Flamingo & Spring
Mountain Roads (369 4008). Bus 301, 302.* **Open**
11am-11pm Mon-Thur, Sun; 11am-midnight Fri, Sat.
Admission $8-$16. **Credit** AmEx, Disc, JCB, MC, V.

Hold on to your toga during this wild 3-D experience.
Four different motion-simulator cinema rides create
the sensation of probing the ocean's depths in a
submarine, riding a runaway rollercoaster, taking
an intergalactic flight or pedalling through a grave-
yard on a bicycle. The rides are relatively short and
pricey (though all four come at a nice discount).

Eiffel Tower

*Paris, 3655 Las Vegas Boulevard South, between
Harmon Avenue & E Flamingo Road (946 7000).
Bus 202, 301, 302.* **Admission** $8; $6 seniors; free under-5s.
Credit AmEx, Disc, JCB, MC, V.

OK, so it's not really a 'ride' and it's only half the
size of the real Eiffel Tower in Paris, but the Vegas
version gives visitors a great view of the Strip and
surrounding mountains. You take a lift to the 46-
storey observation deck – a good spot for watching
the Bellagio fountain show across the street. Go at
dusk to watch the Strip suddenly light up as if
someone's flicked a switch.

GameWorks

*Showcase Mall, 3785 Las Vegas Boulevard South,
between E Tropicana & Harmon Avenues (432
4263). Bus 301, 302.* **Open** 10am-2am Mon-Thur,
Sun; 10am-4am Fri, Sat. **Admission** free; *1hr game*

*Have a roaring time at the **Lion Habitat**.*

Real gondolas for hire at the Venetian.

pass $20; *2hr game pass* $30; or pay for individual
games. **Credit** AmEx, Disc, MC, V.

If you'd rather shove quarters into a video game
than a slot machine, GameWorks is for you. The
brainchild of movie mogul Steven Spielberg, this
huge madhouse is the ultimate arcade and a good
place for trying out the latest video game creations
(50¢-$5). Vertical Reality will take you on a ski lift-
like ride as you wipe out the bad guys in your quest
for Mr Big, while Game Arc straps you into a cockpit
where you'll battle the forces of evil in mock warfare.
There are more than 250 arcade games, all the latest
video games and a 75ft (23m) high indoor rock
climbing wall – the world's largest. Attendants help
climbers with helmets and rigging, and collect fees
($6 halfway, $10 to the top).

Gondola rides

*Venetian, 3355 Las Vegas Boulevard South, south of
Sands Avenue (414 1000). Bus 203, 301, 302.*
Open 10am-11pm Mon-Thur; 10am-midnight Fri,
Sat. **Tickets** $10; $5 under-12s. **No credit cards.**

Purchase your tickets at St Mark's Square, then take
a gondola ride through canals that weave between
faux Venetian architecture. The wooden gondolas
are authentic, the singing gondoliers are tuneful,
but the backdrop of tourists gawking at you will
dampen any hope of a romantic moment.

Grand Adventures Theme Park

*MGM Grand, 3799 Las Vegas Boulevard South, at
E Tropicana Avenue (891 7777). Bus 201, 301, 302.*
Open *summer* 10am-10pm daily; *winter* 10am-6pm
Mon,Thur-Sun. **Admission** free; *rides* $12 each.
Credit AmEx, DC, Disc, MC, V.

Touted as Las Vegas's first and only theme park,
Grand Adventures has become MGM's grand aggra-
vation. Built to lure families with children, it's never
caught on – with tourists or locals – and has shrunk
considerably from its early days, taken up by the
Convention Center, relocated pool and additional
hotel rooms. Inspired by MGM's famous back lot in
Los Angeles, it has a variety of hokey movie-set
buildings and streets where cartoon characters stroll
and entertain.

Most of the rides are geared toward kids, so they
tend to be on the tame side. Expect to get wet on
the water rides (bumper boats, free-floating rafts
and log flume). A more challenging addition is the

Casino Legends Hall of Fame: page 84.

Sky Screamer (*see p88*), and among the open-air theatre attractions is a stunt pirate show with break-away masts, exploding towers, hungry sharks and hand-to-hand combat. Other outdoor stages feature pop and R&B bands, and the indoor Gold Rush Theatre showcases an energetic percussion show. Though the admission price entitles you to unlimited rides and shows (except the Sky Screamer), bring plenty of dosh if you plan to spend much time here; the multitude of shops and food stops can empty your pockets in a hurry.

Speedworld

Sahara, 2535 Las Vegas Boulevard South, at E Sahara Avenue (737 2750). Bus 204, 301, 302. **Open** *summer* 10am-11pm Mon-Thur, Sun; 10am-midnight Fri, Sat; *winter* 10am-10pm Mon-Thur, Sun; 10am-11pm Fri, Sat. **Admission** free; *individual rides* prices vary. **Credit** AmEx, Disc, JCB, MC, V.

A variety of virtual racing thrills, prime among them Virtual Reality Racing: eight people, eight minutes, eight bucks each. Alternatively, there's a 3-D 'motion theater': 3-D, three minutes and three bucks for a passenger's-eye race simulation. Everything is the highest of high-tech.

Star Trek: The Experience

Las Vegas Hilton, 3000 Paradise Road, between Karen Avenue & E Desert Inn Road, East of Strip (732 5111). Bus 108, 112. **Open** 11am-11pm daily. **Admission** $15.95. **Credit** AmEx, DC, Disc, JCB, MC, V.

A Valhalla for Trekkies, this space-age attraction promises to 'boldly go where no entertainment experience has gone before'. Although your trip includes a visit to the bridge of the Starship Enterprise and a ride in a virtual shuttle, most of your time is spent looking at costumes, props and weaponry from every Trek incarnation. Unusually tall Ferengi and unusually friendly Klingons roam through the Experience, happy to pose for photos and chat about their last trip through the Gamma Quadrant. There's also the Spacequest casino, which uses dozens of TV monitors disguised as portholes in order to create the illusion of orbiting Earth. If you're not interested in throwing your money away on twenty-fourth-century slot machines, at least stop into Quark's Bar & Restaurant for some out-of-this-world exotic drinks. Big surprise – the management also found room for a couple of souvenir shops.

Wet 'n Wild

2601 Las Vegas Boulevard South, between Sahara Avenue & Convention Center Drive (737 3819). Bus 204, 301, 302. **Open** *June, July* 10am-8pm, *May, Aug, Sept* 10am-6pm, daily; closed Oct-Apr. **Admission** $25.95 visitors over 4ft (1.22m) tall; $19.95 visitors under 4ft (1.22m) tall; free under-3s. **Credit** AmEx, MC, V.

During the summer, this 26-acre (10.5ha) water park is the coolest place on the Strip. You can swim, float on rafts, challenge the monster wave-making machine, take a plunge down the world's tallest waterslide or just try to cope with the screaming hordes of teenagers who inevitably overrun the place during school holidays. The picnic area at the rear of the water park is a welcome place to spread a blanket and escape the crowds. Wet 'n Wild closes for the winter at the beginning of October and opens again at the end of April.

Film specials

IMAX Theater

Luxor, 3900 Las Vegas Boulevard South, between W Tropicana Avenue & Russell Road (262 4000). Bus 201, 301, 302. **Open** 9am-midnight daily (films usually on the hour). **Admission** $8.95; both films $13.50. **Credit** AmEx, DC, Disc, JCB, MC, V.

The Luxor's IMAX is impressive: a big screen and a big sound system, and the films (one is standard dimension, one is 3-D) seldom match the medium. There's also a state-of-the-art games arcade.

Omnimax Theater

Caesars Palace, 3570 Las Vegas Boulevard South, at W Flamingo Road (731 7110). Bus 202, 301, 302. **Open** 2-10pm Mon-Thur, Sun; noon-10pm Fri, Sat (films on the hour). **Admission** $7; $5 Caesars Palace guests, seniors, 2-12s. **Credit** AmEx, DC, Disc, JCB, MC, V.

This futuristic movie theatre built under a gigantic dome is designed to surround audiences with sound and pictures: it has about 100 speakers and several projection screens, even on the ceiling. The 70mm movies are typically nature films, so expect to soar across the Continental Divide, plunge over waterfalls,

Don't miss!

If you haven't time to trek through 65 casinos or hike the eight miles up and down the Strip, these are a few of the sights and spectacles you shouldn't miss.

Bellagio's fountain shows
Who'd have thought that plumes of water dancing hundreds of feet into the air to recorded music could be so beautiful? A truly magical sight.

Buccaneer Bay pirate battle
Treasure Island's full-size sinking naval ship, dramatic pyrotechnics and hammy theatrics make this one of the best Strip-side spectacles. *See photo.*

Eiffel Tower
The Vegas version might only be half the size of the real thing, but it's worth eight bucks to ride to the top for a superb view of the Strip and of the surrounding city spreading in all directions towards the mountains.

Fremont Street Experience
The light-and-sound shows on the overhead canopy are pretty impressive, but nothing beats the vintage neon on the casinos beneath.

GameWorks
The video arcade meets the rave in this huge, techno-themed environment. All the newest video games are here, along with a climbing wall, a bar with pool tables and live music at the weekends.

Magic & Movie Hall of Fame
Valentine Vox's collection of sideshow props, movie effects, carnival games, and the like are far more creepy than kitsch. Weirdness prevails.

Manhattan Express rollercoaster
Send your heart into a spin and your stomach into your shoes as you twist and turn around New York-New York's skyscrapers. It's a short but scary trip. *See photo.*

Mirage's volcano
OK, it's rather small and low-key compared to more modern spectacles, but the shooting flames, burning water and pina colada-scented explosions are still pretty impressive.

Star Trek: The Experience
Small and expensive, but the theming is seamless and Disney-like in quality. If nothing else, you will be amazed by the 'beaming aboard' special effect.

Casino freebies

Offering free attractions to gamblers is not a new idea. The practice started in the 1950s, when casinos plied their players with free drinks and cigarettes. Of course, the free scotch and sodas did more than lure the hapless gambler to the table. They also loosened his inhibitions – not to mention his wallet. Soon to follow were the casino lounges and buffets (known as chuck-wagons), where you could see a top entertainer for the price of a drink, and gorge yourself on the bargain-priced all-you-can-eat food.

While the lounges and buffets remain today, they simply no longer have the sex appeal to constantly attract new visitors. Therefore, the casinos have had to think up new promotions to entice patrons. These include streetside spectacles to literally stop vistors in their tracks as they pound their way up and down the Strip, as well as extravagant crowd-pullers inside the casinos.

Some provide more of a whimper than a bang: here are a few of the better ones, as well as a selection of time-tested favourites.

Bellagio

3600 Las Vegas Boulevard South, at W Flamingo Road (693 7111). Bus 202, 301, 302.
Shows every 30 mins 3-7pm, every 15 mins 7pm-midnight, daily.
The eight-acre (3.25ha) lake fronting the Bellagio hotel is the site of incredible daily fountain shows (*pictured*) choreographed to music ranging from Pavarotti to Sinatra. The 1,200 water 'cannons', arranged in lines and circles, seem to dance and sway to the music, and shoot as high as 240ft (73m). The best seats are in the Bellagio restaurants, but you also get a great view from the sidewalks out front, which have alcoves and trees but, unfortunately, no benches. The top of the Eiffel Tower at Paris, opposite, is also a good viewing point. Inside Bellagio, don't miss the glass-domed Conservatory, which lies beyond the hotel lobby and is home to thousands of exotic plants and flowers.

Caesars Palace

Caesars Palace, 3500 Las Vegas Boulevard South, at W Flamingo Road (893 4800). Bus 202, 301, 302. **Open** 10am-11pm Mon-Thur, Sun; 10am-midnight Fri, Sat.
Under the ever-changing 'sky' of the Roman-themed Forum Shops complex alongside Caesars Palace, animated statues – including Bacchus, a lyre-playing Apollo and Venus – come to life every hour for a bizarre seven-minute revel with dancing waters and laser lights. In addition, the anima-tronic Atlantis attraction atop an aquarium near Virgin Records offers a lights and special effects drama – actually, rather laughable – every hour

on the hour. Outside Caesars, just to the north of the main fountain, the one that Evel Knievel's son vaulted with his motorcycle in 1989, is a small and pretty open-air Brahma shrine, where visitors from the East worship and leave offerings of fruit and flowers in exchange for luck. It's a tranquil place to pause while walking along the Strip.

Circus Circus

Circus Circus, 2880 Las Vegas Boulevard South, at Circus Circus Drive, between Desert Inn Road & W Sahara Avenue (734 0410). Bus 301, 302.
Shows every 25 mins 11am-midnight daily.
The casino under the pink big top actually has free circus acts high above the casino floor – although the cramped space and shabby décor lessen the spectacle. Let's face it, it's only there so Mom and Pop can go gamble away the rent money. But it's a surreal spectacle watching a trapeze artist in spangled tights fly overhead.

Excalibur

3850 Las Vegas Boulevard South, at W Tropicana Avenue (597 7777). Bus 201, 301, 302. **Shows** *summer* 8pm-1am, *winter* 6pm-midnight, daily.
A fire-breathing dragon does battle with knights and Merlin the Magician at this fairytale castle casino. Other attractions include comedy and dance acts, and strolling musicians at the Medieval Village. But it's all a bit tame – you're better off catching the antics at Treasure Island.

Flamingo Hilton

3555 Las Vegas Boulevard South, at E Flamingo Road (733 3111). Bus 301, 302. **Open** 24hrs daily.
During its expansion completed in 1998, the Flamingo levelled Bugsy Siegel's old suite, which was equipped with secret passageways and bullet-proof walls. In its place are lush grounds and winding pathways that take you past penguins, Chilean flamingos, Mandarin ducks and koi fish swimming in ponds under three-storey high waterfalls. If it weren't for the tennis courts, pool and spa, it would almost look like a wildlife habitat.

Hard Rock

4455 Paradise Road, at Harmon Avenue, East of Strip (693 5000). Bus 108. **Open** 24hrs daily.
Yes, we know music memorabilia can get a bit tired unless you're a rock 'n' roll train spotter, but the Hard Rock's collection is not only impressive but impressively up to date. Classic memorabilia from Hendrix, Gaye, Presley (a fabulous white jumpsuit) and the Beatles, among others, is supplemented by pieces from contemporary icons such as Kurt Cobain, Sheryl Crow, Courtney Love and 'The Artist Formerly Known As...'. Michael Hutchence donated his guitar after playing the Hard Rock's Joint venue a couple of months before his death. There's also some interesting old Vegas paraphenalia in Mr Lucky's restaurant.

Mirage

3400 Las Vegas Boulevard South, between W Spring Mountain & Flamingo Roads (791 7444). Bus 203, 301, 302. **Shows** every 15 mins dusk-midnight daily.
In 1989, the Mirage introduced the first large-scale free spectacle to Las Vegas: an erupting volcano atop a mountain in the middle of a lagoon, next door to the Strip. Even though the 'volcano' is rather small, lacks a cinder dome and looks more like a granite wall, the ten-minute spectacle is worth stopping for, spewing fire, black smoke and a pina colada scent into the palm trees, waterfalls and lagoon. Inside the Mirage, you can see Siegfried & Roy's white tigers looking bored in a glass-enclosed compound, have a cocktail in a tropical rainforest and view pygmy sharks and multicoloured fish in a large aquarium behind the hotel registration desk.

Rio

3700 W Flamingo Road, at Valley View Boulevard, West of Strip (252 7777). Bus 202. **Shows** noon, 2pm, 4pm, 6pm, 8pm, 10pm, daily.
In 1996, the calypso-themed Rio added Masquerade Village, a shopping, dining and entertainment complex, to its already hectic and confusing casino. The Masquerade Show is a kind of Mardi Gras Parade in the Sky in which floats glide high above the floor to an orchestration of music and dance (*pictured*). A cast of dozens – from aerialists to stilt-walkers – adds to the festivities, and guests can participate by hopping on one of the airborne floats. It's quite a spectacle: hardened gamblers have been known to take their eyes from the slot machines to watch the party.

Treasure Island

3300 Las Vegas Boulevard South, at W Spring Mountain Road (894 7111). Bus 203, 301, 302.
Shows 4pm, 5.30pm, 7pm, 8.30pm, 10pm, daily.
Treasure Island underscores its pirate theme with a full-scale mock sea battle every day after dark. The battle pits a pirate galleon against a British frigate in a blue-water lagoon. The show fills the sidewalk with onlookers who stare slack-jawed at the cannons blazing, masts toppling, powder kegs exploding and stunt actors leaping into the lagoon as the Brits' ship sinks beneath the waves.

ride rapids, explore the atom or stand on the rim of an erupting volcano.

The Planetarium

Community College of Southern Nevada, 3200 E Cheyenne Avenue, between Las Vegas Boulevard North & Van Der Meer Street, North Las Vegas (651 4759). Bus 110. **Shows** 3.30pm, 8.30pm Fri, Sat. **Admission** $4; $2.50 seniors, students, 5-12s. **Credit** AmEx, Disc, MC, V.

Star-gazers will enjoy interesting and educational movies and presentations in a small cinema with a 360°, wrap-around screen. After the last performance, you can scan the sky through the planetarium's telescopes (weather permitting).

Museums & collections

The new **Bellagio Gallery of Fine Art** contains casino mogul Steve Wynn's impressive collection of impressionist and post-impressionist works by the likes of Van Gogh, Picasso, Cezanne, Gauguin and Monet. It's rather pompous, but worth a look. For details, *see page 196* **Culture**.

Casino Legends Hall of Fame

Tropicana, 3801 Las Vegas Boulevard South, at E Tropicana Avenue (739 5444). Bus 201, 301, 302. **Open** 7am-9pm daily. **Admission** $4; $3 seniors; no under-18s allowed. **No credit cards**.

Mostly a tribute to past entertainers and casino moguls, the Hall of Fame has hundreds of historical photos, documents and audio and video displays covering such subjects as the Mob involvement in Vegas, old-time stage acts and hotel implosions. There's also a bronze statue of flamboyant casino mogul Bob Stupak, a collection of commemorative

See through the **World of Coca-Cola** *(p86).*

liquor decanters, and more than 8,000 gambling chips, many of which are from casinos that no longer exist. Although there is an admission charge, you can usually find free-admission coupons in tourist magazines or at various locations inside the Tropicana casino.

Guinness World of Records Museum

2780 Las Vegas Boulevard South, between Circus Circus Drive & W Sahara Avenue (792 3766). Bus 301, 302. **Open** 9am-6pm daily. **Admission** $4.95; $3.95 seniors, students; $2.95 5-12s; free under-5s. **Credit** AmEx, Disc, MC, V.

Displays, replicas and videos highlight some of the world's most meaningless records. How about the tallest, fattest, oldest or most married man? Or the most tattooed woman? They're all here, revelling in their forgettability. The Vegas computer databank gives you fun facts about Sin City (such as which stars were wed here), and quirky historical facts.

Imperial Palace Auto Collection

Imperial Palace, 3535 Las Vegas Boulevard South, between Sands Avenue & Flamingo Road (731 3311). Bus 301, 302. **Open** 9.30am-11.30pm daily. **Admission** free (with entry pass from the casino).

You don't need to be a car freak to appreciate the classic and historic vehicles here. If you can find the museum in the parking garage at the rear of the hotel, you'll discover about 200 rare and speciality cars (part of a rotating collection of 750). Among them are Hitler's 1936 Mercedes, JFK's 1962 Lincoln

Wax lyrical about **Madame Tussaud's**.

and vehicles that once belonged to Al Capone, WC Fields and such Las Vegas icons as Howard Hughes, Liberace and Elvis Presley. Among the vintage classics are a 1947 Tucker (one of just 51 manufactured), a 1910 Thomas Flyer and an entire room of about two dozen Duesenbergs.

Liberace Museum

Liberace Plaza, 1775 E Tropicana Avenue, between Maryland Parkway & Spencer Street, University District (798 5595). Bus 201. **Open** 10am-5pm Mon-Sat; 1-5pm Sun. **Admission** $6.95; $4.50 seniors; $3.50 students; $2 6-12s. **Credit** AmEx, Disc, MC, V.

Unless you have a pathological aversion to camp, don't miss this place. A testament to Las Vegas's dedication to ersatz, it's like a costume jewellery boutique run wild: on display are Mr Showmanship's rhinestones, stage jewellery, sequinned jackets, hotpants and more. The Rolls-Royce is genuine, however, and decorated with thousands of mirror tiles. Liberace liked to collect rare and unusual pianos, and about 15 of his finest antiques are displayed here. In an age when Las Vegas is trying to be everything but itself, this shrine to excess and bad taste is a kitschy reminder of the city's heritage.

King Tut's Tomb & Museum

Luxor, 3900 Las Vegas Boulevard South, between W Tropicana Avenue & Russell Road (262 4000). Bus 201, 301, 302. **Open** 9am-11pm Mon-Thur, Sun; 9am-midnight Fri, Sat. **Admission** $5. **Credit** AmEx, DC, Disc, JCB, MC, V.

If you want to walk like an Egyptian, check out the Luxor, a 30-storey black glass pyramid at the south end of the Strip, worth a look in its own right and containing several paid attractions. King Tut's Tomb & Museum is hardly like seeing the real thing,

but it's worth a visit for the full-size re-creation of Tutankhamen's burial chamber and his golden throne and sarcophagus – hand-crafted by Egyptian artisans in historically correct materials. **In Search of the Obelisk** (open 9am-11pm daily; admission $6) uses flight-simulator technology to take the audience on a *Raiders of the Lost Ark*-style action adventure about the Luxor archeological dig.

Madame Tussaud's Celebrity Encounter

Venetian, 3355 Las Vegas Boulevard South, south of Sands Avenue (367 1847). Bus 203, 301, 302. **Open** 10am-10pm daily. **Admission** $12.50; $10.75 seniors; $10 4-12s; free under-4s. **Credit** AmEx, Disc, MC, V.

Opened in mid-1999, this is the first US incarnation of London's top tourist trap – except that in Las Vegas, the waxworks are of American celebrities rather than British royalty. Think of it as a 3-D version of *People Magazine*, with more than 100 wax celebs in various settings. In the Hollywood VIP party, you'll see perky versions of Whoopi Goldberg, Brad Pitt, Jerry Springer and Oprah Winfrey. Other settings feature sports figures (Babe Ruth, Joe Montana, Muhammad Ali), rock stars (Elton John, Tina Turner, James Brown) and Las Vegas legends (Tom Jones, Frank Sinatra, Bugsy).

Movie & Magic Hall of Fame

O'Shea's, 3555 Las Vegas Boulevard South, between Sands Avenue & E Flamingo Road (737 1343). Bus 301, 302. **Open** noon-10pm Tue-Sat. **Admission** $9.95; $3 5-12s; free under-5s. **Credit** AmEx, Disc, MC, V.

Located in O'Shea's casino, next to the Imperial Palace, this display of show business history has exhibits from the golden age of conjuring along with a smattering of movie memorabilia. Big-name

Hey presto! The history of showbiz is revealed at the **Movie & Magic Hall of Fame.**

Fremont Street Experience

In 1995, a five-block section of Fremont Street between Las Vegas Boulevard and Main Street was converted to a pedestrian mall and covered by a 90ft (27m) high, white lattice space frame. The Fremont Street Experience, as it's known, was supposed to be Downtown's saviour, by attracting tourists who had forsaken Vegas's roots in favour of the glitzy Strip resorts. Certainly, the canopy's computer-programed light-and-sound shows are worth seeing.

There are about four different seven-minute shows, from streaking jets and tumbling dice to boot-scooting country dancers. It can be a bit awkward to watch; the images are directly overhead so you really need to be lying on your back – the best place to stand is right in the middle, outside the front doors of Binion's Horseshoe. The best addition has been the periodic staging

of free concerts featuring local bands and nearly forgotten groups from the 1960s and '70s.

Fremont Street is also home to some of Las Vegas's most enduring icons: Vegas Vic, the neon cowboy, waves atop the Pioneer Club, while Vegas Vickie, the neon cowgirl, perches above the Girls of Glitter Gulch gentlemen's club. The Golden Gate Hotel (the city's oldest hotel) still serves a 99¢ shrimp cocktail in classic tulip glasses.

The street got a shot in the arm in late 1999 when **Race Rock** (*see below*), a NASCAR-themed restaurant and logo shop, opened at the corner of Las Vegas Boulevard. The adjacent **Neonopolis**, a three-level dining, shopping and entertainment complex currently under construction, is expected to open in late 2000 and should help revitalise the Downtown scene.

---

illusionists and magicians are celebrated here, including levitation master Harry Kellar and Mephistophelian Dante, who concocted the terms 'hocus pocus' and 'abracadabra'. Another section is full of antique arcade games such as fortune-telling machines, nickelodeons and music boxes. Its real glory is a collection on the art and history of ventriloquism unrivalled anywhere in the world. Run by British ventriloquist and scholar Valentine Vox, it's well worth the admission price (you can also pick up a discount coupon in the casino), and includes a show by Vox himself.

Race Rock

495 Fremont Street, at Las Vegas Boulevard, Downtown (382 7223). Bus 301, 302. **Open** 11.30am-11pm Mon-Fri, Sun; 11.30am-midnight Sat. **Admission** free. **Credit** AmEx, Disc, MC, V.
More than just a themed restaurant, Race Rock, which opened in autumn 1999, is a two-level shrine to auto racing. Among the dozens of exhibits are race car simulators, NASCAR cars, Indy racers, Formula One cars, dragsters, motorbikes and speedboats. A unique feature of the restaurant is its 'track'

with a dozen cars once driven by greats such as Richard Petty, Jeff Gordon and Dale Earnhardt, as well as outlaw and sprint cars, dirt bikes, road racers and Big Foot, the largest monster truck in the world. There are plenty of souvenirs to pick up.

Titanic Exhibit

Rio, 3700 W Flamingo Road, at Valley View Boulevard (252 7776). Bus 203. **Open** 10am-10pm daily. **Admission** $15.95; $9.95 6-14s; free under-5s. **Credit** AmEx, Disc, JCB, MC, V.
Several hundred artefacts from the *Titanic* surface in this exhibition, which opened at the end of 1999 to display many objects for the first time ever. Among them are a ship's whistle, fine china, money, jewellery, personal letters, clothing, suitcases, a pair of shoes and an unopened bottle of olives. Many of the ship's rooms have been recreated for the exhibit, and interactive audio displays provide background information on the artefacts. Although overpriced, it's worth a look – if a bit chilling.

The World of Coca-Cola

Showcase Mall, 3785 Las Vegas Boulevard South, between E Tropicana & Harmon Avenues

It will take up a full city block and, on the street level, some 30 vintage neon signs will be laid out in a kind of neon walking museum. The signs will include several from Las Vegas's colourful past, as well as distinctive signs from other cities.

Although the Experience has helped to stabilise the Downtown casinos, old-time Vegans complain that it has over-sanitised Fremont Street, driving away the hookers, panhandlers and drug dealers – and destroying much of the area's character in the process. If you long for the old days, walk east on Fremont Street, between the El Cortez and the Western Hotel, for a seedy blast from the past. But watch your back.

To reach Fremont Street, take bus 107, 301.

(270 5965). Bus 301, 302. **Open** 10am-10pm Mon-Thur, Sun; 10am-11pm Fri, Sat. **Admission** $3.50; free under-4s. **Credit** AmEx, Disc, JCB, MC, V.

The 100ft (30m) high neon bottle on the exterior sets the tone – this is a shrine to Coke. And a thinly disguised marketing tool: much of the attraction consists of shopping space for Coke-logo merchandise and rather lacks fizz. If you want to look at products other than mugs, caps, T-shirts and key chains, try the mezzanine for better quality, including fine jewellery, Mont Blanc pens, leather jackets and accessories. For a small fee, you can tour the Coke museum – basically a promenade of retro shops (a 1930s soda fountain, 1950s appliance store and 1960s garage) equipped with vintage clocks, TVs, gas pumps, coolers and other Coke-branded gadgets. There's also a theatre for viewing Coke commercials (people actually videotape them and sing along to the jingles) and a fountain where you can sample Coke soft drinks from around the world. Try the Colombian Coke – soft drink, that is – a sweet concoction not unlike cream soda.

Thrill rides

Betting the farm not scary enough for you? Now you can gamble with your coronary health, too – the 1990s saw increasingly scary rides join the fray to compete for tourists' non-gambling dollars. Why not give them a whirl – you have nothing to lose but your lunch.

AJ Hackett Bungy

Circus Circus, 810 Circus Circus Drive, between Las Vegas Boulevard South & Industrial Road, West of Strip (385 4321). Bus 301, 302. **Open** *summer* 2-10pm Mon-Thur, Sun; noon-midnight Fri, Sat; *winter* 11am-9pm Mon-Thur, Sun; 11am-11pm Fri, Sat. **Tickets** $49. **Credit** AmEx, MC, V.

Bungee jumpers leap from a steel tower 210ft (64m) above the Strip and drop with heart-stopping speed towards a sparkling pool. For your trouble, you get a T-shirt and certificate with your first jump.

High Roller & Big Shot

Stratosphere, 2000 Las Vegas Boulevard South, at St Louis Avenue, between Charleston Boulevard & Sahara Avenue, Stratosphere Area (380 7777). Bus 301, 302. **Open** 10am-1am Mon-Thur, Sun; 10am-2am Fri, Sat. **Tickets** (incl admission to the Stratosphere Tower) *High Roller* $9; *Big Shot* $10; *both* $14. **Credit** AmEx, DC, Disc, JCB, MC, V.

If you're afraid of heights, stay well away from the 1,150ft (350m) high Stratosphere Tower. Those with cast-iron stomachs can try the High Roller roller-coaster that circles above the observation deck in a series of tight twists and rolls. Because of the limited space don't expect high speeds; you may, however, experience vertigo or even a nosebleed. More invigorating is the Big Shot, also open-air, which rockets you 160ft (49m) up the tower's spindle under a force of 4Gs; at the top you experience a stomach-lurching moment of weightlessness and float off your seat before free-falling back to the launch pad. If your eyes aren't scrunched up in fear, you get a magnificent view of the city from the top.

Flyaway

200 Convention Center Drive, between Las Vegas Boulevard South & Paradise Road, East of Strip (731 4768). Bus 301, 302. **Open** 10am-7pm daily. **Tickets** $35. **Credit** AmEx, MC, V.

Skydiving without an aeroplane? Well, sort of: you can free-fall in one of only three skydiving simulators in the world, an indoor 21ft (6.5m) high vertical wind tunnel that generates air speeds of up to 115mph (71kph). After 15 minutes of instruction you get 15 minutes of flying time shared with five others. Your experience is – what else? – videotaped and you can buy a copy. It's brilliant fun, and not at all nauseating.

Manhattan Express

New York-New York, 3790 Las Vegas Boulevard South, at W Tropicana Avenue (740 6969). Bus 201, 301, 302. **Open** 10.30am-10.30pm Mon-Thur, Sun; 10.30am-midnight Fri, Sat. **Tickets** $5. **No credit cards.**

*Pass the sick bag: great views, if you can stomach them, from the **Big Shot**. See page 87.*

Gotham never saw anything like this – a rollercoaster soaring around skyscrapers and Miss Liberty. The Manhattan Express twists, loops and dives at breakneck speeds, and features the first ever heart-line roll, which creates the sensation a pilot feels when going through a barrel roll in an aeroplane. Try really hard to smile in the last section, as this is where the photos are taken.

Sky Screamer

Grand Adventures Theme Park, MGM Grand, 3799 Las Vegas Boulevard South, at E Tropicana Avenue (891 7777). Bus 201, 301, 302. **Open** *summer* 10am-10pm daily; *winter* 10am-6pm Mon,Thur-Sun. **Tickets** *single* $35; *two people* $30 each; *three people* $25 each. **Credit** AmEx, DC, Disc, MC, V.
The challenging Sky Screamer hooks you up to a line, then lifts you 250ft (76m) between two mammoth towers and sends you free-falling, much like a pendulum. Flyers are instructed to pull their own rip cords to begin their 70mph (43kph) dive. Reservations – no pun intended – are required on the day of the flight.

Henderson factory tours

If you think your vacation's over because you've run out of gambling money, think again. Nearby Henderson has four food and toy factories – in lieu of themed casinos or mega-resorts – that you can tour for free. They're not the most fascinating places on the planet, but you do get plenty of free goodies. The factories are relatively near one another and best visited in the week. To get to Henderson, drive east on Tropicana Avenue, turn right on to Mountain Vista Street and go two miles to Sunset Way; turn left into Green Valley Business Park and you'll soon see Ethel M Chocolates and its cactus gardens, a good spot to begin.

Cranberry World

1301 American Pacific Drive, at Stephanie Street, Henderson/Green Valley (566 7160). Bus 217. **Tours** 9am-5pm daily.
The message at this Ocean Spray juice processing plant is that cranberries are more than a mere Thanksgiving side dish. The tour and brief show about the tasty red berries leads to the sampling room where you can quaff free juice – 44 flavours at the last count – and wolf down cranberry-soaked baked goods. You can also taste-test various products from Ocean Spray's gourmet line (cranberry mustard, salsa and others).

Ethel M Chocolates

2 Cactus Garden Drive, at Sunset Way & Mountain Vista Street, Henderson/Green Valley (433 2500). Bus 217. **Tours** 8.30am-5pm daily.
If you're a sweet-eater, Ethel M's is definitely for you. The M stands for Mars, as in Forrest Mars, who was one of the world's wealthiest men and creator of the Mars Bar, Milky Way, 3 Musketeers, Snickers and M&Ms. Ethel M Chocolates are named after his mother and produced exclusively in this factory. Most of the activity takes place on weekday mornings, when you can watch the chocolates being made, then sample some of the mouth-watering butter creams, truffles, caramels or nut clusters. Next door is a cactus garden, rich with 300 species of cacti, succulents and desert plants, all beautifully lit up at Christmas. Be sure to heed the rather ominous sign: 'Please be careful. Cactus bite.'

Favorite Brands Marshmallow Factory

1180 Marshmallow Lane, just off Gibson Road, just north of Lake Mead Drive, Henderson/Green Valley (393 7308). No bus. **Tours** 9am-4.30pm Mon-Sat.
If the chocolates haven't given you a sugar high, drive to the marshmallow factory and watch how corn starch and various polysyllabic ingredients are

rolled smooth, cut into shapes, bounced in a drum and boxed into cartons. The reward for your attention is free samples – kids especially love this bit.

Ron Lee's World of Clowns Factory & Tour

330 Carousel Parkway, at Warm Springs & Gibson Roads, Henderson/GreenValley (434 1700). Bus 217. **Tours** 9am-5pm Mon-Sat.

If you've ever seen a Hobo Joe clown statue, it was made here, where they produce more than 50,000 ceramic and pewter statuettes every year, including the ubiquitous figurines of Disney and Warner Brothers characters. Take a factory tour to learn how they're made. Kids can ride on an authentic Chance carousel ($1 a go).

Guided tours

Tour operators do a brisk business in Las Vegas, with most of the trips taking tourists to nearby mountains, lakes and wilderness areas. Only a few offer tours of the city, and none of the casino-resorts explores its own property (so you can forget about being taken behind the scenes at a casino). Here are some of the more interesting options; most tour outfits provide pick-up from and return to your hotel. It's also worth checking the Friday edition of the *Review-Journal* (under 'Jaunts' in the 'Neon' section).

Adventure Photo Tours

889 8687. **Credit** AmEx, Disc, MC, V.

Take a guided full- or half-day photo safari to wilderness spots such as Red Rock Canyon National Conservation Area ($75 per adult, $56.25 per child for a four-hour tour), a Joshua Tree forest in the Spring Mountains, the Goodsprings Valley ghost mines, Valley of Fire State Park, El Dorado Canyon and the Logan Wash.

Website: www.adventurephototours.com

Casino Travel & Tours

1-800 835 5160/Bally's 796 6020/Excalibur 798 7020/3020/Mandalay Bay 632 6131/New York-New York 740 6413/Paris 731 6161. **Credit** AmEx, Disc, MC, V.

Casino Travel & Tours offers professionally guided tours around the city, to Hoover Dam, the Grand Canyon's West Rim, Red Rock Canyon and Spring Mountain Ranch, and Lake Mead. It can arrange reservations at Las Vegas's top golf courses and tickets for shows (except at Mirage Resorts' properties), and has a small fleet of chauffeur-driven limos, sedans and luxury buses. Finally, it's also a full-service travel agency and a booking agent for most of the other tour operators in town.

Website: www.casinotravel.com

Desert Eco-Tours

647 4685. **Credit** AmEx, MC, V.

If you're a hiker, backpacker or rock hound, check out these jeep tours, run by the Southern Nevada Zoo, into the nearby wilderness areas. The half-day ($129 per person, minimum two) or full-day ($179)

tours are conducted year-round with naturalists to geological or gem-collecting sites, ancient Native American sites, ghost towns and Area 51.

Website: www.lvrj.com/communitylink/zoo

Drive-Yourself Tours

565 8761. **Credit** AmEx, Disc, MC, V.

Perhaps the most interesting city tour is offered by this local mom-and-pop operation, which came up with a 90-minute audio tape and road map that you use on a self-guided tour ($14.95; three for $35). Points of interest include the obvious tourist attractions and landmarks, but there are also several gems that even local residents may not know about. For instance, you can visit an elaborate underground house built by Mary and Jerry Henderson, whose family founded cosmetics company Avon, and the estate-like home of Nevada's Lieutenant Governor Lonnie Hammargren, a brain surgeon (yes, really) who has a penchant for building and collecting oddities for his home (a mini-railroad in his backyard, for one). The tour includes celebrities' homes and hangouts, museums, parks and historic buildings. Other tours cover places such as the Hoover Dam and Red Rock Canyon.

Website: www.drive-yourselftours.com

Gray Line Tours

384 1234. **Credit** AmEx, Disc, MC, V.

This venerable tour operator will take you on a 2½-hour city tour ($25 per person) that includes the Strip, the Fremont Street Experience and wedding chapel row. The night-time tour costs $28.

Website: www.pcap.com/grayline.htm

Helicopter & aeroplane tours

Papillon Grand Canyon Helicopters

1-800 528 2418/736 7243. **Credit** AmEx, Disc, MC, V.

Papillon offer only three basic flights – a 12-minute Strip Tour ($68), Grand Canyon flyover and Grand Canyon Champagne Brunch ($307) – but its showmanship is tops. All helicopters have state-of-the-art sound systems and patented viewing windows.

Website: www.papillon.com

Scenic Airlines

638 3300. **Credit** AmEx, Disc, JCB, MC, V.

When you've had enough glitz and want to get back to nature, Scenic Airlines will fly you to various National Parks in the Southwest, such as the Grand Canyon ($218 per person for a seven-hour tour), Bryce Canyon and Monument Valley.

Website: www.scenic.com

Sundance Helicopters

1-800 653 1881/736 0606. **Credit** AmEx, Disc, MC, V.

With 17 tours to offer, Southern Nevada's largest helicopter tour operator has the flight to fit anyone's desires. Experience the neon jungle from above on the city tour ($79). Take a quick jaunt over Red Rock Canyon and the Spring Mountains to the Pahrump Winery. Or take one of four Grand Canyon flights.

Website: www.helicoptours.com

Las Vegas by Area

Beyond the Strip, low-rise Las Vegas sprawls in all directions. Get your bearings here.

A TALE OF TWO CITIES

Las Vegas is the largest (some say only) major US city founded in the twentieth century. The layout of Vegas has almost always been influenced by two factors: its location in the American West near Los Angeles (and therefore its reliance on and fetishism of the automobile), and Nevada's formal legalisation of gambling in 1931.

Unlike great planned cities such as Washington, DC and Paris, Las Vegas's layout is evolutionary rather than revolutionary. A boomtown since its inception, the city has never had time to seriously consider its infrastructure, only frantically to fail to keep up with demand. Flanked by the Spring Mountains to the west and the Sheep Mountains to the east, the inhabited Las Vegas Valley spreads like spilt batter between them. The Valley does not reluctantly 'endure' urban sprawl; rather, it is defined by it.

Two distinct but informally delineated areas and populations define Las Vegas – tourist and resident. Traditionally, the two have always remained separate, despite the many neighbourhood casinos that have sprung up in the past decade. Residents typically prefer to live in homes away from tourist areas, while most tourists are blissfully unaware of the absurdly normal city surrounding Glitter Gulch and the Strip.

Servicing these two unique and often disparate populations has always been the challenge of Las Vegas; at times, more than 250,000 non-residents – the population of a largeish city – may be visiting, each seeking a good time and a chance to relinquish responsibilities. This places quite a strain on an under-realised infrastructure, and has resulted in decades of concentric rings of suburban development moving further and further away from the central tourist areas.

With the obvious financial advantages of gambling combined with the population's aversion to making it a part of their daily lives, a traditional downtown shopping district has never had a chance to evolve, especially given the rapid growth that has characterised the whole of Vegas's history. For a time, until the late 1960s and early 1970s,

Downtown Las Vegas sported some traditional city-centre indicators – movie theatres, department stores and doctors' and lawyers' offices among them. Most of these were relegated to suburban shopping malls and industrial parks as the Downtown area filled with more casinos, touristy souvenir shops and attractions.

This developmental pattern, combined with the American West's relentless attachment to the car and aversion to urban housing and public transport, has resulted in a relatively thinly spread populace covering a geographical area 20 times the size of San Francisco with roughly the same number of residents.

ORIENTATION

The Valley is divided into quarters by two freeways that cross each other: I-15 coursing north-south through the centre of town on its way from Los Angeles to Salt Lake City, and US 95 (aka I-515), a north-south Canada-Mexico freeway that cuts east-west across the central Las Vegas area before returning to its standard directional path. On a map, these two approximate a twisted pinwheel shape, with its pivot just north-west of Downtown Las Vegas. In 2003, the much-needed Las Vegas Beltway will encircle the Valley, connecting with these freeways.

The 'centre' of Las Vegas (and the whole valley), where street numbering starts, is at the junction of Fremont and Main Streets in Downtown. From the Plaza Hotel at 1 S Main Street, numbers increase as you travel in any direction from this intersection. Streets use an even-odd system, with even-numbered addresses on one side and odd on the other. Main Street eventually ends at its intersection with Las Vegas Boulevard South at the base of the Stratosphere Tower, and everything either east or west of the Main Street/Las Vegas Boulevard artery is tagged accordingly.

North-south delineations are more complicated, as they're based on three arteries: Fremont Street, East Charleston Boulevard and US 95. Imagine a line from Fremont Street east to Charleston, then following Charleston all the way east to Sunrise

*Looking north up the **Strip**, with Bellagio to the left and Paris's Eiffel Tower to the right.*

Mountain; in the other direction it starts at Fremont and Main and continues along US 95 to the west.

The wide geographic area of metropolitan Las Vegas is made up of four official jurisdictions: Las Vegas, North Las Vegas, Henderson and unincorporated Clark County. Within and overlapping these jurisdictions are a number of 'areas'. Their sheer physical size calls for a naming system of some type, but one hesitates to term them 'neighbourhoods' as they often lack any distinctive identity. Some are easily recognisable; others blend in with the surrounding stucco.

The Strip

Since mobster Bugsy Siegel opened his Flamingo Hotel in 1946 on a spot far from the developed areas of town (the closest resort then was the original El Rancho, on the south-west corner of the Strip and Sahara Avenue), the Las Vegas Strip has been a shining oasis of decadence in the desert, beckoning travellers with its gaudy imagery and irresistible temptations. You won't find 'the Strip' in any street index – it's not an official designation, but a universally used nickname for the nearly four-mile (6.4-kilometre) stretch of Las Vegas Boulevard South that runs from Sahara Avenue in the north all the way to the famous 'Welcome to Las Vegas' sign, greeting travellers arriving by road from the south. The following description runs south to north.

Russell Road to Tropicana Avenue

Near Russell Road look out for the very few remaining tiny motor inns of the 1950s and '60s, replete with neon signs far flashier than the inns themselves. To the east is the **Little Chapel of the West**, a part of the Old Frontier Hotel and site of many celebrity weddings. The chapel has been moved several times, most recently from the front lawn of the Hacienda casino, which was imploded on New Year's Eve 1996, to its new spot just south of the **Glass Pool Inn**. Notable for its above-ground pool with giant glass portholes in the sides, and the site of many movie scenes, the Glass Pool Inn was originally named the Mirage, until that name was sold to casino magnate Steve Wynn to be used for his trendsetting mega-resort further north.

Across from the Glass Pool Inn is the former Hacienda site, on which now sits the twin resorts of **Mandalay Bay**, a South Seas-themed mega-resort, and the non-gaming **Four Seasons** – the first Las Vegas hotel to win the coveted five-diamond award. Just north is the unmistakable pyramid of **Luxor**, with laser lights shooting up the sides and a beacon beckoning to the ancient gods of the sky.

At the first main intersection (with Tropicana Avenue), you are within an easy walk of more hotel rooms than in all of San Francisco. On the south-east corner are the white towers of the tropical **Tropicana**. The old boy on the block, the Trop was built in 1957. Across Tropicana Avenue to the north is the size-conscious **MGM Grand** – the largest hotel in the world, now sporting the world's largest bronze sculpture (its signature lion) above the entrance. The old angular lion's head was replaced, it is rumoured, because Asian gamblers refused to walk into a lion's mouth. To the north-west is **New York-New York**, whose Statue of Liberty replica is hosed down regularly by mock fire boats. And at the south-west corner sits the oldest of the new, the medieval-themed **Excalibur**, built in 1990 but already starting to show its age. All around the intersection the seething crowds spill on to street corners and squeeze through the pedestrian overpasses.

Tropicana to Harmon Avenue

Continue north and pass the **Showcase Mall** to the east, notable for its Times Square-style giant neon Coke bottle (in competition with New York-New York's Pepsi sign across the street) and a huge, upscale games arcade, **GameWorks**, with the world's tallest indoor climbing wall. Further on is the jumping **Club Utopia** and two tasty quick food stops – **Fatburger** and **Big Mama's Soul Food** – followed by the pink and mauve **Polo Towers** hotel and shopping plaza. Due west are the European flair and fountains of the **Monte Carlo**, flanked on the south by a Vegas landmark and locals' favourite – a petrol station with a neon sign offering gamblers 'free aspirin and tender sympathy' – and on the north by the boardwalk-style façade of the Steve Wynn-owned, and eventually doomed, **Holiday Inn Boardwalk** casino (the rides are for show only). The block ends, on the east, with the **Harley-Davidson Café**, complete with oversized motorcycle protruding from the front.

Silver City casino at the Strip's north end.

Harmon to Flamingo Road

The new **Aladdin**, due to open in summer 2000, stands to the east, totally engulfing the original Aladdin Theatre for the Performing Arts with new construction. If the recently announced plans for Harmon Avenue to be extended across the Strip and I-15 go ahead, the Aladdin will soon sit on a corner lot. The west side of the Strip is largely unspectacular: a helipad for airborne city tours and a mall of T-shirt shops leads to the time-share **Jockey Club**, which looked horribly out of place even when it was built in the 1970s. It is the only major hold-out between Steve Wynn and block-long Strip-front domination.

To the north of the Aladdin is the spectacular (but small, by Vegas standards) **Paris** casino, with its half-scale Eiffel Tower, spot-on architectural replicas, grand fountains and streetside café. A little skip north brings you to the original 'Four Corners' at Flamingo Road. On the south-west side, bizarre light-and-water tunnels – oddly disconnected in style from the classy hotel – lead into **Bally's**. To the north sits the wedged-in **Barbary Coast**, home of Drai's Supper Club. The opulent **Caesars Palace** commands attention with its striking blue-white lighting and huge fountains on the north-west side, while across to the south is the upscale drama of the bell-towered **Bellagio** – whose large replica of Lake Como comes alive every night with a most impressive streetside fountain and music show.

Flamingo to Spring Mountain Road

Next to the Barbary Coast on the east is some of Las Vegas's best remaining and most oft-photographed neon, located on the **Flamingo Hilton** (Bugsy's original Flamingo, though nothing of the original remains). The smaller **O'Sheas** and the right-up-to-the-asphalt oriental-looking **Imperial Palace** follow. Across the street is the romanesque arch leading to the **Forum Shops** at Caesars Palace, and immediately to the north begins the block-long tropical paradise created by the **Mirage** (with its regular pina colada-scented volcano eruptions) and **Treasure Island**, whose Caribbean façade and pirate ships are straight out of the Robert Louis Stevenson handbook. The Brits painfully lose it all several times nightly in a dramatic sea battle.

Back on the east side, **Harrah's** sports a tired 'carnavale' look, sinking into the background of the surrounding overkill. Writers take note: further on is the centre-Strip **Denny's**, located in **Casino Royale** and feeding a 24-hour parade of hungry Las Vegas characters like no other. Past this is the ghost of the Rat Pack's Sands casino, today replaced by another imposing Euro-mimic, the **Venetian**, home of the only Madame Tussaud's outside London. Beyond this lies a series of strip malls and the old **Vagabond Inn**. Don't bother trying, as many do, to see the pirate battle at Treasure Island from here: six lanes of noisy traffic will frustrate your attempt.

Spring Mountain to Convention Center Drive

The **Fashion Show Mall** on the west is a good stop for a snack or a sit-down meal and shopping of all kinds; you can't miss Spielberg's theme eaterie, **Dive!**, obvious from the giant waterfall and life-sized submarine tail bursting from its side. Further along is the **New Frontier**, formerly the site of the longest labour strike in US history, but currently under new ownership and contract. As expected by many Vegas observers, the New Frontier is the next property scheduled for implosion (in summer 2000), to be replaced by a San Francisco-themed casino.

Due east is the revamped high-roller palace and former home of Howard Hughes, the **Desert Inn**, with the only golf course on the Strip (though another is scheduled to open soon) and a classy touch – separate *porte-cochères* for hotel and casino guests. From here you pass almost unknowingly over the Desert Inn Super Arterial – an east-west auto express bypassing both the Strip (by tunnelling under) and I-15 (by flying over). To the east is the **Guardian Angel Cathedral**, a huge Catholic church set back from the Strip whose themed stained-glass windows are one of the few places left where you can see old Vegas icons like the Landmark Hotel.

Across from the Cathedral is the purple neon hue of the **Stardust**, whose dramatic neon and fibre-optic sign is perhaps the most impressive in the city. The east side of the Strip continues with a series of strip malls, notable for several fast-food outlets, a palmist and a full-sized **Starbucks** coffeehouse with plenty of outdoor seating.

*Vintage neon in the **Stratosphere Area**.*

Convention Center to Sahara Avenue

A cluster of development greets the visitor northeast of here, with a tacky-looking two-storey shopping mall giving way to the small **Silver City** casino. Don't look now, but San Francisco developer Luke Brugnara, owner of the Silver City and the shopping mall, also has plans for a San Francisco-themed resort. Hopefully, such plans will not interfere with the squat 1970s rotunda-styled **Peppermill's Fireside Lounge** next door – one of the best places for late-night food and romantic relaxation. Next to the Peppermill is the **La Concha Motel**, a funky building-as-sign development, the lobby made up of a series of exaggerated arches.

It's back to the big neon at the 1955 **Riviera**, whose façade and sign almost constitute overkill, even in Vegas; don't miss the life-sized cast bronze statues of the *Crazy Girls'* derrières, just in front of the casino. Rub 'em for good luck! Across the street are the neon umbrellas of **Slots-o-Fun** – infamous as the site where Vegas's New Year's Eve crowds first became so large that they spilled into the street, way back in the early 1990s. The clown sign of the original family fun palace, **Circus Circus**, still stands, and has been upgraded with a fibre-optic reader board. Nothing can compare with the hotel's night-into-day *porte-cochère*. Continuing across Riviera Boulevard, you pass the **Candlelight Wedding Chapel**, open 24 hours for those romantic emergencies. Next is a strip mall, anchored by the **Algiers Hotel**, one of the few old-time small motels remaining on the Strip, its 'bleeding brick' walls and kidney-shaped swimming pool intact.

From here, the Strip gets a little dark, starting with the decaying hulk of the 'new' **El Rancho**, formerly the Thunderbird. The hotel and its ownership were recently embroiled in a good old-fashioned organised crime scandal involving the property's former owners, some potential investors and the US Securities and Exchange Commission – unsettled as this guide went to press. The hotel's darkened Old West façade makes it look hauntingly like a ghost town, and is an eerie reminder of what all of Las Vegas would look like if the bottom suddenly fell out of the gambling market.

On the east side is a Travelodge motel, followed by a strip mall, a gas station and an Arby's fast-food joint, behind which is the **Guinness World of Records Museum**. Then it's a bit of a wasteland until you reach Sahara Avenue, the corner of which is the site of the original El Rancho Vegas, built in 1941 and later destroyed by fire. Long considered the most expensive piece of undeveloped property in Nevada, the land has been the subject of on-again, off-again development deals for years. Huge trees left over from the El Rancho days still dot the acreage.

The west side finishes brightly, however, with water park **Wet 'n Wild** (that near-vertical water slide is 'Der Stuka') sidling up to the revamped **Sahara Hotel**, whose animated camels on a new fibre-optic sign usher customers into a bright new *porte-cochère*. According to most residents, the Strip begins and ends right here.

Stratosphere Area

Facing north at the corner of Sahara Avenue and Las Vegas Boulevard , you can literally hear the screams emanating from the top of the **Stratosphere Tower**. A quick look up will show you why: at the top of the tallest building in the state of Nevada is the Big Shot, a ride that propels the daring up to the very tip of the needle of the tower – enough to make anyone scream.

Building the tower was enough to make Bob Stupak scream; the former owner of Vegas World (which used to occupy the Stratosphere site) suffered a series of financial and construction setbacks that forced him to do anything he could to get the tower completed. Now that it's done, the Stratosphere has suffered from a poor location (on the edge of the down-at-heel 'Naked City' area) and poor planning and was forced into reorganisational bankruptcy. Still, it's hard to make a tower this big simply go away, even if it is stuck in the nether region between the Strip and Downtown. So the area is gradually becoming known as the Stratosphere Area.

North from Sahara is the unmissable **Holy Cow** casino and microbrewery to the east. Across from here is the **Bonanza**, claiming to be the world's largest gift shop, where you'll find cheap and tacky souvenirs of all kinds. Further north is **Diversity**, a one-stop tattoo and piercing shop. Approaching the Stratosphere, the east side has the **Holiday House Motel**, a holdover from the old days notable for its wacky animated neon sign and Palm Springs-like motor court design.

The Stratosphere is where Main Street and Paradise Road cross Las Vegas Boulevard and turn into each other by way of St Louis Avenue. Beyond here, at the intersection of Oakey Boulevard, is **White Cross Drugs**, with one of the few remaining drugstore food counters in the city. Further down is the 24-hour **Odyssey Records**, a good spot to pick up free newspapers and city guides, and east is the two-storey white building of the **Olympic Garden** topless club. Just east on Oakey Boulevard, behind the Arco gas station, is **Luv-It Frozen Custard**, a Vegas stalwart offering incredibly rich desserts from a drive-up window. Further east is one of the older, posh neighbourhoods in the city, which is filled with modest, well-kept, single-storey, ranch-style homes with circular driveways.

Just past Oakey is the 'Gateway to Downtown' (you'll need to imagine the planned archway), where Fourth Street intersects and leads you, one-way, right to the heart of Downtown. The two-storey **Tod Motor Motel** on the west side and the **Little White Wedding Chapel** on the east, where Joan Collins and Jon Bon Jovi were married (not to each other), lure you closer to Charleston Boulevard. You'll pass **Thai Town** (a small shopping centre with a Thai grocer, restaurant and atmospheric cocktail lounge) and **Talk of The Town** adult bookstore and, on the west, the **Las Vegas International Hostel**, the city's only backpacker hostel. At Charleston Boulevard, the Stratosphere Area ends, becoming Downtown and the **Gateway**

Las Vegas Boulevard en route to Downtown.

District (*see page 96*). The best view of this area is from I-95 to the west, from where you can see landmarks such as the **Holsum Bakery** on West Charleston and the architecturally striking **Clark County Government Center**.

Downtown

In 1905, officials of the San Pedro, Salt Lake and Los Angeles Railroad stood on land that is now the Plaza Hotel and auctioned 1,200 lots to settlers and speculators, jump-starting the rapid and haphazard development that would characterise Las Vegas's history. Believe it or not, the bustling city of neon casinos and gated communities standing today evolved from what was, less than 100 years ago, just a dusty railroad settlement centred on Main and Fremont Streets.

As in most cities, Downtown has suffered some deterioration. With the big resort development all happening at the south end of the Strip, Downtown desperately needed a gimmick to encourage visitors. Spearheaded by Golden Nugget-owner Steve Wynn, Downtown hoteliers sought answers through various redevelopment proposals, finally settling on the **Fremont Street Experience**. The FSE pedestrianised the Glitter Gulch section of Fremont Street, covering it with a canopy of light and sound. Still, Downtown manages to retain an honest Vegas appeal that no amount of lightbulbs can dispel, though in terms of glamour its casinos are far outdone by their cousins on the Strip.

Standing near the canopy – a somewhat ridiculous attempt to outdo the lights that symbolised Glitter Gulch for more than 40 years – at the intersection with Fourth Street, you are within easy walking distance of all the major casinos in Downtown. On the south, **Fitzgeralds'** Irish style leads the way, followed by the billowing **Four Queens** sign, the white and gold **Golden Nugget** (the nicest Downtown hotel and home of the best mid-price buffet) and the red-brick **Golden Gate**, the oldest operating hotel in the city. To the north is **Neonopolis**, a flashy retail and restaurant development, currently under construction, and the

NASCAR-themed **Race Rock** restaurant. Beyond this are the **Fremont** and **Binion's Horseshoe** (made up of the original Binion's and the annexed Mint). Also under the canopy is a strip club, which opted to retain the Vegas Vickie neon sign already in place, becoming the **Topless Girls of Glitter Gulch**. At the far west end stands the **Plaza** hotel.

Walking east along Fremont Street from its intersection with Fourth leads away from the Fremont Street Experience canopy. The street remains pedestrian-only until you reach Las Vegas Boulevard, and is worth walking along to see the interesting (if slightly confusing) **Neon Museum**, a small but growing collection of classic old Vegas neon signs, restored and placed atop poles.

Across Fourth Street is perhaps the only neon 7-11 convenience store sign in the world, and further east is the **El Cortez** casino, a must-visit if only for a taste of Old Vegas and its denizens. The **Metropolitan Police Department** building is directly to the south, where topless dancers and blackjack-dealers alike must get background checks for the required sheriff's department work cards.

Further east on Fremont Street, beyond the FSE's controlled influence, Downtown gets seedy, littered with low-rent hotels and drug dealers. Still, this makes for a great drive at night to see the vintage neon signs of the many old motels; just remember to lock your car doors. On the north side of Fremont Street, at Seventh Street, look for the notable 1960s-mod **City Center Motel**, followed by **Fergusons Motel** and the kitschy motor court of the **Gables**.

Back to Las Vegas Boulevard and heading north from Fremont takes you to Stewart Avenue; on the north-west corner is the half-moon-shaped **City Hall**. Heading west on Stewart Avenue will take you past the original courthouse building – now the Downtown **Post Office** – and the **Downtown Transportation Center** (the CAT bus and trolley stop), straight into the turn-of-the-century-styled **Main Street Station** casino. A left on Main leads past the Plaza to the **Greyhound bus station** (on the west). Further on, you will quickly pass the **Gamblers General Store** showroom to the west and the tiny **El Sombrero Café** to the east.

Conversely, heading south on Las Vegas Boulevard from Fremont Street takes you into the heart of the business area of Downtown. At Bridger Street is the **Foley Federal Building** to the west, while the new federal building takes shape across the way. One street east (Sixth), the venerable French restaurant **André's** – operated by long-time restaurateur André Rochat – is visible, while two streets east, at Seventh Street and Bridger, the sprawling campus of the city's original high school starts. A little further south on Seventh Street, but before Charleston, is the heart of **'Lawyers' Row'**, a collection of attractive, early-century bungalows on Sixth, Seventh and Eighth Streets, most occupied by attorneys and creative businesses.

Going east on Charleston Boulevard takes you towards one of Las Vegas's few distinctive neighbourhoods, the **Huntridge District**, filled with charming bungalows. At Ninth Street, you'll pass **Harley E Harmon Insurance** to the south, a two-storey white home-turned-office, once known for its Christmas decorations. And at Maryland Parkway (which should be named 13th Street but isn't, due to superstition) is the Huntridge liquor/drugstore/food counter combo, followed by the **Huntridge Theatre** itself, a Las Vegas institution.

*Race Rock restaurant: one of the newer attractions in **Downtown**.*

The Gateway District

The revitalisation of Downtown, away from Fremont Street, has been a hot issue for nearly a decade. Mayor Oscar Goodman has come out strongly in favour of the type of redevelopment that would bring middle-class residents back to the city's core. In the triangle of mostly empty land west of the Plaza Hotel (bound by US 95, I-15 and Charleston Boulevard), a new county government office building stands. Talk of more office space, shops, mixed-use residential buildings, a cultural centre and a sports arena to fill the remaining land

induces both dreamy eyes and frustrated responses from locals. Many are pushing for and participating in redevelopment of the general Downtown area, focusing on what is called the Gateway District – still as much a movement as a reality.

Loosely bordered by Charleston Boulevard, Las Vegas Boulevard, Carson Avenue and Main Street, the Gateway District takes its name from the Gateway Motel, which sits at Charleston and Las Vegas Boulevards. The district was so named by Lenadams Dorris, co-proprietor of the Enigma Garden Café on Fourth Street.

Within the Gateway District are several businesses that fall into the loose category of 'cultural retail' – the district is rapidly becoming the arts centre that Las Vegas has always lacked. On

Charleston at Casino Center sits the **Arts Factory** (*see page 206* **Culture**), a two-storey collection of offices filled with photography shops, architects, graphic artists and galleries; the **Nevada Institute for Contemporary Art** relocated here in 1998, a major coup for the district. Across the street and slightly east in the Urga Building is the **Iowa Café** and **Liquid 303**, an independent record store.

Fourth Street, the city's one-way thoroughfare into Downtown, already bustles north of Charleston Boulevard with the **Enigma Garden Café** (*pictured*), **Doña Maria's Mexican Food** (rear entrance) and **Chicago Joe's** Italian restaurant, a Vegas classic. To the west on Main Street, the original 1951 **El Sombrero Café** and the **Attic**, a huge two-storey vintage clothing, furniture and appliance store, keep the scene alive, vibrant and connected to history.

This is one of Vegas's oldest neighbourhoods, just blocks from where it all began, and that historic connection is a critical component of any cultural centre. Offering Las Vegans a living connection to the city's past by converting the area into a workable part of daily Vegas life – instead of allowing it to fall prey to the usual 'implode and rebuild' syndrome – is a primary objective of the Gateway District movement.

Off-Strip

As both construction activity and land prices on the Strip began reaching new heights, resort development spread to the east and west of the famed thoroughfare, resulting in off-Strip corridors that house some places of interest.

East of Strip

The most obvious area of off-Strip encroachment, the Paradise Road corridor (also known as the Convention Area), flanking the Strip to the east, has been the site of development since 1969, when the Landmark and the International opened just south of Sahara Avenue. The International, on the east side, has long been known as the **Las Vegas Hilton**; the showroom has hosted everyone from Elvis Presley to the cast of *Cats*. Across from the Hilton is **Turnberry Place**, a tiny high-rise condo

development currently under construction, where many Vegas luminaries, among them Steve Wynn, have already purchased homes. Further south on Paradise is the **Arco** service station that doubled as the Shell gas station in the James Bond film *Diamonds Are Forever* (the Hilton itself was the film's Whyte House Hotel).

Back on the east side, from the south end of the Hilton all the way to Desert Inn Road, is the **Las Vegas Convention Center** – which is said to be the largest convention facility in the world. On the west side at Convention Center Drive is a parking lot – not the most respectful way to treat the former site of the Landmark.

South of here is a huge bar and nightclub, the **Beach**, a favourite conventioneers' haunt, followed by a handful of business traveller hotels. A skip west on Convention Center Drive heading back towards the Strip, on the right, is the **Flyaway** indoor skydiving centre, where people too scared to jump out of a plane can jump into the slipstream of a giant jet engine instead.

Further south on Paradise Road are the coveted homes lining the **Desert Inn Country Club** golf course. Just past Twain Avenue begins the fledgling 'Restaurant Row', a high-density collection of restaurants. The **Hughes Center** collection of office towers is to the west, followed by university student fave **Gordon Biersch** microbrewery. To the east you'll find delicious Southwestern eating at **Z'Tejas** and a strip mall with several good restaurants including **Marrakesh**, a Moroccan eaterie where seating is on floor pillows, and belly dancers entertain nightly. At the north-west corner with Flamingo Road sits **Freddie G's Diner, Cozymel's** and **Lawry's The Prime Rib. PF Chang's** is to the south-west, the shuttered **Continental Hotel** to the south-east and a strip mall containing **Gandhi's Indian Cuisine** and **Hamada of Japan** to the north-east.

Further south, the junction of Harmon Avenue is the centre of hipster attractions, with the **Hard Rock Café**'s giant guitar sign and the Miami Beach-styled **Hard Rock Hotel** to the north-west. Beckoning further south is the Gay Triangle, home to gay-oriented bars, clubs, cafés and shops, and to the east is the University District.

West of Strip

This corridor is developed primarily at the intersections of Valley View Boulevard with Flamingo Road and Sahara Avenue. At Flamingo, the ultra-fresh **Rio** hotel-casino, with its mirrored main building and new tower, is to the north-east, while the gaudy **Gold Coast** (with cheap movies and a bowling alley) is to the north-west. Valley View then goes north through a semi-residential, semi-industrial district.

An easterly turn at Sahara leads past malls ad infinitum until reaching the train-themed **Palace Station** on the south side, just before I-15. On West Tropicana Avenue (past Valley View), the **Orleans**, notable for its movie theatres with stadium-style seating, is situated among industrial development. Note that Valley View is not continuous between Tropicana and Flamingo.

The rest of the city

Using the maps and listings elsewhere in this book, and the following overview as a general field guide, a visitor should be able to take a tour of the 'other' Las Vegas that few tourists see. For this, a car is a must; doing it by bus, though possible, would be prohibitively time-consuming. The areas are arranged anti-clockwise. Remember that the entire valley is rapidly filling with new housing developments, so construction delays and detours are possible. Also, these area designations, while based upon the general consensus of residents, are our own, and are not to be taken as official names seen on signposts.

South-west Las Vegas

South-west Las Vegas is one of the older, more established suburbs of the city, and easily accessible by travelling west on Tropicana Avenue. Most of the area is unremarkable in the sense that, like much of Vegas, it is made up of middle-class suburban homes surrounded by strip malls. At the far west end of Tropicana, almost as far as the mountains, are the ultra-posh residential developments of **Spanish Trail** and **Spanish Hills**. Many of Las Vegas's most notable residents live behind the walls of these pricey, immaculate communities and, though you can't get inside, you can gaze longingly at the dramatic elevations and landscaping provided for André Agassi and others. At the junction of Tropicana Avenue and Rainbow Boulevard, **Panini**, a fantastic mid-priced Italian restaurant sits on the north-west corner. Heading north, the main artery of Rainbow will lead you through one of the city's older neighbourhoods, **Spring Valley**, though you won't see the modest homes unless you turn off.

North-west Las Vegas

Continuing north on Rainbow eventually leads to Sahara Avenue. Just 15 years ago, this intersection was dark and nearly empty, save for the 7-11 on the south-east corner. Today, it is surrounded by residential and heavy commercial development. An east turn here will lead past countless car dealerships and

The **UNLV campus**, *just east of the Strip.*

Drive-by history tour

Las Vegas constantly recasts itself to anticipate the wants of its patrons. The city roared into the twenty-first century on a slew of demolitions and phoenix-like rebirths that both razed historic standbys and raised new casino-resorts in their stead. In most instances, the famous (or infamous) Strip hotels of the Mob era and Rat Pack past are long gone. Likewise, throughout the city, unrecognised landmarks have disappeared with a similar disregard for their historical significance. A few have survived, however – a side benefit of the city's leapfrog expansion or, in some cases, a simple lack of funds. If you have the time and transport, this drive-by tour will open your eyes to a vision of Vegas past. It is in roughly south-east to north-west geographical order.

Green Shack

2504 E Fremont Street, at Charleston Boulevard, East Las Vegas.
In continuous operation since the 1930s until its closure in July 1999, the Green Shack restaurant evokes decades of memories: construction workers building Hoover Dam stopped by here; the politicos and powerful lunched here; newspaper reporters held down bar stools here; even Bugsy Siegel ate in the place. But history is yesterday and, in Vegas, yesterday is long gone. At the time of writing, the building is a sad and empty shell, its historic fixtures sold at auction, awaiting an unknown future.

Huntridge Performing Arts Theater

1208 E Charleston Boulevard, at Maryland Parkway, Downtown.
This 1943 art deco remnant of Old Vegas was built to serve the surrounding Huntridge neighbourhood. The building may be architecturally dull, but take a look at the integrated tall neon signage and imagine the gracefully curved marquee board lit up with the names of the stars who attended premières here: Frank Sinatra, Jerry Lewis, Marlene Dietrich. It was resurrected in the mid-1990s by the dedicated efforts of Huntridge neighbourhood alumnus and businessman Richard Lenz. Today, the theatre is used primarily as the city's main all-ages performance centre (*see p233* **Nightlife: Music**).

Downtown residential district

Sixth, Seventh, Eighth & Ninth Streets, north from Oakey Boulevard to Bridger Avenue, Downtown.
Although most of residential Las Vegas is unimaginatively cast in the same faux-Mediterranean stucco form, this Downtown neighbourhood is a good example of architectural diversity and small-town homeliness. Well-kept single-storey homes with large yards and wide driveways are typical. Heading south from Charleston on any of the named streets will take you past 1940s bungalows first, then 1950s and 1960s inspirations. Heading north leads into 'Lawyers' Row', where many of the smallish plaster-walled and wood-floored homes have been purchased and restored by ad agencies, graphic arts studios and attorneys.

Las Vegas Academy of International Studies & Performing Arts

315 S Seventh Street, at Bridger Avenue, Downtown.
The original campus of the since-relocated Las Vegas High School, the city's first high school. While today's prison-like US schools are designed with student control in mind, this sprawling open campus spreads itself over two blocks. Check out the three-storey art deco main building facing Seventh Street and the separate performance centre on Eighth, complete with sunken orchestra pit. Slated for destruction, the campus was saved by the intervention of several prominent Nevada citizens who graduated from the school, and turned into a public performing arts high school.

---

chain restaurants and eventually to the **Sahara-Decatur Pavilions**, at the intersection of Decatur Boulevard. Here, four corners of development offer a full day's eating and shopping. Most notable is the north-east side, with food ranging from **Baja Fresh** (Mexican) to **Habib's** (Persian) to **Jamba Juice** (smoothie and juice bar), and shops that include **Borders Books & Coffee**, the **Tower-Good Guys-Wow!** superstore and dozens of small speciality shops.

Heading west on Sahara beyond Buffalo Drive leads past **Rosemary's**, named the best new restaurant in a local newspaper poll in 1999. Past Durango Drive is **The Lakes**, home of the eclectic **Mermaid Café** and lakeside homes with boating

and fishing. The Lakes area is for the most part accessible by car, but facilities are for residents only. At the far west reaches of Sahara Avenue, nestled at the base of the mountains, lies the new **Red Rock Country Club**, a Scottsdale-inspired desert golf community seemingly a galaxy away from the Strip.

Heading north from Sahara on Durango to Charleston Boulevard and then turning west towards the mountains leads to **Summerlin**, the best selling corporate planned community in the nation. Continue west for a mere ten minutes to reach beautiful and wild **Red Rock Canyon Conservation Area**, or turn north to tour clean and somewhat snobby Summerlin – a planned community that includes housing (ranging from

Scotch 80s neighbourhood

Bordered by Charleston Boulevard, Rancho Drive, Oakey Boulevard & I-15, North-west Las Vegas.

Navigating busy Charleston Boulevard, visitors would never guess that a southerly turn on to Shadow Lane will reveal this old-money enclave (*pictured*). This tiny neighbourhood is but a dice throw from Downtown, yet homes are nestled in a quiet, winding labyrinth of tree-lined streets and one-acre homesites with tennis courts, and huge ranch estates. Low-slung trees reveal the area's former swampy nature. Most of the city's original who's who (including current mayor Oscar Goodman) either lives or lived here.

Las Vegas Springs Preserve (aka Big Springs)

Loosely bordered by US 95, Valley View Boulevard & Alta Drive, North-west Las Vegas.

The largest area of undeveloped land in the central city, the 180-acre Big Springs is where legendary Old West explorers Kit Carson and John Fremont parked their horses in the mid-1800s. Huge cottonwoods and natural scrub fill the area and surround an early-century well house, while wild animals – including coyotes and foxes – roam behind the freeway fencing. The land is owned and administered by the Las Vegas Valley Water District and has survived both fire and the threat of being paved over in the name of freeway expansion. Plans were unveiled in 1999 for formal development of the area into a historical learning centre and natural preserve.

Binion Ranch

North side of Bonanza Road, just east of Rancho Drive, North-west Las Vegas.

The Binions are a legendary gambling and ranching family, and their Downtown casino – the Horseshoe – is still recognised as offering the best-quality steak special in town. Family patriarch Benny Binion once lived in this long-boarded-up, two-storey block-and-timber ranch house. With Lonnie 'Ted' Binion's mysterious death in 1998, the place takes on even greater historical significance (though the death did not occur here). As recently as the 1990s, horses and cattle were still kept on the property. Lately, some big old trees were removed, stealing some of the Old West ambience.

Moulin Rouge

900 W Bonanza Road, just west of I-15, North-west Las Vegas.

In the bad old days, Las Vegas hotels forced African-American entertainers – pivotal in the city's growth as an entertainment capital – to flee the Strip after showtime and take refuge at the Moulin Rouge hotel-casino – once disparagingly called 'the Mississippi of the West'. What resulted was a short-lived but legendary stint of black entertainers (Sammy Davis Jr, Nat King Cole) joined on stage by Frank Sinatra and other Strip players in a daring after-hours ritual. The city's racial segregation finally ended with an agreement signed with Strip casino bosses at the Rouge in 1960. Plans to revive the place have fallen flat, though more are now in the pipeline.

Mormon Fort

500 E Washington Avenue, at Las Vegas Boulevard North, North Las Vegas (486 3511). **Bus 403. Open** *8am-4.30pm daily.* **Admission** *$1; 50¢ under-13s.*

Built by Mormon missionaries in 1855, then abandoned to become part of the Las Vegas Ranch, this is Vegas's pioneer settling site and the city's oldest building. Though only remnants remain from the original structure, a restoration and reconstruction of the compound should be finished by May 2000.

$60,000 condos to multimillion-dollar homes), businesses, schools, parks, churches – a regular prefab life. The infrastructure is magnificent, but the overall *Stepford Wives* effect is somewhat disconcerting.

Several miles further north, you pass the older ranch homes of those who tried to get away from it all 20 years ago and are now subsumed by the ever-encroaching stucco. For a deeper taste of old north-west Las Vegas, take Rancho Road north from Sahara. This will lead past the **Scotch 80s** – a swanky neighbourhood of large-lot homes built mostly in the 1950s and 1960s, bordered by Rancho Drive, Oakey and Charleston Boulevards and I-15. This is where Mayor Oscar Goodman resides; entertainer Shecky Greene once lived here, too, as

did Nevada's first African-American neurosurgeon, Dr Frederick Boulware. The gardens are beautifully tended and surprisingly lush, owing to a supply of underground water that makes it almost swampy.

The route also passes **Rancho Circle** to the west, perhaps the most exclusive old neighbourhood in the city, where BB King once lived (and Bob Stupak and Phyllis McGuire still do), at the north-west corner of Rancho and Alta.

Continuing north on Rancho and passing under US 95 will take you through some very old areas, with the primarily African-American area of West Las Vegas spreading out north-east from Bonanza Road (turn right to see the **Moulin Rouge**, Las Vegas's first interracial casino) and **Twin Lakes** (the site of Lorenzi Park, whose ponds were once spring-fed). Further north, a west turn at Vegas Drive leads to the palatial home of master illusionists Siegfried and Roy, just across from the municipal golf course. It's on the north side, and certainly quite gracious, though you can't see much. Look for the white adobe walls and the wrought iron gate bearing the initials S and R.

Rancho Road eventually leads past the **Hilltop House Restaurant** (a classy supper club), **Bob Taylor's Ranch House** and the **Texas Station**, **Fiesta** and **Santa Fe** hotel-casinos, en route to Floyd Lamb State Park and Mount Charleston.

North Las Vegas

After suffering years of public opinion that placed it as a grimy little sister to Las Vegas, North Las Vegas – a city unto itself – has experienced a limited renaissance, a result of the tremendous growth in the Valley as a whole. Residential and business development in an area known as the Golden Triangle nearly mirrors that of the pricier north-west. New homes and shops have sprung up to fill previously undeveloped land between Rancho Road, US 95 and I-15. In reality, the shiny new Golden Triangle area seems somewhat removed from most of North Las Vegas, a working-class city that grew primarily from the **Nellis Air Force Base**, especially since the areas are physically separated by the interstate.

North Las Vegas is home to the majority of the ethnic population of the Valley, as well as the main campus of the **Community College of Southern Nevada** (which has a great planetarium). African-American, Asian and Mexican residents have moved in as Anglos have moved out, turning North Las Vegas into a melting pot of ethnicities, with business signs often printed in native languages. The older area, largely untouched by redevelopment, carries with it more of the historical and urban flavour generally associated with modern cities that Las Vegas proper seems to lack. This can all make for an authentic experience for the adventurous traveller. (It's not particularly dangerous, but you should take the usual urban precautions.)

A good way to reach these areas is to turn off either US 95 or Rancho Road at Craig Road, heading east, which will take you through the Golden Triangle. A southward turn at Las Vegas Boulevard North will lead back towards Downtown, past ethnic eateries, the **Palomino Club**, **Jerry's Nugget** (with desserts to die for), **Forest Lawn Cemetery**, the **Paiute Indian Reservation**, the architecturally interesting **Las Vegas Library**, **Cashman Field** sports ground, the old **Mormon Fort** and the **Las Vegas Museum of Natural History**.

East Las Vegas

East Las Vegas is a large, older section of town, once characterised by ugly quick-build housing tracts and trailer parks, but again unable (and probably unwilling) to avoid the incursion of new development. The most notable part of this area is

Sunrise Mountain, which in the 1960s and '70s was where the independently minded rich would forgo spots in the Scotch 80s to build desert-style homes with panoramic views of the city, often from backyard pools. Following this lead, most new housing development in the area has been focused on and around Sunrise Mountain. Also of note is the **Latter Day Saints Temple**, near the eastern end of Charleston Boulevard, near the mountain. Non-Mormon visitors are not allowed inside, but it is a sight to behold, especially when lit up at night.

Heading back towards Downtown on Charleston, you pass **Donut Tyme**, a 24-hour sugar palace and home of the best doughnuts in town. Closer to Fremont Street on the north side is old-timer **Ralph Jones Display**, a retail-display supplier that often has illuminated Christmas displays in its windows regardless of the season. Parts of the Boulder Highway (Fremont Street, south of Charleston) also fall into East Las Vegas, including the **Showboat Hotel** and the now-closed (despite being listed on the National Register of Historic Places) **Green Shack** restaurant, both just south of Charleston.

University District

Heading south on Maryland Parkway from Charleston, you pass the Huntridge neighbourhood to the east. Just past Oakey Boulevard, on the east, is the **Catholic Bishop Gorman High School** and, at the corner of Sahara Avenue, you're within walking distance of the old **Commercial Center** to the south-west, featuring restaurants and interesting ethnic and boutique shopping. Travelling south, you pass the popular **Boulevard Mall** to the east and, at Twain Avenue, the **Underground**, Las Vegas's oldest independent/alternative music store, to the west. At Flamingo Road, the University District officially begins, with businesses sticking mostly to Maryland Parkway and the rest of the area filled with apartments.

Points of interest here are too numerous to list; suffice it to say that the entire area has something to offer. On the south-west corner of Flamingo is a shopping centre with **Record City**, selling used

Masterplanned community **Summerlin**.

Lake Las Vegas: *a new, upscale resort community on the edge of Lake Mead.*

CDs, and the **Mediterranean Café & Market**. Across the way is **Tower Records** and the used/vintage clothing superstore **Buffalo Exchange**. Also here are more ethnic eateries and savvy clothing outlets, and the **Clark County Library** is just to the east. Further along Maryland Parkway, the **University of Las Vegas-Nevada** (UNLV) campus starts to the west, while two shopping centres filled with cafés, pizza joints, bars, music stores and copy shops line the east side all the way to Tropicana Avenue. Any one of these places provides a great opportunity to tune into the youth culture of Las Vegas – nightclubs, poetry readings, live music – and the natives are usually friendly.

Green Valley & Henderson

A tale of two cities within two cities is the history of Henderson and Green Valley. Founded in 1941 as a company town housing employees of the then-new Basic Magnesium plant, **Henderson** naturally developed a reputation as an industrial town. This reputation was well deserved; in the 1980s the town generated over half of Nevada's industrial output and Las Vegas residents joked about the 'Henderson Cloud', a foul-smelling haze that lingered over the city, attacking the nose of anyone venturing along Boulder Highway towards Lake Mead.

The haze cleared when smokestack scrubbers were installed in the area's factories, but the industrial nature of Henderson could not be so easily expunged. This was proven in 1988 when an earth-shaking ammonium perchlorate (an ingredient in rocket fuel) explosion at the now-relocated Pepcon plant levelled two factories and shattered windows across the Valley.

Today, Henderson proper is an interesting town, with an original downtown and two of the newest and most dynamic suburban developments in Southern Nevada. **Lake Las Vegas** (across Boulder Highway, on Lake Mead) is an impressive high-dollar resort community with hotels, golf courses, residential developments and more, all surrounding a vast man-made lake that empties into Lake Mead. The development is set in a striking desert environment of various elevations and homes start at a chilly half-million dollars; opulent, but somewhat obscene, at least for environmentalists. The first hotel – the Hyatt Regency – opened in December 1999.

Green Valley, to the north-west of Henderson, was the Valley's first masterplanned community. Separated by US 95 from the rest of Henderson, Green Valley, like Summerlin, is home to a massive corporate development of homes in all price ranges, plus shops, schools, parks and more. To reach the area, take Sunset Road west from Boulder Highway to the intersection of Green Valley Parkway.

Green Valley has developed a local reputation for snobbishness, and perhaps rightfully so. So many of the area's residents hail from Southern California that it is often referred to as 'Little LA'. At one point, residents unsuccessfully fought for independence from low-rent Henderson. Others have taken to wearing shirts emblazoned with 'Green Valley 89014', a pretentious take on the TV series, *Beverly Hills 90210*. Conversely, many Green Valley residents participate in cultural activities and offer them significant financial support, and this is reflected in the types of businesses that survive and thrive there. Ethnic eateries, creative retail classes (such as pottery), cinemas and the like do a booming business, and community-sponsored cultural events are well attended. Green Valley community leaders, businesses and residents have achieved a sense of cultural synergy of which others in the metropolis are undoubtedly envious.

Visit the **Green Valley Town Center**, a mall and plaza on the north-west corner of Sunset at Green Valley Parkway, the perfect example of the mall as community focus, or the area surrounding the **Galleria Mall** further east on Sunset. Near here is **Sunset Station**, a neighbourhood casino with a fabulous, Gaudi-inspired interior design. Heading west on Sunset leads past Wayne Newton's home (south-west corner of Russell Road) and the huge **Sunset Park** (at Eastern), eventually returning you, once again, to the inescapable lure of the Strip.

Las Vegas by Season

From poker contests to rodeos to film festivals, Las Vegas's desert climate and party spirit mean year-round festivities.

Whatever the holiday, you can expect a big blowout in the Entertainment Capital of the World. The year 2000 was ushered in with glamorous parties and flamboyant shows. Bette Midler, Barbra Streisand, the Eagles, Carlos Santana, Rod Stewart, Tina Turner and Elton John were among the celebrities who kicked things off in style. Though Y2K and terrorism fears kept visitor counts down and street celebrations to a minimum, the city is poised to return to its previous **New Year's Eve** greatness in December 2000 – you can expect to see at least 250,000 revellers in the streets, almost as many as you'll find in New York City or San Francisco. So you're definitely better off walking or leaving the driving to a professional (buses and taxis), if you're out on the town.

There are other days that are special in Las Vegas. The city's role as the nation's wedding centre means that on **Valentine's Day**, the city is packed with loving couples trying to get hitched in wacky ways – at quickie wedding chapels, drive-thru wedding windows or in lavish environments fit for royalty. **Nevada Day** (31 October) is the day Nevada officially joined the Union and became a state in 1864. Since it also happens to be **Hallowe'en**, the celebrations in Las Vegas multiply. There are numerous parties in casinos and bars around town, and two annual charity balls that put anything most other cities have to offer to shame. Many people have the day off work. All city, county and state offices are closed, but federal offices remain open.

Those looking for multicultural events will not be disappointed. The city's diverse population provides a variety of parties: in the **Jamaican Independence Day Festival** (386 7022); the **Chautauqua Native American Festival** (294 6224); the **Greek Food Festival** (221 8245); the **Mexican Independence Day Celebration** (649 8553) and the **Las Vegas International Mariachi Festival** at Mandalay Bay (632 7777); **Oktoberfest Harvest Festival** (649 8503); and the **Fruits of Africa Festival** (454 1212). The world is at your doorstep – or your hotel lobby – in Las Vegas.

NATIONAL HOLIDAYS

New Year's Day (1 Jan); Martin Luther King Jr Day (third Mon in Jan); President's Day (third Mon in Feb); Memorial Day (last Mon in May); Independence Day (4 July); Labor Day (first Mon in Sept); Columbus Day (second Mon in Oct); Election Day (first Tue in Nov); Veteran's Day (11 Nov); Thanksgiving Day (fourth Thur in Nov); Christmas Day (25 Dec).

CLIMATE

Las Vegas sits bang in the middle of the Mojave desert and consequently has a typical dry desert climate. In summer, although the days sizzle with thermometers reaching their peak around 120°F (49°C), the temperature can drop by 20°F at night. In winter, the city cools off dramatically – it can get as cold as 25 to 35°F (-3 to 1°C) at night; the days average in the high 50°Fs – and some visitors have even witnessed a rare but not impossible hailstorm or snow flurry.

Although the temperatures do vary, you are almost always guaranteed a clear day: Las Vegas averages 307 sunny days a year. The rain, such as it is – average rainfall is four inches (ten centimetres) a year – falls mainly in January and February. Spring and autumn are the best times to visit.

That said, Vegas occasionally experiences freak weather conditions. On 8 July 1999, for example, the Valley was struck by a 100-year flood. Even though the official measure of 1.29 inches (3.28 centimetres) of rain in less than six hours was more than a quarter of the average annual rainfall, the big story was found in pockets around the metropolitan area. More than three inches (7.6 centimetres) of rain fell in a four-hour period over parts of the Valley, sending rivers of mud rushing through the city, destroying buildings and property and killing several people.

Then, on 16 October, an early morning magnitude-7 earthquake, centred in the Mojave desert in Southern California, rattled homes and swayed taller buildings, waking residents and quieting casinos – but only for a moment. No injuries or damage were reported in that incident.

*Watch the world's best compete in the **Pro Bull Riders Tour** in October. See page 105.*

Spring

Big League Weekend
Information 386 7184. Cashman Field, 850 N Las Vegas Boulevard, at Washington Avenue, North Las Vegas. Bus 106, 113. **Date** early Mar.
Las Vegas is without a major league baseball team, so b-ball fans take advantage of this chance to cheer on their favourite professional teams from around the league in pre-season exhibition games.

Las Vegas 400 NASCAR Winston Cup Race
Information 644 4444. Las Vegas Motor Speedway, 7000 N Las Vegas Boulevard, North Las Vegas. Bus 113A. **Admission** $50-$110. **Date** mid-Mar.
Motor racing enthusiasts can get their fill of excitement during this stop on the NASCAR circuit. The newly inaugurated Sam's Town 300 Busch Series Grand National Division race precedes the big event. You'll need to order tickets early, so call the box office on 1-800 644 4444. The LVMS also hosts the IRL Las Vegas 500, an open-wheel race with Indy-style cars, and drag racing.

St Patrick's Day
Date 17 Mar.
If you're looking for green beer and plenty of 'craic', the following pubs will give you a taste of the old country: **Paddy's Pub & Eatery** (4160 S Pecos Road; 435 1684); **The Irish Porker** (1945 Las Vegas Boulevard South; 731 3468); and **JC Wooloughan** (648 0300), an authentic Irish pub brought over brick by brick from Ireland to the Resort at Summerlin. The Sons of Erin also sponsor a lively Downtown parade.

UNLVino
Information 876 4500. Bally's, 3645 Las Vegas Boulevard South, at E Flamingo Road. Bus 202, 301, 302. **Admission** $25-$40. **Date** late Mar.
Sponsored by the University of Nevada, Las Vegas, this wine-tasting event brings California's best wine growers to town. It gets rowdier by the hour, so go early for the best selection of wines, the shortest lines and the least hassle.

Clark County Fair
Information 594 3247. Clark County Fairgrounds, Logandale, Nevada. No bus. **Date** early Apr.
Southern Nevada's only old-time county fair offers four days of food, rides, rodeo events and three stages with continuous entertainment at the county fairgrounds on the I-15, one hour north of Vegas.

NHRA Drag Racing
Information 644 4444. Las Vegas Motor Speedway, 7000 N Las Vegas Boulevard, North Las Vegas. Bus 113A. **Date** Apr.
With the new dragstrip finally complete at the LVMS, this event has been added for the 2000 season and beyond. The oldest and most prestigious straight-line racing organisation in the world, the NHRA sanctions $1/4$ mile standoffs in cars ranging from street-legal sedans to jet-powered dragrails.

King of the Beach Invitational Volleyball Tournament
Information 693 5000. Hard Rock, 4455 Paradise Road, at Harmon Avenue, East of Strip. Bus 108. **Date** Apr.
Tons of fine beach sand cover the parking lot of this Miami-styled hotel, as players from the pro

volleyball circuit dig deep and spike hard for more than $200,000 in prize money.

Gay Pride Parade
Information 733 9800/225 3389. Sunset Park, 2601 Sunset Road, at S Eastern Avenue, East Las Vegas. Bus 110, 212. **Date** Apr or May.
Come out and support the gay and lesbian community at this annual parade and picnic, with food booths, games, workshops and entertainers. It's quickly gaining a reputation as one of the top Gay Pride parades in the west.

Professional Bowling Association (PBA) National & Senior Tour
Information 385 9123/1-303 836 5568. Showboat, 2800 Fremont Street, at Boulder Highway, East Las Vegas. Bus 107, 206. **Date** end Apr.
Nine championship rounds of (televised) bowling and other events for big prize money.

World Series of Poker
Information 382 1600. Binion's Horseshoe, 128 Fremont Street, at Second Street, Downtown. Bus 107, 301. **Admission** free; buy-in for $2,070-$10,000. **Date** Apr-May (finals in May).
The very best poker players in the world get down to serious business during this three-week event with more prize money ($100 million) up for grabs than at any other major sporting event. The final can be watched from small stands around the game itself or on numerous TV screens.

Craft Fair/Rib Burn-Off/Car Show
Information 455 8206. Sunset Park, 2601 Sunset Road, at S Eastern Avenue, East Las Vegas. Bus 110, 212. **Date** May.
This two-day weekend event spreads itself over the sprawling grounds of Sunset Park, offering live music, a classic car show and acres of vendors hawking everything from freshly sizzled ribs and burgers to jewellery and other handicrafts.

Liberace Birthday Celebration & Play-Alike Contest
Information 798 5595. Liberace Museum, 1775 E Tropicana Avenue, at Spencer Street, University District. Bus 201. **Admission** $6.95; $2-$4.50 concessions. **Date** mid-May.
To commemorate Mr Showmanship's birthday, the Liberace Museum sponsors an impersonation contest for amateurs and professionals, who are judged on their technique, costume and presentation by a panel of celebrity judges.

EAT'M Festival
Information 792 9430. Mirage, 3400 Las Vegas Boulevard South, between Spring Mountain & W Flamingo Roads. **Admission** free-$10. **Date** mid-May.
Two years old, the Emerging Artists & Talent in Music festival is a four-day event that gives up-and-coming bands the opportunity to display their skills to recording executives, talent developers and fans. The Mirage hosts the event, with other showcase stages at the Hard Rock, Gilley's, Imperial Palace, Tommy Rocker's and Treasure Island.
Website: www.eat-m.com

February is **Marathon** month: see p106.

Helldorado Days & Rodeo
Information 870 1221. Thomas & Mack Center, 4505 S Maryland Parkway, at E Tropicana Avenue, University District. Bus 201. **Admission** free-$10. **Date** end May or early June.
A time-honoured Las Vegas tradition, this tribute to the Old West features rodeos, a bull riders' competition, carnival rides, barbecues, dancing and live country music. The event separates the 'old-timers', who spend the entire week in cowboy costumes, from 'new' Las Vegans. Lots of fun for all, however.

Summer

Junefest
Information 895 3900. Silver Bowl Park, Sam Boyd Stadium, 7000 E Russell Road, at Boulder Highway, Henderson. Bus 201. **Admission** $15-$30. **Date** first weekend in June.
A day-long concert featuring classic rock 'n' roll groups. When it gets hot, the crowd gets hosed off!

Independence Day & Damboree Days Festival
Information 293 2034. Bicentennial Park, at Colorado Street & Nevada Highway, Boulder City. Bus 116. **Date** 4 July weekend.
Damboree Days in Boulder City is the best Independence Day celebration in the area. The weekend is packed with outdoor contests, dancing and a fireworks display. In Las Vegas itself, some of the neighbourhood casinos host barbecues and small fireworks shows. A bigger show can be found at Desert Breeze Park, while the Firemen's Benefit Association presents the biggest fireworks extravaganza at Sam Boyd Stadium.

Las Vegas International Film Festival
Information 547 0877. Orleans, 4500 W Tropicana Avenue, at Arville Street, South-west Las Vegas. Bus 201. **Date** early June.
Inaugurated in 1998, this ten-day festival is geared towards a local audience and focuses more on independent films than its CineVegas counterpart (*see below*). For more information on both festivals, *see* p199 **Culture: Film**.

Autumn

Grand Slam for Children

Information 891 7777. MGM Grand, 3799 Las Vegas Boulevard South, at E Tropicana Avenue. Bus 201, 301, 302. **Tickets** concert $35, $50, $75 from TicketMaster (474 4000). **Date** early Sept.

Much-beloved tennis star Andre Agassi invites a group of his closest celebrity friends (Elton John, Kenny G, Faith Hill and Tim McGraw and the like) to town for a huge auction and dinner event followed by a stadium-seated concert at the MGM Grand Garden, which is open to the general public. It's rumoured that the event won't happen in 2000.

Las Vegas Street Fair

Information 286 4944. Open lot across from Gold Coast & Rio, 3700 W Flamingo Road, at Valley View Boulevard, West of Strip. Bus 202. **Date** mid-Sept.

This eclectic event includes an international food festival, arts and crafts, karate demonstrations, carnival rides and lots of live bands.

Shakespeare in the Park

Information 263 4963. Foxridge Park, Valle Verde Drive, off Warm Springs Road, Henderson. Bus 217. **Admission** free-$25. **Date** end Sept.

The best outdoor theatre event in town: a travelling troupe presents a Shakespeare play (usually a comedy one year, a tragedy the next). Mimes, madrigal singers and jugglers complete the spectacle.

Art in the Park

Information 294 1611. Bicentennial Park, at Colorado Street & Nevada Highway, Boulder City. Bus 116. **Date** first weekend in Oct.

Hundreds of artists and craftmakers from throughout the Southwest set up shop for this strolling art show in the park.

Las Vegas Jaycees State Fair

Information 457 2147. Cashman Field, 850 N Las Vegas Boulevard, at E Washington Avenue, North Las Vegas. Bus 113. **Date** early Oct.

Enjoy live music, contests, carnival rides, exhibits, delicious food and a host of other activities at this six-day fair, which draws a crowd of about 60,000. Old-fashioned fun for all the family.

Italian Festival

Information 252 7777. Rio, 3700 W Flamingo Road, at Valley View Boulevard, West of Strip. Bus 202. **Date** second weekend in Oct.

Authentic Italian food from the city's best restaurants will damage everyone's waistlines. Pile on the inches at the spaghetti-eating contest and work them off again at the grape-stomping competition.

Professional Bull Riders Tour

Information 1-719 471 3008. Thomas & Mack Center, 4505 S Maryland Parkway, at E Tropicana Avenue, University District. Bus 201. **Admission** $20-$50. **Date** mid-Oct.

For those of you who can't wait for the rodeo in December, check out this event sponsored by Caesars Palace. The top 45 bull riders in the world

arrive in Las Vegas to compete over three days for $1 million and the title of World Champion Bull Rider. For tickets, call TicketMaster (474 4000).

Great Duck Derby

Information 597 1107. Sunset Park, 2601 Sunset Road, at S Eastern Avenue, East Las Vegas. Bus 212. **Date** late Oct.

Thousands of rubber ducks race across the lake in Sunset Park in a competition to raise money for a local disability charity. A weird but wonderful sight.

PGA Las Vegas Invitational

Information 242 3000. **Admission** $15-$20. **Date** late Oct.

This four-day golf tournament, held at three area courses including the Desert Inn Golf Club on the Strip, is one of the most exciting events on the PGA Tour. It brought Tiger Woods his first PGA victory in 1996.

Las Vegas Balloon Classic

Information 434 0848. Silver Bowl Park, Sam Boyd Stadium, 7000 E Russell Road, at Boulder Highway, Henderson. Bus 201A. **Date** end Oct.

Hot-air balloons fill the sky during a weekend of flying competitions. The Saturday sundown 'balloon glow' demonstration is a must-see.

Hallowe'en

Check local publications for details. **Date** on and around 31 Oct.

Hallowe'en is big news in Las Vegas. Shopping centres offer 'safe street' trick-or-treating for the kids (try the Boulevard Mall at the corner of Maryland Parkway and Desert Inn Road), and adults get decked out in elaborate costumes for parties at most of the local nightclubs – Ra at the Luxor, Utopia, and Baby's at the Hard Rock Hotel are particularly wicked. Top of the party list, however, are the Fetish & Fantasy Hallowe'en Ball and the celeb-studded 35-year-old Beaux Arts Ball, held at the MGM Grand. Check local papers for Hallowe'en events. *See also p228* **Nightlife: Gay & lesbian**.

Turkey Trot

Information 367 1626. Call for route details. **Date** early Nov.

Nevada's largest charity run (usually about 900 people take part) features a three-mile fun walk and a competitive 10km run.

LPGA Tour Championship

Information 1-888 254 4653. Desert Inn Golf Club, 3145 Las Vegas Boulevard South, between Sands Avenue & Desert Inn Road. Bus 203, 301, 302. **Admission** $10-$15. **Date** late Nov.

The top 30 professional women golfers tee off in this season-ending tournament for a purse of $750,000.

Nutcracker Holiday Market

Information 732 1638. Convention Center, Riviera, 2901 Las Vegas Boulevard South, at Riviera Boulevard. Bus 301, 302. **Date** late Nov.

A holiday shopping extravaganza in a village setting, plus performances by local ballet company Nevada Dance Theater.

The Magical Forest

Information 259 3741. Opportunity Village, 6300 W Oakey Boulevard, between Jones & Rainbow Boulevards, South-west Las Vegas. Bus 102, 205. **Date** end Nov to Christmas.
A Christmas display with two million lights and a castle complete with Santa, giant candy canes and a forest of decorated trees.

CineVegas Film Festival

Information 1-800 548 0323. Paris, 3655 Las Vegas Boulevard South, between Flamingo Road & Harmon Avenue. **Tickets** $6; $5 concessions. **Date** early Dec. Launched in 1998, this week-long festival includes world premières, classic cinema and short films by UNLV students and local producers. Movies are shown at Paris and other screens around the city. *Website: www.cinevegas.com*

Billboard Music Awards

Information 891 7777. MGM Grand Garden, 3799 Las Vegas Boulevard South, at E Tropicana Avenue. Bus 201, 301, 302. **Date** early Dec.
Stars of the music world gather to honour the number-one performers of the year as determined by record charts and radio play. It's a great night for star-gazing. Get tickets via TicketMaster (474 4000).

National Finals Rodeo

Information 895 3900. Thomas & Mack Center, 4505 S Maryland Parkway, at E Tropicana Avenue, University District. Bus 201. **Admission** $24-$38. **Date** early Dec.
Top cowboys and girls set Las Vegas ablaze with country-oriented entertainment. For nine days the city goes rodeo mad and tickets are notoriously hard to come by. Get your stylish Western duds at the Cowboy Christmas Gift Show (260 8605) at the Las Vegas Convention Center and get ready to party all night at Dylan's (451 4006) and Rockabilly's (641 5800). Contact the Professional Rodeo Cowboys Association (1-719 593 8840) for more information.

Parade of Lights

Information 293 2034. Lake Mead Marina, Lake Mead National Recreation Area. No bus. **Date** mid-Dec.
Boats covered with lights sail around Lake Mead. A good viewing spot is near Boulder Beach.

New Year's Eve

Check local publications for details. **Date** 31 Dec.
The Strip turns into one big street party as 250,000 visitors arrive to celebrate New Year and the city lays on extra ambulances, police and portable toilets. Expect headline performers, a party at every casino, firework displays – and a shortage of hotel rooms.

Las Vegas International Marathon

Information 876 3870/459 8314. **Date** second weekend in Feb.
Some 6,000 runners participate in this 5km run and half-marathon along the old Los Angeles Highway. It starts in Jean, south of Vegas, and ends at the Vacation Village hotel at the south end of the Strip.

Don't miss!

In a city where gambling, drinking, merry-making and sporting events are the norm, every day offers fun and adventure. However, there are a few special events that add a little extra electricity to Las Vegas's glowing skyline. If you're in town at the right time, check out the following:

Las Vegas 400 Winston Cup & Sam's Town 300

Date mid Mar.
Two of Nevada's biggest auto races will quench your need for speed at the Las Vegas Motor Speedway north of town.

UNLVino

Date late Mar.
Taste the best Californian wine and mingle with the highbrow, all in a good cause.

King of the Beach Invitational Volleyball Tournament

Date Apr.
Pretend you're on a beach in Southern California as pro volleyballers do their thing outside the Hard Rock Hotel.

World Series of Poker

Date Apr-May.
A gathering of legendary poker players, major celebrities and vast amounts of cash.

Craft Fair/Rib Burn-Off/Car Show

Date May.
Lounge around Sunset Park, at this family-friendly event, with music, food and old cars.

Liberace Play-Alike Contest

Date mid May.
Professional and amateur pianists tinkle the ivories and strut their stuff in honour of the flamboyant entertainer's birthday.

Shakespeare in the Park

Date end Sept.
An outdoor performance of one of the bard's well-known plays, plus minstrels and other 'authentic' entertainment.

Professional Bull Riders Tour

Date mid Oct.
The world's best bull riders battle it out for the title of World Champion.

National Finals Rodeo

Date early Dec.
When the rodeo rides into town, it brings the nation's top cowboys… and a stampede of the most popular country musicians and comedians around.

Children

Although the casinos may not welcome children with open arms, there's still plenty to keep the kids amused.

Mini-golf for mini-folk at **Scandia** (p109).

When Las Vegas was built, it was meant to be an adult playground. Gambling, drinking, ogling showgirls, living it up – that's what people did, and still do, in Sin City. It's only in the past decade that Las Vegas has attempted to market itself as the 'ultimate tourist destination' and added more family-oriented attractions.

However, even though there are now a number of things for children to do, Las Vegas is inherently not a child-friendly place. Let's face it, casinos and children do not mix. The four newest resorts have little to offer children beyond their themed environments. **Bellagio** deliberately discourages children – it has no special attractions for kids and will not even allow under-18s on the premises unless they are guests of the hotel – while the **Venetian**, **Mandalay Bay** and **Paris** are also more appropriate for adults, aiming to attract business travellers and high-rollers.

Although this sounds ungracious, do not despair. Ironically, one of the most lavish, adult-oriented resorts, the prestigious **Four Seasons**, bordering the Mandalay Bay property, has some special incentives for kids. Milk and cookies are sent to all young guests on arrival, and staff print special T-shirts and create packages filled with beach amenities for kids to use by the pool.

Some other casinos are family-friendly and offer quite reasonably priced rooms, restaurants and attractions, which can be helpful when paying for four or more people. Circus Circus Enterprises (now called Mandalay Bay Resorts), in particular, has historically accommodated families. It owns **Circus Circus**, at the north end of the Strip, and **Excalibur** and **Luxor**, at the southern end.

The **MGM Grand**, **Rio** and **Treasure Island** also welcome kids, and **Caesars Palace**, though more pricey than the others, has always been a top destination for families visting Las Vegas. Finally, the new **Hyatt Regency Lake Las Vegas** boasts Camp Hyatt, an impressive kids' day-care programme. For more information on suitable hotels, *see chapter* **Accommodation**.

CHILDREN & THE LAW

Parents bringing children to Las Vegas should be aware that state law forbids those under 21 from being on casino floors. Children are allowed to pass through the casino area when accompanied by an adult, but cannot linger by any of the gaming tables or machines. A security guard is likely to ask them politely to move outside the casino. Also, a Clark County curfew means that unaccompanied under-18s are not allowed on the streets after 10pm (Mon-Thur, Sun) and after midnight on weekends (Fri, Sat) and during school holidays.

Young children

Babysitters

There are several reliable babysitting agencies in Vegas offering licensed and bonded babysitters who have been cleared through the sheriff's department and the FBI. The sitters, often equipped with toys, games, books and videos, come directly to your hotel room. Rates for up to two children for four hours (the usual minimum) start at $25-$30. Sitters are often available around the clock, but you'll have to give advance notice.

A1 Babysitting Service

382 0432. **Open** 24hrs daily. **Rates** $35 for 4hrs. **Credit** AmEx, MC, V.

After four hours, there is a charge of $8 for each additional hour.

Four Seasons Babysitting Service

384 5848. **Open** 24hrs daily. **Rates** *1-2 children* $24 for 4hrs ($5 per additional hr); *3-4 children* $30 for 4hrs ($7 per additional hr). **No credit cards.**
Not connected to the hotel of the same name.

Grandma Thompson's Romp 'n' Play

1804 Weldon Place, at St Louis Street, Stratosphere Area (735 0176). Bus 301, 302. **Open** 24hrs daily. **Rates** $4 per hr (minimum 5hrs). **No credit cards.**
Drop your child off at this home away from home.

Kids Care Connection

255 0003. **Open** *office* 8.30am-5pm Mon-Fri. **Rates** $8 per hr (minimum 4hrs). **No credit cards.**

Nurseries & activity centres

Many of the largest resorts – even those with family attractions – don't have childcare facilities, but a couple of smaller local hotel-casinos do. The **Gold Coast** (4000 W Flamingo Road, at Valley View Boulevard, West of Strip; 367 7111) runs a free nursery for children aged two to eight. The **Orleans** (4500 W Tropicana Avenue, at Arville Street, South-west Las Vegas; 365 7111) takes kids from three months to 12 years, but charges $5 per hour. Both have movies, toys, crafts and licensed supervisors, are open from 9am to midnight daily and impose a time limit of three-and-a-half hours.

The nursery at the **Santa Fe** (4949 N Rancho Drive, at Lone Mountain Road, North Las Vegas; 658 4900) caters for kids aged from six months to eight years (9am to midnight Wed; 10am to 11pm the rest of the week). You pay a one-off registration free of $10 and then $2 per hour up to a maximum of three hours.

Sam's Town (5111 Boulder Highway, at Flamingo Road, East Las Vegas; 456 7777) has a new childcare facility called the Playroom. Kids aged three to eight are looked after for free from 9am to midnight Mon-Thur and from 5pm to midnight Fri-Sun. A three-hour time limit applies.

At all four places, you don't have to be staying at the hotel, but you do have to be on the premises while your child is in the nursery.

Kids Quest

Boulder Station *4111 Boulder Highway, at E Desert Inn Road, East Las Vegas (432 7777). Bus 107, 112.*
Sunset Station *1301 W Sunset Road, at Stephanie Street, Henderson (547 7773). Bus 212, 217, 402.*
Texas Station *2101 Texas Star Lane, at N Rancho Drive, between Lake Mead Boulevard & Vegas Drive, North Las Vegas (631 1000). Bus 106, 208.*
All **Open** 9am-11pm Mon-Thur, Sun; 9am-1am Fri-Sat. **Admission** $5.25 per hr Mon-Thur; $6.25 per hr Fri-Sun. **Credit** Disc, MC, V.
Located at three of the popular neighbourhood Station Casinos properties, Kids Quest has everything from a Barbie area to computer games. The big cliff and the jungle area are also very popular. Children aged six weeks to 12 years can be dropped

*All-day fun at the **All-American SportPark**.*

off for up to five hours (three-and-a-half hours at Boulder); parents must remain on the premises.

MGM Grand Youth Activity Center

MGM Grand, 3799 Las Vegas Boulevard South, at E Tropicana Avenue (891 3200). Bus 201, 301, 302. **Open** 11am-11pm daily. **Admission** $7 MGM guests; $9 non-MGM guests. **Credit** AmEx, Disc, MC, V.
Youngsters aged three to 12 can check in for up to five hours at a time. The centre has crafts, toys, air hockey, Super Nintendo, a pool and close supervision by enthusiastic staff. It also organises supervised tours of the Grand Adventures theme park.

Services

Baby's Away

1760 Nuevao Road, Henderson (1-800 560 9141/ 458 1019). **Open** 24hrs daily. **Rates** $10 delivery plus rental cost. **Credit** AmEx, Disc, MC, V.
If you're travelling with a baby or young child, it's easy to forget some things. Baby's Away delivers and picks up baby supply rentals including strollers, cribs, car seats and even VCR and Nintendo games. *Website: www.babysaway.com*

Teenagers

Teenagers probably have the roughest time when it comes to planning a night out in Las Vegas. Until you're 21, you can't drink or gain admission to the majority of the city's bars, clubs and showrooms. However, Las Vegas has some decent cinemas (*see chapter* **Culture: Film**), and games arcades are a popular hangout for young adults.

You'll find state-of-the-art arcades in most of the major hotels – however, do be discriminating. In some hotels the arcade amounts to little more than a mid-size room with a few video games (the Monte Carlo, the Rio and the Riviera all fall into this category). Good arcades are located at **Bally's**, **Caesars Palace**, **Luxor**, **Mandalay Bay** and the **Stratosphere**. Some superlative arcades that include not only video games but other types of booths and midway entertainment are at the **Excalibur** (on the 'Fantasy Faire' level), **Circus Circus** (whose games surround a central ring featuring free circus acts), the **Las Vegas Hilton**, the **MGM Grand** and three of the Stations Casinos (**Boulder Station**, **Sunset Station** and **Texas Station**). The very best arcades are at the **Coney Island Emporium** and **GameWorks**, as noted below.

Note that a Clark County ordinance prohibits under-18s from being in arcades after 10pm on weekdays or after midnight at the weekend unless they are accompanied by an adult.

Coney Island Emporium

New York-New York, 3790 Las Vegas Boulevard South, at W Tropicana Avenue (736 4100). Bus 201, 301, 302. **Open** *9am-2am daily.*
This fun-filled arcade and family amusement centre recreates the atmosphere of the original Coney Island. It features over 200 video and midway games, the wacky Bumper Cabs, a prize redemption counter and ooey, gooey cotton candy.

GameWorks

Showcase Mall, 3785 Las Vegas Boulevard South, between E Tropicana & Harmon Avenues (432 4263). Bus 301, 302. **Open** *10am-2am Mon-Thur, Sun; 10am-4am Fri, Sat.* **Admission** *free; 1-hr game pass $20; 2-hr game pass $30; or pay for individual games.* **Credit** AmEx, Disc, MC, V.
This entertainment centre offers great technology, games and social interaction in a club setting. Along with 250 arcade games of all types, there's a 75ft (23m) rock climbing structure, an Internet lounge and two restaurants. Live music is usually offered on Friday and Saturday nights.

All age groups

Attractions

Nearly every place that's listed in our **Attractions** chapter is suitable for children. In particular, try the theme parks **Wet 'n Wild**, **MGM Grand Adventures** and the **Adventuredome** at Circus Circus; the free casino attractions such as the Buccaneer Bay pirate ship battle at **Treasure Island** and the fountain displays at **Bellagio**; and the factory tours in **Henderson**.

Thrill rides and rollercoasters can also be found in abundance on the Strip. The Manhattan Express rollercoaster at **New York-New York** twists, loops and dives around the resort's perimeter, while the

Inverter at **Circus Circus** flips thrillseekers around 360°, while exerting a constant G-force; it's unlike anything in any amusement park in the country.

All-American SportPark

121 E Sunset Road, at Las Vegas Boulevard South (798 7777). Bus 212, 301, 302; free shuttle bus from some Strip hotels. **Open** *varies depending on time of year, so phone first.* **Admission** *individual games $3-$12 each; all-day wristband $19.95-$24.95.* **Credit** AmEx, Disc, MC, V.
Step up to the plate at Slugger Stadium, where 16 batting stations offer pitches ranging from slow softball to 80mph (129kph) hardball. Feed your need for speed at one of the three officially licensed NASKART tracks. There's also a nine-hole, indoor championship putting course, an indoor climbing wall, an interactive sports arcade, pool tables, shuffleboard, darts, a foodcourt and more.

Las Vegas Mini Gran Prix

401 N Rainbow Boulevard, at Vegas Drive, Northwest Las Vegas (259 7000). Bus 101, 209. **Open** *10am-11pm Mon-Thur, Sun; 10am-midnight Fri, Sat.*
This place features four go-kart tracks ($4 a ride) where you can race against friends or against the clock, plus a video-game arcade and snack bar.

M&M's World

Showcase Mall, 3769 Las Vegas Boulevard South, between E Tropicana & Harmon Avenues (740 2525). **Open** *10am-midnight Mon-Thur, Sun; 10am-1am Fri, Sat.*
This is a four-level chocolate lover's paradise. Check out M&M's Academy, an interactive entertainment attraction showing visitors how these cute chocolate candies earn their trademark. 'Graduates' of the attraction even get a diploma.

Primadonna Casino Resorts

Off I-15, at Primm (382 1212/reservations 1-800 386 7867).
About 40 miles (64 km) south of Vegas at Primm (formerly known as Stateline), just before the California border, is a trio of resorts created by the Primm family empire: **Buffalo Bill's**, **Whiskey Pete's** and **Prim Valley**. For $6 at Buffalo Bill's you can experience a breathtaking 225ft (68m) drop on the Desperado, one of the world's highest and fastest rollercoasters. Alternatively, the Turbo Drop ($5) lifts riders into the air and lets them plunge sickeningly to the ground at 45mph (30kph). $12 wristbands entitle thrillseekers to unlimited rides.
Website: www.primadonna.com

Scandia

2900 Sirius Avenue, just south of Sahara Avenue, between Rancho Drive & Valley View Boulevard, West of Strip (364 0070). Bus 401. **Open** *June-Sept 24hrs daily; Oct-May 10am-10pm Mon-Thur, Sun; 10am-11pm Fri, Sat.* **Admission** *individual games $3.95-$5.95 each; unlimited wristband $15.95.* **Credit** MC, V.
Fun for the whole family with batting cages, three miniature golf courses, bumper boats, Indy race cars and lots and lots of arcade games.

Museums

Luckily for kids, Las Vegas's museums are not old-fashioned operations with dusty exhibits hidden in glass cases but tend to be more colourful, less serious tributes to popular culture. Kids will enjoy the **Guinness World of Records Museum** (though their parents will probably be bored rigid), **King Tut's Tomb & Museum** at the Luxor and the **Movie & Magic Hall of Fame** at O'Shea's. Take car-crazy children to one of the world's largest collections of classic cars at the **Imperial Palace Auto Collection** or to the **Shelby Museum** (643 3000) at the Las Vegas Motor Speedway. One of the newest sights in town is **Madame Tussaud's Celebrity Encounter** at the Venetian, the first US version of the London wax museum. For details, *see chapter* **Attractions**.

Lied Discovery Children's Museum

Las Vegas Library, 833 Las Vegas Boulevard North, between Washington Avenue & Bonanza Road, North Las Vegas (382 5437). Bus 113. **Open** 10am-5pm Tue-Sat; noon-5pm Sun. **Admission** $5; $4 12-17s, seniors; $3 3-11s; free under-3s. **Credit** MC, V.

A stimulating interactive museum for kids, designed along the lines of the famous Exploratorium in San Francisco, the Lied features dozens of scientific exhibits that make the viewer a part of the demonstration. It's the sort of place that adults would go to by themselves if they thought they could get away with it, and is infinitely more edifying than Circus Circus's Adventuredome.

Parks & zoos

Numerous parks and recreational areas dot the Las Vegas Valley. **Sunset Park** (below the airport, at E Sunset Road and Eastern Avenue) and **Lorenzi Park** (at W Washington Avenue and N Rancho Drive) are two large parks with rolling green grass, lakes, and volleyball, tennis and baseball facilities. Call 455 8200 for details of both.

Children will appreciate the animal habitats that have popped up in several resorts. The **Mirage** has not one but three animal attractions: Siegfried & Roy's royal white tigers in the Tiger Habitat, rare breeds in the Secret Garden and bottlenose dolphins in the Dolphin Habitat. At the **MGM Grand**, visitors can walk through a glass tunnel to watch the beasts in the Lion Habitat. The reconstructed Wildlife Walk at the **Tropicana** is home to a variety of unusual creatures including pygmy marmosets and toucans. At the Forum Shops at **Caesars Palace**, a saltwater aquarium is filled with rare fish (including sharks) from around the world. The **Flamingo Hilton** has a beautifully landscaped pool area where you'll find pink flamingos and penguins along with other tropical birds and fish, from spring to autumn.

If you're in the mood for a real zoo, the **Southern Nevada Zoological Park** houses a collection of endangered species including apes, chimpanzees, eagles and every species of venomous reptile native to Southern Nevada. Alternatively, outside the city, near Red Rock Canyon, kids can spend the day horse riding or enjoying the petting zoo at **Bonnie Springs/Old Nevada** (*see page 237* **Sport & Fitness**). There's also a reproduction Wild West town with enough shoot-outs and gory hangings to suit the most bloodthirsty child.

For more information, *see chapter* **Attractions**.

Shows

Shows in Las Vegas range from comedians and celebrity headliners to large-scale production revues. Each showroom will have a different policy specifying the minimum age for admission (ask before booking tickets). Parents will find this useful since many shows contain topless dancing and sexually explicit material. Tickets to most shows are in great demand, which means the casinos can usually charge full price, even when a child is occupying the seat.

The best shows – such as Cirque du Soleil's *Mystère* at **Treasure Island** and *O* at **Bellagio** and *EFX* at the **MGM Grand** – can cost close to $100 a ticket, so this can be an expensive family outing. However, *Tournament of Kings* at the **Excalibur** and *Lance Burton: Master Magician* at the **Monte Carlo** are both reasonably priced shows suitable for the whole family.

Small-scale magic shows include Rick Thomas (at the **Tropicana**) and Dixie Dooley (at **Gaughan's Plaza** in Downtown). Thomas performs at 2pm and 4pm daily, except Fridays (tickets $12.95), while Dooley's daily show at 4pm costs $14.95. For free entertainment, try **Circus Circus**'s big top and the **Excalibur**'s 'Medieval Village', with strolling music, juggling, comedy and dance acts. For more information, *see chapter* **Casino Entertainment**.

Sport

For other family-friendly suggestions, including ice-skating, bowling alleys and miniature golf courses, *see chapter* **Sport & Fitness**.

Crystal Palace In-Line Skating & Hockey Complex

9295 W Flamingo Road, at Fort Apache Road, South-west Las Vegas (253 9832/7). Bus 202. **Open** 7-9.30pm Tue-Thur; 10am-5pm Fri; 7-11pm Sat; 12.30-5pm Sun. **Admission** $7; $9 with skates; $10 family of four Tue. **Credit** MC, V.

You can rent or bring rollerskates and rollerblades to this fast-paced rink – or, if you're feeling really adventurous, sign up to play on a roller hockey team. Public sessions are offered most evenings from 7pm. **Branches:** 4680 Boulder Highway (458 7107); 3901 N Rancho Drive (645 4892); 1110 E Lake Mead Drive, Henderson (564 2790).

Consumer

Accommodation

With more than 125,000 rooms to choose from, it helps to have some advice on where to stay. Here it is.

In Las Vegas, the stakes just keep going up. And so do the casino-hotels. Since the previous edition of this guide, the city's Strip has seen the opening of the $950-million **Mandalay Bay** and adjoining **Four Seasons** (3,733 rooms), $1.6-billion **Bellagio** (3,005 rooms), $1.4-billion **Venetian** (3,036 rooms) and $760-million **Paris** (2,900 rooms). Sometime in the summer of 2000, the newly rebuilt $826-million **Aladdin** (2,600 rooms) is due to add its name to the list.

For those who prefer to be far from the madding crowd, the new **Resort at Summerlin** (541 rooms) and **Hyatt Regency at Lake Las Vegas** (496 rooms) have provided upper-end accommodation away from the Strip. The latest building boom has upped the city's hotel room inventory to about 125,000, a staggering 25 per cent increase from two years ago.

Two significant features mark the latest wave of construction: resorts are becoming more and more luxurious and they are relying far less on frivolous, Disney-like attractions. The result is a much greater range of hotel choices for the upscale traveller. The newest hotels tempt guests with large shopping malls, internationally known restaurants, full-scale health spas, elaborate pool complexes and star-quality entertainment. It's now possible to spend a vacation here, with a full slate of activities, and (heaven forbid!) never gamble.

WHERE TO STAY

If you want to stay on the Strip, remember it's a 3½-mile (5.6-kilometre) hike from one end to the other, so you could spend a lot of time tramping from casino to casino – consider whether you want to be based at the north, centre or south.

At the north end (above Spring Mountain Road) you'll find the **Desert Inn**, **Stardust**, **Circus Circus**, **Riviera** and, a long block north, the **Sahara**. Further north still, off the Strip proper and on its own, stands the **Stratosphere**.

The centre of the Strip has the biggest cluster of hotel-casinos – **Treasure Island** and its neighbour the **Mirage**, which is opposite the new **Venetian**; **Harrah's**, **Imperial Palace** and the **Flamingo Hilton**; **Caesars Palace**, **Barbary Coast**, **Bellagio** and **Bally's**, which are all at the intersection with Flamingo Road; **Paris** (adjoining Bally's), the soon-to-open **Aladdin** and the **Monte Carlo**.

Bellagio*'s spectacular lobby (page 116).*

At the southern end, the four corners of the Strip/Tropicana Avenue intersection are occupied by four large casinos: **New York-New York**, **MGM Grand**, the **Tropicana** and **Excalibur**. Further south you'll find the **Luxor** and the new **Mandalay Bay** (now the southernmost casino) and the adjoining **Four Seasons**.

There are plenty of established favourites in which to hang out. Many of the 'old' Strip hotels, such as the Flamingo, Stardust, Riviera, Sahara and Caesars Palace, have undergone expansions or upgrades that make them nearly as attractive as the newest hotels, while retaining a charm that hints of old Las Vegas. The cluster of Downtown casino-hotels do a good job with accommodation, although their dining and entertainment options are more limited than those on the Strip.

Of course, you don't have to stay in a casino. Off the Strip, in the area surrounding the Convention

Center, rooms are aimed at the business traveller and are generally unencumbered by noisy casinos. The new, very upmarket Four Seasons doesn't even have a casino (although Mandalay Bay's extensive gambling facilities are next door); the Resort at Summerlin is aimed at golfers rather than gamblers; and the Hyatt at Lake Las Vegas has a small casino that opens only in the evening. There's also a smattering of old-fashioned, intimate hotels and numerous cheap chain motels.

WHAT TO EXPECT

Because the majority of casinos continue to use amusement as a means of inducing people into their fleecing pens, their attractions – the thrill rides, virtual reality dens, magic shows and belt-popping prime-rib buffets – take precedence over guest rooms. As a result, but with a few lively exceptions, most Las Vegas hotel rooms tend to be of the Holiday Inn variety – clean and modern but nothing that would rival a Ritz-Carlton.

Generally, however, they do a good job and typically include valet parking, cable TV with pay movies, dry cleaning/laundry service, room service (usually 24 hours), swimming pool, rooms adapted for disabled visitors (except in the older hotels) and no-smoking rooms (an increasing trend – two-thirds of Bellagio's rooms are no-smoking). Mini-bars, refrigerators and VCRs are usually only available in suites, though you can always request one (for a charge). Some hotels offer an airport shuttle service: ask when you book. Otherwise, for information on getting to and from the airport and your hotel, *see chapter* **Getting Around**.

RATES

The influx of high-end resort-casinos has tended to push up room prices. In fact, moguls at the Venetian and Bellagio have stated they are trying to maintain the city's highest average room rates – about $160 per night, which is nearly double the citywide daily average. No longer does Las Vegas enjoy a 20 to 30 per cent advantage in room rates over other major cities. Overall, room rates are less than elsewhere, but by only 15 to 20 per cent.

Expect to pay (for a double room, per night) from $50 to $75 in a budget hotel, $60 to $150 in a mid-range hotel and from about $180 in a first-class property, plus hotel tax (currently at 11 per cent Downtown and 9 per cent elsewhere). Note that rates fluctuate hugely. They are typically lower from Sunday to Thursday, when it is also easier to find a room, and higher during holidays and special events, such as Easter, New Year's Eve and Super Bowl weekend, and during the busiest conventions, like Comdex and the Consumer Electronics Show (*see chapter* **Resources** for dates of the major conventions). Rates vary seasonally, too. From Thanksgiving to Christmas and during January, rooms are usually cheaper and

easier to find. The city is busiest in March during Spring Break, when room rates may be driven up considerably. And bear in mind that the room rates listed below are based on information received from the hotels and are subject to change.

RESERVATIONS

At the time of writing, there were more than 125,000 hotel rooms in Las Vegas, the most of any US city. With so many rooms it should not be difficult to find a place to sleep. But because of the city's continuing increase in tourists (to more than 30 million a year) and weekend visitors from Southern California, hotels can and do sell out. Book in advance as much as possible to get the greatest choice of rates. Nearly all casinos have websites and you can often book by e-mail via the website. There are several reservation agencies, some of which claim to be able to get a better rate than the hotel quotes. In our experience there's little difference, but they can advise on the current best deals. Alternatively, browse prices online at **www.lvol.com/lvoleg/hotels/lvtravel/**, which, usefully, has visitor comments on specific hotels.

Las Vegas Convention & Visitors Authority

3150 Paradise Road, opposite Convention Center Drive, Las Vegas, NV 89096 (1-800 332 5333/ 892 0711/fax 892 824). Bus 108.
Open 8am-5pm Mon-Fri.
Website: www.lasvegas24hours.com

Reservations Plus

2275A Renaissance Drive, between Tropicana & Eastern Avenues, Las Vegas, NV 89119 (1-800 805 9528/fax 795 8767). Bus 110, 201.
Open 7am-10pm Mon-Sat; 7am-6pm Sun.
Website: www.houseol.com

The opulent **Caesars Palace** *(page 116).*

The upmarket **Desert Inn** *has the only golf course on the Strip. See page 117.*

Casino hotels

The Strip

Aladdin
3667 Las Vegas Boulevard South, at Harmon Avenue, Las Vegas, NV 89109 (736 0111). Bus 301, 302.
Scheduled to open in summer 2000, the Aladdin is the last in the most recent wave of mega-hotels to rise on the Strip. The hotel's first phase consists of 2,600 guest rooms, a 100,000sq ft (9,300sq m) casino and a 500,000sq ft (46,500sq m) dining, shopping and entertainment complex called Desert Passage. The new Aladdin, which replaces the original hotel built in the mid-1960s and imploded in 1998, also has a 7,000-seat Theater of the Performing Arts, a holdover from the old hotel. The second phase of the project (no timetable released) will include a 1,000-room, music-themed tower and casino and bring the total cost of construction up to $1.3 billion. Guest rooms are decorated in soft pastels and dark wood furnishings, with luxurious marble bathrooms that include separate soaking tubs and showers. Other hotel amenities include a health spa, a 24-hour business centre, convention facilities and the London Club – a separate European-style casino-within-a-casino for high-end players. At the time of writing, room rates were not known.
Website: www.aladdincasino.com

Bally's
3645 Las Vegas Boulevard South, at E Flamingo Road, Las Vegas, NV 89109 (reservations 1-800 634 3434/front desk 739 4111/fax 739 4405). Bus 202, 301, 302. **Rates** *single or double $90-$160; suite $289-$739.* **Credit** *AmEx, DC, Disc, JCB, MC, V.*
In 1980, Bally's (then called the MGM Grand) was the site of the city's worst disaster – a fire swept through the hotel, killing 87 and injuring 700. The tragedy forced Vegas to modernise its safety codes. The hotel's 2,814 guest rooms (including 265 suites) are now among the largest in town; most have a California-modern feel with overstuffed furniture and mushroom coffee tables, while the predominant colours are subdued teal, mauve and earth tones. The swimming pool area, one of the most appealing in town, features a beautiful palm-fringed sun deck and cabanas with their own refrigerators, TVs, rafts and private phones.
Hotel services *Beauty salon. Business centre. Car rental desk. Concierge. Gym. Pool. Spa. Tennis courts. Tour desk.* **Room services** *Cable TV with pay movies. Dataport. Room service (24hrs). Safe. Voicemail.*
Website: www.ballyslv.com

Barbary Coast
3595 Las Vegas Boulevard South, at E Flamingo Road, Las Vegas, NV 89109 (reservations 1-800 634 6755/front desk 737 7111/fax 737 6304/ info@barbarycoastcasino.com). Bus 202, 301, 302. **Rates** *single or double $89-$150; suite $200-$400.* **Credit** *AmEx, DC, Disc, MC, V.*

Water babies will love the aquatic attractions at **Mandalay Bay**. *See page 120.*

Don't be dismayed by the penitentiary-like exterior; inside, the motif is turn-of-the-century San Francisco. The Barbary Coast is very small by Las Vegas standards – only 200 rooms; if you can get one, you'll be charmed by the Victorian wallpaper and paintings, floral carpets, etched mirrors and white lace curtains. Some even have four-poster brass beds, mini-bars and whirlpools. This place is also home to Drai's, one of the city's best supper clubs (*see p162* **Bars & Cafés**).
Hotel services *Concierge. Tour desk.*
Room services *Cable TV with pay movies. Dataport. Room service (24hrs).*
Website: www.barbarycoastcasino.com

Bellagio

3600 Las Vegas Boulevard South, at W Flamingo Road, Las Vegas, NV 89109 (reservations 1-888 987 6667/front desk 693 7444/fax 693 8546). Bus 202, 301, 302. **Rates** *single or double $159-$499; suite $250-$1,250.* **Credit** AmEx, DC, Disc, JCB, MC, V.
In a city that doesn't know the meaning of restraint, Bellagio is positively demure. Steve Wynn's newest mega-resort kicked off the latest building splurge that emphasised upscale accommodation: Bellagio boasts luxuriously appointed standard rooms (3,005 in total, including 400 suites), a bustling, attractive casino, a very impressive collection of restaurants – and Prada, too.

The $1.6-billion project from Mirage Resorts is an adult-oriented resort: under-18s are not allowed on the property unless they're staying there. Ask for a room with a view over the resort's huge lake with its effervescent fountain shows. Bellagio's elegant pool terrace, among the most beautiful on the Strip,

was inspired by Italian gardens and includes mature pine trees transplanted from the old Dunes golf course that used to occupy the property.
Hotel services *Beauty salon. Business centre. Car rental desk. Concierge. Gym. Pool. Spa. Tour desk.* **Room services** *Cable TV with pay movies. Dataport. Room service (24hrs). Safe. Turndown. Voicemail.*
Website: www.bellagioresort.com

Caesars Palace

3570 Las Vegas Boulevard South, at W Flamingo Road, Las Vegas, NV 89109 (reservations 1-800 634 6661/front desk 731 7110/fax 731 6636). Bus 202, 301, 302. **Rates** *single or double $100-$180; suite $250-$750.* **Credit** AmEx, DC, Disc, JCB, MC, V.
Since 1966, Caesars Palace has been the quintessential Vegas pleasure dome and, unlike many of the other themed resorts, its splendidly ridiculous amenities extend from the casino to its rooms and suites, which are among the most luxurious in town. Features include wooden wardrobes, European-style bathrooms (double sink, separate enclosure for the toilet, marble and tiles), dressing rooms, velvet chaise longues and platform beds. The even fancier suites have circular beds, private dining rooms, wet bars, in-room saunas, steam rooms and elaborate audio-visual systems. And for its best customers (ie biggest gamblers), Caesars provides ultra-luxurious accommodation such as the Via Suites with a lush Italian garden atmosphere and the two-storey Roman and Greek 'fantasy suites'. Caesars also has a magnificent pool and sun deck area, aptly named the Garden of the Gods. A rather ugly, 29-storey tower opened in December 1997, adding 1,200 rooms (bringing the grand total to 2,500), furnished with

Greco-Roman art, sculptures, columns and marble tubs; the tower also has a health spa and meeting rooms. You'll find mini-bars and refrigerators in the newer rooms.
Hotel services *Beauty salon. Concierge. Gym. Pool. Spa. Tennis courts.* **Room services** *Cable TV with pay movies. Room service (24hrs). Voicemail.*
Website: www.caesars.com

Circus Circus

2880 Las Vegas Boulevard South, at Circus Circus Drive, between Desert Inn Road & W Sahara Avenue, Las Vegas, NV 89109 (reservations 1-800 634 3450/front desk 734 0410/fax 734 5897).
Bus 301, 302. **Rates** *single or double $45-$85.*
Credit AmEx, DC, Disc, MC, V.
Circus Circus is the number-one hotel choice for families with children, thanks largely to its free circus acts, carnival midway, arcade games and Adventuredome theme park. It was the first of the classless, 'low-roller' casinos to hit the Strip – and its rooms are still among the cheapest in town. After several expansions there are now 3,800 rooms and suites, mainly decorated with soft blue carpeting, pastel bedspreads and upholstery, and light wood furniture, while the circus theming is restricted to just a few hot-air balloons painted on the walls. The West tower is the newest (built in 1997), while the cheapest (and oldest) rooms are in the motel-like Manor section, where you can park at your door. Ask for a south-facing room in the Skyrise tower for the best view of the Strip. Other amenities include pools and a 365-space RV park (*see p131* **RV parks**).
Hotel services *Beauty salon. Business centre. Car rental desk. Pool. Tour desk.* **Room services** *Cable TV with pay movies. Dataport. Room service (24hrs). Safe.*
Website: www.circuscircus-lasvegas.com

Desert Inn

3145 Las Vegas Boulevard South, at E Desert Inn Road, Las Vegas, NV 89109 (reservations 1-800 634 6906/front desk 733 4471/fax 733 4774).
Bus 301, 302. **Rates** *single or double $175-$215; suite $215-$550.* **Credit** AmEx, DC, Disc, JCB, MC, V.
Until the opening of the Four Seasons and the Resort at Summerlin in 1999, the recently remodelled Desert Inn was Las Vegas's only true resort-hotel and is still definitely aimed upmarket. The 715 rooms (three-quarters of which are no-smoking) are among the best on the Strip, with chaise longues, wooden wardrobes and English country furnishings, all in cool lavenders or quiet pastels. Bathrooms are just as posh, and large, tastefully decorated in black and grey granite with double sinks and separate toilet and shower enclosures. Some rooms have their own mini-bars and terraces. Topping the list of the Desert Inn's country club amenities is its famous 18-hole golf course; recent additions include an 18-hole putting course and clubhouse. Other recreational facilities at the 200-acre (81ha) resort are five lit tennis courts, jogging track, workout room and spa. The rooms in the 14-storey tower have nice views of both the peaceful golf course and the ever-bustling Strip, but for a taste of the hotel's glamorous past, try the rooms in the older garden wing.

Hotel services *Beauty salon. Business centre. Car rental desk. Concierge. Golf course. Gym. Pool. Spa. Tennis courts.* **Room services** *Cable TV with pay movies. Refrigerator. Room service (24hrs). Voicemail.*
Website: www.thedesertinn.com

Excalibur

3850 Las Vegas Boulevard South, at W Tropicana Avenue, Las Vegas, NV 89109 (reservations 1-800 937 7777/front desk 597 7700/fax 597 7040/ excres@terminus.intermind.net). Bus 201, 301, 302. **Rates** *single or double $135.*
Credit AmEx, DC, Disc, JCB, MC, V.
Behind the white, pink and blue fairytale castle exterior, Excalibur offers you a standard, Y-shaped hotel tower slab, containing a staggering 4,032 guest rooms (remember that Excalibur is under the same ownership as Circus Circus, so the body count is all-important). Mercifully, the medieval knights theming doesn't spill into the rooms, which are decorated in bold reds, blues and greens, and feature dark wood furniture and wrought-iron fixtures. Among the hotel's amenities are a wedding chapel, beauty salon and two swimming pools. It's more downmarket than some of the other casinos, but a good choice for budget travellers and well located, opposite the MGM Grand and New York-New York.
Hotel services *Beauty salon. Car rental desk. Pool. Tour desk.* **Room services** *Cable TV with pay movies. Dataport. Room service (24hrs). Voicemail.*
Website: www.excalibur-casino.com

Flamingo Hilton

3555 Las Vegas Boulevard South, at E Flamingo Road, Las Vegas, NV 89109 (reservations 1-800 732 2111/front desk 733 3111/fax 733 3353).
Bus 202, 301, 302. **Rates** *single or double $69-$200; suite $250-$580.* **Credit** AmEx, DC, Disc, JCB, MC, V.
This place has changed a lot since Bugsy Siegel built his tropically themed oasis in the desert, and all that remains in remembrance of the Chicago-mobster-turned-Vegas-hotelier is a stone pillar and small plaque in the rose garden behind the casino. For the past ten years the hotel has been in a state of constant renovation. The result is 3,642 rooms in six towers, which surround a pool area reminiscent of Hawaii's Waimea Canyon – 15 acres of tropical plants, waterfalls, streams, gardens, koi ponds and a grove of 2,000 palm trees on a luxurious expanse of lawn. The tropical theme is carried throughout the hotel, but the rooms have a more Hilton influence, done in conservative blues and greens with modern wood and rattan furnishings.

Water enthusiasts will find five pools, water slides, jacuzzis and legions of lounge chairs. And in the middle of this mini-paradise is an open-air wedding chapel for those willing to take the ultimate plunge. Among the health club's numerous services are massage, salt glow and oxygen pep-up, for that post-losing depression.
Hotel services *Beauty salon. Business centre. Car rental desk. Gym. Pool. Spa. Tennis courts. Tour desk.* **Room services** *Cable TV with pay movies. Dataport. Room service (24hrs). Safe. Voicemail.*
Website: www.hilton.com/hotels

Harrah's

3475 Las Vegas Boulevard South, between Sands Avenue & E Flamingo Road, Las Vegas, NV 89109 (reservations 1-800 392 9002/front desk 369 5000/ fax 369 5008). Bus 301, 302. **Rates** *single or double* $50-$200; *suite* $90-$300. **Credit** AmEx, Disc, DC, JCB, MC, V.

For years, Harrah's main building looked like a giant Mississippi riverboat, complete with a promenade deck and twin red smokestacks. But a renovation in 1997 (worth $200 million) torpedoed the paddle-wheeler theme and replaced it with a hackneyed 'Carnival around the World' motif. It also added a 35-storey tower and nearly 1,000 rooms and suites, bringing the total to 2,700. Guest rooms are bright and festive with light wood furniture, brass lamp fixtures and cheerful, multicoloured drapes and bed-spreads. Some rooms have whirlpools. It's a good option if you want to be in the middle of the Strip action – it's within walking distance of the Mirage, Treasure Island, Caesars Palace and the Venetian.
Hotel services *Beauty salon. Car rental desk. Gym. Pool. Spa. Tour desk.* **Room services** *Cable TV with pay movies. Dataport. Room service (24hrs). Voicemail.*
Website: www.harrahsvegas.com

Imperial Palace

3535 Las Vegas Boulevard South, between Sands Avenue & E Flamingo Road, Las Vegas, NV 89109 (reservations 1-800 634 6441/front desk 731 3311/ fax 735 8328/ip@imperialpalace.com). Bus 301, 302. **Rates** *single or double* $60-$95; *suite* $150. **Credit** AmEx, DC, Disc, MC, V.

The small, blue-roofed pagoda facing the Strip is only the tip of the iceberg in this sprawling 2,700-room complex that appears to be built in tiers, each one further from the main drag. The hotel carries an oriental theme – the entrance is marked by crystal, jade, bamboo and curved wood accents, and the cocktail waitresses wear side-split skirts à la Suzie Wong. Standard guest rooms are just that, but party animals should try one of the 'luv tub' rooms: an oversized room with a mirror over the bed and still more mirrors surrounding the deeply decadent 300-gallon sunken bath. Other amenities include a wedding chapel, health club and Olympic-sized pool. Some rooms have mini-bars, whirlpools and terraces.
Hotel services *Beauty salon. Business centre. Car rental desk. Gym. Pool. Spa. Tour desk.* **Room services** *Cable TV with pay movies. Dataport. Room service (24hrs).*
Website: www.imperialpalace.com

Best for...

Children

Circus Circus Despite the statue of a naked woman at the front, the venerable big top-themed hotel is Valhalla for kids with its circus acts, video game arcade, carnival midway and Adventuredome theme park.

Swimming pool

Bellagio Forget about the sandy beaches, wave pools and lazy river rides. Bellagio's pool area is reminiscent of an Italian villa with its garden-like setting and 300 pine trees swaying in the breeze.

Business travellers

Las Vegas Hilton For starters, it's next door to the Convention Center (no chasing taxis), and there's a handy on-site business centre to handle faxes, FedEx, e-mail and other fiscal pursuits.

Old Vegas

El Cortez Avoid the tower and take one of the walk-up rooms that are part of the original adobe brick wing. The sounds of the slots and drunken revellers that funnel up the staircase and rattle around the wooden hallway will transport you to the 1940s, when the El Cortez was the hotspot of Downtown Las Vegas.

High rollers

Las Vegas Hilton The Hilton's biggest gamblers (whose credit line extends into the millions of dollars) stay in one of three gargantuan penthouse suites. They contain every conceivable amenity: objets d'art, period furniture, private swimming pools, Italian marble spas, butlers, chefs… and a partridge in a pear tree.

View

Stratosphere While virtually every hotel has a view of something, the perch atop the tower offers a good view of everything. It's especially impressive at night, when you can watch, at eye level, the line of planes approaching McCarran Airport.

Romance

Desert Inn Even though most of this upmarket property has been expanded and remodelled over the years, the rooms with their country English furnishings retain a cosy ambience crying out for that special rendezvous.

Extended stay

Marriott Residence Inn If you're going to be in town for a while, these condo-like units are large, tastefully decorated and stocked with microwaves, VCRs, dishwashers, refrigerators and a back-to-reality alarm clock.

Campy fun

Caesars Palace The original Vegas pleasure dome hasn't lost its allure with its Roman columns and statuary, posh Garden of the Gods pool area, cocktail goddesses in togas and Olympic Casino, the city's most exciting gambling pit.

Luxor

*3900 Las Vegas Boulevard South, between
W Tropicana Avenue & Russell Road, Las Vegas,
NV 89109 (reservations 1-800 288 1000/front desk
262 4000/fax 262 4404/luxorres@e1.com). Bus 301,
302.* **Rates** *single or double* $50-$250 (weekdays);
$99-$299 (weekends); *suite* $99-$800. **Credit** AmEx,
DC, Disc, MC, V.

The 2,427 rooms in the Luxor's glass pyramid are
reached by 'inclinators,' elevators that rise at a 39°
angle, making you feel like you're on an enclosed ski
lift. Each room (with rampant Egyptian theming)
has a sloping wall and bank of windows with views
of the Strip and surrounding mountains, and a
door that opens to overlook the pyramid's interior
atrium. Note that some views are partially blocked
by the recently completed tower just north of the
pyramid, which houses another 1,950 rooms. Avoid
the pyramid if you like to soak in a bath; most rooms
have a stall shower and no tub. There are several
wading pools and date palms growing out of the
main swimming pool; a cabana comes with rafts,
loungers, cable TV, phones, ceiling fans and a refrigerator stocked with various juices and bottled water.
Hotel services *Beauty salon. Business centre.
Car rental desk. Gym. Pool. Spa. Tour desk.*
Room services *Cable TV with pay movies. Room
service (24hrs). Safe. Voicemail.*
Website: www.luxor.com

Mandalay Bay

*3950 Las Vegas Boulevard South, between
W Tropicana Avenue & Russell Road, Las Vegas,
NV 89119 (reservations 1-877 632 7000/front desk
632 7777/fax 632 7011). Bus 301, 302.*
Rates *single or double* $89-$299; *suite* $189-$399.
Credit AmEx, DC, Disc, JCB, MC, V.

Weathered stone idols stand watch throughout this
60-acre (24ha), tropical-themed luxury property,
which opened in March 1999 and has quickly
become one of the hotspots in town. Except for the
garish gold Y-shaped tower, it's hard to believe this
is a product of the people who brought Las Vegas
Circus Circus and the Excalibur. Given the hotel's
heritage, the interior is surprisingly elegant and spacious. A huge and beautiful lobby, high ceilings
throughout, great carpets and a casino big enough
to host a soccer match make the common areas an
unexpected delight. The well-appointed standard
rooms average 500sq ft (46sq m); larger Vista suites
command spectacular views of the Strip or the
mountains. It's also a haven for beach freaks; the 11-
acre (4.5ha) water park – probably the best in town
– has a lazy river and a wide sandy beach with wave
machine, and there's also a full-service spa. But the
real draw is the restaurant area, which includes
top-end restaurants such as Aureole, China Grill,
Shanghai Lilly, Red Square and the wildly popular
Rumjungle nightclub and is, uniquely, separated
from the casino and its hustle and bustle.
Hotel services *Beauty salon. Business centre.
Car rental desk. Gym. Pool. Spa. Tour desk.*
Room services *Dataport. Room service (24hrs).
Voicemail.*
Website: www.mandalaybay.com

MGM Grand

*3799 Las Vegas Boulevard South, at E Tropicana
Avenue, Las Vegas, NV 89109 (reservations 1-800
646 7787/front desk 891 1111/fax 262 4404/
reservations@mgmgrand.com). Bus 201, 301, 302.*
Rates *single or double* $69-$119 (standard), $79-$129
(concierge level with breakfast); *suite* $99-$2,500.
Credit AmEx, DC, Disc, JCB, MC, V.

The 5,035 rooms in the MGM Grand – the world's
largest resort hotel – are honeycombed in its four
emerald-green towers. They are decorated in four
distinct motifs, the best of which are the Hollywood
rooms done in two-tone wood, with gold-flecked
walls, gilded mouldings and beds backed by
mirrors. Of the 750 suites, about half are really oversized guest rooms with a sofa and two TVs; others
perch on the 29th floor and are huge, split-level in
design and served by one butler and up to 27 telephones. The Mansion, a separate high-roller complex
with 30 suites, has replaced some of the Grand
Adventures theme park.
Hotel services *Beauty salon. Business centre.
Car rental desk. Gym. Pool. Spa.* **Room services**
*Cable TV with pay movies. Dataport. Room service
(24hrs). Voicemail.*
Website: www.mgmgrand.com

Mirage

*3400 Las Vegas Boulevard South, between Spring
Mountain & W Flamingo Roads, Las Vegas, NV
89109 (reservations 1-800 347 9000/front desk 791
7444/fax 791 7446). Bus 301, 302.* **Rates** *single or
double* $79-$400 (Mon-Thur, Sun), $159-$399 (Fri, Sat);
suite $250-$3,000. **Credit** AmEx, DC, Disc, JCB, MC, V.

The Mirage is a striking example of Las Vegas
hotels' emphasis on dramatic public spaces at the
expense of guest rooms, which tend to be identical
and unmemorable. In fact, many of its 3,049 rooms
had to be remodelled within a year of opening
because the closets were too small. The casino's
Polynesian-jungle theming is carried into the rooms,
which are decorated with tropical colour schemes
and have rattan and cane furnishings and floor-to-
ceiling headboards made from white louvred
panels. More recently, some have been redecorated
with rather more subtle taupe, beige and peach
colour schemes and the bathrooms spruced up with
Spanish and Indonesian marble. The pool area
comprises a series of blue lagoons, inlets and waterfalls, plus two islands exotically landscaped with
various palms and tropical flowers.
Hotel services *Beauty salon. Business centre.
Car rental desk. Concierge. Golf course. Gym. Pool.
Spa. Tour desk.* **Room services** *Cable TV with pay
movies. Dataport. Room service (24hrs). Safe.
Turndown. Voicemail.*
Website: www.themirage.com

Monte Carlo

*3770 Las Vegas Boulevard South, at Rue de Monte
Carlo, between W Flamingo Road & Tropicana
Avenue, Las Vegas, NV 89109 (reservations 1-800
311 8999/front desk 730 7777/fax 739 7200).
Bus 201, 301, 302.* **Rates** *single or double* $69-$199
(weekdays), $99-$269 (weekends); *suite* $150-$350.
Credit AmEx, DC, Disc, MC, V.

Experience a touch of Old Vegas at the atmospheric **Algiers Hotel**. *See page 129.*

Vegas glitz meets European refinement at the Monte Carlo, where the architecture is laden with stately columns, cascading fountains and Renaissance-style statues, yet resists lapsing into overstated baroque. Most of the hotel's attractions were designed for guests who like to participate: sun worshippers can bask in the glow of six pools (including a wave pool) in a lush garden setting, or take a leisurely raft ride in the Easy River water park. Next to the park are four lit tennis courts and a pro shop for rentals and lessons. The 3,002 rooms include 256 suites and are tastefully decorated with cherry furniture and turn-of-the-century décor, with brass fixtures, Italian marble and polished granite.
Hotel services *Beauty salon. Business centre. Car rental desk. Gym. Pool. Spa. Tennis courts. Tour desk.* **Room services** *Cable TV with pay movies. Dataport. Room service (24hrs). Voicemail. Website: www.monte-carlo.com*

New York-New York

3790 Las Vegas Boulevard South, at W Tropicana Avenue, Las Vegas, NV 89109 (reservations 1-800 675 3267/front desk 740 6822/fax 740 6700). Bus 201, 301, 302. **Rates** *single or double* $89-$129; *suite* $200-$500. **Credit** AmEx, DC, Disc, JCB, MC, V.

In a triumph of camouflage, New York-New York's dozen skyscraper-like towers are fairly authentic, scaled-down re-creations of NYC landmarks: the Empire State building, Chrysler building, Century building, CBS building and others. The towers range in height from 29 to 47 storeys (Las Vegas's tallest) and house 2,034 guest rooms and suites. Rooms come in a variety of floorplans and themes, though the décor is pretty standardised and doesn't reflect

the character of the different towers. Most use warm earth tones, with polished chrome lamps and light wood furniture. The hotel's health club is little more than a workout room and the pool is small by resort standards. Check when you book that the external rollercoaster doesn't pass your window or you will be continually disturbed by the screams of riders.
Hotel services *Beauty salon. Business centre. Car rental desk. Gym. Pool. Spa. Tour desk.* **Room services** *Cable TV with pay movies. Dataport. Room service (24hrs). Safe. Voicemail. Website: www.nynyhotelcasino.com*

Paris

3655 Las Vegas Boulevard South, between Harmon Avenue & E Flamingo Road, Las Vegas, NV 89109 (reservations 1-888 266 5687/front desk 946 4222/ fax 946 3830). Bus 202, 301, 302. **Rates** *single or double* $129-$369; *standard suite* $350-$650; *one-bedroom suite* $750-$1,250; *two-bedroom suite* $979-$1,219. **Credit** AmEx, DC, Disc, JCB, MC, V.

The City of Lights comes to Las Vegas, with the blessing of its French counterpart: Paris dimmed the lights on the real Eiffel Tower in honour of the Vegas opening in September 1999. Probably the most eye-catching of the new casino resorts, Paris has a façade that incorporates famed Parisian landmarks and a half-scale replica of the Eiffel Tower. The smallish guest rooms (2,900 in total), decorated in French style, are housed in a 34-storey, mansard-roofed tower that was modelled on Paris's Hotel de Ville. They feature crown mouldings, rich fabrics and a European-style armoire. The spacious marble bathrooms have a large vanity unit, a make-up mirror, linen hand towels and European fixtures.

*The **Resort at Summerlin** offers secluded luxury and lots of golfing. See page 127.*

Guests can make use of the tennis courts and other facilities at Bally's next door.
Hotel services *Beauty salon. Business centre. Car rental desk. Concierge. Gym. Pool. Spa. Tour desk.* **Room services** *Cable TV with pay movies. Dataport. Room service (24hrs). Safe. Voicemail. Website: www.paris-lv.com*

Riviera

2901 Las Vegas Boulevard South, at Riviera Boulevard, Las Vegas, NV 89109 (reservations 1-800 634 6753/front desk 734 5110/fax 794 9451). Bus 202, 301, 302. **Rates** *single or double* $69-$95; *suite* $125-$600. **Credit** AmEx, DC, Disc, JCB, MC, V.

When the Riviera opened in 1955, it changed the face of the Strip. Not only was it the first high-rise (nine storeys, 200 rooms), but it also broke with the city's prevailing dude-ranch architecture. Since then the Riv has expanded to 2,067 guest rooms, the best of which are in the newer Monaco and Monte Carlo towers (15 and 18 storeys respectively). The tower rooms are small but not cramped, and decorated with dark wood furniture and burgundy or teal bed-spreads with matching gold-tasselled curtains. About half the rooms have views overlooking the pool, the rest face the surrounding mountains. The rooms in the original nine-storey wing (now the Mediterranean tower) were remodelled in 1996 with light wood furniture and flower-print fabrics. They're closer to the casino action, but the views are dismal (plumbing, air ducts, backs of signs). Hotel amenities include a large pool (flanked on all sides by hotel towers – the sun disappears early), two

night-lit tennis courts, a well-equipped health club and a convention centre.
Hotel services *Beauty salon. Business centre. Car rental desk. Gym. Pool. Spa. Tennis courts. Tour desk.* **Room services** *Cable TV with pay movies. Room service (24hrs). Safe. Voicemail. Website: www.theriviera.com*

Sahara

2535 Las Vegas Boulevard South, at E Sahara Avenue, Las Vegas, NV 89109 (reservations 1-800 634 6666/front desk 737 2111/fax 791 2027). Bus 204, 301, 302. **Rates** *single or double* $55-$85; *suite* $200-$600. **Credit** AmEx, DC, Disc, JCB, MC, V.

Through several expansions, the Sahara has taken on a fresh look. Its famous vertical sign has gone and new towers and Moroccan-style arches, along with palm trees and cascading fountains, have replaced the original two-storey garden buildings. The renovations have helped revitalise the ageing resort, and made it a popular destination for tour groups and conventioneers. It has also boosted the room count to 1,720, including 63 suites. The reno-vated and new rooms have a sunny disposition with tan carpeting and drapes, earth-tone upholstery and wooden desks with brass lamps. Hotel amenities include two pools, one with landscaped gardens and a thatched-hut bar.
Hotel services *Beauty salon. Business centre. Car rental desk. Pool. Tour desk.* **Room services** *Cable TV with pay movies. Dataport. Room service (6am-midnight). Voicemail. Website: www.saharahotelandcasino.com*

Stardust

3000 Las Vegas Boulevard South, at Stardust Drive, between W Sahara Avenue & Desert Inn Road, Las Vegas, NV 89109 (reservations 1-800 824 6033/ front desk 732 6111/fax 732 6257). Bus 301, 302. **Rates** *single or double* $36-$90 *(motor inn rooms),* $60-$160 *(tower rooms); suite* $250-$1,000. **Credit** AmEx, Disc, DC, JCB, MC, V.
The Stardust – with its famous neon sign – has exemplified Las Vegas style and flash for more than 40 years; an adult playground (albeit rather dowdy now) unencumbered by family attractions. Like almost every Strip hotel, it has expanded its accommodation, opening a 32-storey tower that brings its room count to 2,431. The new rooms are among the better buys on the Strip and are decorated with dark carpets, red and black upholstery, glass or marble tables and light wicker furniture. Rounding out the Stardust's amenities are eight bars, two pools and a video games arcade.
Hotel services *Beauty salon. Car rental desk. Pool.* **Room services** *TV with pay movies. Room service (24hrs). Safe. Voicemail.*
Website: www.stardustlv.com

Treasure Island

3300 Las Vegas Boulevard South, at Spring Mountain Road, Las Vegas, NV 89109 (reservations 1-800 944 7444/front desk 894 7111/fax 894 7446). Bus 203, 301, 302. **Rates** *single or double* $49-$350; *suite* $149-$650. **Credit** AmEx, DC, Disc, JCB, MC, V.

Venetian: *large rooms, and gondolas too.*

Like the Mirage, its glamorous cousin next door, Treasure Island's rooms are housed in a Y-shaped configuration, formed by three coral-coloured, 36-storey towers. The casino's dashing pirate theme is evident in the lobby's flamboyant gold trimmings, black corkscrew pillars, marble floors covered with oriental rugs and even a chandelier made of gold-plated skull and bones. The 3,000 guest rooms are decorated with brass fixtures, whitewashed wood furniture, copies of eighteenth-century nautical paintings and floor-to-ceiling windows, many of which offer views of the lively boulevard below. Hotel amenities include a well-equipped spa, a beauty salon, spacious swiming pool area with a long slide (ideal for kids) and cabanas, as well as the inevitable two wedding chapels.
Hotel services *Beauty salon. Business centre. Car rental desk. Concierge. Gym. Pool. Spa. Tour desk.* **Room services** *Cable TV with pay movies. Dataport. Room service (24hrs). Safe. Turndown. Voicemail.*
Website: www.treasureislandlasvegas.com

Tropicana

3801 Las Vegas Boulevard South, at E Tropicana Avenue, Las Vegas, NV 89109 (reservations 1-800 468 9494/front desk 739 2222/fax 739 2469). Bus 201, 301, 302. **Rates** *single or double* $75-$129; *suite* $109-$249. **Credit** AmEx, DC, Disc, JCB, MC, V.
Polynesia in the desert might describe the Tropicana – though it's all looking rather in need of repair now. The 1,800-plus guest rooms continue the island flavour with colourful prints and wood-and-bamboo furnishings. A water park stretches between the hotel's twin towers with three pools (featuring swim-up blackjack in the summer), a waterslide, five spas, two lagoons, tropical plants, lots of exotic flowers, oh, and some live pink flamingos. Other amenities include a wedding chapel and health club.
Hotel services *Beauty salon. Business centre. Car rental desk. Gym. Pool. Spa. Tour desk.* **Room services** *Cable TV with pay movies. Dataport. Room service (24hrs). Safe. Voicemail.*
Website: www.tropicanalv.com

Venetian

3355 Las Vegas Boulevard South, south of Sands Avenue, Las Vegas, NV 89109 (reservations 1-888 283 6423/front desk 414 1000/fax 414 2122). Bus 203, 301, 302. **Rates** *suite* $109-$399; *deluxe suite* up to $1,000. **Credit** AmEx, DC, Disc, JCB, MC, V.
The owners of the Venetian were wiping egg from their faces in May 1999 when the hotel flung open its doors to the public while the place was still under construction. But now the shops, pool area, Canyon Ranch Spa Club and restaurants are all completed, and the architecturally splendid resort has proved itself worth the wait and inconvenience. Standard guest suites (no 'rooms' here), are much larger than the Vegas norm, averaging 700sq ft (65sq m) and the most comfortable and sumptuously appointed in town (even the telephone in the bathroom has a dataport). From the marble foyer to crown mouldings and wrought-iron railings, few amenities have been omitted.
Unbelievably, the vast Venetian is merely phase one of billionaire Sheldon Adelson's plan. Phase two

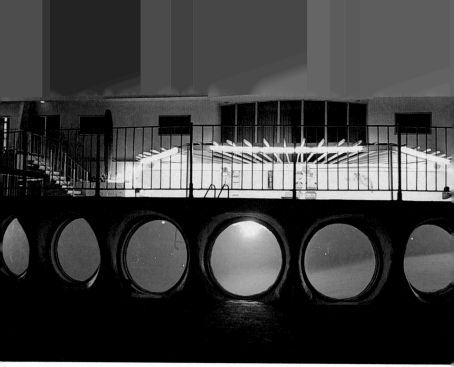

*See-through swimming at the famous **Glass Pool Inn**. See page 129.*

(construction has not yet started) will add another 3,000 guest rooms – making it larger than the MGM Grand – as well as more shops and casino space and a further 15 restaurants.
Hotel services *Beauty salon. Business centre. Car rental desk. Climbing wall. Concierge. Gym. Pool. Spa.* **Room services** *Cable TV with pay movies. Dataport. Fax. Mini-bar. Room service (24hrs). Safe. Voicemail.*
Website: www.venetian.com

Stratosphere Area

Stratosphere

2000 Las Vegas Boulevard South, at St Louis Avenue, between Charleston Boulevard & Sahara Avenue, Las Vegas, NV 89104 (reservations 1-800 998 6937/front desk 380 7777/fax 383 5334). Bus 113, 301, 302. **Rates** *single or double $29-$259; suite $59-$325.* **Credit** *AmEx, Disc, DC, JCB, MC, V.*
Sadly, there are no rooms atop the Stratosphere's imposing 1,149ft (350m) high tower, but you can enjoy the view, nevertheless, in the Top of the World Lounge. The hotel is a conversion of the mid-rise old Vegas World hotel. The rooms have been upgraded with swanky new carpets and curtains, art deco paintings, black lacquer furniture, safes and dataports. Unfortunately, because of its somewhat seedy location away from the main stretch of the Strip, the Stratosphere has suffered from financial difficulties and the new wing is currently only half completed.

Hotel services *Business centre. Car rental desk. Concierge. Gym. Pool. Tour desk.* **Room services** *Cable TV with pay movies. Dataport. Room service (24hrs). Safe. Turndown. Voicemail.*
Website: www.stratlv.com

East of Strip

Hard Rock Hotel

4455 Paradise Road, at Harmon Avenue, Las Vegas, NV 89109 (reservations 1-800 473 7625/front desk 693 5000/fax 693 5010). Bus 108. **Rates** *single or double $75-$250 (weekdays), $145-$300 (weekends); suite from $250.* **Credit** *AmEx, DC, Disc, MC, V.*
The Hard Rock's Miami-style curving hotel block is one of the nicest places to stay in Las Vegas, surprisingly elegant and tasteful for those expecting rock 'n' roll tat. It's also pretty intimate by Vegas standards (be sure to book ahead), with only 340 original rooms and suites, and 317 new rooms. The décor is subdued, classy and masculine, the TV extra-large and the room service top quality – acres of linen, vases of fresh flowers, gleaming serving domes and designer cruet, all for an $8 hamburger. Ask for a room overlooking the pool area, which reflects a Southern California influence, with a sandy beach lagoon and hillside gardens plus a row of tent cabanas. Amphibian gamblers will like the swim-up blackjack table. You'll also find spas and whirlpools, a waterslide and rock music piped underwater. The expansion enlarged the pool area

and added some convention rooms, as well as four restaurants, including an outpost of New York's famed sushi heaven, Nobu.
Hotel services *Concierge. Gym. Pool. Spa.*
Room services *Cable TV with pay movies. Dataport. Room service (24hrs). Voicemail. Website: www.hardrockhotel.com*

Las Vegas Hilton
3000 Paradise Road, between Karen Avenue & Convention Center Drive, Las Vegas, NV 89109 (reservations 1-800 732 7117/front desk 732 5111/ fax 732 5805). Bus 108. **Rates** *single or double* $95-$280; *suite* $350-$850. **Credit** AmEx, DC, Disc, JCB, MC, V.
Located about a block from the Strip, the 3,000-room Hilton is one of Las Vegas's premier vacation resorts. The outdoor recreation deck has six tennis courts, a putting green, shuffleboard and a large pool area. The hotel's long registration desk and lobby area is magnificently decorated with tropical colours, Grecian bas-reliefs, crystal chandeliers and neon rainbows. As you might expect, the rooms are first-rate, with upholstered easy chairs, marble-top dressing tables and deep closets. Some rooms have mini-bars, terraces, fireplaces and whirlpools. Colours tend toward cool blue and green pastels. One of the Hilton's attractions, Star Trek: The Experience, includes a space-age casino and Quark's Bar & Restaurant, and is one of the most popular must-sees in town.
Hotel services *Beauty salon. Business centre. Car rental desk. Gym. Pool. Spa. Tennis courts.*
Room services *Cable TV with pay movies. Room service (24hrs). Safe. Turndown. Voicemail. Website: www.hilton.com/hotels*

West of Strip

Rio
3700 W Flamingo Road, at Valley View Boulevard, Las Vegas, NV 89103 (reservations 1-800 752 9746/ front desk 252 7777/fax 252 8909). Bus 202.
Rates *standard suite* $65-$450; *Masquerade suite* $250-$1,000. **Credit** AmEx, DC, JCB, MC, V.
The constantly expanding, carnival-themed Rio is an all-suite property, with 2,563 in total, split between its original tower and the 41-storey tower in the Masquerade Village wing – a $200-million shopping, dining, entertainment and gambling complex, which also has wedding chapels and two honeymoon suites. It doesn't really matter which tower you're in: the rooms are practically identical and the views the same, though the original tower retains some two-storey suites with curving staircases and giant bathrooms. Otherwise, the suites are actually oversized rooms, with rich colours, tropical prints, smoked glass tables, velour furnishings in the sitting area and floor-to-ceiling windows for panoramic city views. The pool area gets rave reviews: a sandy beach lies at the edge of a tropical lagoon, complete with waterfalls and three swimming pools. There's also an entertainment gazebo and two sand volleyball courts. The Rio Spa has workout facilities, steam room and whirlpools.

Hotel services *Beauty salon. Business centre. Concierge. Golf course (1-888 867 3226). Gym. Pool. Spa.* **Room services** *Cable TV with pay movies. Refrigerator. Room service (24hrs). Safe. Voicemail. Website: www.playrio.com*

Downtown

El Cortez
600 Fremont Street, between Sixth & Seventh Streets, Las Vegas, NV 89101 (reservations 1-800 634 6703/front desk 385 5200/fax 385 1554/ reservations@elcortez.net). Bus 107, 301, 302.
Rates *single or double* $32-$40; *suite* $44. **Credit** AmEx, DC, Disc, JCB, MC, V.
Built in 1941, the El Cortez is the oldest casino hotel in town and was once owned by Benjamin 'Bugsy' Siegel, who sold his interest when he needed to raise cash for his 'Fabulous' Flamingo Hotel on the Strip. The south-west wing is the original adobe brick building. A 14-storey, 200-room tower has been added since, but the original rooms with wooden floors and tile baths remain. Nowadays, El Cortez caters mostly to budget travellers, seniors and die-hard slot fanatics.
Hotel services *Concierge. Hair salon.* **Room services** *Room service (6am-11pm). Voicemail. Website: www.elcortez.net*

Golden Nugget
129 Fremont Street, at Casino Center Boulevard, Las Vegas, NV 89101 (reservations 1-800 634 3454/ front desk 385 7111/guestservices@golden nugget.com). Bus 108, 205, 207, 401. **Rates** *single or double* $58-$160; *suite* $275-$375; *apartment* $500.
Credit AmEx, DC, Disc, JCB, MC, V.
The 1,805 guest rooms at Mirage Resorts' Golden Nugget (the only Downtown hotel without a neon sign) include 27 luxury apartments and six penthouse suites, and are among the most luxurious in town. The elegant lobby features leaf-glass chandeliers, white marble floors and columns, gold and brass accessories and red oriental rugs. In the rooms, you'll find cream carpets and wallcoverings, light wood tables and club chairs, tropical print bedspreads and curtains. The misted pool deck is huge, but because it is surrounded by buildings, catching rays is limited to a few midday hours. The whirlpool spas are a nice touch, as are the marble swans and bronze sculptures. There's also a health club.
Hotel services *Beauty salon. Business centre. Car rental desk. Gym. Pool. Spa. Tour desk.*
Room services *Cable TV with pay movies. Dataport. Room service (24hrs). Safe. Turndown. Website: www.goldennugget.com*

Fremont
200 Fremont Street, at Casino Center Boulevard, Las Vegas, NV 89101 (reservations 1-800 634 6460/ front desk 385 3232/fax 385 6270). Bus 108, 205, 207, 401. **Rates** *single or double* $35-$80.
Credit AmEx, DC, Disc, JCB, MC, V.
Built in 1956, the Fremont Hotel was Downtown's first carpet joint (as opposed to the rural, wooden-floor-and-sawdust joints). Today, its block-long

Golden oldie

For a glimpse of Las Vegas before it became a high-tech spectacle, go to the Golden Gate Hotel in Downtown. Built in 1906 at the corner of Fremont and Main Streets, it is the city's oldest hotel and also a reminder of Vegas's frontier heritage, before reality became virtual and hype replaced history. Better hurry, though; this town likes to blow up its landmarks.

When the hotel first opened, it was called Hotel Nevada. Rooms cost $1 a night and had windows, electric lighting and steam-heat radiators, there was no air-conditioning and guests had to share a bathroom at the end of the hall. The ground floor had a lobby and offices but no casino, yet there was gambling – a roulette wheel and a few poker tables – until it was outlawed in 1909.

The hotel was renamed Sal Sagev ('Las Vegas' spelled backwards) in the 1930s and then the Golden Gate in 1955, when a group of San Francisco investors took over. They opened the casino and introduced the city to the shrimp cocktail – a tasty little treat they'd discovered in an Oakland deli. The dish caught on and has been a Golden Gate tradition ever since – you can still sample one, served with a wedge of lemon in a tulip glass, though the price has soared to 99¢. In the 1950s and 1960s, the Golden Gate became a gathering place for local news reporters, judges, lawyers and businessmen.

While the Golden Gate has modernised to keep up with the times, it manages to retain much of its historic charm. Many of the original ten-foot-by-ten-foot guest rooms remain, though they've been updated with air-con, private baths, cable TV, coffeemakers, voicemail and even

computer ports. The rates have been bumped up to just over $50 a night, but the mahogany doors, plaster walls and tiled bathroom floors are a reminder of the joint's more basic past; plus they throw in breakfast and a newspaper.

In the downstairs lobby area, the décor is turn-of-the-century San Francisco: all mahogany, brass and chequerboard tiles. Nearby, a black baby grand piano sings out its snappy tunes from around noon every day. At times the place sounds like an old silent movie house with the piano player pounding out melodies that rise and fall with the film's plot.

Perhaps some of the best reminders of the hotel's golden years are the patrons who still come here. Among them you might find a 95-year-old woman who traditionally starts off her week with a pancake breakfast and a few pulls on a one-armed bandit, or a couple celebrating their wedding anniversary, as they have done every year since they were married here in 1946. In a town that places little value on history, the Golden Gate has withstood the test of time, and endured the whims and ravages of a market-driven economy. For Las Vegas, it's a welcome step backward.

Golden Gate Hotel

1 Fremont Street, at Main Street, Las Vegas, NV 89101 (reservations 1-800 426 1906/front desk 385 1906). Bus 108, 205, 207, 401. **Rates** *single or double* $38 Mon-Thur, Sun; $53 Fri, Sat. **Credit** AmEx, Disc, DC, MC, V.

neon sign helps light up the Fremont Street Experience. Like its sister hotel across the street, the California, it features a tropical island motif: appropriate, since it caters to a large contingent of travellers from Hawaii. The hotel's 447 guest rooms (including 23 suites) are modern and comfortable and feature floral patterns in hues of emerald and burgundy. There is no swimming pool.

Room services *TV with pay movies. Room service (6am-10am). Safe.*
Website: www.fremontcasino.com

North-west Las Vegas

Resort at Summerlin

221 N Rampart Boulevard, at Summerlin Parkway Las Vegas, NV 89145 (reservations 1-877 869 8777 US only/front desk 869 8777/fax 869 7771). No bus.
Rates *single or double $195-$300; suite $400-$2,100.*
Credit AmEx, DC, Disc, JCB, MC, V.
Calling all golfers: this brand-new 54-acre (22ha) spa-resort is for you. Located in the masterplanned residential suburb of Summerlin (a Howard Hughes Corporation development), about a 25-minute drive from the Strip, the resort looks out over the Red Rock Canyon Conservation Area and has access to tee times at six nearby golf courses, including TPC at the Canyons across the street. It comprises two hotels: the Regent Grand Spa (286 rooms) and the Regent Grand Palms (255 rooms), both managed by Regent International Hotels. Linked by a casino, restaurant and shopping complex, the two hotels operate semi-independently. The Regent Grand Spa, decorated in Spanish revival style, features the state-of-the-art Aquae Sulis spa. The Regent Grand Palms is more formal in décor and has Parian, a high-end restaurant with an ambitious wine list.
Hotel services *Beauty salon. Business centre. Car rental desk. Concierge. Gym. Pool. Putting green. Spa. Tour desk.* **Room services** *Cable TV with pay movies. Dataport. Mini-bar. Refrigerator. Room service (24hrs). Safe. Turndown. VCR. Voicemail. Web TV with e-mail.*
Website: www.resortatsummerlin.com

*Understated elegance at the **Four Seasons**.*

Non-casino hotels

Since casinos subsidise their hotel rooms to provide themselves with a resident pool of gamblers, the non-casino hotels have a hard time competing and thus rates may be slightly higher, though the price differential is not as significant as it used to be. What it buys you is a refuge from the madness and a little more individuality. Generally, the closer to the Strip, the higher the prices.

The Strip

Four Seasons

3960 Las Vegas Boulevard South, between W Tropicana Avenue & Russell Road, Las Vegas, NV 89119 (reservations 1-888 632 5000/front desk 632 5100/fax 632 5195). Bus 301, 302.
Rates *single or double $150-$350; suite $350-$950; speciality suite $900-$3,900.* **Credit** AmEx, DC, Disc, MC, V.
The Four Seasons is Las Vegas's first upmarket hotel without gambling facilities. Well, sort of. Admittedly, there's no gaming in the actual hotel but it's bang next door to the Mandalay Bay mega-resort – in fact, from the outside, it's hard to tell the two apart – so it's only a step along a corridor to a very large casino. Small by Vegas standards, the Four Seasons' 424 rooms (including 86 suites) are located on floors 35 to 39 of Mandalay Bay's gold tower and accessed by separate elevators. The design of the interior – all golden wood panelling, antique furniture and paintings and huge floral displays – creates an air of understated elegance and exclusivity. You'll almost forget you're in Vegas – until you look out of your window at the Strip stretching away to the north. Rooms are not huge (500sq ft/46sq m), but they're luxurious enough, with all sorts of extras – mini-bar, bathrobes, coffeemaker, overnight shoeshine – that you don't usually get in the main hotel-casinos. Guests have their own separate pool within the Mandalay Bay pool complex, complete with lounge chairs and private cabanas, plus a top-class spa and health club. The First Floor Grill is the signature restaurant, but you're probably better off nipping next door to sample Mandalay Bay's more varied dining facilities.
Hotel services *Business centre. Car rental desk. Concierge. Gym. Pool. Spa.* **Room services** *Cable TV with pay movies. Dataport. Mini-bar. Room service (24hrs). Safe. Turndown (twice daily). Voicemail.*
Website: www.fourseasons.com

Near the Convention Center

All the following hotels are near the Convention Center, and therefore handy for the action on the Strip as well as for delegates visiting the many trade shows that take place in Las Vegas. Some hotels cater especially for business people, with fax machines, meeting rooms and so on.

Alexis Park

*375 E Harmon Avenue, between Koval Lane &
Paradise Road, Las Vegas, NV 89109 (reservations
1-800 582 2228/front desk 796 3300/fax 706 0766/
admin@alexispark.com). Bus 108, 213.* **Rates**
1-bedroom suite $99-$139; 1-bedroom loft suite
$179-$249; *larger suite* $350-$1,500. **Credit** AmEx,
DC, Disc, JCB, MC, V.

The Alexis Park was originally built as as a complex
of townhomes and apartments and later transformed
into a hotel. It doesn't have a casino, although the
owners have been seeking a way out of its zoning
stipulations so they can get a gaming licence.
Situated amid lush greenery, streams and waterfalls,
the Mediterranean-style villa is a welcome retreat
from the concrete and steel hotels on the Strip. The
lobby suggests European elegance with its Spanish
tiled floor, overstuffed chairs and French telephones.
The 500 suites are available in ten floorplans.
Furnishings range from Victorian (flower-print
ottomans, mahogany dining tables and chairs) to
Southwest modern (adobe walls, macramé wall-
hangings, club chairs). Some of the larger units (up
to 1,200sq ft/112sq m) have fireplaces and jacuzzis;
all units have refrigerators, mini-bars and VCRs.
Recreational facilities include three swimming pools,
tennis courts and a spa.
Hotel services *Beauty salon. Business centre.
Concierge. Gym. Pool. Spa. Tour desk.*
Room services *Cable TV with pay movies.
Mini-bar. Refrigerator. Room service (7am-1am).
Voicemail.*
Website: www.alexispark.com

Carriage House

*105 E Harmon Avenue, between Las Vegas
Boulevard South & Koval Lane, Las Vegas,
NV 89109 (reservations 1-800 221 2301/front desk
798 1020/fax 798 1020 ext 118). Bus 213.* **Rates**
studio (1 or 2 people) $135; *1-bedroom unit* (up to 4
people) $165; *2-bedroom unit* (up to 6 people) $275.
Credit AmEx, DC, Disc, MC, V.

For some reason, the Carriage House is often overlooked by visitors. It's a pity because the tasteful,
moderately priced rooms are among the best buys
in town, with luxurious plush carpeting, Midwest
tiles, grass-paper wallcoverings and overstuffed
sofas and love seats. The relaxing lobby is decorated in cool greys and blues and furnished with
country-style sofas and tables. The ninth-floor
restaurant, Kiefers, has unobstructed views of the
city and the MGM Grand's theme park. Outside,
the tennis court, pool and sun deck are landscaped
with pine trees.
Hotel services *Concierge. Basketball court. Pool.
Tennis court. Tour desk.* **Room services** *Cable TV
with pay movies. Dataport. Kitchenette. Refrigerator.
Safe. Voicemail.*
Website: www.carriagehouselasvegas.com

Courtyard by Marriott

*3275 Paradise Road, at E Desert Inn Road, Las
Vegas, NV 89109 (reservations 1-800 321 2211/
front desk 791 3600/fax 796 7981). Bus 108, 112.*
Rates *single or double* $109-$119; *suite* $120-$140.
Credit AmEx, DC, Disc, MC, V.

Just across the street from the Convention Center,
Courtyard is popular with business travellers
because of the readily available fax machines, the
well-equipped meeting rooms, and the large work
desks in the 149 rooms. The comfortable lobby is
accented by light wood and brass fixtures and has
a marble fireplace and club chairs. The rooms, decorated in muted tones, range from spartan single-
bed quarters to spacious suites with separate living
rooms. Some units have terraces. The cable TV has
first-run pay movies and the phones are cordless.
After a full day's gambling or doing business, relax
by the pool or in the pavilion in the pretty courtyard.
Hotel services *Gym. Pool.* **Room services**
*Cable TV with pay movies. Dataport. Room service
(4.30-11pm). Turndown. Voicemail.*
Website: http://courtyard.com/LASCH/

La Quinta Inn

*3970 Paradise Road, at E Flamingo Road, Las
Vegas, NV 89109 (reservations 1-800 777 1700/
front desk 796 9000/fax 796 9000 ext 410).
Bus 108, 202.* **Rates** (including continental
breakfast) *single or double* $85-$99; *suite* $115-$125.
Credit AmEx, DC, Disc, MC, V.

The Mediterranean-style building with its white
stucco walls, red tile roof and black ironwork, all
surrounded by tall palm trees, is popular with
vacationers as well as conventioneers. The lobby,
which lingers between Swiss chalet and country
farmhouse, has exposed beam ceilings, a tiled floor,
arched windows and leather wing chairs. The

La Quinta Inn: *handy for conventions.*

three-storey building contains 251 rooms (many renovated in 1999), decorated with a country French flavour, with plush teal carpeting and pastel upholstered furniture. All have coffeemakers; some have whirlpool tubs. The suites have private balconies, microwaves, refrigerators and whirlpool tubs. The courtyard is heavily landscaped with trees, plants and a picturesque fountain and pool.
Hotel services *Free local calls. Gym. Pool.*
Room services *Cable TV with pay movies. Dataport. Voicemail.*
Website: www.laquinta.com

Residence Inn by Marriott

3225 Paradise Road, at Convention Center Drive, Las Vegas, NV 89109 (reservations 1-800 331 3131/front desk & fax 796 9300). Bus 108, 112. **Rates** *(including continental breakfast) studio* $90-$120; *townhouse* $110-$220. **Credit** AmEx, DC, Disc, MC, V.
Like its stablemate (Courtyard) next door, the Residence Inn is a hot item during busy conventions, and its spacious, condo-like units are specifically designed for guests on extended visits. All the rooms and suites are tastefully decorated in earth-tone colour schemes with Danish modern furnishings and modern art, and have balconies or patios, large bathrooms and kitchens complete with microwaves and dishwashers. You can actually relax in the quiet lobby with its wing chairs and fieldstone fireplace. Rounding out the hotel amenities are a swimming pool, three jacuzzis and a grocery shopping service. Guests can use a nearby fitness centre, and, unlike most Vegas hotels, pets are allowed.
Hotel services *Pool.* **Room services** *Cable TV with pay movies. Dataport. Kitchen. Refrigerator. Room service (4-10pm). Voicemail.*
Website: http://residenceinn.com/LASNV/

Old Vegas

Algiers Hotel

2845 Las Vegas Boulevard South, at Riviera Drive, Las Vegas, NV 89109 (reservations 1-800 732 3361/front desk 735 3311/algiers@travelbase.com). Bus 301, 302. **Rates** *single or double* $35-$125; *suite* $70-$150. **Credit** AmEx, Disc, DC, MC, V.
Built in 1953, the Algiers retains much of the style that characterised Vegas during the Frank-and-Dino Rat Pack days. The motorcourt-style inn is a two-storey garden affair; pink, 'bleeding brick' buildings with aqua trim surround a large kidney-shaped pool. Stretch out in a lounge chair under the towering palms and you'll feel like you're back in the Hollywood-high-life oasis of the 1950s. The 105 rooms are clean and well kept, with white panelled walls, light wood furniture, dressing areas and tiled bathrooms. The swag lamps are a reminder of the Algiers' retro polyester heritage. The service is friendly and homey without the hustle of newer establishments, but the hotel lets its near neighbours (Stardust, Circus Circus etc) do the entertaining.
Hotel services *Car rental desk. Pool.*
Room services *Cable TV.*
Website: www.algiershotel.com

Hotel chains

The following hotel and motel chains have branches in Las Vegas, many of them conveniently situated along or near the Strip:

Mid-range
Holiday Inn 1-800 465 4329
Howard Johnson 1-800 446 4656

Budget
Best Western 1-800 528 1234
Budget 1-800 752 1501
Comfort Inn, Econo Lodge, Quality Inn & Rodeway Inn 1-800 221 2222
Days Inn 1-800 325 2525
Motel 6 1-800 466 8356
Ramada Inn 1-800 272 6232
Super 8 1-800 800 8000
Travelodge 1-800 578 7878

Glass Pool Inn

4613 Las Vegas Boulevard South, between E Tropicana Avenue & Russell Road, Las Vegas, NV 89119 (reservations 1-800 527 7118/front desk 739 6636). Bus 301, 302. **Rates** *single or double* $24-$119. **Credit** AmEx, MC, V.
Opened in 1951, the Glass Pool Inn, at the southern end of the Strip, is famous for its unique, elevated swimming pool with windows. According to the owners – who originally called the motel the Mirage but sold the name to Steve Wynn in 1988 – the pool was built to attract passing motorists, parched and dusty after driving for hours across the desert. The rooms – many with exposed beam ceilings, plastic dinette-style furniture and tiled baths – are now somewhat rundown and rented mostly to long-term visitors such as construction workers, and people relocating to Vegas. A popular film location in recent years, the motel has appeared in *Casino, Leaving Las Vegas, Indecent Proposal*, the TV series *Vegas* and *Crime Story*, as well as dozens of commercials, various documentaries and rock videos.
Hotel services *Pool.* **Room services** *Cable TV with pay movies.*

Victory Hotel-Motel

307 S Main Street, at Bridger Avenue, Las Vegas, NV 89101 (387 9257). Bus 108, 205, 207. **Rates** $24-$35. **No credit cards.**
This whitewashed mission-style hotel hasn't changed much since it was built in 1910. The two-storey building has an upstairs balcony overlooking the street and a veranda where guests once sat and watched trains steam into the depot opposite. The 32 rooms are spartan but clean, and surround a modest courtyard. The lobby is equally basic with a TV set that never turns off, an obscure park bench and a deer head mounted on a knotty pine wall.
Hotel services *Pool.* **Room services** *Cable TV with pay movies.*

Outside Las Vegas

Hyatt Regency Lake Las Vegas

*1600 Lake Las Vegas Parkway, Henderson,
NV 89109 (reservations 1-800 554 9288/front desk
567 1234/fax 567 6067). No bus.* **Rates** *single or
double* $175-$245; *suite* $450-$1,800. **Credit** AmEx,
DC, Disc, JCB, MC, V.

Hyatt Hotels' first venture into Las Vegas opened in
December 1999 as a posh, full-service resort that
is unlike the Vegas norm. For a start, the resort is
nearly 30 minutes' drive from the Strip, in a private,
picturesque lakeside community near Lake Mead.
Second, the casino is just a 'part-time' amenity – it's
small by most standards and open only from 10am
to 2am. The major attractions are the water sports,
the Jack Nicklaus-designed golf course and Camp
Hyatt, the chain's renowned daycare programme for
kids. Other hotel amenities include two restaurants,
including a fine dining room, Japanego, modelled on

International Hostel: *cheap and cheerful.*

its namesake in La Jolla, California. The 496 guest
rooms are large and offer views of either the lake or
surrounding mountains. Designs evoke a Moorish
ambience through desert colours, accent mouldings
and carpet border patterns. If you want to forget
you're in Vegas, it's ideal; if not, it's too far from the
Strip to be convenient.

Hotel services *Babysitting & childcare. Beauty
salon. Car rental desk. Concierge. Golf course. Gym.
Pool. Spa.* **Room services** *Cable TV with pay movies.
Dataport. Room service (24hrs). Safe. Turndown.
Voicemail.*
Website: http://lakelasvegas.hyatt.com

Budget

Casino rooms offer such good value that the budget
accommodation sector is relatively small. In addition to the hostel listed below, there are any number
of fading 1950s motels cluttering up the more
unfashionable stretches of Las Vegas Boulevard,
together with their modern counterparts, the chain
cheapies (*see page 129* **Hotel chains**). **Budget
Suites** (*see below*) also rents on a daily and weekly
basis, at competitive rates.

Las Vegas International Hostel

*1208 Las Vegas Boulevard South, between
Charleston & Oakey Boulevards, Las Vegas, NV
89104 (385 9955). Bus 301, 302.* **Rates** *dorm* $14;
private room $28. **No credit cards.**

Backpackers take note: this elderly, two-storey brick
building is the only hostel in town – and therefore
almost always much in demand. Rooms are of the
prison-cell variety – four walls and a bed – while the
dorms have six beds. All bathrooms are shared;
many are in various stages of disrepair so check
them out before renting. Guests can make use of a
communal kitchen and a lounge complete with TV,
VCR (and tapes), books and magazines. AYH and
AAIH members receive a $2 discount per night,
making it very good value. The hostel is in rather a
seedy location, so take extra care when walking
around at night.

Extended stay

Budget Suites

*3684 Paradise Road, at Twain Avenue, Las Vegas,
NV 89019 (reservations 1-800 752 1501/front desk
699 7000). Bus 108, 203, 213.* **Rates** *day* $49.50
Mon-Thur, Sun; $69.50 Fri, Sat; *week* $179.50-$189.50.
Credit AmEx, MC, V.

Located in various places around the Valley – but
usually within walking distance of casinos – every
room at these 220- to 300-unit complexes is a mini-
suite with a living room/kitchen, cable TV and free
local phone calls. The buildings are laid out like
large apartment complexes, with two dozen or so
units in each three-storey block. Maid service is
available, but you can save on this extra expense if
you bring your own linen and towels.

All Budget Suites have studios and one-bedroom
suites, but two bedroom set-ups are available only
at some locations, including the handily placed 3655
West Tropicana outpost – a good place from
which to explore the south end of the Strip. The
small pool areas all have barbecue pits shaded by
palm trees, and there's plenty of parking.

Budget Suites are good places to take children and
keep them happy in the city. They're also popular
with people relocating to Las Vegas. Call 1-800 752
1501 for further details of all locations.
Branches: 3655 W Tropicana Avenue, at Industrial
Road, Las Vegas, NV 89103 (739 1000); 4205
Tropicana Avenue, at Valley View Boulevard,
Las Vegas, NV 89121 (889 1700); 1500 Stardust
Road, between Las Vegas Boulevard South &
Industrial Road, Las Vegas, NV 89109 (732 1500);
2219 N Rancho Drive, at Lake Mead Drive,
Las Vegas, NV 89130 (638 1800); 4625 Boulder
Highway, at Indios Avenue, Las Vegas, NV 89121
(454 4625).

The Meridian

*250 E Flamingo Road, at Koval Lane, Las Vegas,
NV 89109 (735 5949/fax 735 3104). Bus 202, 301,
302.* **Rates** *per month 1-bedroom* $1,470; *2-bedroom*
$1,740; *3-bedroom* $2,200. **No credit cards.**

You can live like a local at this 685-unit apartment
complex, half a mile east of the Strip, which has 100

units available for short-term rent (by the day, week or month; 30-day advance booking advised). One- and two-bedroom luxury flats come with all the creature comforts: fully equipped kitchens, house-wares, linen, answerphones, washing machines and dryers. The apartments have high ceilings and private balconies and are ensconced inside security gates. There are leisure facilities, too – two rather lovely lagoon-style pools and spas, tennis and racquetball courts and a health club. Weekly maid service is available.

Polo Towers

3745 Las Vegas Boulevard South, between E Harmon & Tropicana Avenues, Las Vegas, NV 89109 (reservations 1-800 935 2233/front desk 261 1000). Bus 301, 302. **Rates** *studio (sleeps 2)* $119 Mon-Thur, Sun; $149 Fri, Sat; *1-bedroom* (sleeps 4) $159 Mon-Thur, Sun; $189 Fri, Sat; *2-bedroom* (sleeps 6) $259 Mon-Thur, Sun; $289 Fri, Sat. **Credit** AmEx, DC, Disc, MC, V.

You and your family can spend days or weeks at this 479-room complex opposite the Holiday Inn. Studio and one-bedroom suites are intended for both business travellers and tourists. Decorated in 1980s bachelor-pad style, each unit has its own small private balcony. All have their own refrig-erator, VCR, stereo, closet safe and dataport, and the one-bedroom flats also have kitchens, fully equipped with cooking and dining utensils. A pool and spa are on the roof above a bar that's primarily notable for its kitsch décor and fab view (endless parties of Japanese tourists keep trooping through). Other facilities, such as a fitness centre, are avail-able in the mall at ground level. Note that Polo Towers is a timeshare operation, so sometimes it can be difficult to get a room.

Home from home: **Budget Suites.**

RV parks

RVers have many diverse ports of call in Las Vegas. Rates are highly competitive, with many costing less than $20 a night. All the parks listed below have full hook-ups and accept pets. Reservations are strongly recommended.

California RV Park

100 Stewart Avenue, at Main Street, Las Vegas, NV 89101 (reservations 1-800 634 6505/front desk 388 2602). Bus 106, 107, 208, 214. **Rates** $12. **Credit** AmEx, Disc, DC, MC, V.

This is a great RV park for Downtown visitors, located close to the junction of the I-15 and US 95 and an easy two-block walk to the Fremont Street Experience and its ten casinos. The 220-space lot is gated and includes a swimming pool, jacuzzi, showers and laundry. Its very reasonable rates make it a popular spot, so it's worth booking ahead.

Circusland RV Park

500 Circus Circus Drive, at Las Vegas Boulevard South, Las Vegas, NV 89109 (reservations 1-800 634 3450/front desk 794 3757). Bus 105, 301. **Rates** $16.96 Mon-Thur, Sun; $19.08 Fri, Sat; $25.44 holidays, special events. **Credit** AmEx, Disc, DC, MC, V.

Just off the Strip next to Circus Circus, this is a firm favourite for families. With the hotel's amusement park just steps away and scores of casinos within easy walking distance, both children and adults will be kept amused, and there's the added bonus that you won't have to do much driving once you pull in. The 365-space facility has a handy monorail to the casino and a fenced run for pets, plus a pool, jacuzzi, supply store and laundry.

Website: www.circuscircus-lasvegas.com

KOA Kampground

4315 Boulder Highway, between Desert Inn & E Flamingo Roads, Las Vegas, NV 89121 (reservations 1-800 562 7782/front desk 451 5527). Bus 107. **Rates** *night* $29.95; *week* $180; *month* $350. **Credit** AmEx, Disc, MC, V.

Set up camp here for a day, a week, a month or more. Discounted long-term rates are available at the 240-space facility, which has a store, showers, pool and jacuzzi. Kids will enjoy the playground while adults will appreciate the free shuttle to the casinos (it's pretty far from the Strip). It's one of the very few RV parks that also allows tents.

Silverton

3333 Blue Diamond Road, at Industrial Road, Las Vegas, NV 89139 (reservations 1-800 588 7711/ front desk 263 7777). Bus 303. **Rates** $18 Mon-Thur, Sun; $21 Fri, Sat. **Credit** AmEx, Disc, DC, MC, V.

If you're arriving from California, this is a good place to drop anchor. Just a couple of miles south of the Strip off the I-15, you can settle in before braving the chaos of Las Vegas's traffic and the dollar-hungry casinos. Silverton's 460 spaces are fairly spacious (60ft by 12ft/18m by 3.6m) and each is cable- and phone-ready. They are fairly modest, but clean and convenient. There's also a mini-mart, pool, showers, laundry and shuttle to the Silverton casino.

Restaurants & Buffets

In the past few years, Las Vegas has moved to the top of the restaurant superleague – so wine, dine and enjoy.

Until as recently as the early 1990s, typical Vegas fare consisted of a cheap buffet or an overpriced meal in a 'continental' restaurant. Things started to improve in 1992, when Wolfgang Puck opened **Spago** in the Forum Shops in Caesars Palace. Puck was swiftly followed by other big-name chefs: Mark Miller (**Coyote Café**, 1994), Emeril Lagasse (**Emeril's**, 1995) and Jean-Louis Palladin (**Napa**, 1997); thus 50 years of mediocrity was swept away within five.

In 2000, it may not be an overstatement to proclaim Vegas as the number one dining destination in the world. As outrageous as this may seem, try finding another city that has opened more first-class restaurants, with world-famous chefs, in the past two years. Even the not-so-humble breads and pastries of Gaston Lenôtre, France's best-known pastry chef, have weathered the transition from the streets of the real Paris to the ersatz hotel bearing its name, and are just as pristine and tasty in the desert as they are on the Right Bank.

Paris is but one of four new mega-resorts that have opened since autumn 1998, each of them a stunning mix of architecture, shopping and fine dining – a mix that now defines Las Vegas. Between them, Bellagio, Mandalay Bay, the Venetian and Paris give visitors a wealth of restaurant choices that only the real Paris and New York come close to. Add the recently expanded Hard Rock Hotel to the mix, with its retro-Rat Pack cool – best experienced at **AJ's Steakhouse** – and you see why the term 'hotel dining' has lost its pejorative ring.

Besides being the hippest hotel in town, the HRH also boasts the *nouveau* sushi creations of Nobu Matsuhisa at **Nobu**. His Matsuhisa restaurant in Los Angeles is consistently ranked as that city's best, and in Las Vegas his Japanese/Peruvian avant-garde creations add an intriguing eclecticism to the culinary mix of the hotel and the town. Just down the block is Julian Serrano's cutting-edge cuisine at **Picasso**, inside Bellagio. Picasso was recently named the number one restaurant in the US by *Esquire* magazine. Combine these high-flyers with the diverse wine and food offerings at other hotels (Caesars Palace, for example, now features 14 restaurants) and you have a gourmet playground at your disposal.

If you need further proof of Las Vegas' exalted dining status, look no further than the Venetian. Where else on earth would four celebrity chefs/restaurateurs have the audacity to open branches of their world-famous restaurants side by side in the same hotel? At the Venetian you will find Piero Selvaggio's **Valentino** next door to Joachim Splichal's **Pinot Brasserie**, adjacent to Steven Pyle's **Star Canyon**, which cosies up to Emeril Lagasse's **Delmonico's** – probably the best steakhouse (in a crowded category) in all of Las Vegas right now. Smack in the middle of this line-up is the **Royal Star** Cantonese restaurant, an offshoot of the famous Ocean Star seafood restaurant in Monterey Park, California.

As famous as these high-flyers are, they are not by any means your only choices at this faux version of the jewel of northern Italy. Within the Venetian are also branches of **Zeffirino** (the venerable Roman restaurant's first outpost outside Italy), Wolfgang Puck's **Postrio** and **Il Canaletto**, which comes by way of San Francisco and the Il Fornaio chain.

As dramatic and wonderful as the restaurants at the Venetian are, many would rank those at the Bellagio even higher. Steve Wynn's ultra luxurious resort has opened no less than nine superstar restaurants, with Picasso and Sirio Maccioni's **Le Cirque** leading the way. Along with John-Georges Vongerichten's **Prime**, Maccioni's **Osteria del Circo**, Michael Mina's **Aqua** and Todd English's **Olives**, this star line-up gives Bellagio probably the strongest collection of high-end eateries in any hotel anywhere in the world.

Not to be outdone, down the street finds Alec Stratta displaying his high-class cuisine at **Renoir** in the Mirage. This gem has been awarded five stars by the prestigious Mobil travel guide, as has Picasso. In fact, Las Vegas now shares the top shelf with New York and Atlanta as being the only US cities having more than one five-star winner.

Equally good, if not as numerous, are the restaurants at Mandalay Bay – which boasts the architecturally dramatic **Aureole** as its centre-piece and also has an outpost of LA's **Border Grill**. Paris, meanwhile, has its **Eiffel Tower Restaurant** (perched on the 11th floor) and **Mon Ami Gabi**, a French bistro/steakhouse. Both have views and people-watching to match the extraordinary food.

This tidal wave of gourmet offerings has even improved the choices off the Strip. Fresh seafood used to be an impossibility in this high desert town, but now **McCormick & Schmick's** brings an astounding (and daily) array of fresh fish and shellfish to its east of Strip location. Head further away from the Strip and you'll find some neighbourhood restaurants with the panache and cooking to challenge the big hitters. **Rosemary's** and **Gabriel's Green Lips** were both started by chefs who cut their teeth at well-known hotel restaurants and now put out food and wine lists that were unseen off the Strip as little as two years ago.

Those in the mood for Chinese food need only travel a mile off Las Vegas Boulevard to the Chinatown Mall on Spring Mountain Road, where a dozen regionally diverse restaurants bring the food of China, Vietnam and Japan to one location. Our favourites include the **Dragon Sushi** restaurant, **Sam Woo** (for Cantonese barbecue) and **1-6-8 Shanghai** for the soups, stews and noodle dishes of eastern China.

With so many kinds of cuisine and so many world-famous restaurants, the choices facing the Vegas diner have never been more dizzying. Forget the long-ago image of Vegas as a cow town for rubes or the 'town that taste forgot'. The level of sophistication will now overwhelm even the most jaded of palates. Keep in mind that most of these famous offshoots in the large Strip hotels are in the very expensive category, with dinner for two easily topping $150. But – unlike the Vegas of old – these gourmet outposts are delivering some fabulous bang for your buck.

Below, we've picked out what we think are the best places, but it's also worth checking out the local papers and free magazines for details of additional eateries, as well as money-saving coupons. **Waiters on Wheels** (735 6325) prints the menus of about 50 restaurants across town and can deliver to your room, for a fee.

OPENING HOURS & PRICES

Note that although the casinos are open 24 hours a day, their gourmet restaurants usually take last orders at around 10.30 to 11.30pm and often don't open for lunch. All casinos have at least a coffee-shop, however, that serves food around the clock. Out of the casinos, restaurants keep surprisingly early hours: several take last orders at 9pm, and 10pm is common. Reservations are usually necessary at the fashionable spots, and you should also check dress restrictions.

Averages given are for a typical meal for that restaurant; thus, at a formal gourmet room they cover three or four courses, at a more casual restaurant two, and at a deli a sandwich and dessert. Drinks are not included.

Restaurants

American & burgers

America

New York-New York, 3790 Las Vegas Boulevard South, at W Tropicana Avenue (740 6451). Bus 201, 301, 302. **Open** 24hrs daily. **Average** $18. **Credit** AmEx, DC, Disc, MC, V.
A huge map of the United States hangs from the ceiling, with each state marked with a symbol of something for which it is known, with Vegas being the brightest. Beneath, the restaurant is large and open, and festooned with old travel posters. The menu features a wide variety of dishes such as a traditional turkey dinner, meatloaf, pastas, salads, burgers, a few seafood choices and all-day breakfast. Great dessert menu, too.

Cheesecake Factory

The Forum Shops, Caesars Palace, 3500 Las Vegas Boulevard South, between Spring Mountain & W Flamingo Roads (731 7110). Bus 301, 302. **Open** 11.15am-11.30pm Mon-Thur, Sun; 11.15am-12.30am Fri, Sat. **Average** $19. **Credit** AmEx, DC, Disc, MC, V.
Just reading the menu here (250+ items, with 28 specials) will exhaust you, but the kitchen (or is it a factory?) pulls it off with above-average results on most dishes. Choices range from the mundane (decent meatloaf and mashed potatoes) to the bizarre (Beverly Hills Thai pizza salad, whatever that is). The California Lite cheesecake, meanwhile, would make any food lover cringe. Still, the place is constantly jammed. Maybe it's the prices (moderate) or the people-watching opportunities (great).

Coffee Pub

The Plazas, 3800 W Sahara Avenue, at Paseo Del Prado, North-west Las Vegas (367 1913). Bus 204. **Open** 7.15am-3pm daily. **Average** $12. **Credit** AmEx, DC, Disc, MC, V.
Smoothies, sandwiches, soups, breakfasts and people-watching fill the bill at this breakfast- and lunch-only place. It's big with politicos and bimbos, so wear your reflector sunglasses and have a ball.

Dive!

Fashion Show Mall, 3200 Las Vegas Boulevard South, at W Spring Mountain Road (369 3483). Bus 203, 301, 302. **Open** 11.30am-9pm Mon-Sat; 11.30am-8pm Sun. **Average** $15. **Credit** AmEx, DC, Disc, MC, V.
A wild and wacky sub shop on steroids. It's not hard to believe that Steven Spielberg co-owns this restaurant-cum-fantasy trip, which has enough eye

A tower of wine at outsized **Aureole**, *p136.*

candy to keep both kids and adults satisfied throughout the meal. Don't be put off by the name: 'Dive' refers to the nautical theme (sub – sandwich, sub – submarine, geddit?), not the atmosphere. As far as the cooking goes, gourmet sandwiches abound, made with quality bread and ingredients. Killer french fries with six dipping sauces are a wicked way to start a meal. Try the five kinds of margarita for $9.

Fat Burger

3765 Las Vegas Boulevard South, between W Tropicana & Harmon Avenues (736 4733). **Open** *restaurant* 10.30am-10pm, *drive-thru* 24hrs, daily. **Average** $16. **No credit cards.**
One of the best fast-food burger chains in the States. Here they make 'em good, with chopped onions and, wait for it, real cheese. The old-time atmosphere offers a taste of true Americana, and the milkshakes are worth trying, too.
Branches: see phone book.

In-n-Out Burger

4888 Industrial Road, at W Tropicana Avenue, West of Strip (all locations 1-800 786 1000). *Bus 201.* **Open** 10.30am-1am Mon-Thur, Sun; 10.30am-1.30am Fri, Sat. **Average** $7. **No credit cards.**
If you want to taste what made the hamburger famous, this California-based chain delivers the goods. You haven't tasted burger heaven until you've tried the Double Double Cheeseburger here. A classic experience, not to be missed.
Branches: see phone book.

Mr Lucky's 24/7

Hard Rock, 4455 Paradise Road, at Harmon Avenue, East of Strip (693 5000). Bus 108. **Open** 24hrs daily. **Average** $17. **Credit** AmEx, Disc, MC, V.
Beyond cool. People-watching at its best, with what is undoubtedly the youngest and hippest crowd in Las Vegas in attendance at all hours. So distracting is the constant stream of MAWs (models-actresses-whatever) that your eyes will be diverted from some fairly classy and upscale food that in no way resembles the coffeeshop fare in most hotels. Some of the specials here are as good as anything at Mortoni's (the hotel's more formal dining room; *see p146*), and at half the price. Just walk in and you'll feel a lot hipper than you actually are.

Tony Roma's 'The Place for Ribs'

620 E Sahara Avenue, at Sixth Street, East Las Vegas (733 9914). Bus 204. **Open** 11am-10pm Mon-Thur, Sun; 11am-11pm Fri, Sat. **Average** $15-$20. **Credit** AmEx, Disc, MC, V.
Ribs done right, and by the US's largest rib franchise at that. The slightly sweet BBQ sauce has a mild pepper bite and the hot sauce lives up to its name. The famous onion ring loaf is huge and satisfying and enough for four people. Skip the steak and seafood choices and go straight for the ribs or chicken. Recent upgrades have these franchises looking better than ever.
Branch: Best of the West 2040 N Rainbow Boulevard (638 2100).

Cajun & Creole

Emeril's

MGM Grand, 3799 Las Vegas Boulevard, at E Tropicana Avenue (891 7349). Bus 201, 301, 302. **Open** 11am-2.30pm, 5.30-10.30pm, daily. **Average** $45. **Credit** AmEx, DC, Disc, MC, V.
Emeril Lagasse's fish house features redfish, black-ened tuna and Cajun seafood. Six oysters baked and served with an intense, hot and smoky Tasso hollandaise sauce are an appetiser for four or a meal for one. It would be hard to come by a richer, deeper flavoured or better seasoned shellfish dish anywhere outside New Orleans. Other can't-miss entrées include the cornmeal-crusted redfish with a spicy (and they mean it) red bean sauce, and the Brannon Farms free-range chicken. Also consistently good is any fish of the day recommended by your server. For dessert, try the banana cream pie.

VooDoo Café & Lounge

Rio, 3700 W Flamingo Road, at Valley View Boulevard, West of Strip (252 7777). Bus 202. **Open** *lounge* 5pm-3am, *café* 5-11pm, daily. **Average** $50. **Credit** AmEx, Disc, MC, V.
Great views – it's at the top of the Masquerade Tower – good service and the wacky décor offset less-than-great renditions of Cajun and Creole food. The big bar scene on weekends makes for fine people-watching, especially of the silicone-enhanced variety. The kitchen's reach generally exceeds its grasp, but the spicy crowd makes up for the menu.

Casino classics

Casino restaurants serving food in a particular cuisine are listed under that subheading. Below are the best of the remaining 'gourmet' rooms, which typically serve French, Italian and continental classics plus steak and seafood.

Aureole

Mandalay Bay, 3950 Las Vegas Boulevard South, between W Tropicana Avenue & Russell Road (632 7777). **Open** 5-10.30pm daily. **Average** $55. **Credit** AmEx, DC, Disc, JCB, MC, V.
Aureole is big. Really big. As in 340 seats and 9,150sq ft (850sq m) big, with the world's largest wine vault, holding 9,000 bottles of wine, stretching up four storeys to the ceiling. Thankfully, the menu is short. A good start for those light of heart and wallet might be a fresh salad of seasonal lettuce and herbs tossed in the lightest and freshest citrus vinaigrette imaginable. Pair this with a sometimes over-salted breast of capon 'Saltimbocca' with sweet garlic or a wood-grilled veal chop, and you are eating big-city cuisine that competes with Charlie Palmer's New York original. If you can't afford a full meal but want to admire the design (by Adam Tihany) and enjoy the vibe, have a snack at the bar.

Buccaneer Bay Club

Treasure Island, 3300 Las Vegas Boulevard South, at Spring Mountain Road (894 7223). Bus 203, 301, 302. **Open** 5-10.15pm daily. **Average** $45. **Credit** AmEx, DC, Disc, JCB, MC, V.
An upscale eaterie featuring the best view of the Treasure Island pirate battle, though the sound isn't great (and it can be disruptive as crowds dash to the window). The kitchen can impress with unusual fare, such as game, pheasant and buffalo prime rib. It all depends on who is manning the stoves that night, or month or year – a typical problem for hotel restaurants. Interesting wine list. For dessert, go for a soufflé. You can ask for a window seat when you book (a week ahead, to be safe), but they can't guarantee one.

Burgundy Room

Lady Luck, 206 N Third Street, at Ogden Avenue, Downtown (477 3000). Bus 107. **Open** 5-11pm Mon, Thur-Sun. **Average** $32. **Credit** AmEx, DC, Disc, MC, V.
A minor gem in an unlikely location, turning out old-fashioned 'continental' fare at reasonable prices in an attractive setting. The mature and well-versed staff keep the tableside preparations flaming and the customers happy, with classics such as beef Wellington, fettuccini Alfredo and steak au poivre. The decent wine and drinks lists make this a good alternative to the overpriced 'gourmet' rooms in other casino-hotels.

Hugo's Cellar

Four Queens, 202 Fremont Street, at Casino Center Boulevard, Downtown (385 4011). Bus 107, 403. **Open** 5.30-10.30pm daily. **Average** $38. **Credit** AmEx, DC, Disc, MC, V.

An outstanding wine list and a knowledgeable sommelier make Hugo's a must for oenophiles, but the food remains hopelessly mired in the 1970s 'continental' genre, and shows no sign of improving. Stick with a seafood speciality or beef to avoid disappointment. Surprisingly, given the dated food and atmosphere, Hugo's remains popular with locals and tourists alike, making a table hard to come by at weekends or other busy times.

Isis

Luxor, 3900 Las Vegas Boulevard South, between W Tropicana Avenue & Russell Road (262 4773). Bus 301, 302. **Open** 5.30-11pm daily. **Average** $39. **Credit** AmEx, MC, V.
This small, romantic, round room, with its large, comfortable booths and star-studded blue ceiling, has all the requisites of a romantic restaurant. Food is typical haute continental/gourmet room fare with just enough nouvelle twists to keep it interesting: seared sesame chicken, lobster with thin sesame sauce, grilled veal escalopes and oysters rubbed in chilli, coriander and basil vinaigrette, to name a few. Not the best of the bunch by any means, but worthwhile if you're staying at the Luxor.

Michael's

Barbary Coast, 3595 Las Vegas Boulevard South, at E Flamingo Road (737 7111). Bus 202, 301, 302. **Open** 6-9.30pm daily. **Average** $70. **Credit** AmEx, DC, Disc, JCB, MC, V.
High-roller heaven that's only worth it if someone else is paying. Stratospheric prices, impossible-to-get reservations and a cool reception to unfamiliar faces make this a must only for dining obsessives. If you get in, try the Dover sole, Florida stone crab (in season) or the milk-fed veal chateaubriand. They won't disappoint.

Top of the World

Stratosphere, 2000 Las Vegas Boulevard South, at St Louis Avenue, between Charleston Boulevard & Sahara Avenue, Stratosphere Area (380 7711). Bus 301, 302. **Open** 5pm-midnight daily. **Average** $40. **Credit** AmEx, DC, Disc, MC, V.
Even if the food (continental) was awful – which it isn't – it would be hard not to adore this revolving skyscraper high above Las Vegas. The tables are mounted on a ring around the edge of the circular space, which rotates the full 360° every hour, giving you an ever-changing view. Well-trained and eager staff will actually have you paying attention to what's on the plate. Go at dusk and watch the sunset for a view of Las Vegas at its most dramatic.

Chinese

Chang of Las Vegas

Gold Key Shopping Center, 3055 Las Vegas Boulevard South, at Stardust Drive (731 3388). Bus 301, 302. **Open** 10am-midnight daily. **Average** $25. **Credit** AmEx, Disc, JCB, MC, V.
The authentic food at this comfortable and elegant restaurant includes the town's best and most interesting dim sum. The seafood and Hong Kong-style

Mon Ami Gabi: *an authentic taste of France, right on the Strip. See page 140.*

dishes are also standouts. Staff are happy to talk westerners through the menu, though the language barrier inevitably results in occasionally erratic service. Just point and eat if you want to get the point of the world's best midday meal. There's another branch of Chang's in Bally's, also open for dinner – but check first because they're closed two days (which usually vary) a week.
Branch: Bally's, 3645 Las Vegas Boulevard South, at E Flamingo Road (967 3888).

1-6-8 Shanghai Restaurant
Chinatown Plaza, 4215 Spring Mountain Road, at Wynn Road, South-west Las Vegas (365 9168). Bus 203. **Open** 11am-9.30pm daily. **Average** $12. **Credit** MC, V.
Eastern Chinese cooking comes to Las Vegas in an informal and sinfully cheap setting that gives the best bang for the buck in town. Noodles, breads, stews and hotpots are highlights of the menu here: the big, swirling Chinese pancake (choose either sweet or savoury) is unique. Amazingly, a table is usually easier to come by here than at some lesser places in Chinatown Plaza.

PF Chang's China Bistro
4165 Paradise Road, at E Flamingo Road, East of Strip (792 2207). Bus 108, 202. **Open** 11.30am-11pm daily. **Average** $22. **Credit** AmEx, DC, Disc, MC, V.
Do not confuse with the real Chang's (*see above*). High-toned atmosphere and toned-down food make this spot more popular than it deserves to be. A happening bar scene (some nights) and lots of pretty Gen-Xers will help you forget about the badly seasoned pseudo-Sichuan dishes and well-meaning but often atrocious service. A second branch has

opened near the new Resort at Summerlin, with an airy atmosphere, halogen-lit replicas of ancient Chinese sculpture and (some say) better food.
Branch: 1095 S Rampart Boulevard (968 8885).

Sam Woo BBQ
Chinatown Plaza, 4215 W Spring Mountain Road, at Wynn Road, South-west Las Vegas (368 7628). Bus 203. **Open** 10am-5am daily. **Average** $12. **No credit cards**.
Not a place for vegans or vegetarians, and not coy about it either. The window display is a carnivorous collage of barbecued pigs and poultry, displayed with justifiable pride – they're very, very good. For a cholesterol-laden overview of what these cooks can do, try the barbecue combi: sweet pork, caramelised duck breast and a whole chicken (share it or regret it). The seafood's great, too.

Delis

Capriotti's Sandwich Shop
324 W Sahara Avenue, between Las Vegas Boulevard South & Industrial Road, West of Strip (474 0229). Bus 203, 301, 302. **Open** 10am-7pm Mon-Sat. **Average** $8. **No credit cards**.
A place of which the Earl of Sandwich would be proud. Capriotti's speciality is the turkey sub, made from turkey roasted on the day, on the premises. It is simply outstanding. Other outstanding sandwiches are also offered, but it's the turkey subs that keep the crowds lined up at the door. Odd-sounding but wonderful-tasting is the Bobbie, a complete Thanksgiving dinner: turkey, stuffing, cranberry sauce and mayonnaise on a sub sandwich roll.
Branch: 450 S Buffalo Drive (838 4904).

Montesano's Italian Deli

*Sahara Village Center, 4105 W Sahara Avenue,
between Valley View Boulevard & Arville Street,
South-west Las Vegas (876 0348). Bus 104, 204.*
Open 10am-8pm Mon-Wed; 10am-10pm Thur-Sat.
Average $12. **Credit** AmEx, MC, V.
A slice of New York deli, Italian-style, in Las Vegas.
This family-run deli/pizzeria/bakery turns out some
of the Las Vegas's best bread and southern Italian
food. On Saturdays, the crowds line up outside
Montesano's for semolina and cheese breads, along
with a wide variety of scrumptious Italian desserts.
Small, informal, cheap and friendly – you gotta
problem with that?
Branch: 4835 W Craig Road (656 3708).

Stage Deli

*The Forum Shops, Caesars Palace, 3500 Las Vegas
Boulevard South, between Spring Mountain &
W Flamingo Roads (893 4045). Bus 202, 301, 302.*
Open 7.30am-10.30pm Mon-Thur, Sun; 7.30am-
11.30pm Fri, Sat. **Average** $14. **Credit** AmEx, DC,
Disc, JCB, MC, V.

A clone of the New York original, offering huge
sandwiches, half-sour pickles, tomatoes, bagels
and blintzes. This is as good as it gets for anyone
needing a kosher fix this far from the East Coast.

French & Mediterranean

André's

*401 S Sixth Street, at Bridger Avenue, Downtown
(385 5016). Bus 113.* **Open** 6pm-closing times vary
Mon-Sat. **Average** $50. **Credit** AmEx, DC, Disc,
JCB, MC, V.
A Las Vegas institution that is very popular with
the expense account crowd. Chef/owner André
Rochat serves upscale French cooking and a world-
class cellar (though it yields few bargains). Expect
strictly haute French cuisine (for those who have
never been to France). There's another branch inside
the Monte Carlo casino, which has a large, plush
cigar and cognac bar for post-prandial relaxation,
and is open daily.
Branch: 3770 Las Vegas Boulevard South (730 7955).

The best of Old Vegas

In a city that destroys its past like there's no
tomorrow, little remains of the Las Vegas of
yore. But there are still a few restaurants that
will give you a taste of the 'good old days'.

El Sombrero Café

*807 S Main Street, between Bridger Avenue &
Charleston Boulevard, Downtown (382 9234).
Bus 408.* **Open** 11am-9pm Mon-Sat. **Average**
$12. **Credit** AmEx, MC, V.
Vegas's oldest Mexican restaurant (it opened in
1950) is housed in a small, nondescript building
on South Main Street, a location in which no
restaurant should be able to survive. However,
the El Sombrero has thrived by feeding Las
Vegans a simple Mexican menu full of fresh fiery
salsas, fresh tortillas and a chilli: choose either
colorado (red) or verde (green). The food is as
good as the restaurant's appearance is unas-
suming. Portions are huge and nothing on the
menu tops $10. Line up a hatful of Mexican and
Latin American songs on the jukebox to get you
in the Sombrero mood.

Hilltop House

*3400 N Rancho Drive, just north of Cheyenne
Avenue, North Las Vegas (645 9904). Bus 106.*
Open 5-9pm Mon, Wed-Sun. **Average** $21.
Credit AmEx, DC, Disc, MC, V.
Walking into this converted home on North
Rancho Drive is like entering a 1950s time warp.
Steaks and chicken are the specialities, at prices
way below joints closer to the Strip. Quite
bizarrely, frog's legs have also found themselves
on the specials list. If the 1950s were your era, or

you're simply curious, this is not a bad place to
grab a simple steak dinner.

Huntridge Drug Store Restaurant

*1122 E Charleston Boulevard, at Maryland
Parkway, Downtown (384 3737). Bus 109, 206.*
Open 8am-6pm Mon-Sat; 9am-1pm Sun.
Average $6. **No credit cards.**
Located inside the Huntridge Drug Store and
looking exactly like it did 30 years ago, this place
serves good, old-fashioned, practically extinct
Chinese-American food. Chop suey and chow
mein appear on the very short menu, as do great
burgers, and nothing costs more than $5.
Chef/owner Bill Fong turns out a mean beef
tomato with vinegar, consisting of yummy, soft
chow mein noodles tossed with chunks of beef
and tomato in a light vinegar sauce. Both the
lunch counter and the surrounding drugstore are
original Vegas artefacts.

Manhattan of Las Vegas

*2600 E Flamingo Road, between Eastern Avenue
& Pecos Road, East Las Vegas (737 5000).
Bus 202.* **Open** 4pm-1am daily. **Average** $31.
Credit AmEx, DC, Disc, MC, V.
If the Rat Pack were intact, this is where they
would be today. Plush booths, tuxedoed waiters
and lots of pinky rings make this a *Goodfellas*
retreat of the first order. The crowd is straight
from a casting, and the food decent enough to keep
the limos lined up at the door on most nights. Veal
is the kitchen's strong suit, with pastas and an
excellent Caesar salad not far behind. For dessert,
what else but cheesecake or a moist, rich tiramisu?

Wolfgang Puck's **Spago** *started Las Vegas's restaurant revolution. See page 144.*

Aristocrat

Smith's Town & Country Center, 850 S Rancho Drive, between W Charleston Boulevard & Palomino Road, North-west Las Vegas (870 1977). Bus 106, 206. **Open** 11am-2pm, 5.30-9pm, daily. **Average** $45. **Credit** AmEx, MC, V.

Small, dark and cosy. This nondescript storefront in a mall features a limited menu of meat, seafood and pastas. The veal chop in Dijon mustard sauce and grilled Atlantic salmon over pasta with raspberry butter are consistent favourites with the legal, medical and political types that keep Aristocrat full. For dessert, try the bread pudding with whisky sauce. Excellent and attentive service has kept this place humming for years, and it's one of the few decent restaurants open for lunch during the week.

Le Cirque: *fine dining at Bellagio, p140.*

Drai's

Barbary Coast, 3595 Las Vegas Boulevard South, at E Flamingo Road (737 0555). Bus 202, 301, 302. **Open** 5-9.30pm daily; *supper club* midnight-6am Thur-Sat. **Average** $40. **Credit** AmEx, Disc, MC, V.

Victor Drai offers lighter-than-average French fare, with an emphasis on delicate compositions, such as fresh tomato, basil and goat's cheese tart, organic carrot and leek soup, and a serious and seriously tasty vegetarian section. As good as these are, it is the fish, chicken and lamb dishes that keep most customers coming back. Roast turbot and fast-seared Maine salmon are two of the regular seafood dishes, both highlighted by the piquant seasonings of southern France. For heavier fare, try the grilled free-range chicken with roasted garlic and perfect french fries or the seven-hour leg of lamb, stewed in red wine. The desserts, especially the orange crème brûlée, are consistently fine.

Eiffel Tower Restaurant

Paris, 3655 Las Vegas Boulevard South, between Harmon Avenue & E Flamingo Road (946 7000). Bus 202, 301, 302. **Open** 5.30-10pm Mon-Thur, Sun; 5.30-11pm Fri, Sat. **Average** $65. **Credit** AmEx, DC, Disc, JCB, MC, V.

The room is drop-dead gorgeous and the view is spectacular, but the food isn't as good as it should be. That doesn't prevent the Eiffel Tower Restaurant from being one of the toughest tables in town to score on weekends. French twists are given to simple and hardy fare such as impeccably fresh herb-crusted Pacific snapper, pristine seafood and shellfish and chicken fricassee – and the French pastries are suitably over the top. But at these prices, you'd

Off the Strip, you can enjoy top-notch nosh at **Rosemary's**. *See page 142.*

expect more innovation on the plate. The wine list is broad, deep and obscenely priced: good luck at finding a decent bottle for under $50.

Le Cirque
Bellagio, 3600 Las Vegas Boulevard South, at W Flamingo Road (693 8100). Bus 202, 301, 302. **Open** 6-11pm daily. **Average** $85. **Credit** AmEx, DC, Disc, JCB, MC, V.
Probably the best restaurant in town right now, with an arsenal of eats, both refined and bourgeois, that is creating a new standard of excellence in French food. Executive chef Marc Poidevin and pastry chef Patrice Caillot push the envelope nightly with such succulent offerings as 'Black Tie' scallops tied with black truffles (geddit?). Consommé de boeuf with foie gras ravioli, salade mesclun, roasted duck with honey spice glaze with figs, and roasted lobster in a port wine sauce are all simple, exotic and perfect. Follow these delights with ethereal desserts such as bomboloni (Italian doughnuts filled with vanilla cream) or a dense and warm chocolate fondant with the richest oozing centre imaginable. You're not even close to what fine dining in Las Vegas used to be, so sit back and enjoy the ride and the fun. None of this excellence comes cheap, however. Jackets and ties are mandatory for men – and they mean it.

Le Montrachet
Las Vegas Hilton, 3000 Paradise Road, between Karen Avenue & E Desert Inn Road, East of Strip (445 8667). Bus 108, 112. **Open** 6-10pm Mon, Fri-Sun. **Average** $52. **Credit** AmEx, DC, Disc, MC, V.
Solid French cuisine served in a small and intimate room in an enormous, impersonal hotel. The kitchen combines classic French preparations with some innovative fare. There is a long (and expensive) wine list for those who can afford it. Exquisite desserts can be sampled in the bar/lounge area.

Mon Ami Gabi
Paris, 3655 Las Vegas Boulevard South, between Harmon Avenue & E Flamingo Road (946 7000). Bus 202, 301, 302. **Open** 11.30am-3.30pm daily; 5-11pm Mon-Fri; 5pm-midnight Sat, Sun. **Average** $20. **Credit** AmEx, DC, Disc, JCB, MC, V.
'Gabi' refers to Gabino Sotelino, friend, chef and consultant to Richard Melman, founder of Lettuce Entertain You Enterprises. The company hails from Chicago, and runs some of the Windy City's most innovative eateries, with Everest as its flagship. In Las Vegas, the Eiffel Tower Restaurant and Mon Ami Gabi fill the bill. Both transcend their roots with solid French food. The Eiffel Tower goes for romance, dazzle and innovation, while Gabi keeps things simple with honest renditions of simple bistro fare. Besides great steak frites (that's a thin-cut French steak with french fries, to you non-Francophiles out there), perfect roast chicken and garlicky escargot, Mon Ami Gabi has portable wine bars, the best people watching outside of the Forum Shops and a dead-on Right Bank décor that echoes Paris (the real one) beautifully. It's also the only restaurant with seating right on the Strip.

Monte Carlo Room
Desert Inn, 3145 Las Vegas Boulevard South, at E Desert Inn Road (733 4524). Bus 301, 302. **Open** 6-10pm Mon, Thur-Sun. **Average** $60. **Credit** AmEx, DC, Disc, JCB, MC, V.

As one would expect from a five-diamond resort, this flagship restaurant is very classy, very French and very expensive. Along with Portofino (*see p147*), this room gives the Desert Inn a one-two punch of high-end eateries that only Caesars Palace, Bellagio and Mandalay Bay can compete with. The traditional haute-cuisine fare – such as striped bass en croûte, tournedos Rossini and duck à l'orange – explains why this remains a big favourite with high-rollers and the big-hair set.

Napa

Rio, 3700 W Flamingo Road, at Valley View Boulevard, West of Strip (252 7961). Bus 202.
Open 6-11pm Tue-Sat. **Average** $60.
Credit AmEx, DC, Disc, JCB, MC, V.
Under the direction of Jean-Louis Palladin (and even when he's not at the helm), the cooks at Napa turn out some of Las Vegas's tastiest and most expensive grub. Palladin's very personal style of cooking emphasises fresh ingredients brought in from all over the globe. He combines them into classic and new wave creations that can astonish with their striking flavours and textures. Native ingredients including Maine peekytoe crab, California quail, Hudson Valley foie gras and Colorado lamb are treated with respect – but always set off against another interesting flavour or two. The Rio's bakery provides a fetching mix of delicious breads at every meal, and the Rio Wine Cellar's list (stocked by the master sommelier Barrie Larvin, previously at the Ritz in London) is hard to match in breadth and depth. The cellar restaurant offers more than 240 wines by the glass, but bottle prices are not for the faint of heart.

Olives

Bellagio, 3600 Las Vegas Boulevard South, at W Flamingo Road (639 7111). Bus 202, 301, 302.
Open 11am-3pm, 5-11.30pm, daily. **Average** $40.
Credit AmEx, DC, Disc, MC, V.
Fans of Mediterranean cuisine will love the latest European-style café to wash up on the Strip, a version of Todd English's original outpost in Boston. Upscale and only slightly pretentious (wives of powerful men often lunch here together), Olives offers the best Greek-style salad in town, irresistible flatbreads and entrées – such as barbecued yellowfin tuna and Israeli couscous carbonara – that are a delightful exercise in contrast. Tables outside overlook Bellagio's man-made lake.

Pamplemousse

400 E Sahara Avenue, just east of Paradise Road, East Las Vegas (733 2066). Bus 204. **Open** 6pm-closing times vary Tue-Sat. **Average** $42.
Credit AmEx, DC, Disc, JCB, MC, V.
Owned by a local, Georges LaForge, Pamplemousse has been serving country-style French fare in a rustic setting to Las Vegans, celebrities and visitors for 20 years. Specialities are duck, veal and seafood, while soufflés are the most sought-after dessert. Pamplemousse is popular with performers on the Strip, making it a good place to indulge in some celebrity-spotting.

Palace Court

Caesars Palace, 3570 Las Vegas Boulevard South, at W Flamingo Road (731 7547). Bus 202, 301, 302.
Open 6-10pm daily. **Average** $56. **Credit** AmEx, DC, Disc, MC, V.
The circular, glass-domed dining room looks out on to the new Caesars tower and its incredible pool area, making this a romantic and visual setting like no other. Like all hotel 'gourmet rooms', quality and innovation can vary. Choose from the huge and ever-varying assortment of home-made desserts, such as passion fruit crêpe, guava tart, almond soufflé with two sauces, and chocolate fudge brownie with pistachio ice-cream studded with salted pistachio nuts. All of this comes at a price, though, paid by people who don't care what things cost.

Picasso

Bellagio, 3600 Las Vegas Boulevard South, at W Flamingo Road (693 7111). Bus 202, 301, 302.
Open 6-9.30pm Mon, Tue, Thur-Sun. **Prices** $75, $85. **Credit** AmEx, DC, Disc, JCB, MC, V.
Of all the celeb chefs appearing in Vegas in the past five years, Julien Serrano took the biggest gamble and has made the biggest splash. He's a permanent fixture in the kitchen, and his glorious and inventive Mediterranean/French cooking has the food press checking their thesauruses for superlatives. Only two menus are offered nightly: a tasting menu and a prix-fixe menu, which is slightly cheaper and offers three choices for each course. And there's a stunning display of Pablo's artworks. It's very expensive, but what a way to spend an evening.

Pinot Brasserie

Venetian, 3355 Las Vegas Boulevard South, just south of Sands Avenue (414 8888). Bus 203, 301, 302. **Open** 11.30am-3pm, 5.30-9.30pm, Mon-Thur, Sun; 11.30am-3pm, 5.30-10.30pm Fri, Sat. **Average** *lunch* $15; *dinner* $45. **Credit** AmEx, DC, Disc, MC, V.
On any night, this place hums with the electricity only fine restaurants can generate, fuelled by tantalising aromas and the musical chimes of silver and china. Chef Joachim Splichal's rich yet casual French bistro offers the lighter tastes of French cuisine, with pastas, seafood, steak and wild game, plus a large rotisserie and oyster bar. The space is decorated with items imported from France, including a wooden French door facade (from a hotel in Lyon).

Renoir

Mirage, 3400 Las Vegas Boulevard South, between Spring Mountain & W Flamingo Roads (791 7223). Bus 301, 302. **Open** 6-10.30pm Mon, Tue, Thur-Sun. **Average** $70. **Credit** AmEx, DC, Disc, JCB, MC, V.
When the Mirage decided to get serious about its food in 1999, it plucked chef Alessandro Stratta from the Phoenician hotel in Scottsdale, Arizona. In nine months, he'd earned Mobil's coveted five-star award. Southern France is in his blood and his cuisine. Stratta manages to be ungimmicky and creative, with intriguing dishes such as baby lamb with fricassee of vegetables, and honey- and vinegar-braised short ribs with spinach. There's some decent art in the room as well, but who wants to look up from the plate?

The best Japanese

Benihana Village

Las Vegas Hilton, 3000 Paradise Road, between Karen Avenue & Convention Center Drive, East of Strip (732 5111). Bus 108, 112. **Open** 5-10.30pm daily. **Average** $28. **Credit** AmEx, DC, Disc, JCB, MC, V.

If you're after an intimate dinner, forget it. Benihana is all about dramatic, and sometimes humorous, hibachi cooking. Selections include beef, chicken, fish or vegetable entrées, accompanied by rice and Asian vegetables. Once the ordering is complete, the show begins, as a chef wheels in a cart brimming with raw ingredients and prepares them with a flourish on the hot-top grill built into the table. Excellent beef and shrimp and a tangy house salad dressing make a meal here delicious fun for adults and kids. It's very popular with groups and families, so book ahead.

Dragon Sushi

Chinatown Plaza, 4215 W Spring Mountain Road, at Wynn Road, South-west Las Vegas (368 4328). Bus 203. **Open** 11.30am-10.30pm daily. **Average** $26. **Credit** AmEx, DC, Disc, MC, V.

At this small local restaurant, friendly staff and a picture-filled menu make sushi and Japanese specialities easy to order for those not familiar with the cuisine. A refreshing addition to Las Vegas's strong contingent of Japanese choices.

Hamada of Japan

598 E Flamingo Road, just east of Paradise Road, East Las Vegas (733 3005). Bus 202. **Open** 5pm-midnight daily. **Average** $26. **Credit** AmEx, DC, Disc, JCB, MC, V.

Sushi and hibachi cooking are given the full treatment here. The chefs slice some of the best toro (tuna) and unagi (freshwater eel), and the sushi hand-rolls are among the most interesting and varied in town. The sushi bar is preferable to the touristy look, feel and quality of the dining rooms. It's popular with Japanese people – always a good sign – and there are also branches in the Flamingo Hilton and the new Resort at Summerlin.
Branches: Flamingo Hilton, 3555 Las Vegas Boulevard South (737 0031); Polo Plaza, 3743 Las Vegas Boulevard South (736 1984); Resort at Summerlin, 221 North Rampart Boulevard (869 7777).

Nobu

Hard Rock, 4455 Paradise Road, at Harmon Avenue (693 5000). Bus 108. **Open** 11.45am-2pm Fri-Sun; 6-11pm daily. **Average** from $40. **Credit** AmEx, MC, V.

Finally, a restaurant that puts a new (and positive) slant on the fusion-confusion that is everywhere nowadays. Nobu's cuisine is best described as Japanese-Fusion-Peruvian. The genius behind the food is Nobu Matsuhisa, celeb chef extraordinaire and probably the best known Japanese chef in the western world. His flagship, Matsuhisa, has been the toughest table in LA for years, and the New York Nobu was proclaimed the best sushi restaurant in town almost from the day it opened. The dishes will startle you with their ingenuity; you won't find more interesting, fresher, or healthier food anywhere. And for goodness sake, do not forget the raspberry-infused sake. *See photo*.

Rosemary's

West Sahara Promenade, 8125 W Sahara Avenue, at Cimmaron Road, North-west Las Vegas (869 2251). Bus 704. **Open** 11.30am-2.30pm, 5.30-10.30pm, Mon-Fri; 5.30-10.30pm Sat. **Average** *lunch* $12; *dinner* $35. **Credit** AmEx, DC, Disc, MC, V.

At last, serious gastronomy comes to the suburbs. Many consider this the best off-Strip restaurant in town, and it's hard to argue with that assessment. Michael and Wendy Jordan have created a top-shelf experience that gives every celebrity chef in town a run for their money. Best of all, they deliver the goods at prices that won't have you groaning. For $100, two people can enjoy a complex array of tasty dishes that are big on flavour with lots of ingredients. Everything from sweetbreads to roasted halibut is given the star treatment here, and Jordan does his mentor Emeril Lagasse proud with homages to Southern cooking.

Suzette's

Santa Fe, 4949 N Rancho Drive, at Lone Mountain Road, North Las Vegas (658 4900). Bus 106. **Open** 5-10pm daily. **Average** $39. **Credit** AmEx, DC, MC, V.

Tucked away in the Santa Fe casino is this jewel box of a restaurant. Suzette's is the closest thing to a classic, haute-cuisine French restaurant in Vegas, at prices below those at the time-worn gourmet rooms in the Strip hotels. Dishes such as lobster thermidor, veal Oscar and steak tartare are a throwback to the heyday of rich, French cooking, and are given the complete, big-deal meal treatment here. In fact, it is only the mediocre and overpriced wine list with too few selections by the glass that keeps Suzette's from being at the top of Las Vegas's restaurant pack.

Fusion

Chinois

The Forum Shops, Caesars Palace, 3570 Las Vegas Boulevard South, between Spring Mountain & W Flamingo Roads (737 9700). Bus 301, 302. **Open** *café* 11.30am-midnight, *restaurant* 6-9.30pm, daily. **Average** *café* $18; *restaurant* $45. **Credit** AmEx, DC, Disc, JCB, MC, V.

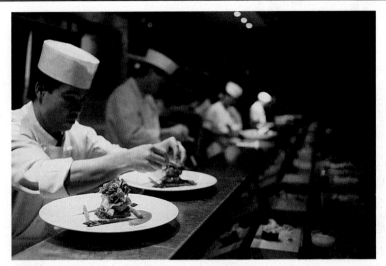

Osaka

4205 W Sahara Avenue, between Sixth Street & Maryland Parkway, East Las Vegas (876 4988). Bus 204. **Open** *11.30am-midnight daily.* **Average** $27. **Credit** AmEx, DC, Disc, MC, V.

Sushi, hibachi cooking and traditional Japanese fare are all done well in Vegas's oldest Japanese restaurant. The newer sister establishment in Summerlin is upscale but comfortable, with a small bar, a large dining room and a teppan (hibachi) grill area – great fun for large groups or gregarious types, as each teppan table seats up to ten. The menu combines traditional fare with a fusion twist. The bilingual staff are most helpful at both places.

Branch: Summerhill Plaza, 7511 W Lake Mead Boulevard (869 9494).

Togoshi Ramen

Twain Center, 855 E Twain Avenue, at Swenson Street, East Las Vegas (737 7003). Bus 203. **Open** *11.30am-11pm daily.* **Average** $9. **No credit cards.**

Cheap and downscale, but don't let that deter you. Ramen and udon noodles come in various guises at unbelievably low prices – this is fast food the way it should be.

Though more Chinese and less cutting-edge than Wolfgang Puck's Chinois in Santa Monica, this clone in the Forum Shops trumps its namesake with some drop-dead (some say overdone) décor. Museum-quality Asian art and sculpture is displayed in a vividly coloured, two-storey setting. Expect flavours and textures that more than compete with the walls. Whole fried fish may be sea bass one night, striped bass another, but never is it less than perfect. The whole roasted Shanghai lobster packs an oily wallop with some serious seasonings. Other standouts include all of the fried rice and vegetable dishes, the dry-fried string beans and super dim sum and sushi.

Gordon Biersch

Hughes Center, 3987 Paradise Road, at E Flamingo Road, East of Strip (312 5247). Bus 108, 202. **Open** *11.30am-midnight Mon, Sun; 11.30am-2am Tue-Sat.* **Average** $23. **Credit** AmEx, DC, Disc, JCB, MC, V.

This is where the beers are. This San Francisco-based brew pub puts out a small list of well-made lagers (no ales) and mixes them with highly seasoned and wide-ranging menu items spanning the globe – everything from Hawaiian sushi to Italian pastas to grilled meats. Pizzas are generally weak (servers will give an honest opinion if asked), but most starters, salads and rotisserie items complement the beers well. Later in the week, if you're single and ready to mingle, and can ignore the din, this is the place to see and be seen. *See also p165* **Bars & Cafés**.

Mayflower

Sahara Pavilion, 4750 W Sahara Avenue, at Decatur Boulevard, South-west Las Vegas (870 8432). Bus 103, 204. **Open** *11am-3pm, 5-10pm, Mon-Thur; 11am-3pm, 5-11pm, Fri, Sat.* **Average** $26. **Credit** AmEx, DC, Disc, MC, V.

Pan-Asian European 'fusion' cooking given by a kitchen that's not afraid to take a few chances. It was at the Mayflower that most Las Vegans first sampled the multicultural fusion creations of the 1980s. Unfortunately, many other spots have now overtaken it, but its popularity, especially with locals, still makes a table hard to come by on weekends, so book ahead.

Head to Downtown for bargain Italian food at **Chicago Joe's**.

Postrio

Venetian, 3355 Las Vegas Boulevard South, just south of Sands Avenue (796 1110). Bus 203, 301, 302. **Open** 11.30am-11pm Mon-Thur, Sun; 11.30am-midnight Fri, Sat. **Average** *patio* $25; *dining room* $35. **Credit** AmEx, DC, Disc, JCB, MC, V.
The omnipresent Wolfgang Puck has opened yet another eaterie – this time in the Venetian. As usual, it offers American cuisine with Mediterranean and Asian influences. Specials include gourmet pizzas, grilled quail with spinach and soft egg ravioli, lamb chops with tamarind glaze, shoestring potatoes and peanut sauce, and Chinese-style duck with mango sauce and crispy fried scallion.Yum.

Spago

The Forum Shops, Caesars Palace, 3570 Las Vegas Boulevard South, between Spring Mountain & W Flamingo Roads (369 6300). Bus 301, 302. **Open** *café* 11am-4pm, 5-11pm, daily; *restaurant* 5-10pm Mon-Thur, Sun; 5-11pm Fri, Sat. **Average** *café* $25; *restaurant* $47. **Credit** AmEx, DC, Disc, MC, V.
When Wolfgang Puck opened Spago in the Forum Shops in 1992, he paved the way for Las Vegas's subsequent embracing of serious, 'celebrity chef' restaurants. An offspring of the famous Los Angeles power haunt, Spago is the quintessential melting-pot restaurant, overlaying America's inherent multicultural cuisine with classical French, Italian and Asian techniques and flavourings. Spago is still one of the best restaurants in town, and continues to deliver an inventive menu, excellent service, an interesting wine list and desserts that never fail to astonish. As you might expect, it attracts the rich and the beautiful.

German

Old Heidelberg German Deli & Restaurant

610 E Sahara Avenue, at Sixth Street, East Las Vegas (731 5310). Bus 204. **Open** 11am-8.30pm Mon-Sat. **Average** $15. **Credit** AmEx, Disc, MC, V.
Hearty German food and scorching Vegas summers would hardly seem to be a match made in heaven, but when the mood strikes, this small storefront will give you a schnitzel fix. Excellent sauerbraten, a good selection of German beers (which do go down nicely on a hot day) and a German delicatessen, actually part of the restaurant, give this place Bavarian charm even when temperatures are rocketing.

Indian

Dosa Den

Tropicana Plaza, 3430 E Tropicana Avenue, at Pecos Road, East Las Vegas (456 4920). Bus 111, 201. **Open** 11.30-3pm, 5.30-9pm, daily. **Average** $10. **No credit cards.**
Dosas are huge Indian crêpes, and this place turns them out beautifully, along with excellent vegetarian Indian food. The soothing yoghurt sauces, piquant spicing and pulse-flour breads suit Las Vegas's desert climate very well. It's a very modest restaurant, with little in the way of décor, in a difficult-to-find location.

Gandhi

4080 Paradise Road, at E Flamingo Road, East of Strip (734 0094). Bus 108, 202. **Open** 11am-2.30pm, 5-10.30pm, daily. **Average** $17. **Credit** AmEx, DC, Disc, JCB, MC, V.

Good northern and southern Indian cuisine plus a selection of vegetarian dishes make Gandhi the best Indian (and possibly even the best vegetarian) restaurant in Las Vegas. With an elegant dining room, in a not-so-elegant shopping centre, located conveniently close to the Strip, Gandhi provides a good alternative to the hotel restaurants when your tastebuds need a jolt. The limited all-you-can-eat-lunch buffet is spicier than the similar buffet at its rival, Shalimar.

Shalimar

Citibank Park, 3900 Paradise Road, between Twain Avenue & E Flamingo Road, East of Strip (796 0302). Bus 108, 202. **Open** 11.30am-2.30pm, 5.30-10.30pm, daily. **Average** $16. **Credit** AmEx, DC, Disc, MC, V.

Shalimar is the longest-lived of Las Vegas's meagre Indian restaurant quota, featuring a bargain all-you-can-eat buffet lunch. You can sample from a reliable, if uninspiring, selection of curries, kormas, biryanis, tandooris, kebabs and vegetable dishes. Somehow, one onion kulcha bread or a nan is never enough. Wash it all down with a drink from the interesting iced tea selection. Shalimar is comfortable, friendly and almost never crowded.

Italian

Battista's Hole in the Wall

Battista's Shopping Center, 4041 Audrie Street, at E Flamingo Road, East of Strip (732 1424). Bus 202, 301, 302. **Open** 4.30-10.30pm Mon-Thur, Sun; 4.30-11pm Fri, Sat. **Average** $20. **Credit** AmEx, DC, Disc, MC, V.

A genuine hoot not too far from the Strip. The casual Italian (cooking, that is) in a kitsch setting will keep both your eye and palate awake. One-price meals, whether they're predicated on pasta, seafood or veal, include unlimited red and white house wine, which, believe it or not, isn't bad. The cioppino (mixed fish stew) is both huge and satisfying; the veal dishes less so. The strolling accordion player (Gordie) and 'celebrity' photos of everyone from Sinatra to obscure TV performers make a meal here unforgettable.

Bertolini's

The Forum Shops, Caesars Palace, 3500 Las Vegas Boulevard South, between Spring Mountain & W Flamingo Roads (735 4663). Bus 301, 302. **Open** 11am-midnight Mon-Thur, Sun; 11am-1am Fri, Sat. **Average** $25. **Credit** AmEx, DC, Disc, JCB, MC, V.

Outdoor dining indoors. Solid, consistent and inspiring Italian food under the artificial skies of the Forum Shops. Pastas and pizzas are the safest bet, but getting a table is never easy: despite its proximity to a huge and noisy fountain, this is one of the best spots in town to watch the parade of worldwide humanity that fills the mall daily. Bertolini's also has a branch in north-west Vegas, which has indoor and outdoor seating and a beautiful, full-length hardwood bar – the perfect place to sip a selection from the extensive wine list.
Branch: 9500 W Sahara Boulevard (869 1540).

Chicago Joe's

820 S Fourth Street, between Gass Avenue & Hoover Street, Downtown (382 5637). Bus 206, 408. **Open** 11am-11pm Mon-Fri; 5-10pm Sat. **Average** $20. **Credit** AmEx, MC, V.

Bellagio's **Osteria del Circo**: *Las Vegas's best Italian restaurant. See page 147.*

For an intimate night out, try the candle-lit **Jazzed Café**, near the university.

Come here for some of the best-priced past as in town. Located in a tiny old brick house, CJ's 23 years in business are a testament to the solid southern Italian cooking of its kitchen. No frills, no dinners over $20 and great service in an intimate setting make Joe's a fantastic bargain – and you'll know you're not in a chain.

Il Canaletto
Venetian, 3355 Las Vegas Boulevard South, just south of Sands Avenue (733 0070). Bus 203, 301, 302. **Open** 11.30am-11pm Mon-Thur, Sun; 11.30am-midnight Fri, Sat. **Average** $32. **Credit** AmEx, DC, JCB, MC, V.
Grasping the essence of Italian cuisine requires knowledge of the culture, and chef Maurizzo Mazzon – a native Venetian – evokes the Venice countryside with his menu of fresh seafood, beef, game and poultry, prepared in wood-fired rotisseries and grills. The operative word is 'fresh'; Italian cooking is more about ingredients than fancy sauces and elaborate presentations. Moreover, Canaletto's two-storey architecture and classic décor replicates the best eateries of design-conscious Milan.

Jazzed Café
Napoli Plaza, 2055 E Tropicana Avenue, between Spencer Street & Eastern Avenue, University District (798 5995). Bus 201. **Open** 6pm-3am Tue-Sun. **Credit** AmEx, Disc, MC, V.
Jazzed opened as a late-night wine and coffee bar, but the owners have since added a stove, boosted the menu with risotto, pasta and salad (all cooked to order) and managed to scrape together an international reputation. One visit to this tiny hangout – cluttered with paintings and candles, acid jazz grooving on the stereo, beautiful people at every table – and you'll understand why everyone from trendsetting Londoners to jaded New Yorkers have proclaimed it the best undiscovered restaurant in Las Vegas. The 50-strong by-the-glass wine menu doesn't hurt, either.

Mortoni's
Hard Rock, 4455 Paradise Road, at Harmon Avenue, East of Strip (693 5047). Bus 108. **Open** 6-11pm daily. **Average** $30. **Credit** AmEx, DC, Disc, MC, V.
This place offers celebrity-watching at its best, plus some solid Italian cooking. Mortoni's is postmodern and neo-hip, with twice the iron-y of a pound of calf's liver. It looks Danish, cooks Italian and oozes cool. Pictures of the ubiquitous Rat Pack line the walls and some pretty good food lines the plates. The portions are in keeping with the huge crockery, and the limited menu successfully combines the mundane with new wave. Like most upscale Italian places in Las Vegas, the pastas are uniformly overpriced and unexciting, so stick with the tasty salads, appetisers and fish specials.

Nora's Pizza & Subs
Flamingo Verde, 6020 W Flamingo Road, at Jones Boulevard, South-west Las Vegas (873 8990). Bus 102, 202. **Open** 11am-2.30pm, 4.30-10pm, daily. **Average** $12. **Credit** AmEx, Disc, MC, V.
A classic Italian family-run pizzeria that serves some outstanding pastas as well. Go for the pasta con sarde (ground olives, sardines and fennel) or puttanesca (redolent of strong capers and green olives). The place is very informal and very small, so bring your own wine, and enjoy some of this town's best pasta at obscenely low prices.

Osteria del Circo

*Bellagio, 3600 Las Vegas Boulevard South, at
W Flamingo Road (693 8150). Bus 202, 301, 302.*
Open 11.30am-2.30pm, 5.30-10pm, daily. **Average**
lunch $35; *dinner* $50. **Credit** AmEx, DC, Disc, JCB,
MC, V.

Currently the best Italian restaurant in Las Vegas
and a place that captures the conviviality of the original restaurant in New York. In a coup that ranks
with Wolfgang Puck's arrival in the Forum Shops
in 1992, Bellagio owner Steve Wynn convinced Sirio
Maccioni and his talented sons to come west in 1998
and bring their ultra-fabulous talent for running
great restaurants with them. This colourful circus
(designed by Adam Tihany, who also created
Mandalay Bay's Aureole; *see p136*) looks out at
Bellagio's lake and inwards to a talented kitchen for
authentic Italian eats like Vegas has never seen.

Panini

*Spring Valley Marketplace, 4811 Rainbow
Boulevard, at W Tropicana Avenue, South-west Las
Vegas (365 8300). Bus 101, 201.* **Open** 11am-
10.30pm Mon-Fri; 5-11pm Sat. **Average** $26.
Credit AmEx, DC, Disc, MC, V.

Interesting pastas, pizzas and salads are presented
by a chef and staff trained at Spago – and it shows.
Both of these neighbourhood-oriented locations
became instantly popular for their quality and very
un-Spago prices. While the older branch on Rainbow
began the dynasty, the larger one on Sunset is sure
to be the destination hotspot for some time to come.
A crowd-pleaser for those who like crowds.
Branch: Sunset Plaza, 3460 E Sunset Road (436 3100).

Piero's

*3555 Convention Center Drive, at Paradise Road,
East of Strip (369 2305). Bus 108.* **Open** 5.30pm-
closing times vary daily. **Average** $37. **Credit**
AmEx, DC, Disc, MC, V.

Overpriced Italian food in a dark, clubby setting. Big
shots and some not-so-big and a few minor celebrities
flock here thinking this is as good as it gets. Big hair
and bad jewellery predominate, and that's just the
men. But if washed-up crooners, minor politicos and
the occasional bent-nose guy are your idea of people-
watching, then grab a booth and be prepared to pay
for the privilege. In fairness, the osso bucco is not bad
and is the sole reason many people visit Piero's.

Hot stuff: **Tacos Mexico.** *See page 150.*

Portofino

*Desert Inn, 3145 Las Vegas Boulevard South,
at E Desert Inn Road (733 4495). Bus 301, 302.*
Open 6-11pm daily. **Average** $42. **Credit** AmEx,
DC, Disc, MC, V.

Perched above the casino floor of the elegant Desert
Inn hotel is this northern Italian heavyweight.
Beautiful surroundings highlight such unique (for
Vegas, at least) offerings as smoked duck ravioli
with basil pesto and Gorgonzola sauce, pappardelle
with wild mushrooms and artichokes, fresh pea
and rosemary soup and a superlative broiled veal
chop with roasted pepper coulis and black truffle
risotto cake. A serious restaurant at serious prices.
Service is dignified, discreet and formal, but has
been known to favour the famous – of whom there
are often a sprinkling.

Spiedini

*Resort at Summerlin, 221 N Rampart Boulevard,
at Summerlin Parkway, North-west Las Vegas
(869 8500). No bus.* **Open** 5-10.30pm daily.
Average $35. **Credit** AmEx, DC, Disc, MC, V.

Gustav Mauler's Spiedini, located in the new Resort
at Summerlin, offers diners a comfortable mix of old-
world charm and modern atmosphere. The menu, a
combination of soups and salads, rich pasta and
over-the-top meat dishes, offers traditional Italian
tastes, while the funky, modernist environment
invokes the palette of Giorgio de Chirico. Come
dressed like you mean it, and leave room for the
tantalising apple tart with vanilla ice-cream.

Terrazza

*Caesars Palace, 3500 Las Vegas Boulevard South,
at W Flamingo Road (731 7568). Bus 202, 301,
302.* **Open** 11.30am-3pm, 5.30-10.30pm, daily.
Average *lunch* $20; *dinner* $42. **Credit** AmEx, DC,
Disc, JCB, MC, V.

Terrazza is huge, high-ceilinged and expensive, not
to mention gorgeous, comfortable, restrained and
one of the best Italian restaurants in town. Dining
alfresco at the edge of the newly renovated Caesars
pool area is one of the most coveted power lunch
spots around. The essences of Mediterranean cuisine – olive oil, capers, olives, rosemary, fennel and
garlic – are used with a light hand in extraordinary
dishes such as rigatoni alla boscaiola, studded with
mushrooms, peas and mascarpone cheese, risotto
with spring vegetables, and succulent rack of lamb
dusted with good Pecorino Romano cheese. Lots of
beautiful people and nary a tomato sauce in sight
make this newcomer a pleasant addition to the
hotel restaurant scene.

Trattoria del Lupo

*Mandalay Bay, 3950 Las Vegas Boulevard South,
between W Tropicana Avenue & Russell Road
(740 5522). Bus 301, 302.* **Open** 11.30am-11pm
Mon-Fri; 10.30am-11.30pm Sat, Sun. **Average** $25.
Credit AmEx, DC, Disc, JCB, MC, V.

Created by the legendary Wolfgang Puck, this new
spot is a signature eaterie developed especially for
Mandalay Bay's 'Restaurant Row'. Lupo (as it is
usually known) offers a traditional northern Italian

Mandalay Bay's **Border Grill** *brings nouvelle Mexican food and a flamboyant interior design*

atmosphere with a menu to match. Still, this is Puck's place, so expect the hostesses to be beautiful, the wine list to be pricey and the hand-made ravioli to be spectacular. Flexibility and spontaneity are key elements– up to four menus are offered at different times during the day.

TreVisi & La Scala
MGM Grand, 3799 Las Vegas Boulevard South, at E Tropicana Avenue (891 7777). Bus 201, 301, 302. **Open** *TreVisi* 11am-11pm, *La Scala* 5.30-11pm, daily. **Average** *TreVisi $20-$40; La Scala $45.* **Credit** AmEx, DC, Disc, MC, V.
The MGM Grand has two Italians: La Scala is the obscenely expensive one and TreVisi is the one worth going to. An informal café, TreVisi offers better service, lower prices and consistently good country Italian fare to hordes of tourists and hotel guests. Great breads, good pizzas and interesting pastas abound at more-than-reasonable prices. At La Scala, metronomic service and astronomical prices prevail for food that isn't worth the effort, though the booths – designed to resemble opera house boxes – are cute.

Zeffirino
Venetian, 3355 Las Vegas Boulevard South, just south of Sands Avenue (414 3500). Bus 203, 301, 302. **Open** 11am-11pm daily. **Average** $45. **Credit** AmEx, MC, V.
The rumour is that Pope John Paul II has a secret passion for Zeffirino's world-famous pesto. You, too, can find out how good it is at this canalside bistro (but bring your own holy water). With a focus on seafood, the specials include filet of sole piccola, lobster tail, soups, salads, 'pizzarettes' and pastas. Enhancing the award-winning cooking are imported speciality oils, pastas, spices, tomatoes and other ingredients from Italy.

Mexican & Southwestern

Border Grill
Mandalay Bay, 3950 Las Vegas Boulevard South, between W Tropicana Avenue & Russell Road (632 7403). Bus 301, 302. **Open** 11am-3pm, 5-11pm, daily. **Average** $32. **Credit** AmEx, DC, Disc, JCB, MC, V.
From a small storefront eatery on LA's Melrose Avenue to one of the newest resorts on the Las Vegas Strip, chefs Mary Sue Milliken and Susan Feniger have come a long way on the strength of their uniquely updated Yucatan-Mexican recipes. Brightly coloured décor enhanced by natural sunlight and potent margaritas are important components of the Border Grill experience, but the food is the main draw.

From the sautéed rock shrimp to the sweet, savoury and spicy plantain empanadas, this is a far cry from the stereotypical Mexican menu. The cheaper café upstairs has a limited menu (tacos, tamales and such), while downstairs features full service, a full menu and outside seating near Mandalay Bay's tropical pool area.

Coyote Café
MGM Grand, 3799 Las Vegas Boulevard South, at E Tropicana Avenue (891 7349). Bus 201, 301, 302. **Open** 8.30am-10.30pm daily. **Average** $38. **Credit** AmEx, DC, Disc, MC, V.
Along with Emeril's (*see p135*), this trend-setting offshoot of the Santa Fe original, gives locals the only reason to get within a mile of the MGM Grand. Despite the long walks, a confusing layout and atrociously ugly décor, the MGM does give Las Vegas two of its best restaurants. Mark Miller and his crew consistently impress with their nouvelle South-western creations – chilli-heads and adventuresome gourmands should rejoice. On the down

to Las Vegas's eating options.

Good cuisine featuring the chillis, soups and stews of Hatch, New Mexico. A wide variety of salsas and a serious nod to authenticity have made this hugely popular with locals and worth a visit by tourists, despite its off-Strip location in the Fiesta casino.

Lindo Michoacan
2655 E Desert Inn Road, between Eastern Avenue & Pecos-McLeod Road, East Las Vegas (735 6828). Bus 112. **Open** 11am-11pm daily. **Average** $17. **Credit** AmEx, DC, Disc, MC, V.
Las Vegas's best Mexican, hands down. Authentic Mexican restaurants abound in California, Arizona and New Mexico, but in Vegas they're harder to find than a flat-chested showgirl. This is the real article: proper Mexican food cooked by a family with pride in its native cuisine. True chilli artistry: the colorado (red) one will blow your head off and yet have you eager to take the next bite. The crème caramel-like flan is pure heaven.

Margaritas
New Frontier, 3120 Las Vegas Boulevard South, at Fashion Show Drive, between W Sahara Avenue & Spring Mountain Road (794 8433). Bus 301, 302. **Open** 11am-10.25pm Mon-Thur, Sun; 3.30-11pm Fri, Sat. **Average** $12. **Credit** AmEx, DC, Disc, MC, V.
A quiet and not-too-crowded Mexican restaurant in an upscale location, serving huge portions at decent prices. For an entrée with a difference, try the Mexican pizza. They also make a killer margarita.

Pink Taco
Hard Rock, 4455 Paradise Road, at Harmon Avenue, East of Strip (693 5000). Bus 108. **Open** 11am-11pm Mon-Thur, Sun; 11am-1.30am Fri, Sat. **Average** $20. **Credit** AmEx, DC, Disc, MC, V.
Part of the Hard Rock Hotel's recent expansion, the Pink Taco is designed to look like a rundown, rustic Mexican watering hole. If you can stop smirking over the double entendres long enough to read the menu, you will discover that famed Mexico City chef Tacho Kneeland (LA's Border Grill) has brought his updated Mexican recipes to Las Vegas. One suspects that the food – despite the low prices and tasty options – is a secondary draw to the huge frozen margaritas and poolside vantage.

Rigo's Tacos #8
2737 Las Vegas Boulevard North, at 11th Avenue, North Las Vegas (399 1160). Bus 117. **Open** 24hrs daily. **Average** $8. **No credit cards**.
Where the other seven are is anyone's guess, but for fast Mexican food done right this is the place. Located well north on Las Vegas Boulevard, Rigo's brings authentic tortillas, tacos and fried pork burritos to this area's Mexican-American population, who know and appreciate the difference between the good, the real and the pathetically franchised. A fantastic salsa bar features freshly made tomato, smoked chilli and green chilli sauces that are not for the faint-hearted. Gringos are thin on the ground, which is the best assurance that you're being served the genuine articles from south of the border.

side, service tends to be below that at other top restaurants. However, the ingenuity of the kitchen usually compensates.

Cozymel's
Hughes Center, 355 Hughes Center Drive, between Koval Lane & Paradise Road, East of Strip (732 4833). Bus 202. **Open** 11am-10pm Mon-Thur, Sun; 11am-midnight Fri, Sat. **Average** $21. **Credit** AmEx, DC, Disc, MC, V.
Yet another franchise Mexican restaurant, albeit an upscale one with large open dining areas and kitchen. The seafood specials are usually the best dishes, with fajitas coming a close second. The house salad and chicken/pozole soup are two more winners. Cozymel's crowded bar scene packs them in late in the week.

Dona Maria's
910 Las Vegas Boulevard South, between Gass Avenue & Charleston Boulevard, Downtown (382 6538). Bus 206, 301, 302. **Open** 8am-10pm daily. **Average** $14. **Credit** AmEx, DC, Disc, MC, V.
This loud and boisterous place serves some of Las Vegas's best Mexican food. The tamales (spicy chopped meat and ground corn, served in a corn husk) are the real draw, but the tortas (sandwiches) and fiery salsas also help keep the place packed, especially at lunch. It's very popular with the city's large Mexican community. Another branch has opened recently in north-west Vegas.
Branch: Dona Maria Tamales Restaurant 3205 Tenaya Way (656 1600).

Garduno's
Fiesta, 2400 N Rancho Drive, between Lake Mead Boulevard & Carey Avenue, North Las Vegas (631 7000). Bus 106, 211. **Open** 11am-3pm, 4-10pm, daily. **Average** $15. **Credit** AmEx, MC, V.

Steaks with attitude at **AJ's Steakhouse**.

Star Canyon

Venetian, 3355 Las Vegas Boulevard South, just south of Sands Avenue (733 5000). Bus 203, 301, 302. **Open** 11.30am-2.30pm, 5.30-10pm daily. **Average** $58. **Credit** AmEx, DC, Disc, MC, V.
Southwest Tex-Mex cuisine with some beautiful twists comes to the Venetian, courtesy of Texas superstar chef Stephen Pyles and his clone of Dallas's Star Canyon. There are displays of cowboy boots, Texas towns (branded on the ceiling) and barbed wire is used as a decorative accessory (probably a first). Intriguing dishes such as spicy rock shrimp taquitos with a killer guacamole, tamale tart with savoury egg custard and Gulf Coast crab meat, and a huge multi-layered vegetable plate with wood-roasted corn typify Pyles' approach. Equally good is the hickory-smoked tenderloin with black pepper zinfandel sauce, which takes the flavour complexity of these seemingly simple ingredients to a new level.

Tacos Mexico

1205 E Charleston Boulevard, at Maryland Parkway, Downtown (385 6806). Bus 109, 206. **Open** 24hrs daily. **Average** $7. **No credit cards**.
Serves good (but not great) soft tacos and huge burritos. Neither the very limited menu nor the very limited parking dissuade this taqueria's fans from keeping it busy day and night. Warning: the hot sauce is lethal.

Viva Mercado

Green Valley Towne Center, 4500 E Sunset Road, at Green Valley Parkway, Green Valley (435 6200). Bus 212. **Open** 11am-9.30pm Mon-Thur, Sun; 11am-10pm Fri, Sat. **Average** $18. **Credit** AmEx, DC, Disc, MC, V.
A solid Mexican restaurant that stands out from the rest, serving authentic Mexican food. Huge burritos, steak asado and lobster or fish tacos are among the specialities. It's locally owned, and very popular with locals – as it should be.

Z'Tejas

3824 Paradise Road, between Twain Avenue & E Flamingo Road, East of Strip (732 1660). Bus 108. **Open** 11am-11pm Mon-Thur, Sun; 11am-midnight Fri, Sat. **Average** $25. **Credit** AmEx, DC, Disc, MC, V.
Food that is not as bad as it could be, nor as good as it should be, in an informally elegant environment. The seared black sesame tuna can be excellent, while the mole sauces are anything but. None of this keeps Z'Tejas ('Zee Tejas', apparently a joke on the original French chef's pronunciation of 'the Tejas') from being a big hit with the business lunch crowd or the margarita maniacs, who tend to come later in the week (the bar can get busy). For an enjoyable time, stick with the simpler dishes, such as Jamaican jerked chicken or crunchy fried catfish, and let the cocktails do their magic.
The new westside location offers indoor seating as well as a covered and misted patio.
Branch: 9560 W Sahara Avenue (638 0610).

Middle Eastern

Habib's

Sahara Pavilion, 4750 W Sahara Avenue, at Decatur Boulevard, South-west Las Vegas (870 0860). Bus 103, 204. **Open** 11am-3pm, 5-10pm, Mon-Sat. **Average** $20. **Credit** AmEx, Disc, MC, V.
This bright and open restaurant on the west side of town serves Middle Eastern food that is unequalled in Las Vegas, including houmous, tabouleh, kebabs and dolma (stuffed vine leaves). Try the khoresht fesenjan (chicken marinated in pomegranate juice, then stewed with pomegranate seeds and crushed walnuts) – a tasty eye-opener to the wonders of Persian cuisine.

Marrakech

Citibank Park, 3900 Paradise Road, between Twain Avenue & Flamingo Road, East of Strip (737 5611). Bus 108, 203. **Open** 11am-11pm daily. **Average** $29. **Credit** AmEx, DC, Disc, MC, V.

Sit on the floor, eat with your hands and learn to appreciate the nuances of Moroccan cuisine. Meals are all fixed price, and the eye candy competes with the shish kebab for some serious attention.

Mediterranean Café & Market
Tiffany Square, 4147 S Maryland Parkway, at E Flamingo Road, University District (731 6030). *Bus 109, 202.* **Open** 9.30am-9.30pm daily. **Average** $11. **Credit** AmEx, DC, Disc, MC, V.
Still going strong in the University District, Paymon Raouf's success was built on serving the kind of ethnic food that the college crowd adores, long before anyone else thought of doing so. With so many Middle Eastern restaurants now open, the café has kept its favoured place by expanding its dining room and extending its hours. Tasty – and cheap – falafel, houmous, braised lamb and more is now available for dinner as well as lunch.

Pizza

California Pizza Kitchen
Mirage, 3400 Las Vegas Boulevard South, between Spring Mountain & W Flamingo Roads (791 7357). *Bus 301, 302.* **Open** 11am-midnight Mon-Thur, Sun; 11am-2am Fri, Sat. **Open** 11am-11pm daily. **Average** $18. **Credit** AmEx, DC, Disc, MC, V.
'Gourmet' pizzas are served at these two frenetic casinos. While the salads, pizzas and desserts are usually well prepared, the pastas are simply not worth it. The Mirage site seems to always be full; an hour's wait is quite common. Note: the Golden Nugget branch closes at 11pm daily.
Branch: Golden Nugget, 129 Fremont Street (386 8190).

Metro Pizza
Paradise Market Place, 3870 E Flamingo Road, at Sandhill Road, East Las Vegas (458 4769). Bus 202. **Open** 11.30am-10pm daily. **Average** $12. **Credit** AmEx, Disc, MC, V.
Decent pizza, very popular with locals, who apparently have never tasted the real thing.
Branches: Renaissance Center West, 4001 S Decatur Boulevard (362 7896); Renaissance Center East, 1395 E Tropicana Avenue (736 1955).

Northside Nathan's
7531 W Lake Mead Boulevard, at Buffalo Way, North-west Las Vegas (255 8822). Bus 210. **Open** 11am-10pm Mon-Thur, Sun; 11am-11pm Fri, Sat. **Average** $6. **Credit** AmEx, DC, MC, V.
It is nearly impossible to find a decent pizza (or pizzeria) in Las Vegas. Never fear, Nathan's is here. With its tinted windows, sports memorabilia lining the walls and giant-screen TV, stepping into Nathan's is a step into the pizzeria's hometown of Detroit. The staff are friendly, the tables clean and the ambience neighbourly.

Pizza Rio
4041 Audrie Street, at E Flamingo Road, East of Strip (733 3950). Bus 202, 301, 302. **Open** 11am-10.30pm Mon-Sat; 1-9pm Sun. **Average** $14. **Credit** AmEx, Disc, MC, V.

Good pizza and beer right off the Strip in the shadow of Bally's. It's owned by the same family as Battista's (*see p145*). Friendly and informal, this is a perfect place to eat once you're fed up with your hotel's choices in fine (and not-so-fine) dining.

Russian

Red Square
Mandalay Bay, 3950 Las Vegas Boulevard South, between W Tropicana Avenue & Russell Road (632 7777). Bus 301, 302. **Open** 5.30pm-midnight daily. **Average** $30. **Credit** AmEx, DC, Disc, MC, V.
Las Vegas loves Russia's vodkas, but not, it seems, Russia's Communist leaders. When Red Square, the trendy South Beach eaterie and bar, opened its Vegas outpost, an enormous statue of Lenin met drinkers at the entrance. Soon after, complaints rolled in and Lenin's head rolled off – removed by Mandalay Bay maintenance. It now sits on the floor of the vodka freezer; rumours say it will be encased and displayed in a solid block of ice. Oh… and they serve 100 varieties of frozen vodka, as well as dinner, in renowned Russian décor.

Salvadorian

Salvadoreño Restaurant
720 Main Street, between Washington Avenue & Bonanza Road, North Las Vegas (385 3600). *Bus 108.* **Open** 10am-9pm Tue-Sun. **Average** $8. **No credit cards.**
The plain but satisfying food of El Salvador: papusas (savoury dumplings), fried plantains, black beans and the like, served in a friendly setting in an unfriendly part of town. For that reason alone, go for lunch.

Steakhouses

AJ's Steakhouse
Hard Rock, 4455 Paradise Road, at Harmon Avenue (693 5000). Bus 108. **Open** 6-10pm Mon-Thur, Sun; 6-11pm Fri, Sat. **Average** $35. **Credit** AmEx, DC, Disc, JCB, MC, V.
The Hard Rock Hotel gets the youngest and hippest crowd in town. AJ's is so swinging, baby, that you expect Bobby Darin to be draggin' on a fag at the neo-hip lounge or Sammy D to be be-boppin' the night away with the inhouse pianist. If you long for a bygone sense of cool, tuck into a martini that's straight from the days of tail fins and bullet bras. Then enjoy a super tender filet smothered in a real Béarnaise sauce, and tell those calories to be damned: it's a classic cholesterol fest and a homage to the classic Vegas of the Rat Pack.

Alan Albert's Steak House
Eppa Shopping Center, 3763 Las Vegas Boulevard South, between E Flamingo Road & Tropicana Avenue (795 4006). Bus 301, 302. **Open** 5-11.30pm daily. **Average** $30. **Credit** AmEx, DC, Disc, JCB, MC, V.

A convenient Strip location (opposite the Monte Carlo) and moderate pricing make this a popular joint for tourists and quite a few locals. Run and owned by the same group responsible for Rosewood Grill (*see p154*), AA is newer, nicer and trying harder.

Bob Taylor's Ranch House
6250 Rio Vista Drive, at Ann Road, North Las Vegas (645 1399). No bus. **Open** 4.30-10pm Mon-Thur, Sun; 4.30-11pm Fri, Sat. **Average** $30. **Credit** AmEx, DC, Disc, MC, V.
A tranquil oasis located just off North Rancho Road, some way out of town, Bob Taylor's used to be surrounded by nothing but empty desert and a few ranches. Now, suburban encroachment threatens to make it yet another casualty of the stucco farms popping up everywhere. Mesquite grilled steaks, cooked at an open grill almost inside the ranch-styled dining room, are the speciality of the house. Memorabilia and movie posters line the walls, and a great spur collection is displayed in the bar, making this a must-see if you're interested in how Vegas looked when it was defined by the Old West rather than fake volcanoes and skyscrapers.

Brown Derby
MGM Grand, 3799 Las Vegas Boulevard South, at E Tropicana Avenue (891 7318). Bus 201, 301, 302. **Open** 5.30-10.30pm daily. **Average** $38. **Credit** AmEx, DC, Disc, MC, V.
The Brown Derby is a huge, Hollywood-themed steakhouse adjacent to Emeril's (*see p135*) in the MGM Grand. This place is crowded, noisy and expensive, with food and service a notch below that offered at other steakhouses. Your best bet is the Sunday brunch, offering better fare than you'll find on the usual menu.

Delmonico's
Venetian, 3355 Las Vegas Boulevard South, just south of Sands Avenue (733 5000). **Open** 11.30am-1.30pm, 5.30-11pm, daily. **Average** $70. **Credit** AmEx, DC, Disc, JCB, MC, V.
Emeril Lagasse has put his Cajun twist on the genre with heavily seasoned selections such as a Cajun rib-eye with real kick, and simple but exquisite steaks that can't be beat – not in this town anyway. Other favourites include a deliciously tender lamb shank on a bed of risotto, and a chateaubriand that melts in your mouth. Seafood offerings are also strong, with shrimp and crab given the full and exotic new American/Cajun treatment. If you still have room, the bread pudding is to die for.

Gallagher's
New York-New York, 3790 Las Vegas Boulevard South, at W Tropicana Avenue (740 6450). Bus 201, 301, 302. **Open** 4-11pm daily. **Average** $35. **Credit** AmEx, DC, Disc, MC, V.
A copy of the real Gallagher's in the real New York City. Choice, not prime, beef in the ersatz New York-New York Hotel, in the ersatz city of all time, Las Vegas. It's good enough, but there are better steakhouses in town for the same price.

Best seafood

Seafood in the desert? You'd be surprised.

Aqua
Bellagio, 3600 Las Vegas Boulevard South, at W Flamingo Road (693 7223). Bus 202, 301, 302. **Open** 6-11pm daily. **Average** $50. **Credit** AmEx, DC, Disc, JCB, MC, V.
Michael Mina, of the flagship restaurant in San Francisco, and chef Mark Lo Russo demonstrate that thrilling seafood can be created 250 miles from the ocean. Clean lines and a smart casual look (by designer Tony Chi) provide the perfect backdrop for the seafood-as-metaphor-for-meat philosophy. Additional eye candy is provided by a Robert Rauschenberg painting. Menu delights include miso-glazed Chilean sea bass, wild turbot with truffle mash potatoes and Maine lobster pie.

Caviarteria
The Forum Shops, Caesars Palace, 3500 Las Vegas Boulevard South, between Spring Mountain & W Flamingo Roads (792 8560). Bus 301, 302. **Open** 11am-11pm Mon-Thur, Sun; 11am-midnight Fri, Sat. **Average** $26. **Credit** AmEx, DC, Disc, JCB, MC, V.
New York's purveyor of all things fishy and fine has come to Vegas. Featuring top-quality caviar, smoked salmon and fine champagnes, this is a place for those who know quality and are willing to pay for it. The beautifully

Golden Steer Steakhouse
308 W Sahara Avenue, between Las Vegas Boulevard South & Industrial Road, East of Strip (984 4470). Bus 103, 204. **Open** 4.30-11.30pm daily. **Average** $40. **Credit** AmEx, DC, Disc, MC, V.
The enormous (and, yes, golden) steer that acts as a sign for the coolest steak place in town also advertises its décor: discreet it is not. Think updated bordello crossed with an Old West saloon and you're almost there. But the less-than-classic décor doesn't detract from the steaks, which are as classic as they come: large, juicy and perfectly grilled. Team it with a huge baked potato and a Caesar salad that remains one of the best around (even if it isn't prepared tableside as it used to be), and you'll be in heaven.

Lawry's The Prime Rib
Hughes Center, 4043 E Howard Hughes Parkway, between Koval Lane & Paradise Road, East of Strip (893 2223). **Open** 5-11pm daily. **Average** $28. **Credit** AmEx, DC, Disc, JCB, MC, V.
In one of the most beautiful dining rooms in the city, Lawry's serves one of the most limited menus. You can have anything you want here, as long as it's prime rib. Some would say that bringing prime rib to Vegas is like taking coals to Newcastle. But it

appointed small space at the end of the Forum Shops is reminiscent of New York's small, elegant restaurants. The only downside is the blaring of the hourly animatronic show, which may detract from the subtle, yet intense, flavours of the imported products used here. The Oscetra caviar is the best buy, the blinis are light, slightly sweet and fantastic, and the Park Avenue smoked salmon pastrami sandwich is the most adventurous item on the menu.

Gabriel's Green Lips

2871 N Green Valley Parkway, at Sunset Road, Henderson (450 3104). No bus. **Open** 11am-2.30pm, 5.30-10.30pm, Tue-Sun. **Average** $22. **Credit** AmEx, DC, Disc, MC, V.
For more than two years, Gabriel Gregoriescu has served some of Vegas's tastiest and best priced food in a teeny-weeny space full of warmth and personality. Seating around 50, this Henderson café fills up quickly with diners who appreciate the fresh and personal cuisine, which can compete with anything at the Strip hotels, at half the price. The menu is rich in shellfish (mussels done five different ways), pan roasted salmon and lemony crab cakes, but the pasta and chicken dishes sparkle, too. For dessert, no one can top the huge apple strudel. Even the small wine list is unique for its eclectic choices at rock-bottom prices.

McCormick & Schmick's Seafood

335 Hughes Center Drive, at E Flamingo Road, East of Strip (836 9000). Bus 202. **Open** 11am-10pm Mon-Fri; 5-10pm Sat, Sun. **Average** *lunch* $20; *dinner* $34. **Credit** AmEx, Disc, DC, JCB, MC, V.

There's something fishy going on at McCormick & Schmick's and it's not the chicken. You can get chicken here, of course, as well as steak, but that's hardly the point at this upscale seafoody grill. This place is serious about seafood in a way that Las Vegas had never seen until it opened its doors two years ago.
No one in town does a better happy hour, with huge platters of top-shelf crab, quesadillas, fish tacos and bar food that are sinfully cheap and shrimply delicious. Try the daily selection of oysters so fresh and briny you'll swear you're on the coast. A limited (and expensive) wine list and some fusion experiments that try too hard to push the creativity envelope are the only detractions from an otherwise solid operation.

Second Street Grill

Fremont, 200 Fremont Street, at Casino Center Boulevard, Downtown (385 6277). *Bus 107, 402.* **Open** 5-10pm Mon, Thur, Sun; 5-11pm Fri, Sat. **Average** $27. **Credit** AmEx, DC, Disc, MC, V.
A silk purse of a restaurant in a sow's ear of a hotel, if ever there was one. Most of Fremont Street has been cleaned up and yuppified, but the Fremont hotel seems to enjoy being the seediest place on all three blocks. Amazingly, someone decided to put an upscale, attractive Pacific Rim seafooder right where the most Hawaiian tourists would bump into it. Ignore the state of the hotel and follow the islanders to some of Vegas's most innovative seafood. The whole fried Thai red snapper is food as both art and architecture. Service and wine could be improved.

works splendidly, and has been a welcome addition to all the fatty low-rent cuts of this much-maligned Vegas dinner staple. Lawry's got started in the 1930s, smack bang in the heart of Beverly Hills, and has been at the pinnacle of America's meat-and-potatoes culture ever since. It still prides itself on doing a few things well: prime rib (three different cuts are carved tableside), whipped potato and a famous spinning house salad that has been made the same way since 1938 with few complaints.

Morton's of Chicago

Fashion Show Mall, 3200 Las Vegas Boulevard South, at W Spring Mountain Road (893 0703). *Bus 203, 301, 302.* **Open** 5.30-11pm Mon-Sat; 5.30-10pm Sun. **Average** $40. **Credit** AmEx, DC, Disc, JCB, MC, V.
As chains go, this is a good one. All that's missing to complete your steak fantasy is a Morton's mascot handing out cholesterol badges to those who manage to consume the tender double porterhouse in one sitting. You are shown your selected dish before it's cooked, still wrapped in cellophane – a somewhat contrived, not to say unappetising flourish: this, and the high prices, are significant downsides. Still, you can dine well on an outstanding house

salad with a sinfully rich blue cheese dressing, perfectly cooked sirloin and reliable salmon, swordfish and other seafood dishes. In keeping with Morton's nationwide reputation, the wine list is lengthy but severely overpriced. Love the souvenir piggy table lamps, though.

Palm

The Forum Shops, Caesars Palace, 3570 Las Vegas Boulevard South, between Spring Mountain & W Flamingo Roads (732 7256). Bus 301, 302. **Open** 11.30am-11pm daily. **Average** $50. **Credit** AmEx, DC, MC, V.
From the bread to the prime steaks and lobsters, Palm consistently outperforms the competition in a very crowded category. The huge, slightly charred grilled lobsters make it good for fish-eaters, too. The service is consistently excellent, and the newly improved wine list includes a good selection by the glass. Only a high noise level and uncomfortable booths keep a meal here from being close to perfect.

Prime

Bellagio, 3600 Las Vegas Boulevard South, at W Flamingo Road (693 7223). Bus 202, 301, 302. **Open** 5-11pm daily. **Average** $55. **Credit** AmEx, DC, Disc, JCB, MC, V.

Definition: first-class, superior, pre-eminent. That pretty much sums up Jean-Georges Vongerichten's take on the American steakhouse. His talented crew, headed by chef Kerry Simon, turn out sophisticated cuisine in a striking royal blue and brown décor that provides a perfect view of Bellagio's spectacular fountain shows. Try for a window seat for the full effect, but even in the main room and alcoves you will be transported by the magic of the world's most exotic beef emporium. Prime steaks are the highlights, but don't overlook the free-range chicken, seared ahi tuna or wood-grilled veal chop, or one of the ten potato or side dishes. There's also a choice of 11 sauces and seven mustards.

Rosewood Grill

3339 Las Vegas Boulevard South, between Sands Avenue & Flamingo Road (792 9099). Bus 203, 301, 302. **Open** 4.30-11.30pm daily. **Average** $29. **Credit** AmEx, DC, Disc, MC, V.
Known for its huge lobsters and amazingly long, eclectic wine list. Otherwise, this older sibling of Alan Albert's (*see p152*) has the look, feel and service of a tourist food factory.

Ruth's Chris Steakhouse

Citibank Park, 3900 Paradise Road, between Twain Avenue & Flamingo Road, East of Strip (791 7011). Bus 108. **Open** 11am-10.30pm daily. **Average** $35. **Credit** AmEx, DC, Disc, MC, V.
Two health warnings before you come here: too much butter could raise your cholesterol level, while

Bellagio's **Noodles***: for a taste of Asia.*

too many à la carte selections could send your blood pressure through the roof (when it's time to get your wallet out). Prime steaks are served in an attractive setting, but most aficionados prefer Palm, Morton's or the Golden Steer (for all, *see above*).
Branch: Cameron Corner, 4561 W Flamingo Road (248 7011).

The Steak House

Circus Circus, 2880 Las Vegas Boulevard South, at Circus Circus Drive, between W Sahara Avenue & Desert Inn Road (794 3767). Bus 301, 302.
Open 5-11pm Mon-Fri, Sun; 5pm-midnight Sat. **Average** $28. **Credit** AmEx, DC, Disc, MC, V.
Mesquite grilled steaks are dished up at prices below those at other beef emporia along the Strip. This strong, musky hardwood imparts a flavour to meat that is nirvana to some, anathema to others. Because of this, or maybe because of the good prices, it can be next to impossible to get a table here.

Thai & Vietnamese

Komol

Commercial Center, 953 E Sahara Avenue, between Sixth Street & Maryland Parkway, East Las Vegas (731 6542). Bus 103, 204. **Open** 11am-10pm Mon-Sat; noon-10pm Sun. **Average** $19. **Credit** AmEx, Disc, MC, V.
Despite its location in a run-down mall, Komol remains hugely popular with locals for its authentic rendering of Thai cuisine. Be sure to designate the degree of heat you wish, and the kitchen will do its best to comply.

Noodles

Bellagio, 3600 Las Vegas Boulevard South, at W Flamingo Road (693 7111). Bus 202, 301, 302.
Open 11am-3am daily. **Average** $18. **Credit** AmEx, DC, Disc, MC, V.
Tony Chi, the world-famous New York-based architect, sketcher of many international award-winning eateries, here offers his take on casual modern elegance. Teak panelling abounds while modern fixtures dominate – though not over the delicious pan-Asian dishes (there's more than just Thai and Vietnamese). Served chilled, the wickedly hot Korean spicy vegetable noodles send a delightfully confusing sensation to your palate, while the Thai noodle soup and congees are superlative. An absolute gem in service, quality and atmosphere. And the prices are good, too.

Saigon

Sahara Pavilion, 4251 W Sahara Avenue, at Decatur Boulevard, South-west Las Vegas (362 9978). Bus 103, 204. **Open** 10am-10pm daily. **Average** $12. **Credit** AmEx, MC, V.
Stick with Vietnamese items and avoid the Chinese-sounding ones. Saigon truly excels at pho dishes – large, hearty bowls of noodle soup – which are sometimes very hot and spicy, sometimes not, but always full of thick rice noodles and made with deeply flavoured broth. The spicy beef noodle soup is a knockout. Pork and shrimp noodle soup and spicy

If you love hogs, you'll love the **Harley-Davidson Café**.

beef with vermicelli and vegetables are also recommended. The latter is more a tangle of white vermicelli with lemon grass, with lime-marinated beef sitting atop, than a traditional soup.

Thai BBQ
Bill Plaza, 4180 Jones Boulevard, at W Flamingo Road, South-west Las Vegas (222 0375). Bus 102, 202. **Open** 11am-11pm daily. **Average** $14. **Credit** AmEx, Disc, MC, V.
This place used to be a real sleeper, but has now been discovered despite a downscale and hard-to-find location. It gets a steady stream of customers who recognise it as one of the best in town. The friendly and helpful service makes both hardcore Thai aficionados and novices feel welcome while they tuck into hearty and huge portions of classic Thai dishes that will blow your head off. Highlights include papaya salad, excellent beef, pork and chicken satay, stuffed chicken – 'Wings of Angel' – and rich, hot and spicy beef noodle soup.

Thai Spice
4433 W Flamingo Road, at Arville Street, South-west Las Vegas (362 5308). Bus 202. **Open** 11am-10pm daily. **Average** $16. **Credit** AmEx, DC, Disc, JCB, MC, V.
A real anomaly among Thai restaurants in Las Vegas, Thai Spice is larger, brighter, nicer and generally better than the others. A short drive or cab ride from the Strip hotels, it serves excellent versions of favourites such as Thai beef salad, pad thai, tom kha gai (hot and sour chicken soup) and fishcakes. Good accessibility, décor and service make this one of Las Vegas's most popular Thai restaurants.

Theme restaurants

Two-course meals at the restaurants listed below average around $12-$20. For a review of **Dive!**, the submarine-themed restaurant, *see page 134.*

Hard Rock Café
4475 Paradise Road, at Harmon Avenue, East of Strip (733 8400). Bus 213. **Open** 11am-midnight Mon-Thur, Sun; 11am-12.30am Fri, Sat. **Credit** AmEx, DC, Disc, MC, V.
Loud, loud, loud, but still fun for rock fans of all ages. The kids will want to stay and soak up the music and memorabilia while most adults will be looking for the exit after less than an hour. Great people-watching and burgers, along with a 30ft (9m) Gibson guitar out front, make this a must-stop on the tourist trail. Only a distant relation, incidentally, of the neighbouring Hard Rock casino-hotel.

Harley-Davidson Café
3575 Las Vegas Boulevard South, at Harmon Avenue (740 4555). Bus 301, 302. **Open** 11.30am-midnight daily. **Credit** AmEx, DC, Disc, JCB, MC, V.
For those who worship the almighty hog, this hyper-themer is a must. For those who worship good food, look elsewhere.

Motown Café
New York-New York, 3790 Las Vegas Boulevard South, at W Tropicana Avenue (740 6440). Bus 201, 301, 302. **Open** 7.30-11.30pm Mon-Thur, Sun; 7.30pm-2am Fri, Sat. **Credit** AmEx, DC, Disc, JCB, MC, V.
Firehouse meatloaf, chicken and waffles (yes, together – try it, you might even like it), strawberry

shortcake and even S'Mores cake make this an artery-hardener if ever there was one. The richness of the grub matches the richness of the vibe that used to be Motown. Once the house R&B group begins its act, all will be forgiven. If you must take in the theme scene, make this the one.

Planet Hollywood
The Forum Shops, Caesars Palace, 3500 Las Vegas Boulevard South, between Spring Mountain & W Flamingo Roads (791 7827). Bus 301, 302. **Open** 11am-11pm Mon-Thur, Sun; 11am-midnight Fri, Sat. **Credit** AmEx, DC, Disc, JCB, MC, V.
For movie buffs, not food buffs. Buy a T-shirt, gawk at the memorabilia and skip the food.

WB Stage 16
Venetian, 3355 Las Vegas Boulevard South, just south of Sands Avenue (414 1699). Bus 203, 301, 302. **Open** 11am-1am daily. **Average** $30. **Credit** AmEx, Disc, MC, V.
This place is not the Bugs Bunny cartoon-themed restaurant one might expect. Warner Brothers has painstakingly recreated sets from movies such as *Batman*, *Casablanca* and the Rat Pack's Vegas classic, *Oceans 11*, in its dining rooms. The food stands up to the 'New Las Vegas' culinary scene with its eclectic continental menu, and the upstairs Velvet Lounge (where appetisers are served until 2am) is a jewel.

Restaurants by area

The Strip
Alan Albert's Steak House (p151); America (p134); Aqua (p152); Aureole (p136); Bertolini's (p145); Brown Derby (p152); Buccaneer Bay Club (p136); California Pizza Kitchen (p151); Caviarteria (p152); Chang of Las Vegas (p136); Cheesecake Factory (p134); Chinois (p142); Coyote Café (p148); Dive! (p134); Delmonico's (p152); Drai's (p139); Eiffel Tower Restaurant (p139); Emeril's (p135); Fat Burger (p135); Gallagher's (p152); Harley-Davidson Café (p155); Il Canaletto (p146); Isis (p136); Le Cirque (p140); Margaritas (p149); Michael's (p136); Mon Ami Gabi (p140); Monte Carlo Room (p140); Morton's of Chicago (p153); Motown Café (p155); Noodles (p154); Olives (p141); Osterio del Circo (p147); Palace Court (p141); Palm (p153); Picasso (p141); Pinot Brasserie (p141); Planet Hollywood (p156); Portofino (p147); Postrio (p144); Prime (p153); Red Square (p151); Rosewood Grill (p154); Spago (p144); Stage Deli (p138); Star Canyon (p150); The Steak House (p154); Terrazza (p147); Trattoria del Lupo (p147); TreVisi & La Scala (p148); Zeffirino (p148).

Stratosphere Area
Top of the World (p136).

East of Strip
AJ's Steakhouse (p151); Battista's Hole in the Wall (p145); Benihana Village (p142); Cozymel's (p149); Gandhi (p145); Golden Steer Steakhouse (p152); Gordon Biersch (p143); Hard Rock Café (p155); Lawry's The Prime Rib (p152); Le Montrachet (p140); Marrakech (p150); McCormick & Schmick's (p153); Mortoni's (p146); Mr Lucky's 24/7 (p135); Nobu (p142); PF Chang's China Bistro (p137); Piero's (p147); Pink Taco (p149); Pizza Rio (p151); Ruth's Chris Steakhouse (p154); Shalimar (p145); Z'Tejas (p150).

West of Strip
Capriotti's Sandwich Shop (p137); In-n-Out Burger (p135); Napa (p141); VooDoo Café & Lounge (p135).

University District
Jazzed Café (p146); Mediterranean Café & Market (p151).

Downtown
André's (p138); Burgundy Room (p136); Chicago Joe's (p145); Doña Maria's (p149); El Sombrero Café (p138); Hugo's Cellar (p136); Huntridge Drug Store Restaurant (p138); Second Street Grill (p153); Tacos Mexico (p150).

North Las Vegas
Bob Taylor's Ranch House (p152); Garduno's (p149); Hilltop House (p138); Rigo's Tacos #8 (p149); Salvadoreño Restaurant (p151); Suzette's (p142).

East Las Vegas
Dosa Den (p144); Hamada of Japan (p142); Komol (p154); Lindo Michoacan (p149); Manhattan of Las Vegas (p138); Metro Pizza (p151); Old Heidelberg German Deli & Restaurant (p144); Osaka (p143); Pamplemousse (p141); Togoshi Ramen (p143); Tony Roma's 'The Place for Ribs' (p135).

North-west Las Vegas
Aristocrat (p139); Coffee Pub (p134); Northside Nathan's (p151); Rosemary's (p142); Spiedini (p147).

South-west Las Vegas
1-6-8 Shanghai Restaurant (p137); Dragon Sushi (p142); Habib's (p150); Mayflower (p143); Montesano's Italian Deli (p138); Nora's Pizza & Subs (p146); Panini (p147); Saigon (p154); Sam Woo BBQ (p137); Thai BBQ (p155); Thai Spice (p155).

Henderson & Green Valley
Gabriel's Green Lips (p153); Viva Mercado (p150).

Buffets

Benjamin Disraeli once proclaimed, 'There is moderation even in excess.' He probably never dined in a Las Vegas buffet. The fact is that Las Vegas's all-you-can-eat buffets are a testament to man's ability to over-indulge, and live to reminisce about it. And like every other decadence in the city, they've become an institution, as much a part of the town's aura as the opulent casinos. Nowhere else can travellers consume so much food for so little money – despite steadily rising buffet prices in recent years. Moreover, surprisingly enough, the quality of food is decent, if not always first-rate. Perhaps not fine enough to nourish a royal family, but fit for any pauper's palate.

Nearly every major casino has a buffet, which typically serves breakfast, lunch and dinner (in separate sittings). Some offer theme buffets highlighting different cuisine such as seafood, steak and shrimp, prime rib or even Haiwaiian food, usually on different nights of the week. Others have brunch buffets, usually on Saturdays and Sundays, while a couple serve elaborate Sunday champagne brunches. Whatever the differences, they all work the same way – you pay one price, sometimes as little as $5.99 for dinner, and you can gorge yourself into oblivion. No trip to Las Vegas would be complete without trying one, if only for the sheer spectacle of seeing how high people can pile their plates.

The idea of the buffet started in the early 1940s at the original El Rancho Las Vegas Hotel, where owner Beldon Katleman was looking for a way to keep customers in his casino after the late stage show. Katleman dreamed up the 'Midnight Chuckwagon Buffet – All you can eat for a dollar'. His idea of treating guests to an elaborate feast for a small price was soon copied by other hotels and the Vegas buffet boom was born. It didn't take long for hotel operators to figure out that if the midnight chuckwagon buffet was such a great grabber, why not offer it at breakfast, lunch and dinner, too? They did, and the rest is history.

Modern buffets barely resemble the old chuckwagon smorgasbords, which typically included heated dishes set up on long banquet tables. Today's buffets feature carving stations (prime rib, ham, turkey), cooking stations (omelettes, stir-fries) and steam tables or kiosks (to ensure food is warm but not dried out). The average dinner buffet features at least 50 food selections: salads, fruit, roast beef, baked ham, roast turkey, fried chicken, vegetables, potatoes, rolls, coffee and all the desserts imaginable. In addition to the standard American fare, many casinos also offer international choices such as Mexican, Brazilian, Chinese and speciality barbecue dishes served at their own kiosks; a few even feature Mongolian grills.

Breakfast buffets provide breakfast meats (ham, bacon, sausage), egg dishes (including omelettes cooked to order), potatoes, waffles, pancakes and the like. There's also usually a salad bar of fresh fruit and vegetables as well as juices and coffee. Lunch buffets can go one of two ways. The first is a subdued version of the dinner buffet – that is, the carving station offers just one or two entrées and the selection of prepared dishes is limited. The second is a nearly exact replica of dinner, and at several dollars off the price, these are great bargains for an already bargain meal.

Buffet prices vary, but at most major resorts they run from $4 to $6 per person for breakfast up to $10 to $13 for dinner, with cheaper rates for kids. Buffet prices have edged higher in recent years (as have most prices in Las Vegas), but so has the quality, especially at the new mega-resorts (Bellagio, Paris) and the highly competitive locals' casinos (Fiesta, Reserve, the Orleans). Bellagio's dinner buffet, at $22.95 a head, is the most expensive in town – but the food is very good. The lunch buffet ($12.50) at the new Resort at Summerlin is also highly praised.

Eating in a buffet has become such a staple of Vegas life that you can even take a course that 'teaches how to make appropriate food choices at buffets'. In addition to pointing out high-protein and low-fat food offerings, the course teaches how to avoid cholesterol-heavy dishes and when to count calories. It even includes a buffet tour and pocket-sized lists of unhealthy food combinations. The $15 course is run by the Health Education and Wellness Department (877 5356). Our own tour takes you through some of the better buffets in town – but you must supply your own nutritionist. We've reviewed the dinner buffets; don't expect the same selection at breakfast or lunch.

Bally's Big Kitchen

Bally's, 3645 Las Vegas Boulevard South, at E Flamingo Road (739 4111). Bus 202, 301, 302. **Buffets** *Breakfast 7-11am, lunch 11am-2.30pm, dinner 4.30-10pm, daily.* **Prices** *Breakfast $9.99; $4.99 under-7s. Lunch $11.99; $5.99 under-7s. Dinner $15.99; $6.99 under-7s.* **Credit** *AmEx, Disc, MC, V.*
From the carpeted and chandeliered dining area to the bountiful kitchen offerings, this is one of the best spreads in town. Diners make their selections in a kitchen manned by chefs and servers, then repair to the split-level dining room, with booths and tables, which overlooks the Strip. As well as standard buffet fare (prime rib, chicken, fish, pasta), you can often choose from leg of lamb, sirloin, king crab legs, peeled shrimp and Chinese specialities such as crispy duck, sweet and sour chicken and barbecued spare ribs (prepared by Asian chefs in their own kitchen). There's also an excellent baked potato bar for people who want less meat. After consuming a 5,000-calorie meal, top it off with a sugar-free dessert, and pretend that over-indulgence is merely a state of mind.

Bally's Sterling Brunch

*Bally's, 3645 Las Vegas Boulevard South, at
E Flamingo Road (739 4111). Bus 202, 301, 302.*
Buffet 9.30am-2.30pm Sun. **Price** $49.95.
Credit AmEx, Disc, MC, V.
So extraordinary are some of the dishes at Bally's
Sterling Brunch – Sundays only – and so upscale is
the clientele that even calling it a Vegas buffet seems
tawdry and inappropriate. All items, from the
breads to the sushi to the pastries, are made in-house,
specifically for this day alone. From the fresh
smoked Nova salmon with (very good) bagels to
caviar with blinis and a cold lamb potato salad with
lime vinaigrette, the 20-plus appetisers and scores
of entrées feature something for everyone on a scale
of quality and taste unthinkable for most buffets.
This is Las Vegas as it used to be: upscale food,
tuxedoed waiters, flowing champagne, all lapped
up by swellegantly dressed guys and dolls.

Bellagio Buffet

*Bellagio, 3600 Las Vegas Boulevard South, at
W Flamingo Road (693 7111). Bus 202, 301, 302.*
Buffets *Breakfast* 7-10.30am, *lunch* 11am-3.30pm,
dinner 4-10pm, daily. **Prices** *Breakfast* $9.95.
Lunch $12.50. *Dinner* $22.95. All free under-3s.
Credit AmEx, Disc, JCB, MC, V.
The price is about double other Strip buffets, but it's
worth it. The tastefully decorated dining room is
well laid out for easy access to the food (mirror-
image food stations serve the two wings of the
sprawling room), and divided into separate smoking
and no-smoking areas. In addition to the usual
buffet fare, offerings include venison, duck breast,
steamed clams, king crab legs, woodland mushrooms and haricots verts. You'll also find desserts
that matter, seemingly made in-house from the
freshest ingredients.

One drawback is the age limit – no one under 18
is allowed unless they're staying as a guest at the
hotel. The same policy applies to the casino and
shopping promenade: don't even attempt to bring in
a stroller unless you have a room key.

The Buffet

*Golden Nugget, 129 Fremont Street, at Casino
Center Boulevard (385 7111). Bus 107, 403.*
Buffets *Breakfast* 7-10.30am, *lunch* 10.30am-3pm,
Mon-Sat. *Dinner* 4-10pm daily. *Brunch* 8am-4pm Sun.
Prices *Breakfast* $5.90; $2.90 under-10s. *Lunch*
$7.25; $3.75 under-10s. *Dinner* $9.95 ($10.95 Sun);
$5.15 under-10s. *Brunch* $10.95; $5.50 under-10s.
Credit AmEx, Disc, DC, MC, V.
You'll find a touch of class in the Buffet's opulent
dining room: marble-top tables, partitioned booths,
etched glass and brass fixtures. The offerings are
near the top of the Vegas food chain, especially the
elaborate salad bar and cold food stations: ultra-
fresh veggies, California chicken salad, pasta and
antipasti salads, mounds of fresh fruit, Waldorf and
pistachio salads and seafood goodies such as crab
legs, shrimp, sushi and oysters. The Nugget eschews
the vogue for multiple serving stations representing
every cuisine known to man, but it does have a
carvery, typically serving turkey and prime rib.

Visit the **Garden Court Buffet** *at Main*

Desserts here beat most other buffets: fresh-baked
tarts, cobblers, cakes, pies and locally famous bread
pudding served on a layer of custard. Typically,
there is a wait to get in, but since this is more like
a sit-down dining experience and less like a mess
hall, it's worth it.

Captain's Buffet

*Showboat, 2800 Fremont Street, at Boulder
Highway, East Las Vegas (385 9123). Bus 107,
206.* **Buffets** *Lunch* 10am-2.30pm Mon-Fri. *Dinner*
4.30-10pm daily. *Brunch* 8am-3.30pm Sat, Sun.
Prices *Lunch* $5.99. *Dinner* $5.99 Mon-Wed;
$11.95 Thur, Fri; $7.95 Sat, Sun; $1 discount
under-12s. *Brunch* $5.99 Mon-Thur; $6.95 Sat, Sun;
$1 discount under-12s. *All* free under-3s.
Credit AmEx, Disc, MC, V.
In this cheerful, New Orleans garden-themed room
the usual American dishes are served (chicken,
prime rib, fish, pork chops), plus make-your-own
tacos and pizzas. On Wednesday nights, you can
feast on all-you-can-eat New York steaks. Unlike
most buffets, you don't have to stand around in
queues staring at the back of other patrons' heads
as the line inches forward – when you check in with
the cashier, you're given a portable beeper that will
go off when your table is ready. Of course, there's a
method to the Captain's madness. With the pager,
you can gamble at the machines or tables while
waiting to be fed.

Carnival World Buffet

*Rio, 3700 W Flamingo Road, at Valley View
Boulevard, West of Strip (252 7777). Bus 202.*
Buffets *Breakfast* 8-10.30am, *lunch* 11am-3.30pm,
Mon-Fri. *Dinner* 3.30-11pm daily. *Brunch* 8.30am-

Street Station for a pretty dining room and Asian specialities. See page 160.

3.30pm Sat, Sun. **Prices** *Breakfast* $8. *Lunch* $11. *Dinner* $14. *Brunch* $14. *All* free under-3s. **Credit** AmEx, Disc, JCB, MC, V.

If you can stand the long queues, you'll be rewarded with a variety of fresh and tasty cuisine, served amid planters of fake tropical blooms and palm-fringed display tables. Choose from Chinese stir-fry, Mexican taco fixings, Japanese sushi and teppan yaki, Italian pasta and antipasti, a Mongolian grill and fish and chips. There's even a barbecue chicken and ribs station, with baked beans and mashed potatoes, and a set-up for hot dogs, burgers, fries and milkshakes. You can also order a steak grilled while you wait, but they cost a few dollars more. Tip: if you join the Rio's slot club, you get to stand in a much shorter line.

Circus Circus Buffet

Circus Circus, 2800 Las Vegas Boulevard South, at Circus Circus Drive, between W Sahara Avenue & Desert Inn Road (734 0410). Bus 301, 302. **Buffets** *Breakfast* 6-11am, *lunch* noon-4pm, Mon-Sat. *Dinner* 4.30-11pm daily. *Brunch* 6am-4pm Sat, Sun. **Prices** *Breakfast* $4.99. *Lunch* $5.99. *Dinner* $7.49. *Brunch* $4.49. *All* free under-3s. **Credit** AmEx, Disc, MC, V.

The large pink room with the circus-tent awnings and paintings of giraffes is the busiest buffet on the Strip, serving more than 10,000 people a day. Although the queues are well managed, you'll inevitably have to wait at peak times, and it can take a while for tables to be cleared. Once you're in, there are exact duplicate stations offering exact duplicate dishes – and lots of them. The ranks and ranks of stainless steel dispensers inevitably evoke an institutional feel, but while the quality is a cut above a

school cafeteria, fill your plate and you'll have the ultimate TV dinner. Exaggeration? Where, other than frozen TV dinners, could you find Salisbury steak, chicken fritters and ravioli and meatballs?

Classic Buffet House

3331 E Tropicana Avenue, between Eastern Avenue & Pecos Way, East Las Vegas (435 2226). Bus 201. **Buffets** *Lunch* 11am-4.30pm, *dinner* 5-9pm, daily. **Prices** *Lunch* $6.95; $3.95 under-8s. *Dinner* $8.95; $5.95 under-8s. **Credit** Disc, MC, V.

This bright and airy buffet restaurant – one of the few not found in a casino – serves first-rate Chinese and Japanese cuisine at bargain prices. Each day more than 50 dishes are served from a possible 200 different recipes. Selections include curry pork, kung pao chicken, shrimp with broccoli, tempura vegetables, Napa cabbage, beef with asparagus, spicy tofu, cashew chicken and Szechuan eggplant, to name a few. At dinner, you can also feast on all-you-can-eat shrimp and crab legs. The friendly staff, including co-owner Sophie, are always willing to help you in evaluating the dishes.

The Feast

Palace Station, 2411 W Sahara Avenue, at Rancho Drive, West of Strip (367 2411). Bus 204, 401. **Buffets** *Breakfast* 7-11am, *lunch* 11am-3pm, Mon-Sat. *Dinner* 3-11pm Mon-Sat; 3.30-11pm Sun. *Brunch* 7am-3.30pm Sun. **Prices** *Breakfast* $4.49. *Lunch* $6.49. *Dinner* $8.99. *Brunch* $8.99. **Credit** AmEx, Disc, JCB, MC, V.

In the late 1980s, the Feast pioneered the Las Vegas buffet 'action' format, at which short-order cooks prepared omelettes, burgers and steaks to order. The Feast was the top buffet in town for several years, until the Rio opened the Carnival World, with its separate serving stations for different ethnic fare. Today, the Feast has been surpassed by many other buffets, but its salad and dessert bars remain among the largest in the city. Specialities on offer include a Chinese stir-fry station, a burger grill and a wide array of side dishes and fresh fruit and vegetables. Sweet-eaters will like the numerous pies and cakes, which are supplemented by frozen yoghurt with homemade fudge, fruit cobblers and cream-filled éclairs. Other casino buffets may be more elaborate, but Palace Station's Feast remains a decent bargain.

Festival Buffet

Fiesta, 2400 N Rancho Drive, at Lake Mead Boulevard, North Las Vegas (631 7000). Bus 106, 210. **Buffets** *Breakfast* 7-11am, *lunch* 11am-3pm, Mon-Fri. *Dinner* 4-10pm daily. *Brunch* 7am-3pm Sat, Sun. **Prices** *Breakfast* $4.99; $2 4-11s. *Lunch* $6.49; $3 4-11s. *Dinner* $9.99; $4.50 4-11s. *All* free under-4s. **Credit** AmEx, Disc, MC, V.

You can rub elbows with the locals at this popular smorgasbord, serving the best barbecue in town. It's away from the Strip, but meat-heads will pronounce it worth the schlepp. Belly up to the Pit for a taste of the Old West: ribs, ham, turkey, beef, sausage and shredded pork, along with all the fixings – beans, cornbread, mashed potatoes and corn-on-the-cob. If you prefer the flavour of the Far East, try the Mongolian Grille, where you select fresh veggies, pork, shrimp and sauces, then watch as chefs custom-prepare your meal. There are also fish and chips, Cajun specialities, a pasta bar, cold cuts for sandwiches and a gourmet coffee bar. The Monday night Hawaiian luau is a monster if you like raw shellfish and fresh Pacific seafood.

Fresh Market Square Buffet

Harrah's, 3475 Las Vegas Boulevard South, between E Sands Avenue & Flamingo Road (369 5000). Bus 203, 301, 302. **Buffets** *Breakfast* 7-11am, *lunch* 11.30am-3.30pm, *dinner* 4-10pm, daily. **Prices** *Breakfast* $7.99. *Lunch* $8.99. *Dinner* $12.99; $4.99 4-11s. **Credit** AmEx, Disc, JCB, MC, V.

With its giant celery and cornstalk columns, over-sized muffins and multicoloured replica fruit, this is an adventure in eating that Lewis Carroll would love. Besides the usual salad bars and food displays, chefs prepare while-you-wait fajitas and chimichangas at the Mexican station, and endless supplies of fettucine, lasagne and sausages are cooked fresh at the Italian station. In keeping with the hotel's New Orleans theme, the American Bounty station serves such dishes as chicken étouffé, red beans and dirty rice, barbecued ribs and meatloaf. You won't find any crayfish, but there's a good seafood selection (served every night, not just Fridays) that includes peel-your-own shrimp, Alaskan king crab legs, oysters Rockefeller and scallops on the half shell. Be sure to save room for the Market Square's signature dessert, Bananas Foster – skillet-heated bananas topped with a caramel-rum sauce.

Garden Court Buffet

Main Street Station, 200 N Main Street, at Stewart Avenue, Downtown (387 1896). Bus 207. **Buffets** *Breakfast* 7-10.30am, *lunch* 11am-3pm, Mon-Fri. *Dinner* 4-10pm daily. *Brunch* 7am-3pm Sat, Sun. **Prices** *Breakfast* $4.99. *Lunch* $6.99. *Dinner* $8.99. *Brunch* $7.99. *All* free under-3s. **Credit** AmEx, Disc, JCB, MC, V.

With its high ceilings, marble-top counters, used-brick walls and tall windows, this is one of the prettiest – and best – buffets in town, with a distinctly non-institutional feel. Main Street Station (along with the nearby California and Fremont Hotels) caters to a large number of Hawaiian tourists, so the best bets here are the Chinese and Polynesian specialities. There's also wood-fired, brick-oven pizza, fresh salsas at the Mexican station, a barbecue rotisserie and a selection of Southern dishes.

Makino Todai Restaurant

3965 S Decatur Boulevard, at Flamingo Road, West of Strip (889 4477). Bus 103, 202. **Buffets** *Lunch* 11.30am-2.30pm, *dinner* 5.30-9pm, daily. **Prices** *Lunch* $12.95 Mon-Fri; $13.95 Sat, Sun; $6.48 children under 5ft (1.52m); $4.95 children under 4ft (1.22m); $2.50 children under 3ft (91cm). *Dinner* $20.95 Mon-Thur; $21.95 Fri-Sun; $10.98 children under 5ft (1.52m); $5.95 children under 4ft (1.22m); $2.50 children under 3ft (91cm). **Credit** AmEx, Disc, MC, V.

For the mother of all Japanese buffets, this hyperactive non-casino restaurant is unlike any in town. The buffet is divided into several sections, of which the most impressive is the sushi section where eight chefs busily replenish 40 different kinds of sushi. You'll also find snow crab legs, sashimi, green lip mussels, poached fresh salmon, cucumber and shrimp salad, marinated mushrooms, calamari salad and other cold plates. You can also dig into chicken teriyaki, lemon chicken, clams with ginger, fried shrimp, steamed beef dumplings, tempura shrimp, Todai roast beef and beef teriyaki and more. Phew.

Mirage Buffet

Mirage, 3400 Las Vegas Boulevard South, between W Spring Mountain & Flamingo Roads (791 7111). Bus 301, 302. **Buffets** *Breakfast* 7-10.45am, *lunch* 11am-2.45pm, *dinner* 3-10pm, Mon-Sat. *Brunch* 8am-10pm Sun. **Prices** *Breakfast* $9.12. *Lunch* $10.19. *Dinner* $15.55. *Brunch* $18.02. *All* free under-3s. **Credit** AmEx, Disc, JCB, MC, V.

Here's another buffet that's usually packed (read: long queues), especially on weekends and holidays. If you're a slot-club member, ask a casino host or pit boss for a comp slip, which will transport you past the mob to the front of the line. Once inside, you'll find a garden setting with palm trees, stone fountains and flower boxes. The food is fresh and well prepared with a lean, oddly enough, towards good nutrition. The salad bar, for instance, is enormous, with dozens of choices to excite any vegetarian's palate. Other cholesterol-friendly selections include tabbouleh, Thai beef, Chinese chicken and seafood salad. There are even sugar- and fat-free cakes and puddings if the first several courses have induced dessert guilt.

Palatium Buffet

Caesars Palace, 3570 Las Vegas Boulevard South, at W Flamingo Road (731 7110). Bus 202, 301, 302. **Buffets** *Breakfast* 8-11.30am, *lunch* 11.30am-3.30pm, Mon-Fri. *Dinner* 4-10pm Mon-Sat. *Brunch* 8.30am-3.30pm Sat, Sun. **Prices** *Breakfast* $7.95; $3.98 7-12s. *Lunch* $9.95; $4.98 3-12s. *Dinner* $14.95, $7.50 3-12s Mon-Thur, Sat; $18.95, $9.50 3-12s Fri. *Brunch* $13.95, $7.50 3-12s Sat; $14.95, $7.50 3-12s Sun. *All* free under-3s. **Credit** AmEx, Disc, JCB, MC, V.

The Palatium Buffet, named after the second-century gathering place of Rome's academy of chefs, is popular with tourists and locals for its Friday night seafood feast. The food is freshly prepared by chefs at open cooking stations, and often includes poached salmon, grilled swordfish, Alaskan crab legs, peeled shrimp and scallops. For an additional $3 you get a whole lobster (the cashier will give you a coupon that you redeem with the chef). While the food here – from the fresh salads and baked breads to carved meats and sculpted desserts – is recommended, the buffet suffers from long and slow-moving lines around the small, semicircular serving area. This is because you must negotiate an old-fashioned queuing system. It's time the Palatium climbed out of the second century and set up separate food stations for its patrons' convenience.

Paradise Buffet

Fremont Hotel, 200 Fremont Street, at Main Street, Downtown (385 3232). Bus 107, 403. **Buffets** *Breakfast* 7-10.30am, *lunch* 11am-3pm, Mon-Sat. *Dinner* 4-10pm daily. *Brunch* 7am-3pm Sun. **Prices** *Breakfast* $4.99. *Lunch* $6.49. *Dinner* $9.99 Mon, Wed, Thur, Sat, Sun; $14.99 Tue, Fri. *Brunch* $8.99. *All* free under-3s. **Credit** AmEx, Disc, JCB, MC, V.

The Paradise Buffet is another great spot for seafood, which is served on Tuesday, Friday and Sunday nights – and at less than half the cost of the Palatium. True to its name, the décor includes palms, birds of paradise and bright tropical flowers. There are even bird calls, Polynesian music and the splash of waterfalls to help the effect. The serving tables are decorated with ice sculptures and laden with lobster claws, crab legs, shrimp, oysters, smoked salmon, clams and entrées such as shrimp scampi and scallops Provencale. Of course, land-lubbers will find the usual selection of chicken, steaks, prime rib and pasta dishes.

Shalimar

3900 Paradise Road, between Sands Avenue & Flamingo Road, East of Strip (796 0302). Bus 108, 203. **Buffet** 11.30am-2.30pm Mon-Fri. **Prices** $7.50; $3.75 under-12s. **Credit** AmEx, Disc, MC, V.

At this off-Strip Indian restaurant, which relies on northern Indian specialities, you'll find tasty tandoori dishes that are flavourful but not incendiary. House favourites include samosas, tandoori-cooked chicken tikka kebab, and boti kebab (marinated pieces of leg of lamb cooked in a clay oven). You can also feast on nice renditions of chicken or vegetable curry, and vegetarian dishes made from aubergine, cauliflower, okra, spinach and tomatoes.

Village Seafood Buffet

Rio, 3700 W Flamingo Road, at Valley View Boulevard, West of Strip (252 7777). Bus 202. **Buffet** 5-10pm Mon-Thur, Sun; 5-11pm Fri, Sat. **Price** $24.95; free under-2s. **Credit** AmEx, Disc, JCB, MC, V.

This seafood buffet is separate from the Rio's Carnival Buffet. In fact, it's on the other side of the casino, in the Masquerade Village tower. It's more expensive than most, but seafood fans will love it. Specialities include steamed clams, swordfish, calamari, salmon, scallops, shrimp and king crab legs. Try the Mongolian Seafood Barbecue, which has a choice of shrimp, scallops, fish or squid.

Best buffets

There are now nearly 50 buffets in town. Most of them are massive feeding operations designed to draw gamblers into casinos, but some are stand-alone restaurants that rely on good food, service and pricing to attract customers. Here are some of the best, most unusual or distinctive buffets in town.

Best food

Bellagio As well as a wide variety of dishes, the quality and freshness are superb – and worth the hefty price.

Best value

Main Street Station's Garden Court Buffet The buffet prices (breakfast $4.99, lunch $6.99, dinner $8.99) are among the cheapest around, while the quality remains high. Under-3s eat for free.

Best seafood

Rio's Village Seafood Buffet The price ($24.95) is among the city's highest, but considering you'd pay that for just a nice salmon fillet, it's within reason.

Best Asian

Makino Todai You'll gawp at the huge counter filled with Japanese specialities, fresh sushi and Chinese dishes.

Best champagne brunch

Bally's Sterling Brunch At $50 a person, it should be the best; everything from caviar to cheese blintzes to steak Diane, served only on Sundays (9.30am-2.30pm) in the Steakhouse.

Best hours

Holiday Inn Casino Boardwalk (3750 Las Vegas Boulevard South, just north of the Monte Carlo; 735 2400). We couldn't find any other buffet that was open 24 hours. The food is mediocre and the décor tacky (though not ghastly), but you can gorge yourself at 2.30am if such is your desire.

Bars & Cafés

Whatever your preferred tipple – cocktails or cappuccinos or both – you'll find no shortage of drinking holes in this 24-hour town.

Bars

Las Vegas has no last call. None. You can drink round the clock, every day of the year. This fact rarely occurs to visitors until they're facing down daybreak from the floor of a taxi, making deals with the deity of their choice to get back to their hotel room without incident.

The city's casinos, lounges and bars take full advantage of this mixed blessing. Most casinos provide free cocktails or other drinks to gamblers and many offer bottled beers and cocktails to non-players for under a dollar, in the hope that they'll get sauced enough to forget themselves and start playing. The downside of this state of affairs is that almost every bar in Las Vegas, from the glitziest casino to the smallest corner dive, is tainted by the sickly glow and clanking din of video poker machines (if you want to play, make it clear to the bartender or ask for a roll of quarters and your drink will be free if you sign a chit). The few bars that don't have video poker machines simply couldn't get a gaming licence.

Despite this handicap, it's possible to enjoy a civilised drink – or an uncivilised drunk, if that's your taste – all over town. Most of the action happens on or near the Strip, where lounges are something akin to Disneyland. The further you go from the Strip, the thinner the tourist mix gets (locals tend to avoid casino bars) – but, unfortunately, so does the quality. Most drinking establishments beyond the tourist reach are generic neighbourhood bars with very little difference in vibe or décor. There are a few diamonds to be found beyond the motherlode, but they require a bit of digging to unearth – we've listed the best of the non-Strip bars below.

Note that the terms 'lounge' and 'bar' are often used interchangeably, although lounges tend to be rather more sedate and upmarket, with plush seating and a live band usually playing pop covers or inoffensive jazz. Casino bars worth visiting in their own right are included here; for casino lounge bars with live music, *see chapter* **Casino Entertainment**.

Inevitably, more noteworthy bars and pubs will open during the life of this guide: check listings papers such as *CityLife* and the *Las Vegas Weekly* for their current selections.

BOOZE & THE LAW

You have to be 21 to consume or buy alcohol in Nevada, and you will be required to produce photo identification, even in casinos. Nevada authorities always take underage drinking and gambling very seriously indeed.

Las Vegas's drink-driving laws are as harsh and uncompromising as in any major US city, and the Metro Police department doesn't let too many woozy fish swim by. Fortunately, you can easily walk back and forth between Strip bars, dip in and out of those on Fremont Street, and a taxi ride to and from the best off-Strip joints costs little, though getting one back to your hotel may be more tricky. Cabs are plentiful around the Strip and the bartender will usually hail one for you if asked. All bars listed below are open 24 hours daily unless specified otherwise.

The Strip

Carousel Bar
Circus Circus, 2880 Las Vegas Boulevard South, at Circus Circus Drive, between Desert Inn Road & W Sahara Avenue (734 0410). Bus 301, 302.
Credit AmEx, DC, Disc, MC, V.
Immortalised in both Hunter S Thompson's book *Fear and Loathing in Las Vegas* and Terry Gilliam's film of the same name, Circus Circus's Carousel Bar represents Las Vegas at its most chilling and sublime. Yes, patrons sit in a slow-turning representation of an amusement park carousel; yes, live trapeze artists spin and dive overhead. The experience is largely what you bring to it – either you'll be intrigued (as Thompson's readers were) or terrified (as Thompson was). Either way, you'll get a unique Vegas experience. And the drinks are cheap, too.

Drai's on The Strip
Barbary Coast, 3595 Las Vegas Boulevard South, at Flamingo Road (737 7111). Bus 202, 301, 302.
Open 5.30-11.30pm daily. **Credit** AmEx, MC, V.
Adjoining a swank restaurant in the basement of one of the most unremarkable hotel-casinos on the Strip, this lounge feels anything but subterranean. Sensually lit by candles, adorned with bookshelves and lined with plush sofas, it looks like a study belonging to an eccentric millionaire with a taste for leopard-print smoking jackets. A quiet jazz combo plays in one corner. The cocktails are among the most expensive in town.
Dress: smart casual; no shorts.

Hot stuff: the signature fire pit at the deliciously kitsch **Peppermill's Fireside Lounge**.

Hamilton's

New York-New York, 3790 Las Vegas Boulevard South, at W Tropicana Avenue (740 6400). Bus 201, 301, 302. **Open** *4pm-2am daily.* **Credit** *AmEx, Disc, MC, V.*

Overlooking a cavernous casino space yet absorbing very little of its attendant din, this swank martini-and-cigar bar is very popular with the Rat Pack-wannabe crowd. A patio faces the stage of the Empire Bar downstairs, where jazz and swing bands throw down nightly. Even though the place runs three-deep in would-be gigolos and standard black cocktail dresses, Hamilton's is worth at least one round of Zombies. On occasion, the proprietor – deeply tanned master thespian George Hamilton – crashes his own party. *See also p211* **Casino Entertainment: Lounges**.
Dress: jackets required; no jeans or T-shirts.

Holy Cow Café & Brewery

2423 Las Vegas Boulevard South, at E Sahara Avenue (732 2697). Bus 205, 301, 302.
Credit *AmEx, Disc, MC, V.*

Las Vegas's oldest microbrewery is hardly its best. Far superior suds are served up at Gordon Biersch, the Triple 7 and Barley's (for all, *see below*), and the bovine motif is obnoxious beyond belief. The only advantage Holy Cow can claim is its central location on the corner of the Strip and Sahara, halfway between the major Strip hotels and Fremont Street.

Peppermill's Fireside Lounge

Peppermill Inn Restaurant, 2985 Las Vegas Boulevard South, just north of Convention Center Drive (735 7635). Bus 301, 302. **Credit** *AmEx, Disc, MC, V.*

This dark lounge, darker than most, is so thoroughly kitsch it can't help but be cool. A giant fire pit anchors the room, with blue flames inexplicably erupting from a pool of water. Waitresses in long, slit dresses serve up outrageous cocktails; the aptly named Scorpion requires a glass the size of a fishbowl. The crowd tends to keep to themselves or paw up their dates, whichever comes naturally.

Red Square

Mandalay Bay, 3950 Las Vegas Boulevard South, between W Tropicana Avenue & Russell Road (632 7777). Bus 301, 302. **Open** *5.30pm-2am daily.* **Credit** *AmEx, DC, Disc, MC, V.*

Red Square restaurant boasts a full menu – much caviar, naturally – and its pre-glasnost theme is charming, but the real attraction is a matchless selection of vodkas, from the standard Stolichnaya to such exotic brands as South Africa's Savanna Royal and Poland's Luksosowa. Drinks are served on a bar that is, literally, a sheet of pure ice – a nice touch. Be warned: the price of a single round at this little slice of Leningrad could flip the old Marxist cleanly over in his mausoleum. Trivia point: the decapitated statue of Lenin outside the restaurant originally had a head, but it was removed (and the fake bird droppings added) after the good citizens of Las Vegas complained; the head now sits on the floor of the restaurant's vodka freezer.

Rumjungle

Mandalay Bay, 3950 Las Vegas Boulevard South, between W Tropicana Avenue & Russell Road (632 7777). Bus 301, 302. **Open** *5.30pm-2am Mon-Thur, Sun; 5.30pm-4am Fri, Sat.* **Credit** *AmEx, DC, Disc, MC, V.*

Rumjungle serves its fullest possible use as a nightclub, but for those with a taste for the Virgin Islands, the bar's selection of more than 100 different rums will drench any tropical fire burning within. The 'real' bar doesn't open until 5.30pm, however, and by the time the giant room cranks up the dance beats, having a civilised drink here is near impossible. Plan accordingly. *See p226* **Nightlife: Dance clubs**.

Get down and dirty at the **Double Down Saloon**, the hippest bar in town.

Stratosphere Area

Top of the World Lounge
Stratosphere, 2000 Las Vegas Boulevard South, between Sahara & St Louis Avenues (380 7777). Bus 301, 302. **Open** 11am-12.30am daily. **Admission** $6 (elevator). **Credit** AmEx, Disc, MC, V.
It is exactly as it sounds: a casino lounge (with no live music or gambling, oddly enough) on the 104th floor of the Stratosphere Tower, the tallest free-standing observation tower west of the Mississippi River. Admission to the tower is $6, though you can beat it by making reservations at the Top of the World revolving restaurant. Worth a stop if you were planning to go up the tower anyway, which you should – the view is quite spectacular.

Downtown

The Bar at Thai Town
Thai Town, 1201 Las Vegas Boulevard South, at Park Paseo Drive, Downtown (388 1682). Bus 301, 302. **Credit** MC, V.
Located directly across the street from the Las Vegas Youth Hostel, the Bar is a decent stop for the legal-age globetrotter. The Far East décor is unobtrusive, a comfortable sofa allows visitors to stretch out a bit and, to clinch the deal, the staff serve one of the best martinis in town. Too many video poker machines, perhaps, but nevertheless a comfortable little joint. The delicious Thai appetisers are highly recommended.

Huntridge Tavern
Huntridge Shopping Center, 1116 E Charleston Boulevard, at Maryland Parkway, Downtown (384 7377). Bus 206. **No credit cards**.
The Tavern has been serving up booze, brews and attitude for more than 30 years. This is everything a dive bar should be: low-estate without being seedy, intriguing without being dangerous. Presumably, the fiftysomethings that warm the stools here go home to their families for an hour or two, every now and again. Get loaded up here before taking in a rock or punk band at the Huntridge Theater, just across the street (*see p233* **Nightlife: Music**).

Mad Dogs & Englishmen Pub
515 Las Vegas Boulevard South, at Bonneville Avenue, Downtown (382 5075). **Credit** AmEx, MC, V.
It's nice to have a pub near Fremont Street, even if Mad Dogs & Englishmen is fairly unremarkable as pubs go; if you're looking for an experience to stir your senses, take a cab to the Crown & Anchor instead (*see below*). Still, Mad Dogs has the standard lagers, stouts and ciders on tap, which makes it an acceptable place to escape the too-bright, too-loud overkill of Fremont. And the mix of characters the place attracts – from high-priced lawyers to higher-priced escorts – makes a stop worthwhile.

Triple 7 Brew Pub
Main Street Station, 200 N Main Street, at Stewart Avenue, Downtown (387 1896). Bus 108, 301, 302, 401, 402, 403. **Open** 11am-7am daily. **Credit** AmEx, DC, Disc, JCB, MC, V.

The Triple 7 serves decent beer and bar munchies (the garlic and herb fries are among the best we've had), but the best reason to visit this microbrewery is to gawk at Main Street's multimillion-dollar collection of antiques and rarities. Only in Vegas: after drinking enough brews, men can stroll to the lavatory and relieve themselves on a portion of the Berlin Wall that's been encased in plastic.

East of Strip

Double Down Saloon
Paradise Plaza, 4640 Paradise Road, at Naples Drive, between Harmon & Tropicana Avenues, East of Strip (791 5775). Bus 108.
No credit cards.
The Double Down is still the hippest bar in Vegas, with no competition in sight. Darkly psychedelic murals cover every surface, the infamous jukebox cranks out an eclectic mix ranging from British punk to American jazz, TV monitors display 1940s adventure serials or midget pornography, and the clientele is deliciously mixed. Former patrons have included film director Tim Burton and late LSD guru Dr Timothy Leary. A giant sign over the front door proclaims the Double Down the 'happiest place on Earth' and more than once they've been right. Don't leave without trying the house beverage, a sweet, blood-red concoction of mysterious origin lovingly dubbed 'Ass Juice'. The Double Down is less than a mile from the Strip; don't miss it. *See also p234* **Nightlife: Music.**

Drink & Eat Too!
200 E Harmon Avenue, at Koval Lane, East of Strip (796 5519). Bus 201, 202, 213. **Open** *Jan-Nov* 8pm-5am Tue-Sat; *Dec* 8pm-5am Thur-Sat. **Admission** $5-$10; women with local ID free. **Credit** AmEx, DC, MC, V.
Drink is less a bar and more an amusement park. Overpriced drinks are served in baby bottles, test tubes and small plastic buckets, offering the illusion of novelty where none exists. The VIP loft (open, in fact, to anyone and his brother) above the cigar room is the only place in the establishment where you can avoid being herded like cattle or brusquely handled by security thugs. With its high ceiling and post-modern furniture, the loft is actually quite pleasant – but getting there without getting shoved or inappropriately fondled is next to impossible.
Dress: smart casual; no cut-off shorts, sweatsuits or tank tops.

Gordon Biersch
3987 Paradise Road, at Flamingo Road, East of Strip (312 5247). Bus 108, 202. **Open** 11.30am-midnight Mon, Sun; 11.30am-2am Tue-Sat.
Credit AmEx, DC, Disc, JCB, MC, V.
San Francisco's prize microbrewery is now one of Las Vegas's most popular pick-up joints. It fills to capacity every night with beautiful people drawn by the fine brew, live music (call for times) and an extensive menu that features such colourfully named appetisers as Angry Prawns. Valet parking is available, and you'll need it.

Viva Las Vegas Lounge
Hard Rock, 4455 Paradise Road, at Harmon Avenue, East of Strip (693 5000). Bus 108.
Credit Disc, MC, V.
The Viva Las Vegas lounge – called 'the Sidebar' by locals, owing to its location on the side of the Hard Rock's bustling casino – is fairly lively around the clock, but really jumps on Friday and Saturday nights, when young singles pack the area to over-flowing. The drinks cost slightly more than they should, but the people-watching more than makes up for this shortcoming – as do the 'lightbulb' suits worn by the Red Hot Chili Peppers at Woodstock number two and now mounted, with straight-faced reverence, behind the bar. Despite being in the Hard Rock Hotel, there's no live music.

West of Strip

VooDoo Lounge
Rio, Masquerade Village Tower, 3700 W Flamingo Road, at Valley View Boulevard, West of Strip (252 7777). Bus 202. **Open** 11am-3am daily.
Admission free Mon-Thur, Sun; $10 Fri, Sat.
Credit AmEx, DC, Disc, JCB, MC, V.
There's a whole lot of gross pretension going on here. After getting a serious up-and-down from a bouncer standing by the elevator you are whisked 41 storeys up to the VooDoo Lounge, where the air is rare, the view spectacular, silicone-enhanced cleavage abounds and the overrated psychedelic cocktails go for the price of an entire steak dinner in Downtown. The VooDoo draws bodies by the thousands to sample its metropolitan quality and to mix with the pretty crowd, but the vibe is empty. Worth a visit for the view, however. *See also p212* **Casino Entertainment: Lounges.**
Dress: 11am-5pm casual, no beachwear; 5pm-2am smart casual, no athletic wear.

University District

Crown & Anchor Pub
1350 E Tropicana Avenue, at Maryland Parkway, University District (739 8676). Bus 109, 201.
Open 11am-5am daily. **Credit** AmEx, Disc, MC, V.
This 'proper' British-style pub serves up pints of Guinness, Newcastle Brown and Blackthorn cider hand over fist and does an equally brisk trade in cocktails (sample one of their James Bond-themed martinis). Split-level seating, when available (the loft closes early), cements the charm of this establishment and you can get standard pub grub. It's also the most likely bet for watching soccer internationals featuring British teams.

Dispensary Lounge
Ocotillo Plaza, 2451 E Tropicana Avenue, at Eastern Avenue, University District (458 6343). Bus 110, 201. **Credit** MC, V.
The kitschy spirit of the 1970s lives and thrives in this dark, quiet, curiously sexy lounge. Its look and vibe, with churning water wheel, wood fixtures and waitresses garbed in tight-fitting Spandex, would fit

Crown & Anchor: *pub life, Vegas style.*

neatly into a Quentin Tarantino movie. If the music at the Dispensary ever includes a song recorded after 1980, let us know.

Moose McGillycuddy's Pub & Café
4770 S Maryland Parkway, between E Tropicana & Harmon Avenues, University District (798 8337). Bus 108, 213. **Open** 11am-3.30am daily. **Credit** AmEx, DC, MC, V.
This chain establishment is quite possibly the most obnoxious – and wildly successful – college bar in Sin City. Dare to stay past 8pm and you'll be buried in waves of clueless hotel management majors, howling jocks and every blonde airhead within a ten-mile radius. If you're looking to hook up with someone who won't remember you tomorrow – or ever again, for that matter – this is the place.

North Las Vegas

Legends Lounge
865 N Lamb Boulevard, at Washington Avenue, North Las Vegas (437 9674). Bus 112, 208. **Admission** free-$5. **No credit cards.**
This far-flung bar is one of a very small number that books live music on a regular basis (hence the occasional admission charge). The owner plays his live Grateful Dead and Phish tapes almost constantly, instilling a peaceful, easy feeling in anyone who stops by. Too far out of town to pop in for casual drinks, but a fine destination if one of Las Vegas's better local bands is rocking the house. *See also p234* **Nightlife: Music.**

Pogo's Tavern
2103 N Decatur Boulevard, between Smoke Ranch Road & Lake Mead Boulevard, North Las Vegas (646 9735). Bus 103. **Open** 9am-3am daily. **No credit cards.**
This quiet joint is the perfect place to escape the gaudy neon overkill of Las Vegas, yet still enjoy its charm. A live swing band, made up of retirees from classic Strip swing bands, plays every Friday to an audience that barely reaches double figures. *See also p235* **Nightlife: Music.**

South-west Las Vegas

Money Plays
West Flamingo Center, 4755 W Flamingo Road, between Polaris Avenue & Decatur Boulevard, South-west Las Vegas (368 1828). Bus 202, 103. **No credit cards.**
The typical sports bar décor is not much to look at, but Money Plays draws a huge party crowd. Live bands play in the back, and anyone and everyone is welcome, wearing whatever the hell they want. *See also p234* **Nightlife: Music.**

North-west Las Vegas

JC Wooloughan
Resort at Summerlin, 221 N Rampart Boulevard, at Summerlin Parkway, North-west Las Vegas (869 7777). No bus. **Credit** AmEx, Disc, MC, V.
Built in Dublin then reassembled here, this Irish pub features authentic Irish antiques, timber, masonry and fixtures. Belly up to the bar and enjoy draught Guinness, Murphy's, Boddington's and Tennent's. You can also imbibe fine Scotch and Irish single malts, including Knappogue 36-Year-Old and Middleton Very Rare. The live entertainment often includes Irish talent.

Henderson

Barley's Casino & Brewing Company
Mountain Vista Shopping Center, 4500 E Sunset Road, at Mountain Vista Boulevard, Henderson (458 2739). Bus 212. **Credit** AmEx, DC, Disc, MC, V.
Henderson residents have a lot to be grateful for in Barley's. The fair-sized but not overbearing casino is packed every night. One of the town's better Mexican restaurants, Viva Mercado's, adjoins the establishment. And the beer is worth writing home about, particularly the Red Rock and Black Mountain lagers. Don't be afraid to sample whatever seasonal brew is on tap. Outdoor seating is available, overlooking a fountain that children run through in summer.

Gaudi Bar
Sunset Station, 1301 W Sunset Road, at Stephanie Street, Henderson (547 7777). Bus 212, 217, 402. **Credit** AmEx, DC, Disc, JCB, MC, V.
Located in the middle of a noisy casino, the Gaudi Bar – named after famed Barcelona architect Antoni Gaudí – is the most colourful bar in Las Vegas and

quite possibly the entire world. Drawing (very) freely from Gaudí's wild designs, it is bright, psychedelic and pleasantly womblike, with right angles at a bare minimum. The cocktails are casino-cheap, service is rapid and the crowd a fairly even mix of tourists and locals.

Boulder City

Backstop Bar
533 Avenue B, at Nevada Highway & Wyoming Street, Boulder City (294 8445). Bus 116.
Open 8am-1am Mon-Thur; 8am-3.15am Fri, Sat.
No credit cards.
By dint of its location, the Backstop Bar offers one bonus that no other Las Vegas bar can claim – gambling is illegal in Boulder City, so there are no video poker machines here. With that diversion removed, you can enjoy the ambience: the bar's rustic quality, the stuffed buffalo heads peering down from the walls and a few stiff drinks with the friendly citizens of the town that built Hoover Dam.

Everywhere

PT's Pub
Locals call PT's 'the McDonald's of bars', owing to their tendency to pop up on every corner. PT's are no-nonsense bars, with cheap American draught beers, seemingly endless happy hours and well-used pool tables and dartboards. Practically anywhere you end up in Las Vegas, there is a PT's nearby. A warning to would-be drunk drivers: many of their outposts are frequented by off-duty policemen.

Branches closest to the Strip: 532 E Sahara Avenue, at Sixth Street, East of Strip (792 4121); Park Place Shopping Center, 3790 Cambridge Street, between Twain Avenue & Flamingo Road, East of Strip (792 4475).

Coffeehouses & cafés

Like much of the city's so-called 'cultural retail', the Las Vegas café and coffeehouse scene has its ups and downs. Along the way, the terms 'café' and 'coffeehouse' have evolved definitions particular to the city. Nothing illustrates this better than a brief history of the city's first java-pusher, Lenadams Dorris. In the early days (the late 1980s), the buzzword was 'coffeehouse' and the place to go was Dorris's very European-styled Newsroom. It was here that a broad mishmash of the city's culturati and intelligentsia would gather to exchange ideas and make conversation over a thin menu of espresso drinks.

Today, the Newsroom is long gone and Dorris runs the Enigma Garden Café – where the food is the main attraction, hence 'café'. The espresso-focused culture that evolved from the Newsroom has been supplanted by the international brand of Starbucks, which, in its quest for worldwide dominance, has increased its local presence from five to more than 20 outlets since 1998.

The best, bar none

Best cocktails
Peppermill's Fireside Lounge
Half the taste of a good cocktail is related to the atmosphere in which it is served. Just imagine how your caipirinha will taste in this sweet, sour and thoroughly intoxicating room.

Best view
VooDoo Lounge
Turn your back on the would-be hipsters and flip-sters at this bar atop the Rio hotel-casino, and you'll be hit in the face with the best view in town – the 'action' part of the Strip, from Caesars Palace to Mandalay Bay.

Best theme
Red Square
Squeezing out the kitschy, far-out Quark's Bar at Star Trek: The Experience by a decapitated head – that of the Lenin statue out front – Red Square makes revolution look cool. Besides, we'll take any chance to wear a parka in the desert.

Best martini
Drai's on The Strip
They cost a bit, but the martinis served in this swank subterranean restaurant and lounge are worth every penny.

Best atmosphere
Double Down Saloon
It's hip, it's frightening, it's lurid – in other words, don't leave town without drinking here.

Best Vegas experience
Carousel Bar
The drinks are cheap, the poker tables are close, there are acrobats flying over your head and, yes, the room really is spinning.

Best beer
Gordon Biersch
The brews at this popular, well-trafficked establishment are as tasty as the attractive punters that suck them down.

The crowd of java junkies has also grown, evolving from mere disaffecteds to the wider population. As is typical of Vegas, the big chains have devoured a sizeable chunk of the local enterprises; contrary to expectation, Las Vegans are not very adventurous but are well known for embracing anything tried and true. Locally owned espresso shops are typically cafés serving a wide menu of soups, sandwiches and the like, while Starbucks offers cosy indoor-outdoor environments with only a small selection of baked goods but very tasty espresso drinks and teas.

The Strip

There are very few places on the Strip, outside of the resort restaurants, to get a simple, decent cup of coffee. Your best bet is to head for the closest branch of Starbucks; otherwise, you will be compelled to drink the thin brown swill that is typically offered at your average casino coffeestand. Case in point: at one café inside the Paris casino (which, as a French-themed place, really should know better), espressos and cappuccinos are served pre-mixed, from a machine.

Starbucks

Polo Towers Plaza, 3743 Las Vegas Boulevard South, at Harmon Avenue (739 9780). Bus 301, 302. **Open** 5.30am-10.30pm Mon-Thur, Sun; 5.30am-midnight Fri, Sat. **Credit** AmEx, MC, V.
Gold Key Shops, 3049 Las Vegas Boulevard South, at Stardust Drive (737 9717). Bus 301, 302. **Open** 6am-10.30pm daily. **Credit** AmEx, MC, V.
Fashion Show Mall, 3200 Las Vegas Boulevard South, at W Spring Mountain Road (794 4010). **Open** 8am-9pm Mon-Fri; 8am-8pm Sat; 8am-6pm Sun. **Credit** AmEx, MC, V.
With its attractive wood and sculpted metal décor, unique floorplans (no two locations are exactly alike) and a wide selection of flavoured coffee drinks, Starbucks' Las Vegas operations are, at the very least, preferable to the noisy, understaffed and just plain awful coffeestands located in the centre of most casino floors. The brewed coffees are not quite as good as the delicious espresso drinks; try the rich, orange-flavoured mocha valencia if nothing else appeals. There are a few pastries and baked goods, but they pale in comparison to the beverages. All drinks can be made non-fat and caffeine-free.
The chain is spreading fast (some would say like the plague): branches are numerous and found all over the city – though there are only three on the Strip, plus a kiosk inside Treasure Island. There are also locations inside Boulder Station and in two Barnes & Noble bookstores; in fact, there seems to be a Starbucks wherever you turn your head.
Branches: 1340 E Flamingo Road (737 9099); 4732 Faircenter Parkway (258 1223); 7541 Lake Mead Boulevard (240 4710); 5215 Sahara Avenue (248 9166); 850 S Rancho Drive (870 6993); Boulder Station, 4111 Boulder Highway (457 3313); and many others (see phone book).

Downtown

Café Neon

The Attic, 1018 S Main Street, just north of Charleston Boulevard, Downtown (388 4088). Bus 206. **Open** 9am-5pm daily. **Credit** Disc, MC, V.
Located on the upper level of vintage clothing and appliance store, the Attic (*see chapter* **Shops & Services**), Café Neon is separated from the second-hand bell-bottoms by a row of fish tanks. It's really just a coffee-and-pastry counter – the funky, disco-era décor and good shopping nearby make it worth a stop, but only if you're in the neighbourhood.

Enigma Garden Café

9182 S Fourth Street, just north of Charleston Boulevard, Downtown (386 0999). Bus 206, 403. **Open** 7am-late daily. **No credit cards**.
A visit to Enigma, still Downtown's premier café, is an absolute must. Set in a pair of early twentieth-century railroad barracks houses and their garden, the Enigma feels wonderfully detached: not part of Las Vegas, or even the world at large. Its beverage menu is the deepest in town, running the gamut from mochas to cappuccinos to chai tea, and the food, though simple, is lovingly prepared (the tabbouleh is recommended). A small art gallery shows local talent; poetry readings happen on select weeknights; live music rocks the garden on weekends. Don't miss a moment. *See also p203* **Culture: Poetry readings**.

Brewed Awakening

East Gate Plaza, 2305 E Sahara Avenue, at Eastern Avenue, East Las Vegas (457 7050). Bus 110, 204. **Open** 6am-6pm Mon-Fri; 7am-5pm Sat; 9am-4pm Sun. **Credit** AmEx, Disc, MC, V.
A tiny coffeehouse with an in-house bakery. The coffee is unremarkable, but the fresh muffins, rolls and pastries more than make up for it. There's live music on Sunday mornings.

University District

Café Copioh

Runnin' Rebel Plaza, 4550 S Maryland Parkway, at Harmon Avenue, University District (739 0305). Bus 109, 201, 203. **Open** noon-midnight Mon; noon-3am Tue-Thur; 3pm-3am Fri; 6pm-3am Sat; 6am-midnight Sun. **No credit cards**.
The best reason to visit Café Copioh is for the crowd: an even mix of arty, pretentious types and honest-to-Goth vampire youth, all enjoying very good coffee and cold coffee 'slush' that cannot be bettered in this hemisphere. The food, though decent, is not always available – the kitchen seems to close down at will. Poetry readings are held on Tuesday evenings; for details, *see p203* **Culture**.

Café Espresso Roma

The Promenade, 4440 S Maryland Parkway, at Harmon Avenue, University District (369 1540). Bus 109, 213. **Open** 7am-10pm Mon, Tue, Thur; 7am-2am Wed; 8am-11pm Fri, Sat; 8am-10pm Sun. **No credit cards**.

Coffee and comfort at **Café Copioh.**

Although essentially an adjunct study hall for UNLV across the street, the venerable (and recently renovated) Roma manages to win you over nonetheless. The coffee drinks are equal parts good taste and nerve – try the four-shot espresso and honey-soaked 'Brain' for maximum firepower – and their policy of '90¢ for any mug of coffee, within the bounds of sanity' has stood since time immemorial. The students are friendly, and local art, poetry and music are represented in rotating shows on designated nights – *see p203* **Culture: Poetry readings** and *p235* **Nightlife: Music**.

Jazzed Café
Napoli Plaza, 2055 E Tropicana Avenue, between Spencer Street & Eastern Avenue, University District (798 5995). Bus 201. **Open** 6pm-3am Tue-Sun. **Credit** AmEx, Disc, MC, V.
Although most seating in this tiny café is reserved for patrons choosing from the selective Italian menu and wine list, Jazzed does have a small bar and couch for those wanting only liquid refreshment. This is the most cosmopolitan café in Las Vegas, hands down, where patrons can learn to swear in Italian while watching proprietors Kirk and Connie Offerle whip up risotto. It's the birthplace of dance group the Vibe (*see p207* **Culture: Theatre & dance**), and is often inhabited by dancers. The management prefers that patrons refrain from asking for 'lemon peels in your espresso or ice for your wine'. Sound advice under any circumstances. *See also* chapter **Restaurants & buffets**.

South-west Las Vegas

Mermaid Café
2910 Lake East Drive, at Lake Sahara, South-west Las Vegas (240 6002). Bus 204. **Open** 11am-11pm Mon, Tue; 11am-midnight Wed, Thur; 11am-2am Fri, Sat; noon-8pm Sun. **Credit** AmEx, Disc, MC, V.
Getting to the Mermaid is a bit of a jaunt – almost 20 minutes by taxi. Truth be told, even some locals have a hard time finding it. Once there, however, the

travel time invested pays off handsomely. The café is quiet and cosy, facing a small (man-made) lake. Good coffee, beer and wine complement a menu of sandwiches and salads. Poets recite purple prose, jazz combos play quietly and, best of all, you'll be outside every part of the Vegas experience for as long as you want – a benefit that, if you stay in town long enough, becomes a necessity.

North-west Las Vegas

Jitters
Pueblo Shopping Center, 8441 W Lake Mead Boulevard, at Rampart Boulevard, North-west Las Vegas (256 1902). Bus 210. **Open** 6am-10pm Mon-Sat; 7am-9pm Sun. **Credit** AmEx, DC, Disc, MC, V.
By the look of things, home-grown mini-chain Jitters desperately wants to be the next Starbucks – a regional stop for java, muffins and delicious sandwiches (try the Garden of Eatin'). The selection of teas is very good – fortunately, because the coffee is unexceptional, though many who like chain consistency prefer Jitters to Starbucks simply because it feels more like a local hangout than an international conglomerate. There are now 15 branches in and around Vegas, including ones inside the Sahara, Riviera and Sunset Station casinos. The Lake Mead Boulevard branch, with patio seating around a rock fountain and great mountain views, is lovely, but the action on weekends is at the Village Square location.
Branches: Ocotillo Plaza, 2457 E Tropicana Avenue (898 0056); 8145 W Sahara Avenue (948 8880); Village Square Center, 9350 W Sahara Avenue (804 0480); Lido Plaza, unit 128, 4343 N Rancho Drive (655 3660); and others (see phone book).

Photos & Flowers Garden Café
Cornerstone Buildings of Meadows Shops, unit 318, 3818 Meadows Lane, at Valley View Boulevard, North-west Las Vegas (258 1554). Bus 104, 207. **Open** 8am-5pm Mon-Fri; 8am-3pm Sat, Sun. **Credit** AmEx, Disc, MC, V.
Photos & Flowers (the flora in the name comes from an on-site hothouse) is one of the more popular lunchtime destinations in the area, yet never feels overcrowded, no matter how many bodies pour in for java and sandwiches. It's a fine place to enjoy afternoon tea, light lunches or that delicious old standard, quiet conversation.

Green Valley

Café Sensations
Athenian Plaza, 4350 E Sunset Road, at Athenian Drive, Green Valley (456 7803). Bus 212. **Open** 7am-8pm Mon-Thur; 8am-9pm Sat; 9am-4pm Sun. **Credit** DC, Disc, MC, V.
Located close to the exclusive Green Valley Athletic Club, Café Sensations hosts more rich souls than poor but remains humble. A full menu of coffee drinks and light meals is available, live jazz groups play intermittently and a variety of interesting shops are within walking distance.

Shops & Services

Calling all lovers of kitsch and followers of fashion – Las Vegas has shopping options galore just for you.

Las Vegas is a city that reinvents itself more often than Madonna. The Vegas you visit this year will be a far cry from last. Four new casinos have taken up residence on the Strip since the first edition of this guide, two of which – Bellagio and the Venetian – have added a host of options to the Vegas retail scene. That scene doesn't compare, of course, with Los Angeles, New York, London or other world shopping destinations, but it's getting there. Most stores are still of the chain variety, however, and in some areas – books, for example, and street fashion – Las Vegas is sadly lacking.

Unlike many other major US cities, Vegas has no clearly defined shopping districts. Most of its stores are grouped together – either on the Strip in malls within the larger casinos-hotels, or in non-casino malls or shopping centres dotted about the city. For a wider selection and some local flavour, get off the Strip and into the neighbourhoods. Though Las Vegans use the Strip, too; the Forum Shops at Caesars Palace is a locals' favourite for its excellent customer service and atmosphere.

Things change quickly here, so it's a good idea to call ahead if your destination is a particular shop. Remember that sales tax – 7.25 per cent in Nevada – will be added to the label price.

One-stop

At the time this guide went to press, plans were afoot for more than four million square feet (372,000 square metres) of new retail space in the Vegas Valley. A quarter of that will be added to the **Fashion Show Mall**, including department stores Bloomingdales and Lord & Taylor. Look for a new addition to the already monumental **Forum Shops** at Caesars Palace. The reborn Aladdin casino-hotel promises the **Desert Passage** retail and entertainment complex, with 136 stores and 14 high-profile restaurants and clubs. It will feature a series of exotic desert settings, including a 'Lost City' modelled after the ancient city of Petra.

But wait, there's more. The MGM Grand has plans for a Grand Canyon-themed shopping area (due for completion in autumn 2000) as part of the

$33-million expansion of the **Showcase** mall. Some 60 tons of fake rock will mimic the canyon's rugged walls, simulated flash floods will gush hourly, accompanied by thunderstorm sounds and special effects, and a helicopter will hover above it all. Finally, a huge shopping mall located between **Mandalay Bay** and the **Luxor** mega-resorts, to be anchored by Nordstrom, is expected by the time 2001 rolls around.

Casino malls

The Forum Shops
Caesars Palace, 3500 Las Vegas Boulevard South, between W Spring Mountain & Flamingo Roads (893 4800). Bus 301, 302. **Open** 10am-11pm Mon-Thur, Sun; 10am-midnight Fri, Sat. **Credit** varies.
More than just a mall, the Forum Shops at Caesars Palace are an experience. Costumed staff, be-pillared décor, the famous ever-changing skies, huge fountains, lush lighting – it's enough to make you believe they really did have chi-chi shopping centres in Ancient Rome. The Forum Shops were extended in 1997 and in order to encourage customers to the extremities, there are attractions at either end: statues coming to life at one end and Atlantis rising from the waves at the other. Concessions have been cannily distributed; though there's no tat, there's plenty that's affordable. Mid-range chain outposts such as the Gap, Banana Republic, Abercrombie & Fitch, Guess and Diesel punctuate a top-rank designer line-up that includes DKNY, Hugo Boss, Armani, Versace, Ralph Lauren, Christian Dior, Fendi, Gucci and Louis Vuitton. There's also some good gift shopping here, from the sweet centre at FAO Schwarz to Caesars' own gift shop to a fridge magnet shop. Brits in search of CDs, way cheaper in the States, should note that this is the site of Las Vegas's Virgin Megastore, which has a quiet upper-storey café if you want to escape the crowds. If not, there are all manner of food stops, from the best of the chains to off-the-scale upscale.

The Grand Canal Shoppes
Venetian, 3355 Las Vegas Boulevard South, just south of Sands Avenue (414 1000). Bus 203, 301, 302. **Open** 10am-11pm Mon-Thur, Sun; 10am-midnight Fri, Sat. **Credit** varies.

*Visit **Via Bellagio** for designer fashion.*

Further proof that Venice really is sinking. The idea of a themed shopping mall – winding canals crossed by bridges, singing gondoliers, fake houses and shops, sky-painted ceilings – has been done before – and better. Half the shops weren't ready when the Venetian opened in May 1999; it's better now, but nothing really stands out, even though they claim the likes of Lladro, Movado and Jimmy Choo. Other names worth seeking out include Banana Republic, Kenneth Cole, bebe and Ann Taylor, but in general, it's a disappointment. The walkways are narrow, the layout unimaginative and, despite the welcome openness of the 'St Mark's Square' area and a few good restaurants, overall this mall leaves you with the feeling of a second-rate Forum Shops.
Website: www.venetian.com

Via Bellagio

Bellagio, 3600 Las Vegas Boulevard South, at W Flamingo Road (693 7111). Bus 202, 301, 302.
Open 10am-midnight daily. **Credit** varies.
In line with Bellagio's upscale, adult-only environment, its small shopping mall contains only the smartest of designer names, including Chanel, Tiffany, Giorgio Armani, Gucci, Prada, Hermès and Moschino. If your wallet can't cope, you can at least enjoy this opulent shrine to materialism and the daylight streaming in through the vaulted glass ceilings.
Website: www.bellagiolasvegas.com

Non-casino malls

Boulevard Mall

3528 S Maryland Parkway, between E Desert Inn Road & Twain Avenue, East Las Vegas (732 8949). Bus 109, 112, 203, 213. **Open** 10am-9pm Mon-Fri; 10am-8pm Sat; 11am-6pm Sun. **Credit** varies.
The first mall of its type in the city, this is a bastion of the Las Vegas shopping world: centrally located, reasonably priced and loaded with stores of every type. When you're weighed down with bags and nearing collapse, check out the Panorama Café's foodcourt for cheap, delicious cuisine from all over the world.

Fashion Show Mall

3200 Las Vegas Boulevard South, at W Spring Mountain Road (369 8382). Bus 203, 301, 302.
Open 10am-9pm Mon-Fri; 10am-7pm Sat; noon-6pm Sun. **Credit** varies.
Bullock's, Neiman Marcus, Saks Fifth Avenue, Robinsons May and the brand-new Bloomingdales and Lord & Taylor are all represented at this very popular mall. There's also a Gap and a handful of other more humble marques. Business is kept humming thanks to the patronage of loaded locals and foot traffic on the Strip. The atmosphere is a bit cold, but we like the scattering of capacious sofas so you can sit back and recover from price shock.

The Galleria at Sunset Mall

1300 Sunset Road, at Stephanie Street, Green Valley (434 0202). Bus 212, 217. **Open** 10am-9pm Mon-Sat; 11am-6pm Sun. **Credit** varies.
The Galleria Mall is in Green Valley, one of Las Vegas's upper-crust neighbourhoods. Geared to fit in with its surroundings, it's elegant but not ridiculously overpriced and crammed with yuppified clothing stores. It also houses some excellent gift and stationery shops, including Papyrus, Spencer Gifts and Natural Wonders.

Meadows Mall

4300 Meadows Lane, between Decatur & Valley View Boulevards, North-west Las Vegas (878 4849). Bus 103, 104, 207. **Open** 9am-10pm Mon-Fri; 10am-7pm Sat, Sun. **Credit** varies.
A typical sprawling honeycomb of more than 140 generic and chain shops, the Meadows is on a par with the Boulevard Mall in terms of price. Though it was recently given a much-needed remodel and facelift, the mall is still utilitarian rather than inspirational. Children will enjoy the Menagerie carousel.

Department stores

Dillard's

Fashion Show Mall, 3200 Las Vegas Boulevard South, at W Spring Mountain Road (733 2008). Bus 203, 301, 302. **Open** 10am-9pm Mon-Sat; noon-6pm Sun. **Credit** AmEx, DC, Disc, JCB, MC, V.
This is perhaps the American West's equivalent to Marks & Spencer: very nice beauty aisles, a good selection of casual and formal women's shoes and a great selection of men's suits at decent prices.

Branches: Boulevard Mall, 3528 S Maryland Parkway (734 2111); The Galleria at Sunset Mall, 1300 Sunset Road (435 6000); Meadows Mall, 4300 Meadows Lane (870 2039).
www.dillards.com

JC Penney
Boulevard Mall, 3528 S Maryland Parkway, between E Desert Inn Road & Twain Avenue, East Las Vegas (735 5131). Bus 109, 112, 203, 213. **Open** 10am-9pm Mon-Fri; 10am-8pm Sat; 11am-6pm Sun. **Credit** AmEx, Disc, MC, V.
This store is as American as apple pie. You'll find updated classic staples for both men and women. The quality is good and prices are down to earth, with plenty of seasonal sales. This branch has an extensive housewares and décor section and a good selection of watches and jewellery.
Branches: The Galleria at Sunset Mall, 1300 Sunset Road (451 4545); Home Store, 771 S Rainbow Road (870 7727); Meadows Mall, 4400 Meadows Lane (870 9182).
Website: www.jcpenney.com

Macy's
Fashion Show Mall, 3200 Las Vegas Boulevard South, at W Spring Mountain Road (731 5111). Bus 203, 301, 302. **Open** 10am-9pm Mon-Sat; noon-6pm Sun. **Credit** AmEx, JCB, MC, V.
Macy's is the king of US department stores, and a good bet for stocking up on Calvin Klein underwear. All outlets offer sturdy, good-quality merchandise at reasonable prices, and clothing ranges from classic to trendy. The Spring Mountain Road branch has great homewares and frequent sales.
Branches: Home Store, 4450 W Spring Mountain Road (731 1111); Meadows Mall, 4300 Meadows Lane (258 2100).
Website: www.macys.com

Neiman Marcus
Fashion Show Mall, 3200 Las Vegas Boulevard South, at W Spring Mountain Road (731 3636). Bus 203, 301, 302. **Open** 10am-8pm Mon-Fri; 10am-7pm Sat; noon-6pm Sun. **Credit** AmEx, MC, V.
This is a great or terrible place to get lost with a credit card, depending on how you look at it. High-end merchandise and a classy atmosphere to match. For a cheaper version, try the discount branch at Primm on the California border.
Branch: Last Call at Neiman Marcus, 32100 Las Vegas Boulevard South, Primm (874 6900).
Website: www.neimanmarcus.com

Saks Fifth Avenue
Fashion Show Mall, 3200 Las Vegas Boulevard South, at W Spring Mountain Road (733 8300). Bus 203, 301, 302. **Open** 10am-8pm Mon-Wed; 10am-9pm Thur, Fri; 10am-7pm Sat; noon-6pm Sun. **Credit** AmEx, DC, Disc, JCB, MC, V.
A shopping experience for those with discriminating taste and a heavyweight bank account. Mens' and womens' apparel sections are especially strong. If you've got the taste but not the money, check out Saks's discount store in Belz Factory Outlet World or the Fashion Outlet of Las Vegas (for both, *see below*).
Website: www.sacsfifthavenue.com

Discount & factory outlets

Belz Factory Outlet World
7400 Las Vegas Boulevard South, at Warm Springs Road, south of Las Vegas (896 5599). Bus 303. **Open** 10am-9pm Mon-Sat; 10am-6pm Sun. **Credit** varies.
Rather than schlepp through high-end mall after high-end mall searching for sales and begging for bargains, head over to Belz where savings are a sure bet. Check out the Calvin Klein outlet, Off Fifth! Saks Fifth Avenue outlet, Nike, Vans, Lenox, Waterford/Wedgwood, Bose, London Fog and many others. An eclectic foodcourt will keep you energised and a giant carousel will keep the kids content.
Website: www.belz.com

Broadacres Open Air Swap Meet
2930 N Las Vegas Boulevard, at Pecos Road, North Las Vegas (642 3777). Bus 111, 113. **Open** 6.30am-6pm Fri-Sun. **Credit** varies.
Now in its 22nd year, this weekend market of selling and swapping is a Las Vegas classic. Just four miles (6.5km) north of Downtown, it offers 40 acres of bargains in both new and used goods. Pop into the beer garden for a sudsy refresher, put the kids on a pony for a ride or just sit in the shade watching the world go by.

Fantastic Indoor Swap Meet
1717 S Decatur Boulevard, between Oakey Boulevard & Sahara Avenue, North-west Las Vegas (877 0087). Bus 103, 205. **Open** 10am-6pm Fri-Sun. **Credit** varies.
Tired of stuffing your bucks into the slots with nary a single payoff? At Fantastic, a buck will not only get you in the door, but might even score you a nice something or other. All merchandise is new, not second-hand. It's not as interesting as Broadacres, but worth a visit nonetheless.
Website: www.fantasticswap.com

Fashion Outlet of Las Vegas
32100 Las Vegas Boulevard South, Primm (874 1400). No bus. **Open** 10am-9pm daily. **Credit** varies.
Designer labels are all the rage at this upscale, fully enclosed outlet mall 35 miles (56km) south of the Strip (there's a free shuttle bus if you don't have a car). Browse discounted merchandise by Donna Karan, Versace, Kenneth Cole, Guess, Pottery Barn and many more, then have a bite at a dozen fast-food and table-service eateries.

Wal-Mart
3075 E Tropicana Avenue, at Pecos Road, East Las Vegas (451 8900). Bus 111, 201. **Open** 24hrs daily. **Credit** AmEx, DC, Disc, JCB, MC, V.
Perhaps *the* definition of one-stop shopping, with toys, appliances, computers and software, video games, sporting goods, electronics, cameras, clothing, groceries, furnishings and healthcare (there's an optician and even a dentist in most Wal-Mart locations). Known for its vast variety and low prices.
Branches: see the phone book.
Website: www.walmart.com

Arts & entertainment

The **Tower Records** superstore (*see page 175*) offers the most interesting and eclectic selection of new books in the city, as well as good music, film, travel, art and erotica sections. For details of **Get Booked**, a friendly book and video shop in the city's Gay Triangle, *see page 227* **Nightlife: Gay & lesbian.**

Books

Albion Book Company

2466 E Desert Inn Road, suite G, at Eastern Avenue, East Las Vegas (792 9554). Bus 110, 112. **Open** 10am-6pm daily. **Credit** AmEx, Disc, MC, V.

The quintessential used bookstore, crammed with obscure offbeat editions alongside classic Dickens and Tolstoy. Prices are low and there's an air of comfortable chaos, with plenty of character, both on the shelves and behind the counter.

Barnes & Noble

3860 S Maryland Parkway, between Spencer Street & Flamingo Road, Henderson (734 2900). Bus 109, 202. **Open** 9am-11pm daily. **Credit** AmEx, DC, Disc, MC, V.

Barnes & Noble is done up in rich, dark wood accents and seems to have a more relaxed 'go ahead and sit and read a chapter or two of that book you probably won't buy' attitude than some

Albion Book Co: *a bibliophile's delight.*

of its competitors. It's also got a nice selection of magazines, periodicals and national papers, but is a bit thin on international news.

Branches: 567 N Stephanie Street, between Sunset Road & Warm Springs Road, Henderson (434 1533); 2191 N Rainbow Boulevard, at Lake Mead Boulevard (631 1775).

Website: www.bn.com

Borders Books, Music & Café

1445 Sunset Road, at Stephanie Street, Green Valley (433 6222). Bus 103, 204. **Open** 9am-11pm Mon-Sat; 9am-6pm Sun. **Credit** AmEx, Disc, MC, V.

A hangout for hip intelligentsia, Borders boasts not only a top-notch book selection, but also music and a café, perfect for discussions on love, war and the meaning of life. The periodical selection is extensive and worth a browse, as are the video aisles.

Branches: 2323 S Decatur Boulevard (258 0999); 2190 N Rainbow Boulevard (638 7866).

Website: www.borders.com

Dead Poet Books

3858 W Sahara Avenue, at Valley View Boulevard, South-west Las Vegas (227 4070). Bus 104, 204. **Open** 10am-6pm Mon-Sat; noon-5pm Sun. **Credit** AmEx, DC, Disc, JCB, MC, V.

A charming hodgepodge of antiquarian books. Specialities include metaphysical cookbooks, military histories and plenty of first editions.

Native Son Bookstore

1301 D Street, between Owens & Washington Avenues, North Las Vegas (647 0101). Bus 214. **Open** noon-7pm daily. **Credit** AmEx.

Go native with a trip to this African bookstore. There's a lot of culture-specific literature, along with history, biographies and fictional brain-candy.

Readmore Bookstore

Sahara Town Square, 2560 S Maryland Parkway, at E Sahara Avenue, East Las Vegas (732 4453). Bus 109, 204. **Open** 9am-8pm Mon-Sat; 10am-5pm Sun. **Credit** Disc, MC, V.

Every magazine known to man (and woman) is sold here, though the selection of books is scanty. Hard-to-find publications such as *Christian Motorsports, Detective, The Quest, Skeptic, Raygun* and many more grace Readmore's shelves, along with scientific journals and an abundance of smut.

Branches: see the phone book.

Cameras & electronics

A word of warning: beware photo processing and film developing services on the Strip. It may be a hassle to go a little out of the way or wait till you're home, but it's better than paying three times the going rate. Instead, use the photo centres at large drugstores such as Walgreens or Sav-On (see Yellow Pages under 'Pharmacy'), where you can often get one-hour processing and find film on sale – or try the stores listed below.

As for electronics, why not check out the many pawn shops? Needless to say, pawning is a popular activity in Las Vegas, and you can often find great

Wax Trax Records: *used vinyl, rock 'n' roll memorabilia and a friendly vibe.*

stuff at up to half its original cost. Besides, they can be really fascinating places. Check the Yellow Pages for conveniently located stores.

Casey's Cameras
Liberace Plaza, 1775 E Tropicana, at Spencer Street, University District (736 0890). Bus 201. **Open** 9am-6pm Mon-Fri; 9am-5pm Sat. **Credit** AmEx, Disc, MC, V.

Conveniently located near the Liberace Museum, Casey's doesn't offer photo processing, but the pros here can advise on almost any camera query. It has an impressive array of professional cameras by the likes of Hasselblad and Leica, as well as collectors' cameras and great deals on used cameras.

Circuit City
4860 Eastern Avenue, at Tropicana Avenue, University District (898 0500). Bus 110, 201. **Open** 10am-9pm daily. **Credit** AmEx, Disc, MC, V.

Electronics and home appliances galore. If, after making a purchase here, you find identical merchandise sold cheaper anywhere in town, Circuit City will pay you the difference.
Branches: 5055 W Sahara Avenue (367 9700); 561 Stephanie Street (451 7111).
Website: www.circuitcity.com

The Good Guys
4580 W Sahara Avenue, at Decatur Boulevard, South-west Las Vegas (364 2500). Bus 103, 204. **Open** 9am-midnight daily. **Credit** AmEx, Disc, MC, V.

Good Guys offers competitive prices, a good selection (especially in computers and related equipment) and non-commissioned sales staff. That means no

one overwhelming you with a barrage of slick sales talk and useless information.
Branches: 621 Mall Ring Circle (451 7790); 3778 S Maryland Parkway (892 9200).
Website: www.thegoodguys.com

Sahara Camera Center
Albertson Shopping Center, 2305 E Sahara Avenue, at Eastern Avenue, East Las Vegas (457 3333). Bus 110, 204. **Open** 9am-6pm Mon-Fri; 9am-5pm Sat. **Credit** AmEx, Disc, MC, V.

Claiming to be 'Nevada's largest full service camera store', this place pretty much has, and does, it all. In business for close to 30 years, it offers rental and repair services, quality new and used equipment, very knowledgeable staff and one-hour photo processing. Prices are fair and many are discounted. The vast array of accessories includes ever-precious video batteries and all kinds of film including 8mm.

Wolf Camera & Video
Belz Factory Outlet World, 7400 Las Vegas Boulevard South, at Warm Springs Road, south of Las Vegas (896 4271). Bus 303. **Open** 10am-9pm Mon-Sat; 10am-6pm Sun. **Credit** AmEx, Disc, MC, V.

Offering a welcome escape from the electronics superstores, Wolf has friendly, well-informed staff, an excellent selection of still and video cameras and one-hour photo processing (black and white takes a week). Bargain-hunting Brits take note: it also stocks UK-compatible PAL camcorders.
Branches: Sahara Pavilion, 2580 Decatur Boulevard (889 1998); 7500 Lake Mead Boulevard (240 9916); Village Square, 9310 W Sahara Avenue (233 9407); Trails Village, 1958 Village Center Drive (240 9936).
Website: www.wolfcamera.com

Music & video

Big B's CDs & Records

4761 S Maryland Parkway, just south of Tropicana Avenue, University District (732 4433). Bus 108, 201. **Open** 11am-9pm Mon-Sat; noon-6pm Sun. **Credit** AmEx, Disc, MC, V.

Big B's buys used CDs and vinyl or offers a trade-in from among its healthy inventory of new and used music. Staff are extremely knowledgeable and friendly, and high turnover keeps the stock current. Highly recommended.
Website: www.bigbsmusic.com

Blockbuster Video

3862 W Sahara Avenue, between Valley View & Decatur Boulevards, South-west Las Vegas (364 1242). Bus 204. **Open** 10am-midnight daily. **Credit** AmEx, Disc, MC, V.

With 30 locations in Vegas, Blockbuster is the most widespread video store, though not the cheapest. Cinephiles take note: the foreign film selection is one of the best in town.
Branches: call 1-800 800 6767 to find your nearest.
Website: www.blockbuster.com

Hollywood Video

Renaissance Center West, 4001 Decatur Boulevard, at W Flamingo Road, South-west Las Vegas (367 0074). Bus 103, 202. **Open** 9am-3am daily. **Credit** AmEx, Disc, MC, V.

$1.99 for a five-day rental is hard to beat, and there's a guaranteed new-release policy so you should always get the film you want. The selection is dizzying, especially for kids' movies.
Branches: see the phone book.
Website: www.hollywoodvideo.com

Odyssey Records

1600 Las Vegas Boulevard South, at Wyoming Avenue, Downtown (384 4040). Bus 301, 302. **Open** 24hrs daily. **Credit** AmEx, Disc, MC, V.

This rap and R&B headquarters has occupied the same location for more than 15 years: a once prominent stretch of Las Vegas Boulevard that is now considered rather seedy. We prefer to think of it as colourful.

Tower Records, Video & Books

4580 Decatur Boulevard, at W Sahara Avenue, South-west Las Vegas (364 2500). Bus 103, 204. **Open** 9am-midnight daily. **Credit** AmEx, Disc, MC, V.

Located in the vast Tower-Good Guys-Wow! superstore, this arm of Tower Records wins the prize for variety: it has videos (for sale and rent, with a refreshingly strong foreign selection), books, magazines and periodicals and, of course, a vast array of CDs, cassettes and vinyl. Pop/rock consumes the majority of space, leaving the R&B section a little thin, but the generous selection of world beat, jazz vocalists and classical is happily noted. If it all becomes too much, have a rest in the café and suck back a latte beneath the mammoth video screen.
Branch: 4110 Maryland Parkway (371 0800).
Website: www.towerrecords.com

Underground

1164 E Twain Avenue, at Spencer Street, East Las Vegas (733 7025). Bus 108, 203. **Open** 11am-8pm Mon-Sat; noon-5pm Sun. **Credit** MC, V.

Plenty of used (and a bit of new) vinyl and CDs, with an emphasis on punk and garage. This place is also a good stop for psychobilly.

Virgin Megastore

The Forum Shops, Caesars Palace, 3500 Las Vegas Boulevard South, between W Spring Mountain & Flamingo Roads (696 7100). Bus 301, 302. **Open** 10am-midnight Mon-Thur, Sun; 10am-1am Fri, Sat. **Credit** AmEx, DC, Disc, JCB, MC, V.

This vast place has everything, and lots of it, so prepare to be overwhelmed. On your way to the indie racks, you're bound to be pulled towards the techno section, and if you're heading for funk, you may be swayed by a movie soundtrack. Prices are steep, but promotions on new releases and some 'nice price' older material can be found throughout. Staff are youthful and perky, and seem happy to help.
Website: www.virginmega.com

Wax Trax Records

2909 S Decatur Boulevard, between Sahara Avenue & Desert Inn Road, North-west Las Vegas (362 4300). Bus 103, 204. **Open** 10am-5pm daily. **Credit** AmEx, MC, V.

Wax Trax offers two storeys of vinyl and memorabilia – bins busting at the seams, fat with old soul and R&B, jazz, doo-wop and rock 'n' roll – plus a mixed selection of used CDs. Walls are covered with photos of the greats, many signed, givin' up love and thanks to owner Rich Rosen. It's almost like a trip to a music museum. Be prepared for some boisterous East Coast conversation, a super friendly house pup and an earful/eyeful of music history.

Sport & outdoor

Desert Outfitters

2101 S Decatur Boulevard, at O'Bannon Drive, North-west Las Vegas (362 7177). Bus 103. **Open** 10am-7pm daily. **Credit** AmEx, Disc, MC, V.

A favourite with locals and those in the know for years. The extremely knowledgeable duo that runs it will rent the gear for a weekend in the wilderness, and offer a bit of desert knowledge, too. Half the store is dedicated to prospecting – there's gold in them thar hills! Take your time, have a cup of coffee, pick up some pointers and maybe a map or a book or both. Recommended.
Website: www.desertoutfitters.com

Desert Rock Sports

8201 W Charleston Boulevard, at Cimarron Road, North-west Las Vegas (254 1143). Bus 206. **Open** 9am-7pm Mon-Fri; 9am-6pm Sat; 10am-6pm Sun. **Credit** AmEx, Disc, MC, V.

Desert Rock specialises in climbing equipment. You can rent the necessary gear (including shoes) and try the wall at the climbing centre next door before buying. It has well-recognised names at upmarket prices – including a large selection of backpacking

The best toy stores

There are branches of the **Disney Store** all over, including the Forum Shops and the Boulevard, Fashion Show and Galleria malls.

The Discovery Store
Fashion Show Mall, 3200 Las Vegas Boulevard South, at W Spring Mountain Road (792 2121). Bus 203, 301, 302. **Open** 10am-9pm Mon-Fri; 10am-7pm Sat; noon-6pm Sun. **Credit** AmEx, DC, Disc, JCB, MC, V.
Operated as part of the nature-driven Discovery Channel TV network, this shop in the Fashion Show Mall is a paradise of learning and thinking toys, games and exploration tools for those – of any age – who seek knowledge.
Branches: The Nature Company, Boulevard Mall, 3528 S Maryland Parkway (792 0877); The Forum Shops, 3500 Las Vegas Boulevard South (733 0787).
Website: www.discoverystore.com

FAO Schwarz
The Forum Shops, Caesars Palace, 3500 Las Vegas Boulevard South, between W Spring Mountain & Flamingo Roads (796 6500). Bus 301, 302. **Open** 10am-11pm Mon-Thur, Sun; 10am-midnight Fri, Sat. **Credit** AmEx, DC, Disc, MC, V.
FAO Schwarz is right up there with Willie Wonka's Chocolate Factory in terms of a child's dream come true. Three storeys of playthings make this one of the largest toy stores in the US. Serious collectors should visit the private room, which sells toys for up to $28,000.
Website: www.faoschwartz.com

Imagination Unlimited
Tropicana Nellis Shopping Village, 4934 E Tropicana Avenue, at Nellis Boulevard, East Las Vegas (434 5696). Bus 115, 201. **Open** 10am-6pm Mon-Thur, Sat; 10am-7pm Fri; 11am-5pm Sun. **Credit** AmEx, Disc, MC, V.
For kids and collectors: timeless dolls and bears, complex models, trainsets and miniatures, and plenty of sturdy Lego and Brio for active toddlers.
Branches: 3175 E Tropicana Avenue (434 7440); 3262 Civic Center Drive (649 3311).

Toys of Yesteryear
2028 E Charleston Boulevard, at Eastern Avenue, East Las Vegas (598 4030). Bus 110, 206. **Open** 11am-4pm Sat. **Credit** AmEx, Disc, MC, V.
Forget the dice clocks and take home a prized piece of Americana from your trip to Vegas. This tiny shop *(pictured)* has all sorts of old-fashioned toys and collectibles – including Kewpie dolls, *Star Wars* toys, cars and books – which are sure to trigger some treasured childhood memories. Check out the great collection of cast-metal toys.

---

and camping stuff – and staff are skilled, well informed and extremely personable.
Website: www.desertrocksports.com

Nevada Bob's
3999 Las Vegas Boulevard South, at Russell Road (451 3333). Bus 301, 302. **Open** 9am-9pm Mon-Fri; 9am-9pm Sat; 10am-9pm Sun. **Credit** AmEx, Disc, MC, V.
The world's largest chain of pro golf shops has several stores in Vegas. Choose from name brands such as Calloway, McGregor and Arnold Palmer – and keep an eye out for Vegas local, Tiger Woods.
Branches: see the phone book.

The Sports Authority
Sahara Pavilion, 2620 S Decatur Boulevard, at Sahara Avenue, South-west Las Vegas (368 3335). Bus 103, 204. **Open** 10am-9pm Mon-Fri; 9am-8pm Sat; 10am-6pm Sun. **Credit** AmEx, Disc, MC, V.
This chainstore in the Sahara Pavilion shopping centre is definitely the authority on selection and price, though staff assistance could do with a bit of fine-tuning. It offers a wide assortment of athletic fashions, plus equipment for every sport in the book, from canoeing to hunting.
Branch: 1431 W Sunset Road (433 2676).

Subskates

3736 E Flamingo Avenue, at Sandhill Road, East Las Vegas (435 1978). Bus 202. **Open** 10am-7pm Mon-Sat; 11am-5pm Sun. **Credit** AmEx, Disc, MC, V.
Snowboarders, bladers, skaters and anyone with a fetish for balancing on a board congregate here to purchase their equipment, plus lots of cool clothing – size XXXL, of course.
Branch: 840 N Rainbow Boulevard (258 3635).
Website: www.subskates.com

Fashion

Don't be fooled by all the tacky Vegas kitsch that pretty much assaults you once you get off the plane. Also, don't try to gauge local fashion by checking out what the tourists on the Strip are wearing. Laugh if you must, but believe this: Vegas has become a major fashion force to be reckoned with. Admittedly, this is largely to do with the increasingly upscale casino shopping malls and their designer marques rather than any homegrown talent.

Spend the rent at the new Via Bellagio on **Gucci**, **Prada**, **Chanel** and **Hermès**. Blow the bank at the Forum Shops at Caesars Palace bagging **Versace**, **Armani**, **Ferragamo**, **Louis Vuitton** and **Dior**. The Fashion Show Mall offers the chance to lighten your wallet at **Saks Fifth Avenue** and **Neiman Marcus**. You'll also have no trouble finding fashionable and cheaper chain-stores. **The Gap**, **Limited** and **Victoria's Secret** occupy space in most shopping malls mentioned in this chapter. Other slightly more upmarket chains, such as **Banana Republic**, **Guess** and **bebe**, can be found scattered among the big-dollar boutiques at the Forum Shops and the Venetian's Grand Canal Shoppes.

Abercrombie & Fitch

The Forum Shops, Caesars Palace, 3500 Las Vegas Boulevard South, between W Spring Mountain & Flamingo Roads (731 0712). Bus 301, 302. **Open** 10am-11pm Mon-Thur, Sun; 10am-midnight Fri, Sat. **Credit** AmEx, Disc, MC, V.
Mid-range casual men's and women's wear with a streetwise twist. Clothes are young, just the right side of trendy and usually nicely cut, too. Shoptalk: A&F doesn't carry anything in black.
Website: www.abercrombiefitch.com

Cache

Fashion Show Mall, 3200 Las Vegas Boulevard South, at W Spring Mountain Road (731 5548). Bus 203, 301, 302. **Open** 10am-9pm Mon-Fri; 10am-7pm Sat; noon-6pm Sun. **Credit** AmEx, DC, Disc, JCB, MC, V.
A class-act store for the upwardly mobile woman. You'll find conservative casual wear, business attire and formals.
Branches: The Forum Shops, Caesars Palace, 3500 Las Vegas Boulevard South (796 3532); The Galleria at Sunset Mall, 1300 Sunset Road (454 0026);

The Grand Canal Shoppes, Venetian, 3355 Las Vegas Boulevard South (733 0242).
Website: www.cache.com

The Men's Wearhouse

Sahara Pavilion, suites 45 & 46, 4570 W Sahara Avenue, at Decatur Boulevard, South-west Las Vegas (878 4330). Bus 103, 204. **Open** 10am-9pm Mon-Fri; 9.30am-6pm Sat; 11am-5pm Sun. **Credit** AmEx, Disc, MC, V.
This national chain is known to be *the* place for designer suits at discount prices. It also carries a varied selection of dress shoes and accessories.
Branches: 3519 Maryland Parkway (734 6150); 509 N Stephanie Street, Henderson (547 0890).
Website: www.menswearhouse.com

Pacific Sunwear of California

The Galleria at Sunset Mall, suite 2653, 1271 Galleria Drive, at Stephanie Street, Henderson (433 0003). Bus 212, 217. **Open** 10am-9pm Mon-Sat; 11am-6pm Sun. **Credit** AmEx, Disc, MC, V.
Surf's up, dude. Most of the merchandise is Pacific Sunwear's own label, but surfing brands, including O'Neill and Quicksilver, are also available.
Branch: Meadows Mall, 4300 Meadows Lane (878 3250); Belz Factory Outlet World, 7400 Las Vegas Boulevard South (897 1723).
Website: www.pacsun.com

Stash

Village Square, 9410 W Sahara Avenue, at Fort Apache Road, South-west Las Vegas (804 1640). Bus 204. **Open** 10am-7pm Mon-Thur; 10am-8pm Fri, Sat; noon-6pm Sun. **Credit** AmEx, Disc, MC, V.
Holding steady as one of the first off-Strip boutiques to offer upscale trend-ware for both men and women, Stash is a favourite with silver spoon-fed locals, transplants and tourists alike. You'll find designer jeans for your derrière, by the likes of Lucky Brand and Big Star, plus labels from Betsey Johnson, Bisou Bisou and Ann Ferriday, to name-drop a few.
Branch: 8876 Eastern Avenue (933 4567).

Structure

The Forum Shops, Caesars Palace, 3500 Las Vegas Boulevard South, between W Spring Mountain & Flamingo Roads (892 0421). Bus 301, 302. **Open** 10am-midnight daily. **Credit** AmEx, Disc, MC, V.
This classy and affordable store stocks men's contemporary wear for both work and play.
Branches: The Galleria at Sunset Mall, 1300 Sunset Road (898 3706); Fashion Show Mall, 3200 Las Vegas Boulevard South (732 2825); The Boulevard Mall, 3528 S Maryland Parkway (735 8355).

Accessories & jewellery

If you've hit the jackpot, you'll no doubt want to celebrate: head to Bellagio to pick up a tiara at **Tiffany & Co** (697 5400).

The Hat Company

Belz Factory Outlet World, 7400 Las Vegas Boulevard South, at Warm Springs Road, south of Las Vegas (897 1666). Bus 303. **Open** 10am-9pm Mon-Sat; 10am-6pm Sun. **Credit** AmEx, Disc, MC, V.

From Indiana Jones hats to Easter bonnets, the Hat Company has them all. The variety is overwhelming: plumed, flowered and ribboned; felt, cloth and straw; name brands such as Stetson, Kangol and Panama.

The Jewelers of Las Vegas

Tropicana, 3801 Las Vegas Boulevard South, at E Tropicana Avenue (798 5522). Bus 201, 301, 302. **Open** 9am-1am daily. **Credit** AmEx, DC, Disc, JCB, MC, V.

A pirate's chest of affordable treasures, with 12 Vegas locations, including ones inside the Tropicana, Las Vegas Hilton, Flamingo Hilton and the Desert Inn casinos. Brand names include Rolex, Piaget, Ebel, Baume & Mercier, Movado and Citizen. Watch repairs are carried out in-house and jewellery can be made to order.

Branches: see the phone book.
Website: www.thejewelers.com

John Fish Jewelers

Commercial Center, 953 E Sahara Avenue, between Paradise Road & Maryland Parkway, East Las Vegas (731 1323). Bus 204. **Open** 9.30am-5.30pm Mon-Sat. **Credit** AmEx, Disc, MC, V.

A hole-in-the-wall that hides some mind-blowing finds with price tags that will put a smile on your face. There's a little bit of everything: antiques, one-off jewellery from estate sales and custom-made modern designs.

Simayof Jewelers

The Grand Canal Shoppes, Venetian, 3355 Las Vegas Boulevard South, just south of Sands Avenue (731 1037). Bus 301, 302. **Open** 10am-11pm Mon-Thur; 10am-midnight Fri, Sat. **Credit** AmEx, DC, Disc, JCB, MC, V.

Looking as if they might have graced the likes of Sophia Loren, the brilliant diamond necklaces that fill the tiny windows at Simayof are stunners. Stand outside, mouth agape and get an eyeful, as diamond cutters perfect their craft right in front of you.

Children

There's a branch of **Gap Kids** in the Fashion Show Mall (796 0010); check the phone book for other locations.

Brats

Fashion Show Mall, 3200 Las Vegas Boulevard South, at W Spring Mountain Road (735 2728). Bus 203, 301, 302. **Open** 10am-9pm Mon-Fri; 10am-7pm Sat; noon-6pm Sun. **Credit** AmEx, DC, Disc, JCB, MC, V.

A kid's fashion boutique for your little prince or princess, with brands including Hollywood Babe, Sarah Sarah, San Francisco Blues, Flapdoodles, Cach-cach, Princess Kids, Guess and DKNY. Sizes are from infant to age 14.

Branch: Monte Carlo, 3770 Las Vegas Boulevard South (795 8350).

Wee Ones

3380 E Russell Road, suite 107, at Pecos Road, Henderson (898 6869). Bus 111. **Open** 10am-6pm Mon-Sat. **Credit** AmEx, Disc, MC, V.

Wee Ones offers thoughtfully recycled kids' clothes, furniture and toys as well as maternity clothing. Familiar and trusted names include Levi's, Playskool and Fisher Price. Merchandise quality is always great and prices are extremely reasonable.

Cleaning & repair

Al Phillips the Cleaner

2201 E Tropicana Avenue, at Eastern Avenue, University District (736 6029). **Open** 24hrs daily. **Credit** MC, V.

Al Phillips is the largest dry-cleaning chain in the Western US, with 15 drive-through Vegas locations. Eight of them are open 24 hours a day, seven days a week, and all provide dry-cleaning, laundry, alterations, shoe repairs (all same-day service) and men's formal wear hire. Suede and leather cleaning is available as well.

Branches: see the phone book.

Cora's Coin Laundry

1097 E Tropicana Avenue, at Maryland Parkway, University District (736 6181). Bus 108, 201. **Open** 8am-9pm daily. **No credit cards.**

Located just two miles off the Strip, Cora's is popular with UNLV folk. It's clean, open seven days a week and near a yummy Thai restaurant. It offers self-service or drop-off laundry, dry-cleaning and, yes, there are video poker machines.

Eldorado Cleaners

3650 S Decatur Boulevard, at Twain Avenue, Northwest Las Vegas (248 2735). Bus 103. **Open** 7am-7pm Mon-Sat. **No credit cards.**

Eldorado's (aka 1.25 Cleaners) sometimes offers coupons in the newspaper for 99¢ dry-cleaning, and for a little more you can opt for same-day turn-around on duds in before 9am.

Branches: 236 S Decatur Boulevard, (880 9701); 3280 E Tropicana Avenue (898 8238).

Discount

Burlington Coat Factory

4750 Eastern Avenue, at E Tropicana Avenue, University District (451 5581). Bus 110, 201. **Open** 10am-9pm Mon-Sat; 11am-6pm Sun. **Credit** AmEx, Disc, MC, V.

The name of this outlet store is a bit deceptive. True, there are coats, plenty of them, in fact, and at great prices – but also linens, baby furnishings, suits, handbags and more. Like most discount stores, there's often a sense of disorder about the place, but good buys are abundant and easy to spot.

Branch: 5959 W Sahara Avenue (247 1268).

Eyewear

Davante

The Forum Shops, Caesars Palace, 3500 Las Vegas Boulevard South, between W Spring Mountain & Flamingo Roads (737 8585). Bus 301, 302. **Open** 10am-11pm Mon-Thur, Sun; 10am-midnight Fri, Sat. **Credit** AmEx, DC, Disc, JCB, MC, V.

Find your favorite eyewear from more than 50 of the world's top designers in this beautiful boutique setting. An optician will assist you with your prescription. Non-prescription eyewear also available.
Branches: see the phone book.

Frame Fixer
3961 W Charleston Boulevard, at Valley View Boulevard, North-west Las Vegas (735 7879).
Bus 206. **Open** 10am-5.30pm Mon-Fri; 10am-4pm Sat. **Credit** AmEx, Disc, MC, V.
Sometimes it's cheaper to repair than replace, and this fast, friendly place is a good bet.

Shoes

There are branches of **Salvatore Ferragamo** in the Forum Shops and the Fashion Show Mall, and of **Kenneth Cole** in the Forum Shops and the Grand Canal Shoppes. Many of the major Strip casino-hotels can arrange shoe-repair service.

Cactus Boot & Shoe Repair
5000 W Charleston Avenue, at Decatur Boulevard, North-west Las Vegas (877 0800). Bus 103, 206.
Open 8.30am-5pm Mon-Fri; 9am-5pm Sat. **Credit** AmEx, Disc, MC, V.
Not exactly next door to the Strip, but if you're mobile, this is a good bet. The kind souls (sorry) who run the place are friendly and fast, and prices are reasonable. Suede cleaning is also available.

Desert Birkenstock
The Village, 3920 W Charleston Boulevard, at Valley View Boulevard, North-west Las Vegas (877 9577).
Bus 104, 206. **Open** 10am-6pm Mon-Sat. **Credit** AmEx, Disc, MC, V.
The only downside to Birkenstocks is that they'll make all your other shoes seem painfully constricting by comparison. Available in myriad styles and colours, they mould to fit the shape of your feet and will last virtually forever.
Branches: 2427 E Tropicana Avenue (454 0114); 2732 N Green Valley Parkway (433 6336).

Hot Foot Shoes
9420 W Sahara Avenue, at Fort Apache Road, North-west Las Vegas (579 9672). Bus 105, 204.
Open 10am-6pm Mon-Thur; 10am-7pm Fri, Sat; noon-5pm Sun. **Credit** AmEx, Disc, MC, V.
A trek out to this classy shoe and accessory shop could save you hours of trudging through casino malls looking at one designer shop after another. Hot Foot Shoes carries the best of the lot, including Kenneth Cole, Via Spiga, Charles David, DKNY and Cole Haan. Seasonal clearances and frequent sales.

Johnston & Murphy Shoe Shop
Fashion Show Mall, 3200 Las Vegas Boulevard South, at Spring Mountain Road (737 0114). Bus 203, 301, 302. **Open** 10am-9pm Mon-Fri; 10am-7pm Sat; noon-5pm Sun. **Credit** AmEx, Disc, MC, V.
Skilfully crafted men's shoes.

Just For Feet
The Forum Shops, Caesars Palace, 3500 Las Vegas Boulevard South, between W Spring Mountain &

Flamingo Roads (791 3482). Bus 301, 302. **Open** 10am-11pm Mon-Thur, Sun; 10am-midnight Fri, Sat. **Credit** AmEx, Disc, MC, V.
Every kind of athletic shoe, with styles by New Balance, Nike, Reebok, Converse, Adidas and more, plus a fair selection of hiking boots and Doc Martens. The Caesars store is a huge, multi-level beast, with a place for shooting hoops upstairs and a giant video screen. Staff are usually overworked and under-interested, but if you know what you want, you'll do fine.
Branch: 4500 W Sahara Avenue (878 7463).

Naturalizer Shoe Company
Boulevard Mall, 3528 S Maryland Parkway, between E Desert Inn Road & Twain Avenue, East Las Vegas (791 0722). Bus 109, 112, 203, 213. **Open** 10am-9pm Mon-Fri; 10am-8pm Sat; 11am-6pm Sun. **Credit** Disc, MC, V.
Who says comfort and fashion don't mix? Here you'll find classic women's high heels, loafers, flats and boots that rival tennis shoes for comfort. Styles are designed for the mature and refined shopper.
Branch: The Galleria at Sunset Mall, 1300 Sunset Road (434 3237).

Red Wing Shoes
4616 W Charleston Avenue, at Decatur Boulevard, North-west Las Vegas (870 4244). Bus 103, 206.
Open 9.30am-7.30pm Mon-Fri; 11am-5pm Sat, Sun. **Credit** AmEx, Disc, MC, V.
Red Wing specialises in work boots and hiking boots. Prices are good, and staff exceedingly helpful: they offer polish and shoe repair and will even break in 'hotspots' before you leave the store.

Wild Pair Shoe Store
Boulevard Mall, 3528 S Maryland Parkway, between E Desert Inn Road & Twain Avenue, East Las Vegas (369 9356). Bus 109, 112, 203, 213. **Open** 10am-9pm Mon-Fri; 10am-8pm Sat; 11am-6pm Sun.
Credit AmEx, Disc, MC, V.
Fun, funky shoes often available at super money-saving prices. A good bet if you need to find kicks for last-minute clubbing, though you might want to look elsewhere for the conservative, 'suit-wearing-job-interview' slip-ons.

Specialist

For information on where to hire wedding outfits, and for the fabulous and venerable **Williams Costume Company**, a Vegas stalwart since 1959, *see page 38* **Weddings**.

Rent-A-Dress & Tux Shop
Sahara Paradise Plaza, 2240 Paradise Road, at Sahara Avenue, East of Strip (796 6444). Bus 108, 204. **Open** 10am-9pm Mon-Sat; 11am-4pm Sun.
Credit AmEx, Disc, MC, V.
Whether you're in search of an elegant evening gown, a flashy cocktail dress, bridal wear or a standard tux, you'll find it in the racks of this diverse store. There's a seamstress on the premises for alterations and adjustments. It also has shoes.
Website: www.weddinginvegas.com

Only in Vegas

Of course, Las Vegas has supermarkets, department stores, auto parts suppliers, chi-chi boutiques and all those other boring, normal retail outlets. But who cares? This city is all about image, and in this instance, image means 'Vegas, bay-bee!'. While the rest of the monied hordes are schlepping through the upscale resort malls, dropping dosh on stuff they can find in any other global city, you will have the inside track on items that really say 'Las Vegas'. And don't think that means cheap, tacky souvenirs. Then again, don't think it doesn't.

A Little Off the Top

3140 S Valley View Boulevard, between Desert Inn Road & Sahara Avenue, West of Strip (222 3599). Bus 104. **Open** 10am-6pm Tue-Fri; 10am-5pm Sat. **Credit** MC, V.

Lovely, lingerie-clad ladies will trim and blow-dry your hair, and even throw in a neck and shoulder massage for a price that'll make you blush. This tiny joint tends to be especially popular with the men. Imagine that.

Website: www.alittleoffthetop.com

Bare Essentials Fantasy Fashion

4029 W Sahara Avenue, at Valley View Boulevard, West of Strip (247 4711). Bus 104, 204. **Open** 10am-7pm Mon-Sat; noon-5pm Sun. **Credit** AmEx, Disc, MC, V.

Whether you're a young stripper weekending in Vegas or an empty nester looking to spice up a lengthy marriage, the boys at Bare Essentials will outfit you the right way with lingerie, bikinis, G-strings, sky-high platforms and even feather boas. The campy gay owners are right when they say that women feel at ease shopping in their store.

Bonanza: The World's Largest Gift Shop

2460 Las Vegas Boulevard South, at Sahara Avenue (385 7359). Bus 204, 301, 302. **Open** 8am-midnight daily. **Credit** AmEx, Disc, MC, V.

If it is Las Vegas-related kitsch you want, behold the jackpot. Roulette-wheel ashtrays, Elvis sunglasses-sideburn combos, slot machine salt-and-pepper sets, coin-filled toilet seats, used playing cards and dice clocks galore fill aisle after aisle.

Chanel

Bellagio, 3600 Las Vegas Boulevard South, at W Flamingo Road (765 5505). Bus 202, 301, 302. **Open** 10am-midnight daily. **Credit** AmEx, DC, JCB, MC, V.

You won't find any cheap trinkets at this boutique from one of the world's most renowned fashion figures. Sure, precious gems can be found anywhere, but not the Priscilla Presley diamond-and-sapphire necklace (which she wore to the Bellagio grand opening), priced at a cool $262,000. Diamonds may be a girl's best friend elsewhere, but in Las Vegas, diamonds are forever.

Elvis-A-Rama Museum

3401 S Industrial Road, at Desert Inn Road, West of Strip (309 7200). Bus 203, 301, 302. **Open** 10am-6pm daily. **Admission** museum $9.95. **Credit** AmEx, MC, V.

Opened in November 1999 behind the Fashion Show Mall, Las Vegas finally has a shrine to one of its most enduring icons. There's a museum, a jam-packed gift shop – supposedly the largest outside Memphis – and you can even get married here. The museum has $3-million worth of Elvis memorabilia, including cars, a boat, a gold lamé suit and other clothes, and every couple of hours an Elvis impersonator performs a 15-minute show.

Website: www.insidervlv.com

Gamblers Book Club

620 S 11th Street, at Charleston Boulevard, Downtown (382 7555). Bus 109, 206. **Open** 9am-5pm Mon-Sat. **Credit** Disc, MC, V.

If this shop is any indication, gambling is still king, the Mob never left and Disneyland might as well keep its influence in Southern California, where they go for that kind of stuff. Supposedly the largest distributor of gambling books in the world, if it contains words about the games, the legendary figures or Las Vegas, it's in the Gambler's Book Club.
Website: www.gamblersbook.com

Gamblers General Store

800 S Main Street, at Hoover Avenue, Downtown (382 9903). Bus 108, 204. **Open** 9am-5pm daily. **Credit** AmEx, Disc, MC, V.
If you can't bear to leave and desperately want to live la vida Vegas when you get home, this is the place for you. All manner of gaming hardware – craps tables, roulette wheels, gaming layouts, poker chips, slot machines – are available, and they'll even ship it for you (though some items cannot be shipped to some places). *See photo.*
Website: www.ggss.com

Judith Leiber Boutique

The Forum Shops, Caesars Palace, 3500 Las Vegas Boulevard South, between W Spring Mountain & Flamingo Roads (893 4800). Bus 301, 302.
Open 10am-11pm Mon-Thur, Sun; 10am-midnight Fri, Sat. **Credit** AmEx, Disc, JCB, MC, V.
In any shape, a Judith Leiber handbag whispers 'great taste!', 'an eye for detail' and 'you must be loaded!'. But when that $2,550 purse is shaped like a valentine and emblazoned with 13,000 Austrian rhinestones depicting the queen of hearts, it can only scream out 'Las Vegas!'. Don't miss the king of spades handbag and dice pillboxes.

Lost Vegas Gallery & Gifts

Arts Factory, 101 E Charleston Boulevard, between Main Street & Casino Center Boulevard, Downtown (388 8857). Bus 113, 206. **Open** 10am-4pm Tue-Sat.
Just because it's a gallery doesn't mean it's a

snooty, kitsch-free zone. Photos and postcards illustrate Vegas's high-rolling, Rat Packing, Elvis-laden atomic-blast past, while the works of local artists primp for buyers. All things Vegas can be found here, in more interesting and whimsical dress than at a standard gift shop. *See photo.*

Paradise Electro Stimulations

1509 W Oakey Boulevard, at Western Avenue, Stratosphere Area (474 2991). Bus 105. **Open** 9am-7pm Mon-Fri. **Credit** AmEx, Disc, MC, V.
Skip the strip shows and charge straight (or not) to the worldwide headquarters for Dant'e Amore's electrically enhanced sex toys. These playthings all have one goal in mind: raising your wattage to a fever pitch. For more details, *see p222* **Nightlife: Adult**.
Website: www.peselectro.com

Red Rooster Antique Mall

307 W Charleston Boulevard, at Martin Luther King Boulevard, North-west Las Vegas (382 5253). Bus 207. **Open** 10am-6pm Mon-Sat; noon-5pm Sun. **Credit** AmEx, MC, V.
A labyrinth of cluttered rooms and dozens of individually run stalls mean dusty magazines hold shelf space next to $100 antique amber bottles. Look carefully and you'll find delightful old casino memorabilia: ashtrays, gaming chips, matchbooks, postcards and much more.

Serges Showgirl Wigs

953 E Sahara Avenue, at Maryland Parkway, East Las Vegas (732 1015). Bus 109, 204. **Open** 10am-5.30pm Mon-Sat. **Credit** AmEx, Disc, MC, V.
Wigs were big in the 1960s, but in Vegas, where hair has always been big, they never went out of style. Serges, the world's largest retailer of wigs, offers thousands of natural and synthetic hairpieces in hundreds of styles and colours. It sells mainly to showgirls, but anyone can browse and buy. *See photo.*
Website: www.showgirlwigs.com

Siegfried & Roy Boutique

Mirage, 3400 Las Vegas Boulevard South, between Spring Mountain & W Flamingo Roads (791 7111). Bus 301, 302. **Open** *summer* 10am-7pm daily; *winter* 11am-6pm Mon-Fri, 10am-6pm Sat, Sun. **Credit** AmEx, DC, Disc, JCB, MC, V.
In the 1950s it was Louis Prima and Keely Smith; in the '70s, Tom Jones and Elvis Presley. Today, it is magicians Siegfried and Roy that the world knows, and the pair obliges that notoriety with a gift shop specialising in all the S&R merchandise you could want: stuffed tigers, books, CDs, pyjamas, even boxer shorts.

Shepler's Western Wear

3025 E Tropicana Avenue, between McLeod Drive & Pecos Road, East Las Vegas (898 3000). Bus 201. **Open** 10am-9pm Mon-Sat; 11am-6pm Sun. **Credit** AmEx, Disc, MC, V.

Whoa, bronco! From boots with fringes to belt buckles the size of solar reflectors, Shepler's stocks the latest in rodeo wear for cowboys, cowgirls and cowkids. Ideal for souvenirs of the Wild Wild West. **Branch:** 3025 W Sahara Avenue (258 2000).

Underwear

You'll find classy lingerie at Neiman Marcus, Lord & Taylor and Macy's. Branches of that underwear staple, **Victoria's Secret**, are in malls all over town; check the phone book for details. *See also page 180* **Only in Vegas**.

Frederick's of Hollywood

3725 S Maryland Parkway, at Twain Avenue, East of Strip (734 2070). Bus 108, 203. **Open** 10am-9pm Mon-Fri; 10am-6pm Sat; noon-5pm Sun. **Credit** AmEx, Disc, MC, V.

The old standby for wild lingerie, although it's actually somewhere closer to mild these days. A recent campaign saw Frederick's trying to be a more couple-friendly store by offering 'classier' lingerie for men and women. Did it succeed? Does it matter? *Website: www.fredericks.com*

Vintage & stylish second-hand

The Attic

1018 S Main Street, just north of Charleston Boulevard, Downtown (388 4088). Bus 206. **Open** 9am-6pm daily. **Credit** DC, Disc, MC, V.

Probably the most popular in the Vegas vintage category, thanks to an eye-catching, colourful store and some savvy advertising. The street-level floor has furniture, appliances and the like, while one level above you'll find clothing, shoes, oddities and accessories. Admission (really!) costs $1, refundable on purchase. Café Neon is located on the upper level of the shop (*see p168* **Bars & Cafés**). The store is often called upon by Hollywood film producers for props and clothing while filming in Vegas. *Website: www.atticvintage.com*

Bricktop & Boris

Commercial Center, 900 E Karen Avenue, at Sahara Avenue, East Las Vegas (735 3007). Bus 204. **Open** 10am-7pm Mon-Sat. **Credit** AmEx, Disc, MC, V.

Picture the estate sale of a rich, eccentric woman and you'll have an idea of the contents of this tiny boutique. A thorough search will often net you a find, or even hundreds of finds if you're into feathers, rhinestones and fake fur.

Buffalo Exchange

Pioneer Center, suite 18, 4110 S Maryland Parkway, at Flamingo Road, University District (791 3960). Bus 109, 202, 213. **Open** 11am-7pm Mon-Sat; noon-6pm Sun. **Credit** MC, V.

One of Vegas's most popular young adult shopping spots, Buffalo Exchange has price tags that fall somewhere between budget and mid-level. The clothing is mainly second-hand with some new items from shop clear-outs, but just as stylish as anything to be found in a mall. *Website: www.buffaloexchange.com*

Retro Vintage Couture

Valley View Plaza, 906 S Valley View Road, at Charleston Boulevard, North-west Las Vegas (877 8989). Bus 104. **Open** 11am-7pm Tue-Fri; 11am-6pm Sat. **Credit** AmEx, Disc, MC, V.

This is one of the first real vintage 'boutiques' in Las Vegas. You're sure to be greeted warmly and made to feel important by proprietress Melina Crisostomo, who has gone the extra step in order to make shopping at this tiny gem a pleasure. This stuff is vintage, not thrift, so prices will be higher than at your local charity shop, but the quality and calibre of the clothing are vastly different as well: beautiful, classically tailored suits and dresses and a generous selection of shoes and accessories. There's a jam-packed rack of sale clothing in front of the store.

Savers Thrift Department Store

5130 W Spring Mountain Road, at Decatur Boulevard, South-west Las Vegas (220 7350). Bus 103, 203. **Open** 9am-9pm Mon-Sat; 10am-6pm Sun. **Credit** Disc, MC, V.

Savers offers no-frills, second-hand shopping in locations that look as if they might have been grocery stores in a previous incarnation. The name is somewhat deceptive: the goods are certainly plentiful, but it can be a bit disconcerting to see the price tag on a pair of violently worn Levi's. Shoppers keep coming back for the daily deals, however, such as department discounts and tag sales.

Branches: 1100 E Charleston Boulevard (474 4773); 3145 E Tropicana Avenue (433 1402); 3121 N Rancho Drive (658 0083).

Food & drink

Bakeries

Byblos Café

Mediterranean Restaurant & Bakery, 4825 W Flamingo Road, at Decatur Boulevard, West of Strip (222 1801). Bus 103, 202. **Open** 10am-10pm Mon-Sat. **Credit** AmEx, DC, Disc, JCB, MC, V.

Treat yourself to a visit to the pastry case here. From the wickedly delicious maamohl (rose water and cream pie encrusted with pistachios) to the decadent shibeeb (filo-wrapped, honey-dipped cream), and the guilt-inducing namora (lightly fried dough, dipped in honey), the possibilities for pleasure are endless.

Diamond Bakery

Chinatown Mall, 4255 W Spring Mountain Road, at Wynn Road, West of Strip (368 1886). Bus 203. **Open** 9am-9pm daily. **Credit** AmEx, Disc, MC, V.

Exotic and enticing offerings, sweet and otherwise: chicken cookies, apple turnovers, ham and cheese rolls, steamed cream buns, fresh fruitcakes and, of course, mile-high wedding cakes and children's birthday cakes. Staff are patient and knowledgeable.

Less crowded than the other boulangerie at Paris and a bit gentler on the nerves, Lenôtre is loaded with luscious éclairs, cakes, cookies and croissants. You still have to order cafeteria-style, but it's bright and spacious and there's plenty to keep the eyes happy while you wait.

Toscano's Baking Co

Rio, 3700 W Flamingo Road, at Valley View Boulevard, West of Strip (364 8724). Bus 202. **Open** 7am-8pm daily. **Credit** AmEx, Disc, JCB, MC, V.
Giant cinnamon rolls and massive muffins, speciality breads, pies and cheesecakes are all freshly baked daily. Not a bargain bakery by any means, but even the smallest expenditure will be rewarding. Toscano's also makes wedding cakes.

Beer & wine

Cost Plus World Market (*see page 187*) has one of the best priced and most varied wine and imported beer selections in town.

La Cave

Paris, 3655 Las Vegas Boulevard South, between Harmon Avenue & E Flamingo Road (946 4339). Bus 202, 301, 302. **Open** 9am-11pm daily. **Credit** AmEx, Disc, DC, JCB, MC, V.
La Cave may well disappoint real wine enthusiasts and if you're looking for a moderately priced bottle to enjoy in your room, you'll probably be disappointed, too; the mark-up on some labels is very steep. However, it's handy to have champagne and sparkling wine available for impromptu windfall and wedding celebrations (Dom Perrignon and Perrier Jouet stand out), and there's an interesting smattering of pâtés and imported cheeses, plus tins of cookies, truffles and other trifles.

Lee's Discount Liquor

3480 E Flamingo Road, at Pecos Road, East Las Vegas (458 5700). Bus 111, 202. **Open** 9am-10pm Mon-Thur; 9am-11pm Fri, Sat; 9am-9pm Sun. **Credit** AmEx, Disc, MC, V.
A combination of old favourites, hard-to-find European wines and liqueurs and dirt-cheap prices make Lee's the best liquor store in town. If it's not stocked, staff can probably order it. Refrigerated coolers offer a surprising sampling of beer from around the planet, and a few hard ciders as well. The selection of hardcore magazines on display very close to the cashier is somewhat distracting – some customers may take offence, and some may take children. Please do neither.
Branches: see the phone book.

Spirits Plus Liquor & Wine Shops

4880 W Flamingo Road, at Decatur Boulevard, South-west Las Vegas (873 6000). Bus 103, 202. **Open** 8am-11pm Mon-Fri; 8am-midnight Sat; 8am-10pm Sun. **Credit** AmEx, Disc, MC, V.
As well as the usual range of alcohol, there's caviar royale and cigars and liquor-catering services. The store also has an underground wine cellar and a sommelier on site from Tuesday to Saturday.

Oh la la! French pastries at **Lenôtre**.

Great Harvest Bread Company

Sunset Mountain Vista Plaza, suite A, 4650 Sunset Road, at Mountain Vista Street, Green Valley (547 1555). Bus 212. **Open** 7am-7pm Mon-Sat. **Credit** MC, V.
Banana walnut, white cheddar garlic, cranberry orange, spinach feta, apple crumble – freshly baked breads for breakfast, lunch, dinner and dessert fill this shop with a truly mouth-watering aroma. Free sample slices – not pieces, but entire slices – are offered daily.

Las Vegas Bakery

4734 E Flamingo Road, at Boulder Highway, East Las Vegas (458 2192). Bus 202. **Open** 8am-7pm Mon-Sat; 8am-2pm Sun.
No credit cards.
This bakery is open seven days a week and specialises in cakes, most notably the oft-requested 'emergency' wedding cake. With as little as two hours' notice, the masterful team of bakers can produce a stunning celebratory cake and save the day. Viva Las Vegas Bakery!

Lenôtre

Paris, 3655 Las Vegas Boulevard South, between Harmon Avenue & E Flamingo Road (946 4341). Bus 202, 301, 302. **Open** 7am-11pm daily. **Credit** AmEx, Disc, DC, MC, V.

The Wine Cellar

*Rio, 3700 W Flamingo Road, at Valley View
Boulevard, West of Strip (247 7962). Bus 202.*
Open 11am-midnight Mon-Thur; 10am-2am Fri, Sat;
10am-midnight Sun. **Credit** AmEx, Disc, DC, JCB,
MC, V.

By far the finest selection of wine anywhere in Las
Vegas, the retail arm of the Rio's impressive cellars
has about 150 kinds of wine on sale, ranging in price
from $8 to $400. A vast selection is available by the
glass in 'tastings' for $6 to $60. Any questions are
addressed by not one, but two resident sommeliers.

Ethnic

Eliseevsky Russian-European Food

*4825 W Flamingo Road, at Decatur Boulevard, West
of Strip (247 8766). Bus 103, 202.* **Open** 10am-8pm
Mon-Sat; noon-6pm Sun. **Credit** MC, V.

Albeit a bit spartan, this family-owned Russian deli
and grocer is a find. The shelves are filled with
cryptically labelled delicacies and sweets in fantastic wrappings, while sodas, juices, sparkling
water and kefir (a yoghurt drink) fill the cooler
alongside rich cakes and cream cheeses. The deli
case houses salads, pirojki, caviar, smoked fish and
hard salamis, and there are also Russian speciality
items, including nesting dolls, bumper stickers
videos, cassettes, books and magazines.

Gee's Oriental Market

*4109 W Sahara Avenue, at Valley View Boulevard,
West of Strip (362 5287). Bus 104, 204.* **Open** 8am-
8pm daily. **Credit** Disc, MC, V.

The place for Chinese, Thai, Vietnamese and
Filipino groceries, with first-rate fresh produce and
seafood. Gee's claim to fame is that it's the only place
in Las Vegas to carry meang da na, a cockroach-like
insect that is considered an oriental delicacy.

India Sweets & Spices

*Commercial Center, 953 E Sahara Avenue, between
Paradise Road & Maryland Parkway, East Las
Vegas (892 0720). Bus 204.* **Open** 11am-8pm daily.
Credit AmEx, Disc, MC, V.

Come here for curry spices, a small array of Indian
and Pakistani groceries and a weekend deli offering
samosas and the like.

International Marketplace

*5000 S Decatur Boulevard, at Reno Street, south of
W Tropicana Avenue, West of Strip (889 2888).
Bus 103, 201.* **Open** 9am-8pm Mon-Fri; 9am-6pm
Sat, Sun. **Credit** AmEx, MC, V.

Hard to miss, this huge building is a warehouse of
imported edibles, goodies and gadgetry of every
kind. Heavy on the Asian influence, it has plenty of
delicacies and oddities in every conceivable package, bag, box and tin, plus a mind-boggling assortment of teas and honey. Prices are on the serious side
of cheap and many items are available in bulk.

Italcream

*3871 Valley View Boulevard, at W Spring Mountain
Road, West of Strip (873 2214). Bus 104, 203.*
Open 8am-4pm Mon-Fri. **No credit cards.**

Magnifico! Giovanni Parente and his family are
Italians with a secret recipe for the best gelato we've
ever tasted. After a visit to Italcream,you'll want to
ditch those trashy souvenirs and stuff your suitcases with ice-cream instead.

Mediterranean Café & Market

*Tiffany Square, 4147 S Maryland Parkway, at
E Flamingo Road, University District (731 6030).
Bus 109, 202.* **Open** *café* 11am-8pm daily; *market*
9.30am-8pm Mon-Fri; 9.30am-5pm Sat. **Credit**
AmEx, Disc, MC, V.

Shop at the excellent grocery/deli for a wide variety
of Arabic, Armenian, Greek and Iranian groceries,
then visit the relaxed next-door café for the best
baklava in town. Warning: you might be distracted
by a lovely belly dancer undulating near your table.

Siena Deli

*Renaissance Plaza, 2250 E Tropicana Avenue, at
Eastern Avenue, University District (736 8424).
Bus 110, 201.* **Open** 10am-6pm Mon-Sat; 10am-4pm
Sun. **Credit** AmEx, DC, Disc, MC, V.

The Italian owner of this deli/restaurant has brought
Italy's finest cuisine to Vegas. Prices may be steep
($144 for aged balsamic vinegar), but the quality and
authenticity are impeccable. Siena also carries a
wide variety of Italian cooking hardware such as
pasta machines.

Branch: 5755 Spring Mountain Road (871 8616).

Gourmet

Village Meats & Wine

*Village East Plaza, 5025 Eastern Avenue, at
E Tropicana Avenue, University District (736 7575).
Bus 110, 201.* **Open** 10am-6pm Tue-Sat.
Credit MC, V.

Caviar, pâté, fine cheeses and aged beef… this is the
place to come for all the trappings of a gourmet feast.
A nice bottle of French wine completes the perfect
ensemble for a romantic evening.

Health food & vitamins

J'n'J Health Foods

*Gold's Plaza, 3776 E Flamingo Road, at Sandhill
Road, East Las Vegas (456 7807). Bus 202.* **Open**
9am-6pm daily. **Credit** AmEx, Disc, MC, V.

This store is designed for muscle men and gym bun-
nies with abs of steel. There's a limited selection of
food and cosmetics, but J'n'J makes up for it with
Vegas's best array of high-tech body-building/ weight-
losing/fat-burning/thigh-sculpting/gut-trimming
bars, shakes and pills. Prices are unbeatable.

Rainbow's End Natural Foods

*1100 E Sahara Avenue, at Maryland Parkway,
East Las Vegas (737 7282). Bus 109, 204.* **Open**
9am-9pm Mon-Fri; 9am-8pm Sat; 11am-6pm Sun.
Credit AmEx, Disc, MC, V.

Rainbow's End offers a broad choice of herbs, vita-
mins and bodycare products, but limited produce
and food. A café full of veggie delights makes up
half the store and is a good place for lunch.

Sugarless Shack

Topaz Plaza, 2570 E Tropicana Avenue, at Topaz Street, East Las Vegas (450 9728). Bus 201. **Open** 9.30am-6pm Mon-Sat. **Credit** AmEx, Disc, MC,V.
A diabetic's fantasy land. Here you can satisfy that pesky sweet tooth with goodies that are, well, almost as good as the real thing.

Wild Oats Community Market

3455 E Flamingo Road, at Pecos Road, East Las Vegas (434 8115). Bus 111, 202. **Open** 8am-9pm daily. **Credit** MC, V.
Wild Oats monopolises the Vegas health food industry, and for good reason. Prices are a bit steep, but its stock of organic produce, health foods, natural bodycare products, homoeopathic medicines and macrobiotic supplies is exemplary. The adjacent café offers fab juices and healthy snacks.
Branch: 6720 W Sahara Avenue (253 7050).
Website: www.wildoats.com

Supermarkets & grocery stores

There are four main supermarket chains in Las Vegas. **Albertson's** has in-store bakeries and a swell selection of other baked goods; it also gets the nod for the best supermarket seafood offerings. **Smith's** stores tend to be older and a little pricier than the others. Some branches house a Chinese kitchen (good for cheap lunches) and some have Goldenswirl, the paragon of frozen yoghurt stands. **Vons** is similar in price to Smiths, with a good health and beauty section and bountiful fresh fruits and veggies. The newcomer is **Raley's**.

This Californian chain offers an extensive health food section and manages to keep prices lower than its competitors. For details of supermarket locations, consult the Yellow Pages.

British Grocery Store

Pioneer Square, 3375 S Decatur Boulevard, at Desert Inn Road, West of Strip (579 7777). Bus 103. **Open** 10am-8pm Mon-Fri; 10am-6pm Sat. **Credit** MC, V.
Reportedly, more than 30,000 Brits now call Las Vegas home. To dispel any lingering homesickness, Lorna Alexander's shop offers copies of the latest *Sunday Times*, as well as marmalade, teas, sweets, fruit squash and so on. The freezers are stocked with steak and kidney pies, sausage rolls, black pudding, scones and more, and the dairy case holds clotted cream and Red Leicester cheese.
Website: www.britishgrocers.com

Trader Joe's

2101 S Decatur Boulevard, at O'Bannon Drive, one block north of Sahara Avenue, North-west Las Vegas (367 0227). Bus 103, 105, 204. **Open** 9am-9pm daily. **Credit** Disc, MC, V.
Trader Joe's emulates the old-time neighbourhood grocery with a twist: the products are all tested to ensure they are 'the best' (it claims) of their kind. The ambience is New Agey, but there's plenty of hedonism to be found among the healthy: delicious imported chocolate and cookies, and decadent party and snack foods. High quality and highish prices.
Branch: 2716 N Green Valley Parkway, Henderson (433 6773).
Website: www.traderjoes.com

Bad hair day? Let the experts at **Diva Salon** *sort you out. See page 186.*

Many of the casinos have lavish full-service spas and beauty salons; for details of some of the best, *see page 243* **Sport & Fitness: Health spas**.

Complementary medicine

Healthy Alternatives

820 Rancho Lane, suite 20, between Tonopah Avenue & Charleston Boulevard, North-west Las Vegas (382 5717). Bus 106, 206, 215. **Open** 10am-6pm Tue-Sat. **Credit** AmEx, MC, V.
Here you'll find consultation, therapy, education and training all in one place. Get help from a naturopathic doctor, advice on Ayurvedics, herbal and supplement recommendations, massage and energy work, even laser therapy. Training is available in meditation, yoga and tai-chi. Note that it's on a small inlet of Rancho Lane, off the main drag.

T&T Ginseng

Chinatown Mall, 4215 W Spring Mountain Road, at Wynn Road, South-west Las Vegas (368 3898). Bus 203. **Open** 10am-8.30pm daily. **Credit** MC, V.
A fascinating store and natural herbal pharmacy. The uninitiated (and those who don't read Chinese), shouldn't be intimidated by the labels – diagnosis and treatment are handled with ancient wisdom and extreme care. An oriental medical doctor and herbalist are on duty daily.

Worton's Palmistry Studios

1441 Las Vegas Boulevard South, at Convention Center Drive (386 0121). Bus 301, 302. **Open** by appointment. **No credit cards**.
Holding hands with Las Vegas since 1958, this wonderful place offers professional palmistry and astrology and then some. It's located on the northern, more eclectic, end of the Strip.

Hair salons

Diva Studio

3159 W Tompkins Avenue, between Polaris Avenue & Industrial Road, West of Strip (736 2011). Bus 201. **Open** 9am-7pm Mon-Sat.
For the down-to-earth diva (or dude) wanting great service at minimal expense in a trendy, neo-classical atmosphere. Treatments include massage, facials, reflexology, waxing, facials, body sculpture, Juliette detox wraps and manicures and pedicures. Great haircuts, too.

Dolphin Court

7581 W Lake Mead, at Buffalo Road, North-west Las Vegas (432 9772). Bus 210. **Open** 8am-9pm Mon-Sat; 9am-6pm Sun. **Credit** AmEx, DC, Disc, MC, V.
This place employs some of the best colourists in Las Vegas. If you're serious about healthy hair, skin and nails, come here to get solid advice and professional care. Yes, it's worth the extra money. Full spa services are available.
Branch: 3455 S Durango Drive (949 9999).
Website: www.dolphincourt.com

Absolute Ink: skin art by Iron Mike.

Euphoria Salon & Day Spas

Monte Carlo, 3770 Las Vegas Boulevard South, at Rue de Monte Carlo, between W Flamingo Road & Tropicana Avenue (895 7600). Bus 301, 302. **Open** 9am-7pm daily. **Credit** AmEx, DC, Disc, JCB, MC, V.
Euphoria is a familiar name in Vegas, with more than half a dozen locations around town. Stylists are competent and haircuts reasonably priced. As for the spa end of it, the hotel-based operations tend to be a bit more luxurious.
Branches: see the phone book.

Southern Nevada University of Cosmetology

Tropicana Plaza, 3430 E Tropicana Avenue, at Pecos Road, East Las Vegas (458 6333). Bus 111, 201. **Open** 8am-4.30pm Tue-Sat. **No credit cards**.
Conserve cash with a visit to the other university in Las Vegas. All work is done by students who are under constant scrutiny, which means they're 50 times more careful than your average stylist, though not as experienced.

Trade Secret

Boulevard Mall, 3528 S Maryland Parkway, between E Desert Inn Road & Twain Avenue, East Las Vegas (731 4669). Bus 108, 203. **Open** 10am-9pm Mon-Fri; 10am-8pm Sat; 11am-6pm Sun. **Credit** Disc, MC, V.
Convenient if you happen to be at the Boulevard Mall already and need a quick trim or some haircare products. This store has a selection of recognised

names like Sebastian and John Freida, and an area at the rear offers the standard salon treatments. The lack of windows make for some unfortunate use of fluorescent lighting.

Branch: The Galleria at Sunset Mall, 1300 Sunset Road (898 1878).

Massage

Alternative Health Choices Wellness Center

5650 W Flamingo Road, between Jones Boulevard & Lindell Way, South-west Las Vegas (220 5995). Bus 203. **Open** 9am-6pm Mon-Sat; by appointment Sun. **Credit** AmEx, Disc, MC, V.

Specialised therapy for whatever ails you. Medical massage for prenatal/infant, whiplash, sciatica and much more. Other services include reflexology and acupressure.

Body Works Massage Therapy

5025 S Eastern Avenue, just south of E Tropicana Avenue, East Las Vegas (736 8887). Bus 110, 201. **Open** 10am-6pm daily. **Credit** MC, V.

Body Works offers the usual wonderful treatments, including Swedish deep tissue and Chinese Mix, as well as muds and salts.

Dahan Institute of Massage Studies

3320 E Flamingo Road, at Pecos Way, East Las Vegas (434 1338). Bus 111, 203. **Open** 1.30-9.30pm Mon-Thur; 9am-9.30pm Fri; 9am-5.30pm Sat, Sun. **Credit** Disc, MC, V.

Well known locally for its outstanding training programmes, Dahan also offers top-notch massage to the public, given by skilled, pre-graduate students. Massages are monitored and prices tend to be better than at the full-service spas.

Branch: 2911 N Tenaya Way (434 1338).

Tattoos

Absolute Ink

1141 Las Vegas Boulevard South, one block south of Charleston Boulevard, Stratosphere Area (383 8282). Bus 301, 302. **Open** noon-10pm Mon-Thur, Sun; noon-midnight Fri, Sat. **Credit** AmEx, Disc, MC, V.

If you want a permanent souvenir of Las Vegas, visit this relaxed, attitude-free tattoo parlour near Downtown. They're serious about their art, and you should be too if you choose to book their time. Piercings start at $20 and they claim the lowest tattoo prices in town. Ask for Iron Mike.

Household

Antiques

Charleston Antique Shops

2014-2026 E Charleston Boulevard, between Burnham Drive & Eastern Avenue, East Las Vegas (386 0238). Bus 205. **Open & credit** varies.

Unbeknownst to many tourists and even some locals is the fact that there are more than two dozen tiny antique shops in converted old houses along the east end of Charleston Boulevard. You'll find fine china, dolls, desks, postcards, Tiffany lamps, telephones, perfume bottles, mirrors, train sets, clocks and more. Dealers are knowledgeable and approachable.

The Sampler Shoppes

6115 W Tropicana Avenue, at Jones Boulevard, South-west Las Vegas (368 1170). Bus 102, 201. **Open** 10am-6pm Mon-Sat; noon-6pm Sat. **Credit** AmEx, Disc, MC, V.

This indoor mall, a converted grocery store, has more than 40,000sq ft (3,700sq m) where 200 dealers display their wares. You'll find antiques, books, collectibles, dolls, furniture, glassware, jewellery, toys and much more. There's also a small café.

Showcase Slots & Antiquities

4305 S Industrial Road, between W Tropicana Avenue and W Flamingo Road, West of Strip (740 5722). Bus 202. **Open** 9am-5pm Mon-Sat; 11am-5pm Sun. **Credit** AmEx, DC, Disc, MC, V.

What could be a more appropriate souvenir of Las Vegas than an antique slot machine? This store at the back of Bellagio has got lots, some from way back in the 1930s and 1940s, as well as new slots, old-fashioned Coca-Cola dispensers, Wurlitzer jukeboxes and other memorabilia.

Website: www.showcaseslots.com

Décor & supplies

Cost Plus World Market

3840 S Maryland Parkway, at E Flamingo Road, University District (794 2070). Bus 109, 202, 213. **Open** 9am-9pm Mon-Sat; 10am-7pm Sun. **Credit** AmEx, Disc, MC, V.

An arty superstore of imported home supplies, furnishings and decorations with a neo-natural feel. It also has a nice selection of imported vino as well as pastas, sauces, curries, candies and such like. The perfect place to pick up a couple of glasses and a bargain-priced bottle of red.

Branch: 2151 S Rainbow Boulevard (638 8844).

Little Baja

3360 S Decatur Boulevard, between W Spring Mountain & Desert Inn Roads, West of Strip (873 5556). Bus 103. **Open** 9am-5pm Mon-Sat; 10am-3pm Sun. **Credit** MC, V.

No one can say this place is hard to find: half of the store is splayed out along Decatur Boulevard. A fenced yard houses hundreds of fountains, big and small, and other ornamental garden goodies. Inside, there's furniture aplenty, primarily in the Southwest/Mexican farm style. There's lots of nice ironwork, wooden carvings, beautiful blown-glass trinkets, cherubs, candelabras, cabinets and so on. Prices run from reasonable to steep.

Pier 1 Imports

4021 Decatur Boulevard, at W Flamingo Road, South-west Las Vegas (876 2233). Bus 103, 202. **Open** 10am-9pm Mon-Fri; 10am-8pm Sat; 11am-7pm Sun. **Credit** AmEx, Disc, MC, V.

Cosmetics & perfume shops

Beauty Center & Salon

6160 W Tropicana Avenue, at Jones Boulevard, South-west Las Vegas (891 8895). Bus 102, 201.
Open 9am-8pm Mon-Fri; 9am-7pm Sat; 9am-5pm Sun. **Credit** AmEx, MC, V.

This great source of high-end haircare products, cosmetics and nails is just two miles off the Strip. It's not quite as expansive as Ulta3, but brands include Sebastian, Joico, Aveda, Redken and Matrix Essentials. The salon area at the back offers professional cuts and colour at reasonable prices.
Branches: see the phone book.

Perfume Depot

5725 Pecos Road, between Russell Road & Patrick Lane, East Las Vegas (454 5059). Bus 111.
Open 10am-7pm Mon-Fri; 10am-6pm Sat; 11am-5pm Sun. **Credit** AmEx, Disc, MC, V.

Perfume Depot has huge quantities of designer fragrances at discount prices.

Sephora

3311 Las Vegas Boulevard South, just south of Sands Avenue (735 3896). Bus 203, 301, 302.
Open 10am-11pm Mon-Thur, Sun; 10am-midnight Fri, Sat. **Credit** AmEx, Disc, MC, V.

Next door to the Venetian, this brand-new 10,000sq ft (930sq m) cosmetics and perfume emporium is the largest and most comprehensive in Las Vegas (*pictured*). Packed with products from Guerlain, Dior and Yves Saint Laurent, its appeal spans many generations, so you'll also find the latest hip offerings from Stila, Anna Sui and Urban Decay. Use the make-up application areas, or let a pro apply the goods to make your mug gorgeous. You can also create your own scent.
Website: www.sephora.com

Ulta3

3776 S Maryland Parkway, at Twain Avenue, East Las Vegas (735 4744). Bus 109, 203, 213.
Open 10am-9pm Mon-Sat; 11am-6pm Sun. **Credit** AmEx, DC, Disc, MC, V.

If you can pump it, dab it, spray it, squirt it, squeeze it or otherwise apply it, Ulta3 has got it. Another plus: it's located inside a full-service beauty salon where professionals will apply your new goodies.
Branches: 2120 N Rainbow Boulevard (631 3556); 543 N Stephanie Street (451 6211).
Website: www.ulta3.com

There's a distinctly global flavour to this unique and tasteful store. African, Asian, European and Indian wares grace the shelves, and there is a small selection of natural-fibre clothing and some jewellery.
Branches: 1419 Sunset Road (451 4511); 3181 N Rainbow Boulevard (645 5534).

Zo Calos

7470 Industrial Road, suite 104, at Warm Springs Road, south of Las Vegas (269 6550). No bus. **Open** 10am-6pm Mon-Sat. **Credit** AmEx, Disc, MC, V.

Furnishings sold here aren't of the typical cheap motel/lone cactus type; this is Old Southwest at its best. Past customers include former Las Vegas mayor Jan Jones and Indy-car racer Jimmy Vasser.

Specialist & gifts

Ca'd'Oro

The Grand Canal Shoppes, Venetian, 3355 Las Vegas Boulevard South, just south of Sands Avenue (696 0080). Bus 301, 302. **Open** 10am-11pm Mon-Thur, Sun; 10am-midnight Fri, Sat. **Credit** AmEx, Disc, JCB, MC, V.

This gorgeous gallery is named after one of the finest façades in Venice, the Palace of Gold. From the hand-blown Murano glass light fittings to the hand-made custom tiles, it's a gem. You'll find very upscale, contemporary creations as well as forever-classic timepieces from the likes of Omega, Tag Heuer, Charriol and Bertolucci.
Website: www.thecadoro.com

Maxters

Village Square, 9420 W Sahara Avenue, at Fort Apache Road, South-west Las Vegas (869 8226). Bus 204. **Open** 10am-6pm Mon-Sat. **Credit** AmEx, DC, Disc, JCB, MC, V.

On the west end of town near the Las Vegas Art Museum, Maxters has an eclectic assortment of collectibles, including jewellery, toys, antiques and memorabilia. Prices are on the high side, but it's great for browsing as well as buying. Stroll from one side of the shop, where vintage silver jewellery and Patek Philippe watches are displayed, to the other, where a fully restored Harley-Davidson motorbike rests near a vintage Coca-Cola cooler. Art and furniture are also offered.
Website: www.maxterslv.com

The Museum Company

Caesars Palace, 3500 Las Vegas Boulevard South, between W Spring Mountain & Flamingo Roads (792 9220). Bus 301, 302. **Open** 10am-11pm Mon-Thur, Sun; 10am-midnight Fri, Sat. **Credit** AmEx, Disc, JCB, MC, V.

This chainstore is, as you might expect, not unlike a gift shop at a local museum (not a Las Vegas museum, of course). It's a good place to find interesting artsy gifts for kids and adults, including cards, books, calendars, music, toys and oddities. If you're about to leave Las Vegas and forgot to buy any presents, don't worry: there's also a branch at McCarran Airport.
Website: www.museumcompany.com

Psychic Eye Bookstores

*3315 E Russell Road, at Pecos Road, East Las Vegas
(451 5777). Bus 111.* **Open** 10am-9pm Mon-Fri;
10am-8.30pm Sat; 11am-6pm Sun. **Credit** AmEx,
Disc, MC, V.

Incense swirls around shelves of tarot cards, crystals,
astrology charts and books on mysticism. Religious
art from India, the Far East, ancient Ireland and elsewhere line the walls. Behind a velvet curtain,
Madame Fortune Teller reads palms.
Branches: 6848 W Charleston Boulevard (255 4477);
4810 Spring Mountain Road (368 7785).

Re Gallerie

*Paris, 3655 Las Vegas Boulevard South, between
Harmon Avenue & E Flamingo Road (792 2278).
Bus 202, 301, 302.* **Open** 9am-11pm daily. **Credit**
AmEx, DC, Disc, JCB, MC, V.

This lovely shop specialises in vintage French
posters and prints recreated on its 100-year-old
press, on display in the adjoining room. Designs
include the art nouveau goddesses of Alphonse
Mucha, the bold geometric designs of European art
deco and Hollywood classics such as King Kong and
Charlie Chaplin. Prices start at $100 for small
posters, $300 for large posters.

Cigar & smoke shops

Mr Bill's Pipe & Tobacco Company

*4441 W Flamingo Road, at Arville Street,
South-west Las Vegas (221 9771). Bus 202.*

Open 9am-9pm Mon-Sat; 10am-9pm Sun. **Credit**
AmEx, Disc, MC, V.

Cigarettes, cigars, pipe tobacco, chewing tobacco –
if there was such a thing as liquid tobacco, Mr Bill's
would carry it. Check out the arty selection of lighters,
as well as rock posters and jewellery. Sssssmokin'!
Branches: see the phone book.

Las Vegas Cigar Co

*3755 Las Vegas Boulevard South, between
E Tropicana & Harmon Avenues (262 6140). Bus
301, 302.* **Open** 8am-9.30pm daily. **Credit** AmEx,
Disc, MC, V.

All cigars here are 100% hand-rolled using imported
tobaccos blended by Cuban masters and cigar
makers. Sweet, natural or maduro wraps are available, plus pipe tobacco and imported cigarettes such
as clove and beedies.

Paiute Tribal Smoke Shop

*1225 N Main Street, between Washington & Owens
Avenues, North Las Vegas (387 6433). Bus 208,
214.* **Open** 7am-8pm Mon-Sat; 8am-7pm Sun.
Credit Disc, MC, V.

The Indians have used their knowledge of Mother
Nature to put together one of Nevada's finest tobacco
collections. You pay taxes to the Paiute nation rather
than the state of Nevada, and prices end up pretty
competitive. There's a cigarette shop (some non-
domestic brands) and a cigar and pipe tobacco room,
which opens an hour later every day.

Tobacco Road

*Juanita Plaza, 3650 E Flamingo Road, at Sandhill
Road, East Las Vegas (435 8511). Bus 202.* **Open**
9am-10pm daily. **Credit** AmEx, MC, V.

Peace, love, Grateful Dead paraphernalia and nico-
tine in all its various forms. Check out the pipes
intended for, ahem, tobacco use only.

Florists

A Rain Forest

*4171 S Maryland Parkway, at E Flamingo Road,
University District (732 9555). Bus 109, 202.* **Open**
7am-7pm Mon-Sat; 8am-4pm Sun. **Credit** AmEx,
MC, V.

When you haven't a clue, flowers will do. From
exotic arrangements to the traditional dozen red
roses, there's something for every occasion here. If
you don't have time to stop by, call 1-800 356 9377
for same-day delivery anywhere in the US. A week's
notice is required for delivery outside the States.

Travel

Prestige Travel

*6175 W Spring Mountain Road, at Jones Boulevard,
South-west Las Vegas (251 5552). Bus 203.* **Open**
7.30am-6pm Mon-Fri. **Credit** AmEx, Disc, MC, V.

If you're tired of long waits on the phone listening
to elevator music, let someone else do the dirty work.
Prestige has 22 locations and will book your airline
tickets, rental cars, cruises, tours and packages.
Branches: see the phone book.

Las Vegas on the Cheap

Las Vegas has always had a reputation as a bargain city, and it still offers plenty of cheap deals – if you know where to look.

One of the long-standing maxims in Las Vegas is this: the way to finance your vacation on 25¢ a day is to put your quarter into the right slot machine – and hit a big jackpot. The fortunes of Lady Luck notwithstanding, the golden era of living it up on pennies a day is ancient history, if not ancient folklore, for mortals who lack such a Midas touch.

Over the past decade, the cost of visiting Las Vegas has increased while the great deals people used to talk about seem to be drying up. This is partly due to the US's strong economy: people may be spending proportionally less of their vacation money on gambling (though the casinos' revenues are constantly on the increase), but they are happy to spend more on other activities such as eating and shopping – and they're less concerned about always getting the cheapest deal. The culture of Las Vegas is also changing: there are an increasing number of high-priced celebrity-chef restaurants, designer shopping promenades and mega-resorts such as Bellagio and the Venetian that insist on charging higher room rates.

Nevertheless, there are still plenty of ways to eat, drink, sleep and gamble cheaply, if you know where to look. Casinos must be competitive to entice gamblers into the fleecing pens. Thus you should find all manner of attractive promotions and be able to keep expenses to a minimum, while having a good time.

Be advised that deals and promotions come and go rapidly. The best way to keep track of them is to get hold of the **Las Vegas Advisor**, a 12-page monthly newsletter that employs a team of researchers to test out the best and cheapest that the casinos offer on all fronts. A year's subscription costs $50 in the US, $60 in Canada and $70 overseas, postage included. Not cheap, but the price does include a first-class coupon book offering deals on everything from car hire (15 per cent off Hertz rentals) to eating out (two for the price of one at many of the major buffets, easily saving you that amount and more in a week's stay. Or, you can buy a single issue (no coupon book) for $5, $8 overseas (postage included).

The *Advisor* is available from Huntington Press, 3687 S Procyon Avenue, Las Vegas, NV 89103 (1-800 244 2224 enquiries and credit card orders). The company also publishes two useful budget-beating guides, among other gambling-related titles: *Comp City: A Guide to Free Las Vegas Vacations* ($19.95) and *The Las Vegas Advisor Guide to Slot Clubs* ($14.95). Postage is extra.

Details of casinos for which no address is given here will be found in our **Casinos** chapter.

Funbooks

Funbooks are probably the best source of freebies and usually contain lucky bucks or match-play coupons, discounts for food, drinks and shows, coupons for souvenirs and other discounts for car rentals, beauty shops and so forth. The best coupons are the ones that say 'free' or 'two-for-one', especially if they're for buffets or restaurants. The souvenirs are usually cheap key rings, playing cards or other trinkets, invariably with the casino's name and logo on them. Many casinos produce their own funbooks, which are available at the main cage (cashier) or the welcome desk (if there is one).

You can just walk in off the street and ask for one; you don't have to be staying at the hotel or gambling. However, if you're staying at the hotel ask the front-desk clerk if there is a funbook for guests; it'll have more valuable coupons than the funbook that anyone can get for the asking. Or, if you're driving into town, stop at any of the visitor centres on the highways leading in – they usually ask for an out-of-Nevada driver's licence since these freebies are designed for tourists. Also, the visitor centres often have tourist magazines stocked with coupons and offers.

Slot clubs

Most casinos run a slot club. Their main purpose is to keep track of a gambler's slot and video poker play, and to retain customer loyalty by providing rewards in the form of points that can be redeemed for cash or merchandise – much like

Westward Ho: *cheap rooms on the Strip.*

supermarket reward cards. You insert your slot club card into a slot on the machine every time you play. The more you spend, the greater the benefits that accrue.

Even if you don't plan to sequester yourself at a slot or video poker machine, you'll benefit from joining as many slot clubs as you can. It doesn't cost anything and many clubs give free gifts or discount tickets (two-for-one buffet deals, for example) and even free money to anyone who signs up. Casino shops and restaurants also frequently offer ten to 15 per cent discounts to card-carrying members. In addition, members are offered room discounts and free meals throughout the year, and can attend special events such as tournaments, parties and barbecues. You'll also receive a slot club newsletter, which usually contains coupons, event dates and the like. You need to show ID to join (there will be a clearly marked booth), although many casinos will also send out a slot-club application form on request so that you can sign up before arrival. Alternatively, you can sign up as soon as you arrive, charge everything to your room while at the same time accruing points in the casino, and then get your room and food comped at the end of your stay.

It's hard to recommend one slot club over another because the benefits change frequently. Sometimes, the casinos offering the best deals are the ones with the least attractive facilities, hence their need to pull the customers in. This isn't always the case; many slot clubs are so good that players become regular customers in order to take advantage of the perks: **Caesars Palace** has been known to offer some excellent slot play benefits; all **Mandalay Resort Group** properties pay top dollar for their slot club cash rebate; the fancy **Resort at Summerlin** gives you points for anything you buy on site (including the morning paper); the **Gold Coast** club has a department store catalogue full of merchandise you can buy with points; members of the **Fitzgeralds** club can check their slot club accounts online; **Circus Circus** lets you use your card for table games; and at the **MGM Grand** you can exchange your points for American Airlines frequent-flyer miles. There are many other examples and the *Las Vegas Advisor* gives updates on who is offering what.

Accommodation

The best prices are in Downtown, where the hotels often charge half the rate of their Strip cousins. Most of the Downtown hotels – including the **California** (12 Ogden Avenue, at First Street; 385 1222), **Fitzgeralds**, **Four Queens** (202 Fremont Street, at Casino Center Boulevard; 385 4011), **Fremont** (opposite the Four Queens; 385 3232), **Golden Gate** (1 Fremont Street, at Main Street; 382 3510), **Las Vegas Club** (18 Fremont Street, at First Street; 385 1664), **Main Street Station** and **Jackie Gaughan's Plaza** – charge less than $50 a night for a room. The **El Cortez**, **Gold Spike** (400 Ogden Avenue, at Las Vegas Boulevard; 384 8444) and **Western Hotel** (899 Fremont Street, at Ninth Street; 384 4620) actually charge under $25 a night.

On the Strip, only a handful of hotels charge less than $50 a night, and these prices are often available only during the week or the off season. If you're still interested, check out the **Aztec Inn** (2200 Las Vegas Boulevard, next door to the Stratosphere; 385 4566), **Bourbon Street** (120 E Flamingo Road, just off the Strip; 737 7200), **Sahara**, **Westward Ho** (2900 Las Vegas Boulevard South, just south of Circus Circus; 731 2900), **Stardust** and **Vacation Village** (6711 Las Vegas Boulevard South, about three miles south of the actual Strip; 897 1700).

The price you pay for a room can be affected by the day of the week, time of year or what event is taking place. Here are some tips on how to make sure you're getting the best rate.
● Room rates follow a seasonal pattern, although 'off-season' is now less clearly defined as the city has broadened its tourist appeal. The period between Thanksgiving and Christmas is the slowest, when occupancy levels and room rates are at their lowest – except the week when the

Save dollars, not calories

Cheap food and drink have been a tradition of this city's resort industry since the 1950s. The all-you-can-eat buffets, $4.99 prime rib dinners and 99¢ shrimp cocktails are now as much a part of the Vegas gestalt as craps, cards and cleavage. The most publicised food deals are the buffets, which now cost $8-$20 per person for the dinner sitting and $4-$7 for breakfast or lunch (for details on the best buffets, *see chapter* **Restaurants & Buffets**).

The least expensive buffets in town include those at the **Sahara**, **Circus Circus**, **Excalibur**, **Holiday Inn Casino Boardwalk** (3750 Las Vegas Boulevard South, just north of the Monte Carlo; 735 2400), **Lady Luck** (206 N Third Street, at Ogden Avenue; 477 3000), **Silverton** (3333 Blue Diamond Road, at the I-15; 263 7777), **Sam's Town** and any of the **Station** casinos.

The once-famous 99¢ breakfast is now an endangered species, but you can find a rib-sticking $1 breakfast at the Emerald Room at the

El Cortez, which serves two eggs, bacon, potatoes, toast and coffee 24 hours a day. The best ham-and-eggs deal is the 'Natural' at the coffeeshop at **Binion's Horseshoe**: two eggs, toast, potatoes, coffee and a slab of ham that covers the plate, for the princely sum of $2.75. The Sourdough Café at **Arizona Charlie's** has been offering a $2.49 steak-and-eggs special for years. Served 24 hours, this artery-clogger comes with a six-ounce sirloin, two eggs, potatoes and toast. Charlie's also serves three 77¢ breakfast specials from midnight to 6am. And for lovers of tradition, the **Golden Gate** hotel still offers its 99¢ shrimp cocktail, served in a tulip glass (*pictured*).

Meat eaters should check out the **Gold Coast** for its $7.95 steak dinner (served 24 hours a day), the **Lady Luck** for its prime rib specials ($5.49 and $10.99), and the **El Cortez** for a no-nonsense slab of prime rib beef for $6.99. If you like seafood, the snow crab legs specials at Kady's in the **Riviera** ($9.95) and at Roberta's

---

National Finals Rodeo is in town (usually early December). July and August are also cheap, largely because it's hot enough to fry an egg on your car.
● It's always easier – and usually cheaper – to book a room during the week (Sunday to Thursday) rather than for Friday and Saturday.
● Always try to book well in advance, and ask for dates that have more favourable rates. Casino staff know their rates up to a year in advance.
● Avoid holidays such as New Year's Eve, the Fourth of July, Memorial Day and Labor Day. Avoid major conventions such as Comdex and the Consumer Electronic Show (for dates, *see chapter* **Resources**), when hotels raise their rates by up to 500 per cent.
● Regardless of when you book, ask about discount rates for auto club members, senior citizens (AARP) or corporate customers. If you plan to gamble, ask about a 'casino rate', which usually runs 50 per cent below prevailing rates. This is available to slot club members and 'rated' gamblers. One way to become 'rated' is to deposit funds with the casino cashier then draw on it as you gamble; you'd probably need to deposit at least $2,000 to get a discount or a full 'comp'.

● If you arrive in town without a booking, call around the biggest and least fashionable properties, which are most likely to have rooms. **Tropicana** and **Circus Circus** are good bets.
● Book a room in a motel. There are plenty of local and chain motels on the Strip or in the streets around Downtown.

Comp rooms

Of course, the best rate is the free or 'comped' room. And they're not as hard to come by as you might think. First, find out if you qualify for a free room. Many writers or journalists (print and broadcast) can get a free room simply by asking the publicity or advertising director. If you're a travel agent or tour operator, call the casino's hotel sales department; at worst they'll probably offer a discount. Hotels with convention facilities (most have them) will often comp a room to anyone who calls the hotel sales manager and claims to be a meeting planner, though they may need to back it up on headed notepaper.

The largest block of free rooms is reserved for gamblers, the casino's best customers. To find out

in the **El Cortez** ($15.95) are probably the best value in town. If you like both, go to the **Hard Rock**'s Mr Lucky's café for a mean steak and grilled shrimp for $5.95, served 24 hours. The Hard Rock also serves up a $2.95 gourmet fire-baked pizza from 1-5am every day. Another great pizza deal is the $1.95 slice at Roxy's Pipe Organ Pizzeria at the **Fiesta**, which also has a $1.95 antipasto bar. 'Graveyard specials' (midnight to 7am) are another cheap way to eat well: the **Riviera**'s Kady's serves sweet and sour pork for $2.99 and all-you-can-eat pancakes for $1.99.

To find out about these and other similar food and drink bargains, check the Friday edition of the *Las Vegas Review-Journal* for restaurant ads and coupons. Also check the various free visitor magazines, such as *Showbiz*, *What's On*, *Today in Las Vegas* and *Vegas Visitor*, which circulate throughout the casinos and hotels.

COMP MEALS

The same rules apply for a comp meal as for a comp room. Your gambling investment determines whether you're entitled to a free meal in the casino's buffet, coffeeshop or gourmet room: check with the casino hosts. If you're a member of a slot club you can probably get a comp meal based on the amount of coins you shove through a machine (they keep track electronically).

how much you must gamble in order to sleep for free, talk to a casino host or pit boss. At the **San Remo**, **Imperial Palace** or the **Stardust** you might be told you have to play blackjack for eight hours at $25 per hand or play the $1 slot machines for the same time-span. If you want to stay at the **Venetian** or the **Mirage**, it might be $100 a hand for 12 hours. During that period, it's possible to drop thousands of dollars, so use common sense – don't spend your child's tuition fee for the sake of a $69 room. An alternative that can work is to flash some cash and then hit up a pit boss in the evening – the casino department always has rooms.

Drinking

It goes without saying that alcohol, that great purse-string loosener, is freely available in the casinos. Cocktail servers supply gamblers with an endless stream of the stuff, so long as they continue to spend. You won't get exotic cocktails, but well drinks (beers and basic spirits) and other non-premium drinks are yours for the asking.

Servers circulate more frequently through the pit than the slot areas, and more frequently among the higher than the lower denomination slots. If you want good service at a machine, watch where the servers are going to fill their tray, take a seat in their path and try to look like a serious gambler. A first-time tip, especially if you're winning, won't do your second-time chances any harm.

Supposedly, free drinks are for gamblers, not gawkers, but there's nothing to stop you leaving your slot stool, glass in hand, the minute you're served. On the other hand, a $2 roll of nickels can last you quite a while on 5¢ video poker – long enough for several drinks, anyway. Probably the best way to get free booze is to buy in for a roll or two of quarters at any video poker bar: keep feeding a machine and toking the bartender and you'll be set up royally. If you're dying for a shot and don't want to buy even a $2 roll of nickels, take a seat in the keno lounge or sports book. You will probably be able to order one drink, no questions asked.

If you don't want to gamble, you'll have to put up with cheap, not free – but there's plenty of that around, too. When you want to drain a few beers, there's a big selection of imported labels at **Binion's Horseshoe** for $1.25. **O'Shea's**, next to the Flamingo Hilton, serves draught Harp or Guinness for $1.25, or you can hunker down in **Casino Royale** (737 3500) opposite the Mirage and watch the volcano erupt while downing 50¢ brews. You can also find 50¢ beers at the nearby Kanpai Bar at **Imperial Palace** and at Nickel Town, inside the **Riviera**. To the west of the Strip, the **Orleans** does dollar draughts.

Finding cheap well drinks is tough, but you can guzzle cocktails for only 75¢ at **Bourbon Street**, or nurse your 99¢ margarita at the **Westward Ho** or in the Guadalajara Bar at the **Palace Station**. Like everything else, drinks are cheaper in Downtown: cocktails cost $1 at **Jackie Gaughan's Plaza** and $1.50 at the **Las Vegas Club**, although you can get a watered-down well drink for 50¢ at the **Gold Spike**.

Entertainment

Of course, there are plenty of free, albeit brief, casino spectacles – the erupting volcano at the Mirage, the pirate battle at Treasure Island, Bellagio's dancing fountains, the Fremont Street Experience in Downtown, to name a few – but after gawping at them in amazement a couple of times, you'll probably be ready for something different. For entertainment value, hang out at casino lounges, which usually host contemporary singers and musicians. Most have no cover charge and no minimum drink purchases: for more information on the best places, *see chapter* **Casino Entertainment: Lounges**.

Nearly all the visitor magazines have coupons for discounts on casino production shows. For cheaper shows, you might get a $3 or $5 discount while the expensive shows sometimes offer two-for-one deals. The ultimate discount is a comp, and the best way to get one is through the casino. Once again, ask a casino host or a pit boss; the show comp can be one of the easiest for gamblers to get. Upper-level slot club members can often swing a show ticket with minimum effort.

If you're in town when a new casino is opened, look out for special launch parties with free entertainment, refreshments (usually hot dogs and beer) and fireworks displays. Throughout the year there are also dozens of community events – from street parades and sporting events to craft fairs in local parks – that are free and worth attending. *See chapter* **Las Vegas by Season** for details of annual celebrations, and check the *Review-Journal*'s Friday supplement, 'Neon', the *Las Vegas Sun*'s Friday 'Accent' or the event calendars in free papers such as *City Life* for listings of special events.

Top tips

● If you gamble, join a slot club or get registered with the pit. The money spent will earn you free food, show tickets, merchandise, cash, rooms, even your air fare – depending on how much you're willing to gamble.

● When possible, book your accommodation during 'off' periods: in the week (Sunday to Thursday), in high summer (July and August) or in the stretch between Thanksgiving and Christmas.

● Use fun books, especially from places such as the **Stardust** casino or visitor centres outside town. They have plenty of free and two-for-one deals.

● Look in the free visitor magazines, such as *Showbiz, What's On* and *Vegas Visitor*, available everywhere, for discount coupons and leads to other casino promotions.

● When playing slots, play in the Downtown casinos. Collectively, the machines there have a higher payback percentage than those located on the Strip.

● When you want to eat big but spend little, go to a lunch buffet. They're cheaper than the dinner buffet and serve practically the same range of food.

● For cheap entertainment, check out the lounges. There's usually no cover charge and only a one- or two-drink minimum. The ones with the best entertainers are at the **Sahara, Riviera, Stardust, Las Vegas Hilton, Caesars Palace** and **MGM Grand**.

Gambling

Most of the locals-oriented casinos hold promotions that reward gamblers with extra payouts or other prizes. At the **El Cortez**, for instance, you may receive a ticket for a draw (for cash prizes worth $200-$2,000) every time you hit a four of a kind on video poker or a minimum jackpot of 300 coins on any slot machine. Plus, the **Sahara** once paid a $1,000 bonus if you scored a royal flush during the first ten minutes of every hour (one day a week). The **Fiesta** often pays double for your second royal flush hit within 24 hours of the first one. Many casinos give away logo jackets as a bonus when you hit a top jackpot. **Sam's Town** gives away a whole house every March. Such promotions come and go quickly: to find out about them, check at the hotel's promotions desk, ask the casino host or read the visitor magazines.

Casinos such as **Slots-A-Fun** (734 0410) next to Circus Circus often stage free spins on a giant slot machine or free hands-on poker machines for the chance of a car or other lofty prize. Most players usually end up with a deck of cards, keyring or other meaningless trinket – but the promotion got you into the casino and that was its purpose. Also popular among locals is the pay-cheque-cashing promotion, which rewards cheque-cashers with a free spin on a wheel or slot machine, free tickets to a buffet or scratch-off tickets. The most popular cheque-cashing events are held by the **Station** casinos and the **Gold Coast**.

Other freebies include match-play coupons (available in casino funbooks) that can be used like money – but only in conjunction with the real thing. For instance, if you have a $5 coupon, you can combine it with your $5 bet for a total bet of $10 on, say, blackjack. If you win, you're paid even money on the $10; if you lose, you've only lost $5. Not a bad deal.

It goes without saying that for these gambling promotions to be worth anything to you, you need to be proficient at the game in question. Otherwise you'll be throwing your own money away in pursuit of the casino's. Always understand what you are trying to win and how much it might cost to do so.

Besides promotions and giveaways, certain casinos offer lower betting minimums that help you prolong your limited bankroll. Blackjack tables on the Strip, for instance, usually require $5 minimum bets, but you can find $1 tables at the **Sahara, Casino Royale** and **Slots-A-Fun**. There are many more of them in Downtown, at the **Las Vegas Club, El Cortez, Gold Spike** and **Western Hotel**. The latter three also offer penny slot machines, sometimes have progressive jackpots exceeding $10,000. If you're looking for cheaper roulette and crap tables, check out the places that offer $1 blackjack tables.

Arts & Entertainment

Culture

Contrary to what you might expect, Las Vegas is not a cultural desert: its arts scene may be small but it's thriving.

As Las Vegas continues to make good its promise to be 'the last great mythic city that Western Civilisation will ever create' (in novelist Michael Ventura's phrase), its ever-struggling but ever-growing artistic and cultural scene looks more and more intriguing. Even if the casinos are unlikely to ever encourage or support a cultural scene that might direct attention away from their establishments, the sheer size of Las Vegas's population (1.6 million and counting) ensures a healthy minority of artists and enthusiasts who find in Vegas the perfect place to pursue their interests. While visitors often remark on the 'surreal' nature of the casinos and the Vegas landscape, those who make the city their home take such 'surrealism' for granted: it's merely a part of living in this unique microcosm of the American Dream of freedom, luck, reinvention and money.

So while Las Vegas will never (thankfully) be Seattle or San Francisco or (despite many attempts to make it so) Los Angeles, it will continue to develop art and culture out of the gaudy collision of pop culture and myth. And if the artistic scene has to be tougher, more savvy and more underground to survive, so much the better. If a lack of wide recognition and full appreciation is unavoidable, it also frees up the Vegas cultural scene to forge ahead in new and interesting directions.

Art galleries

As art critic and Las Vegan Dave Hickey observed, aesthetically, Las Vegas is a rather Catholic town; the icons of worship to the twin gods of the American Dream (money and the 'freedom' to be whatever you want to be) are writ large in the cavalcade of spectacles that parade past the visitor's dazzled eye. To be an artist in such an environment can be daunting – and enormously challenging and liberating. While it has not spawned any movements or schools, Las Vegas has attracted a rich diversity of visual artists, such as Rita Deanin Abbey, Mary Warner, Robert Beckmann, Susanne Foresteri, Jeffrey Vallance, Jim Stanford, Kathleen Nathan, Jack Hallberg, Yek, and dozens of others.

Fortunately, there are now many public and private galleries to serve them (many are located together in the **Arts Factory**, Las Vegas's own

one-stop arts complex – *see page 206*), along with shows by regional, national and international artists. Marc Chagall, Salvador Dali, Herbert Bayer, Peter Alexander and John McCracken are some of the names recently seen on gallery and museum walls, along, of course, with the heavy hitters of modernism and impressionism that grace the walls of Steve Wynn's little gift to the cultural credibility of Vegas: the **Bellagio Gallery of Fine Art**.

Admission to most of the galleries listed below is free. You can also find art at the **Las Vegas Art Museum** and the **UNLV Barrick Museum** (*see page 202* **Museums**).

Bellagio Gallery of Fine Art

Bellagio, 3600 Las Vegas Boulevard South, at W Flamingo Road (693 7722). Bus 202, 301, 302. **Open** 8am-11pm daily; children admitted 9-11am daily. **Admission** $12. **Credit** AmEx, Disc, JCB, MC, V.

Thanks to the collision of Mirage Resorts owner Steve Wynn's enthusiasm for art with his shrewd resort-business instincts, the Strip now enjoys the works of impressionist, post-impressionist and modernist masters. Minor (along with a few major) works by Picasso, Renoir, Miró, Monet, Cezanne, Gauguin, Van Gogh, Pollack and others hang on the unusual black walls of the Bellagio Gallery of Fine Art. And, yes, these masterpieces are indeed for sale (just in case you won a few million at the tables the night before).

The tremendous public response to the collection has resulted in the gallery moving from its original, cramped two-room space in the Conservatory to larger quarters near the pool. Now throngs of tourists (as well as hordes of grateful local art lovers) have plenty of room to put the audio tour (narrated by Wynn himself) to their ears while they enjoy what amounts to Las Vegas's only major art collection. As you might expect, there's a large gift-shop next door to the gallery.

Website: www.bellagiolasvegas.com

City of Las Vegas Galleries

Charleston Heights Art Center *800 S Brush Street, between W Charleston Boulevard & Evergreen Avenues, North-west Las Vegas (229 6388). Bus 206.* **Reed Whipple Cultural Center** *821 Las Vegas Boulevard North, between Washington Street & Bonanza Road, North Las Vegas (229 6211). Bus 113.*

Both **Open** 1-9pm Mon, Thur; 10am-9pm Tue, Wed; 10am-6pm Fri; 9am-5pm Sat; 1-5pm Sun.

A wide range of intriguing and well-curated student and professional work, from MFA candidates to painters such as Peter Alexander and Karen Carson, is shown on the UNLV campus. It's one of the most spacious galleries in town, with an upstairs gallery overlooking the main floor.

Classical music

After many years of union strife and a lack of artistic direction on the part of the now-defunct Nevada Symphony Orchestra (formerly the city's principal classical organisation), the classical music scene has been re-energised by the emergence of the new **Las Vegas Philharmonic** (895 2728). The Philharmonic had its première season in 1999 and initial impressions suggest it has all the marks of becoming the city's pre-eminent orchestra. The **Nevada Chamber Symphony** (433 9280) has also made great strides in presenting programmes that are distinctive and adventurous. Other groups of note are the **Las Vegas Youth Camerata Orchestra** (385 8948), featuring some of the city's best young players, and the **Southern Nevada Musical Arts Society** (451 6672). The **Nevada Opera Theater** (436 7140) performs mostly light operettas and small-scale productions.

Picasso's Portrait of Dora Maar *(1942).*

The cultural affairs division of the city's Department of Parks & Leisure organises exhibitions of a consistently high quality at its two galleries, one at the CHAC and one at the Reed Whipple. Formerly a branch library, the CHAC has been transformed into a neighbourhood arts centre with a small gallery that has been put to excellent use, showing both regional and local artists. It's a bit off the beaten path, but usually worth the effort. The Reed Whipple is older, far larger and easily accessible from Downtown, but lacks the CHAC's intimacy.

Las Vegas-Clark County Library District Galleries

The vast majority of Las Vegas's public art galleries are in local libraries, and continue to be the first places where many residents and local artists are able to interact, in spite of the district's current avowed hostility to the arts. The quality of exhibitions varies widely. Your best bet is to visit any library, look at a current schedule and pick whichever show sounds most intriguing. Some galleries are also architecturally interesting, such as the Rainbow branch with its curving, high-walled, conical space.

For listings, *see p199* **Libraries**; note there's no gallery at the Las Vegas Boulevard branch.

UNLV Donna Beam Fine Arts Gallery

Alta Ham Fine Arts Building, 4505 S Maryland Parkway, between E Flamingo Road & Tropicana Avenue, University District (895 3893). Bus 109, 201, 202. **Open** *9am-5pm Mon-Fri; 10am-2pm Sat.*

In terms of venues, the main one for both local and national artists remains the **Artemus W Ham Concert Hall** (4505 S Maryland Parkway; 386 7100), on the UNLV campus. This excellent venue was designed specifically for acoustic music, and has hosted everything from the Bolshoi Ballet to national and international orchestras. It's also home to UNLV's **Charles Vanda Master Series** (895 2787), held from autumn to spring. For many years, this event has brought numerous classical solo and ensemble performers, along with dance productions, to Las Vegas.

Other venues where classical music can be found include the intimate and pleasant, if rather remote **Nicholas J Horn Theatre** on the Community College of Southern Nevada campus in North Las Vegas (3200 E Cheyenne Avenue; 651 5483), the **Clark County Library Theater** (1401 E Flamingo Road; 733 7810) and the **Winchester Community Center Theater** (3130 S McCleod Drive; 455 7340), an intimate space in East Las Vegas that specialises in smaller, modern presentations such as the Mandolin String Quartet and woodwind groups.

Visitors to Las Vegas in the summer months have the opportunity to enjoy the **Las Vegas Music Festival** (361 4684). For nine seasons, this event has brought together top professional and student talent from around the city and the nation for a series of concerts at various venues, under the direction of well-known, Harvard-educated Nevadan conductor Evan Christ.

Film

Viva Las Vegas, Ocean's 11, Casino, Honeymoon in Vegas, Aria, Indecent Proposal, Con Air, Fear and Loathing in Las Vegas, Showgirls, Diamonds are Forever, Rain Man, Godfathers I & II, Hoffa, Swingers, Mars Attacks, Go: the list of films using Las Vegas as their backdrop continues to grow, even if most of these films are second-rate and inaccurate (like the overrated Leaving Las Vegas, most of which was actually shot in Reno). The endless visual fascination of Las Vegas, along with the natural beauty of its surrounding desert landscape, will no doubt make it a favourite of directors for many years to come. In fact, a six-month period cannot pass without the appearance of an article touting Vegas as the 'New Hollywood' or news of yet another attempt to build a permanent studio facility. If there's an emblematic image that springs to mind, it's of Warren Beatty as Bugsy Siegel in Bugsy, raising his arms in epiphany as he sees his vision for Las Vegas springing up out of the little railroad town's surrounding wastes. Whether a 'New Hollywood' really does finally burst into being remains to be seen.

For film fans, however, options to enjoy movies get better and better, with well-equipped multiplexes popping up everywhere and not one but two international film festivals vying for local cinephile eyes. Foreign and independent films now routinely play in town (albeit only for a week at a time) and visitors are able to get a movie fix with little difficulty. **Charleston Heights Arts Center** (see page 196 **Art galleries**) hosts a varied and inexpensive series of documentaries and foreign films every spring and autumn.

For film listings information, check the Las Vegas Sun, Neon or CityLife. Alternatively, you can phone 222 3456 for listings, but note that this service uses zip codes to direct callers to their nearest cinema.

Cinemas

These are the best and most interesting movie houses in town.

Regal Cinemas

Recorded information 221 2283. **Admission** $7.75; $4.75 3-11s, seniors and all matinées. **No credit cards**.
Boulder Station 11 Boulder Station, 4111 Boulder Highway, at Desert Inn Road, East Las Vegas. Bus 107.
Colonnade 14 8880 S Eastern Avenue, at Pebble Road, Green Valley. No bus.
Sunset Station 13 Sunset Station, 1301 W Sunset Road, at Stephanie Street, Green Valley. Bus 212, 217.
Texas Station 18 Texas Station, 2101 Texas Star Lane, at Rancho Drive, North Las Vegas. Bus 106, 208.
Village Square 18 9400 W Sahara Avenue, at S Fort Apache Road, North-west Las Vegas. Bus 105.

Regal Cinema at Boulder Station.

For the highest quality in sound, projection and comfort, the Regal Cinemas – three of which are located in the neighbourhood Station casinos – simply cannot be beaten. In addition, each has a touch of the old movie palace in its design: the Boulder cinema evokes an art deco train station with its enormous lobby clock, while the Sunset takes its cue from the tilework of Barcelona architect Antonio Gaudi. While the Regal cinemas are a bit of a trek, they'll be worth it to the film purist who demands wide screens and good prints.

Most independent and art films that come to town are shown at the Village Square, a gargantuan, 18-screen facility located at the Valley's far west end at the Lakes. It's also the only cinema for this rapidly growing area of town, which means long lines and crowded theatres – but at least there are plenty of shopping and dining facilities nearby.

Century Orleans 12

Orleans, 4500 W Tropicana Avenue, at Arville Street, South-west Las Vegas (227 3456). Bus 201. **Admission** $7.75; $4.75 3-11s, seniors and all matinées. **No credit cards**.
The Orleans hotel-casino's 12-screen cineplex features full THX on all screens and was the first to provide stadium-style staggered seating – if you cannot abide someone's head in front of you, this is the cinema for you. The sound and projection rivals the Regal theatres, and the Orleans' proximity to the Strip makes it the best bet for visiting film buffs. It's also the home of the Las Vegas International Film Festival, held every summer.

Gold Coast Twin
Gold Coast, 4000 W Flamingo Road, at Valley View Boulevard, West of Strip (367 7111). Bus 202. **Admission** $7; $4 matinées. **No credit cards.**
For many years, the intimate Gold Coast Twin was the closest to an art house that Las Vegas had. It still shows a mix of small films and Hollywood blockbusters, but these days leans more heavily on the latter. The snack counter is outrageously cheap, with tubs of popcorn for a measly $1.50.

Las Vegas Drive-In
4150 Smoke Ranch Road, at Rancho Drive, North Las Vegas (646 3565). Bus 106. **Open** 6-10pm Mon-Thur; 6-10.30pm Fri, Sat. **Admission** $5.50; free under-13s. **No credit cards.**
Alas, only one drive-in remains in Las Vegas, down from a half-dozen or so in the glory days in the 1960s. Located just north of Rancho Drive (aka US 95), its six screens still provide an authentic drive-in movie experience, though it's slightly marred by the intense light from the towering sign of the nearby Fiesta casino.

United Artists Showcase
Showcase Mall, 3785 Las Vegas Boulevard South, between E Tropicana & Harmon Avenues (740 4911). Bus 301, 302. **Admission** $7.75; $4.75 children & all matinées. **No credit cards.**
The UA Showcase is the only cinema on the Strip, tucked into a side alley next to the MGM Grand's parking garage. Its location is definitely an advantage, although the sound and projection are merely competent. Filmgoers can park for free in the Showcase garage with validation.

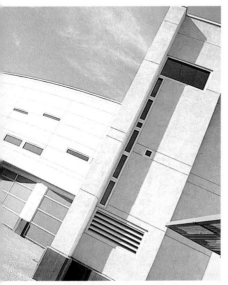

The innovative **Sahara West Library** *(p202).*

Film festivals

For years, local cinephiles bemoaned the lack of an international film festival, especially as the population broke the million mark and the marriage between Vegas glitz and movie glamour became more and more obvious to everyone. In the late 1990s, film lovers got their wish in spades: now there are not one, but two annual film festivals competing for both native and visiting eyes.

The **Las Vegas International Film Festival** (PO Box 18000-185 Las Vegas, NV 89114; 547 0877), held in early June at the Orleans' movie theatres, is the grittier and more devotedly independent of the two. Recent showings included premières of *The Red Violin* and *Desert Blue*; a tribute to horror producer/director Roger Corman; a retrospective of the films of Truffaut; and a whole slew of independent features and documentaries. While aimed more at locals than tourists, the ten-day festival nevertheless has drawn audiences from both camps.

The more glamorous, week-long **CineVegas International Film Festival** (477 7530; www. cinevegas.com), held in December at the Paris hotel-casino, features mainstream films from Hollywood (the world première of *Star Trek: Insurrection* was held at the inaugural festival in 1998) as well as films from around the world. Films are usually grouped into categories (new French independents, new Latino films, new Asian cinema), and the festival also features Le Prix Cristal, an award honouring outstanding achievements by women in film.

Both festivals are in a fledgling stage, and while CineVegas has more money and a higher profile, there's no reason why the growing Vegas metropolis cannot support both ventures. Their presence on the cultural scene is another clear signal that Vegas is at last developing on a par with other cities in terms of options in the arts.

Long before the big festivals rolled into town, the **UNLV International Film Series** (895 3547) has quietly been screening foreign films every autumn in a small auditorium on the UNLV campus. Films are usually subtitled and a couple of years' old, and are attended by students and academics – though all are welcome.

Libraries

Thanks to the vision of former Las Vegas-Clark County Library District director Charles Hunsberger, Las Vegas has some of the newest and most architecturally significant libraries in the region. They also boast facilities that go beyond traditional library services to offer theatres, concert halls, galleries, museums and more. The **Summerlin Library & Performing Arts**

Folk art masks on display at the **UNLV Barrick Museum**. *See page 202.*

Center, the **Whitney Library & Recital Hall**, the **Rainbow Library & Amphitheater**, the **Sahara West Library & Fine Arts Museum** were all built in the past ten years. While some of these structures' potential as cultural centres for the Valley has yet to be fully realised, it's only a matter of time (and a few changes in shortsighted policy) before they take up the slack caused by the absence of a central performing arts centre. If you attend a performing arts event off the Strip, it will probably be held in one of these new libraries.

Beyond the cultural events offered at the libraries, their real attraction is their design: they represent some of the best architecture you'll find away from the Strip. The **Clark County Library** on East Flamingo Road was designed by internationally renowned architect (and designer of inexpensive housewares) Michael Graves, and its striking, postmodern, neo-classical labyrinth has been dubbed 'the pastel mausoleum'. The dramatic entrance to the **West Charleston Library** resembles Stonehenge with the top sliced off at an angle by a giant butter knife.

But the **Sahara West** branch in North-west Las Vegas is undoubtedly the finest of all; a grand marriage of form and function, complete with a simulated grotto (although the overall effect has been slightly lessened by the removal of the water feature) and vast, airy galleries that put one in mind of an elegant ocean liner stranded upon the high desert seas. For more details, *see also chapter* **Architecture**.

All libraries are open 9am-9pm Mon-Thur; 9am-5pm Fri, Sat; 1-5pm Sun.

Clark County
1401 E Flamingo Road, between Maryland Parkway & Eascondido Drive, East Las Vegas (733 7810). Bus 110, 202.

Enterprise
25 E Shelbourne Avenue, at Las Vegas Boulevard South, East Las Vegas (269 3000). Bus 303.

Green Valley
2797 N Green Valley Parkway, at Sunset Road, Green Valley (435 1840). Bus 212.

Las Vegas
833 Las Vegas Boulevard North, between Washington Avenue & Bonanza Road, North Las Vegas (382 3493). Bus 113.

Rainbow
3150 N Buffalo Drive, at W Cheyenne Avenue, North-west Las Vegas (243 7323). Bus 210.

Sahara West

9600 W Sahara Avenue, between S Fort Apache Road & Grand Canyon Drive, North-west Las Vegas (360 8000). Bus 204.

Spring Valley

4280 S Jones Boulevard, between W Flamingo Road & Rochelle Avenue, South-west Las Vegas (368 4411). Bus 202.

Summerlin

1771 Inner Circle, between Summerlin Parkway & Town Center Drive, North-west Las Vegas (256 5111). Bus 211.

Sunrise

5400 Harris Avenue, at Nellis Boulevard, North Las Vegas (453 1104). Bus 115.

West Charleston

6301 W Charleston Boulevard, at Torrey Pines Drive, South-west Las Vegas (878 3682). Bus 206.

West Las Vegas

951 W Lake Mead Boulevard, at Martin Luther King Boulevard, North Las Vegas (647 2118). Bus 105.

Whitney

5175 E Tropicana Avenue, between Nellis Boulevard & Boulder Highway, East Las Vegas (454 4575). Bus 115, 201.

Museums

While Las Vegas still suffers from a lack of major museums, there are plenty of smaller institutions with unique and enlightening offerings, especially when it comes to the history of Southern Nevada. As any traveller knows, the most amazing and informative things can sometimes be discovered in smaller museums like these.

The **Liberace Museum** is a must-see; for years, it was derided for being the stereotypical Vegas museum, but, frankly, as an artefact of our celebrity-worshipping culture, it's just as illuminating as any Warhol film – and twice as much fun. For details, *see chapter* **Attractions** – where you'll also find several 'attraction' museums, many of which are located inside casinos. For the fabulous **Lied Discovery Children's Museum**, *see page 110* **Children**.

Clark County Heritage Museum

1830 S Boulder Highway, between Horizon Drive & Wagon Wheel Avenue, Henderson (455 7955). Bus 107. **Open** 9am-4.30pm daily. **Admission** $1.50; $1 3-15s, seniors; free under-3s. **Credit** MC, V.

Long before Las Vegas was a resort mecca, it was just another Western railroad town. Here you'll find an assortment of exhibits relating to Southern Nevada's past: a recreated city street featuring

Discover leopard sharks at the Las Vegas Natural History Museum. See page 202.

*Literary wannabes take the stage at the **Enigma Garden Café**.*

historic area homes with period furnishings, a 'time-line' mural, and a 1918 Union Pacific steam engine and caboose. It's quite a long way from town, on the outskirts of Henderson, but handy for combining with an excursion to the unmissable Hoover Dam and/or Boulder City.

Las Vegas Art Museum

Sahara West Library, 9600 W Sahara Avenue, between S Fort Apache Road & Grand Canyon Drive, North-west Las Vegas (360 8000). Bus 204. **Open** 10am-5pm Tue-Sat; 1-5pm Sun. **Admission** free.
Recently ensconced in this fabulous, Smithsonian-specified museum space attached to the Sahara West Library, the LVAM aims to make a quantum leap from its former identity showing 'watercolour-league' artists to become the city's premier visual arts organisation. To that end, a hotshot curator was hired, who regularly writes turgid screeds pro-claiming Las Vegas to be the home of 'post-post-modernism' (whatever that means). Nevertheless, the museum has slowly raised its profile, featuring exhibits of minor works by Chagall and Dali, and it's worth the trip out to the western edge of the Valley, if only to admire the architectural beauty of the library itself.

Las Vegas Natural History Museum

900 Las Vegas Boulevard North, at Washington Avenue, North Las Vegas (384 3466). Bus 113, 208. **Open** 9am-4pm daily. **Admission** $5; $4 seniors, students; $2.50 4-12s; free under-4s. **Credit** AmEx, Disc, MC, V.

The Marine Life Room features small sharks in a large tank, the Wild Nevada Room has exhibits on the flora and fauna of Nevada and the Young Scientist Center is full of interactive displays. But the big draw are five, huge, roaring, robotic dinosaurs, including a 35ft (11m) long Tyrannosaurus Rex. What more could a kid want? Combine a visit here with a trip to the nearby Lied Discovery museum and you have the perfect family excursion – and it's undoubtedly cheaper than a day in an arcade.

Nevada State Museum & Historical Society

Lorenzi Park, 700 Twin Lakes Drive, at Washington Avenue, North Las Vegas (486 5205). Bus 108, 204. **Open** 9am-5pm daily. **Admission** $2; free under-18s. **No credit cards.**
Located not far from Downtown in a pretty park with a large duck pond, the Nevada State Museum has permanent exhibits on the natural and anthro-pological history of the region, from the ancient Paiute Indians to nineteenth-century pioneers to the men and women of the Nellis Gunnery School in World War II. The standout exhibit tells the story of Bugsy Siegel's Flamingo Hotel, complete with interactive recordings of Bugsy (played by an actor) threatening business partners with bodily harm.

UNLV Barrick Museum

4505 S Maryland Parkway, between E Flamingo Road & Tropicana Avenue, University District (895 3381). Bus 109, 201, 202. **Open** 8am-4.45pm Mon-Fri; 10am-2pm Sat. **Admission** free.

The Barrick is technically UNLV's natural history museum and also contains some fine permanent displays on ancient and modern Las Vegas history, including a wonderful collection of folk art masks. Of late, it has also become one of the city's finest art exhibition spaces. Several excellent group and individual shows have graced its front rooms, drawing from the best of UNLV's art faculty and regional sources. A must for any gallery crawl; call for details of current exhibitions.

Poetry readings

Touring poets, whether of the highly literary variety like Diane di Prima or Robert Creely or of the performance slam variety like Beth Lisick or Hal Sirowitz, are always amazed by the size and enthusiasm of poetry audiences in Las Vegas. As well they should be: who could possibly have guessed that Vegas would develop such a strong and vibrant poetry scene?

For readings by bards passing through town, check *CityLife*. Listed below are weekly open readings that will give visitors a taste of what local poets and spoken-word artists have to offer. And if you're brave enough, there's room on the sign-up sheet for you, too.

Imaginary Garden Society

Enigma Garden Café, 918A S Fourth Street, just north of Charleston Boulevard, Downtown (386 0999). Bus 301, 302, 401. **Time** *7.30pm Wed.*
Founded in 1995, the Imaginary Garden Society reading, led by Patti Morello and Noah Abrahamson, takes advantage of the Enigma café's pretty garden to create an open, round-robin poetry reading that has become Vegas's best-known literary gathering. The parade of regional and national poets (Beth Lisick, Marci Blackman, Thea Hillman, Daphne Gottlieb, Kevin Sampsell, Ritah Parish, Whitman McGowen and Margery Snyder, to name but a few) that performs there on a regular basis makes the Enigma 'poetry central'.

Perks Reading

Borders, 2323 S Decatur Boulevard, at W Sahara Avenue, South-west Las Vegas (258 0999). Bus 103, 105, 204. **Time** *7.30pm Sat.*
Recently relocated to what has become Las Vegas's favourite bookstore is one of the nicest and most open of local readings. Hosted by poet and scene-whirlwind Danna Botwick, Perks has a different theme every week (such as 'Skin', 'Red' or 'Lunch') and local poets usually rise to the challenge with amusing results. The move from a smaller coffee-house to Borders may present some new challenges in the choice of themes, since many young children are present in the shop.

Poetry at the Café Copioh

Café Copioh, Runnin' Rebel Plaza, 4550 S Maryland Parkway, at Harmon Avenue, University District (739 0305). Bus 109, 201, 202. **Time** *8-9.15pm Tue.*
If your idea of a poetry reading is of crazed Beat types spewing words through clouds of thick smoke, look no further than the Tuesday-night reading at this popular café in the University District. The crowd is young, Goth and tragically hip, and the energy level is cranked up accordingly. If you want to see the next wave of spoken-word artists (and to see the occasional slam professional trying out material), this is the place.

Train of Thought

Café Espresso Roma, The Promenade, 4440 S Maryland Parkway, at Harmon Avenue, University District (369 1540). Bus 109, 213. **Time** *8pm Mon.*
The oldest, semi-continuous open poetry venue in town, the Reading Formerly Known as Poetry Alive is now hosted by Alan Nation (or, on occasion, by poet/police officer Harry Fagel). The Roma reading has undergone many ups and downs, but eventually every local poet returns to the scene of their first literary crimes. Recently, it has suffered a drain of talent and audience to other local readings, so if you're a nervous first-timer, the low-key Roma scene is a safe place to start. *See also p168* **Bars & Cafés**.

Theatre & dance

Thanks to the sudden and swift success of Broadway shows such as *Chicago* and *Rent* on the Strip, the Las Vegas theatrical landscape is shifting away from hackneyed production shows and into the brave new world of legitimate theatre. Even performance art has gained a toehold that would have been unthinkable just five years ago, with the signing of the avant-garde Blue Man Group to an extended run at the Luxor, starting in February 2000.

Both amateur and professional theatre are thriving like never before, with several brand new (and, amazingly enough, competent) theatre companies taking to the boards all over Vegas. The success of UNLV's MFA Playwriting programme has energised not only the university theatre department, but feeds such companies as **The Asylum** and **Our Backs to the Walls Players**. New plays by local and regional playwrights, inventive and offbeat productions and, yes, the perennial Neil Simon play by small community groups, are all turning the Vegas theatre scene into a lively place.

Local dance, oddly, has diminished somewhat in recent years; odd because of the sheer number of professionals drawn to Las Vegas in search of employment with hotel-casino productions. Companies include a mix of former and current Strip performers moonlighting for the love of their art, along with a handful of ballet dancers who resist the lure of big showroom paychecks.

UNLV Dance Theatre's production of Metamorphosis by Carole Rae. See page 207.

Venues

Most theatre and dance companies operate out of a hodgepodge of facilities. Three come under the banner of the local library district: the **Summerlin Library & Performing Arts Center Theater**, the **West Las Vegas Library Theater** (both of which seat around 300 and have proscenium stages) and the **Clark County Library Theater** (a 500-seater with a thrust stage). These are the newest venues in town, with excellent sightlines and acoustics. *See page 199* **Libraries** for details.

UNLV (*see page 206*) has three venues: the 550-seat **Judy Bayley Theater** for major shows, the smaller **Paul C Harris** theatre and the **Black Box** for intimate, workshop-style shows. Companies also use the more limited facilities offered by city-run spaces **Charleston Heights Arts Center Theater** and the **Winchester Community Center Theater**. For details of performances, check *CityLife*'s calendar of events or phone the individual companies.

Theatre companies

Actors' Repertory Theater
647 7469. **Tickets** $12-$25. **Credit** AmEx, Disc, MC, V.

Now in its 13th season, ART is the only Equity company in Las Vegas and probably the most professional. Seasons are divided between mainstream musicals (*Oliver, The King and I*), farces (*The Importance of Being Earnest, Run for Your Wife*) and topical dramas such as Tom Stoppard's *Rough Crossing* and Tony Kushner's controversial *Angels in America: Millennium Approaches*. Usually staged in the Summerlin Library & Performing Arts Center, ART's productions are always well mounted, and show a particular talent for classical farce.

Miller's *Death of a Salesman* have proved. The department is committed to giving exposure to academic classics as well as presenting newer plays.

Las Vegas Little Theater
Schiff City, 3844 Schiff Drive, at Spring Mountain Road & Valley View Boulevard, South-west Las Vegas (362 7996). Bus 104, 203. **Tickets** around $12. **No credit cards**.
The pre-eminent amateur company in town, the LVLT has the distinct advantage over other companies of having its own theatre. It's also notable for tackling less-than-sure-fire crowd-pleasers, dramas such as *Ordinary People* and plays by Athol Fugard and Wendy Wasserman (along with the usual Noel Coward comedies). LVLT makes a virtue of its modest production values by presenting straightforward, serious shows.

Nevada Theatre Company
873 0191. **Tickets** up to $10.
The newest and strongest company on the scene, the Nevada Theatre Company, founded in 1998, has drawn highly positive notices for its recent productions of Pierre Corneille's *The Illusion; And Then They Came for Me: Remembering the World of Anne Frank* – a collective, multimedia piece; and *Balitmore Waltz* by Paula Vogel. Led by artistic director Deanna Dupelchain, the company has created quite a buzz among theatre fans, winning several local 'Best Theatre Company' polls in a very short time. So far, it has used the Clark County Library Theater and the UNLV Black Box for most of its productions.

Off-Broadway Theater
Commercial Center, 900 Karen Avenue, suite D116, between Sixth Street & Maryland Parkway, East Las Vegas (737 0611). Bus 109, 204. **Tickets** $13; $11 seniors, students and all matinées. **Credit** MC, V.
The Off-Broadway company has its own 99-seat theatre in the dilapidated Commercial Center strip mall and specialises in 'wholesome' productions, usually light comedies in the vein of Neil Simon. Recent taglines for its comedies include such inducements as 'Not only side-splitting but front-and back-splitting as well!'.

Our Backs to the Wall Players
254 0735. **Tickets** up to $10.
As the name implies, Our Backs is a somewhat avant-garde company dedicated to innovative and unusual theatre. Its début production in spring 1998 was a well-received version of Eric Bogosian's *Suburbia*, followed by a fascinating, apocalyptic multimedia version of 'the Scottish play' entitled *Macbeth: An Urban Tragedy*, which was performed on the steps of the 1930s art deco Las Vegas Academy. Under artistic director Linsey Hamilton, it promises to become the city's most vital alternative company.

Rainbow Company Children's Theatre
Reed Whipple Cultural Center, 821 Las Vegas Boulevard North, between Washington Street & Bonanza Road, North Las Vegas (229 6211). Bus 113. **Tickets** $5; $3 seniors, students; $2 under-12s. **No credit cards**.

The Asylum
Winchester Community Center Theater, 3130 S McCleod Drive, just north of E Desert Inn Road, East Las Vegas (455 7340). Bus 108, 111. **Tickets** up to $10. **No credit cards**.
The Asylum, run by local actress and theatre maven Maggie Winn-Jones, is one of the newer companies in town and focuses on bringing the work of Las Vegan and regional playwrights to a wider audience. It also features PlayPen, a staged reading series that encourages audience feedback.

CCSN Theater
3200 E Cheyenne Avenue, between N Pecos Road & Campus Drive, North Las Vegas (651 5483). Bus 111, 218. **Tickets** up to $20. **Credit** AmEx, DC, MC, V.
The Community College of Southern Nevada's theatre department is off the beaten track in northeast Las Vegas, but occasionally worth the trip, as recent, engaging productions of Eric Bogosian's *Drinking in America*, Euripedes' *Medea* and Arthur

Las Vegas's oldest theatre company (it's been going strong for 23 years) is, to some minds, also its best. Housed in its own space in the Reed Whipple, its consistent high quality has brought it a reputation as the place for young actors and directors to hone their craft. The company prides itself on creating children's theatre that doesn't insult young people's intelligence, and its productions are always highly creative and well designed. Shows are usually aimed at four-year-olds upwards.

UNLV Department of Theatre Arts
4505 S Maryland Parkway, between E Flamingo Road & Tropicana Avenue, University District (895 3666). Bus 109, 201, 202. **Tickets** up to $20. **Credit** AmEx, DC, Disc, MC, V.
UNLV presents classic drama and recent musicals during spring and autumn in its unappealing Judy Bayley Theater, but its most lively and interesting productions are often found in the Black Box, where the MFA Playwriting programme runs workshops on one-act plays by students and the faculty. The annual series of student one-acts, held in the Black Box in spring and autumn, is usually good for a gem or two; the quality of acting and directing can be surprisingly accomplished.

Dance companies

Las Vegas Civic Ballet
Reed Whipple Cultural Center, 821 Las Vegas Boulevard North, between Washington Street & Bonanza Road, North Las Vegas (229 6211). Bus 113. **Tickets** $5; $3 seniors, students; $2 under-12s. **No credit cards**.
The city's ballet company, with its own space at the Reed Whipple, remains one of the primary training grounds for aspiring young dancers before the lure

The Arts Factory

For a long time, the primary barrier to the development of a viable arts scene in Las Vegas was the lack of a central area or neighbourhood to nurture it. The development of the Gateway District – a section of Downtown dating from the 1920s and 1930s that lies south of Fremont Street and north of Charleston Boulevard – was a long time in coming, each step patiently taken one at a time, by various artists and entrepreneurs.

That development took a quantum leap forward a few years ago, when commercial photographer Wes Isbutt created the Arts Factory. Isbutt was looking for a space for his photographic business, Studio West, and wound up reclaiming a block-long 1940s building on Charleston Boulevard. It now houses more than a dozen galleries, studios and creative businesses.

Isbutt decided to buy the whole building and set up a community of creative forces, both commercial and non-profit, that would energise each other and centralise the incipient arts scene; perhaps even create a 'mini-Soho' for the Gateway District. 'Arts communities flourish in warehouse districts because the only people willing to fix up cool old spaces are artists: funky people for funky buildings,' says Isbutt. 'We hope that many of the buildings around the Arts Factory follow our lead.'

The Arts Factory's two floors now house the city's two foremost non-profit galleries, along with the city's best commercial galleries, an architecture studio, two graphic design firms, a frame shop, individual artists' studios and a foreign film club; not to mention Lost Vegas, a gallery/shop devoted to all sorts of Sin City kitsch and souvenirs (*see chapter* **Shops & Services: Only in Vegas**). Any visitor interested in what's happening with local artists now has an excellent, almost comprehensive first stop.

On the Factory's opening night, Isbutt created a swank and swinging parody of the Last Supper with a photo shoot that placed an Elvis impersonator in the central role. At the end of the shoot, Elvis jumped on the table to belt out a rendition of 'Viva Las Vegas' to the watching crowd: a suitable blessing for Sin City's new era in the arts.

The Arts Factory
103 E Charleston Boulevard, between Main Street & Casino Center Boulevard, Downtown. Bus 113, 206.

Contemporary Arts Collective Gallery
Suite 102 (382 3886). **Open** noon-4pm Mon-Sat.
The CAC continues its mission as the only artist-run, non-commercial, high-calibre gallery in town – and also the only one that shows experimental and Polaroid photography. It walks the fine line between an edgy, grassroots aesthetic and academic polish (many of its members are associated with UNLV) with great success. The collective's members, drawn from all walks of the artistic community, form the core of the best artists in town, and shows by regional artists as well as hometown favourites are always fun and provocative.

Nevada Institute for Contemporary Arts Gallery
Suite 101 (434 2666). **Open** 10am-5pm Tue-Fri; noon-5pm Sat.
With NICA's relocation to the Arts Factory in 1999, the laser-like focusing of the city's arts scene

of employment on the Strip becomes too strong to resist. Although the quality of productions tends to vary, the LVCB takes risks and provides a valuable showcase for local choreographers.

Nevada Ballet Theater
243 2623. **Tickets** up to $48. **Credit** AmEx, Disc, MC, V.
Associated with UNLV, the NBT is the city's only fully professional ballet company and tends towards classical works and certified crowd-pleasers, such as its recent hit adaptation of Bram Stoker's *Dracula* and its annual version of *The Nutcracker*. Shows are held at UNLV's Judy Bayley Theater.

UNLV Dance Theater
4505 S Maryland Parkway, between E Flamingo Road & Tropicana Avenue, University District (895 3827). **Bus** 109, 201, 202. **Tickets** $10; $8 seniors, students. **Credit** varies with venue.

Many devotees of dance consider the UNLV student dance department to be the best in town, particularly because of the many fine guest artists who come here from around the world. Both classical ballet and modern work are well represented in its productions, usually mounted at the Artemus W Ham Concert Hall or the Judy Bayley Theater.

The Vibe
798 5995. **Tickets** $15. **No credit cards**.
Another company (run by Kirk Offerle, proprietor of the Jazzed Café, *see p169* **Bars & Cafés**) that prides itself on inventive choreography and innovative ideas, the Vibe is made up of Strip performers and local dancers who collaborate every year on a couple of well-attended showcases (usually held late at night to accommodate showroom performers' schedules). The shows also draw upon the talents of local visual artists, poets and musicians.

into one structure is nearly complete. NICA is the city's most high-profile non-profit gallery, and is dedicated to raising awareness of the visual arts in Southern Nevada by showcasing a mix of well-known local and regional artists. The NICA's shows tend to be more on the academic side compared with the Contemporary Arts Collective, but they are usually no less compelling and sometimes superior.

M(9) Gallery
Suite 108 (845 7907). **Open** phone for details.
This small space next to the back entrance of the Arts Factory is the brainchild of local painter Jerry Misko II (*pictured*), who uses the gallery as a showcase for work by edgy local painters, both established artists and emerging talents.

The George L Sturman Fine Arts Gallery
Suite 204 (384 2615). **Open** 11am-4pm Mon-Fri.
This intimate gallery features connoisseur George Sturman's collection of drawings and prints by artists such as David Hockney, Franz Kline, Claes Oldenberg and others, plus some wonderful pieces of African folk art and a few Disney animation cells.

The Smallworks Gallery
Suite 201 (388 8857). **Open** 10am-2pm Tue-Sat.
Possibly the 'hippest' commercial gallery in Vegas, Smallworks has played host to a number of nationally known artists such as Barbara Kasten and Robert Beckmann, along with first-rate group shows by local artists. Its most recent coup was a stunning exhibition of works by famed Bauhaus artist Herbert Bayer.

Casino
Entertainment

From lounge acts to comedy clubs to showroom extravaganzas, all the world's a stage in Las Vegas.

Las Vegas may lack a certain modesty in billing itself 'The Entertainment Capital of the World', but it does indeed offer something for every pleasure-seeking night crawler. Most of the city's nightlife is inevitably focused on the casinos and their lavish stage productions, comedy shops, celebrity concerts, topless revues and free lounge shows. On any given night you can choose from about 70 different stage shows and headliners, plus another 60 lounge acts.

Casino shows range from star-studded productions, such as *The Great Radio City Spectacular* starring Maurice Hines and *EFX* with Tommy Tune, to awesome stage spectaculars like Siegfried and Roy's space-age magic fantasy and Cirque du Soleil's surreal *Mystère*. There are also some less ostentatious revues, such as the thoroughly entertaining *Forever Plaid*, an endearing 1950s musical at the Flamingo Hilton. Shows with a magic theme are popular (*Siegfried & Roy* still leads the pack in this category), as are so-called 'tribute' or celebrity impersonator shows (*Legends in Concert, American Superstars*) that feature lookalike impressionists who perform live or lip-sync to recordings of their famous alter-egos.

For audiences who can live without the sequins and G-strings, Broadway shows such as the Tony award-winning *Chicago* (indefinite run at Mandalay Bay) and *Rent* (limited engagement at the Las Vegas Hilton), as well as off-Broadway hits such as *Blue Man Group* (starting February 2000 at the Luxor), have become increasingly popular. Of course, staging Broadway hits in Vegas is not new. Over the years Strip and Downtown casinos have hosted renditions of popular musicals such as *Can Can, Mame, South Pacific, Sweet Charity, Funny Girl* and *Oklahoma*, to name a few. With the popularity of *Chicago* and others, entertainment directors are looking at importing other productions such as *Miss Saigon, Buddy* and *Cabaret* in 2000 and beyond.

As an alternative to the stage extravaganza, some casinos continue the Las Vegas tradition of booking celebrity headliners such as Natalie Cole, George Carlin, Johnny Mathis, Reba McEntire,

Tony Bennett, Ricky Martin, Huey Lewis & the News – the list eventually includes anyone in mainstream show business, past or present. The goal, of course, is to pack the showroom and, thus, pack the casino. The practice was kickstarted during the early days of the Rat Pack – that ultra-hip symbol of Las Vegas in 1960 – made up of Frank Sinatra, Dean Martin, Sammy Davis Jr, Joey Bishop and Peter Lawford. The Rat Pack would ad lib and clown around, often until the showroom closed, then carry on in the lounges. Their routine was simple: Davis played the 'kid' to Sinatra's 'swinger' and Martin's 'drunk'. Vegas impresarios understood then, as they do now, that stars in the showroom meant full houses. And there were no bigger stars in 1960 than Sinatra and his Rat Pack.

Despite the cornucopia of entertainment choices, the traditional production show, with its schlocky themes, contemporary music, dancers, jugglers, parlour magicians and brigades of statuesque showgirls, continues to carry the banner of Las Vegas entertainment. Since the 1950s, when Vegas floor shows were highly stylised versions of vaudeville schtick, productions have become bigger, louder, more sophisticated and, it goes without saying, a great deal more expensive to produce. A typical example is Bally's *Jubilee!*, which opened in 1981 and continues in updated incarnations. The latest rendition features, in the first few minutes alone, the destruction of a temple and the sinking of a giant model of the *Titanic*, complete with pyrotechnics, cascading water, fire-spewing blast furnaces and 80 topless dancers who drop from the ceiling, ascend from elevators or stroll on stage from the wings. Overall, *Jubilee!* includes about two dozen production numbers and a number of speciality acts – a magician, juggler and gymnasts.

For more casual entertainment, practically every casino has at least one lounge, which usually features some type of live performer. The kind of act you'll find in a lounge varies, from sloppy ventriloquists to one-woman bands to polished groups like the Fortunes and the Coasters. Most of the time, the lounge act is an up-and-coming musician or singer putting on an entertaining show for

The Rat Pack and two blonde lovelies: casino entertainment in the 1960s.

the price of one or two drinks. Gone are the days when lounges served as launching pads for future headliners or showcased top-notch late-night performers such as Louis Prima and Keely Smith.

INFORMATION & TICKETS

Though the information given here is as accurate as possible, unsuccessful shows do close, and new ones open. To check what's on and who's appearing in town, look at the entertainment supplement 'Neon' in the Friday edition of the *Review-Journal.* You'll find the same information in visitor magazines such as *Showbiz* and *What's On,* and the free weeklies, such as *Las Vegas Weekly* and *CityLife.* If you're out of town, call the **Las Vegas Convention & Visitors Authority** (892 0711) to ask for a free copy of its 'Showguide' or check its website (www.lasvegas24hours.com).

You can buy tickets at the box office where the show is being staged or through ticket agencies such as **TicketMaster** (474 4000) and **Allstate Ticketing** (597 5970). There are ticket brokers in nearly every casino, but, like the agencies, they often charge a commission (sometimes called an entertainment tax) on top of the face value of the tickets. It's best to deal with the show's own box office because you can sometimes pick up free two-for-one coupons or other discounts. If you book by phone, pick up the tickets at the 'will call' window.

Admission prices to production shows range from about $26 for *Forever Plaid* at the Flamingo Hilton to $110 for Cirque du Soleil's water spectacular *O* at Bellagio. Celebrity concerts usually fall somewhere in between – you can pay $39.50 for ZZ Top and $65 for Natalie Cole. Comedy clubs charge from $16 to $22 for a 60-minute show, and prices usually include one or two drinks. Sometimes ticket prices include tax; sometimes it goes on top. Expect to pay higher prices on holidays and during some conventions.

Reduced-price kids' tickets are rare, although children over five (sometimes three) are allowed in to most shows (if nudity is involved, the limit is 18 or 21). Only the really big shows (*EFX, Mystère, O, Siegfried & Roy*) sell out early – it's best to book two to six weeks ahead for these. But it's always worth calling the box office, especially midweek, or you could queue for last-minute cancellations.

Following a trend that started earlier in the decade, most tickets are for specific seats, thus all but eliminating the worn-out practice of greasing the captain's palm for a better seat. At the few showrooms that still use maitre d' seating, you'll have to arrive early and stand in line if you want a good seat. If you're not satisfied with your seat's location, discreetly tip the maitre d' or the captain, from $10 to $20. If you'd prefer to sit in a booth than at a long table with chairs that face the wrong direction, you might have to shell out $50 or more.

For rock music and other entertainment options, *see chapters* **Nightlife** and **Bars & Cafés**.

Comedy clubs

The city's comedy clubs are a by-product of the cable TV and Comedy Store craze that swept the nation in the 1980s. Before gaining their own venue, comedians in Las Vegas mostly worked in lounges or as opening acts for headliners in the main showroom, where they functioned as a kind of high colonic, loosening up the audience for the marquee attraction to follow. Today's comedy clubs follow the same format: two or three stand-up comics deliver their jokes, then the featured comedian closes out the show. Headliners are often known for their work on TV or movies (Chris Rock, Robert Schimmel, Jimmie Walker and Willie Tyler & Lester), while many of the country's biggest comedians (Jerry Seinfeld, Drew Carey, Paula Poundstone) who once played the Vegas comedy shops now return for the large audiences (and paycheques) of the casinos' main showrooms.

Bourbon Street Comedy Theater

Bourbon Street, 120 E Flamingo Road, just east of Las Vegas Boulevard South, East of Strip (228 7591). Bus 202, 301, 302. **Shows** 8.45pm Tue-Thur; 6.45pm, 9.45pm Fri, Sat. **Admission** $32.95; no under-18s. **Credit** AmEx, Disc, MC, V.
The ongoing show in this intimate club is Dr Naughty, the X-rated comedy hypnotist. Drawing on subjects (victims?) from the audience, Dr Naughty induces people to say and do bawdy things, either by themselves or in tandem with fellow volunteers.

Comedy Stop

Tropicana, 3801 Las Vegas Boulevard South, at E Tropicana Avenue (739 2714). Bus 201, 301, 302. **Shows** 8pm, 10.30pm daily. **Admission** $16 includes two drinks. **Credit** AmEx, DC, Disc, MC, V.
One of the oldest venues for comedy in Las Vegas, the Comedy Stop is also one of the largest, with more than 400 seats. Seating is at large tables; it can be hard to see the stage from the back of the room. Typically, three comedians are presented twice nightly. Thursdays are two-for-one appreciation nights for locals.

The Improv

Harrah's, 3475 Las Vegas Boulevard South, between Sands Avenue & E Flamingo Road (369 5111). Bus 301, 302. **Shows** 8pm, 10.30pm Tue-Sun. **Admission** $19.95; no under-18s. **Credit** AmEx, DC, Disc, MC, V.
The Budd Friedman-owned club, part of a nationwide chain, traces its roots to the old cellar comedy stores of New York and Chicago. It presents three or four comedians twice nightly except Mondays.

Riviera Comedy Club

Riviera, 2901 Las Vegas Boulevard South, at Riviera Boulevard (794 9433). Bus 301, 302. **Shows** 8pm, 10pm Mon-Thur, Sun; 8pm, 10pm, 11.45pm Fri, Sat. **Admission** $20.38 general; $28.63 VIP seats; both prices include two drinks. **Credit** AmEx, DC, Disc, JCB, MC, V.
The Riviera Comedy Club presents three or four comics twice nightly (a third late show is staged on Friday and Saturday nights). To its credit, the Riviera has ventured into new waters with its all-gay comedy revues, and its XXXtreme Comedy – mostly shock comedians who talk nasty about bodily functions and social diseases.

Lounges

The glory days of the fabulous casino lounge entertainers (Shecky Greene, Don Rickles, Wayne Newton, Louis Prima and Keely Smith) ended in the 1970s, when casinos began to book the better lounge acts into the main showrooms (where they could charge real money), and customers began to find other interests (sleeping?) to occupy them until five in the morning.

Although lounges have made a comeback, they are no longer mini-showroom-type venues. Instead, they are smaller and open to the casino, and typically feature homogenous acts that serve best as background noise or a respite from the tables. Nevertheless, many lounges are used as testing grounds for up-and-coming musicians and singers, so it's possible you could stumble on the next Tom Jones in a dimly lit corner of some off-Strip hotel. There are even a few lounges actually dedicated to showing you a good time. Here are the best ones.

Bourbon Street Cabaret

Orleans, 4500 W Tropicana Avenue, at Arville Street, West of Strip (365 7111). Bus 201, 301, 302. **Open** 24hrs daily; live music from 6.30pm. **Admission** free with 2-drink minimum. **Credit** AmEx, DC, Disc, JCB, MC, V.
With the quiet feel of a courtyard club in New Orleans's French Quarter, the Bourbon Street Cabaret, located a few blocks west of the Strip, is a nice spot to enjoy your favourite drink while listening to classic jazz, blues and zydeco. The club's décor includes replicas of grand and baby grand pianos suspended from the ceiling.

Coral Reef Lounge

Mandalay Bay, 3950 Las Vegas Boulevard South, between W Tropicana Avenue & Russell Road (632 7777). Bus 301, 302. **Open** 24hrs daily. **Admission** free. **Credit** AmEx, DC, Disc, MC, V.
Though this comfortable lounge's location – at the intersection of Mandalay Bay's so-called Restaurant Row and the casino floor – may be distracting to some, it is perfectly aligned with the traditional lounges of Las Vegas past, offering a quick but not permanent diversion from the gambling action. It has a secluded, tropical feel, a large and often crowded dancefloor and live bands (usually 9pm-3am) playing everything from pop to salsa.

Cleopatra's Barge

Caesars Palace, 3570 Las Vegas Boulevard South, at W Flamingo Road (731 7110). Bus 202, 301, 302. **Open** 9pm-4am Tue-Sun. **Admission** free; 2-drink minimum Fri, Sat. **Credit** AmEx, DC, Disc, MC, V.
For one-on-one encounters, climb aboard Cleopatra's Barge and dance to live bands, usually playing rock or R&B. This lively lounge is more like a crayon-coloured Viking boat, complete with oars, furled sails and a buxom mermaid figurehead, but it floats in real water and bobs up and down when the

Cocktails and cigars: relax in style at **Hamilton's** *in New York-New York.*

dancefloor action heats up. Be careful when cross-ing the gangplank: inebriated revellers have been known to take a dive into the drink.
Dress code: smart casual; no jeans.

Hamilton's
New York-New York, 3790 Las Vegas Boulevard South, at W Tropicana Avenue (740 6400). Bus 201, 301, 302. **Open** 4pm-2am daily. **Admission** free. **Credit** AmEx, Disc, MC, V.
The brainchild of legendary tan-meister George Hamilton, this art deco joint serves good cigars, single malts, chilled martinis and a musical diet of Nat King Cole crooners and Rat Pack wannabes. You can also sup Beluga caviar, smoked trout salad and a canapé plate of salmon, shrimp and ham. *See also p163* **Bars & Cafés**.
Dress code: jackets required; no jeans or T-shirts.

La Playa
Harrah's, 3475 Las Vegas Boulevard South, between Sands Avenue & E Flamingo Road (369 5000). Bus 301, 302. **Open** 8.30pm-2.30am daily. **Admission** free. **Credit** AmEx, Disc, JCB, MC, V.
La Playa's tropical flavour works well with Harrah's carnival motif. The indoor-outdoor lounge has multi-coloured palm trees, a nine-screen video wall and festive fibre-optic lighting throughout. Live music – everything from salsa to rock – plays every day.

Lagoon Saloon
Mirage, 3400 Las Vegas Boulevard South, between Spring Mountain & W Flamingo Roads (791 7111). Bus 301, 302. **Open** 10am-4am daily. **Admission** free with 2-drink minimum. **Credit** AmEx, Disc, JCB, MC, V.

There might not be a lagoon, but the tropically themed lounge is set amid flowing waterfalls and lush foliage from the casino's rainforest atrium. It also comes with parrot-style chairs and a seashell-studded bar top. The music is usually of the easy listening variety, and is nearly always accompanied by the incessant screech of parrots.
Dress code: no tank tops.

Las Vegas Hilton Nightclub
Las Vegas Hilton, 3000 Paradise Road, between Karen Avenue & E Desert Inn Road, East of Strip (732 5111). Bus 108, 112. **Open** 8pm-4am daily. **Admission** free with 2-drink minimum. **Credit** AmEx, DC, Disc, MC, V.
Perhaps Vegas's best live entertainment bargain, with singer/dancer/performer Louie Louie, plus dancing until 4am. Art deco styling, superb lighting and an up-to-the-minute sound system are all part of the deal in this upscale club. *See also p231* **Nightlife: Gay & lesbian**.

Le Bistro Lounge
Riviera, 2901 Las Vegas Boulevard South, at Riviera Boulevard (734 5110). Bus 301, 302. **Open** 6pm-1am Tue-Fri, Sun; 6pm-3am Mon, Sat. **Admission** free with 2-drink minimum. **Credit** AmEx, Disc, MC, V.
The lounge, slightly elevated above the casino, has a New York-style ambience with ribbons of red neon, chrome columns and brass accents. If you like jazz, stop by on Monday nights for Don Menza's jam session, which often includes well-known guest artists. Other regulars are Susan McDonald, who blends country with Top 40 numbers, and the ageing Freddie Bell, a scratchy-voiced throwback to the old-time crooners, who punctuates his songs with one-liners.

Loading Dock Lounge

Palace Station, 2411 W Sahara Avenue, at Rancho Drive, West of Strip (367 2411). Bus 204, 401.
Open 5.30pm-1am Mon-Thur, Sun; 8.30pm-2am Sat, Sun. **Admission** free with 2-drink minimum. **No credit cards.**

A popular spot with local hotel and casino workers who like to hang out here after work. The bands begin playing in the afternoon, usually rock or R&B numbers, but the dancefloor doesn't really heat up until mid-evening.

Mambo's Lounge

Rio, 3700 W Flamingo Road, at Valley View Boulevard, West of Strip (252 7777). Bus 202.
Open 8pm-1am Mon-Thur, Sun; 8pm-2.30am Fri, Sat. **Admission** free. **Credit** AmEx, JCB, MC, V.

If you have a taste for a Latin beat – or even if you don't – check out the salsa and merengue sounds at Mambo's in the Rio. The live bands perform with flair and gusto, and they've recently expanded the lounge to accommodate flashy lambada-style dancers. While the music and clientele are authentic, the Mambo's décor lapses into Vegas's version of a Jimmy Buffet Bar – thatched roofs, rice-paper fans and bamboo furnishings.

Monte Carlo Pub & Brewery

Monte Carlo, 3770 Las Vegas Boulevard South, at Rue de Monte Carlo, between W Flamingo Road & Tropicana Avenue (730 7777). Bus 201, 301, 302.
Open 11am-2am Mon-Thur; 11am-4am Fri; 10am-4am Sat; 10am-2am Sun. **Admission** free. **Credit** AmEx, JCB, DC, Disc, MC, V.

Even if you're not an avid beer drinker you'll like the atmosphere – huge copper beer barrels, antique furnishings, live piano entertainment every night and a pleasant outdoor patio that overlooks the hotel's lavish pool area. Visitors can even roam the microbrewery's catwalk and gaze down on the brewing process. Six different styles of Monte Carlo-labelled beer are produced, including an IPA, an American-style, unfiltered wheat ale, an Irish stout and a rich amber ale. You can soak it all up with a choice of delicious brick-oven pizzas, sausage platters, salads and sandwiches.

Naughty Ladies Saloon

Arizona Charlie's, 740 S Decatur Boulevard, at Alta Drive, South-west Las Vegas (258 5200). Bus 103, 207. **Open** 9.15pm-1.30am Tue-Sun.
Admission free. **Credit** AmEx, Disc, MC, V.

Old West hospitality is the fare at this saloon that looks as though it's straight from a *Gunsmoke* set. There's no Miss Kitty tending the bar, only frontier-style Western music from (who else?) the Naughty Ladies, who get the place whooping and hollering. Attire is mostly tight jeans, boots and Peterbilt trucker caps, but the place is friendly and the drinks are deliciously cold.

The Railhead

Boulder Station, 4111 Boulder Highway, at E Desert Inn Road, East Las Vegas (432 7777). Bus 107, 112. **Open** 24hrs daily; live music from 7pm.
Admission free. **Credit** AmEx, Disc, MC, V.

There's always something happening in this intimate cabaret-style lounge on the Boulder Strip. The booking agent shows no favouritism when choosing his acts, which have included retro rock stars like Chubby Checker, R&B's Sonny Turner and country's Charlie Daniels. When headliners aren't lighting up the stage, customers can take to the spotlight themselves during the frequent karaoke nights.

Royal Street Theater

Jerry's Nugget, 1821 Las Vegas Boulevard North, at Main Street, North Las Vegas (399 3000). Bus 113.
Open 8pm-2am daily. **Admission** free.
Credit AmEx, DC, Disc, MC, V.

This intimate lounge and dance hall has split-level seating and space-age lighting, and frequently hosts live entertainment such as Magaly and the Vamps – when it isn't staging a Latin dance party.

Starlight Lounge

Stardust, 3000 Las Vegas Boulevard South, at Stardust Drive, between W Sahara Avenue & Desert Inn Road (732 6213). Bus 301, 302. **Open** 24hrs daily. **Shows** usually 11pm, but times vary.
Admission free-$10. **Credit** AmEx, Disc, MC, V.

Even though the lounge lizard has become an endangered species in recent years, you may spot one or two here, crouching in the corner, cigarette in one hand, martini in the other. The Starlight is a throwback to the old-time Vegas lounge – dark, smoky and lacking all political correctness. The entertainment is quite good and often includes the Maxx and Chuy's Company.

Texas Station

2101 Texas Star Lane, at N Rancho Drive, between Lake Mead Boulevard & Vegas Drive, North Las Vegas (631 1000). Bus 106, 208. **Open** 24hrs daily.
Admission free. **Credit** AmEx, DC, Disc, MC, V.

The cosy confines of Texas Station offer several lounge options. Crazy Mary's is known for its Bloody Marys, while you can catch margarita madness at the Laredo Cantina, which usually has the retro sounds of cover band Love Shack (9pm Thur-Sat) or pianist Jerry Tiffe (Sun). On the other hand, if you're feeling slightly more sophisticated, point your upturned nose to the Garage for cognac and fine cigars.

VooDoo Lounge

Rio, Masquerade Village Tower, 3700 W Flamingo Road, at Valley View Boulevard, West of Strip (252 7777). Bus 202. **Open** 11am-3am daily; shows 9pm. **Admission** free Mon-Thur, Sun; $10 Fri, Sat.
Credit AmEx, DC, Disc, MC, V.

From its perch on the 41st floor of the Masquerade Village Tower, the VooDoo Lounge has the best panoramic view in town. The décor is minimalist black and the juggling bartenders serve up potent potables to the punters. To keep things humming, better-than-average bands offer everything from swing to jazz and Brazilian rhythm. *See also p165* **Bars & Cafés**.

Dress: 11am-5pm casual, no beachwear; 5pm-2am smart casual, no athletic wear.

Production shows & showrooms

Las Vegas's original stage productions were called 'floor shows'. When Sophie Tucker performed at El Rancho and Jimmy Durante played the Flamingo in the 1940s and 1950s, they were always preceded by a line of girls, a comedian or magician, and a speciality act such as a juggler or ventriloquist. In 1958. the specs for the Vegas floor show changed radically with the introduction of the spectacular production show *Lido de Paris* at the Stardust. It was all production and no headliner. The show was the star.

With its big spectacle and topless showgirls, the Stardust packed them in and set the stage for other productions: *Folies Bergere*, *Jubilee!*, *City Lites*, *Splash!* and others followed. Soon other genres were developed: magic, impersonators, hypnotists, even *Tournament of Kings*, complete with jousting knights and Merlin the magician (at Excalibur). Occasionally, casinos will book Broadway shows such as the Pulitzer Prize-winning *Rent* and Tony award-winning *Chicago* (currently at Mandalay Bay). Past productions include *Sweet Charity*, starring Juliet Prowse, *A Chorus Line*, *Ain't Misbehavin'* and *42nd Street*. But they rarely last. Andrew Lloyd Webber's *Starlight Express* ended its run at the Las Vegas Hilton after just a couple of years.

Today's formula for a successful production show seems to involve contemporary music and dance, dynamic special effects (even pyrotechnics), a comedian, jugglers, a few motorcycles and dozens of feathered showgirls. Storylines, such as they are, exist as mere pretexts for parading brigades of suggestively costumed women who jiggle through clouds of pastel-coloured smoke as over-amped pop tunes blare. Cheesy glamour to be sure, but one of a kind, nonetheless.

Most production shows have at least some topless scenes (typically in the later of the two evening shows), but few casinos stage ongoing adult revues (currently, there's only the Riviera's *Crazy Girls* and the Luxor's *Midnight Fantasy*). You'll find a few more during the male-dominated conventions (such as Comdex, in November), but most of the adult shows (topless and all-nude) take place in men's clubs throughout the city – for details, *see chapter* **Nightlife: Adult**.

Adult revues

Crazy Girls
Riviera, 2901 Las Vegas Boulevard South, at Riviera Boulevard (794 9433). Bus 301, 302.
Shows 8.30pm, 10.30pm Tue-Fri, Sun; 8.30pm, 10.30pm, midnight Sat. **Admission** $24.78-$33.03; no under-18s. **Credit** AmEx, DC, Disc, MC, V.
The long-running topless show was launched in 1985 and continues to jiggle twice nightly in the hotel's Mardi Gras Plaza. The show features eight girls who dance to canned music and act out silly

Crazy Girls, *crazier tourists: bronze bums advertise the Riviera's famous topless show.*

Don't miss!

Vegas production shows are renowned as tacky spectacles with schlocky themes, built around troupes of showgirls draped in feather boas and not much else. True enough – but you'll also find award-winning Broadway musicals and mind-blowing, higher-than-high-tech circus shows. Try to see at least one big-scale show for a true only-in-Las-Vegas experience. These are the best shows currently running in town.

Chicago (Mandalay Bay)

This six-time Tony award-winning musical is probably the least typical of a Vegas stage show, but is perhaps the most satisfying theatrical event in town. It could also signal a change in the type of show casinos will book as we head into the twenty-first century.

EFX (MGM Grand)

EFX blends music and grand illusion to create a high-tech musical odyssey through time and space. The show is enormous in scale, but this doesn't detract from the talented cast and the diverse musical score.

Jubilee! (Bally's)

This long-running spectacle is a prototypical production show – a musical extravaganza with a huge cast of dancers and showgirls, and some dizzying stage effects ranging from sinking the *Titanic* to a World War I aerial battle.

Mystère (Treasure Island)

The most artistic and visually impressive of the city's big shows. Canadian circus empire Cirque du Soleil presents a surrealistic celebration of music, dance, acrobatics, gymnastics, mime and comedy.

O (Bellagio)

Cirque du Soleil's latest water-based show takes circus skills into a new realm of fantasy and awesome technical wizardry – even if the set is more astonishing than the human performers.

Siegfried & Roy (Mirage)

For more than 25 years, Siegfried and Roy have set the standard for illusionists in this city. They may be past their prime, but their show is still full of grand illusions, special effects and time-tested showmanship.

---

skits on a small stage. There are, however, some talented cast members. Debra Sills is a gifted singer, who even sings live on stage, and Karen Raider – the leader of the pack – is an accomplished real estate broker. As you would expect, the clientele consists mainly of high-testosterone frat boys and Asian businessmen.

Les Trix

San Remo, 115 E Tropicana Avenue, between Island & Duke Ellington Drives, East of Strip (597 6028). Bus 201, 301, 302. **Shows** 8pm, 10.30pm Tue-Sun. **Admission** $25.99 includes one drink; no under-18s for late show. **Credit** AmEx, DC, Disc, MC, V.
A variation of the old *Showgirls of Magic* that once played here, this is an eclectic blend of comedy, cockatoos and cleavage. Comedian Joe Trammel provides the jokes (he's actually pretty good), while Clint Carvalho supplies the cockatoos, parrots and other feathered friends in a fast-paced bird act. The stars of the show, however, are the topless magicians, who sing, dance and show off their illusions as well as their physical attributes.

Midnight Fantasy

Luxor, 3900 Las Vegas Boulevard South, between W Tropicana Avenue & Russell Road (262 4400). Bus 301, 302. **Shows** 10pm Mon, Wed-Fri, Sun; midnight Sat. **Admission** $29.95; no under-21s. **Credit** AmEx, DC, Disc, JCB, MC, V.
The Luxor is the latest Strip casino to toss its G-string into the topless revue ring. The show has a cast of nine lithe dancers (including two who sing

live to taped tracks), who perform predictable numbers such as *Some Like It Hot* and *Sexual Healing*. The show leans towards the old school of topless revues: namely, the women begin the number in flowing costumes that are designed for quick removal.

Celebrity impersonators

American Superstars

Stratosphere, 2000 Las Vegas Boulevard South, at St Louis Avenue, between Charleston Boulevard & Sahara Avenue, Stratosphere Area (380 7711). Bus 113, 301, 302. **Shows** 7pm Mon, Tue, Sun; 7pm, 10pm Wed, Fri, Sat. **Admission** $22.95; $16.95 5-12s. **Credit** AmEx, DC, Disc, MC, V.
This rock 'n' roll celebrity tribute treats you to impersonations of Madonna, Diana Ross, Michael Jackson, Gloria Estefan and the Spice Girls (complete with Ginger), with support from a live band and dancers. Children's tickets are available.

Danny Gans: The Ultimate Variety Performer

Mirage, 3400 Las Vegas Boulevard South, between Spring Mountain & W Flamingo Roads (791 7111). Bus 301, 302. **Shows** 8pm Tue-Thur, Sat, Sun. **Admission** $67.50; no under-5s. **Credit** AmEx, DC, Disc, MC, V.
Now installed in his very own 1,250-seater theatre at the Mirage, Danny Gans continues to stage one of the hottest shows in town. His new show contains

many favourites from his long stint at the Rio, but he is now supported by a multimillion-dollar sound-and-light system and an expanded band. Once called the man with a thousand voices, Gans does remarkable singing impressions from a repertoire of some 200 voices. He's also adept at mimicking celebs and has a spontaneous comedy style that audiences love.

Lasting Impressions

Luxor, 3900 Las Vegas Boulevard South, between W Tropicana Avenue & Russell Road (262 4400). Bus 301, 302. **Shows** 7.30pm daily. **Admission** $29.95. **Credit** AmEx, DC, Disc, MC, V.
Bill Acosta's show is reminiscent of the variety acts that used to appear on the old *Ed Sullivan Show*. There's an old-school air to his tributes to late, great celebs such as Frank Sinatra, Sammy Davis Jr, Nat King Cole and George Burns, to name a few. His act is supported by dance impressionist Jay Fagan, as well as the ubiquitous bevy of showgirls.

Legends in Concert

Imperial Palace, 3535 Las Vegas Boulevard South, between Sands Avenue & Flamingo Road (794 3261). Bus 301, 302. **Shows** 7.30pm, 10.30pm Mon-Sat. **Admission** $34.50. **Credit** AmEx, DC, Disc, MC, V.
This venerable revue has been cloning entertainer lookalikes since the mid-1980s. The secret to its success is the believable performers who spookily re-create the likes of Elvis, Roy Orbison, Buddy Holly, Liberace, Madonna, the Blues Brothers and the recently added Rod Stewart. Unlike some shows, the impersonators sing live – rather than lip-sync – and are backed by a live band. Adding sparkle are the obligatory showgirl dancers, back-up singers and a red laser and projection system that creates mystifying patterns and special effects.

Dinner shows

Caesars Magical Empire

Caesars Palace, 3570 Las Vegas Boulevard South, at W Flamingo Road (731 7333). Bus 202, 301, 302. **Shows** 4.30pm, 9.30pm Tue-Sat. **Admission** $75.50; $37.75 5-10s. **Credit** AmEx, DC, Disc, JCB, MC, V.
Breaking from the format of traditional stage shows, this is a multi-chambered magical mystery tour that blends fine dining with the world of illusion. It begins with an intimate supper show, where a magician performs for about 15 diners. After feasting, you are guided through subterranean catacombs to a seven-storey Sanctum Secorum where you can explore the Forbidden Crypt of Rameses, watch a brief Lumineria show or quench your palate in the Sanctum bars. You then move on to one of two theatres where magicians perform on rotating schedules. The price includes a three-course dinner, and just as well – this is as much hokum as magic.

Tournament of Kings

Excalibur, 3850 Las Vegas Boulevard South, at W Tropicana Avenue (597 7600). Bus 201, 301, 302. **Shows** 6pm, 8.30pm daily. **Admission** $34.95. **Credit** AmEx, DC, Disc, MC, V.

The *Tournament of Kings* is a medieval-themed dinner show in a multi-tiered theatre, with magic acts, singers and laser special effects. There's even jousting, as armour-clad knights thunder across the stage on huge steeds before doing battle with axes and swords. It's all, of course, irredeemably Vegas – maidens dance in Broadway-style formation and a courtly king bursts into a version of *Viva Las Vegas*. The medieval theme means you can eat the Cornish game hen with your fingers.

Drag shows

An Evening at La Cage

Riviera, 2901 Las Vegas Boulevard South, at Riviera Boulevard (794 9433). Bus 301, 302. **Shows** 7.30pm, 9.30pm Mon, Wed-Sun. **Admission** $28-$36. **Credit** AmEx, DC, Disc, MC, V.
The city's most popular drag show stars Frank Marino as a catty Joan Rivers and also features lip-sync impersonations of Liza Minnelli, Dionne Warwick, Madonna, Diana Ross and others. A great moment is the 'Sister Act', when a dozen hip-hopping 'nuns' bound on and off the stage. The show is superbly choreographed (the supporting female dancers are great) and the taped music and lighting tastefully enhance the show.

The Kenny Kerr Show

Jackie Gaughan's Plaza, 1 Main Street, at Fremont Street, Downtown (386 2444). Bus 108, 403. **Shows** 8pm, 10pm Tue-Sat. **Admission** $31.85. **Credit** AmEx, Disc, JCB, MC, V.
Long-time Vegas female impersonator Kenny Kerr presents his *Women of Hollywood*, a slightly sinful drag show that pays tribute to the likes of Barbra Streisand, Cher, Diana Ross and Marilyn Monroe. Kerr's underrated flair for comedy superbly sets up his 'boys-will-be-girls' cast as they celebrate their favourite female stars in inimitable style.

Magicians & magic shows

Lance Burton: Master Magician

Monte Carlo, 3770 Las Vegas Boulevard South, at Rue de Monte Carlo, between W Flamingo Road & Tropicana Avenue (730 7777). Bus 201, 301, 302. **Shows** 7.30pm, 10.30pm Tue-Sat. **Admission** $44.95-$49.95. **Credit** AmEx, DC, Disc, JCB, MC, V.
Although magicians are now commonplace in Vegas, Lance Burton remains the city's premier illusionist. His show is an entertaining blend of intimate cabaret and high-powered extravaganza. There are usually 17 illusions in the show: highlights include a levitating and disappearing white Corvette, and Burton's 'off to the gallows' stunt in which he somehow escapes the noose and ends up in the middle of the audience. A winsome sextet of dancers helps out.

Siegfried & Roy

Mirage, 3400 Las Vegas Boulevard South, between Spring Mountain & W Flamingo Roads (791 7777). Bus 301, 302. **Shows** 7.30pm, 11pm Mon, Tue, Fri-Sun. **Admission** $95. **Credit** AmEx, DC, Disc, MC, V.

The hottest ticket in town is also, at $95 a ticket, one of the most expensive. But then S&R are an institution par excellence – where else can you catch a fire-breathing dragon, white tigers, a vanishing (and reappearing) elephant and any number of eye-rubbing illusions? While some are variations of time-tested tricks (men get levitated, women are sawn in half), they are performed with great flair. The magicians (imagine, if you dare, a hybrid of Liberace, Marlin Perkins, David Copperfield and Arnold Schwarzenegger) are supported by a large-scale production company of dancers and acrobats, as well as impressive state-of-the-art sound, lighting and special effects.

Steve Wyrick, World Class Magician

Lady Luck Hotel, 206 N Third Street, at Ogden Avenue, Downtown (385 4386). Bus 107, 301. **Shows** 7.30pm, 10.30pm Tue-Sun. **Admission** $32.95. **Credit** AmEx, Disc, JCB, MC, V.
A welcome addition to the entertainment-starved Downtown area, Steve Wyrick's tightly knit magic show may be something of an economy version of Lance Burton, but many of his illusions are dramatic enough to keep audience members on the edge of their seats. Wyrick has supposedly struck a deal that will take him from his current home at the Lady Luck to the Sahara on the Strip some time in 2000.

Takin' It Uptown

Harrah's, 3475 Las Vegas Boulevard South, between E Sands Avenue & Flamingo Road (369 5222). Bus 301, 302. **Shows** 7.30pm, 10pm Mon, Tue, Thur, Sat; 9pm Wed, Fri. **Admission** $44.95. **Credit** AmEx, DC, Disc, MC, V.
Mexico's leading illusionist Joaquin Ayala (star of the *Spellbound* show) left town at the end of 1999, to be replaced by contemporary singer Clint Holmes. Holmes' show, Takin' It Uptown, blends classical, jazz and even samba, backed by a live band. It often takes on a concert-like approach, where no two shows are alike. Holmes enjoys dialogue with the audience and frequently invites celebrities to the stage, joining him in impromptu duets or skits. Shonica Roland, a 'breaking talent', brings a fresh new face to the jam sessions.

Production shows

Chicago

Mandalay Bay, 3950 Las Vegas Boulevard South, between W Tropicana Avenue & Russell Road (632 7580). Bus 301, 302. **Shows** 7.30pm Tue-Fri, Sun; 7pm, 10.30pm Sat. **Admission** $55, $65, $80. **Credit** AmEx, Disc, JCB, MC, V.
Currently in the middle of an indefinite run, the Bob Fosse musical is one of the most compelling theatrical productions to hit the Strip. The bawdy, burlesque-inspired satire of American justice is dark, sassy, sensual and delightful. To stay fresh, it rotates its cast members. Ben Vereen, Chita Rivera, Marilu Henner, Hal Linden and Jasmine Guy are among the Broadway and TV veterans who have had starring roles. Note: the front-row seats are not the best in the house – aim for three or four rows back.

EFX

MGM Grand, 3799 Las Vegas Boulevard South, at E Tropicana Avenue (891 7777). Bus 201, 301, 302. **Shows** 7.30pm, 10.30pm Tue-Sat. **Admission** $49.50-$70; $35 5-12s. **Credit** AmEx, DC, Disc, MC, V.
Starring Tommy Tune, *EFX* is a high-tech musical odyssey through time and space, in which Tune embarks on a jokey, emotional journey to rediscover his power of imagination. Along the way he also discovers worlds beyond reality and encounters such well-known faces as Harry Houdini, HG Wells and Merlin the Magician. The diverse musical score incorporates everything from Gregorian chants and traditional Irish music to hard rock and Broadway ballads. The show's special effects, derived from film and theme-park technology, are spectacular.

Folies Bergere

Tropicana, 3801 Las Vegas Boulevard South, at E Tropicana Avenue (739 2411). Bus 201, 301, 302. **Shows** 8pm, 10.30pm Mon-Wed, Fri-Sun. **Admission** $49.75-$59.75; no under-16s. **Credit** AmEx, DC, Disc, MC, V.
Las Vegas's longest-running production show, *Folies* was revamped in 1997 with new numbers, costumes and sets – but has kept the city's most exquisite showgirls. The show is a tribute to Parisian music hall as well as a romp through 100 years of French fashion, music and social mores: there's a royal ballroom sequence, a beach scene set on the French Riviera in the 1920s, a jazzy 1950s number and a 'Contemporarily Yours' finale that catapults the show into the present day. Other highlights include a 1940s jukebox number with jitterbugs and flying acrobats, a Hollywood glamour number from the 1930s and, of course, a signature can-can routine from turn-of-the-century Paris.

Forever Plaid

Flamingo Hilton, 3555 Las Vegas Boulevard South, at E Flamingo Road (733 3333). Bus 202, 301, 302. **Shows** 7.30pm, 10pm Tue-Sun. **Admission** $25.65. **Credit** AmEx, DC, Disc, JCB, MC, V.
This former off-Broadway show had everything against it when it opened in 1994 – no showgirls, no magic acts, no pyrotechnics, outdated music and a quirky, if not bewildering, plot. To wit: four glee clubbers – the Plaids – return from the dead (they died in a car collision with a bus carrying girls from a Catholic school), and seek to perform the perfect show while overcoming their own shortcomings. Perhaps inevitably, the show is now a cult hit. Part of the allure is the late 1950s and early 1960s music, performed live in the intimate, 200-seat Bugsy's Celebrity Theater.

The Great Radio City Spectacular

Flamingo Hilton, 3555 Las Vegas Boulevard South, at E Flamingo Road (733 3333). Bus 202, 301, 302. **Shows** 7.45pm Mon-Thur, Sun; 7.30pm, 10.30pm Fri, Sat. **Admission** $42.50-$62.50. **Credit** AmEx, DC, Disc, JCB, MC, V.
The high-kicking Radio City Rockettes star in this whimsical tribute to New York's Radio City Music Hall, with Maurice Hines as guest star. Among the

more interesting variety acts are comedy juggler Nino Frediana, magicians Tim Kole and Jenny Lynn, and Stacy Moore and his madcap mutts.

Jubilee!

Bally's, 3645 Las Vegas Boulevard South, at E Flamingo Road (967 4567). Bus 202, 301, 302. **Shows** 7.30pm, 10.30pm Wed-Mon. **Admission** $49.50-$66. **Credit** AmEx, DC, Disc, MC, V.

This long-running show, revamped with new costumes, sets and production numbers in 1997, is a musical extravaganza with a huge cast of dancers and dizzying stage effects ranging from the sinking of the *Titanic* to a World War I aerial dogfight and Samson destroying the Temple of the Philistines. The 16-minute opening number, based on Jerry Herman's *Hundreds of Girls*, sets the pace with dozens of dancers and singers in beaded costumes and feathered headdresses. This is turned-on-tacky at its best.

Michael Flatley's Lord of the Dance

New York-New York, 3790 Las Vegas Boulevard South, at W Tropicana Avenue (740 6815). Bus 201, 301, 302. **Shows** 7.30pm, 10.30pm Tue, Wed, Sat; 9pm Thur, Fri. **Admission** $59 Mon-Thur, Sun; $68 Fri-Sat; no under-5s. **Credit** AmEx, DC, Disc, MC, V.

This high-energy *River Dance* clone is ignited by talented young performers (ages 16-22), one singer and two violinists. The uninspiring storyline follows a Celtic version of *West Side Story*, but the rousing dance numbers are enough to keep the audience's attention from straying, even if the signature tap-dancing sounds are enhanced with recordings.

Mystère

Treasure Island, 3300 Las Vegas Boulevard South, at Spring Mountain Road (894 7111). Bus 203, 301, 302. **Shows** 7.30pm, 10.30pm Wed-Sun. **Admission** $74.80. **Credit** AmEx, DC, Disc, JCB, MC, V.

Another creation of the genre-stretching Cirque du Soleil, this show is a surrealistic celebration of music, dance, acrobatics, gymnastics, mime and comedy, taking audiences on a metaphorical journey that starts at the beginning of time – symbolised by a blast of Japanese Taiko drums sent from the heavens – and follows with a blend of music, dance and stunning displays of athleticism. Showstopping moments include the mesmerising aerial bungee ballet, the dazzling Korean plank, the precision Chinese poles performance and some awesome trapeze artists. Spectacular stuff.

Notre Dame De Paris

Paris, 3655 Las Vegas Boulevard South, between Harmon Avenue & E Flamingo Road (967 4567). Bus 202, 301, 302. **Shows** 7.30pm, 10.30pm Tues-Sat. **Admission** $69.50; no under-8s. **Credit** AmEx, DC, Disc, JCB, MC, V.

Opened in January 2000 and scheduled to run for five years, *Notre Dame De Paris* is a twenty-first-century pop-rock adaptation of Victor Hugo's classic, *The Hunchback of Notre Dame*. The show that has taken Paris by storm, and has set box-office records in France, is likely to win many new admirers in this English-language version.

O

Bellagio, 3600 Las Vegas Boulevard South, at W Flamingo Road (1-888 488 7111/693 7111). Bus 202, 301, 302. **Shows** 7.30pm, 10.30pm Wed-Sun. **Admission** $93.50-$110. **Credit** AmEx, DC, Disc, JCB, MC, V.

It's hard to imagine Cirque du Soleil outdoing itself, but its production of *O* comes close. This awesome spectacular, which opened in October 1998, has a cast of 74 trapeze artists, contortionists, divers, synchronised swimmers and others who navigate an unbelievable stage that transforms from the Arctic Ocean to an African watering hole practically instantaneously. As with *Mystère* at Treasure Island, *O* is performed in a specially built theatre. The use of water – as a character in its own right and not just a theatrical prop – gives fluidity to a show that is like a parade of haunting images with a slightly Fellini-esque quality. The experience of watching the show is rather like climbing inside a Salvador Dali painting.

Oh, what a circus, oh, what a show: Cirque du Soleil's stunning **O** *at Bellagio.*

A **Splash!** *of neon at the Riviera.*

Splash!

*Riviera, 2901 Las Vegas Boulevard South,
at Riviera Boulevard (794 9433). Bus 301, 302.*
Shows 7.30pm, 10.30pm daily. **Admission** $46.75-
$57.75; no under-18s. **Credit** AmEx, DC, Disc, MC, V.
Splash! was the original aquatic revue, staged
around a 20,000-gallon aquarium complete with
mermaids, high divers and synchronised swimmers
– good, but not as good as its publicity suggested.
Its popularity peaked in the early 1990s but after 15
years the aquatic revue was beginning to look water-
logged. So the producers scrapped the water tank
and installed an ice-rink instead, updated the
production numbers and introduced a new *Splash!*
at the end of 1999. Ice-skaters feature in the opening
and closing numbers, and once again a variety of
speciality acts perform in between. The show continues to ride pop culture, but tired Michael Jackson
and Madonna standards have been replaced with
tunes such as Cher's *Believe* and Prodigy's *Smack
My Bitch Up*. The motorcyclists riding in a 16ft (5m)
steel globe continue to thrill audiences, who also
appreciate the contribution of juggler and talented
contortionist Underarmaa Darihuu.

Wayne Newton

*Stardust, 3000 Las Vegas Boulevard South, at Stardust
Drive, between W Sahara Avenue & Spring Mountain
Road (732 6325). Bus 301, 302.* **Shows** 9pm Mon-
Thur, Sun; 8pm, 11pm Sat. **Admission** $44.95.
Credit AmEx, DC, Disc, JCB, MC, V.
The Stardust's production show *Enter the Night*,
with its explosive dance numbers, dynamic music,
variety acts and incredible laser special effects,
closed permanently at the end of 1999. Since January
2000, the casino's showroom has been taken over by

Wayne Newton (who reputedly signed the most
lucrative contract in Vegas history). He will perform
at the Stardust for 40 weeks each year.

Showrooms

Circus Maximus Showroom

*Caesars Palace, 3570 Las Vegas Boulevard South,
at W Flamingo Road (731 7333). Bus 202, 301,
302.* **Shows** usually 8pm, 11pm Thur-Sun.
Admission $55-$100. **Credit** AmEx, DC, Disc,
JCB, MC, V.
This is one of the few remaining old-style Vegas
showrooms. From Jack Benny and Judy Garland to
Diana Ross and Jerry Seinfeld, the roster of head-
lining celebs in Caesars' Circus Maximus room has
included the best that the world of showbiz has to
offer. In the past, the 1,000-seat room has also put
on productions such as *Sweet Charity*, with Juliet
Prowse, and the original *Odd Couple*, starring Tony
Randall. Broadway shows are no longer staged here,
but it hosts TV specials such as NBC's *World's
Greatest Magic*.

Congo Showroom

*Sahara, 2535 Las Vegas Boulevard South, at
E Sahara Avenue (737 2111). Bus 204, 301, 302.*
Shows usually 8.30pm daily. **Admission** from $30;
no under-18s. **Credit** AmEx, DC, Disc, JCB, MC, V.
The Sahara's Congo room has showcased four
decades of Las Vegas entertainers. From Mae West,
George Burns and Judy Garland to Tina Turner, it's
hosted them all – even the Beatles in 1964. Today,
it's searching for an identity to carry it into the
twenty-first century. After a few failed attempts at
production shows, the Sahara seems content to offer
B-grade and seen-better-days headliners, such as
Judy Tenuta, Rich Little and Jackie Mason.

Copacabana Showroom

*Rio, 3700 W Flamingo Road, at Valley View
Boulevard, West of Strip (252 7777/reservations
1-888 746 7784). Bus 202.* **Shows** 7.30pm Tue,
Thur, Fri, Sun; 7pm, 9.30pm Wed, Sat. **Admission**
$58 incl 1 drink. **Credit** AmEx, DC, Disc, MC, V.
New for January 2000, *At the Copa* stars David
Cassidy and Sheena Easton singing old favourites
from the age of swing to the 1970s, to the grand
accompaniment of an 18-piece orchestra. Keep your
ears open for Cassidy-classic *I Think I Love You*,
and Bond theme *For Your Eyes Only*, by Ms Easton.

Hollywood Theatre

*MGM Grand, 3799 Las Vegas Boulevard South, at
E Tropicana Avenue (891 7777). Bus 201, 301, 302.*
Shows daily; times vary. **Admission** $37-$70.
Credit AmEx, DC, Disc, JCB, MC, V.
This intimate theatre in the MGM Grand has an old-
fashioned movie house entrance and 630 seats
arranged in a tiered, horseshoe around the stage.
Randy Travis, Sheena Easton, Smokey Robinson,
Rita Rudner and the Go-Gos have all played here,
and it's home to Jay Leno and his *Tonight* Show for
Las Vegas tapings. Performers are usually booked
for a two-week run.

Nightlife

Mega dance clubs are the new tip in after-hours Vegas, but if you want to see sexy strippers, you can can.

Neon naughties on Fremont Street: the **Girls of Glitter Gulch**. *See page 221.*

Adult

Never mind the image; Las Vegas is deeply conflicted when it comes to the moral issues of sexy entertainment. Though many travellers expect Las Vegas to be a non-stop orgy of adult excess, those expectations outpace the reality. Despite what you've heard and perhaps hoped for, modern Las Vegas is not the uninhibited sexy playground of legend. Visitors seeking to indulge are typically redirected to the hedonism of pricey, over-the-top food, accommodation and shopping. It is more politically correct to dump one's rent money on Wolfgang Puck and a day at the spa than on a bevy of jiggling beauties. The rapid residential growth of the past two decades is partly responsible for this; recent transplants blindly expect a similar moral climate to what they had in their previous hometown. Though cab-top advertisements remain plastered with competing sells for topless bars and sexy showgirls, some residents are fighting to eliminate or restrict the ads.

Prostitution is illegal in Clark County (in which Las Vegas sits) and bawdy shows are officially frowned upon. While the G-stringed buttocks of the Riviera's *Crazy Girls* beckon you in bronzed immortality from a statue in front of the resort, officials are frantically trying to cover the very same cheeks, shown on billboards, with pasted-on ruffles; and while the lure of legal prostitution is just an hour's drive away, across the Nye County line in Pahrump, officials are enforcing regulations that prohibit its advertisement in Clark County.

During Vegas's reign as America's adult playground during the 1950s to '70s, every casino was expected to offer scantily clad showgirls shaking their things while ribald comedians told jokes that would make most of today's visitors blush. A few (notably the Riviera) still offer sexy showgirls and the occasional late-night dirty comic, but today's showroom is more likely to offer headliners, variety acts and avant-garde performance troupes than Parisian-style burlesque. As a barometer of this change, look no further than the Stardust, whose feather-and-sequin revue *Enter the Night*

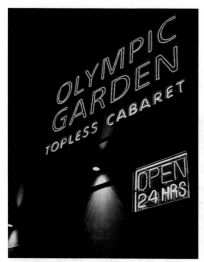

Las Vegas's biggest topless bar.

was replaced in January 2000 with headliner Wayne Newton.

Yet even with the attempts to restrict or even eliminate adult-styled entertainment under the guise of 'family friendliness' (a dismal marketing failure), there are still plenty of opportunities to liberate the libido. After developing a bad reputation in the 1980s for a dodgy collection of adult clubs that misled visitors into believing sex was for sale within the city, today's Las Vegas adult entertainment scene is heavily regulated and, for the most part, on the up-and-up.

Live adult entertainment in Las Vegas is principally geared towards the heterosexual male. There are more than 35 places where nude or nearly nude ladies (aged 18-plus) dance for dollars, but just one (Olympic Garden) where women can see men do the same. And the less obvious is nearly impossible to find. Women are prohibited by strict house rules from entering strip clubs without a male escort, purportedly to discourage both prostitution and jealous outrage. Consequently, women interested in seeing other women wiggle – while permitted the same freedoms as men when tipping dancers and buying lap-dances – often find themselves bringing along a male friend as an escort. Gay men must resort to slipping tips in the G-strings of the go-go boys at gay disco Gipsy.

Adult entertainment in twenty-first-century Las Vegas falls into four categories: casino revues; topless or nude bars and clubs; adult book/toy stores; and swingers clubs. Still, even with all of these goings-on, it is likely that you'll find the city's adult entertainment tame when compared with

San Francisco, New York or Dallas – and playfully timid in the shadow of mainland Europe.

It is important to note than when taking a cab, be sure to specify which club you want to visit; cabbies are often paid kickbacks to drop tourists at certain clubs, regardless of their quality. Unless otherwise stated, admission prices for bars and clubs apply at all times. For more info, see ads in free local weeklies *CityLife* and *Las Vegas Weekly*.

Casino revues

Most casinos have cleaned up, homogenised or scrapped altogether their adult-oriented shows in favour of headliners and family-friendly perfor-mances. The **Riviera**, which bills itself as 'the adult alternative', has not. Its recently updated *Splash!* show still offers topless dancers as part of a large-scale Vegas extravaganza, and *Crazy Girls* is straight ahead tan-and-sexy topless burlesque. The casino's comedy club also hosts XXXtreme Comedy, where the comedians all go blue. **Bally's** *Jubilee!*, a traditional Vegas feather-and-sequin show, retains its topless beauties, as does the **Tropicana**'s *Folies Bergère*. For full details, *see chapter* **Casino Entertainment**.

Topless bars

Topless bars are dark, loud and crowded – especially on Friday and Saturday and during conventions. A non-stop parade of entertainers shimmies to a DJ's music, stripping down to a G-string, a pair of six-inch platform shoes and, if you're lucky, a smile. The dancers are much more chatty than those in nude clubs, and the bars all serve alcohol and are open to those aged 21 and above. There are many more clubs than the ones listed below, but these offer the best atmosphere and dancers.

Cheetahs Topless Club

2112 Western Avenue, between W Oakey Boulevard & Sahara Avenue, Stratosphere Area (384 0074). *Bus 105, 204, 205.* **Open** 24hrs daily. **Admission** $10 8pm-5am daily. **Credit** AmEx, Disc, MC, V. This is Vegas's most relaxed topless bar, and the place with the best overall experience. Large enough to have five stages working at once yet as intimate as a neighbourhood sports bar, Cheetahs has a rep-utation as the locals' hangout. The place is packed during American football season, when Monday Night Football parties offer $5 'touchdown dances'. The gals are deliciously varied in style and there is much less silicone here than at other clubs. Bouncers and bartenders are very friendly, and the VIP room has hosted cosy lap-dances for everyone from sport and rock stars to actresses. A word of warning: you're better off catching a cab if you arrive or leave this place when it's dark – the area can be dodgy. *Dress: casual.* *Website: www.cheetahstoplessclub.com*

Club Paradise

*4416 Paradise Road, between Flamingo Road &
Harmon Avenue, University District (734 7990).*
Bus 108, 202. **Open** 4pm-6am Mon-Fri; 6pm-6am
Sat, Sun. **Admission** $10. **Credit** AmEx, DC, Disc,
MC, V.
A hyperbolic exercise in the popular 'gentlemen's
club' genre, Paradise has all the trappings (classy
exterior, open interior with plush carpeting and
pampering seating, no dancer poles) and high-
dollar luxuries (expensive champagnes, cigars and
even dinner service) you might expect. All dancers
must wear similarly styled long evening gowns
instead of the inspirational variety of sensual-to-
sluttish costumes you'll see elsewhere. This is
clearly an effort to maintain the conjured air of
subdued class, but instead results in dozens of
lookalike gals doing lookalike moves on stage.

Crazy Horse Too Gentlemen's Club

*2476 Industrial Road, at Sahara Avenue,
Stratosphere Area (382 8003). Bus 105, 204.*
Open 24hrs daily. **Admission** $10 6.30pm-4.30am
daily. **Credit** AmEx, DC, MC, V.
Following a much-needed face-lift and an $800,000
expansion, the Crazy Horse Too has reasserted itself
as one of the top topless joints in the city. Long
known as a rowdy place perfect for a frat house
reunion, the welcome renovations have brought a
Romanesque theme (including Caesars-like outfits
for the waitresses) to a formerly down-at-heel club.
Poles on the main stage encourage acrobatic finesse,
though some dancers ignore them. Well known for
attracting weekending strippers from California and
Arizona, be wary of the hustlers here. It is wise to
observe the dancers' stage skills before settling on
one for a lap-dance – good advice at any club.
Website: www.crazyhorsetoo.com

Girls of Glitter Gulch

*20 Fremont Street, between Casino Center & Main
Street, Downtown (385 4774). Bus 107, 108, 301,
302.* **Open** noon-4am Mon-Thur, Sun; noon-6am
Fri, Sat. **Admission** 2-drink minimum. **Credit**
AmEx, MC, V.
Located in the family-friendly and security-sani-
tised area beneath the Fremont Street Experience
canopy, this hold-out from the old days still draws
in the punters, day and night. You too can stroll in
after watching the extravagant free light and music
show and experience – for rather more money – a
performance with nearly as many lights and a different kind of sizzle. Heavily advertised on billboards and cabs all over town, Glitter Gulch
features average-looking women with enormous
breasts lap-dancing for men with enormous wallets.
The location tends to draw a touristy crowd.

Olympic Garden Cabaret

*1531 Las Vegas Boulevard South, at Wyoming
Avenue, Stratosphere Area (385 8987). Bus 301,
302.* **Open** 24hrs daily. **Admission** $5 8pm-4am
daily. **Credit** AmEx, DC, MC, V.
On the Strip near the Stratosphere, this is the largest
and most visible of Las Vegas's adult entertainment

venues. Two storeys of multiple rooms present a
nice variety of hard-working dancers in what can
only be described as a warehouse of sexuality. The
main room has large, pole-less circular stages
surrounded by stageside seating, couches, booths,
the DJ stall and the main bar. Opposite is a darker,
more intimate and luxurious room with a runway
and two circular stages. Upstairs, a VIP room
awaits, where Vegas's longest-running male exotic
dance revue is presented to the delighted shrieks of
women gone wild (call for a schedule). The atmosphere is fairly comfortable, though the incessant
strobe lights and loud sound system can be overwhelming. The number of physical enhancements
have earned Olympic Garden the nickname 'Silicone
Valley' among local dancers, but the sheer number
of performers on the roster (more than 300 on a busy
night) will keep the visitor happy.
Dress: no tank tops.

Spearmint Rhino

*3340 Highland Drive, at W Desert Inn Road, West of
Strip (734 7336). Bus 105.* **Open** 24hrs daily.
Admission $5 after 10pm. **No credit cards**.
Part of a renowned California chain of nude clubs,
Spearmint Rhino boasts one of the most chic,
modern interiors in the city (for adult clubs). Opened
as a totally nude juice bar (no alcohol), management
soon tried to circumvent city law by buying the bar
next door and erecting a glass partition between the
two. When that practice was stopped, Spearmint
Rhino gave in, went topless and now offers a full bar
and restaurant. Though Rhino has the expected
stage and lap-dancing, what makes this place unique
is that late at night (around 3am), the bar gets a
little wacky, hosting after-hours parties that draw
anyone and everyone – couples, singles, gays, you
name it. Definitely worth a try for the bar crowd
seeking something a little different and daring.
Note: if you're driving, you can't turn into
Highland Drive from Desert Inn Road; you have to
access it either from the south, off Spring Mountain
Road, or from the north, off Sahara Avenue.

Nude clubs

Nude clubs, in which the girls go bare-assed naked
(sometimes even without shoes), are similar to topless bars with an important difference – they're
prohibited from serving alcohol. This results in a
strange twist: most nude clubs are open to patrons
18 and older (except the **Palomino**, the only nude
bar in town permitted a liquor licence and therefore restricted to over-21s). As a result, nude clubs
attract a different type of patron (younger and less
affluent) and a different kind of dancer (younger
and more money-hungry) – a combo that leads
to an annoying, anxious synergy. A pocketful of
dollars and an assertive attitude will overcome this
in many instances. For some reason, nude dancers
try to take their 'art' more seriously than topless
dancers, when, in fact, most patrons just wanna see
them wiggle, spread and show some personality.

Déjà Vu Showgirls

3247 Industrial Road, between Spring Mountain Road & Sahara Avenue, West of Strip (894 4167). Bus 105, 203. **Open** 11am-6am Mon-Sat; 6pm-4am Sun. **Admission** before 6pm $10; bar minimum after 6pm $10. **No credit cards.**

'Hundreds of beautiful girls and three ugly ones, coast-to-coast' is this national chain's slogan (yes, America has national nude club chains!). The dancers lean towards the pretty end of the scale and each possess a uniqueness that is difficult to come by in the land of silicone sameness. Déjà Vu's claim to fame is a series of theme nights – from Amateur Nights to oil and Jell-O wrestling to shower parties and more – lending them a kind of frat-house-party-with-strippers ambience.
Dress: no tank tops.

Little Darlings

1514 Western Avenue, just north of Wyoming Avenue, Stratosphere Area (366 1141). Bus 105. **Open** 11am-6am Mon-Sat; 6am-4am Sun. **Admission** $20 men; free women. **Credit** MC, V.

Stark lighting, annoying DJs and plastic drink cups are immediate challenges to the success of Little Darlings. Add that most patrons are high-school grads in backwards baseball caps and you're wondering why we've listed the place. It's simple: most of the girls are gorgeous, and barely legal age-wise (if that's your thing). Body piercings – in the most inaccessible of places – and wax jobs are all the rage. Stage dancers pick their own music (anything from Sisters of Mercy to Blue Oyster Cult), so you'll get a hint of their personalities before committing to a private lap-dance. These dances can get pretty wild, though planting your hands solidly at your side will avoid problems with kneed-in groins and vice cops. Dancers are not at all chatty here; either cough up for a lap-dance or they move on. This works both ways, though, so sweetly say 'no thanks' if you have your eye on another.
Dress: no tank tops.
Website: www.showgirl.com

Palomino Club

1814 Las Vegas Boulevard North, just north of Main Street, North Las Vegas (642 2984). Bus 113. **Open** 2pm-4am daily. **Admission** $10. **No credit cards.**

The most atmospheric nude club (it's amazing what liquor profits can do) may not be as 'world-famous' as the advertising slogans suggest, but the granddaddy of Las Vegas strip clubs has earned a reputation – even if only as the only nude bar in town. The Palomino is no mere strip joint; instead, it offers a true cabaret atmosphere. Downstairs, a runway stage juts into the audience and an MC (not just a DJ) performs his fairly funny comedy act between floor shows. Upstairs, dancers work a small round stage with a pole. The main runway showcases only 'feature dancers' (adult-film actresses, centrefolds, published models). These uniformly beautiful burlesque artists all have fully

fledged fantasy costumes (cowgirl, cheerleader, nurse and so on), of which every stitch is gracefully and sexily removed until they are completely naked, right down to their polished toenails.

Adult book & toy stores

Typically, adult bookstores are seedy locales with porn mags, adult videos for rent or sale and all sorts of rubber and leather novelties lined up in rows of dirty-floored aisles. There are, however, a few that are clean, nicer or notable in some way – we've listed the best below.

Adult Superstore

3850 W Tropicana Avenue, at Valley View Boulevard, West of Strip (798 0144). Bus 201. **Open** 24hrs daily. **Credit** AmEx, Disc, MC, V.

Although there are four locations of this locals' favourite, the one you must visit is the 'mega-super-store' on West Tropicana Avenue. It truly lives up to that designation, with more than 8,000sq ft (744sq m) – on two levels – of every size, shape and texture of adult entertainment. There are magazine and video sections devoted to every fetish and fantasy legal in Nevada, while the selection of rubber toys, fetish gear and even sexy food items (check out the penis pasta) is unequalled. A huge selection of party items also makes this a favourite stop for those planning hen or stag nights. While it has the requisite 'video arcade' (private movie-viewing booths), it is also the only place left in Las Vegas where you can view adult films on the big screen. Take a friend and make a night of it.

Paradise Electro Stimulations

1509 W Oakey Boulevard, at Western Avenue, Stratosphere Area (474 2991). Bus 105. **Open** 9am-7pm Mon-Fri. **Credit** AmEx, Disc, MC, V.

Discard any preconceptions of adult playthings before entering. PES (aka the Studio) is known the world over for something entirely different: electrically operated muscle stimulation devices. That's right, folks – dildos, plugs, sheaths, you name it – all composed of striking crystal-clear plastic, and all attachable to an electrical impulse control unit that purportedly stimulates the user from the inside out. Add the architecturally appealing 'Chair' (which, as well as offering restraining devices, will accept many of the toys as attachments), and you've got quite a collection of industrial-strength sexual enhancers with a decidedly postmodern flair. Featured nationwide on HBO's *Reel Sex*, PES is truly an experience for the sexually adventurous; call ahead for a private viewing.
Website: www.peselectro.com

Rancho Adult Entertainment Center

4820 N Rancho Drive, at Lone Mountain Road, North Las Vegas (645 6104). Bus 106. **Open** 24hrs daily. **Credit** AmEx, MC, V, Disc.

The best of the small adult bookstores has something for everyone: a large variety of always-new videos, magazines and vibrating toys, S&M gear, leather and vinyl, massage oils and more. If you can't find what you're looking for, the friendly staff – including several women – will help or order it for you. All this contributes to a very comfortable atmosphere, one that makes this the place for couples – men and women, gays and straights. You'll often see pairs sheepishly walking the aisles, discussing the merits of one toy over another, or small groups of women stopping off for novelty gifts on the way to hen nights or divorce parties.

Showgirl Video

631 Las Vegas Boulevard South, at Bonneville Avenue, Stratosphere Area (385 4554). Bus 206, 301, 301. **Open** 24hrs daily. **Credit** AmEx, MC, V.
This otherwise unappealing adult bookstore is notable for its live dancer fantasy booths. While the one-on-one booths are always on the action, feature dancers (adult-film and magazine starlets) rule the place during the trade convention season. A few blocks south of Showgirl is its sister store, Talk of the Town, which is a similar operation, though slightly larger and more accommodating to couples. If you enjoy adult videos, the live shows viewed from the booths will make for an interesting heavy-breather – especially if you're willing to shove enough cash through the glass.

Swingers clubs

Swingers clubs are legal adult gathering spots where consenting adults of all sexual proclivities and relationship arrangements have the opportunity to mix, mingle and more. The clubs do not offer gambling or alcohol (though you can bring your own), but do have the other amenities that are associated with nightclubs, such as dancefloors and music. You pay an entrance fee only.

Hide 'n' Seek

3084 S Highland Drive, between Desert Inn Road & Sahara Avenue, West of Strip (650 2747). Bus 105. **Open** 7pm-4am daily. **Credit** MC, V.
Billed as a fully licensed, right-in-the-city 'alternative nightclub', Hide 'n' Seek has a dancefloor and an entertainment area. Looking for couples, singles, bisexuals? You'll find them all here, enjoying a little partying, playing and perhaps petting, if the vibe is right. Theme nights are offered (call for details) and admittance is generally limited to couples or single women, though a few single men can get in depending on the crowd mix. Staff 'hostesses' will dance for you for a fee, but if you're really looking for dances, you'd be better off at a couples-friendly strip club. *Website: www.hnslv.com*

The Red Rooster

451 6666; call for further details.
The city's oldest swingers club. Located in the huge home of hosts Mike and Chris out in a remote area of old Henderson, the Rooster is a bizarre mix of private nightclub and sex extravaganza. It's not unusual to see a crowd of 100 boogieing on the dancefloor, a small group of men playing eight-ball

on one of the many pool tables or couples relaxing around the straight-from-the-1970s sunken fire pit. Then again, it's also not unusual to see people giving and getting oral sex right at the bar, either. There is a pool, several hot tubs, private play rooms and an upstairs area for 'committed couples' only. Sodas and snacks are provided, but BYOB. *Website: www.vegasredrooster.com*

Dance clubs

Las Vegas has never been a clubbing city – until now. Unlike other American metropolises, Vegas's nightlife is dominated by the powerful lure of casino resorts, each offering their own brand of tempting diversions with the primary purpose of attracting and keeping the bottom-line business of gambling within their respective doors. In a town where money can be made quickly and easily by anyone with a gaming licence, chancing the fickle club scene was once a risk Vegas was not willing to take. Not any more.

In the 1990s, a dramatic shift occurred in the Vegas nightlife landscape. Longtime off-Strip locale the Shark Club (formerly Paul Anka's Jubilation disco in the 1970s) was demolished to make room for another as-yet uninitiated resort project, and the on-Strip Metz Club finally failed after many short-lived incarnations as a high-rent touristy nightclub. Sensing opportunity, the Rio opened its main showroom – with sound and lighting systems already in place – as a late-night dance club. Meanwhile, underground promoters brought the house and techno scene to Las Vegas via Los Angeles. Suddenly, a glittering nightlife renaissance was afoot.

The decisive moment occurred in February 1996, when the late nightclub promoter Aaron Britt assembled a team of enthusiasts to create **Club Utopia** in the old Metz spot on the Strip. Like nightclubs throughout the world, Utopia lifted techno and other progressive dance sounds from the underground and thrust them into a mainstream nightclub environment. After a rocky first year, Club Utopia evolved into an internationally recognised venue, inspiring a clubbing rebirth that is now a major movement on the Strip.

As club music and fashion styles congealed in the late 1990s into what many have called the 'Rebirth of Disco', and younger visitors descended upon Vegas, opening casino nightclubs became less of a risk and more of a necessity. Flighty trends no longer make the scene unstable; rather, it has come full circle. Techno hippies happily skank to remixes of disco hits, hip hoppers revisit breakdance moves to Fatboy Slim and conventioneers bounce gleefully to the crushing beats of Vegas's own international superstars, the Crystal Method. Dancing is back and bigger than ever.

Now recognised as a low-risk customer draw and publicity generator, several major new clubs have opened since the last edition of this guide, all but one in a casino. DJs are hailing 2000 as the year Las Vegas – with no last call and sun-rising parties every night – breaks into the top five clubbing cities in the world.

Note that all the clubs listed below admit over-21s only. The exception is the **Sanctuary**: a live music and dance club open to those aged 18 and over. Located in the city's historic Huntridge district just behind the venerable theatre to which the neighbourhood owes its name, it has a full bar (which requires proper ID) and live music (from hot local bands to smaller national acts) or DJs almost every weekend. *See page 233* **Music** for more details.

Gay dance club **Gipsy** (*see page 231* **Gay & lesbian**) is also very popular with non-gays, while the **House of Blues** (*see page 233* **Music**) offers after-hours dancing most weekend nights. It's an excellent live music venue, but only a decent nightclub (the sound system is fabulous, but the lighting is quite unsuited to the dancefloor).

Some clubs have no fixed closing time. Call before setting out as times and prices may change. Women with local ID often get in free.

Bouncing **Baby's** *at the Hard Rock Hotel.*

Baby's

Hard Rock, 4455 Paradise Road, at Harmon Avenue, East of Strip (693 5000). Bus 108, 213. **Open** 10pm-5am daily. **Admission** $7-$15. **Credit** AmEx, DC, Disc, MC, V.

Sin City's celebrated nightlife got a lot hipper in 1999 with the addition of Baby's, where *Austin Powers* meets *Logan's Run* two storeys beneath the Hard Rock Hotel. A combined effort of Peter Morton and LA restaurateur Sean Macpherson, the secluded, subterranean hideaway – past an indiscriminate doorway and down two flights of stairs – encourages the frolicking friskiness of today's Mod Squad. Far more retro than rave, dark wood panelling and velveteen upholstery greet clubsters in the small aquarium room, where acid jazz sets the mood. Around the corner is the main room, all done up in retro-futurist fancy. Here, DJ Funkler spins deep lounge, house and jungle, and the waitresses burst forth from barely zipped vinyl. *Website: www.hardrock.com*

The Beach

365 Convention Center Drive, at Paradise Road, East of Strip (731 1925). Bus 108. **Open** *cabana & sports bar* 24hrs daily; *dance club* 10pm-4am Mon-Thur, Sun; 10pm-6am Fri, Sat. **Credit** AmEx, Disc, MC, V.

Described by one observer as 'Gidget Goes to Studio 54' (a reference to the series of campy American beach movies of the 1960s), the Beach is a two-storey fun stop playing heavily on the sun-and-surf theme. This 'meet market' features surfboard and grass hut décor, complete with bartenders and waitresses in beachwear and bikinis, who sometimes get up on the bar to do slightly suggestive dances. Thanks to its location across from the Convention Center, the Beach also has a cabana and sports bar that is open during the day, and has hosted special performances, including the one Pink Floyd is reputed to have given Microsoft chairman Bill Gates. *Dress: smart casual. Website: www.beachlv.com*

C2K

Venetian, 3355 Las Vegas Boulevard South, south of Sands Avenue (948 3007). Bus 203, 301, 302. **Open** 11pm-dawn Wed-Sun. **Admission** $10 men; $5 women. **Credit** AmEx, Disc, MC, V.

This multifaceted entertainment venue – a concert hall in the early evening, a skull-pounding dance party after hours – has space for 1,400 seated patrons and who knows how many grooving on the dancefloor. Narrow but tall, C2K's two upper storeys (including private skyboxes) offer nice views of the party going on below. Despite drawbacks such as bars foolishly placed on the dancefloor and drinks priced on the gold standard, the club is already hosting some of the city's best club nights (Naked Hollywood, Hedonism). Racy and risqué, C2K has live video projections of the mayhem throughout the club, thus offering exhibitionists and voyeurs equal pleasure. Go-go dancers groove enticingly on the stage and, after the conventioneers clear out at about 1.30am, the hardcore clubbers take over and things get truly spicy. *Dress: no athletic shoes, baggy trousers, jeans, beach attire or hats. Website: www.clubczk.com*

Club Rio

*Rio, 3700 W Flamingo Road, at Valley View
Boulevard, West of Strip (252 7727/252 7777). Bus
202.* **Open** from 10.30pm Wed-Sat. **Admission** $10
men; $5 women. **Credit** AmEx, DC, Disc, JCB, MC, V.
Las Vegas's original casino nightclub operates in the
Copa showroom after David Cassidy and Sheena
Easton pack up for the evening. The surroundings
are wide-open and plush, with plenty of booths and
seating under the high ceilings. The crowd is decidedly older for a nightclub. Drawing mostly tourists,
single conventioneers and middle-aged couples, Club
Rio has succeeded where the Metz Club failed. Disco
cover band Boogie Nights appears on Wednesdays;
Thursday is the 'Latin Labeatoh' salsa night.
*Dress: smart casual; no shorts, collarless shirts,
tennis shoes or excessively baggy or ripped clothing.
Website www.playrio.com*

Club Utopia

*The Epicenter, 3765 Las Vegas Boulevard South,
between Harmon & E Tropicana Avenues (740 4646).
Bus 301, 302.* **Open** 9pm-10am Thur-Sat. **Admission**
from $10 Thur, Fri; $15 Sat. **Credit** AmEx, MC, V.
The innovator when Vegas dance clubs were still
stuck in pop-land, Utopia sparked a music and night-
clubbing revolution. The club has rave-friendly
music from techno and house to breakbeat and more,
spun by local and imported international DJs. There
are three rooms, two levels, a huge dancefloor,
an upstairs outdoor patio, great sound and atmospheric enhancers. Though the vibe has been diluted
since the early days and rumours of its ultimate
demise persist (the land is highly coveted), it's still
the king of Vegas dance clubs. *See also p233* **Music**.
Website: www.clubutopia.com

Drink & Eat Too!

*200 E Harmon Avenue, at Koval Lane, East of Strip
(796 5519). Bus 201, 202, 213.* **Open** *Jan-Nov*
8pm-5am Tue-Sat; *Dec* 8pm-5am Thur-Sat.
Admission $5-$10. **Credit** AmEx, DC, MC, V.
This two-storey alcohol palace, known locally as
'Drink', has been the place for Vegas's university
student, young lawyer and model-actress wannabe
crowd since opening in 1995. Half the fun is finding
your way around the labyrinthine space to order
drinks at one of the numerous bars. The dancefloor
is large, though it's made to look and feel like
cobblestones – a high-heeled lawsuit waiting to
happen. The drinks menu, featuring odd serving
containers such as jars and baby bottles, is exhaus-
tive, and the music a mix of popular techno, disco
and modern rock. Locally, Drink draws its notoriety
from being built in the middle of a cluster of apartment complexes, and having battled their residents
ever since. Reggae band Bonafide performs on
Saturday nights. Note: the bouncers are notoriously
testy. *See also p165* **Bars & Cafés**.
*Dress: smart casual; no tank tops, cut-offs or
excessively baggy clothing.*

The Hop

*1650 E Tropicana Avenue, between Maryland
Parkway & Spencer Street, University District
(310 5060/736 0042). Bus 201.* **Open** from 7pm
Wed-Sat. **Admission** $5 Wed, Fri; $10 Thur, Sat.
Credit AmEx, Disc, MC, V.
Like a hybrid of something from *Casablanca* and
Ocean's 11, the Hop is a classic speakeasy in the
Vegas style. Low ceilings mask the spacious interior:
a multi-tiered room filled with plush velvet booths

Run wild at Mandalay Bay's hot new nightclub **Rumjungle**. *See page 226.*

and chairs so comfortable you could lie down in one and do what comes naturally. All seats face the stage, and the stage fronts the dancefloor. Dancing to live music, ranging from oldies to big band, happens several nights a week, with each night promoted by a different group.

Dress: smart casual; no blue jeans, athletic wear or excessively baggy clothing.

Pink E's

3695 W Flamingo Road, at Valley View Boulevard, West of Strip (252 4666). Bus 202. **Open** 24hrs daily. **Admission** free Mon; $1-$3 Tue-Fri, Sun; $6-$8 Sat; free women Thur. **Credit** MC, V.

Is it a nightclub? Is it a pool bar? It it a video arcade? Whatever it is, Pink E's is the most popular weekend gathering spot for the local rock 'n' roll crowd. Dozens of pink-felt pool tables (free on Sundays) are available for that eight-ball fix, and more than a fistful of pinball machines and electronic games await your skills. All of this, plus a constant blast of rock music, keeps the tight-pants girls happy, and that keeps the motorcycle-riding guys smiling, too. Watch for the occasional night of live rock from local and national bands, and don't miss the restrooms – trust us. *See also p242* **Sport & Fitness**.

Dress: casual; no cut-offs, biker wear, gang wear or excessively baggy trousers.

Ra

Luxor, 3900 Las Vegas Boulevard South, between W Tropicana Avenue & Russell Road (262 4000). Bus 301, 302. **Open** 10pm-6am Wed-Sat. **Credit** AmEx, DC, Disc, MC, V. **Admission** $10 men; $5 women.

Ra is intimate in comparison with some of the more excessive spaces in town, but the elaborate Egyptian theming is seamless and impressive. Now one of the 'oldest' (opened 1997) of the new clubs, Ra is still one of the best in terms of atmosphere, packing 'em in with excellent lighting and sound and a furious promotions schedule. Special theme nights include Pleasuredome (underground dance, Wednesdays) and Turning Trixxx (decadent and sexy London club night, monthly). Cage dancers get their groove on to keep the crowd moving, and live concerts on the venue's stage also mix it up, with big-name spinners such as DJ Skribble and DJ Rap making guest stops.

Dress: no tank tops, baggy trousers, shorts, sport wear, jeans, T-shirts or hats.
Website: www.luxor.com

Red Dragon Lounge

Mandalay Bay, 3950 Las Vegas Boulevard South, between W Tropicana Avenue & Russell Road (893 3388). Bus 301, 302. **Open** 10am-4pm Wed. **Admission** $10. **Credit** AmEx, DC, Disc, MC, V.

Currently staged in the China Grill, a funky modernist restaurant straight out of the pages of *Wallpaper** magazine, this midweek neo-Asian affair is the product of veteran Vegas club scenesters. An instant hit with those in the know, Red Dragon has that ultimate, hard-to-find, big-city underground-yet-upscale vibe. Deep-lounge DJs are flown in weekly to complement the house spinner, DJ Funkler.

Website: www.reddragonlounge.com

Rumjungle

Mandalay Bay, 3950 Las Vegas Boulevard South, between W Tropicana Avenue & Russell Road (632 7777). Bus 301, 302. **Open** 10.30pm-2am Mon-Thur, Sun; 10.30pm-4am Fri, Sat. **Admission** $10 Mon-Wed, Sun; $15 Thur; $20 Fri, Sat. **Credit** AmEx, DC, Disc, MC, V.

Not since the loss of the Shark Club has the raging-hormones crowd had such a jumping nightspot in which to get jiggy. By day, Rumjungle is a pleasantly hip restaurant with a world-friendly menu and pocket-friendly pricing. But late night, it gussies up and morphs from Meat Market to Meet Market. A DJ spins music heavy on Latin house and techno, and thundering bass pours from the entrance as a long line of partygoers waits to be admitted. Once past the velvet ropes and the steaming 50ft (15m) high fire-and-water wall, clubbers indulge in an environment so atmospheric you'll swear you landed in Rio de Janiero. The dancefloor is tiny compared with the rest of the club, but this does little to quell the spirits of the young and beautiful.

Dress code: smart casual. No shorts.
Website: www.mandalaybay.com

Studio 54

MGM Grand, 3799 Las Vegas Boulevard South, at E Tropicana Avenue (891 1111). Bus 201, 301, 302. **Open** 10pm-3am Tue-Sat. **Admission** men $10 Tue-Thur; $20 Fri, Sat; women free. **Credit** AmEx, DC, Disc, JCB, MC, V.

With everyone from teenage technoids to new grand-mas dancing to disco, recreating the famed Studio 54 was an obvious move for the city of replication. The upscale warehouse-styled club has four levels, each of them featuring its own dancefloor, seating and a bar tended by the prettiest boys this side of *An Evening at La Cage*. There's also great lighting and sound, sexy go-go dancers (men and women) and a fun, high-energy mix of music from the 1970s to 2000. Though its initially strict 'are you hip enough?' admission policy has been relaxed a bit, the high cover charge and chi-chi VIP lounges still result in an odd mix of club kids and high-rollers sharing dancing space with baby boomers reliving their glory days. MGM hotel guests get in for free Tuesdays to Thursdays.

Dress: smart casual. Men: collared shirts, sport coats, no baggy jeans or tennis shoes.
Website: www.mgmgrand.com

Gay & lesbian

Touted as the City of Sin, a modern Sodom and Gomorrah, Las Vegas is perhaps one of the last places on earth where you can truly lose your inhibitions (and your shirt) for a night or a weekend without getting caught. But it's also politically and morally steeped in its Mormon history. Only certain 'sins' are accepted, and as a result many local homosexuals are still very closeted. Nevada laws banning sodomy were repealed only in 1995, thanks to continual lobbying by local gay and

Get Booked: *for all your gay reading needs.*

lesbian activists (it's now legal for anyone over the age of 18). However, this advance threatens to be stifled by a year 2000 petition to legally define marriage in the state as a 'union between one man and one woman'.

But fear not, queer tourist: remember that this is also the city that Liberace built. The **Liberace Museum** (*see page 85* **Attractions**) is a sparkling must-see Vegas treasure – a grand rhine-stone-encrusted tribute to the Queen who was the jewel on the crown of this desert oasis for decades. Feeling more at home already now, aren't you? This is the land that good taste forgot, where 'excessive' is a compliment and high kitsch rules supreme. Make the obligatory pilgrimage to the larger-than-life double bust of Siegfried & Roy. Bare chested and surrounded by gigantic, phallic crystals, this outrageous and overt monument to the illusionists' own brand of excess and camp narcissism occupies a place of honour in front of Treasure Island.

Las Vegas's burgeoning gay district, the 'Gay Triangle', or 'Fruitloop' as it is affectionately referred to by locals, is easily found by first-time visitors. Its epicentre is at the corner of Naples Drive and Paradise Road, just south of the Hard Rock Café. There you'll find **Get Booked** for all your literary needs and a host of bars including **Gipsy**, Las Vegas's oldest and most popular gay dance club.

One of the newest additions is **Key's** piano bar on Sahara Avenue. Key's and its neighbours are creating a gay area of their own at the north end of the Strip, for those seeking the company of locals. Across Sahara, in the Commercial Center, you'll find the **Spotlight** – Las Vegas's largest gay locals' hangout – as well as **Badlands**, the **Las Vegas Lounge**, the **Apollo Health Spa** and **Second Time Around** thrift store, which raises money Aid for AIDS of Nevada (*see below*).

For details of the annual **Gay Pride** celebration, *see page 104* **Las Vegas by Season**.

Resources

Resources

Gay & Lesbian Center of Las Vegas
912 E Sahara Avenue, between Sixth Street & Maryland Parkway, East Las Vegas (733 9800/ fax 733 9075). Bus 204. **Open** 10am-8pm Mon-Fri.
A support organisation for gay men and lesbians. Different groups meet here daily at various times, including a gay men's discussion group (5.30pm Fri), a lesbian group (7pm Fri) and a youth group (5pm Thur). There are also free and confidential HIV tests (3-5.30pm Thur). Call ahead, though, because the schedule of meetings might change. Note that the centre can be tricky to find: it's on a little cul-de-sac off Sahara Avenue, opposite the Commercial Center. *Website: www.lasvegasglbtcenter.org*

Get Booked
Paradise Plaza, 4640 Paradise Road, at Naples Drive, between Harmon & Tropicana Avenues, East of Strip (737 7780). Bus 108, 213. **Open** 10am-midnight Mon-Thur; 10am-2am Fri; noon-2am Sat; noon-midnight Sun. **Credit** AmEx, Disc, MC, V.
This small store, selling books, magazines, greetings cards and videos (for rent or sale) is Las Vegas's only gay and lesbian bookstore.

HIV & AIDS

At the risk of stating the obvious, Nevada is a unique state with legalised gaming and limited legalised prostitution in some counties. It ranks 12th in the nation for AIDS cases per capita and second for alcohol consumption. Combine these sobering statistics with the fact that Las Vegas's thriving tourist industry attracts more than 32 million visitors annually, and it soon becomes obvious that Vegas is not only a pleasure zone but a danger zone, too. To restate the obvious, always practise safe sex.

For more specific information on HIV/AIDS, local resources and various support groups and free tests, contact **Aid for AIDS of Nevada**, the state's largest and most comprehensive AIDS service provider, or the AIDS information line at the **Clark County Health District**.

Aid for AIDS of Nevada (AFAN)
Sahara Rancho Medical Center, 2300 S Rancho Drive, suite 211, between Sahara Avenue & Oakey Boulevard, West of Strip (382 2326). Bus 201. **Open** 8am-5pm Mon-Fri.
In addition to offering free advice and testing, this support group raises money and awareness through three big-scale annual events: the Black & White Party, the Beaux Arts Ball (*see box p228*) and a sponsored walk up and down the Strip, which attracted 5,000 participants in 1999.
Website: www.wizard.com/afan

AIDS Information Line
Clark County Health District, 625 Shadow Lane, annex A, just north of Charleston Boulevard, North-west Las Vegas (383 1393). Bus 206, 401. **Open** 8am-4.30pm Mon-Fri.

You shall go to the ball

While Las Vegas is known as a party town where anything goes, it has not forsaken all morals in search of hedonism. A growing awareness of the importance of assisting those in need has helped one local AIDS service organisation raise funds, while playing host to two of the most fabulous parties of the year.

Each September, Aid for AIDS of Nevada (AFAN) holds the **Black & White Party**, poolside, at the Hard Rock Hotel. This elegant yet fun cocktail party attracts a true cross-section of close to 3,000 of the city's culturati. Guests dress in casual to sophisticated black and white, with many in creative, flamboyant attire. The entrance fee is either non-perishable food worth $25 or $35 in cash – the donations keep AFAN's foodbank stocked for several months. Food is provided by local restaurants cooking on site, and drinks are free. Many local performers from shows on the Strip provide top-notch entertainment throughout the evening.

The second big party is at Hallowe'en. In a land where drag queens and impersonators queue with you at the grocery store on any given day, such a holiday could pass by relatively unnoticed. But for more than 35 years the **Beaux Arts Hallowe'en Ball** (*pictured*) has been ensuring that Hallowe'en in Vegas is an unforgettable occasion – the party that local entertainers and nationally recognised celebrities prepare for year round. Its legendary Costume Contest has been judged by every famous name that has ever performed on a Vegas stage, from Sammy Davis Jr to Liza Minelli.

Held at the star-studded Studio 54, inside the MGM Grand, the ball is also a fundraiser for AFAN and is open to the public. The rare combination of Joe Public and the entertainment industry's elite creates a unique and memorable event. Tickets cost $15 in advance and $20 at the door. Contact AFAN on 382 2326 for more information on both events.

Media

For information on what's happening in and around the bars or for special events, local gossip and personal ads, pick up the *Las Vegas Bugle*. It's free, published twice a month and available at all local gay bars, coffeehouses, bookstores and other gay-owned or gay-friendly businesses, including most of those listed in this section.

Out Las Vegas is a new gay entertainment magazine with some articles but mainly adverts for escorts, bars and some special events. Geared primarily towards men, it also includes ads for women and many for transsexuals.

Also check out **www.gayvegas.com**, which is operated by the *Bugle*.

Spiritual

The **Las Vegas Metropolitan Community Church**, the city's only gay church, meets every Sunday at 10am at the Huntridge Theatre (1208 E Charleston Boulevard, at Maryland Parkway) and every Wednesday at 6pm at 1140 Almond Tree Lane, suite 301, at Maryland Parkway; call 369 4380 for more details.

Accommodation

Although it is widely known that a significant segment of the gay and lesbian communities virtually runs the hotels here (as well as a long list of other industries), don't rush up to the check-in desk and announce that you're queer – the Vegas tourist industry is only just beginning to wake up to the power of the gay dollar. However, many hotels are willing to help direct you and answer questions if you ask in a discreet manner.

The **Riviera** is generally considered the most openly gay-friendly hotel on the Strip and occasionally brings in nationally recognised gay and lesbian comics and musicians. However, it's in need of renovation and many visitors prefer the newer, glitzier and more youthful hotels such as the **Hard Rock**, **MGM Grand**, **Mandalay Bay** and **Luxor**, all of which have spectacular restaurants, are closer to the more active end of the Strip, feature top-name entertainers and have nightclubs that are fun and packed every weekend. For details of all, *see chapter* **Accommodation**.

Chapman Guesthouse

1904 Chapman Drive, off Sahara Avenue, just east of Maryland Parkway, East Las Vegas (312 4625). Bus 204. **Rates** $59-$79. **Credit** AmEx, MC, V.
This exclusively gay male guesthouse has five rooms, pool, jacuzzi, sundeck and off-street parking. The mailing address is PO Box 46193, Las Vegas, NV 89114, and booking is recommended.
Website: www.chapmanguesthouse.com

The Ranch

1110 Ralston Drive, near Martin Luther King Boulevard & Washington Avenue, North Las Vegas (631 7013/fax 631 7723). Bus 105, 208. **Rates** *summer* $75 per person; *winter* $150 per person; call for weekend and weekly rates. **No credit cards**.
The one lesbian-owned B&B in Las Vegas has three private, no-smoking rooms, swimming pool, spa, full country breakfast and lots of fresh air. The staff will pick you up at the airport if you ask.

Nightlife

One unique attribute of Las Vegas is that nearly everything is open and available 24 hours a day, 365 days a year – including the dozen or so gay bars and a few that identify themselves as 'alternative' and therefore gay-friendly. However, like the city itself, the Las Vegas nightlife scene is experiencing the joys and despairs of its own growing pains. Visitors who are looking for a big-city club experience similar to New York or Los Angeles are likely to be disappointed, for Las Vegas is, in many ways, still in its adolescence.

Although the gay clubs are well attended, the new trend is for the more 'sophisticated' and less closeted members of the gay community (and numerous 'experimenters') to visit the big clubs in the newer hotel-casinos. The most popular at the time of writing were: **Ra** at the Luxor, **C2K** at the Venetian, **Club Utopia** next to the MGM Grand and **Studio 54** inside the MGM Grand, all of which attract a good mix of gay and straight partygoers. For more information, *see page 223* **Dance clubs**.

A special note to female readers: don't be discouraged by the apparent lack of activities for lesbians and their friends. All the 'mixed' bars mentioned here draw a healthy, attractive crowd of women (of all ages), especially at the weekend and for special events.

Of the production shows, Norbert Aleman's *An Evening at La Cage* at the Riviera stands out. This female impersonation review stars Frank Marino as Joan Rivers and features the most incredible gowns this side of Chicago. The *Kenny Kerr Show* is still going strong, having moved to Jackie Gaughan's Plaza in Downtown. Flanked by a crew of gorgeous, scantily clad male dancers and a cast of flawless impersonators, Kenny has been the undisputed queen of queens for more than 25 years. For more information on both shows, *see page 215* **Casino Entertainment**.

Finally, many cafés and coffeehouses in Las Vegas are either gay-owned and operated or gay- and lesbian-friendly. Of those listed in our **Bars & Cafés** chapter, the **Enigma Garden Café** and **Mermaid Café** have particular gay appeal.

Admission to the bars and clubs listed below is free unless otherwise stated.

Bars

Backdoor Lounge

1415 E Charleston Boulevard, at 15th Street, Downtown (385 2018). Bus 206. **Open** 24hrs daily. **Admission** $3 Fri. **No credit cards**.
A haven for local gay men, the Backdoor boasts 'the friendliest bartenders in town', occasional slot and video poker tournaments and regular drink specials.

Backstreet Bar & Grill

5012 Arville Street, between W Flamingo Road & Tropicana Avenue, South-west Las Vegas (876 1844). Bus 104, 201, 202. **Open** 24hrs daily. **No credit cards**.
A favourite haunt of all the cowboys and cowgirls of Las Vegas (of which there are quite a few) and the home of the Nevada Gay Rodeo Association, Backstreet has the busiest Sunday afternoon beer bust in town. Attention, ladies: if you want to meet women of all ages and interests, git yerself down to the Backstreet Bar & Grill every Thursday night at 7pm for line dancing lessons. Non-dancers are welcome, too.

Badlands Saloon

Commercial Center, 953 E Sahara Avenue, unit 22B, between Sixth Street & Maryland Parkway, East of Strip (792 9262). Bus 204. **Open** 24hrs daily. **No credit cards**.
Yet another locals' bar, with country music, pool tables and not a woman in the place.

The Buffalo

Paradise Plaza, 4640 Paradise Road, at Naples Drive, between Harmon & Tropicana Avenues, East of Strip (733 8355). Bus 108, 213. **Open** 24hrs daily. **No credit cards**.

Visit gay club **Gipsy** for go-go boys, drag shows and a jumping crowd.

Las Vegas's legendary Levi-leather bar, where only the boldest of lesbians dare to cross the threshold. Once in, you'll find the usual pool-playing, recipe-swapping, friendly crowd of guys (and a few gals) dressed to look meaner than they really are.

Las Vegas Eagle
Tropicana Plaza, 3430 E Tropicana Avenue, at Pecos Road, East Las Vegas (458 8662). Bus 111, 201. **Open** 24hrs daily. **No credit cards.**
Famous for its Underwear Nights (Wed & Fri), this is primarily a men's Levi-leather bar, with liquor/beer busts twice a week and nightly drink specials.

Las Vegas Lounge
900 E Karen Avenue, between Paradise Road & Maryland Parkway, East of Strip (737 9350). Bus 108, 109. **Open** 24hrs daily. **No credit cards.**
A mixed venue: mostly queens, transsexuals, cross-dressers and their friends, fans and appreciators. There are regular live shows and drinks promotions.

Snick's Place
1402 S Third Street, between E Charleston Boulevard & Wyoming Street, Stratosphere Area (385 9298). Bus 301, 302. **Open** 24hrs daily. **No credit cards.**
Las Vegas's oldest gay men's bar, a historical 'must-see' neighbourhood landmark.

Spotlight
957 E Sahara Avenue, at Commercial Center, East Las Vegas (696 0202). Bus 204. **Open** 24hrs daily. **No credit cards.**
Very much a locals' hangout, Spotlight aims to be the 'friendliest gay bar in Las Vegas'. It hosts regular liquor/beer busts, free dinners at the weekend and 'Jock Night' on Saturdays.

Clubs

Spearmint Rhino (*see page 221* **Adult**) is a strip club for the most part, but also has great, very mixed, after-after-hours parties from about 4am that can last past noon.

Angles/Club Lace
4633 Paradise Road, at Naples Drive, between Harmon & Tropicana Avenues, East of Strip (791 0100). Bus 108, 213. **Open** 3pm-6am daily. **No credit cards.**
This was at one time the city's sole women's bar. It's now a mixed dance bar, with ladies' nights (for 'Womyn Only') on Thursdays and Fridays. Saturday nights are dominated by a male African-American crowd grooving away to house and hip hop music.

Flex Lounge
4371 W Charleston Boulevard, at Arville Street, North-west Las Vegas (385 3539). Bus 206. **Open** 24hrs daily. **Admission** $2 Fri, Sat; $5 Sun. **No credit cards.**
One of Las Vegas's few truly mixed clubs, the Flex Lounge on Charleston Boulevard is a favourite because of its drink specials and great dancing. There are karaoke nights on Mondays, go-go boys and DJs from Wednesday to Saturday and a Latino drag show on Sundays.

FreeZone
610 E Naples Drive, at Paradise Road, between Harmon & Tropicana Avenues, East of Strip (794 2300/2310). Bus 108, 213. **Open** 24hrs daily. **No credit cards.**

A 'Fruitloop' newcomer, FreeZone (located opposite Gipsy) caters for women on Tuesday nights, men on Thursdays, mixed karaoke fans on Sundays and Mondays, and has some of the best drag shows in town on Fridays and Saturdays. It's also home to Celebrations! restaurant.

Gipsy

4605 Paradise Road, between Harmon & Tropicana Avenues, East of Strip (731 5171). Bus 108, 213. **Open** from 10pm daily. **Admission** $5 Mon, Tue, Thur, Fri, Sun; $6 Sat. **No credit cards.**
Gipsy draws a decidedly gay crowd, with about a 3:1 ratio of men to women. Until recently, it was the only place to go for a taste of the 'live and let dance' attitude prevalent in most metropolitan nightclubs, and it still draws more than just gays. After a recent renovation, the club now sports a video wall and more seating – though it is still small (tiny, even) by most standards. By 2am on a Saturday night, Gipsy is a heaving wall-to-wall sweatfest with no room to move. Music ranges from techno to R&B to the gay-friendly neo-disco heard around the globe, while scantily clad go-go boys work the corners of the dancefloor. Don't miss the incredible Toni James's strip show at 2am on Tuesday and drag show on Thursday. Monday features Latin iconess Cha Cha, and there's a retro night with drinks promotions on Wednesday.

GoodTimes Bar & Nightclub

Liberace Plaza, suite 1, 1775 E Tropicana Avenue, at Spencer Street, University District (736 9494). Bus 201. **Open** 24hrs daily. **No credit cards.**
Although it's open throughout the week, GoodTimes is the only place to be on a Monday night, when a lively mixed crowd and plenty of younger party-goers take advantage of the best liquor bust in town while dancing into the morning on the only stainless steel dancefloor in Las Vegas.

Key's of Las Vegas

1000 E Sahara Avenue, at Maryland Parkway, East Las Vegas (731 2200). Bus 204. **Open** *bar* 10am-4am daily; *restaurant* 6-11pm Mon-Thur, Sun; 6pm-midnight Fri, Sat. **Credit** AmEx, Disc, MC, V.
Key's bills itself as 'the hottest little piano bar in town' and is busy with a largely professional, over-30s crowd. Reservations are recommended for the hugely popular live entertainment night – 'Dining with the Divas' – on Wednesdays at 8pm. Key's also houses a good-value restaurant that offers pizza, buffalo wings, steak and the like, for around $10 a head. A good champagne brunch buffet is available for $7.95 between 10.30am and 2.30pm on Sundays. *Website: www.keys-lv.com*

Las Vegas Hilton Nightclub

Las Vegas Hilton, 3000 Paradise Road, between Karen Avenue & E Desert Inn Road, East of Strip (732 5111). Bus 108, 112. **Open** 8pm-4am daily. **Credit** AmEx, DC, Disc, MC, V.
OK, it's not really a gay club, but the lounge at the Las Vegas Hilton now features Louie Louie, a high-energy pop singer/dancer/performer, accompanied by two percussionists and some amazing black divas (back-up singers). Together, they blow the roof off the place every Friday and Saturday night. All pretty incredible for a free show, with just a two-drink minimum. For more information, *see also p211* **Casino Entertainment**.

Cruising

Las Vegas boasts a veritable plethora of adult bookstores, theatres and video-store-cum-arcades, which are the city's prime spots for cruising. Any of the several **Adult Superstores** (*see page 222* **Adult**) are a must-visit: the one at Tropicana and Valley View is the largest adult-oriented enterprise on the West Coast, offering a 200-channel arcade and a two-screen theatre. If you prefer a man in uniform, try **Desert Books**, located near Nellis Air Force Base.

The **Apollo Heath Spa** is known worldwide – not for its lavish pamperings, mind, but for the notoriety of its former co-owner, Doc Ruehl. Doc owned the houseboat in Miami where gay serial killer Andrew Cunanan took his own life, thus backing up the theory that most infamous criminals all have connections with Las Vegas at some time during their lifetime of transgression.

There is a 'clothing optional' **gay men's beach** just outside Las Vegas at Lake Mead. Even though the location falls under federal jurisdiction, there is a state law against nudity 'with sexual intent' – so cruise with caution, boys!

Apollo Health Spa

Commercial Center, suite A19, 953 E Sahara Avenue, between Sixth Street & Maryland Parkway, East Las Vegas (650 9191). Bus 109, 204. **Open** 24hrs daily. **Admission** $21-$30. **Credit** MC, V.
During the media frenzy created by his link to Andrew Cunanan, former co-owner Doc Ruehl returned to his homeland, Germany. The Apollo, however, still enjoys local celebrity status, as well as a healthy crowd most nights, many of them tourists. Recently remodelled, it has a heated pool, jacuzzi, steam room, sauna and video room plus a new gym and a maze (darkroom) area. *Website: www.apollospa.com*

Desert Books

4350 N Las Vegas Boulevard, at Craig Road, North Las Vegas (643 7982). Bus 113, 115. **Open** 24hrs daily. **Credit** MC, V.

Gay beach

Head east on Lake Mead Boulevard (Highway 147) until you hit the lakeside road: turn left (north) towards Calville and Overton Bays. At the eight-mile marker, turn right on to a dirt road; stay left at all forks, making all left turns. Park where it seems obvious, then head left over the hills and continue along the path: gays to the left, straights to the right. But beware: park rangers are on the look out to cite homosexuals.

Music: rock, folk & jazz

Las Vegas is so rich in live music that it is nearly impossible to avoid it. It pours from every casino lounge, it fills every showroom and theatre and sometimes – usually while the annual EAT'M conference is in session – live bands even play on the Strip itself (*see page 104* **Las Vegas by Season**). It wasn't always so. Just a few years ago, casino operators downplayed their musical attractions, and some resorts even closed their lounges. Showroom productions eschewed live musicians in favour of pre-recorded scores, and, as a result, Las Vegas's local artists and bands struggled – as they do to a lesser degree even today – in near-anonymity.

Then the tide turned, so quickly and decisively it startled even the most jaded locals half-out of their wits. The Hard Rock Hotel opened a theatre, the **Joint** in March 1995, which drew and continues to draw major talents (the likes of the Rolling Stones and Lenny Kravitz). A few years later, in March 1999, the Mandalay Bay resort saw the opening of a **House of Blues** venue with a show by Bob Dylan, and the chase was on. Between these two venues and others such as **Sanctuary**, the **Huntridge Theatre** and the **MGM Grand Garden**, nearly every touring musician in the world has either played Las Vegas or will soon enough. And the local talent has benefited from the new entertainment boom as well – many local bands have had the opportunity to play the larger venues in opening slots and a few have even been signed to recording contracts.

To find a band or venue that suits your taste, pick up one of Vegas's many free arts and entertainment publications. The 'alternative' weekly newspapers, *Las Vegas Weekly* and *CityLife*, both feature live music and event calendars, as does the tourist publication *Showbiz*. And there are also some websites – top among them **www.vegas com** and **www.lvlocalmusicscene.com** – that boast calendars of live music and special events that are updated daily.

Because of licensing laws, under-21s are limited in their choice of venue. But they are welcome at the Huntridge, the Joint (depending on the performer), House of Blues (also conditional – call ahead), the major arenas and all the coffeehouses and cafés. Admission prices throughout the venues vary depending on the act; there may be no charge in bars and cafés. Unless otherwise stated, venues do not accept credit cards.

For details of musical entertainment in casino lounges, see the **Casino Entertainment** chapter. Information on classical music venues are given in the **Culture** chapter.

Prices for tickets at the major venues range from around $20 for a local show at the House of Blues to more than $40 at the MGM Grand Garden. Tickets for all these venues can be bought through **TicketMaster** (474 4000) for a fee.

Rock, punk, hip hop, pop & rave

The past few years have seen some breakout rock and pop talents leave Vegas for richer pastures. Techno/rave duo the Crystal Method (Ken Jordan and Scott Kirkland, who met while working as volunteer DJs at UNLV's community radio station KUNV) scored a giant hit with their debut album, appropriately titled *Vegas*. And hot R&B trio 702 honed their talents as students at the Las Vegas Academy, a public school catering for the artistically gifted.

Meanwhile, the local talent keeps patiently working the openings. It has much to compete with: who wants to watch a local band while a volcano is erupting in front of a nearby hotel? And yet, for a town with mile-high distractions, there's an amazing variety of talented groups – Home Cookin', Inside Scarlet, 12 Volt Sex, Los Trios De Nada, the Nines and Phatter Than Albert chief among them – that cannot be easily labelled, with influences ranging from Tom Waits to P-Funk.

Major venues

Aladdin Theater for the Performing Arts

Aladdin, 3667 Las Vegas Boulevard South, at Harmon Avenue (736 0111). Bus 301, 302.
Credit AmEx, Disc, MC, V.
Las Vegas's best midsize venue is out of commission until at least summer 2000 (locals reckon a winter reopening is more likely), while the surrounding hotel is rebuilt from scratch and the theatre is refitted. As long as the crisp acoustics remain unaffected by the remodelling process, the Aladdin should continue to be a fine place to see and hear everything from Pearl Jam to the Bolshoi Ballet.

*Find a musical haven at the **Sanctuary**.*

The Joint

*Hard Rock, 4455 Paradise Road, at Harmon
Avenue, University District (693 5000). Bus 213.*
Tickets from $30. **Credit** AmEx, DC, Disc, MC, V.
This 1,400-capacity, two-level room is rapidly
becoming the most significant venue in the western
US, owing to its sterling sound, swanky ambience
and location inside 'the world's first rock and roll
casino'. Playing the Joint has now become a mark of
stature, one that countless bands – from the Pet
Shop Boys to Garbage to Sting – have felt compelled
to claim. The venue's biggest drawbacks are its high
ticket prices (seldom do they drop under $30) and
the management's annoying habit of overloading
the room. Not that these caveats matter at all when
the drink is flowing and the beats hit you.
Website: www.hardrock.com

House of Blues

*Mandalay Bay, 3950 Las Vegas Boulevard South,
between W Tropicana Avenue & Russell Road
(632 7600/tickets 632 7666). Bus 301, 302.*
Tickets from $20. **Credit** AmEx, Disc, JCB, MC, V.
Just like every other House of Blues venue in the US?
Not really. Vegas's House of Blues, a 1,900-capacity,
three-level room, is such a thoughtfully planned and
richly soulful venue that it feels as if it's been part of
the Strip forever (in fact, it opened in March 1999).
There's not a surface in the HOB that's not painted,
textured or otherwise covered with striking 'outsider'
folk art and, odd as it may seem, the look of the room
somehow improves the quality of the experience. It's
a pretty high-quality affair to begin with: the sound
system is state-of-the-art, and there are very few bad
seats in the house (beware the pillars on the main
floor). Recent visitors have included the Offspring,
Bryan Ferry and Orbital.
Website: www.hob.com

MGM Grand Garden

*MGM Grand, 3799 Las Vegas Boulevard South, at
E Tropicana Avenue (891 1111). Bus 201, 301, 302.*
Tickets from $40. **Credit** AmEx, DC, Disc, JCB,
MC, V.
Modelled after New York City's Madison Square
Garden, the Grand Garden is the best arena-sized
venue in town. The sound at Buffalo Bill's Star of
the Desert arena may be superior, but its location in
Primm – some 30 miles outside town – makes it
impractical for bands and fans alike. The Grand
Garden's crisp acoustics have served the likes of
Lauryn Hill, the Who and Janet Jackson very well
indeed – warming up the sound when warmth is
needed and chilling 'cold' beats until they snap.
Website: www.mgmgrand.com

Thomas & Mack Center

*4505 Maryland Parkway, at E Tropicana Avenue,
University District (895 3801). Bus 108, 109, 201.*
Tickets from $30. **Credit** AmEx, Disc, MC, V.
The Thomas & Mack is primarily a sports venue,
built for UNLV's win-some, lose-more basketball
team. A recent refitting corrected some acoustic
problems, and not a minute too soon – with the
opening of Mandalay Bay's similar-sized Events

Centre, the improved acoustics give the T&M a
much-needed edge. The sound at the Events Center
is as bad as the T&M's was a year ago.

Clubs & smaller venues

Boston Grill & Bar

*Mountain View Center, 3411 S Jones Boulevard, at
Spring Mountain Road, South-west Las Vegas (368
0750). Bus 102, 203.* **Open** 24hrs daily. **Shows**
9pm Mon-Thur, Sun; 10pm Fri, Sat. **Admission** free.
If you've ever searched for the elusive 'Vegas Sound',
this is the place to find it. Called simply 'the Boston'
by regulars, the Boston Grill & Bar features live
local music seven nights a week. Though its surroundings and ambience could politely be called
dank, local rockers and funksters play the Boston
by the busload – from quirky jazz-rockabilly outfit
King Cartel to the amazingly inventive jazz-metal
ensemble Native Tongue and earnest singer/song-
writer Mark Huff.

Club Utopia

*The Epicenter, 3765 Las Vegas Boulevard South,
between Harmon & E Tropicana Avenues (740
4646). Bus 301, 302.* **Open** 10pm-6am Wed-Sat.
Shows usually 11pm; phone for a schedule.
Admission from $10 Thur, Fri; $15 Sat.
Club Utopia plays host to every travelling techno
and big-beat outfit that rolls through Sin City. BT,
Expansion Union, Juno Reactor and Moby have all
taken the large circular stage, and Vegas's native
sons Crystal Method shot their *Busy Child* video
inside the enormous discotheque. Guest DJs – the
likes of Sasha and Paul Oakenfold – stop by when
they feel inclined to spin for gamblers. The club has
plans to open on Tuesday nights; phone to check.
See also p225 **Dance clubs**.
Website: www.clubutopia.com

Huntridge Performing Arts Theatre

*1208 E Charleston Boulevard, at Maryland Parkway,
Downtown (477 7703/info hotline 471 6700).
Bus 109, 206.* **Open** 10am-2pm daily.
Shows times and days vary; phone hotline for details.
Admission from $6.
Las Vegas's oldest venue, built at the height of World
War II, began life as a movie house where Frank
Sinatra and Judy Garland once hosted premières.
Today, the Huntridge Theatre hosts so many punk,
hardcore, rap and metal bands that locals have
tagged it – unofficially – 'the Punktridge'.
The sound mix is good and loud, the beer good
and cold and if you avoid the 'orchestra' pit (where
a number of teenage boys are beating the living day-
lights out of each other at this exact moment) you
should have a good evening's worth of entertainment. Tickets for national acts here and at the
Sanctuary are available from TicketMaster.

Sanctuary

*1125 S Maryland Parkway, at Charleston Boulevard,
Downtown (477 7703/info hotline 471 6700).
Bus 109, 206.* **Open** office 10am-2pm daily.
Shows usually 8pm or 9pm; phone hotline for a
schedule. **Admission** $3-$10.

Located behind the Huntridge Theatre (with which it shares phonelines) in a converted 1950s post office, Sanctuary offers a variety of music that is pretty much unmatched. One night may find a jazz combo backing up performance poets, beatnik-style; the following evening, a thrash or punk band could be whipping the crowd into a lather. A fine place to see local and touring acts, with but one caveat: during packed shows, the room heats up quickly and stays uncomfortably warm. Cool down on the back patio.

Legends Lounge

Lamb Square, 865 N Lamb Boulevard, at Washington Drive, North Las Vegas (437 9674). Bus 112, 208. **Open** 24hrs daily. **Shows** 9pm Wed-Sat. **Admission** $3.

The Grateful Dead paraphernalia on the walls is a bit misleading. You're just as likely to find Dead or Phish fans listening to old bootlegged tapes as a live band, but when performers are featured the programme is deliciously varied. It could be the earthy funk of locals Mama Zeus, the folk-rock explorations of Mark Huff, the straight-up rockabilly of Dragstrip 77 or travelling 'jam' bands such as the Disco Biscuits and Jive Talkin' Robots. Legends may be small, but its sound and ambitions are big.

Money Plays

Flamingo Center, 4755 W Flamingo Road, between Cameron Street & Decatur Boulevard, South-west Las Vegas (368 1828). Bus 103, 202. **Open** 24hrs daily. **Shows** 10pm Sat. **Admission** free.

Money Plays features local rock almost every weekend. The only drawback is that you'll have to squeeze your way into a seething crowd of drunken college kids to get anywhere near it.

Blues

Clubs close frequently in Las Vegas for various reasons, the most common being plain bad luck. It's usually the blues that suffers first, running from venue to venue like a refugee. The following places have displayed an admirable tenacity in booking live blues bands on a regular basis, even when the crowds aren't there to support it. Legendary performer BB King maintains a Vegas residence and plays (very) infrequent gigs around town, usually at casino venues.

Double Down Saloon

Paradise Plaza, 4640 Paradise Road, at Naples Drive, between Harmon & Tropicana Avenues, East of Strip (791 5775). Bus 108. **Open** 24hrs daily. **Shows** 10pm Wed. **Admission** free.

This art-infested dive hosts live blues; call ahead for times and dates. *See also p165* **Bars & Cafés**.

Sand Dollar Blues Lounge

3355 Spring Mountain Road, at Polaris Street, West of Strip (871 6651). Bus 203. **Open** 24hrs daily. **Shows** 10pm daily. **Admission** $3 Mon-Thur, Sun; $5 Fri, Sat.

This venue is able to harbour at least one band, sometimes two, a night. The room runs thick with smoke and atmosphere, the cover charge never exceeds $5 and an active fan base supports, with genuine fervour, shows by local heroes the Ruffnecks and the Moanin' Blacksnakes.

Country

Las Vegas's country and western scene is like a bear – it hibernates most of the year, only waking up for the National Finals Rodeo in early December. Around that time, nearly every popular country artist that's not nailed down or currently serving time comes to Vegas to roost. When country artists play Vegas, they tend to gravitate toward the **Silverton** hotel-casino (1-888 588 7711; 263 7777), the **House of Blues** (*see page 233*) and the **Star of the Desert Arena** (box office 386 7867 ext 7145), located in Buffalo Bill's casino in Primm, at the California border.

Larry's Hideaway

3369 Thom Boulevard, at Rancho Drive, North Las Vegas (645 1899). Bus 106. **Open** 11am-2am Mon-Sun; 11am-5am Fri, Sat. **Shows** 7pm daily. **Admission** free.

This modest establishment features live bands every night, playing country classics to a packed dancefloor. Expect excellent service, friendly staff and some serious honky-tonkin'.

Folk

Las Vegas has enjoyed a rich legacy of folk and acoustic music ever since one Paul Summers Jr started a floating folk club called the Acoustic Asylum in 1993. Summers has since relocated to Portland, Oregon, and the Asylum fizzled out a few years after he left, but the stage was set. Quite a few of the musicians playing folk/acoustic nights today either played with Paul or have a stage to play on because of his benevolence. Nearly every live music venue in town features folk performers from time to time, most notably the **Legends Lounge** (*see above*), home to shows by local folk booster organisation Worldfolk.

If you fancy a java or juice fix with your folk music, try the **Enigma Garden Café** (386 0999; http://radiant.org/enigma) in Downtown or the far-flung **Mermaid Café** (240 6002; www.cafe mermaid.com) in South-west Vegas. The former offers live music in its pretty courtyard at the weekend as well as a poetry evening on Wednesdays. Although bookings reflect a wide range of musical tastes, folk is usually the star attraction, with travelling folkies such as Danielle Howle making the Enigma their sole Vegas stop. Alternatively, the Mermaid has folk/acoustic music several nights a week, and quite a few of Las Vegas's up-and-coming folk voices – from Secondhand Rose to Michael Soli – seem to have settled here. For further details of both venues, *see chapter* **Bars & Cafés**.

Rockin' the house: great sounds at the **House of Blues.** *See page 233.*

Jazz & swing

Las Vegas's jazz scene has improved markedly in recent years, but is still a few years away from consolidating its position. Big-name jazz musicians such as Branford Marsalis and Nicholas Payton have been known to play one-night stands, but if you walk into any casino lounge hoping for a shot of the real stuff, be prepared to hear the artform set back some 15 years. Most of the live jazz on the Strip is of the saccharine variety; to find the real jazz, you'll need to drive or take a cab. As well as the venues listed below, **Gordon Biersch** (*see page 165* **Bars & Cafés**) features live local rock and jazz groups on an irregular basis.

Good swing bands are somewhat easier to find. Several major venues feature live big bands – some, like Uncle Sugar and the Sweet Daddies, are even locally grown – but on a basis that could kindly be called irregular. Sometimes the town is packed with swing bands; other times, you won't find one for miles. The **Hard Rock**, the **Hop** (*see page 225* **Dance clubs**), the **Sunset Brewing Co** brewpub at Sunset Station (547 7777) and the **Empire Bar** at New York-New York (740 6969) have been known to lurch when the horns blow. Check local calendars for details.

Café Espresso Roma
The Promenade, 4440 S Maryland Parkway, at Harmon Avenue, University District (369 1540). Bus 109, 213. **Open** 7am-10pm Mon, Tue, Thur; 7am-2am Wed; 8am-11pm Fri, Sat; 8am-10pm Sun. **Shows** Fri, Sat. **Admission** free; donations $3-$5 are welcome.

This one-time home to Vegas's folk and acoustic music scene now features a variety of bands. Most are local rock outfits, but you can catch a hardcore troubadour every now and again. The café also hosts open-mike poetry evenings and has DJs spinning acid jazz and drum 'n' bass. The schedule is flexible, so call for details. *See also p168* **Bars & Cafés** and *p202* **Culture.**

Pogo's Tavern
2103 N Decatur Boulevard, between Smoke Ranch Road & Lake Mead Boulevard, North Las Vegas (646 9735). Bus 103. **Open** 9am-midnight daily. **Shows** 8pm Fri.

The only weekly swing night that has endured is at Pogo's Tavern, a tiny dive bar on the north-west side of town. The nameless band is made up of old-timers, veterans of a dozen or so big bands that shook Sin City when swing was the undisputed king of the Strip. Hearing the stories these gentlemen have to tell is reason enough to make a night of it and – unlike most of the new-generation poseurs who added horns to what was once a garage-punk band three short years ago – this band will honour every request. *See also p165* **Bars & Cafés.**

Gigi's Southern Cuisine
2590 Maryland Parkway, at Sahara Avenue, East of Strip (939 4444). Bus 109, 204. **Open** 11am-9pm Mon-Thur, Sun; 11am-11pm Fri, Sat. **Shows** 9pm Fri, Sat. **Credit** AmEx, MC, V.

Located some ten minutes off the Strip, this soul-food restaurant offers live jazz combos every Friday and Saturday night in a dark, cosy and intimate setting. It's best to call ahead to ensure that a band is playing; just dropping by may land you in the middle of a karaoke session.

Sport & Fitness

If you're bored with the indoor sports played at the casinos, try a different kind of gaming.

Cards and dice, not racquets and balls, are the tools of trade for the most famous games people play in Las Vegas. But there's a whole other world out of doors and a few miles away from the resort corridors. When the cards turn against you, take advantage of the Valley's year-round sunshine and temperate climate. From golf and tennis to more extreme sports, such as rock climbing and skydiving, there is never a shortage of things to do. Try skiing in the winter at Mount Charleston, water-skiing at Lake Mead or make the most of the abundance of hiking and biking trails through the beautiful natural scenery surrounding the city.

Outdoor activities

Las Vegans say, 'It's a dry heat.' Tourists just say, 'Damn, it's hot!' During summer, the temperature outside will top 90°F (32°C) before breakfast and climb into triple digits by afternoon. Even the locals stay inside between June and August, but that's no reason to limit your outdoor activities, as long as you take the proper precautions: wear a cap or some protection for your head, use sunblock (at least factor 15) and carry plenty of water.

Boating

You can rent all kinds of boats – from fishing boats to houseboats – at the marinas bordering Lake Mead. For details, s*ee chapter* **Day Trips**.

Bungee jumping

For that free-fallin' feeling, head for the aptly named Sky Screamer at **MGM Grand** or AJ Hackett Bungy at **Circus Circus** (for details, *see page 88* **Attractions**).

Cycling

Sure, you can ride a bike down the Strip, but it's not recommended. Distracted drivers in rented cars are a potential hazard to pedestrians and any-one using two-wheeled transport. Instead, head west on Charleston Boulevard to **Escape the City Streets** to rent a bike, then pedal on to **Red Rock Canyon National Conservation Area** (visitor centre 363 1921). There, you'll find a one-way scenic road that loops past breathtaking sandstone cliffs. The sight of roadrunners streaking

through the desert will make you feel like you're in a Warner Bros cartoon – beep beep! For more on Red Rock, *see chapter* **Day Trips**.

Also within reach of Escape the City Streets are the wide, marked bike lanes of the sparkly new corporate-planned town of **Summerlin**. To explore, start at the junction of Charleston Boulevard and Rampart Boulevard and head north on Rampart to Pueblo Park. You can ride west in the park for several miles along paved paths that are separated from the traffic (watch out for pedestrians, who share the paths).

Other popular routes include the **Cottonwood Valley Loop**, an eight-mile off-road trail near Red Rock: head west from town on Highway 160 and look for a dirt road 5.9 miles (9.5 kilometres) past the junction with Highway 159. The **River Mountain Peak** is a ten-mile (16-kilometre) route on the border between Vegas and Henderson. To get to the head of the trail, drive along I-93/95 to Equestrian Drive, turning east.

An unofficial bike trail exists at the north-west corner of Tropicana Avenue and Decatur Boulevard. This challenging and well-worn trail runs through one of the few undeveloped parcels of land in the urban area – power your bike up and down steep standstone formations and across a natural wash. Though used often by local gear-heads, it is unsanctioned, so bike safely.

Escape the City Streets

8221 W Charleston Boulevard, unit 101, between Buffalo & Durango Drives, North-west Las Vegas (596 2953/bike@escapeadventures.com). Bus 205, 206. **Open** *10am-6pm Mon-Fri; 9am-5pm Sat, Sun.* **Bike hire** *from $26 per day.* **Credit** *AmEx, Disc, MC, V.*
Located en route to Red Rock Canyon, this outfit conducts various road and off-road tours in Red Rock or will provide bikes, maps and supplies if you'd rather go it alone. Items for rent include road bikes, mountain bikes, tandems and children's trailers, and it also offers guided bike tours to the national parks of Utah, Arizona and California. *Website: www.escapeadventures.com*

Fishing

There's superb fishing year round at Lake Mead. The lake is stocked with half a million rainbow trout every year, and there's also black bass, bluegill, crappie and striped bass, some as big as

All-American SportPark: baseball cages, a climbing wall and much more. See page 238.

50 pounds (23 kilograms). To fish from the Nevada shore, you'll need a Nevada fishing licence ($12 plus $4 per additional day); to fish from a boat, you'll need a licence from Nevada and a special-use stamp from Arizona (the two states share jurisdiction over the lake). All the necessary documents are available from most marinas. Professional fishing guides are available to direct you to the hottest spots: try **Fish-Inc** (1500 Palomino Drive, Henderson; 565 8396) or **Karen Jones Fishing Guide Service** (1018 Cutter Street, Henderson; 566 5775).

You can also fish within the city in the lake at **Sunset Park** (Sunset Road and Eastern Avenue) and at pretty **Floyd Lamb State Park**, which is 15 miles (24 kilometres) from Downtown (for details, *see chapter* **Day Trips**).

Frisbee golf

Frisbee golf is just what it sounds like: golf played with a frisbee, except that the disc is a little smaller than the traditional frisbee and made from a softer, heavier rubber. You throw the frisbee into 'holes' – not holes in the ground but above-ground containers.

Frisbee golf course

Sunset Park, 2601 E Sunset Road, at Eastern Avenue, East Las Vegas (455 8200). Bus 110, 212. **Open** 7am-11pm daily. **Admission** free.
The city's only frisbee golf course has 18 holes. Try to play during the week, as the park can get very crowded on weekends.

Hiking

For information on the best hiking areas near Las Vegas, *see chapter* **Day Trips**.

Horse riding

Bonnie Springs/Old Nevada

1 Gun Fighter Lane, off Highway 159, Red Rock Canyon (875 4191). No bus. **Open** *summer* 10.30am-6pm, *winter* 10.30am-4.30pm, daily. **Rates** $20 per person. **Credit** MC, V.
One-hour guided rides leave from this quaint Wild West theme park in Red Rock Canyon.

Cowboy Trail Rides

One mile south of visitor centre, Red Rock Canyon National Conservation Area (249 6686).
Ride a genuine mustang on rustic mountain trails through Red Rock Canyon. The most popular rides are the Sunset BBQ ride ($139 per person) and the two-hour Rim Canyon Ride ($89). All rides are accompanied by a cowboy guide, and first-time riders are welcome. Booking is advisable.

Hunting & shooting

Call the **Nevada Department of Wildlife** (486 5127/www.state.nv.us/cnr/nvwildlife) for information on hunting dove and quail, and waterfowl in the Lake Mead area. Limited deer hunting is also available. Special seasons are scheduled for elk, antelope and bighorn sheep. The **American Shooters Supply & Gun Club** (3440 Arville Street, between W Desert Inn & Spring Mountain

*Feed the need for speed at the **Las Vegas Motor Speedway**. See page 243.*

Roads; 362 1223) has the only 50-yard (45-metre) indoor shooting range in Las Vegas. A hunting licence for non-residents is $111. The **Las Vegas Gun Club** (9200 Tule Springs Road, behind Floyd Lamb State Park; 645 5606) has an outdoor range, where scenes from *Viva Las Vegas* were filmed.

Rafting

Down River Outfitters in Boulder City (1-800 748 3702/293 1190) and **Jerkwater Canoe & Kayak Company** in Topock, Arizona (1-800 421 7803/1-520 768 7753/www.jerkwater.com) offer canoe/raft delivery and retrieval for trips on the Colorado River.

Black Canyon River Raft Tours

1-800 696 7238/293 3776. **Rates per person** *River tour $64.95; with hotel pick-up $79.95.* **Credit** Disc, MC, V.
One-day guided raft trips along the Colorado River, from just below the Hoover Dam to Willow Beach, through a waterfall and hot springs. There are a few splashes along the way, but no rapids. Based in Boulder City, the company will pick up groups from most Las Vegas hotels. Lunch is usually included. *Website: www.rafts.com*

Rock climbing

The outstanding rock climbing opportunities around Las Vegas are one of the area's most under-publicised attractions. There are also various indoor climbing walls in the city.

All-American SportPark

121 E Sunset Road, at Las Vegas Boulevard South (798 7777). Bus 212, 301, 302; free shuttle bus from some Strip hotels. **Open** *varies depending on time of year, so call first.* **Admission** *individual*

games $3-$12 each; all-day wristband $19.95-$24.95. **Credit** AmEx, Disc, MC, V.
Try the indoor sport-climbing wall before heading outside to the real thing. Individual and group instruction is available.

Red Rock Canyon

Visitor centre 363 1921. Head west on W Charleston Boulevard (20 miles from the Strip). **Open** *visitor centre 8am-4.30pm, scenic loop 7am-dusk, daily.*
Most visitors are content to hike, cycle or drive the 13-mile/21km loop (vehicle entrance $5) that winds through some of the most scenic parts of Red Rock Canyon, but the area also offers some of the best year-round climbing in the States. Call the visitor centre for information on climbing regulations and stop off at **Desert Rock Sports** (8201 W Charleston Boulevard; 254 1143) en route to the park, for climbing, backpacking and camping equipment. It also has a huge indoor climbing wall. The best guide to routes is *Red Rock Select* by Todd Swain (Chockstone Press; $25).

Sky's the Limit

1270 Calico Drive, Red Rock (1-800 733 7597/ 363 4533/info@skysthelimit.com). **Open** *office 9am-5pm Mon-Fri.* **Rates** *from $169.* **Credit** AmEx, Disc, MC, V.
Based at Red Rock Canyon (take the Calico Basin/ Red Springs exit off W Charleston Boulevard), this is the best outfit for beginners' climbing courses as well as guided scrambles, technical climbs and advanced alpine courses. Prices start at $169 for a half-day introductory course. Sky's the Limit will arrange transport from the city if needed. *Website: www.skysthelimit.com*

Vegas Rock Gym

3065 E Patrick Lane, suite 4, at McLeod Drive, East Las Vegas (434 3388/rock@skylink.net). Bus 111, 212. **Open** *noon-10pm Mon-Fri; 11am-10pm Sat;*

11am-8pm Sun. **Rates** $10 per day; equipment $6; lesson $5. **Credit** Disc, MC, V.

Indoor training facility with specially designed climbing walls and professional instructors.

Scuba & skin diving

Scuba divers should head to Lake Mead, where visibility averages 30 feet (nine metres) and can reach up to 60 feet (18 metres) in winter. There are some unusual underwater sights, including plenty of boat wrecks and Hoover Dam's asphalt factory. The most popular diving area is **Scuba Park**, adjacent to Lake Mead marina.

American Cactus Divers

Annie Oakley Plaza, 3985B E Sunset Road, at Annie Oakley Drive, Henderson (433 3483). Bus 114, 212. **Open** 9am-6pm Mon-Fri; 9am-4pm Sat, Sun. **Rates** beach dives $25; equipment rental $37 per day. **Credit** AmEx, Disc, MC, V.

Blue Seas Scuba Center

4661 Spring Mountain Road, between Arville Street & Decatur Boulevard, South-west Las Vegas (1-800 245 2036/367 2822). Bus 203. **Open** 11am-7pm Mon-Fri; 9am-5pm Sat; noon-5pm Sun. **Rates** equipment rental $35-$70 per day. **Credit** AmEx, Disc, MC, V.

Desert Divers Supply

5720 E Charleston Boulevard, at Nellis Boulevard, East Las Vegas (438 1000). Bus 115, 206. **Open** 10am-7pm Mon-Fri; 8am-6pm Sat, Sun. **Rates** equipment rental $35 per day. **Credit** AmEx, Disc, MC, V.

Drew's Dam Divers

1-800 291 2650/293 5558/damdivers@aol.com **Rates** $70 per person. **Credit** AmEx, Disc, MC, V. Based in Boulder City, this outfit operates a diving charter service, with two boats on Lake Mead.

Skiing

Visitors might feel odd packing their skis for the desert, but there are two first-class skiing areas located within day-trip distance of the city. The ski season is usually from November to April.

Las Vegas Ski & Snowboard Resort

Mount Charleston (645 2754/snow conditions 593 9500). **Day lift pass** $28; $21 children. **Credit** AmEx, MC, V.

Just 47 miles (75km) from downtown Las Vegas, the ski area at Mount Charleston's Lee Canyon has a terrain breakdown of 20% beginner, 60% intermediate and 20% expert, and snow-making equipment in case nothing falls the old-fashioned way. The Las Vegas influence is evident in the naming of the runs: High Roller, Blackjack, Keno, the Strip and the Line, among others. New additions include a half-pipe and terrain park, and sledding, snowmobiling and cross-country skiing are available further down the mountain. There's no accommodation at the resort itself, but there's a free bus from town and the day

lodge (open 9am-4pm daily) has a ski school, rental shop, coffeeshop and cocktail lounge. There's night skiing on Saturdays (4-10pm). For more on Mount Charleston, *see chapter* **Day Trips**.

Website: www.skilasvegas.com

Brian Head Ski Resort

Brian Head, Utah (454 7669). I-15 north to exit 75, then Highway 145. **Day lift pass** $35; $22 children, seniors. **Credit** AmEx, Disc, MC, V.

It's a three-hour drive to this first-rate resort in Utah, but the skiing is terrific and there is plenty of lodging if you want to stay the night. Brian Head extends over two mountains: Brian Head Peak reaches 11,307ft (3,465m); across the valley are the intermediate and beginner runs on Navajo Peak – a total of 53 trails in all. Terrain Peak features jumps, berms (moguls) and other obstacles for advanced skiers and snowboarders. **Escape the City Streets** (*see p236*) runs buses from Las Vegas to Brian Head on Wednesdays and Saturdays.

Website: www.brianhead.com

Skydiving

Both skydiving centres listed below offer freefall and tandem jumping, and both are 30 or so miles south of Vegas. If you haven't quite got the nerve to jump out of a real plane, try the vertical wind tunnel at **Flyaway** (*see page 87* **Attractions**) for the next best thing.

Las Vegas Skydiving Center

Jean Airport, 23500 Las Vegas Boulevard South, Jean (877 1010). No bus. **Open** 8am-dusk daily. **Rates** around $159. **Credit** AmEx, Disc, MC, V.

Skydive Las Vegas

1401 Airport Road, Boulder City (1-800 875 9343/ 293 1860/skydive@skylink.net). No bus. **Open** 8am-7pm daily. **Cost** around $159. **Credit** AmEx, Disc, MC, V.

Swimming

Almost every hotel and motel in Las Vegas has a swimming pool, which is fortunate since most of the city's public pools are located in neighbourhoods that tourists would prefer not to visit. The majority of resort pools close at twilight, which might seem odd considering the balmy evening temperatures in Las Vegas between April and October, and don't open at all in winter. The reason, though the hotels are reluctant to admit it, is they'd rather have their guests in the casino than lounging poolside.

The pools are for hotel guests only: although you can sometimes just wander in, you'll need to show a room key to receive a towel and a cushion for the lounge chairs. Many are worth a peek even if you've left your cossie at home: the **Caesars Palace** pool area is as opulent as a Roman villa; the **MGM Grand**'s pools look big enough to float an ocean liner; and the **Rio**'s pool has a sandy

Golf courses

Las Vegas has about half the golf courses it needs to meet the demand of tourists and residents. For decades, new course construction was limited by the high cost of land and low supply of water, and the city has been playing catch-up ever since. Of the 30 courses in the area, a third are private, which means you'll have to know a club member to get through the gate. That leaves 20 or so 18-hole tracks for one million residents and 30 million tourists – no wonder finding a tee time can be tougher than finding a generous slot machine.

Expect to pay $100 or more per round on any of the better golf courses. If you can stand the desert heat, some places offer discounts on July and August afternoons. To be certain of getting a tee time, it's best to call up to two weeks in advance. **Las Vegas Preferred Tee-Times** (1-888 368 7833) will make reservations for you at a number of courses in the area.

There are two kinds of golf courses in the city: the standard 18-hole designs similar to those found throughout the States, and desert golf, or 'target' courses, where only the tee boxes, fairways and greens are maintained and the surrounding natural desert landscape is left intact. The water that keeps the fairways green and the water hazards full is chemically treated and recirculated; it's perfectly safe, but don't drink it.

The **Desert Inn**'s fine but overpriced course is currently the only one on the Strip, but it will soon be joined by another course south of Mandalay Bay, near Russell Road. The most exclusive course is **Shadow Creek**, built by

Mirage Resorts owner Steve Wynn. Designed by Tom Fazio, this exclusive golfing experience is available only to visiting dignitaries and the highest of high-rollers at Wynn's casinos.

Most courses are open from 7am to dusk. Other ones in the area worth trying are **Angel Park** (254 4653), **Craig Ranch** (642 9700), the **Legacy** (897 2108) and **Wildhorse** (434 9000). For information on golfing tournaments, *see* chapter **Las Vegas by Season**.

Badlands

9119 Alta Drive, at Rampart Drive, West Las Vegas (363 0754). Bus 211. **Price per round** $125 Mon-Thur; $165 Fri-Sun. **Credit** AmEx, Disc, MC, V.
This target layout designed by Johnny Miller is one of the most unforgiving tracks in Las Vegas. Failure to hit the ball straight will lead to an up-close and personal experience with one of many natural washes, arroyos and canyons. Help is available from golf carts equipped with the Sky-Links system, which provides the exact distance to the hole from any lie. *See photo.*
Championship; 6,926yds; par 72.
Website: www.americangolf.com

beach for volleyball. **Mandalay Bay**'s fantastic pool complex comes complete with fake beach, wave machine, lazy river and zillions of palm trees – and there are rumours that the owners are building a similar pool area, on the vacant land south of the property, which will have a shark tank and be open to non-hotel guests.

Water-skiing

Tom's Water Sports

433 3263/tomswatersports@sprint.com. **Credit** AmEx, DC, Disc, MC, V.
From April to October, Tom's Water Sports rents equipment, organises half-day ($84 per person) and full-day ($134) trips to Lake Mead and offers lessons in water-skiing, wakeboarding and tubing. In the winter, trips are arranged on demand. You can rent ski boats at marinas on the lake.
Website: www.tomswatersports.com

Participation sports

Bowling

A number of neighbourhood casinos have bowling alleys. The **Showboat** (2800 Fremont Street; 385 9153) has 106 lanes with automatic scoring and is open 24 hours. The Showboat Invitational Bowling Tournament, one of the oldest competitions on the Professional Bowling Association's tour, is held there every January. The 56-lane bowling facility at **Sam's Town** (5111 Boulder Highway; 454 8022) is also open all night. The 60 lanes at the **Santa Fe** (4949 N Rancho Drive; 658 4995) feature Bowlervision, a system that tracks the speed and path of the ball from release until it strikes the pins. The bowling alley at the **Gold Coast** (4000 W Flamingo Road; 367 4700) has 72 lanes, while the **Orleans** (4500 W Tropicana Avenue; 365 7400) has 70.

Desert Pines Golf Club

315 E Bonanza Road, at Pecos Road, East Las Vegas (366 1616). Bus 111, 215. **Price per round** $95 Mon-Thur; $115 Fri-Sun. **Credit** AmEx, MC, V.

Voted one of the best public courses in the US by *Golf Digest* magazine, Desert Pines' tight, challenging layout has narrow, tree-lined fairways and nine holes on water. The practice facility, featuring a two-tier driving range with automatic ball placement, is the best in Las Vegas. *Championship; 6,810yds; par 71.*

Highland Falls

10201 Sun City Boulevard, at Lake Mead Boulevard, North-west Las Vegas (254 7010). Bus 210. **Price per round** *winter* $101 before 1pm; $59 after 1pm; *summer* rates vary. **Credit** AmEx, Disc, MC, V.

A narrow layout that favours the sand player. With all the large, imposing traps that dot this 18-hole landscape, a bit of wedge wizardry might be the difference between par and double bogie. A well-maintained, reasonably priced course that still hasn't been discovered by most locals…yet. *Championship; 6,512yds; par 72.*

Las Vegas Golf Club

4300 W Washington Avenue, between Valley View & Decatur Boulevards, North Las Vegas (646 3003). Bus 103, 208. **Price per round** $16.75; $25.75 with cart; $5 seniors; $14 with cart. **Credit** AmEx, DC, Disc, MC, V.

A recent price hike had locals grumbling, but 'the Municipal' is still a bargain. It's a good beginners' course, with wide-open fairways and large greens. It's well maintained considering how much play it receives, and a good choice if you're on a budget or prefer to walk rather than rent a cart. Pack a lunch, though, because it's busy from sunrise to sunset and you'll probably be there all day. *Championship; 6,631yds; par 72.*

Las Vegas Paiute Resort

10325 Nu-Wav Kaiv Boulevard, at US 95, north-west of Las Vegas (658 1400/teeup@lvpaiutegolf. com). No bus. **Price per round** $130 Mon-Thur; $135 Fri-Sun. **Credit** AmEx, MC, V.

Unspoiled desert scenery surrounds these two Pete Dye-designed courses, built on land belonging to the Paiute Indian tribe. Choose the Snow Mountain course, which has earned raves from *Golf Digest.* You'll need at least half an hour to drive there (take exit Snow Mountain Road east), but it's worth the extra effort. *Championship; 7,158yds; par 72.* *Website: www.lvpaiutegolf.com*

Painted Desert Golf Club

5555 Painted Mirage Road, between I-15 & Ann Road, North-west Las Vegas (645 2568). No bus. **Price per round** $100 Mon-Thur; $125 Fri-Sun. **Credit** AmEx, MC, V.

Keep the ball straight on this rugged, target-style layout, where the houses surrounding the course were built a little too close to the fairways. The greens are always in excellent shape and the practice facilities are outstanding. *Championship; 6,840yds; par 72.*

Primm Valley

I-15 south, exit Yates Well Road, at the Nevada border (679 5510). No bus. **Price per round** *guests of Primm Properties* $95 Mon-Thur; $105 Fri-Sun; *guests of MGM Grand and New York-New York* $120 daily; *others* $130 Mon-Thur; $160 Fri-Sun. **Credit** AmEx, Disc, MC, V.

Those who can't get to play at Shadow Creek (which would be just about everybody) might find Primm Valley the next best thing: Tom Fazio designed the Lakes Course here with the same general layout. The fairways are forgiving to a point, but the course is still a formidable challenge, especially from the back tees. *Championship; 6,945yds; par 72.*

Ice-skating

Chill out at Las Vegas's two ice arenas. Both offer rentals for public ice-skating throughout the year as well as hockey leagues and lessons for kids.

Sahara Ice Palace

Commercial Center, 953 E Sahara Avenue, at Maryland Parkway, East Las Vegas (862 4262). Bus 109, 204. **Open** noon-2.45pm, 3-5pm, Mon-Wed; noon-2.45pm, 3-5pm, 7.30-9.30pm, Thur; noon-2.45pm, 3-5pm, 8-10pm, Fri; 1-4pm, 8-10pm, Sat; 1-4pm Sun. **Admission** $5; $4 under-12s; $2 skate rental; $3 incl skates Thur nights. **Credit** AmEx, Disc, DC, MC, V.

Santa Fe Ice Arena

Santa Fe, 4949 N Rancho Drive, at Lone Mountain Road, North-west Las Vegas (658 4991). Bus 106. **Open** noon-2pm Mon, Wed; 3-5pm Tue, Thur; noon-2pm, 8pm-midnight, Fri; 2-4pm, 8pm-midnight, Sat;

2-4pm Sun. **Admission** $5; $4 under-16s; $1.50 skate rental. **Credit** AmEx, DC, Disc, MC, V.

Miniature golf

The **All-American SportPark** (*see page 238* for listings) has an indoor, nine-hole 'natural' putting course, complete with water hazards.

Mountasia Family Fun Center

2050 Olympic Avenue, between Mountain Vista Boulevard & Sunset Road, Henderson (898 7777). Bus 212. **Open** 3-10pm Mon-Thur; 3pm-midnight Fri; 10am-midnight Sat; 10am-10pm Sun. **Admission** $5.50; $4 4-12s. **Credit** AmEx, MC, V. Mini-golf, go-karts, bumper boats and rollerskating.

Scandia

2900 Sirius Avenue, just south of Sahara Avenue, between Rancho Drive & Valley View Boulevard, West of Strip (364 0070). Bus 401. **Open** *June-Sept*

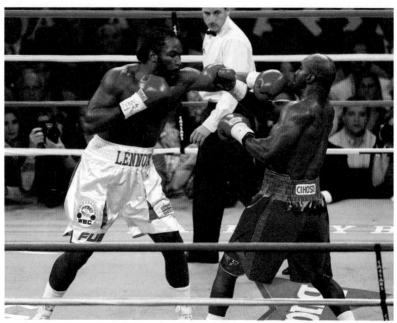

Lewis v Holyfield: Las Vegas is the home of championship boxing. See page 244.

24hrs daily; *Oct-May* 10am-10pm Mon-Thur, Sun; 10am-11pm Fri, Sat. **Admission** *individual games* $3.95-$5.95 each; *unlimited wristband* $15.95. **Credit** MC, V.

Three miniature golf courses, plus baseball batting cages, go-karts and a video arcade.

Pool & billiards

Pink E's

3695 W Flamingo Road, at Valley View Boulevard, West of Strip (252 4666). Bus 202. **Open** 24hrs daily. **Cost** free-$3. **Credit** AmEx, MC, V.

A bright, colourful spot with a café, dancing and 50 pool tables (with pink playing surfaces). No under-21s are allowed.

Tennis

Many hotels have tennis courts that are open to the public, though hotel guests receive priority. These include **Bally's** (ten courts, six lighted), **Desert Inn** (five lighted courts), the **Flamingo Hilton** (four lighted courts), the **MGM Grand** (four lighted courts) and the **Monte Carlo** (four lighted courts). If you're staying elsewhere, you can play for $5 on **UNLV**'s 12 lighted courts (4505 S Maryland Parkway; 895 4489). Free tennis on two lighted courts is available at **Paradise Park** (4770 S Harrison Drive; 455 7513) and on

eight lighted courts at **Sunset Park** (260 9803), located south-east of McCarran Airport. *See also page 244* **Health clubs**.

Spectator sports

Las Vegas Mayor Oscar Goodman has set his sights on bringing a professional sports team to the city before 2005. The locals are eager, but the owners of baseball, football and basketball have expressed concern that players might be tempted to bet on (or against) their own team. Still, all of the most prominent American sports are represented locally, through exhibition games, minor league teams and teams from UNLV. And two or three times a year, the focus of the entire sporting world centres on Las Vegas for championship boxing. With the rich and famous amassed in the first few rows, the show in the audience is sometimes more interesting than the action in the ring.

American football

The UNLV football team plays at the **Sam Boyd Stadium** on Boulder Highway and Russell Road (895 3900), and in the shadow of the college's more prominent basketball team. However, the hiring of former National Football League coach John Robinson has re-energised the programme and fan support is picking up. The season runs from September to December. Tickets cost $12 to $20; there are usually plenty of good seats available.

Monday night pro football is also an institution in a town built on betting. Although Las Vegas has no pro team of its own, nearly every drinking establishment – casino, neighbourhood tavern, topless bar – offers big-screen television viewing of Monday's games.

Auto racing

Las Vegas Motor Speedway

7000 Las Vegas Boulevard North, North Las Vegas (644 4444). No bus. **Admission** $50-$110. **Credit** AmEx, Disc, MC, V.

Opened in 1996, this 1,500-acre (607ha) motorsports entertainment complex can accommodate up to 107,000 spectators. Located just east of Nellis Air Force Base, it presents drag races, NASCAR events, short track races, motocross and a variety of other contests. The highlights of the local racing calendar are the annual Las Vegas 400, a Winston Cup event held in March (*see p103* **Las Vegas by Season**) and the Indy Racing League's open-wheel Las Vegas 500, in April.
Website: www.lvms.com

Baseball

The Las Vegas Stars, the AAA farm team of the major league San Diego Padres, play their home games at **Cashman Field** (850 Las Vegas Boulevard North, at Washington Avenue) from April to September. The 12,000-seat stadium, one of the nicest in the minor leagues, is rarely full,

Health spas

A few hours at a health spa can seem like a vacation within a vacation. Several Strip casino-hotels have elegant spa facilities that rival the best in Palm Springs and Scottsdale, and most are open to non-guests. Basic services include a variety of massage therapies (Swedish, shiatsu, aromatherapy) and skin care programmes (loofah, exfoliation), plus a sauna, steam room, whirlpool and fitness rooms. The spas listed below have mixed fitness facilities and beauty salons, but single-sex steam rooms, saunas and jacuzzis. Reservations are advised.

Bellagio Spa

Bellagio, 3600 Las Vegas Boulevard South, at W Flamingo Road (693 8080). Bus 202, 301, 302. **Open** 6am-8pm daily. **Rates** $25 Mirage Resorts guests only. **Credit** AmEx, Disc, JCB, MC, V.

Bellagio's classy spa offers personal training and standard pampering delights (massages, facials and body-wraps) in a deluxe Mediterranean-style environment – but it's open only to guests of Mirage Resorts.

Canyon Ranch Spa Club

Venetian, 3355 Las Vegas Boulevard South, just south of Sands Avenue (414 3600). Bus 203, 301, 302. **Open** 5.30am-10pm daily. **Rates** $25 guests and non-guests. **Credit** AmEx, Disc, JCB, MC, V.

At 64,000sq ft (5,950sq m), Canyon Ranch is one of the largest spa and fitness centres in the city, with 24 treatment rooms, classes and a climbing wall. Aromatherapy treatments are a speciality.

Four Seasons Health Club & Spa

Four Seasons, 3950 Las Vegas Boulevard South, at Russell Road (632 5000). Bus 301, 302. **Open** 6am-9pm daily. **Rates** free guests; free with treatment non-guests. **Credit** AmEx, Disc, JCB, MC, V.

Like the small but exclusively intimate Four Seasons Hotel itself, this spa (*pictured*) offers its guests personal attention and expert service. The best part: staff leave a 15-minute interlude between every appointment so you won't be rushed off after your relaxing massage.

Grand Spa

MGM Grand, 3799 Las Vegas Boulevard South, at E Tropicana Avenue (891 3077). Bus 201, 301, 302. **Open** 6am-8pm daily. **Rates** $20 guests; $25 non-guests (Mon-Thur only). **Credit** AmEx, Disc, JCB, MC, V.

Renovated in 1998, this 30,000sq ft (2,790sq m) spa features state-of-the-art equipment, 30 massage treatment rooms and two suites for couples.

The Spa at the Desert Inn

Desert Inn, 3145 Las Vegas Boulevard South, at Desert Inn Road (733 4571). Bus 203, 301, 302. **Open** 6am-7pm Mon-Fri; 7am-7pm Sat, Sun. **Rates** $20 guests; $25 non-guests. **Credit** AmEx, Disc, JCB, MC, V.

The Desert Inn's spa, with its Italian marble statues, Greek columns, vaulted ceilings and hand-painted murals, has set the local standard for stress relief amid luxurious surroundings. Avoid the wait usually associated with treatments from several different therapists by booking a day of beauty with a single expert.

though the Stars have ranked among the most consistently successful teams in the Pacific Coast League. Try to go on a promotion night, when you might receive free merchandise or see a concert after the game. Call 386 7200 for tickets ($4-$7).

Basketball

From 1977, when they first made it to the Final Four, through to 1990, when they captured the national championship, the UNLV Runnin' Rebels men's basketball team were the hottest ticket in town. Though the team's fortunes faded steadily for several years following NCAA sanctions in the early 1990s, the past two seasons have again shown potential. Games are played at the recently remodelled **Thomas & Mack Center** on the university campus (4505 Maryland Parkway; 895 3900; website www.thomasandmack.com) from November to May. In October, NBA teams play exhibition games at the Thomas & Mack as well, but the tickets ($10-$25) disappear quickly.

UNLV's women's basketball team, the Lady Rebels, play at the same venue, and have been posting as many wins as the men's team in the past few seasons. Tickets are just $4, one of the cheapest ways in town to spend two hours.

Boxing

Las Vegas evolved into a boxing mecca primarily because fight fans like to bet on who's going to win, and for years Vegas was the only place they could do that (legally, anyway). Since 1960, the city has played host to some of the most celebrated – and the most bizarre – boxing events in the sport's history. Among the recent headline-makers was Mike Tyson's infamous ear-nibbling of Evander Holyfield during their heavyweight-title bout and Oscar De La Hoya's controversial loss to Felix Trinidad. Championship fights are usually held at **Caesars Palace**, the **MGM Grand** or the **Mirage**. Ringside seats can cost as much as $1,500; the 'cheap' seats fall into the $100 to $200 range, depending on the event and venue. Order well in advance through the hotel or Ticketmaster (474 4000). Some boxers open their workout and training sessions to the public free of charge; for information contact the hotel hosting the fight.

Rodeo

Held every December, the National Finals Rodeo (see p106 **Las Vegas by Season**) is the sport's most prestigious event. Finalists compete in seven different events during the nine-day competition at the **Thomas & Mack Center** at UNLV (895 3900). Tickets cost $24 to $38. Cowboys from all over the US converge on Las Vegas to attend and to watch the superstars of country music perform on the Strip after the ridin' and ropin' is done.

Wrestling

OK, technically it's not a sport, but where else can we classify it – culture? Las Vegas hosts half a dozen or so World Wrestling Federation (WWF) and World Championship Wrestling (WCW) events every year. WCW's 'Halloween Havoc' is held every October at the MGM Grand; other event schedules vary: check the local newspapers or the websites of the WWF (www.wwf.com) or WCW (www.wcwwrestling.com) for details. On Monday and Thursday nights, fans of Sting and Goldberg gather at the Nitro Grill on the second level of the Excalibur to watch the live action on TV.

Health clubs

Many hotels, including **Bally's**, **Caesars Palace**, the **MGM Grand**, the **Tropicana** and the **Mirage**, have health club facilities that are free to guests and open to the public for a fee. Away from the Strip, there are several clubs that offer day- or short-term passes.

24 Hour Fitness

2605 S Eastern Avenue, at E Sahara Avenue, East Las Vegas (641 2222). Bus 110, 204. **Admission** day $10; week $25. **Open** 24hrs.
Feel the urge to pump some iron at 2am? 24 Hour Fitness is – as you might have guessed – open all night, seven days a week. The aerobics studio is larger than most.

Gold's Gym

Gold's Plaza, 3750 E Flamingo Road, at Sandhill Road, East Las Vegas (451 4222). Bus 202. **Admission** day $10; week $35; month $50. **Open** 24hrs daily.
Touted as a no-frills fitness gym, Gold's offers all the free weights, weight machines and cardio equipment an exercise buff could ever handle. Both branches also have aerobic classes and shops.
Branch: Sahara Pavilion, 4720 W Sahara Avenue, North-west Las Vegas (877 6966).

Las Vegas Athletic Club

2655 Maryland Parkway, at Karen Avenue, East Las Vegas (734 5822). Bus 109. **Admission** day $10; week $25. **Open** 24hrs daily.
Five locations throughout Las Vegas, each with swimming pools, saunas, jacuzzis, racquetball courts, Nautilus, free weights and more than 200 weekly aerobics classes, including dance, step and cardio. This is the only 24-hour branch.

Las Vegas Sporting House

3025 S Industrial Road, between Sahara Avenue & Stardust Drive, West of Strip (733 8999). Bus 105. **Admission** day $15; week $50. **Open** 24hrs daily.
Located just west of the Strip, directly behind the Stardust, the Sporting House offers aerobics, Cycle Reebok, ten racquetball courts, two tennis courts, indoor and outdoor swimming pools, basketball, personal training, yoga, t'ai chi and a restaurant.

Trips Out of Town

Trips Out of Town

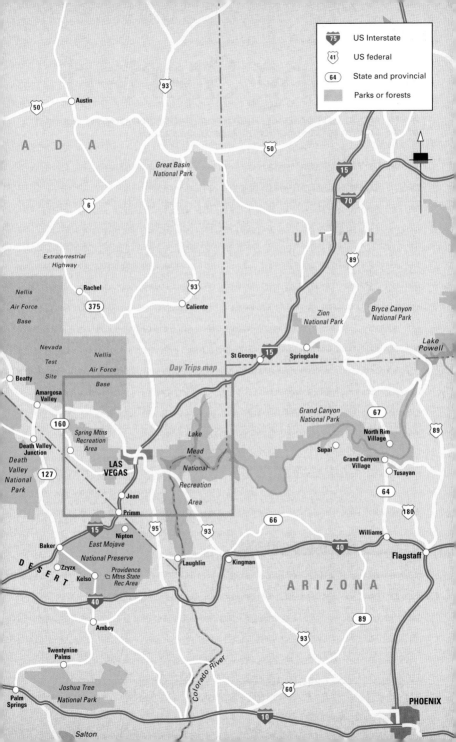

Getting Started

North, south, east or west: whatever direction you choose, the best of the Southwest's spectacular landscapes await.

One of the best things about Las Vegas is how easy it is to leave it. When the 24-hour razzle-dazzle begins to grow wearying and you yearn for sunlight rather than neon, head outside the city. The options for day trips are plentiful; within 50 miles (80 kilometres) of the city you'll find peaceful desert parks (**Red Rock Canyon**, **Valley of Fire**), boating and fishing (on **Lake Mead**), man-made marvels (**Hoover Dam**) and even somewhere to ski (**Mount Charleston**).

Further afield lie more possibilities. Las Vegas's position in the southernmost tip of Nevada means it is close to three states packed with interesting destinations – to the south and west lies California, to the east is Arizona and to the north-east Utah – while to the north, of course, is the rest of Nevada. Some of the best-known natural sights in the US, including the **Grand Canyon**, **Death Valley** and **Zion National Park**, are within easy reach.

This is the land of the automobile, so the easiest – usually the only – way to get anywhere is by car. Fortunately, road connections are good, with interstates and federal highways leading off at all points of the compass. The I-15 takes you south-west (towards Los Angeles) and north-east (towards Salt Lake City); US 93 and US 95 head north into Nevada and south into Arizona and California, respectively. The I-40 is also nearby. The I-15 can be unpleasantly crowded, especially heading into California, but, in general, you'll be travelling roads that are fast, empty and surrounded by spectacular desert scenery. On many trips, the drive itself is as much of an experience as the destination.

The desert

Desert lovers are drawn to the very starkness and nakedness that others find so repellent. Compared to wetter, greener areas, deserts are very easy to read: the 'bones' of mountains are laid bare before you; views are long and unobscured; plants are sparse in form and coverage; the cloudless skies and intense sunlight can bleach out colours but also create fabulous shadows and vivid hues, especially towards dusk.

And Las Vegas is one of the best places in the US from which to explore the country's dramatic desertscapes. It lies slap bang in the middle of one – the **Mojave** – and close to two others – the **Great Basin** and the **Sonoran** (also known as the Colorado desert). Only the Chihuahan desert, which covers part of southern New Mexico and much of Mexico, is too far away for easy access.

The usual definition of a desert is that it receives less than ten inches (25 centimetres) of precipitation a year and has high evaporation (curiously, temperature doesn't come into it, although deserts are usually thought of as hot), but this is a pretty wide definition, allowing much room for variation. Lack of cloud cover is also important, because it causes heat to reradiate – go back into the sky – very rapidly at night, hence the often high variation between day and night temperatures. Other crucial factors are how and when precipitation occurs, and elevation. All three of the deserts near Las Vegas share characteristics, but they also exhibit great differences in landscape, vegetation and wildlife.

The **Mojave** is the smallest, covering the lower quarter of Nevada and part of Southern California, a total of 54,000 square miles (140,000 square kilometres). It is deemed a 'hot' desert, with low average elevations (Las Vegas is at 2,200 feet/670 metres) and precipitation falling as rain, usually in winter. It includes some of the most dramatic landscapes to be found in the North American deserts and also the lowest absolute elevation and maximum temperature recorded in the US (both in Death Valley, California). Unless you venture far from Las Vegas, most of your driving will be in the Mojave desert and you'll soon learn to recognise characteristic plants: the spidery creosote bush predominates but its signature plant is the bizarre Joshua tree.

The **Great Basin**, which covers the northern three-quarters of Nevada plus the western half of Utah, is the largest desert in the US, covering more than 158,000 square miles (409,000 square kilometres). It is described as a 'cold' desert because more than half its annual precipitation occurs in winter in the form of snow, and its northern position and high base elevations (usually above 4,000 feet/ 1,220 metres) mean it experiences lower average temperatures than areas to the south. It was named by nineteenth-century explorer John C Fremont because its rivers lack outlets to the sea – though the name is misleading in that its shape is nothing like a basin. It doesn't look much like a desert, either: silvery green

The Joshua tree

The weird, multi-branched Joshua tree is the most distinctive plant in the Mojave desert. Many think it ugly – explorer John C Fremont considered it 'the most repulsive tree in the vegetable kingdom' – though rock group U2 liked it enough to call an album after it. Early Mormon pioneers named it after the Biblical character Joshua as its branches resembled upstretched arms beckoning them to the promised land.

This 'tree' is, in fact, a yucca (*Yucca brevifolia*) and a member of the lily family: its stem is pith rather than wood. Joshuas grow very slowly and live up to 900 years, with an average height of 20-30 feet (6-9m). In the spring, the tips of the branches carry large clusters of creamy flowers, which open for one night only and smell like mushrooms. After blossoming, the branch forks, eventually giving the Joshua its many-limbed form. Though not exclusive to the Mojave, it is abundant there, at elevations between 2,000 and 4,500 feet (600 to 1,370 metres). However, the most extensive forests are found in Joshua Tree National Park and the East Mojave National Preserve (*see chapter* **Into California**).

sagebrush, the dominant plant (and Nevada's state plant), blankets vast areas, and many desert plants of popular imagination – such as large cacti, agaves and yuccas – are conspicuous by their absence.

The transition between the Great Basin and the Mojave deserts occurs roughly around a line drawn to the north-west of Las Vegas, between Beatty and Caliente; the transition zone itself is marked by the existence of blackbrush, a small, dark, round shrub. You'll notice the change in vegetation if you drive north from Vegas to Reno.

The **Sonoran** desert extends over part of southern California and the south-western quarter of Arizona. Like the Mojave, it is both lower and hotter than the Great Basin, and rain falls in both summer and winter. Unless you drive as far south as Joshua Tree National Park, you won't cross into the Sonoran.

There's also the **Colorado Plateau**, an area of semi-desert that includes the canyon country of south-eastern Utah and the north-eastern portion of Arizona. Geologically, it is very different from the nearby desert, its landscape made up of colourful layers of sedimentary rock that erosion has carved into dramatic rock formations and stunning canyons – of which the Grand Canyon is the most magnificent and famous example. It includes many of the plants found in true desert areas as well as grassland and woodland species.

Desert survival

The desert is a dangerous place, especially in high summer when temperatures rocket and frazzled skin and dehydration are real possibilities. Don't be fooled into thinking that an air-conditioned automobile will keep you safe: cars break down. Treat the desert with the respect it deserves; here are a few tips for your journey.

● **Water**: Carry plenty of drinking water, in your car and with you when hiking. In summer, allow at least one gallon (four litres) per person per day.

● **Dress up**: Wear suitable clothing, including a broad-brimmed hat, sunglasses and a shirt. Carry sunscreen – and use it. Temperatures can plummet at night, even in summer, so carry warm clothing if necessary.

● **Avoid the midday sun**: In summer, hike in the early morning or late afternoon. Wear long trousers and tough walking boots to protect you from the sun, spiky plants, snakes and uneven terrain; sandals are not adequate for most desert trails.

● **Watch for signs of dehydration**: If you feel dizzy, nauseous or develop a headache, get out of the sun immediately and drink plenty of water. Dampen your clothing to lower your body temperature.

● **Be prepared**: Take a compass and a good topographic map if you're heading off-trail into remote areas or exploring back roads. Distances are deceptive and it's easy to get lost. Carrying a torch is also a good idea.
● **Weather alert**: Look out for changes in the weather, especially in summer when storms and flash floods are common. Never park or camp in washes (dry creek beds).
● **Road conditions**: Check with a park ranger or visitor centre before you set out, especially if you're planning to drive on any unpaved roads. If you break down, stay with your car.
● **Watch vehicle gauges**: Turn off air-conditioning on uphill grades to lessen engine strain and, if the engine overheats, slowly pour water over the surface of the radiator to cool it – do not open the radiator. Leave a window slightly open if you park the car for any length of time in the heat.
● **The desert is a fragile place**: Stick to marked trails if possible and don't trample vegetation, soil crusts or animal burrows. Don't place your hands or feet where you can't see them: snakes and scorpions may be lurking.

Useful information

For details of outfits offering tours to sights outside Las Vegas, *see page 89* **Attractions**

Driving & transport

For details of car and RV rental companies, *see* chapter **Getting Around**. Driving around Las Vegas means you're frequently crossing from one state to another and back again, so remember that speed limits may change from state to state.

American Automobile Association (AAA)
3312 W Charleston Boulevard, just west of Valley View Boulevard, Northwest Las Vegas (870 9171). **Open** 8.30am-5.30pm Mon-Fri.
The fabulous Triple A provides excellent maps, guidebooks and campground listings – and they won't cost you a penny if you're a member or belong to an affiliated organisation, such as the British AA. There are branches in Summerlin, Henderson, Carson City and Reno in Nevada, St George in Utah and throughout California. Many motels offer discounts to AAA members.

Greyhound
200 S Main Street, at Carson Street, Downtown (384 9561/central information 1-800 231 2222). *Bus 113, 207.* **Open** 24hrs daily. **Credit** AmEx, Disc, MC, V.
A long-distance bus service to over 2,000 destinations nationwide, including Los Angeles ($34.50 one-way, $60.75 round-trip, 5-7hrs) and Reno ($68 one-way, $135.50 round-trip, 9hrs). Reservations are not accepted.

Road conditions
Arizona 1-520 573 7623; **California** 1-916 445 1534; **Nevada** 486 3116; **Utah** 1-801 964 6000.

Outdoors

For weather information phone lines, *see chapter* **Essential Information**.

Bureau of Land Management
4765 Vegas Drive, Las Vegas, NV 89108 (647 5000). **Telephone enquiries** 7.30am-4.15pm Mon-Fri.
Website: www.nv.blm.gov

National Park Service
601 Nevada Highway, Boulder City, NV 89005 (293 8906). **Telephone enquiries** 8.30am-4pm Mon-Fri.
Website: www.nps.gov

Nevada State Parks
District VI headquarters, 4747 W Vegas Drive, Las Vegas, NV 89108 (486 5126). **Telephone enquiries** 8am-5pm Mon-Fri.
Website: www.state.nv.us

Sierra Club
PO Box 19777, Las Vegas, NV 89132 (recorded info 363 3267; membership Walter Barbuck 735 9411).
The grandaddy of environmental outfits, the Sierra Club organises regular guided hikes (open to non-members) in Red Rock Canyon, Mount Charleston and the Lake Mead area. Call for information on upcoming hikes, monthly meetings, other activities and membership.
Website: www.sierraclub.org

US Forest Service
2881 S Valley View Boulevard, suite 16, Las Vegas, NV 89102 (873 8800). **Open** 8am-4.30pm Mon-Fri.
Website: www.fs.fed.us/htnf

Tourist information

Call the following offices for visitor information, maps and accommodation advice in each state. The Nevada office is particularly good, sending out a comprehensive – and free – information pack.

Arizona Office of Tourism
1-602 230 7733.
If you're in Britain, you can get a free information pack by calling 01426 946334.
Website: www.arizonaguide.com

California Division of Tourism
1-800 862 2543/1-916 322 2881.
Call the 1-916 number (in Sacramento) if you need information sending overseas.
Website: www.gocalif.ca.gov

Nevada Commission of Tourism
1-800 638 2328.
Website: www.travelnevada.com

Utah Travel Council
1-801 538 1030.
Website: www.utah.com

Day Trips

Ninety minutes' drive, tops, and you can choose between desert, mountain and lake, all equally spectacular.

Hoover Dam

Half an hour's drive south-east of Las Vegas lies the engineering miracle that ensured the city's survival and made possible its phenomenal growth. The Hoover Dam, built at the height of the Depression, is a mind-boggling structure. Without it, much of the Southwest would not exist. Constructed and still run by the Bureau of Reclamation, it controls the turbulent and flood-prone Colorado River, providing electricity and water to more than 18 million people in California, Nevada and Arizona. It keeps the neon aglow in Vegas, irrigates cotton fields and date plantations in Southern California, allows film stars to water their lawns in Beverly Hills and makes it possible for huge cities and rich farmland to flourish in one of the driest, hottest and most inhospitable regions of the world.

The bare facts are impressive enough. It's big, very big – 726 feet (221 metres) high, 660 feet (200 metres) thick at its base, 40 feet (12 metres) at the top, 1,244 feet (379 metres) wide at its crest. Its reservoir, the 110-mile (177-kilometre) long and 500-foot (152-metre) deep Lake Mead, is the largest man-made lake in the US and can hold enough water to cover the entire state of Nevada, six inches (15 centimetres) deep. The dam swallowed up enough concrete to pave a highway between San Francisco and New York (and then some). Its two flood-control spillways can each handle the equivalent of the Niagara Falls.

And building it was an equally mammoth task. The concrete would have taken a hundred years to set if left under normal conditions: the cooling process was speeded up by pouring ice-cold water through a network of pipes laid into each block of concrete. Vast, 30-foot (nine-metre) diameter pipes (known as penstocks) were lowered, section by section, from an overhead cableway 800 feet (244 metres) above the canyon floor and squeezed into tunnels blasted out of the side walls. An army of workers, 16,400-strong, laboured for four years night and day, finishing in February 1935 – an amazing two years ahead of schedule.

Named after US president Herbert Hoover, the dam straddles the border between Arizona and Nevada: two clocks on the intake towers show the time difference. On the Nevada side are the main, multi-storey car park ($2) and escalators leading to the subterranean visitor centre; there's more parking (and stunning views of the whole structure) on the Arizona side. You can walk around at the top of the dam, but be careful when crossing busy US 93.

Don't miss the sculptures (by Norwegian-born artist Oskar Hansen) on the Nevada side. A bronze bas-relief commemorates the 96 workers who died during the dam's construction – 'they died to make the desert bloom' – and two huge, bronze-winged figures flank a flagpole above a terrazzo floor inlaid with a celestial map, marking Franklin D Roosevelt's dedication of the dam in September 1935. The white mark on the shoreline indicates the flood level in 1983 when spring run-offs from the Colorado were double the average and Lake Mead rose to within seven feet (two metres) of the top of the dam; the two spillways were used for the first time since they were tested in 1941.

The visitor centre, which opened in 1995, cost a stonking $123 million – although you wouldn't know it from the exhibits upstairs, which are badly laid out and uninformative. And there's no book-shop, although you can buy copies of old photos of the dam's construction ($1 each black and white, $3 colour). The theatre shows three films in succession (about 35 minutes in total), one of which is a short 1930s film on the building of the dam with great footage and gung-ho narration. There's a top-floor observation deck and, across the road, a snack bar and poorly stocked gift shop. But, of course, the highlight of any visit is getting down into the dam itself.

There are two tours, a regular tour and a 'hard hat' tour (so-called because everyone gets to don a hard hat). The dam receives more than a million visitors a year, so expect to queue for tickets and then to queue for your tour; it's best to go early in the morning or late in the afternoon to avoid the worst of the rush. Space is limited on the hard hat tour so it's a good idea to book.

The 35-minute regular tour (which starts about every ten minutes) takes you in an elevator 520 feet (158 metres) down through the volcanic canyon wall to the power plants housing the gargantuan turbines, through the central office building and to the base of the dam, where the tamed Colorado bubbles out green and furious.

The hard hat tour (leaving every half-hour) is pricey but more detailed (it takes an hour) and with

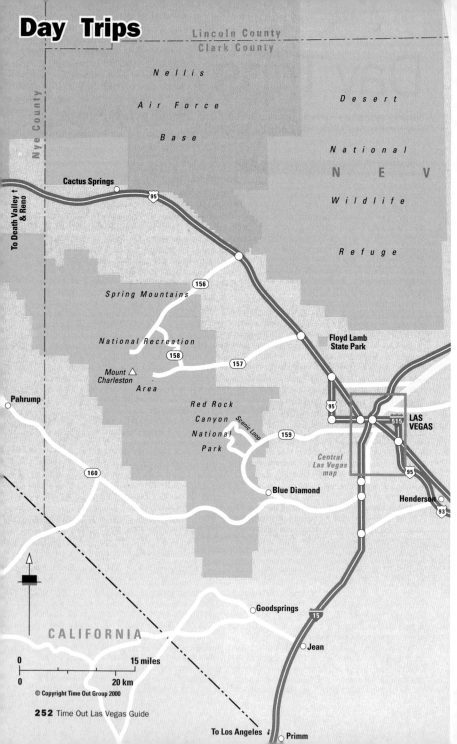

Day Trips

Lincoln County
Clark County

Nye County

Nellis

Air Force

Base

Desert

National

N   **E**   **V**

Wildlife

Refuge

To Death Valley ↑ & Reno

Cactus Springs

95

156

Spring Mountains

National Recreation

158

Mount △ Charleston

Area

157

Floyd Lamb State Park

95

515

LAS VEGAS

Pahrump

Red Rock

Canyon

Scenic Loop

National

Park

159

Central Las Vegas map

160

Blue Diamond

Henderson

95

93

Goodsprings

15

CALIFORNIA

Jean

↑

0   15 miles

0   20 km

© Copyright Time Out Group 2000

To Los Angeles ↓ Primm

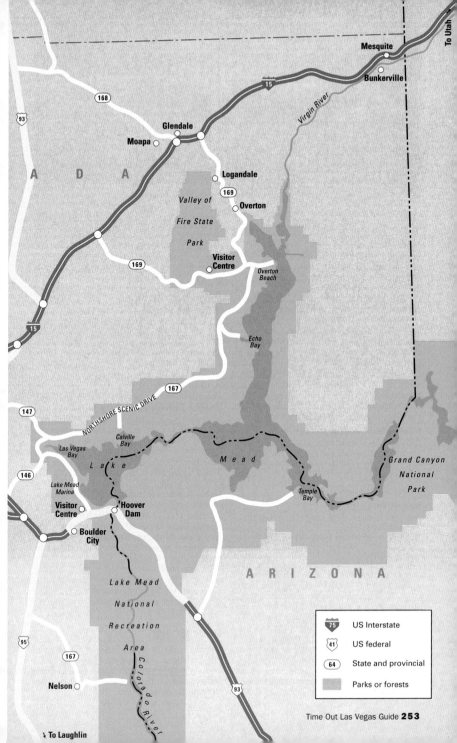

*Experience the extraordinary engineering of the **Hoover Dam** on a 'hard hat' tour.*

smaller groups: 15 people, as opposed to 80 on the regular tour. You see the original staircase, 982 steps snaking all the way from the top to the bottom of the dam, and also get to peek out of a ventilation inlet halfway up the dam face. The art deco detailing is fabulous: look for abstract Indian symbols inlaid in the black and white terrazzo floor in the office building and the huge fluted brass doors to the toilets at the top of the dam. If you really want to find out exactly how the dam was built and works, it's worth the extra dosh; and, hey, you get to keep your hard hat.

You can also take a cruise on Lake Mead on the three-deck paddlewheeler **Desert Princess** (an hour-and-an-half round trip): you join the boat at Lake Mead Cruises Landing on the Lake Mead shoreline (*see opposite* **Lake Mead** for details of breakfast and dinner cruises). The boat used to dock at the Hoover Dam, but at the time of writing, the high water level makes this impossible.

Hoover Dam Visitor Center
294 3523. **Open** 8am-5.45pm daily. **Admission** *exhibits only* $4; *plus regular tour* $8, $7 seniors, $2 6-16s; *plus hard hat tour* $25; free under-5s. Tour times can vary during the year, so it's a good idea to phone first. *Website: www.hooverdam.com*

Desert Princess
293 6180. **Cruises** 10am, noon, 2pm, 4pm daily. **Tickets** $16; $6 2-11s. The 4pm cruise is from 1 Apr-Oct 31 only.

Boulder City

A few miles from the Hoover Dam is the green and pleasant town of Boulder City, built from scratch in 1931 to house the dam workers. Triangular in shape, it was the first 'model city' in the US, built according to progressive planning theories. The Bureau of Reclamation, government buildings and a park sit at the apex of the triangle, with the workers' houses radiating down from there. It was not intended as a permanent settlement, but though the population dropped after the dam was finished, it recovered during World War II and the town is now flourishing, with a population of 14,500.

Driving down US 93, you pass some small, old-fashioned motels and stalls selling Mexican pottery and other handicrafts. Only slowly do you realise that something's missing: there are no casinos. Boulder City is the only town in Nevada where gambling is illegal: maybe the reason for its quiet and civilised atmosphere.

Take a detour through the US 93 business loop to view the historic district, full of tree-lined streets and grassy parks. The **Boulder Dam Hotel** (turn right at Arizona Street) is the white and green building with tall cypresses outside. You can't stay the night here but it does have a gift shop, two art galleries, a restaurant and the **Chamber of Commerce** (open 9am-5pm Mon-Fri; 293 2034), where you can pick up a map and a guide to walking tours of the historic district. The hotel is also home to the recently renovated **Hoover Dam/Boulder City Museum** (open 10am-5pm daily; admission $2; 294 1988), which has social history exhibits and shows a film on the building of Boulder City and the dam.

Down the street from the hotel, past the city's newspaper office and the cinema, is **Evans Old Town Grille** (294 0100), which serves American food and has outdoor seating. On US 93, **Two Gals** (1632 Nevada Highway; 293 1793) is a good spot for a light lunch with omelettes and a wide selection of vegetarian sandwiches, while the **Happy Days Diner** (512 Nevada Highway; 293 4637), one of the city's oldest restaurants, is decorated in classic 1950s diner style and serves suitably classic diner food.

If you're heading from Boulder City towards the dam, you get a spectacular view of Lake Mead as you rejoin US 93 before you start descending through twisty canyons covered with pylons and power lines.

Getting there

For the Hoover Dam, take US 93 south for 32 miles (51 kilometres); Boulder City is seven miles (11 kilometres) before the dam. To see Boulder City's historic district, turn off at the business loop, which then rejoins US 93.

Lake Mead

Lake Mead is the second most popular recreation spot (after Las Vegas, of course) in Nevada: 9.6 million visitors (the vast majority of them locals) come to its 550 miles (885 kilometres) of shoreline every year to boat, fish, swim, water-ski, camp, picnic and generally enjoy watery pleasures in the middle of the desert. It's completely artificial, created when the natural flow of the Colorado River was blocked by the Hoover Dam, and is certainly an incongruous sight: a large blue splodge surrounded by barren mountains, with just very tops of canyons peeking above the water. It's the centrepiece of the huge Lake Mead National Recreation Area, which also includes Lake Mohave to the south (created when the Colorado River was stemmed again in 1953 by the Davis Dam) and the surrounding desert east to the edge of Grand Canyon National Park and north to Overton.

Lakeside Scenic Drive (which becomes Northshore Scenic Drive) skirts the western side of Lake Mead for nearly 60 miles (96 kilometres): it's not particularly scenic and you rarely see the lake, but it's the access road for the five concession-operated marinas along the Nevada shoreline (the Nevada/Arizona border runs through the centre of the lake). Planted with palms, eucalyptus and (very poisonous) oleander, these are green havens in the stark landscape.

Lake Mead (next to Boulder Beach) and **Las Vegas Bay** are the largest and closest marinas to Las Vegas and therefore the busiest; further north are **Calville Bay**, **Echo Bay** and **Overton Beach**, while **Temple Bay** is a less accessible and quieter marina on the Arizona side. There are a couple of other boat landings and many small dirt roads (some suitable for 4WD vehicles only) leading to the lake edge. Head straight for one of the marinas or first visit the **Alan Bible Visitor Center** (293 8990; open 8.30am-4.30pm daily), a few miles west of the Hoover Dam: it's rather basic, but you can pick up a useful map and information on fishing and other activities.

The best way to explore the lake is, of course, by boat. There are numerous secluded coves, sandy beaches and narrow canyons accessible only by water, and the warm, clear lake is ideal for swimming: the water temperature averages 78°F (26°C) in spring, summer and autumn. You can rent large ski boats, patio boats, small fishing boats and Sea-Doos (wave runners) for a few hours or a whole day; the larger marinas offer more choice. The clarity and warmth of the water also make the lake ideal for scuba diving, and although you can't hire equipment at the lake, dive shops in Las Vegas rent gear and run courses (*see page 239* **Sport & Fitness**).

All the marinas have small ranger stations (which are not always open), grocery stores and restaurants; some have additional facilities such as swimming beaches (without lifeguards), picnic sites, motels, showers, laundries and petrol stations. If you have more time to spare and want to spend a few days investigating the further reaches of the lake, you can rent a houseboat at Echo Bay and Calville Bay, although you'll need a group of at least six to make it worth the money. Houseboats are popular, so be sure to book well in advance during the summer.

Lake Mead also offers some of the best year-round sport fishing in the country, particularly for striped and largemouth bass. Head for the upper Overton Arm of the lake for crappie, blue gill, green sunfish and catfish. Most marinas sell fishing licences ($12, plus $4 per additional day), bait and tackle, while some even rent rods. If you fish from a boat, you must have a fishing licence from either Arizona or Nevada and a special-use stamp from the other; note that you can't fish within harbour areas. Check at a ranger station for the current hot fishing spots.

If you don't want to pilot your own craft, the paddlewheeler **Desert Princess** offers breakfast, dinner and dinner-dance cruises, as well as tours to and from the Hoover Dam. The boat leaves from Lake Mead Cruises Landing (between Boulder Beach and Las Vegas Bay).

A 19-mile (30-kilometre) drive south of the Hoover Dam, the Willow Beach landing on the Colorado River is the best place for trout fishing in the area. Lake Mohave, even further to the south, is narrower than Lake Mead and attracts far fewer visitors. It has two marinas and is another good spot to fish for rainbow trout, especially in its upper reaches in Black Canyon.

Boat rental

Note that rates, choice of boats and rental conditions vary from marina to marina.
Rates *ski boat* two hours $100, per day $300;
patio boat two hours $40-$70, per day $120-$210;
fishing boat two hours $20-$40, per day $60-$120;
wave runner one hour $50, per day $250;
waterskiing gear $18 per day.

*Take to the water at **Lake Mead**.*

Desert Princess cruises

293 6180. **Cruises** *breakfast* 10am Sat, Sun; *early dinner* 6.30pm Mon-Thur, Sun (Nov-Mar 5.30pm Sun only); *dinner-dance* (no children) 7.30pm Fri, Sat. **Tickets** *breakfast* $21, $10 2-11s; *early dinner* $29, $15 2-11s; *dinner-dance* $43.

Where to eat

Most marinas have some form of restaurant or bar. Try the one on the water at family-run **Las Vegas Bay** (565 9111) or the grander **Tail O' The Whale** restaurant at Echo Bay (394 4000), with its dark interior and heavy nautical theming overlooking the water. Both of them serve the usual burgers, sandwiches and fish, although the latter are not, as you might expect, from the lake.

Where to stay

If you want to stay on land, **Seven Crown Resorts** runs motels (rooms cost $43-$89) at Echo Bay, Boulder Beach and Temple Bar. There are campgrounds at all marinas except Overton and Willow Beach: sites are available on a first-come, first-served basis and cost $10 per night.

Houseboat rental

All houseboats have a fully equipped kitchen, TV and video, barbecue and sun deck. Echo Bay has about 80 boats in four sizes: the smallest sleeps six, the largest 14. Calville Bay's 55 boats can be driven from the lower or upper deck and come in three sizes, each sleeping ten. Note that you can only board on certain days of the week, depending on the length of the rental.

Calville Bay

Forever Resorts 1-800 255 5561/565 4813. **Rates** (for standard 56ft/17m boat). Boats can be rented for three, four, five or seven days.

Mid Oct-Apr three days $995, seven days $1,695; *May* three days $1,595, seven days $2,195; *June-Labor Day* three days $2,295, seven days $3,495; *Labor Day-mid Oct* three days $1,795, seven days $2,595. **Website:** *www.foreverresorts.com*

Echo Bay

Seven Crown Resorts 1-800 752 9669/394 4000. **Rates** (for smallest boat, sleeping six). Boats can be rented for three, four or seven days. *Memorial Day weekend, mid June-mid Sept* three days $950, seven days $1,550; *mid Sept-mid June (except Memorial Day weekend)* three days $650, seven days $1,150. **Website:** *www.sevencrown.com*

Getting there

The Alan Bible Visitor Center is situated 27 miles (43 kilometres) south of Las Vegas on US 93, at the junction with Lakeshore Scenic Drive. To reach Las Vegas Bay, Boulder Beach and Lake Mead marinas without going to the visitor centre, take Boulder Highway south and turn left at Lake Mead Drive (Highway 147) or take Lake Mead Boulevard east (also Highway 147): both join the shore road. For Cottonwood Cove on the east shore of Lake Mohave, take US 95 south from Las Vegas for 70 miles (113 kilometres).

Red Rock Canyon

A mere 20 miles (32 kilometres) from the gaming tables of Vegas is one of Nevada's most popular and beautiful outdoor areas. The cool, deep-cut canyons of the Red Rock Canyon National Conservation Area make it a popular hiking spot all year round, while climbers come from all over the world to enjoy some of the best rock climbing in the US.

*The Calico Hills in **Red Rock Canyon**, a mecca for rock climbers.*

Part of the Spring Mountains, the centrepiece of the park is a nearly sheer escarpment of Aztec sandstone, the remnant of ancient sand dunes that covered this area some 180 million years ago. About 65 million years ago, the Keystone Thrust Fault pushed older grey limestone over younger sandstone, reversing the normal layering and resulting in today's dramatic – and unique – landscape. The red and cream Calico Hills to the east are more rounded, as they are not protected from erosion by a higher limestone layer.

Because of the availability of water in the area – there are more than 40 springs and many natural catchment basins (known as *tinajas* or tanks) – Native Americans have used Red Rock Canyon since about 3,500 BC: evidence remains in the form of rock art (etched petroglyphs and painted pictographs), as well as occasional artefacts such as arrowheads and ceramics. Roasting pits – circular areas of piled-up limestone that were used as ovens – are most common and very distinctive: some are large mounds several yards high. Animals are also drawn to the area's water. More than 45 mammal species inhabit the park – among them mountain lions, kit foxes, coyotes, kangaroo rats, mule deer and the near-mythical desert bighorn sheep – but you'll be lucky to spot any.

The most visible animals are probably the non-native burros (donkeys). About 50 live around Red Rock Canyon, and they're often seen along the roadside, especially in the early morning and late afternoon. Remember that these are wild animals, which can bite and kick: observe them from a distance and never try to feed them. Humans are also a danger to burros; if they are encouraged to congregate at roadsides, some will inevitably be hit and killed by vehicles.

Head first for the newly expanded **Bureau of Land Management Visitor Center** (363 1921; open 8.30am-4.30pm daily) for information and a map; it's also got a good selection of books and gifts. The centre is at the start of the one-way, 13-mile (21-kilometre) scenic drive: it's open from 7am to dusk daily and costs $5. There are picnic sites at Willow Spring, Red Spring and Red Rock Vista, and a new campground ($10). The drive is popular with cyclists and gives access to numerous hiking trails, which range from an easy, half-mile loop to a strenuous, 13-mile there-and-back hike to the top of Bridge Mountain. Many trails are not clearly marked and involve scrambling over rocks, so it's a good idea to take a topographic map (available from the visitor centre) and a compass.

A good introduction to the Calico Hills that line the start of the scenic drive is the two-and-a-half mile (four-kilometre) **Calico Tank** trail. Park at Sandstone Quarry and walk past the remains of the quarry, an agave roasting pit and then into a side canyon, over eroded sandstone slopes and gullies until you reach a large natural water tank.

You have been warned!

Added steps make it easier for novice hikers, but note that sandstone can be soft, crumbly and slippery, especially when wet. Just above the tank is a fine view (smog permitting) of the valley and the Strip's casino monoliths.

Good short summer hikes include **Ice Box Canyon** and **Pine Creek Canyon**, which heads past the foundations of a 1922 homestead to a green canyon with a stream and ponderosa pines. There are scores of other trails: for further details, pick up a copy of the BLM's trail leaflet, or Branch Whitney's *Hiking Las Vegas*, which also covers Mount Charleston. Guided hikes are led by park staff on weekends and some weekdays (ask at the visitor centre) and by the Sierra Club (363 3267). For information on climbing in the area, *see page 238* **Sport & Fitness**.

If you'd prefer something less physical, head further west on Highway 159 to the green and pretty oasis of **Spring Mountain State Park** (admission $5), situated at the base of the dramatic Wilson Cliffs. You can tour the New England-style ranch house (open noon-4pm Mon-Fri, 10am-4pm Sat, Sun), stroll around the historic buildings in the white fenced grounds (look for the old fig tree by the blacksmith's shop) and picnic on a grassy meadow under shady trees. There are regular guided walking tours (Friday to Monday), open-air theatre performances during the summer and 'living history' programmes in the autumn; more information is available on 875 4141.

A few miles on is **Bonnie Springs/Old Nevada**, a mock Wild West town (entrance $6.50 adults, $4 children) with a melodrama, gunfight and hanging staged daily (usually 11.30am, 2pm and 4pm). It's rather dilapidated, but good fun, and there's also a free petting zoo, restaurant and bar (open 8am-11pm daily), horse rides and a motel (875 4400) on site.

Getting there

Head west for 20 miles (32 kilometres) on Charleston Boulevard. If you're staying near the southern end of the Strip, it's probably quicker to drive south on the I-15, then take Highway 160 towards Pahrump and turn right on to Highway 159.

Valley of Fire

Bored of the man-made wonders of Las Vegas? Head north 50 miles to discover a natural marvel whose eroded red sandstone formations are just as spectacular as the neon-clad casinos on the Strip. The aptly named Valley of Fire State Park is bounded by the grey limestone Muddy Mountains to the south and west and was Nevada's first state park (entrance is $5). It's easily explored in a day and could be combined with a trip to Lake Mead: Overton Beach, at the northern end of the lake, lies a few miles east of the park.

Summer highs top 110°F (43°C); as such, the best times to visit are (as is usual in the desert) spring and autumn. The cactus and wildflower blooms are usually at their peak in mid-April. If you're lucky you may catch a glimpse of a desert tortoise (Nevada's state reptile); you're sure to see antelope ground squirrels (chipmunks to you and I), which are common and a nuisance if you're camping or picnicking. Don't feed them and don't pet them: they may be carrying bubonic plague.

Although most sights are visible from your car, you'll experience much more if you get out and walk. Marked trails are few and very short but hiking is permitted throughout the park: ask for advice at the visitor centre. The main attractions are the fiery Aztec sandstone formations, created from sand dunes deposited 135-150 million years ago and sculpted by wind and water into bizarre, often anthropomorphic shapes, as their names reflect: look for the **Beehives**, **Elephant Rock** and **Seven Sisters** along Highway 169, the main east-west road through the park. Short walks lead to some ancient petrified logs and three stone cabins, constructed by the Civilian Conservation Corps in the 1930s to provide primitive shelter for travellers. A two-mile (five-kilometre) scenic loop road takes you past some of the park's most dramatic rock formations. Nestled in among them

are two campgrounds ($12); campsite B has the best sites. Back country camping is not allowed in the park.

Set halfway along Highway 169, the visitor centre (1-702 397 2088; open 8.30am-4.30pm daily; website www.desertusa.com/nvval/) is a gem, with superb displays on the area's geology, ecology, flora and fauna and human history, all of which compensate for a feeble bookshop. The road north from the centre offers a panoramic view of multi-coloured sandstone at Rainbow Vista and ends at the White Domes picnic area. An easy three-mile (seven-kilometre) trail from Rainbow Vista leads to yet more spectacular and colourful rocks at **Fire Canyon**, from where you can see the spot where Captain Kirk met his doom in the movie *Star Trek: Generations*. A popular movie location, the Valley of Fire provided a backdrop to the classic *One Million Years BC* as well as numerous Westerns, including Peckinpah's *The Ballad of Cable Hogue*.

Humans have lived in the area for about 4,000 years and Indian rock writings are common throughout the park. **Atlatl Rock** on the scenic loop road has an impressive number of petroglyphs, while others are visible on the short trail to **Mouse's Tank**, a natural water basin used in the 1890s as a hideout by a renegade Indian known as Mouse. Visit the **Lost City Museum** (open 8.30am-4.30pm daily; 1-702 397 2193) in Overton, eight miles (13 kilometres) north of the park, to learn more about the Indian inhabitants, from the ancient Basketmaker people and the Puebloans (Anasazi) to the Paiute, whose present-day descendants still live in Southern Nevada.

Getting there

Head north on the I-15 for 33 miles (53 kilometres) to Highway 169: it's 17 miles (27 kilometres) to the park's western entrance. You can also enter the park from Lake Mead, off Northshore Scenic Drive.

*Sandstone sculptures against a desert blue sky in the **Valley of Fire**.*

Mount Charleston

It's true: you can jet-ski near Las Vegas in the morning and snow ski in the afternoon. Forty-five minutes north-west of the city lies the Spring Mountain Recreation Area, commonly known as Mount Charleston. It's part of the massive Spring Mountain range, which is dominated by Charleston Peak, the highest point in Southern Nevada at 11,918 feet (3,633 metres). In the winter, you can ski and snowboard at Lee Canyon; in the summer, you can hike around the forested slopes, which are substantially cooler than the city. There are also picnic sites and several campgrounds ($10, open mid-May to mid-October) in the area.

Watch the vegetation change as you climb into the mountains, moving from creosote, bursage and Joshua trees on the lower slopes to piñon and Utah juniper, through ponderosa pine and mountain mahogany, and finally to gnarled bristlecone pines where the tree-line peters out at 10,000 feet (3,000 metres). Due to the isolation of the Spring Mountain Range, about 27 species of flora and fauna are unique to this 'sky island'.

There are two roads into the area, both off US 95. Nearest to Las Vegas is Highway 157 (Kyle Canyon Road), which ascends through winding canyons and wooded slopes – very pretty in autumn – to **Mount Charleston Hotel** (872 5500), a grand, rustic-style lodge with a huge green lobby warmed by an open fireplace. Eat in the cavernous dining room or stay in one of its 63 rooms (ask about ski and lodging packages). The road continues for another few miles, past a small park information office (872 5486; open 9am-4pm daily in summer; Wednesday to Sunday only in winter), terminating at **Mount Charleston Lodge** (1-800 955 1314/872 5408). Here, you'll find a 24-hour bar, a restaurant, riding stables and some posh log cabins.

Then, backtrack to the hotel and turn on to Highway 158 (Deer Creek Highway), which connects with Highway 156 (Lee Canyon Road), the other road into the area off US 95. Seven miles (11 kilometres) down Highway 158, the short **Desert View Trail** leads to a spectacular view of the valley below and the mountains in the distance. In the 1950s, when the atomic era was at its height, locals came here to view the mushroom clouds billowing up from the Nevada Test Site. Now the most spectacular views on offer are the admittedly stunning sunsets.

At the junction with Highway 156, turn left for the ski area, which is open between Thanksgiving and Easter. The elevation here is 8,500 feet (2,600 metres), with three chairlifts leading up another 1,000 feet (300 metres) to 13 slopes (for further details of skiing in the area, *see page 239* **Sport & Fitness**). Drive back to US 95 on Highway 158 for a fine view of the desert below.

The US Forest Service prefers hikers to stick to its designated trails. However, there are numerous unmarked hikes, too (take a compass); a good guide is *Hiking Las Vegas* by Branch Whitney, which also covers the Red Rock Canyon area. The six-mile (ten-kilometre) **Bristlecone Trail** provides good views of limestone cliffs and bristlecone pines, while the short trail to **Mary Jane Falls** is more strenuous, with hikers climbing 900 feet (274 metres) towards a waterfall. The mother of all hikes, though, is the 18-mile (29-kilometre) round-trip to Mount Charleston Peak: best attempted by experienced walkers, it's a difficult and demanding trail, not clear of snow until July. The South Loop takes you up through grassy meadows, above the tree-line and past a 1955 plane wreck to the summit, from where you can enjoy a stunning view of southern Nevada, eastern Californian and southern Utah: return by the same route or via the North Loop. For all hikes, you'll need warm clothing and water.

En route to Mount Charleston

Near Mount Charleston are two other places of interest, both off US 95 to the east. Fifteen miles (24 kilometres) from the city is **Floyd Lamb State Park** (486 5413; admission $5; open 8am-sunset daily), former site of Tule Springs Ranch. Its lush lawns, shady cottonwoods and four lakes make it a popular, year-round picnicking and fishing spot, although it's best to avoid weekends and Easter Sunday in particular if you don't like crowds. It's extremely serene during the week, though, with peacocks wandering around the white buildings that remain of the ranch built by Jacob Goumond in the 1940s. As well as raising cattle and growing alfalfa, Goumond catered for prospective divorcees waiting out the six-week residency required to get a divorce in Nevada (the shortest in the nation). The old stables are back in use; rides cost $20 per hour, $15 per half-hour. Don't be alarmed if you hear gunshots; the Las Vegas Gun Club is next door.

Further to the north is the **Desert National Wildlife Refuge**, established in 1936 to protect the desert bighorn sheep and its habitat. A gravel road leads to a self-service information centre, where you can pick up a leaflet on the refuge and stroll around the ponds of Corn Creek Springs. The refuge occupies 1.3 million acres (526,500 hectares) and receives about 20,000 visitors a year: if you like your desert solitary, this is where to come. The western half is used by the Nellis Air Force Range as a bombing area and is closed to the public, while the rest is a nature reserve, accessible by two unmaintained dirt roads: you'll need a high clearance or 4WD vehicle. Summer is the best time to spot the elusive bighorn sheep and the wildflowers are usually in bloom from March to May; call 646 3401 for more information.

Where to stay

Apart from **Mount Charleston Hotel** and **Lodge** (*see above*), try **Almost Heaven** (123 Rainbow Canyon Boulevard, Mount Charleston, NV 89124; 1-888 636 5398/872 0711/website www. almostheaven_lv.com), an upmarket B&B that's owned by a former cocktail waitress from the Mirage. Almost Heaven is popular with high rollers and Las Vegas celebrities; prices per night ($165-$349) include a gourmet breakfast and 24-hour butler service.

Getting there

Take US 95 north; Highway 157 is about 35 miles (56 kilometres) from Downtown. In winter, you'll need snow chains on the mountain roads.

Laughlin

Wedged into the far southern tip of the Nevada portion of Tristate (the Nevada/Arizona/California border region), Laughlin has no right to exist, even by Nevadan standards. This is one of the hottest spots in one of the hottest states in the Union, with midsummer temperatures that can sizzle all the way up to 120°F (47°C). Yet when Don Laughlin, a Las Vegas club owner, bought the failing bait shop, bar and motel that stood here in 1969, he had a vision of a mini-Vegas by the Colorado River. In the last two decades, that dream has become reality: nine major casino-hotels line the two-mile strip, Casino Drive, making Laughlin Nevada's third biggest gambling centre.

The sophisticates of Las Vegas may sniff at Laughlin's (not entirely justified) reputation as a hick, low-roller resort, but it's a relaxed, friendly place and enjoys two major advantages over its flashier neighbour to the north-west: extremely cheap hotel rooms (book ahead), and its riverside location. When casino claustrophobia takes hold, stressed-out gamblers can cruise or jet-ski on the Colorado, stroll along the riverside walk, relax on Harrah's public beach, feed the ducks by the Riverside or gaze at the monster carp outside the **Edgewater** (1-800 677 4837/1-702 298 2453). And if you fancy a casino crawl, leave the car in the garage and hop on the water taxi, which costs a mere $2 per journey.

With the exception of the **Colorado Belle** (1-800 477 4837/1-702 298 4000), a faux Mississippi paddlesteamer, the casinos lack the architectural chutzpah found in Vegas, although each one has its own charms. Nostalgic gamblers pack out Don Laughlin's **Riverside** (1-800 227 3849/1-702 298 2535), with its gold, glass and wood décor, vintage car collection and a six-screen cinema; floor-to-ceiling windows ensure fine views from the **Hilton Flamingo** (1-800 352 6464); while effective theming characterises low-rise **Wild**

West Pioneer (1-800 634 3469/1-702 298 2442), south-of-the-border **Harrah's** (1-800 427 7247) and the turn-of-the-century railroad **Ramada Express** (1-800 243 6846/1-702 298 4200).

Laughlin, to be polite, is not renowned for its food. Stuff-your-face bargain buffets, surf'n'turf combos and steak deals of uninspiring quality dominate the scene. If you're prepared to pay for a little more class, then the **Lodge** at **Gold River** (1-702 298 2242) and **William Fisk's Steakhouse** at Harrah's (1-702 298 4600) both offer good fare in tranquil surroundings. The pick of the pack, however, is probably Colorado Belle's the **Boiler Room** (1-702 298 4000), which is impressively decked out as – surprise, surprise – a ship's boiler room, and is Laughlin's only brew pub. Finally, for more information about the town, Laughlin's visitor centre is located at 1555 Casino Drive (1-702 298 3321).

Around Laughlin

Laughlin's boom times are under threat from an audacious (though slow-moving) plan conceived by the Fort Mojave Tribe, which owns 33,000 acres (13,300 hectares) of land along the Colorado to the south. A planned community of 40,000 people – to be called Aha Macav ('the people by the river') – will include 11 casinos that threaten to siphon off some of Laughlin's five million annual visitors. At the time of writing, however, Aha Macav consists of one casino (**Avi**; 1-702 535 5555) and lots of empty space.

Something of the history of the Fort Mojave Tribe (and what little history there is of Laughlin) can be gleaned from the delightfully eclectic and interesting displays in the **Colorado River Museum** (1-520 754 3399), half a mile north of the Laughlin bridge on the Arizona side. The museum also contains information on the petroglyphs to be found in **Grapevine Canyon** across the river, which can be reached by heading a couple of miles up a dirt road (follow the signposts to Christmas Tree Pass) off Highway 163.

The **Davis Dam**, a mile to the north of Laughlin, was completed in 1953, spawning the Arizonan settlement of Bullhead City and creating long, thin **Lake Mohave**. It's inaccessible by road for most of its length; the best spot from which to sail and plunder the lake's copious and famously huge striped bass is **Katharine Landing**, a couple of miles north of the dam on the Arizona side. In addition to campgrounds and the usual resort facilities, a ranger station (1-520 754 3272) provides information and offers nature hikes in the surrounding area.

Getting there

Head south on US 95, then take Highway 163 east for about 90 miles (145 kilometres).

Into Nevada

Home of gambling, ghost towns, extraterrestrials and miles and miles of wide open space.

Las Vegas, in case you hadn't realised, is not typical of anywhere, least of all Nevada. The state is the seventh largest in the Union but has a population of only 1.85 million, of which nearly 1.3 million live within 40 miles (64 kilometres) of Las Vegas. Take away the population (250,000) of the other main urban area, Reno/Sparks, and that leaves very few people scattered across a large and sparsely settled state.

Reno itself, more than 400 miles (644 kilometres) to the north-west, is smaller, greener and less brash than its loud southern cousin, but still has enough glitzy casinos to entertain even the most dedicated gambler. En route to Reno, you'll cross numerous north-south mountain ranges and sagebrush-covered valleys, typical of the Great Basin desert. You'll also pass a few once-prosperous mining towns such as **Goldfield** and **Tonopah**, and the evidence of Nevada's other great money-maker, the US military: the south end of the massive Nellis Air Force Range lies just north of Las Vegas, while the north end extends all the way to Tonopah. In the 1950s, curious onlookers came to watch the nuclear tests that were conducted there at the Nevada Test Site; nowadays, visitors are drawn in droves to the (literally) otherworldly sights and delights of the **Extraterrestrial Highway**, by the many extraordinary tales of UFO sightings and other sinister goings-on at the base's infamous **Area 51**.

The road to Reno

Driving north to Reno on US 95 takes you almost entirely through classic Nevada scenery: Great Basin desertscapes, boom-and-bust mining towns and huge, off-limits military bases. Leaving Las Vegas, US 95 passes the high peaks of Mount Charleston to the west and, for nearly 200 miles (321 kilometres), skirts the edge of the vast Nellis Air Force Range to the east. You pass **Amargosa Valley**, **Beatty** (watch your driving speed here; this is a notorious speed trap) and **Scotty's Junction**, all gateways to Death Valley National Park just over the California border (*see chapter* **Into California**). Near Beatty (on the Nevada side) lies the photogenic ghost town of **Rhyolite**. Established in 1905 after gold and silver were discovered in the Bullfrog Hills, its population peaked at 10,000 but the town was deserted by 1912. Now you can wander past ghost sculptures and

Old-time **Tonopah**. *See page 262.*

various crumbling brick buildings, including the town jail, train depot and school, and the famous bottle house, constructed when building materials were scarce but there was no shortage of empty beer bottles from the town's 50 saloons. The Friends of Rhyolite (PO Box 85, Amargosa Valley, NV 89020) was set up to protect and preserve the town and presents 'living history' events at the annual Rhyolite Resurrection Festival, held in March.

Walker Lake: *a welcome glimpse of blue in the desert.*

About 30 miles (48 kilometres) north of Scotty's Junction is **Goldfield**, a classic example of Nevada's once-grand mining towns. Gold was discovered here in 1902: by 1907 the population had passed 10,000. At the height of the boom in 1910, it was easily the largest town in the state, with a population of 20,000, but the gold ran out and a fire in 1923 destroyed 53 square blocks: now there are less than 300 inhabitants in Goldfield. Several grand brick buildings, including the abandoned Goldfield Hotel and high school, along with the occupied county courthouse, are poignant reminders of the town's heyday. Drop into the **Santa Fe Saloon** (turn right at Fifth Avenue) for a taste of the past: it's a rickety structure with a long wooden bar and signed photos of boxer and ex-miner Jack Dempsey.

About 200 miles (321 kilometres) from Las Vegas is **Tonopah**. In 1900, prospector Jim Butler discovered silver here: almost $150 million of ore had been dug by the time the lode ran out in 1915. Small mines still dot the surrounding area, but it survives mainly as a convenient crossroads town, at the junction of US 95 and US 6, and through the jobs provided by the **Tonopah Test Range**, where top-secret military planes are test-flown (listen for the sonic booms).

Choose from numerous motels along the main street or try the old-fashioned, slightly shabby **Mizpah Hotel** (1-775 482 6200): the creaky lift has its original brass and mirror fittings and there's a walk-in strongroom at the back of the lobby; rooms cost $37 to $59.95 with breakfast. The **El Marques** restaurant (1-775 482 3885) down the street serves decent, good-value Mexican food.

The large **Station House casino** (1-775 482 9777) at the southern end of town has a dark, cramped gaming area, rooms ($35.50 for two people), a restaurant and a wonderful collection of old chrome slot machines in the basement next to the toilets. Next door is the **Central Nevada Museum** (open summer 9am-5pm daily; winter

11am-5pm Mon-Sat; 1-775 482 9676). It is a fascinating, if haphazardly arranged, place: photos of Tonopah and Goldfield in their glory days line the walls, clothing, household goods and other artefacts are crammed into glass cases, and there's a 'purple glass' collection (manganese used in early glass turns purple in sunlight). Rusting mining equipment sits outside. For more details about Tonopah, contact the **Chamber of Commerce** (1-775 482 3859).

From Tonopah there's 100 miles (161 kilometres) of gloriously empty road until **Hawthorne**, the next town of any size. As you approach the town, you see one, then two, then thousands of strange, half-buried, oblong structures jutting out of the desert floor, looking like they belong in a *Mad Max*-style movie. Since the 1930s, Hawthorne has been home to the US Army's ammunition depot, and these half-buried bunkers are in fact full of bullets, bombs and weapons. The town has a number of motels and one casino (the El Capitan); Maggie's Restaurant (on US 95) is a clean, pink, but rather soulless place serving reasonable steak, burgers, salad and sandwiches.

Just north of Hawthorne, the road skirts the western edge of the 30-mile (48-kilometre) long **Walker Lake**, a remnant of an ancient lake that once covered most of western Nevada (and a small portion of eastern California). The lake has dropped 100 feet (30 metres) since 1930, and its fish are slowly dying because the Walker River has been diverted for irrigation, but it's still a popular spot for swimming, boating and fishing: there are picnic sites and one campground (Sportsmans Beach) off US 95. At the northern end of the lake is the **Walker River Indian Reservation**, which belongs to the Southern Paiute, who have lived in Nevada for more than 700 years.

About 30 miles (48 kilometres) north of Hawthorne, you have the choice of taking the 'alternate' US 95 north-west to Fernley, where it joins the I-80, or continuing on the main US 95 north to Fallon to join the US 50. Take main US 95 if you plan to head back east into Nevada on US 50 or I-80, otherwise alternate US 95 provides a useful shortcut to Carson City or Reno and is the more interesting route. It takes you through the attractive oasis of **Yerington**, surrounded by big trees in the fertile Mason Valley; rest your eyes on all that green after miles of scrubby desert. You can visit **Fort Churchill Historic State Park** (1-775 577 2345), which houses the ruins of an 1860s US army outpost, a visitor centre, picnic sites and a campground. At I-80, head west: it's a fast 30 miles (48 kilometres) into Reno.

Reno

Though few people outside the American West are aware of it, Las Vegas isn't the only large gambling city in Nevada. Reno, 440 miles (708 kilometres) north-west, is the 'original' Las Vegas. Las Vegas could never have become Las Vegas if Reno hadn't been Reno first. But in the 1950s, Reno took one look at what was happening to Las Vegas and made a deliberate decision to limit the spread of gambling to the downtown core along Virginia Street. This 'redline' remained in effect till 1978; even today, only a handful of casinos are found outside downtown.

You could comfortably fit four Renos inside Las Vegas. It's not only smaller, it's also slower and prettier. The Truckee River runs right through the middle of downtown, giving the city a more natural and rural flavour. Also unlike Las Vegas, Reno experiences four distinct seasons: in winter, skiers jam the slopes of more than 20 ski resorts within an hour of town; summers are balmy and every weekend some special event closes off Virginia Street for a block party. More in line with it brash cousin, however, is the planned implosion of the historic Mapes Hotel, a 47-year-old art deco building that was the first in the nation to house a hotel, casino, restaurant and live entertainment under one roof; preservationists are fighting this as the guide goes to press.

Look out for **Hot August Nights**, the classic-car equivalent of a Grateful Dead gig. Up to 60,000 people come to town to join in the fun: cruisin', drag races, cool car contests and live music. **Street Vibrations**, in mid-September, is the Harley-Davidson equivalent, attracting thousands of bikers on their 'hawgs'.

Compared to brazen Las Vegas, sedate Reno is one of the best-kept secrets in the West.

Downtown

The venerable **Reno Arch** spans Virginia Street in the heart of downtown. This is the fourth such arch; the first was erected in 1926 to celebrate the completion of a transcontinental highway that passed through Reno, while the second, built in 1938, stands outside the **National Automobile Museum** at Lake and Mill Streets a few blocks away. The arch proudly proclaims Reno the 'Biggest Little City in the World', as opposed to Las Vegas, which is one of the littlest big cities in the world.

For a few blocks on either side of the current 13-year-old arch there are souvenir shops, pawn shops and old hotels, as well as half a dozen major casinos – Circus Circus, Silver Legacy, Eldorado, Fitzgeralds, Harrah's, Cal-Neva Virginian – and a couple of minor ones. The railroad tracks bisect Virginia Street and every day two passenger and several freight trains still close the street to traffic, as they have for the past 130 years.

Along the riverfront is a two-block plaza that leads to two downtown parks: Wingfield, on an island in the middle of a bulge in the river, connected to the mainland by pedestrian bridges; and Riverside, three acres of grass, with tennis and basketball courts and a playground.

Cal-Neva Virginian

140 N Virginia Street, at E Second Street (1-775 323 1046). **Rooms** $32-$69.
Credit AmEx, Disc, MC, V.
The sprawling Cal-Neva opened in 1962 and is still under the same ownership. It's home to the famous 24-hour 99¢ breakfast (3,000 served every day), a $1.50 hot dog and Heineken (the Cal-Neva is Heineken's largest US account) and the best prime-rib special in northern Nevada.

There's good gambling, too: the action here is rammin' jammin', smoky and loud. The poker room and race and sports books are the busiest in town. In 1999, the Cal-Neva took over the shuttered Virginian next door, adding 300 hotel rooms, its first rooms in 37 years.

Circus Circus

500 N Sierra Street, at W Fifth Street (1-800 648 5010/1-775 329 0711). **Rooms** $39-$79.
Credit AmEx, DC, Disc, JCB, MC, V.
With big-top acts performed continuously through-out the day and a midway of carnival games, the Circus Circus casino draws consistently large crowds of low-rollers, gawkers and kids. Thanks to a refit, its rooms are bright, clean and appealing. The eating and drinking facilities have also been successfully updated and they now include a fab Southwestern restaurant.

Eldorado

345 N Virginia Street, at E Fourth Street (1-800 648 5966/1-775 786 5700). **Rooms** $40-$750.
Credit AmEx, DC, Disc, MC, V.
The Eldorado casino is owned and operated by the locally well-known Carano family. It's justly renowned for its classy restaurants – including the only microbrewery in downtown and a stellar Friday seafood buffet in the convention centre. The Eldorado also offers good bar-top video poker and a classy showroom.

Fitzgeralds

255 N Virginia Street, at W Second Street (1-800 648 5022/1-775 785 3300). **Rooms** $28-$200.
Credit AmEx, DC, Disc, MC, V.
Fitzgeralds is named after the early Reno casino operator Lincoln Fitzgerald. The predominant theme is Irish green; the Fitz installs all-green lightbulbs on the Reno Arch in honour of St Patrick's Day. You can bypass the railroad tracks using the skywalk one floor above the ground level.

Flamingo Hilton

255 N Sierra Street, at W Second Street (1-800 648 4882/1-775 322 1111). **Rooms** $59-$219.
Credit AmEx, DC, Disc, MC, V.
The big pink Flamingo Hilton has a rockin' casino, a large show lounge and showroom and the Top of the Hilton restaurant on the 21st floor. This offers the finest dining in downtown, including Reno's best Sunday brunch, and is the only restaurant in town with a view.

Harrah's Reno

219 N Center Street, at E Second Street (1-800 427 7247/1-775 786 3232). **Rooms** $49-$325.
Credit AmEx, DC, Disc, MC, V.
Harrah's has dominated downtown Reno for more than 50 years since William Harrah opened the first joint in 1946. It boasts two casinos, a large race and sports book, remodelled restaurants (including one of the best buffets in town), a small showroom, and one of the two kid's arcades in downtown.

National Automobile Museum

10 Lake Street South, at Mill Street (1-775 333 9300). **Open** 9.30am-5.30pm Mon-Sat; 10am-4pm Sun. **Admission** $7.50; $6.50 seniors, disabled; $2.50 6-18s; free under-5s.
Housed in a $10-million building reminiscent of a sleek metallic-flake and chrome 1950s Chrysler, the National Automobile Museum houses nearly 200 classic and unique cars, from an 1890 Philion to one of Elvis's custom Cadillacs.

National Bowling Stadium

300 N Center Street, at E Fourth Street (1-775 334 2695/2600). **Open** 9am-5pm daily.
This $35-million stadium, the only one of its kind, opened in 1995 and made Reno the Bowling Capital of the World. It features 80 lanes, a 100-seat geodesic Omnimax cinema, Kicks nightclub (owned by Paul Revere of Paul Revere and the Raiders fame) and the downtown visitor centre. There's no public bowling – the stadium is reserved for national tournaments – but you can tour the building for free when there's no action or for a small admission charge when a tournament is on.

Silver Legacy

407 N Virginia Street, at W Fourth Street (1-800 687 8733/1-775 329 4777). **Rooms** $49-$159.
Credit AmEx, DC, Disc, MC, V.
Opened in June 1995, Silver Legacy is one of Reno's two Las Vegas-style mega-resorts. Although it's the second largest resort in Reno, it would only be the 26th largest in Vegas. It does, however, claim the

world's largest composite dome, which houses a 120ft (37m) high mining rig that mints silver dollars once an hour. Skywalks connect the Legacy with the Eldorado on one side and Circus Circus on the other. Antiques and a stunning silver service (including a 58-candle candelabra and a solid silver wine cooler bucket) adorn the Victorian lobby. These treasures were part of a half-ton lot shipped across to Tiffany in New York in the 1870s by John Mackay, one of the Comstock Kings.

Outside downtown

There are four major casinos scattered around the basin in which Reno sits. You can see the monstrous and central **Reno Hilton** (2500 E Second Street; 1-800 648 5080/1-775 789 2000) from all over town. With 2,000 rooms, it's the largest hotel-casino north of Las Vegas, and comes with five restaurants (the breakfast buffet is a fresh, low-priced delight), a 2,000-seat showroom, lounge, comedy club, nightclub, two cinemas, 50-lane bowling alley, video arcade, eight tennis courts, his-and-hers health clubs, Olympic-sized swimming pool, golf driving range and – phew! – a 452-space RV park.

At the east end of the valley, in Reno's sister city Sparks, is John Ascuaga's **Nugget** (1100 Nugget Avenue, at Victorian Square and I-80 east; 1-800 648 1177), with 1,920 rooms, 800-seat showroom and fine restaurants, including the best oyster bar this side of Fisherman's Wharf in San Francisco. Across the street from the Nugget is the **Silver Club** (1040 Victorian Avenue, 1-800 905 7779), the second largest casino in Sparks, with the only all-the-steak-you-can-eat buffet in the area and the popular Rail Bar on the mezzanine level.

On Virginia Street a couple of miles south of downtown are the **Peppermill** (2707 S Virginia Street, at Grove Street; 1-800 282 2444), which has enough indoor neon, silk flowers and ferns and noise for five casinos; and **Atlantis** (3800 S Virginia Street, at Peckham Lane; 1-800 723 6500), with a tropical setting, including a 30-foot/nine-metre high waterfall and thatched roofing over the pits. The new skywalk casino has an oyster bar, a coffeebar that spans Virginia Street between the casino and parking lot, and glass elevators (for a fun little thrill ride with a good view).

Sightseeing

Stop off at the **Liberty Belle Saloon** (4250 S Virginia Street, at Peckham Lane; 1-775 825 1776) in order to peruse its outstanding exhibit on the development of slot machines. Owners Marshall and Frank Fey are the grandsons of Charlie Fey, who invented the first slot machines in 1898. You can also head into the hills east of Reno to **Virginia City** (south on US 395 for eight miles/13 kilometres, then east on Highway 341 for another

The Reno Arch welcomes visitors to Nevada's ritzy-glitzy northern town.

eight miles/13 kilometres), one of the most authentic (albeit touristy) historic mining towns in the American West, where the famous Comstock Lode was unearthed. Visit museums, saloons and gift shops, tour two underground mines and take a ride on a railway powered by a steam engine, or seek out a historic mansion tour for a more authentic, less touristy experience.

An hour north of Reno is the turquoise expanse of **Pyramid Lake**, a large and beautiful natural desert lake. A remnant of ancient Lake Lahontan, which once covered much of Nevada, it's the only home of the prehistoric cui-ui (pronounced 'kwee-wee') sucker fish, and is considered sacred by the Native American Paiute who look after it. Fifty miles (80 kilometres) to the north is the small town of Gerlach, gateway to the large and very flat **Black Rock Desert**. This was the site of Richard Noble's successful bid to set a new land speed record in 1997 of 764 miles per hour (1,230 kilometres per hour), which broke the sound barrier on land for the first time in history. The Black Rock Desert is also the home of the annual and infamous Burning Man festival, now the largest outdoor art extravaganza in the world, attracting 23,000 celebrants in 1999.

If you still have time, drive into the mountains to the west of Reno to **Lake Tahoe** (drive south on US 395 for eight miles/13 kilometres, then take Highway 431 west for 25 miles/40 kilometres). Lake Tahoe is one of the greatest alpine lakes in the world and the undisputed crown jewel of western Nevada.

About 30 miles (48 kilometres) south of Reno on US 365 lies **Carson City**, a picturesque and quaint historical town that also happens to be the Nevada state capital. Historically home to many of the state's politically powerful families. Carson is also site of the state legislature building, the Governor's Mansion, the state supreme court, and the Nevada State Museum, housed in the old mint building.

Where to eat & drink

Until 1999, the family-value, family-style, family-run Santa Fe topped the list of places to eat in Reno. This traditional Basque restaurant stood on the same spot for more than 50 years, until an unexplained family feud closed it down. All that remains is **Louie's Basque Corner** (301 E Fourth Street, at Evans Avenue; 1-775 323 7203). Food is served 11.30am-2.30pm and 5-9.30pm daily. Louie's continues to serve the Santa Fe's signature Pecan Punch cocktail but, all in all, the place is no substitute for the original.

Two European-style coffeehouses serving good food, beer and great coffee are the **Pneumatic Diner** (Truckee River Lodge, 501 W First Street; 1-775 786 8888 ext 106; open 11am-11pm daily) and **Deux Gros Nez** (249 California Avenue; 1-775 786 9400; open 6am-midnight Mon-Wed, Sun; 6am-1am Thur-Sat).

Reno's bar scene is limited, but check out **Reno Live**, on the lower level of Eddie's Fabulous Fifties club in downtown (45 W Second Street; 1-775 329 1950; open 9pm-5am daily), where you'll find

Great gambling, fine dining and a fab view – the **Flamingo Hilton** has it all. See page 264.

'Reno's hottest party' from Thursday to Sunday, with perpetual promotions and discounts, such as 'Show Me Your Boxers' night, free draught beer at certain times and free cocktails for ladies (usually Fridays). **Big Ed's Alley Inn** (1036 E Fourth Street; 1-775 322 4180; open 8am-9pm Mon-Thur; 8am-10pm Fri, Sat; 8am-3pm Sun) is a local institution, now owned by Reno's most popular DJ, Bruce Van Dyke (he's the morning jock at KTHX, 100.1 FM). Big Ed's offers raucous concerts nearly every weekend, good beer and great food, including the best bar pizza in town.

There's also fun to be had at the 24-hour **Li'l Waldorf Saloon** (1661 N Virginia Street; 1-775 323 3682), a barbaric college bar across from the university. The **Great Basin Brewing Co** in Sparks (846 Victorian Avenue; 1-775 355 7711; open until 10.30pm Mon-Thur, Sun; until 1am Fri, Sat) is within walking distance of a host of other bars.

Two new arrivals in town are also worth a visit. Just south of downtown in an up-and-coming neighbourhood, the **Midtowne Marketplace** (121 Vesta Way, at Holcomb Avenue; 1-775 323 7711) is Reno's first truly trendy restaurant outside a hotel-casino. It serves modern Italian cuisine and top Californian wines in a roomy industrial setting, with an outdoor balcony and courtyard seating. It's open 11am-10pm Mon, Sun; 11am-midnight Tue-Thur; 11am-2am Fri, Sat.

Nestled in a refurbished Victorian mansion, the **Silver Peak Restaurant & Brewery** (124 Wonder Street, at Holcomb Avenue; 1-775 324 1864; open 11am-midnight daily) offers eight in-house draught beers and a hearty menu that ranges from gourmet pizza to steaks and chops.

Where to stay

Roughly 25,000 rooms are available in Reno, running the gamut from dirt-cheap to sky-high. The hotel-casinos above fall into the medium price range. Prices peak in August but can be rock-bottom during winter. Call the **Reno Convention & Visitors Authority** hotel reservation service on 1-800 367 7366 for further information.

Tourist information

Downtown Visitor Center

National Bowling Stadium, 300 N Center Street, at E Fourth Street (1-775 334 2695/2600).
Open 9am-5pm daily.
Call the Bowling Stadium and ask to be put through to the visitor centre, or call the automated info line at the Reno Convention & Visitors Authority (1-800 367 7366).

Getting there

By car

See p261 **The road to Reno**.

By bus

One bus operated by K-T Bus Lines (1-775 322 2970) runs in each direction daily, leaving Reno at 7am, arriving Las Vegas at 4pm, and leaving Las Vegas at 8am, arriving Reno at 5.15pm. The trip costs $72 one-way, $136.80 round trip.

By air

A round trip from McCarran International Airport on American (1-800 433 7300), Southwest (1-800 435 9792) and America West (1-800 235 9292) costs $88-$184 depending on the time of year.

ET Highway

If you think Las Vegas is strange, just wait until you drive along the 87 miles (140 kilometres) of Highway 375, also known as the Extraterrestrial Highway and a mecca for UFO freaks and tourists. It's a beautiful, lonely desert road, typical of Nevada's range and basin landscape, that cuts across mountain ranges and through 20-mile (32 kilometre) long valleys. The real reason for its fame is that it skirts the north-eastern edge of **Nellis Air Force Range**, the vast and sinister military complex that covers a big swathe of south-central Nevada. As well as housing the Nevada Test Site (where numerous atomic bombs were exploded above ground in the 1950s and below ground through the early 1990s) and the Tonopah Test Range (test site for the B-2 Stealth bomber in the 1980s), the complex is the home of **Area 51**, the top-secret R&D facility whose existence the US government still refuses to acknowledge.

Mystery surrounds and rumours abound about Area 51, specifically concerning the dry beds of Groom Lake and Papoose Lake. The US military is said to be experimenting with new-tech aircraft including a hypersonic spy plane dubbed Aurora and, if you believe the more outrageous claims, also conducting tests on alien spaceships and holding at least a couple of aliens in cold storage, some say the self-same aliens that dropped in on Roswell, New Mexico, in 1947.

Speculation reached fever pitch in 1989, when physicist Bob Lazar appeared on a Las Vegas news show, claiming he had worked at Papoose Lake and seen nine flying saucers in camouflaged hangars: he even said he'd seen one briefly in flight. Numerous UFO sightings have since been reported along Highway 375, notably near the 'black mailbox' (much to the disgust of the mailbox's owner). The latest rumour is that the military has effectively closed down Area 51 and moved testing to locations in Utah and Colorado.

The road was officially designated ET Highway in 1996 to coincide with the launch of the movie *Independence Day*. All but one of the official state 'Extraterrestrial Highway' signs along the route have since been stolen.

The only settlement on the highway is **Rachel** (population 80), a straggly collection of mobile homes, and location of **The Little A'Le'Inn** – alien: geddit? (1-775 729 2515). You can't miss it: there's a bug-eyed alien painted on the side and a parking sign on the roof with a picture of a flying saucer. It's the only motel on the road, and also serves food (an Alien Burger costs $2.75). There's alien-related literature and UFO photos on the walls, as well as a pool table, video poker machines (this is Nevada, after all) and a bar area bedecked with Republican posters: don't get into a conversation about gun control unless you're against it.

At the other end of Rachel, fill your tank at the highway's only petrol station and visit the **Area 51 Research Center** (1-775 729 2648), set up by Glenn Campbell to highlight the government's shenanigans around Area 51 rather than to attract alien enthusiasts. Campbell now spends most of his time in Las Vegas, where he runs an Area 51 website (www.ufomind.com). The black mailbox is now painted white and located south of Rachel, between mileposts 29 and 30.

Whatever the truth about Area 51, there is certainly no end to the bizarre goings-on in the skies above the ET Highway. But whether the reports of strange lights, odd-shaped craft and unconventional flying patterns are due to visitors from outer space or wishful thinking is open to debate. Given the number of military planes, commercial jets, flares, weather balloons, satellites and general airborne activity in the region, you would expect to see something unusual overhead. Rachel attracts plane spotters, obsessed with the latest military hardware, as well as UFO geeks.

Novice sky-gazers should note that the B-2 stealth plane looks like a classic flying saucer when viewed from the front or rear, and at night even a car's headlights in the distance can look spooky. Sadly, the closest (and potentially most dangerous) encounter you're likely to experience is with a cow wandering into the middle of the road while you're feverishly scanning the sky for spaceships.

Since 1995, when the military annexed more land, the only view of Area 51 is from **Tikaboo Peak**, 26 miles (42 kilometres) from the base. You get superb views of the surrounding desert, but all you'll see of the (supposedly non-existent) base is a few distant buildings. It's a strenuous, high-altitude hike, best done in summer (snow can last until April) and early in the morning, before heat haze distorts the view. Make sure you and your vehicle are properly equipped; conditions are harsh and there are no park rangers out here. Take binoculars.

The best route (usually accessible by a non-4WD vehicle) is via a dirt road off US 93 at milepost 32.2, south of Alamo. It's just over 22 miles (35 kilometres) to Badger Spring and then a two-hour hike to the summit, but it's easy to get lost. For a detailed description, read Chuck Clark's *Area 51 Viewer's Guide* ($15), available from the Area 51 Research Center. Guided tours in your own vehicle (1-775 729 2529; $99 for four) to Tikaboo Peak are also available from Rachel; other tours visit the 'black mailbox' and Groom Lake Road as well as the wreckage of a US Air Force plane crash.

Take care when approaching Area 51. Armed guards patrol the border, and you can be sure that someone is watching your movements. Do not, repeat, *do not* cross the boundary into the military zone: you will be arrested, questioned and fined at least $600. The guards are also authorised to use 'deadly force' on trespassers. The problem is that the border is not accurately marked on maps and often hard to detect: it's defined by orange posts, some topped with silver globes, and occasional 'restricted area' signs, but no fence.

If you'd like to look inside the Nellis Air Force Range without facing possible arrest, consider the Department of Energy-sponsored guided tour to the bomb-cratered **Nevada Test Site**. The tour takes place once a month; reservations should be made six weeks in advance.

The test site is also home to **Yucca Mountain**, proposed site of the only permanent repository for high-level nuclear waste in the US. Not surprisingly, it's a controversial subject: many Nevadans are unhappy about the prospect of tons of spent radioactive fuel travelling by rail and road past their front doors, to be dumped in their backyard. Guided tours to the Yucca Mountain site run six times a year. You can also visit the Department of Energy's **Yucca Mountain Science Center** in Las Vegas. For more information about the centre, and the tours to both the Test Site and Yucca Mountain, *see page 11* **History**.

Where to stay

The Little A'Le'Inn
HCR 61 Box 45, Rachel, NV 89001 (1-775 729 2515). **Rates** double $31.50 .

Rooms are located in cosy, if dilapidated trailers: you get a shared bathroom, a communal kitchen-cum-living room and yet more UFO photos.

Getting there

Take US 93 north for 107 miles (172 kilometres) to the junction with ET Highway (Highway 375). Rachel is 36 miles (58 kilometres) to the north-west of the junction.

Home on the range

Nevada contains all kinds of towns: casino towns, border towns, farming towns, ranching towns, mining towns, railroad towns, boomtowns, even a UFO town. But it will soon boast a new kind of town that's not only unique to the state but to the whole country. A gun town.

Forty-five miles west of Las Vegas, near Pahrump, a $25-million masterplanned and themed resort community is under construction on 550 acres of desert scrub. It's called Front Sight – appropriately enough – and is headed by Dr Ignatius Piazza, a former chiropractor and gun enthusiast in his late 30s. Think of it as a typical golf resort, with grand homes and townhouses on the outskirts, a full staff of instructors, a clubhouse with pro shop, repair shop and storage facilities, and a steady stream of players coming and going, honing their skills. Only instead of golf, the focus is firearms.

In a country where gun control is a political hot potato, such a development is inevitably controversial: some see it as more depressing evidence of the increasing violence of American society; others as the best way to prevent the violence – and for citizens to protect themselves in the event of it.

Certainly, Front Sight is perfectly located for its purposes. Nye County is pro-development and has liberal zoning policies. Nevada is an 'open-carry' state, meaning you can legally walk around most places with a sidearm strapped to your belt, and a 'shall-issue' state, meaning you can get a concealed-carry permit just by asking for it (and taking a cursory safety course and passing a shooting test). Nevada also allows private citizens to own sub-machine guns (California doesn't). Best of all for Piazza and his students, the attractions of the Las Vegas Strip are only 40 minutes away.

Front Sight is aimed at anyone who wants to become more proficient in the use of firearms; everyone from SWAT cops to soccer moms have been trained there. There are training ranges for dry-practice (unloaded guns) and live-fire (loaded guns), and large canvas tents provide shade for lectures. A gunsmith shop and armoury, a pro-shop, underground training tunnels, permanent classrooms, even a gourmet restaurant overlooking a man-made lake (this is Vegas, after all) are scheduled to open by the end of 2000. The resort is subdivided into 177 one-acre homesites (at last count, more than 30 of them had been sold). Upwards of 350 condos, a school, church, airstrip and big front gate are also planned.

Two- and four-day classes in handgun, shotgun, rifle or sub-machine gun are offered ($500-$1,200), with one-day and half-day classes also planned. Visitors provide their own weapon and ammunition. For more details, call 1-800 987 7719, email info@frontsight.com or check the website (www.frontsight.com). Call before you visit.

Getting there
From Las Vegas, head west on Highway 160 (take the Blue Diamond exit off I-15) for 38 miles (61km) towards Pahrump. Turn left on the Tecopa road and drive four miles (6.5km), then go right at the Front Sight sign and drive another four miles on a gravel road.

Into Arizona

Holes in the ground don't come any larger than the Grand Canyon.

Parts of north and west Arizona are easily reached from Las Vegas, although its major cities – Phoenix and Tucson – are too far to visit comfortably in a couple of days. The jewel in Arizona's crown is, undoubtedly, the **Grand Canyon**, a relatively short five-hour drive away.

Grand Canyon National Park

Everything you've heard about the Grand Canyon is true: it's stunning; overwhelming; mind-blowing; one of the great natural wonders of the world. And, fortunately, it's only a few hours' drive or a short flight from Las Vegas.

Most of the park's annual five million visitors head for the **South Rim** and the accommodation, restaurants, shops and sights of **Grand Canyon Village**, perched on the edge of the canyon lip. Inevitably, it's crowded, but remains remarkably untouristy. The national park is 277 miles (446 kilometres) long, most of which is difficult to reach and rarely visited; just a tiny portion of it is accessible from the South Rim. The canyon is also misnamed: it's not just one rip in the earth but rather a series of canyons surrounding the central gorge cut by the Colorado River – a staggering 5,000 feet (1,524 metres) from top to bottom.

From the South Rim you can see lightning forks hit the **North Rim** ten miles (16 kilometres) away across the canyon, but to reach it you'll have to hike down to the bottom and up again, drive 200 miles (322 kilometres) or catch the rim-to-rim bus. The North Rim is 1,000 feet (305 metres) higher and only open mid-May to mid-October; it has fewer facilities and is less accessible than the South Rim, so doesn't get as many visitors. Even so, it can still get pretty crowded and you'll need to book ahead for lodging. The South Rim is closer to the Colorado River and has much better views into the canyon. Call Trans Canyon Shuttle (1-520 638 2820) for details of the bus service between the two rims; the journey takes about five hours.

Entrance to the park is $20 per car and you'll need to stay at least two nights to give yourself enough time to explore the village, rim drives and various lookout points and to venture into the canyon itself – and drive back to Vegas. If you want to take a mule trip, air tour or hike to the bottom of the canyon, you'll need longer. At an average elevation of 7,000 feet (2,134 metres), the South Rim is not unbearably hot in summer but

the canyon bottom, a mile down, can push 110°F (43°C). April, May, September and October are probably the best months to visit; most of the rainfall occurs in summer, and from December to March, temperatures plummet and the upper canyon is usually snowbound.

Head first for the surprisingly small visitor centre (open summer 8am-6pm daily; winter 8am-5pm daily) for books, trail guides and to pick up a copy of *The Guide*, the park's newspaper, which has comprehensive info on sights, facilities and activities and a rather feeble map; the map provided by AmFac (which runs the park's accommodation) is better.

Two roads lead out from the village along the canyon rim: the eight-mile (13-kilometre) **West Rim Drive** passes various observation points on the way to its end at Hermit's Rest; the **East Rim Drive** goes 23 miles (37 kilometres) to **Desert View**, site of the amazing **Watchtower** and the park's eastern entrance, and offers the clearest views of the Colorado River. The centrepiece of the Watchtower – a circular, 70-foot (21-metre) high re-creation of an ancient Indian tower – is the Hopi Room, which is decorated with vividly coloured Hopi designs depicting various gods and legends. The tower is fitted with black-mirror reflectoscopes that condense and simplify the views of the canyon, while also intensifying its colours. It was built by the remarkable Mary Colter, architect and designer for the Fred Harvey Company, which set up some of the first tourist facilities at the canyon.

Three miles (five kilometres) west of Desert View, there's an 800-year-old ruin of an Anasazi pueblo and rather scanty information on the history and culture of the canyon's Native American inhabitants at **Tusayan Museum**. Both roads are worth exploring because each provides very different views into the canyon. You can also walk along the very edge of the rim, on the pedestrian-only Rim Trail, which parallels the West Rim Drive; the first one and a half miles (2.4 kilometres) through the village are paved; it then gets pretty rocky.

From mid-March to mid-October, a free shuttle bus service operates three loops – around the village, along the West Rim Drive and along the East Rim Drive as far as the South Kaibab trailhead and Yaki Point. During these months, the West Rim Drive is closed to private vehicles. The West Rim shuttle stops at every overlook on its way out, but only at Mohave Point and Hopi Point on its return.

If you're planning to watch the sunset, check the time of the last bus before you leave – if you miss it, you'll have a long, dark walk back to the village. A 24-hour taxi service runs between the village and the airport, trailheads and other destinations (for more information, call 1-520 638 2822 or 1-520 638 2631 ext 6563).

Although the yawning chasm of the Grand Canyon is obviously the main attraction, there is plenty of human history to interest the visitor. Travellers have been coming to gawp at the Grand Canyon since the nineteenth century and the village is dotted with historic buildings (many built by Mary Colter) – among them the luxurious **El Tovar Hotel**, which cost a cool quarter of a million dollars when built in 1905. A leaflet describes a self-guided walking tour around the village's historic district. Walking west from the hotel along the Rim Trail, you pass **Bucky O'Neill's cabin** from the 1890s (the oldest surviving building on the rim), **Bright Angel Lodge**, the **Lookout Studio** and the **Kolb Brothers' Studio**. Pioneering photographers Ellsworth and Emery Kolb started snapping mule riders venturing into the canyon in 1902; the lack of water on the rim meant they had to hike halfway down the canyon to their developing tent at Indian Gardens, process the photos and get back to the top before the mules returned. (All water at the South Rim is still pumped up from inside the canyon; look out for the transcanyon pipeline on the Bright Angel trail.) The Kolbs were also the first to film a boat trip down the Colorado in 1912. The studio now houses a bookstore and gallery.

However limited your time, try to hike at least part-way into the canyon. As jaw-dropping as the views are from the rim, it's almost too huge to take in: you need to get closer to really appreciate the stunning colours of the cliffs; to identify the different geological layers; to watch the vegetation gradually change from pine trees to cacti as you descend; to see the turbulent brown waters and hear the roar of the Colorado.

Two maintained trails – **Bright Angel** and **South Kaibab** – lead to **Phantom Ranch** at the bottom of the canyon, where they connect with the **North Kaibab** trail from the North Rim. Hikers share the trails with mule riders (note that mules have priority), and the upper sections especially can get overcrowded. Remember it will probably take you twice as long to walk up as down (though walking down is harder on your knees and feet); do not attempt to hike to the river and back in one day. Water supplies below the rim are very limited, so carry plenty (allow one gallon per person per day in summer) and ample food. A few granola bars or a bag of trail mix is not enough for a day's arduous hiking – you do not want to add to the statistics of dehydrated or exhausted hikers picked up by rangers (the number of search and rescue missions each year regularly tops the 400 mark). Wear proper hiking boots and take a ten-minute rest every hour; raising your legs above the level of your heart will aid recovery. There is little shade on either trail, so avoid hiking at midday.

The nine-and-a-half-mile (15.3 kilometre) Bright Angel trail follows the line of a wide geological fault, which creates a natural break in the cliffs and means views into the canyon are good from the very top. The fault shifted the usual layering of the rock strata; as you descend you can see that the layers on the left are much higher than those on the right. Water is usually available from May to September at the **resthouses** one and a half miles (2.4 kilometres) and three miles (five kilometres) from the trailhead. These are good day hike destinations; more experienced hikers could head for the campground at **Indian Gardens** (four and a half miles/7.2 kilometres), whose tall cottonwoods, planted by prospector Ralph Cameron in the early 1900s, are easily identifiable from the rim. The South Kaibab trail is shorter (6.3 miles/ten kilometres) but steeper than Bright Angel trail and has no campground or water; hike to the tree-dotted plateau of **Cedar Ridge** (1.5 miles/one kilometre) if you're short of time.

If you want to camp overnight below the rim, you'll need a $10 permit (plus $5 per person per night), available by mail, fax (1-520 638 2125) or in person from the Backcountry Office, Grand Canyon National Park, PO Box 129, Grand Canyon, AZ 86023; you can also join the waiting list for next-day cancellations. Phone 1-520 638 7875 for further information about permits (no permits are issued by phone). For general information on trip planning, call the office on 1-520 638 7888. Note that the number of permits is limited.

In addition to Indian Gardens, there are campsites at **Bright Angel** (next to Phantom Ranch) and **Cottonwood Springs** (open May to October, accessible from the North Rim on the North Kaibab trail). Hikers who stay at Phantom Ranch do not need permits; non-guests can also eat there but must book meals in advance.

You can also visit one of the most beautiful and remote corners of the Grand Canyon in the **Havasupai Indian Reservation**, which lies adjacent to the park to the south-west. To reach the village of Supai, where you'll find the tribal headquarters (1-520 448 2731), the tourist office (1-520 448 2141/2121) and lodging (1-520 448 2111/ 2201), drive 70 miles (113 kilometres) on Highway 18 (which is off Route 66 east of Peach Springs). From the parking area, it's then an eight-mile (13-kilometre) hike or horse ride to Supai. **Peach Springs** is within the **Hualapai Indian Reservation** and site of the Hualapai tribal headquarters (1-520 769 2216), where you'll find lodging and general information about Colorado River trips.

The beautiful, awe-inspiring **Grand Canyon** *– once seen, never forgotten.*

Future plans for the Grand Canyon are inevitably concerned with minimising the damaging impact of the ever-increasing number of visitors. The park service intends to ban private vehicles from high-use areas including the Grand Canyon Village and rim overlooks, expand public transport (using light rail and electric and gas-powered buses), bicycle and pedestrian systems and build a new orientation and transport centre at Mather Point. At the North Rim, meanwhile, it is likely that visitor numbers will be limited in order to try and provide a low-key, uncrowded atmosphere in this haven of natural beauty.

En route to the Grand Canyon

Sixty miles (97 kilometres) south of the national park, at the junction with the I-40, is the small and friendly town of **Williams**, named after legendary mountain man 'Old' Bill Williams, whose huge statue stands at the west end of town. It has the distinction of being the last town on Route 66 to be bypassed by the freeway system (in 1984) and is still a mecca for Route 66 enthusiasts, lured by numerous souvenir shops and regular classic car rallies. The centre of town is lined with impressive, turn-of-the-century brick buildings and old-style concrete street lamps; visit the shop and headquarters of *Route 66 Magazine* (323 W Route 66; 1-520 635 4322) for some great memorabilia and have breakfast at **Old Smoky's** on the nearby corner (624 W Route 66; 1-520 635 2091). For details on lodging, restaurants and other facilities, stop at the **visitor centre** in the old Santa Fe Freight Depot (200 W Railroad Avenue; 1-520 635 4061; open 8am-5pm daily) or check the town's website (www.amdest.com/az/williams/williams yellowpages.html).

The **Grand Canyon Railway** also operates out of Williams; it's a tourist train, running daily trips to the old Santa Fe Railway station in the heart of Grand Canyon Village, and is pulled by a turn-of-the-century steam engine during the summer. There are various 'classes of service' in an assortment of historic carriages, and musicians and characters in Western costume entertain passengers on the journey. The train leaves from Williams at 10am and arrives at the village at 12.15pm; return fares start at $49.95, $24.95 under-16s, plus $8 park fees for adults (no fees for children or seniors). More details on 1-800 843 8724/1-520 773 1976 and on its website, www thetrain.com.

Flagstaff, 35 miles (56 kilometres) east of Williams, is also a good jumping-off point for the Grand Canyon: it's 80 miles (129 kilometres) from Grand Canyon Village via Highway 180 and Highway 64. Situated at the base of the San Francisco Peaks (the highest mountains in Arizona), this pleasant university and railroad town has numerous motels, interesting museums, good restaurants and brewpubs and the **Lowell Observatory** (from where the planet Pluto was first spotted in 1930). The atmosphere is laid-back and the historic downtown area is full of small coffeehouses, shops and restaurants. Route 66 runs through the centre of town. More information from the Chamber of Commerce (101 E Route 66; 1-520 774 4505).

Where to eat

There are three restaurants, two self-service cafés and a takeaway snack bar in the Grand Canyon Village, all open daily. The splendid, dark wooden dining room with its large Indian murals at the **El Tovar Hotel** is very popular – you have to take your luck at breakfast (6.30-11am) and lunch (11.30am-2pm) but must book for dinner (5-10pm); hotel guests take priority over non-guests. Nearby are the less formal **Bright Angel Lodge** dining room (6.30am-10pm) and **Arizona Steakhouse** (Mar-Dec, from 5pm). **Maswik Lodge** has a friendly sports bar and inexpensive cafeteria (6am-10pm) serving burritos, burgers, pasta and sandwiches, and there's a larger cafeteria at **Yavapai Lodge** (Mar-Oct 6am-10pm). The cocktail lounge in the El Tovar was decorated by Mary Colter, who also designed the Bright Angel Lodge with its fabulous 'geological' fireplace. Stone from the bed of the Colorado River forms the hearth, with the design mimicking the different layers of rock in the Grand Canyon, right up to the uppermost Kaibab limestone layer at the top.

There's also a snack bar at **Hermit's Rest** (summer 8am-6.30pm; winter 9am-5pm) and a cafeteria at **Desert View** (summer 8am-6pm; winter 9am-5pm).

Where to stay

There's plenty of accommodation (run by AmFac) in Grand Canyon Village, but rooms can be

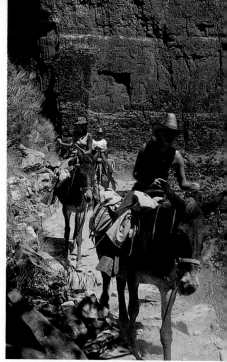

Mule rides are very popular, so book ahead.

reserved 23 months in advance, and often are, especially for the summer – so book as far ahead as you can.

The hunting lodge-style **El Tovar Hotel**, with its grand lobby adorned with stuffed animal heads, offers the most splendid lodging in the village; try to get one of the rooms with a spacious private balcony overlooking the rim. The pioneer-style, 1930s **Bright Angel Lodge** and more modern, motel-style **Kachina** and **Thunderbird Lodges** are also near the edge of the canyon. **Maswik** and **Yavapai Lodges** are further away and less expensive. Also within the village are **Mather campground** with 320 sites ($12-$15 – book on 1-800 365 2267) and a trailer village for RVs ($19). The rustic log and stone cabins and more modern dorms at **Phantom Ranch**, at the bottom of the canyon, are often booked to capacity months in advance.

A few miles south of the village, just outside the park, is **Tusayan**, where you'll find a number of motels: **Moqui Lodge** (also run by AmFac; open Mar-Nov), **Red Feather Lodge** (1-800 538 2345/1-520 638 2414), **Best Western** (1-800 528 1234/1-520 638 2681), **Holiday Inn** (1-800 465 4329/1-520 638 3000) and **Quality Inn** (1-800 221 2222/1-520 638 2673). A free shuttle-bus service runs between Tusayan and the village. There are also plenty of motels in Flagstaff and Williams, where the friendly, British-run **Norris Hotel** (1-800 341 8000/1-520 635 2202; rooms from $28) is easy to spot: there's a Union Jack flying from the roof.

On the North Rim, **Grand Canyon Lodge** (also run by AmFac) has rooms and cabins (and a spectacular dining room); there's also a campsite. Outside the park, there's accommodation at **Kaibab Lodge**, 18 miles (29 kilometres) north (1-520 638 2389) and **Jacob Lake Inn**, 45 miles (72 kilometres) north (1-520 643 7232).

Grand Canyon Village
Reservations 1-303 297 2757/same-day reservations 1-520 638 2631/fax 1-303 297 3175. **Rates** *El Tovar Hotel* $114-$279; *Bright Angel Lodge & cabins* $44-$229; *Thunderbird & Kachina Lodges* $109-$119; *Maswik Lodge* $60-$113; *Yavapai Lodges* $85-$99. **Credit** AmEx, Disc, JCB, MC, V.

Tours

AmFac operates mule and coach trips within the park; call 1-303 297 2757 for reservations or visit the transportation desks at Bright Angel, Maswik and Yavapai Lodges and the visitor centre.

By mule
Year-round *one-day trip to Plateau Point* $106.60; *overnight trip to Phantom Ranch* $294.78 one person; $523.60 two people. **Mid Nov-Mar** *two-night trip to Phantom Ranch* $408.44 one person; $684.98 two people. Prices include accommodation and all meals.

Riding into the canyon perched on the back of a mule may be less strenuous than hiking, but it's not really a soft option; easier on the legs, perhaps, but not on your backside. The one-day (7hr) trip takes you down 3,200ft (975m) on the Bright Angel trail to the edge of the Tonto plateau, from where you get great views of the inner canyon and Colorado River. The two-day trip goes into the canyon on the Bright Angel trail, overnights at Phantom Ranch and returns on the South Kaibab trail. Trips are very popular, so book in advance if possible (up to 23 months ahead). Alternatively, put your name on the waiting list at the Bright Angel transportation desk, but cancellations are rare. There are also mule rides (half-day and one-day) from the North Rim but they do not go all the way to the river.

By coach
Choose from various sightseeing trips along the West and East Rim Drives, including the popular 90-minute trip to watch the sunset from Mohave Point (May-Oct; $12 per person). Yaki Point is a good place to watch sunrise. You can also take tours outside the park to places such as Monument Valley.

By air
Various outfits run plane rides ($65-$180 per person) and helicopter rides ($90-$165) over the canyon's rim, operating out of Grand Canyon Airport just south of Tusayan. Try **Air Grand Canyon** (1-800 247 4726/ 1-520 638 2686); **Grand Canyon Airlines** (1-800 528 2413/1-520 638 2407); **Papillon**

Helicopters (1-800 528 2418/1-520 638 2419); **Airstar Helicopters** (1-800 962 3869/1-520 638 2622) or **Kenai Helicopters** (1-800 541 4537/1-520 638 2412/638 2764). For sightseeing flights from Las Vegas, *see p89* **Attractions**.

By river
You can follow in the wake of one-armed scientist and explorer Major John Wesley Powell, the first man to navigate the length of the Colorado River by boat (in 1869), by taking a river trip through the rapids of the Grand Canyon. You'll need at least eight days, which is the time it takes to travel the 277 miles (446 kilometres) downriver from Lees Ferry, the official start of the Grand Canyon, to Pearce Ferry on Lake Mead.

Numerous commercial river runners offer trips in a range of vessels, but the season is limited, as is the number of boats permitted, so they are often full. Operators include **Canyon Explorations** (1-800 654 0723/1-520 774 4559), **Arizona Raft Adventures** (1-800 786 7238/1-520 526 8200) and **Grand Canyon Expeditions** (1-800 544 2691/ 1-435 644 2691). **Canyoneers** (1-800 525 0924/1-520 526 0924) offers three-day trips to Bright Angel Beach, near Phantom Ranch – but you have to hike out from the bottom of the canyon. *The Guide* has a list of river concessioners.

Outside the park, **Hulapai River Runners** in Peach Springs (1-800 622 4409/1-520 769 2210) offers one- or two-day trips within the Havasupai Indian Reservation, and **Aramak-Wilderness River Adventures** (1-800 528 6154/1-520 645 3279) runs one-day smooth-water raft trips from Glen Canyon Dam to Lees Ferry. You can also book this trip through the AmFac transportation desks.

Tourist information

Check out the Grand Canyon's excellent website at **www.thecanyon.com/nps** for information on accommodation, hiking, backcountry permits, maps of the area and so on – all you need to know to plan your trip.

Getting there

By car
To reach the South Rim, head south on US 93 to the I-40, then turn left on to Highway 64. It's 290 miles (467 kilometres), about 5½hrs from Vegas. For the North Rim, head north on the I-15, then east on Highway 9, Highway 59 and US 89A to Highway 67, which leads into the park: it's a slightly shorter route, but will take longer.

For information on road conditions in the park, call 1-520 638 7888.

By air
Several companies offer scheduled flights from North Las Vegas airport to Grand Canyon airport at Tusayan: try **Scenic Flights** (1-800 634 6801/ 739 1900. The flight takes 1hr 15mins and a return ticket costs $160-$200.

Into California

Welcome to a state of contrasts: from blistering desertscapes to the streets of Los Angeles.

A short drive from the concrete and neon of Las Vegas into California will bring you to some of the US's most spectacular and accessible desert scenery. Heading south on the I-15, the main road between Las Vegas and Southern California, you quickly leave any signs of habitation behind and enter a world of barren mountains and sloping valleys with only creosote bushes and Joshua trees to provide relief from the brownish-pink landscape.

You can throw the dice one last time at the mini-gambling resort of **Jean**, a few miles north of the border, and on the border itself at tiny **Primm**, essentially three casinos and a rollercoaster. Just across the border lies the vast, empty expanse of the **Mojave National Preserve** and, less than a hundred miles (160 kilometres) further south, is **Joshua Tree National Park**, where the Mojave desert joins the Sonoran desert. California is also the home of America's most infamous desert area, the starkly beautiful **Death Valley National Park**. Remember that these are remote, largely uninhabited areas, so take the usual precautions for desert driving and hiking (*see page 248* **Getting Started**): you don't want to discover what it's like to run out of petrol in the middle of Death Valley in high summer.

Of course, you can just drive through the desert without stopping. Have breakfast in Las Vegas and lunch on Venice Beach: the beaches, bars and beautiful people of **Los Angeles** are a mere five-hour drive away (traffic permitting) on the I-15.

Jean & Primm

Catering primarily for Californian gamblers whose habits can't wait until Las Vegas for gratification, Jean and Primm are dedicated casino encampments that straddle the I-15.

Jean, 40 miles (64 kilometres) south of Las Vegas, is the older of the two, and feels like it. Its two resorts, **Gold Strike** (1-800 634 1359/477 5000) and **Nevada Landing** (1-800 628 6682/387 5000) have an agreeably old-time aura; their casinos, small by Las Vegas standards, are kitted out in red, gold and glittering glass. Nevada Landing is marginally the more appealing: its blue and white, paddlesteamer-beached-in-the-desert exterior morphs into a barrel-vaulted casino hall with enormous scrolled beams, lit by what look like the largest chandeliers in the world.

Located right by the Nevada/California state line and as such in a prime location to get first dibs on those desperate inbound gamblers, **Primm** is a three-resort cluster of an altogether more modern aspect. The success of the Primm family's first casino-hotel here, **Whiskey Pete's**, was so great that they followed it with **Primadonna** and **Buffalo Bill's** (reservations for all three resorts on 1-800 386 7867). Buffalo Bill's is the most impressive of the three, with its silo-like exterior ringed by the Desperado, the world's tallest rollercoaster. The interior, modelled on an Old West mining town, is as impressive a piece of theming as any found in Las Vegas: the high-ceilinged, somewhat gloomy halls contain tiny mock steam trains, old-style shopfronts, trees and a section of the rollercoaster and log flume rides.

The visitor centre (874 1360) behind the Gold Strike in Jean provides information on Jean, Primm and other Nevada attractions, such as the nearby ghost town of **Goodsprings**. Founded in the 1860s, the town hit the headlines in 1942 when Clark Gable stayed there awaiting news of the plane crash that killed his wife Carole Lombard. It is currently enjoying something of a revival, with a population of more than 100. The **Pioneer Saloon** (1-702 874 9362; open 11am to late daily), with walls and ceiling made of pressed tin, has been in business since 1913.

Mojave National Preserve

A wedge-shaped area bordered by two interstates (the I-15 to the north and the I-40 to the south), the 1.6 million acres (648,000 hectares) of the Mojave National Preserve are sparsely inhabited – you can drive for miles without seeing another car – but conveniently close to Las Vegas for exploration in a day. Good paved roads and myriad dirt roads (some of which can only be driven in a 4WD vehicle) criss-cross the area, and the weird Joshua tree, popular symbol of the Mojave, is abundant at higher elevations.

Although mines and ranches still operate in the area (obey all 'no trespassing' signs) and hunting is allowed, half the preserve is designated as wilderness. Signs of human habitation, past and present, are scattered about in isolated pockets, serving to emphasise how vast and empty the desert can be. The best times to visit are either in

Majestic desert scenery in the **Mojave National Preserve**.

the spring or the autumn; it's achingly hot between mid-May and mid-September, when temperatures spiral well over 100°F (38°C). Try to be there in the late afternoon, when the shadows are long and the mountains at their most beautiful.

A good starting point is the small town of **Baker** on the I-15, proud home of the tallest thermometer in the world, which towers 134 feet (40 metres) above the desert floor: you can see it from miles away. Visit the fabulous **Mad Greek Diner** for houmous and spanakopita (1-760 733 4354; open 6am-midnight daily) and don't forget to fill up on petrol and drinking water: there are no services in the preserve. The **Desert Information Center** (under the thermometer) has good maps, books and updates on road conditions.

If you have only a few hours, drive from Baker via the Kelbaker Road, Kelso-Cima Road and Cima Road, to rejoin the I-15: the 67-mile (107-kilometre) circuit is a good introduction to the preserve's sights, both natural and man-made.

You pass the reddish humps of over 30 young volcanic cones before reaching **Kelso**, which used to be a major passenger stop on the Union Pacific Railroad; now only freight trains, looking like long silver caterpillars, pass through. The grand, Spanish Mission-style depot, built in 1924 and finally closed in 1985, may eventually become a visitor centre. At Kelso, turn left on to the Kelso-Cima Road, which runs parallel to the 7,000-foot (2,130-metre) high Providence Mountains. At Cima, little more than a collection of wooden shacks, take the Cima Road back towards the I-15: you'll head past the gently swelling **Cima Dome**, which has the largest stand of Joshua trees anywhere in the world. The species found here (*Yucca brevifolia jaegeriana*) is shorter and has more branches than that found in the Joshua Tree National Park.

If you want to detour to the 500-foot (150-metre) high Kelso sand dunes, continue on Kelbaker Road at the Kelso-Cima turn-off and turn right after about seven miles on to a signed dirt road. Formed 10,000 to 20,000 years ago, the dunes support a remarkable variety of plant and animal life, including the rarely seen desert tortoise. You may hear the dunes 'booming' when dry sand grains slide down the steep upper slopes.

If you have more time, particularly if you're in the area during the blistering summer, head for the **Providence Mountains State Recreation Area**, significantly cooler than the desert floor. Multi-branched cholla, spiky Mojave yucca, round barrel cactus, spindly Mormon tea and the flat pads of prickly pears share the upland slopes with juniper and piñon trees, creating a stunning geometric display. There are great views south from the visitor centre. The park also houses the dramatic limestone **Mitchell Caverns**, which remain a cool 65°F (18°C) year round. There are guided tours of the caves ($6 adults; $3 children) at 1.30pm from Monday to Friday and at 10am, 1.30pm and 3pm on Saturday and Sunday from Labor Day to Memorial Day, and at 1.30pm on Saturday and Sunday only the rest of the year – call 1-760 928 2586 for reservations.

Also worth visiting is the tiny settlement of **Nipton** (population 40), located just outside the northern edge of the preserve. There's a railroad crossing, an old-fashioned country store selling souvenirs, books and some groceries, a town hall and a charming hotel. One of the hotel's rooms is named after silent film star Clara Bow, whose husband owned a ranch nearby and who used to entertain Hollywood guests at the hotel. If you head back towards Las Vegas from Nipton via Searchlight, you pass an impressively huge forest of Joshua trees.

*Waiting for the train at **Nipton**.*

Other sights include **Zzyzx**, also known as Soda Springs, on the edge of the white expanse of Soda Dry Lake. It has been used as an Indian campsite, a military outpost, and a health resort by early radio evangelist Curtis Howe Springer, and is now a study centre.

If you're still hungry for more desert, head south-east to **Joshua Tree National Park** ($10 entrance fee), which occupies a transitional zone between two desert ecosystems. The western half is in the Mojave, and has large Joshua-tree forests and jumbled piles of massive granite boulders, which are popular with climbers. The eastern half is in the Colorado desert, and is lower, drier, a bit hotter and dominated by creosote; you'll also see numerous types of cholla and the distinctive 20- to 30-foot (six- to nine-metre) high ocotillo, which is most striking when in bloom (usually in March). There are two entrances from the north and one from the south; the main visitor centre (open 8am-4.30pm daily) is off Highway 62, near the military town of **Twentynine Palms**. A scenic drive through the park gives access to viewpoints, a few marked trails, campgrounds and picnic sites; call 1-760 367 5500 for more information or check the park service website (www.nps.gov/jotr).

Where to stay

Baker has a number of motels and restaurants; contact the **Chamber of Commerce** (1-760 733 4469) for details. Inside the preserve are two campgrounds ($10), with a limited water supply. Set among juniper and piñon woodland, the Mid-Hills campground is usually significantly cooler than Hole-in-the-Wall – and much prettier. Campsites are issued on a first come, first served basis.

Hotel Nipton

HCR 1, Box 357, Nipton, CA 92634 (1-760 856 2335/ hotel@nipton.com). **Rates** $55 including tax and continental breakfast.
The nicest place to stay near the preserve. Fronted by a cactus garden, it has four rooms, a jacuzzi and a large verandah with views across the Ivanpah Valley. Reservations recommended.
Website: www.nipton.com

Tourist information

Desert Information Center
72157 Baker Boulevard, Baker (1-760 733 4040).
Open 9am-5pm daily.
Website: www.nps.gov/moja

Getting there

Baker is 90 miles (145 kilometres) south on the I-15. It's a beautiful drive, but this is the main road between Las Vegas and Los Angeles so traffic can be heavy and accidents frequent. To reach Joshua Tree National Park, take the Kelbaker Road through the preserve and continue south via Amboy (visit the Route 66 diner) to Twentynine Palms; it's about 130 miles (210 kilometres) from Baker to the park entrance.

Los Angeles

West of Baker, the I-15 continues through stark desert terrain until it reaches **Barstow**, 63 miles (101 kilometres) further on, an unattractive and sprawling town notable primarily for its vast factory mall and railroad depot. Should you wish to stop over, Barstow offers a full complement of cheap motels and the usual chain restaurants. The freeway then continues through the pine-capped wilderness country of the San Bernadino Mountains before hitting the Los Angeles sprawl.

If you haven't been to the Los Angeles before, first thing you need to know is that it doesn't really exist as an identifiable place. Los Angeles is a city, a county and a region; the county contains 88 cities merged into a vast agglomeration over 100 miles (160 kilometres) wide, of which the City of Los Angeles is the nominal heart. LA's sights are spread throughout the region and the essential LA experience – driving the freeways – has no precise location. If you only have a short time, you should focus on the area between Downtown and the ocean, known as the LA basin, which includes the best-known beach areas, the burgs of the rich and famous, Hollywood and Sunset Strip.

Areas

Beverly Hills, Bel Air & Rodeo Drive

Whether you're a hard-core shopper or a sociologist, don't miss a walk or drive down **Rodeo Drive**. In the very heart of **Beverly Hills**, these few blocks, where some of the superswanky shops require appointments for entrance, embody conspicuous consumption at its best or worse. Trinkets sell for thousands and men, women and children don furs, silks and giant gemstones for a regular afternoon outing. It attracts an odd mix of tourists and very wealthy Angelenos, many of them residents of Beverly Hills' tree-lined streets of mansions with perfectly manicured gardens. Beverly Hills became a city in 1880, before which it was known chiefly for its crops of robust lima beans. The houses are big, as expected, and built in every style imaginable. Drive off the main drag and explore the side streets to get the full effect. But beware of the zealous Beverly Hills police, who sometimes stop strangers to check why they might be walking.

Bel Air, also home to the rich and famous, is a posh hillside community that lies west of Beverly Hills. Known for their privacy and pretty views, the houses in this gated neighbourhood are visual feasts, but, unfortunately, visitors driving along the meandering roads won't see much save the names of these grand mansions written on the mailboxes, as the best houses are hidden from sight.

Downtown

Downtown LA is an odd stew of old and new, vibrant and stagnant, beautiful and ugly. It's made up of the skyscraper-studded financial downtown, El Pueblo de Los Angeles – the site of the original settlement, now a buzzing pedestrian area based around Olvera Street – City Hall, Chinatown and Little Tokyo. Much of it can be explored on foot during the day, but be careful after dark as some parts can be rough (many homeless people take to the streets at night).

Some of LA's most stunning architecture is found downtown, such as the romantic **Union Station**, where you almost expect to see Bogie and Bergman kissing a star-crossed goodbye. Other landmarks include the **Bradbury Building** (304 South Broadway), as featured in *Blade Runner*, and the space-age **Westin Bonaventure Hotel** (404 South Figueroa Street). Also of note are the **Music Center**, whose lavish Dorothy Chandler Pavilion often hosts the Oscar ceremony, the **Museum of Contemporary Art** (MOCA), the **Angels Flight** funicular railway (Hill Street, between Third and Fourth Streets) and **Broadway**, a thriving Mexican shopping street. In the 1940s, LA's Community Redevelopment Agency developed **Little Tokyo** and **Chinatown** to the east, which have since blossomed into thriving, bustling communities, great spots for food, shops and religious shrines. A new addition to downtown is the vast **Staples** arena, at 1111 Figueroa Street (on the corner of Figueroa and 11th Streets), home to basketball, ice-hockey and pop concerts. It's worth driving by at night when the arena is bathed in a lurid purple glow.

Hollywood Boulevard

Gone are the dream-come-true days of fur-wrapped starlets and tuxedoed leading men. Over the past few decades, Hollywood Boulevard has descended into a sink of X-rated cinemas, tacky tourist shops, vagrants and unrealised dreams. To say it is anticlimactic would be an understatement, but there are nevertheless a few places on this long street well worth a stop: the historic **Mann's Chinese** and **El Capitan Theaters**, the old **Roosevelt Hotel**, beautifully designed **Pantages Theater**, **Musso & Frank's Grill** and **Frederick's of Hollywood** lingerie store among them. Furthermore, the strip is now undergoing a facelift. The street has been cleaned up; an open-air mall and purpose-designed

theatre for the Oscar ceremony are being built above a new subway at the corner of Hollywood and Highland; grand old cinemas, such as the Egyptian, have been restored; and restaurants and cafés have opened in the area. Many locals consider the Hollywood neighbourhood to be a gritty antidote to some of LA's more sterile environments.

The **Walk of Fame**, with bronze stars embedded in the pavement paying tribute to more than 2,500 Hollywood greats (and not-so-greats, so long as they had a good publicist and some spare cash), extends in all directions from the junction of Vine Street and Hollywood Boulevard, with the longest stretch running westwards to La Brea Avenue.

Melrose Avenue & Los Feliz

It's slightly less cutting-edge than it used to be, but Melrose Avenue is still a mecca of LA trendiness. Locals and tourists throng to it like ants on an anthill, especially the stretch between La Brea and Fairfax Avenues. Lined with funky restaurants, art galleries, theatres, comedy clubs and shops selling everything from vintage clothes and used Levi's to designer sunglasses and art, it attracts mainly young trendoids and the punk-grunge hippies with its adrenaline pulse. A few happenin' highlights: **Aardvark** for vintage clothing, **Caffe Luna** for espresso and mouthwatering tiramisu, the **Wound & Wound Toy Company** for wind-up toys and music boxes, and the **Groundlings Improv Theatre**, where many of the *Saturday Night Live* greats served their apprenticeship.

Melrose Avenue suffers from a lack of parking, a fact that may have contributed to the emergence in recent years of other trendy shopping streets that are a bit more accessible: try **Robertson Boulevard** in Beverly Hills for upmarket clothing stores, and **La Brea Avenue** between Beverly and Sixth for modernist furniture and clothing. **Los Feliz**, the stretch of Vermont Avenue between Hollywood and Franklin Boulevards in particular, has become a rival to Melrose; it even boasts **Wacko**, a famous goofy games and cards store that left its long-time home on Melrose and is now on Hollywood at Rodney. **Sunset Boulevard**, east of Hillhurst, is also a magnet for the would-be bohemian denizens of East Hollywood and Silverlake.

Santa Monica

Beautifully framed by mountains and sea, affluent Santa Monica is the jewel of LA's Westside. Known locally as 'the people's republic of Santa Monica', it is the heart of bourgeois liberalism, noted for its environmental causes, rent control, tolerance of the homeless – and great shopping and restaurants. At its heart is **Third Street Promenade**. Created in the late 1980s for pedestrians only, its four blocks are at their best on weekend nights, when the street performers are out, cafés, bars, restaurants and some shops open late and vendors fill the street with carts selling silver jewellery, organic cotton clothes and bonsai trees. Almost anything you could ask for is at hand: good food, shops both practical and whimsical, several multiscreen cinemas, an indoor mall and pavement tables. Although it's not only tourists who come here, some find it rather contrived and antiseptic. However, any visitor daunted by the magnitude of the city will be reassured by the very blandness that others find off-putting. Third Street Promenade is also handy for the beach, and there's ample parking on Second and Fourth Streets. There is also very good shopping and food to the south on Main Street between Edgemar and Rose Avenue.

Sunset Strip
The famous Sunset Strip is the section of Sunset Boulevard that runs from Doheny Drive to Laurel Canyon in West Hollywood. Studded with billboards and bright lights, it has been the centre of LA nightlife since the 1920s. Along its length are such landmarks as the **Whisky A-Go-Go** and **House of Blues** music clubs, the **Comedy Store** and the **Viper Room** nightclub, as well as swinging hotels such as the **Mondrian**, the **Standard** and the perennially glamorous **Chateau Marmont**. Lots of restaurants and shops, too.

Venice
At the turn of the century, builders, government and, most notably, tobacco magnate Abbot Kinney transformed this area into the 'Venice of America', complete with canals, bridges, imported gondolas, meandering streets and a bohemian spirit. The canals were condemned in 1940 and some filled with concrete, but the remaining ones have since been restored and gentrified into an idyllic residential neighbourhood, complete with quacking ducks. Only those with relatively robust wallets can live along the quaint waterways, but everyone is free to wander among them. Enter the network by turning south off Venice Boulevard on to Dell Avenue, about a quarter of a mile back from the beach. Venice as a whole is a mixed and magnetic community of post-1960s hippies, the elderly, artistic and free-spirited, with a bit of gang territory thrown in (watch yourself and your car in inland areas, especially after dark). **Abbot Kinney Boulevard** is a good place to window-shop or enjoy a coffee or meal at a local café or restaurant. And then, of course, there's **Venice Beach** (*see below*).

Beaches
Locals will tell you two things about LA's beaches: one, just because it's the Pacific, don't expect the ocean to be warm, and, two, the further away you are from Santa Monica Bay, where waste is pumped into the water, the cleaner the water. The public beaches are usually open from dawn to sunset. Most welcome children but not dogs and have parking (though it's at a premium in high season), showers, restrooms, volleyball courts and rental stands for inline skates and bicycles.

Venice Beach is the place to go for people-watching – every category of life is represented among the throngs that descend here. Ocean Front Walk (popularly known as the Boardwalk) offers shops, restaurants, food stands and Muscle Beach, the outdoor gym where you can watch would-be

Arnies tone up. **Santa Monica Beach** is often crowded and has a summer-holiday feel to it, enhanced by its pier, three city blocks in length and packed with engagingly low-tech diversions, including the famous carousel – fun, but not the main attraction. The best beaches in **Malibu**, north up the coast, are private, but the public ones are nonetheless popular, especially with surfers, even if they don't match up to the imagined Malibu. Further north still are **Zuma Beach** – quintessential California sun and sand – and **El Matador**, small, beautiful and dominated by rocky outcrops, hence the steep walk down. The beaches also extend to the south, where the best are **Manhattan**, **Huntington** and **Hermosa**.

Sights
There are a million things to see and do in LA; if you have limited time, try the following.

Disneyland
1313 Harbor Boulevard, Anaheim, Orange County (1-714 999 4565/1-714 781 4560/recorded information 1-714 781 4565). I-5, exit Harbor Boulevard. **Open** daily; hours vary, so call in advance. **Admission** $39; $37 seniors; $29 3-11s. **Credit** AmEx, MC, V.
Called 'the happiest place on earth', Disneyland is all it's cracked up to be – if you like that kind of thing – though it's beginning to seem a bit small. This immaculate world (deliveries and rubbish removal are all done underground) will take you to Tomorrowland, Fantasyland, Frontierland and Adventureland; through the middle of it all runs Main Street, always busy but positively throbbing on parade days. Although new rides come on line with movie-studio productivity, some of the old favourites still draw enormous crowds: Space Mountain, the Matterhorn, the Haunted Mansion and Pirates of the Caribbean. If you hate having a song stick in your head, skip It's a Small World, which has an inane tune. But if you want to see Disneyland at its most quaint and enchanting, then don't miss it – a boat trip around the world in what might be 80 minutes, given the delightfully slow pace of the ride. Disneyland is good fun, but get there early to beat the crowds, be prepared to queue and pace yourself – it's big.
Website: www.disneyland.com

J Paul Getty Center
1200 Getty Center Drive, at the I-405, Brentwood (1-310 440 7300). I-405, exit Getty Center Drive. **Open** 11am-7pm Tue, Wed; 11am-9pm Thur, Fri; 10am-6pm Sat, Sun. **Admission** free. **Parking** $5; booking compulsory – book 2 weeks in advance. **Credit** AmEx, MC, V.
The new and much-fêted Getty museum has finally given Los Angeles the cultural kudos that it has long desired. The $733 million it cost to build and stock (over and beyond what was transferred from the original Getty) shows; as well as fabulous collections of art and artefacts from antiquities to modern

For a view of Los Angeles beach life, pay a visit to **Santa Monica** pier.

masters, it has world-class archives. The views over the city are also fabulous. 'Your Getty' claimed the opening publicity campaign, an exhortation that LA took so much to heart that it's often overrun with visitors (even the supposedly off-limits areas), though the limited parking space acts as a natural filter. If you didn't book in advance, park in Santa Monica and take the number 14 Big Blue Bus. *Website: www.getty.edu*

Six Flags California

Magic Mountain Parkway, off the I-5, Valencia (1-661 255 4100/recorded information 1-661 255 4111). I-5, exit Magic Mountain Parkway. **Open** days and hours vary, so call in advance; Hurricane Harbor closed in winter. **Admission** *Magic Mountain* $39; $20 over-55s; $19.50 children under 48in (122cm). *Hurricane Harbor* $19; $12 children, seniors. **Credit** AmEx, Disc, JCB, MC, V.
Six Flags theme park comprises Six Flags Magic Mountain and its new cousin, Six Flags Hurricane Harbor Water Park. Both give you rides, rides and more rides, and spectacular rides at that – roller-coasters and water rides for every level of screamer, the most famous of them being the Colossus, the largest wooden-framed rollercoaster ever built. Set scenically on the hip of the San Fernando Mountains and created for kids and adults, Six Flags is fun with a screamingly huge capital F.
Website: www.sixflags.com

Universal Studios Hollywood & CityWalk

100 Universal City Plaza, Universal City (1-818 508 9600). US 101, exit Universal Center Drive. **Open** daily; hours vary, so call in advance. **Admission** $34 seniors; $29 3-11s. **Credit** AmEx, DC, Disc, MC, V.
Although you can opt to attend animal acts, stroll round the Lucille Ball museum, experience the Back to the Future flight simulator, go on rides such as Jurassic Park or watch scripted shows inspired by recent TV programmes or movies, the best way to see Universal is to take the tram. The ride takes you

through the backlot of the working studio, where you will see the likes of King Kong, the shark from *Jaws*, the parting of the Red Sea and the *Psycho* house, plus glimpses of studio life. Allow a full day and start early. The complex also houses Universal CityWalk, a Los Angeles-themed shopping and eating 'street'. Mobbed most of the time, the City-Walk is at its glitzy best at night when the two blocks of collaged LA architecture come alive.

Hiking in the mountains

All this sanitised fun can make you forget there's a natural LA out there. A favoured pastime of Angelenos is hiking in the the Santa Monica Mountains, which frame the LA Basin). **Will Rogers Park** and **Temescal Canyon**, both off Sunset Boulevard, west of the I-405, are two favourite places where you can be out of sight and sound of the city within minutes of starting. For details of trails; check the *Time Out Los Angeles Guide* or hiking guides available in LA bookstores.

Star-spotting

Celebs are everywhere. But they're not usually at the addresses on the star maps sold on Hollywood street corners, which are horribly out of date. Most celebs live in Hollywood Hills, Beverly Hills, Bel Air, Brentwood, Santa Monica, Malibu and, now, Los Feliz (Madonna among them). Some are so famous everyone knows where they live.

If you want to spot TV mogul Aaron Spelling or his *Beverly Hills 90210* actress daughter Tori, you could go and hang outside their mansion in Bel Air. Take Sunset Boulevard west through Beverly Hills and Bel Air and make a left on Mapleton Drive. Take it all the way to the end. That last huge house on the left is the place. OK, you can't see the private ice-rink or cinemas – and definitely not the present-wrapping room – but it still looks impressive. A much better bet is the little-discussed Broad Beach, home to the likes of Steven Spielberg, Kurt Russell and Goldie Hawn, Robert Downey Jr, Ali MacGraw, Sylvester Stallone, Mel Gibson and Sting (when he's in town). These people like to say they live in Malibu, which throws stargazers off the (beaten) track slightly, as Broad Beach is actually part of Zuma Beach further up the coast.

Of course, seeing a celebrity's home isn't the same as seeing a real live person. However, in these days of stalkers, that might be considerably more difficult. If you can be bothered, you could hang out at some of the gourmet supermarkets in the swankier districts, shop (or pretend to) at the likes of Barneys of New York or the Beverly Center or eat at celeb haunts – the fashionable ones change monthly, but perennial favourites include Mortons, Musso & Frank, Formosa Café and Spago.

The only reliable way to stake out a star is to pick a dead one: Humphrey Bogart, Clark Gable, Walt Disney and Spencer Tracy push up the daisies in the Forest Lawn Cemetery in Glendale, Cecil B DeMille, Rudolph Valentino and Peter Lorre are in the Hollywood Memorial Cemetery at 6000 Santa Monica Boulevard, and Marilyn Monroe, Natalie Wood, Roy Orbison and Buddy Rich can be found at the Westwood Memorial Cemetery at 1218 Glendon Avenue.

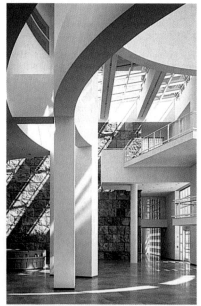

*The splendid **Getty Center**: see page 278.*

Where to eat & drink

Los Angeles was once a gastronomic wasteland, lagging far beyond the rest of California. But in the 1980s, a string of high-concept restaurants appeared, characterised by inventive décor, food and presentation, which won the city a place on the culinary map. Now, superchefs have become big business in the city and foodie mania is rife, with the result that Los Angeles has so many good restaurants that singling any out in a review here would be inappropriate.

All the major tourist districts have everything from branches of the fast-food chains to seriously upscale restaurants, as well as numerous coffee-houses and ethnic eateries (for more detail, consult the *Time Out Los Angeles Guide*, which lists a full selection). Another foodie delight are the farmers markets, scattered throughout the region, where chefs and home-cooks buy their supplies of local organic vegetables and freshly baked bread.

Where to stay

For a list of places to stay in LA, contact the **Los Angeles Convention & Visitors Bureau** or **Preferred Hotels & Resorts**. Contact numbers for the main US chain hotels are given on *page 129* **Accommodation**.

Preferred Hotels & Resorts Worldwide

10877 Wilshire Boulevard, suite 403, LA, CA 90024 (1-888 755 9876/fax 1-310 374 7025).

Tourist information

The essential guidebook to LA is the *Time Out Los Angeles Guide*, published by Penguin ($14.95/£9.99). The website www.at-la.com has the best internet links.

Los Angeles Visitor & Convention Bureau

685 S Figueroa Street, between Seventh Street & Wilshire Boulevard, Downtown, LA, CA 90017 (1-213 689 8822). I-110, exit Ninth Street east. **Open** 8am-5pm Mon-Fri; 8.30am-5pm Sat. Call or write for a visitor information pack.

The Janes House, Janes Square, 6541 Hollywood Boulevard, at Hudson Avenue, Hollywood (1-213 689 8822). US 101, exit Hollywood Boulevard west. **Open** 9am-5pm Mon-Sat.

Getting there

By car

Los Angeles is 293 miles (471km) from Las Vegas; the journey takes 5-6hrs, plus stops, depending on the traffic.

By bus

Greyhound operates a frequent service (every 30 mins to 1hr during the day) between Las Vegas and LA, costing $37 one-way, $72 return.

Welcome to the end of the earth? **Death Valley National Park.**

By air

Numerous airlines, including **United**, **Northwest** and **America West**, ply the oversubscribed LA route. Fares vary tremendously (from about $80 to $200 return) according to availability and time of year, but in general, the earlier you book, the better the price. Night flights are usually cheaper.

Death Valley National Park

The near-naked mountains, vast white salt lakes and blistering climate of Death Valley National Park are otherworldly, but then that's the point. This is a land of extremes. It is one of the hottest and driest places on earth: precipitation averages less than two inches (five centimetres) a year and the highest temperature in the US (and the world, for several years) – a mind-numbing 134°F (57°C) – was recorded here in 1913. The lowest point in the western hemisphere is here – near Badwater, at 282 feet (86 metres) below sea level – only 100 miles (160 kilometres) from the highest point in the US, the 14,494-foot (4,420-metre) high peak of Mount Whitney in the Sierra Nevada. An annual bicycle race takes place between the two.

Enlarged and redesignated as a national park under the 1994 Desert Protection Act, Death Valley is now the largest national park outside Alaska, covering more than 3.3 million acres (1.3 million hectares). Usually it's only Europeans who are mad enough to venture out here in the height of summer, when it can be hot enough to literally take your breath away and turn walking 20 yards from the air-conditioned safety of your car into a major ordeal. The air temperature in July and August

often tops 120°F (49°C) – the ground temperature can be 50 per cent higher – and lows average 90°F (32°C); now you know why Furnace Creek got its name. The best months to visit are October to March, though it can approach freezing at night in December and January. Entrance is $10 per car.

Although Death Valley is misnamed (only one pioneer actually died while trying to cross it), its reputation as a savage and life-threatening place is well deserved. It is reassuring to know that all the major car manufacturers test their vehicles in the extreme conditions here, but keep an eye on gauges and make sure you have enough petrol (available at Furnace Creek, Stovepipe Wells, Scotty's Castle and Panamint Springs). Roadside storage tanks hold radiator water. Check road conditions at the visitor centre, especially if you plan to drive any unpaved roads. Always carry plenty of water and take desert survival very seriously.

The visitor centre, with its 1950s exhibits and great bookshop, is at **Furnace Creek**, near the park's main accommodation and many of its best-known sights. A short drive east, you can walk around the ruins of **Harmony Borax Works**, from where the famous 20-mule teams used to haul wagons 165 miles (266 kilometres) across the desert to the nearest railroad. The eroded golden hills of nearby **Zabriskie Point** (named, rather prosaically, after a borax mine superintendent) are best seen at sunrise. Further south is the white expanse of **Badwater** (the mountainside sign marking sea level shows how low you are) and the road to the cool heights of **Dante's View**, which provides a spectacular view across blindingly white salt lakes to the Panamint Mountains.

Fifty miles (80 kilometres) north of Furnace Creek is the extravagant mansion of **Scotty's Castle**, built in the 1920s as a winter retreat for Chicago millionaire Albert Johnson. The castle is named after Johnson's eccentric and flamboyant friend Walter Scott, more commonly known as 'Death Valley Scotty'. Costumed rangers give tours of the interior (1-760 786 2392). Admission costs $8 for adults and $4 for children aged six to eleven. The tours are extremely popular, so while you wait your turn, you can explore the landscaped grounds containing Scotty's grave. Nearby is the 500-foot (152-metre) deep volcanic **Ubehebe Crater**. Other sights include the 700-foot (213-metre) high **Eureka sand dunes**, the **Wildrose charcoal kilns** and **Racetrack Valley**, a dry mud flat covered in faint trails left by large, probably wind-blown, boulders.

Although it's often too hot to hike in Death Valley, there are plenty of trails, short and long, including the strenuous 14-mile (23-kilometre) round-trip to the 11,000-foot (3,353-metre) high summit of **Telescope Peak**. A good summer hike (remember the higher you climb, the cooler it gets), the trail starts at Mahogany Flat campground and climbs 3,000 feet (914 metres) to spectacular views of Mount Whitney. In winter it should only be attempted by experienced climbers equipped with ice axes and crampons.

The Death Valley area is also littered with ghost towns and abandoned mines (watch your step). If you're heading into California on Highway 178, be sure to drop in on the tiny ghost town of **Ballarat**, set on the edge of the beautiful Panamint Valley.

En route to Death Valley

Leaving Las Vegas on Highway 160, you pass the straggly settlement of **Pahrump**, Nevada's fastest-growing rural town, home of the infamous Chicken Ranch whorehouse (Pahrump is just over the Nye County line, where prostitution is legal). Pahrump boasts three casinos, three motels, one traffic light and not much else, although you might want to visit **Pahrump Valley Vineyards** (1-775 727 6900), Nevada's only winery. To reach it turn right off Highway 160 at 3810 Winery Road (just past the town sign): the winery is the blue-roofed white building.

Opened in 1990, the vineyard produces almost 20,000 cases a year, mainly with grapes imported from California. You can join a free, half-hour tour and tasting (10am-4.30pm daily), eat in the good-value restaurant (open noon-3pm, 5-9pm, Wednesday to Sunday) or buy some wine ($7-$16 per bottle): best-seller is the white Symphony.

For more information on the area's numerous attractions, contact the friendly and helpful staff at the Chamber of Commerce (1-775 727 5800), also on Highway 160.

Where to eat

The Furnace Creek Inn's dining room is open to non-guests for breakfast, lunch and dinner (book for dinner) and afternoon tea is served daily in the lobby lounge. There are restaurants at Furnace Creek Ranch (open year round), Stovepipe Wells Village and Panamint Springs.

Where to stay

The main accommodation is at **Furnace Creek**. Further north **Stovepipe Wells Village** also has 83 rooms (1-760 786 2837; $53-$76), and at Death Valley Junction, you can stay at the atmospheric if shabby **Amargosa Opera House** (1-760 852 4441; $49-$59.95) and watch ballet performances by eccentric owner Marta Becket.

Furnace Creek Inn & Ranch Resort

PO Box 1, Death Valley, CA 92328 (Inn 1-760 786 2361/ranch & reservations 1-760 786 2345). **Rates** *Inn* $155-$350; *ranch cabins* $94-$99; *ranch rooms* $124-$149.
Set into the hillside above Furnace Creek Wash, the 1930s inn is the most luxurious place to stay in Death Valley, with 66 rooms, a swimming pool surrounded by date palms, a grand dining room and four tennis courts. Down the road, the more rustic Ranch has nearly 200 rooms and 28 cabins, an 18-hole golf course (the lowest in the world), a swimming pool, stables (open Oct-May), tennis courts, a bar, restaurant and store. Non-guests can use some of the facilities. Rates are cheapest from mid-May to mid-October.
Website: www.furnacecreekresort.com

Campgrounds

There are nine campgrounds in the park (some are accessible only by 4WD). Furnace Creek, Mesquite Spring and Wildrose are open all year. Most cost $10 per night. Check with the visitor centre for rules about backcountry camping.

Tourist information

Death Valley Visitor Center

Furnace Creek, Death Valley National Park, CA 92328 (1-760 786 2331). **Open** 8am-6pm daily. *Website: www.nps.gov/deva*

Getting there

There are a number of entrances to Death Valley from Nevada. From Las Vegas, the shortest route is south via the I-15 and Highway 160; a few miles after Pahrump take State Line Road to Death Valley Junction and Highway 190 into the park (120 miles/193 kilometres). Alternatively, head north on US 95, entering the southern end of the park from Amargosa Valley (via Highway 373 and Death Valley Junction), the centre from Beatty (via Highway 374) or the north from Scotty's Junction (via Highway 267). From the Mojave National Preserve, head north from Baker on Highway 127.

Into Utah

Refresh body and soul with the heavenly landscapes of Zion.

Utah, home to the Mormons and Little Jimmy Osmond, is an enormous state, with its capital, Salt Lake City, and upriver canyon country too far away to contemplate as day trips from Las Vegas. Despair not, for **Zion National Park** offers enough awe-inspiring landscapes to make even the most jaded pause for thought.

Zion National Park

A few hours north from Las Vegas on the I-15 lies Zion National Park, a glorious introduction to the spectacular canyon country of south-east Utah. Zion's 2,000-foot (610-metre) high cliffs and towering rock formations were discovered by early Mormon travellers in the 1880s. Originally called Mukuntuweap (loosely meaning 'like a quiver', a description of the shape of Zion Canyon), its name was changed to Zion in 1919 when it became a national park. Spring and autumn are ideal times to visit, with the wild flowers usually at their peak in May. In July and August, daytime temperatures can exceed 110°F (43°C) and brief thunderstorms are common in the afternoon. Winters are usually mild, with snow falling at higher elevations but rarely in Zion Canyon itself.

The main entrance to the park is in the south, at the small, pretty town of Springdale. Admission costs $20 per car, and the park's two campgrounds, new visitor centre (which opened in May 2000) and administrative offices lie just beyond the entrance.

Most of the sights and trails are accessible or visible from the six-mile (ten-kilometre), dead-end scenic drive through the gorge of Zion Canyon, along the edge of the Virgin River. The names of the vividly coloured Navajo sandstone monoliths along the drive echo the religious sensibilities of the area's first visitors: look out for the **Great White Throne**, the **Three Patriarchs**, **Angel's Landing**, the **Pulpit** and the **Temple of Sinawava**. Scan the rock faces and you may see tiny, ant-like figures clinging to the sheer cliffs: Zion is popular with climbers. Climbing routes are detailed in Eric Bjourstad's *Desert Rock – Rock Climbs in the National Parks* (Chockstone Press).

Entering the park from the east takes you through a completely different landscape from Zion Canyon. This is slickrock country: vast white, orange and pink rock formations, eroded into domes and buttes and marked with criss-cross patterns, loom next to the road. You can't miss the huge white monolith of **Checkerboard Mesa**. The twisting Zion-Mount Carmel Highway, an engineering miracle when it was built in 1930 and still very impressive, leads through two long, narrow tunnels to link up with the scenic drive. **Kolob Canyons**, in the north-western corner, and separate from the main park, has its own entrance (at exit 40 off the I-15), visitor centre and a five-mile (eight-kilometre) drive with some spectacular views of the red 'finger' canyons.

With more than 2.5 million visitors a year, most travelling in private cars, Zion is crowded all year round, but can be unbearable in summer. Vehicles wider than 7ft 10in (2m 39cm) or higher than 10ft 4in (3m 15cm) must be escorted ($10 per vehicle) through the Zion-Mount Carmel tunnel, which adds to delays. You don't so much hike as queue along the more popular trails.

To cope with the volume of visitors, half of whom spend less than four hours in the park, and to minimise pollution, noise and damage to vegetation, a new transport plan was implemented in May 2000. From March to October, the scenic drive is closed to private vehicles. Visitors have to leave

Zion Canyon and the Virgin River.

their cars at the south entrance or in Springdale, and then catch a (free) shuttle bus into the park. Guests of **Zion Lodge** (*see below*) are permitted to drive as far as the lodge. There are two bus loops, one with nine stops in Zion Canyon, the other with six stops in Springdale – you can get on and off as often as you want. The **Pa'rus Trail**, a short cycle path along the Virgin River, connects Zion Canyon to the visitor centre and the campgrounds.

There are plenty of maintained hiking trails off the scenic drive; the short easy routes along the valley floor (such as **Weeping Rock** and the **Riverside Walk**) are the busiest; head upwards to get away from the crowds. You get a fine view of lower Zion Canyon and Springdale at the end of the two-mile (3.2-kilometre) **Watchman** trail; shade is minimal, so go in the early morning or late afternoon. Many trails involve tough climbs and steep drop-offs. Don't attempt the five-mile (eight-kilometre) trail to **Angel's Landing** if you're afraid of heights; the last half mile follows a steep, narrow ridge fitted with chains – but the view is worth the heart palpitations.

Many people hike the **Narrows**, a section of the Virgin River where the canyon walls are up to 2,000 feet (610 metres) high and at times only 20 to 30 feet (six to eight metres) apart. The spectacular hike always involves wading, sometimes swimming, through cold water and can be dangerous in mid-summer when flash floods are likely. Late June, early July and September are the best months, but always check conditions at the visitor centre first. Hiking as far as Orderville Canyon takes about two hours from the end of the Riverside Walk; you need a permit for all-day or overnight hikes.

Horse rides are available at Zion Lodge and you can rent bikes in Springdale – try **Bike Zion** (1-435 772 3929; $23-$35 per day) – to explore the off-road trails and the nearby ghost town of **Grafton**, used in the movie *Butch Cassidy and the Sundance Kid.*

Where to eat

Springdale has plenty of cafés and restaurants but a shortage of bars (this is Utah, after all). Zion Lodge is open to non-guests; book for dinner.

Bit & Spur

1212 Zion Park Boulevard, Springdale (1-435 772 3498). **Open** (summer only) *restaurant* 5-9pm, *bar* 5pm-midnight, daily.
Smart Mexican restaurant with covered, outdoor seating. It offers the closest thing to a bar that you'll find in Springdale.

Oscar's Café & Deli

948 Zion Park Boulevard, Springdale (1-435 772 3232). **Open** *Mar-Nov* 7am-9pm daily; *Dec-Feb* 8am-8pm daily.
Friendly, laid-back little café just off the main drag. Pizzas, pastries, good coffee and six types of breakfast burrito ($5.50-$6.50). A good place for breakfast; sit on the patio and take in the views.

Where to stay

There are numerous places to stay in Springdale, ranging from cheap to top-dollar. Contact the **Zion Chamber of Commerce** (PO Box 331, Springdale, UT 84767; 1-888 518 7070) for details. Its website – www.zionpark.com – provides lots of useful information on sightseeing, dining and other activities, as well as a list of accommodation options. Inside the park are two campgrounds ($14) and Zion Lodge. Book in advance.

Cliffrose Lodge & Gardens

281 Zion Park Boulevard, Springdale, UT 84767 (1-800 243 8824/1-435 772 3234). **Rates** *May-Oct* $119-$145.
A pricey but pretty place, with gardens stretching down to the Virgin River and a large swimming pool. Child-friendly. Rates are 50% less in winter.

El Rio Lodge

995 Zion Park Boulevard, PO Box 204, Springdale, UT 84767 (1-888 772 3205/1-435 772 3205/ elrio@infowest.com). **Rates** *May-Oct* $47-$52; *Nov-Apr* $35-$39.
A ten-room, two-storey motel run by a friendly local couple. There's no garden, but prices are good and the views great.
Website: www.elriolodge.qpg.com

O'Toole's Under the Eaves

980 Zion Park Boulevard, Springdale, UT 84767 (1-435 772 3457/otooles@southernutah.com). **Rates** *Mar-Oct* $60-$125; *Nov-Feb* $55-$95.
This cute, clean B&B (open year round) has six rooms, including a splendid en suite studio attic and a cabin in the back garden. Rates include breakfast.
Website: www.otooles.com

Zion Lodge

Reservations 1-303 297 2757/front desk 1-435 772 3213/fax 1-435 772 2001). **Rates** *motel* $85; *cabin* $95; *lodge suite* $116.
This rustic-style lodge is set in the centre of the park. Built in 1925 by the Union Pacific Railroad, it was renovated in the 1980s. There are also 40 cabins and a motel – 121 rooms in all. For rooms from April to October, book about five months ahead.
Website: www.amfac.com

Tourist information

Zion Canyon Visitor Center

Springdale, UT 84767 (recorded information 1-435 772 3256). **Open** *summer* 8am-7pm daily; closes earlier in winter.
Website: www.nps.gov/zion

Getting there

To reach the main entrance to the park (164 miles/ 264 kilometres from Vegas), take the I-15 north through the pleasant Mormon town of St George and turn right on to Highway 9. To visit the Kolob Canyons area of the park, continue for 25 miles (40 kilometres) on the I-15.

Directory

Directory

Las Vegas facts and figures: essential information for every visitor.

For information on the abbreviations used in this guide, *see page vi* **About the Guide**. If you're calling from outside Nevada, you will need to prefix all telephone numbers in Clark County with 1-702 and numbers in the rest of the state with 1-775. All 1-800 numbers given are free within Las Vegas, most are free within the US and many are available from outside the country (though you will be charged for the call).

Getting Around

Unless, like almost half of visitors to Las Vegas, you drive your own car into town, you will need to decide whether or not to rent one. The main factors in your decision should be the time of year (walking more than a short distance in summer is uncomfortable at best), whether you plan on visiting any out of town destinations (few are served by public transport) and where you are staying. If you're based on the Strip (Las Vegas Boulevard South), and don't plan to venture far from it, a combination of walking, buses, taxis and shuttle services will get you around pretty cheaply and efficiently, and save you from the tourist traffic. On the other hand, car hire is usually relatively cheap, both self- and valet parking are free and outside rush hour you can get from one end of town to the other in 30 minutes.

It's almost impossible to get lost in Las Vegas, especially at night, when the lights of the Strip casinos are visible for miles in any direction. You soon learn to get your bearings from the Stratosphere Tower at the far north of the Strip, the green-lit MGM Grand to the south and the squat pink and purple Rio to the west. Cross streets are clearly marked with overhead signs that indicate the street numbers to either side. It

also helps that four of the major east-west thoroughfares – Tropicana Avenue, Flamingo Road, Desert Inn Road and Sahara Avenue – are named after the hotels located where those streets cross the Strip.

Free city maps are available from most hotels, rental car agencies and visitor centres. The *Rand McNally Las Vegas EasyFinder* ($5.95) has larger print than most maps and is laminated, for easy folding and unfolding. Although maps are updated frequently, remember they may not show all the newest casinos or roads. Compass's Las Vegas map is one of the more recent.

Knowing where to go is one thing; getting there can be something else entirely. The construction of highways and the expansion of surface streets haven't kept pace with the unprecedented increase in both residents and visitors flocking to Las Vegas, resulting in some serious rush-hour congestion. In a tourist destination where most of the major attractions are located on one of two streets (the Strip and Fremont Street), you might expect to find a subway running beneath the gridlocked traffic – but you don't. A monorail system has been in development for more than a decade, but political squabbling over the cost, the route and which casinos will

get the stations has resulted in perpetual delays. However, the city's bus service is constantly expanding, supplemented by a variety of hotel shuttles.

To & from the airport

Las Vegas has grown so fast that **McCarran International Airport** (261 5211/www. mccarran.com), unlike most airports attached to major cities, now finds itself in the centre of town, just five minutes from the south end of the Strip. This makes arriving in Las Vegas thankfully free of the usual headaches of getting from airport to hotel. Clean, modern and well designed, McCarran comes on as an aeronautically themed casino, taking first (and last) tilt at the tourist dollar with halls full of slot machines and video poker. It added 26 new gates in 1998.

International flight service into Las Vegas is still limited. Currently, there are five direct weekly flights from Tokyo to Las Vegas aboard **Japan Air**, and **Virgin Atlantic** starts twice-weekly flights from the UK's Gatwick Airport on 8 June 2000. For airline phone numbers, *see page 290* **Airlines**.

Buses

Public bus routes 108 and 109 run north from the airport, but neither go up the Strip. If you're heading for the area east of the Strip, the 108 heads north up Swenson Street and stops at the Las Vegas Hilton; the 109 goes along Maryland Parkway.

Private shuttle buses to the Strip and Downtown hotels are available outside the arrivals terminal and run 24 hours daily. Reservations are advised for the trip from the airport (just pick up the appropriate courtesy phone on arrival) and required for the trip back. Fares are less than $5 each way to the Strip and slightly more to Downtown. Call **Bell Trans** (739 7990) or **Gray Line** (739 5700).

Taxis & limousines

Bell Trans also runs a limo service. Taxis can be found immediately outside the arrivals terminal: expect to pay $9-$12 to get to most hotels on the Strip, about $15 to Downtown.

Public transport

The only form of public transport is the bus system, run by **Citizens Area Transit** (**CAT**), with 45 scheduled routes throughout the Las Vegas Valley and the outlying cities of Laughlin and Mesquite. Buses run 24 hours between Downtown and the Strip; from about 5.30am to 1.30am on other routes. For route and schedule information, call 228 7433 or visit the **Downtown Transportation Center** (**DTC**) at Stewart Avenue and Casino Center Boulevard (open 6am-10pm Mon-Fri; 6am-6pm Sat, Sun), the central transfer point for many routes.

CAT buses are safe and as comfortable as a bus can get and relatively comprehensive in their coverage of the city. All can take both bicycles and wheelchairs. Racks inside the front of buses carry maps/ timetables, although they're often empty.

Bus routes

The CAT bus network is scrambling frantically to keep pace with the growth of the city, and services are continually being added or frequency improved. Routes tend to go along one street without deviation, either north-south or east-west, so you will probably have to change buses if you're going from one corner of the city to another.

The most useful bus for tourists is the 24-hour **301**, which travels the length of Las Vegas Boulevard from Downtown in the north to Vacation Village hotel at Sunset Road in the south, stopping in front of all major hotels. It leaves the DTC at ten-minute intervals from 5.30am to midnight, and at 15-minute intervals thereafter. As is the way of buses everywhere, 301s tend to get bunched up in the traffic, so you may have to wait longer. When one does come, you may not be able to get on: they are often overcrowded, especially in the late afternoon/ early evening. The **302** evening express service (every 15 minutes, 6pm-1am) follows the same route along the Strip but makes fewer stops.

For detailed info, check the website **www.rtc.co.clark. nv.us/cat/cat.htm**. For a **bus route map**, *see page 313*.

A more colourful alternative is the privately run **Strip Trolley**, which runs every 20 minutes from 9.30am to 2.30am down the Strip, stopping at all major hotels, the Fashion Show Mall, Wet 'n' Wild water park and the Las Vegas Hilton. Unlike the CAT buses, the trolley picks up and drops off passengers at the front door of some hotels, instead of on the street outside. They are no less crowded than the city buses, but the experience has a more congenial, 'touristy' feel, if that's what you want. Call 382 1404 for more information.

For details of free hotel shuttles, *see page 288* **Shuttles & monorails**.

Fares & bus stops

Most CAT routes cost $1.25 for adults and 60¢ for seniors, 6-17s and disabled passengers. Exact fare is required, as, irritatingly, are photocards for all concessions (available from the DTC with the appropriate certification). The 301-302 route along the Strip costs $2 for all passengers. Transfers are free; you must ask for one when you pay the fare. Bus stops are marked by white, green and purple signs bearing the feline CAT logo; most have shelters to provide relief from the scorching summer sun, though they're often full.

An exact fare of $1.50 is required for the Strip Trolley. Ask at your hotel front desk if it is on the trolley route; if so, it will stop at the main entrance.

Tokens & passes

Most visitors aren't in town long enough to justify the purchase of a 30-day reduced fare pass but they are available for $30 either in person from the DTC or by mail (processing takes seven to ten days, money order only). Tokens are a better bet for short-term visitors: they're sold in bags of 40 for $20; you need two for an adult fare (four on the 301 or 302 buses) and one for children, saving about 25 per cent.

Taxis & limos

There are taxi ranks outside most hotels and throughout tourist areas, and restaurants and bars will be happy to call a cab for you. Note that taxis are tougher to find when there's a major convention in town and on New Year's Eve and holiday weekends, and there may be a long wait if you're calling from outside the tourist areas. Technically, you can't hail a

Shuttles & monorails

Instead of taking the bus or driving, you can travel around Las Vegas for free on numerous hotel shuttle buses and four monorails. If they don't take you direct to the casino you want, they'll take you within walking distance.

For instance, the most useful monorail links **Bally's** and the **MGM Grand** (9am-1am daily). If you disembark at Bally's, you'll be within striking distance of the Barbary Coast, Caesars Palace and the Flamingo Hilton. And from the MGM, you can walk to the Excalibur, New York-New York, the Tropicana and Luxor. The other monorails operate 24 hours and link **Monte Carlo** and **Bellagio**; the **Mirage** and **Treasure Island**; and the **Excalibur**, **Luxor** and **Mandalay Bay** – but in all cases, it's often quicker to walk.

As for shuttle buses, the **Barbary Coast** has a shuttle to the Gold Coast, a mile west of the Strip on Flamingo Road (and opposite the Rio), and to the Orleans in South-west Las Vegas. The **Rio**'s own shuttle runs from a small building on the east side of the Strip, just south of the Aladdin.

The **Stratosphere**, aware of its out-of-the-way location, runs a shuttle to and from the Strip, while the **Hard Rock**'s shuttle travels in a loop to the Stardust, Fashion Show Mall, Forum Shops, Tropicana and back to the Hard Rock. Useful places to pick up shuttles are the **Fashion Show Mall** and the **Tropicana**. The **Sam's Town** shuttle bus is the most efficient and gives you access to just about every other shuttle in town.

taxi from the street, although it's acceptable to approach an empty cab with its light on if it's stopped in traffic. Meters start at $2.20, and increase by $1.50 per subsequent mile. The most prominent taxi firms in town are **Checker**, **Star**, **Yellow Cab** (all on 873 2000) and **Whittlesea** (384 6111).

Limousines vary from the basic black stretch at about $40 an hour to flamboyant party-venues-on-wheels complete with a fully stocked bar, TV and VCR and formally dressed chauffeur. Companies include **Bell Trans** (385 5466), **Las Vegas Limo** (1-888 696 4400) and **Presidential** (731 5577). Many limos are available for hire outside hotels as well, and if you are in a large group on a busy night, the cost is worth avoiding the long taxi line.

Driving

If you're visiting Las Vegas for two or three days and wander only from one casino to another (as most tourists do), it's possible to get by on foot and bus. For exploring the rest of the city or travelling out of town, you'll need to rent a car.

Though many streets in Las Vegas are smoother and wider than in most urban centres, growth rates mean you'll have to navigate construction zones in every corner of the city. Streets get very congested in the morning and evening rush hours (7-9am, 4-7pm). At weekends, the number of visitors increases dramatically and traffic is much heavier in tourist areas after 4pm. The Strip is slow-going most of the time and turns into a virtual parking lot when the town is crowded: avoid it if possible after 6pm on weekends and keep in mind that many of the cars you're sharing it with are driven by other visitors who are equally unfamiliar with their surroundings.

Locals never drive the Strip unless that's their destination, and tourists in a hurry would do well to do the same. The nearby parallel streets – Industrial Road to the west and Paradise Road to the east – move a bit faster, and provide access to the back entrances of several casinos. For north-south journeys that are longer than a block or so, it's often worth getting on the I-15, which runs

parallel to the Strip. If you're trying to get across town, aim for the fast-moving Desert Inn arterial, a mini-expressway that runs under Las Vegas Boulevard and over the I-15 (no junctions at either).

The north-south I-15 intersects with the east-west US 95 just north-west of Downtown at the always-congested and confusing 'Spaghetti Bowl' (though major improvements are under way). US 95 connects to the 53-mile (80km) beltway under construction, which will eventually (by 2003) transport commuters around the entire Las Vegas Valley. Portions of the beltway (such as the I-215 airport connector) are already in use.

Rules of the road

You can turn right on a red light after stopping, if the street is clear. U-turns are not only legal (unless otherwise specified) but often a positive necessity given the long blocks and, on the Strip at least, few breaks in the median. Speed limits throughout town are 35mph (56kph), unless otherwise marked. School zones and construction zones, marked by signs and sometimes flashing lights, are strictly enforced and fines are doubled.

Parking

Self-parking is plentiful, and free, at every Vegas resort and attraction (Downtown casinos require a validation stamp). Most hotels also have valet parking, which is convenient, safe and free (apart from the $1-$2 tip to the valet on your way out). If you see a sign saying valet parking is full, and you're driving a Jag, Mercedes or other luxury car, stay put: chances are they'll find an empty spot. If you're a guest of the hotel, you will also get preferential treatment. Alternatively, flash your cash – a $5, $10 or $20 bill (depending on how busy it is) will get you a spot no matter what the sign says.

Self-parking lots vary in their convenience. Some, such as Caesars', lead you directly to the action; some, such as at the Rio and Sahara, require a fair schlepp. Valeting is therefore the best option if time is a factor; if, for example, you're going to see a show – but bear in mind that you'll have to wait longer to have your car returned if hundreds of people disgorged from the same showroom are waiting in line (tips when handing in your ticket will help here, too).

Car rental

Most of the major car rental agencies are located at or near McCarran Airport, with other branches scattered around town. Call around to find the best rate, and book well in advance if you're planning to visit over a holiday weekend or to attend a major convention – the city has been known to run out of cars. Conversely, at times when business renters are scarce, you should get a good rate – and it's definitely worth asking for an upgrade.

If your hotel has a car-rental desk, start there; if not, ask the concierge, who can often get a good rate from a local firm (the car will be delivered to you, or, more likely, a shuttle will take you to the lot).

Almost every rental agency will require a credit card and a matching driver's licence, and few will rent to anyone under 25. The price quoted will not include tax, liability insurance or collision damage waiver (CDW), which could double the daily rental rate. Ask about discounts, available to members of the AAA (which extend to British AA members), AARP and other corporations and organisations. Travel agents often get a particularly worthwhile discount. Also keep an eye out for coupons.

National car rental companies

Alamo *1-800 327 9633*
Website: www.freeways.com
Avis *1-800 331 1212*
Website: www.avis.com
Budget *736 1212*
Website: www.budgetrentacar.com
Dollar *739 8408*
Website: www.dollarcar.com
Enterprise *1-800 736 8222*
Website: www.pickenterprise.com
Hertz *1-800 654 3131*
Website: www.hertz.com
National *1-800 227 7368*
Website: www.nationalcar.com
Thrifty *896 7600*
Website: www.thrifty.com

Local car rental companies

Some local companies have more flexible policies than their national counterparts, and sometimes offer better rates. **A-Fairway Rent-A-Car** (369 8533) and **X-Press International** (795 4008) accept cash deposits instead of a credit card, and have no age restriction. And for those who want to make their Vegas entrance in appropriately flashy style, **Rent-A-Vette** (736 2592) rents Corvettes, Porsches, Vipers, Ferraris and the like. Well-reputed local company **Allstate** (736 6147) is strong on heavy-

duty off-road vehicles and pick-up trucks. The Las Vegas franchise of **Rent-A-Wreck** (474 0037) has year-old models at great prices, and offers the cheapest insurance we found.

Motorcycle rental

If you're planning on getting off the Strip and into the desert during your visit (and you really should), what better way to do it than on a hog? Many of these places listed below are located on the Strip or at the airport, or both. Most offer unlimited mileage, insurance, helmets and anything else you'll need to get your motor runnin' so you can head out on the highway.

Eaglerider *876 8687;* **Easyriders** *368 7808;* **Harley-Davidson of Southern Nevada** *431 8500;* **North American Motorcycle Tours** *434 0200.*

RV rental

Renting an RV will cost about $400 for three days and between $800 and $1,000 for a week, depending on the size of the vehicle. **Cruise America** (456 6666) has everything from 18ft (5.5m) camper homes to 30ft (9m) RVs. Call ahead for a brochure, which comes with a ten per cent money-off coupon. **RVN4Fun** (254 0770/www.rvn4fun.com) has 125 US and Canada locations.

Walking

No one would call Las Vegas a foot-friendly city. Pedestrians are rarely seen off the Strip, and even there they face more dangers than they should have to, resulting in some nasty accident statistics (48 pedestrians, many of them tourists, were killed in Clark County in 1999). Walking the Strip, they are constantly crossing entrance and exit roads; crossing from one side to another, they have the choice of a long walk to the next cross

Directory

street or a dangerous dash across ten lanes of traffic. The practice is so deadly that police issue jaywalking citations on a regular basis. From one Strip hotel to the next, walking is perfectly possible, but can be frustrating: trying to take a short cut often gets you trapped in a maze of service roads.

Fortunately, pedestrian bridges across the Strip are being built at a rapid rate. There is a bridge between Bellagio and Bally's and, at the intersection of the Strip with Tropicana, you can only cross by pedestrian bridges, which (of course) guide you past the entrances of the four casinos on its corners.

Don't underestimate distances if you're walking along the Strip, especially on hot days. You are, after all, in the desert.

Cycling

Las Vegas was recently named one of the 'Top 10 Worst Bicycling Cities in the Nation'. The road system (except in Summerlin) is designed solely for the car driver, and bikes are such a rarity that drivers forget to check for their existence. The only people who cycle here are security guards and people with a death wish. Bike rental outlets are aimed at leisure riders planning out-of-town excursions – there are some great desert rides in the vicinity (*see page 236* **Sport & Fitness**).

Resources A-Z

Emergencies

Ambulance, fire, police (emergency)
911 (free from public phones)

Police (non-emergency)
795 3111

Rape Crisis
366 1640

Suicide Prevention
731 2990

Poison Control Center
732 4989

Airlines

Air Canada
1-800 776 3000

American Airlines
Domestic 1-800 433 7300

America West
1-800 235 9292

British Airways
1-800 247 9297

Canadian Airlines International
1-800 426 7000

Continental Airlines
domestic 1-800 523 3273/ international 1-800 231 0856

Delta Airlines
domestic 1-800 221 1212/ international 1-800 241 4141

Northwest Airlines
domestic 1-800 225 2525/ international 1-800 447 4747

Reno Air
1-800 736 6247

Southwest Airlines
1-800 435 9792

TWA
1-800 221 2000

United Airlines
1-800 241 6522

US Airways
1-800 428 4322

Virgin Atlantic
1-800 862 8621

Attitude & attire

Despite a glamorous past, Las Vegas the tourist city is as formal or informal as you want it to be, and universally friendly. During the warmer months, shorts and T-shirts are accepted wear along the Strip and in most casinos, though in recent years, dressing up to a minimum of smart-casual has again become the norm for a night out. Some higher-end lounges and restaurants have dress codes (sports shoes, T-shirts and baggy jeans are not popular), and dining can be quite formal.

Business

Las Vegas used to be a one-industry town, if you can call hedonism an industry. Gambling and tourism remain the city's most prominent enterprises, in both revenue and employment. The casinos and resorts are open around the clock and require thousands of workers on three eight-hour shifts. As a result, grocery stores, dry-cleaners and gas stations are open 24 hours, to accommodate the workers who have to do their chores in the middle of the night.

Though tourism has been thriving for more than a decade, the Las Vegas business community has recognised the need for economic diversification, and its efforts have been successful, particularly in manufacturing – from wood, plastic and rubber products to, not surprisingly, gambling equipment – trade and distribution. The state's economic development authorities have attracted hundreds of companies to Southern Nevada – the climate and favourable tax structure argue eloquently on their behalf. Recent arrivals include Citibank and Ocean Spray.

In general, the business approach is less aggressive than in New York or Los Angeles. There is no provincial favouritism, because nine out of ten Las Vegans are originally from somewhere else. For some reason, though, it's difficult to get a phone call returned, so don't feel reluctant about calling twice in the same day.

For details of the **Las Vegas Chamber of Commerce** and the **Las Vegas Convention & Visitors Authority**, *see page 299* **Tourist information**.

Nevada Development Authority

Hughes Center, 3773 Howard Hughes Parkway South, between Sands Avenue & E Flamingo Road, East of Strip (791 0000). Bus 108, 203. **Open** 8am-5pm Mon-Fri. *Website: www.nevadadevelopment. org*

Communications

Accurate Communications
2101 S Decatur Boulevard, suite 21, between W Sahara Avenue & Oakey Boulevard, South-west Las Vegas (259 1520). Bus 103, 204. **Open** *office* 8am-5pm Mon-Fri. **No credit cards.**
Users can call in and receive messages from a secretary or voicemail box. AC will also fax messages to a specified location, or relay them to an pager.

Cellular City
4720 S Polaris Avenue, at Tompkins Avenue, West of Strip (873 2489). Bus 203. **Open** *office* 8.30am-5pm Mon-Fri; *phone lines* 24hrs daily. **Credit** AmEx, DC, Disc, JCB, MC, V.
Rents cellular phones by the day or week, and will even deliver the phone to your hotel.

Computer rental

Bit-by-Bit
3400 Desert Inn Road, at Polaris Avenue, West of Strip (474 6311). Bus 105. **Open** 9am-5pm Mon-Fri. **Credit** AmEx, MC, V.
The place to rent PCs, Macs, notebooks, LCD panels and printers. Same-day delivery. *Website: www.bit-by-bit.com*

Inacom Computer Rentals
3111 S Valley View Road, West of Strip (1-800 999 9899/367 6742). No bus. **Open** 8am-5pm Mon-Fri. **Credit** AmEx, MC, V.
Daily, weekly and monthly rates, with local installation, set-up and pick-up. *Website: www.inacomrentals.com*

Conventions

Several cities, among them New York and Chicago, have claimed to be the 'Convention Capital of the World', but when judged by sheer volume of convention business, Las Vegas has no competition. The numbers speak for themselves: in 1998 (the last year for which figures are available), the city played host to nearly 4,000 trade shows, attended by 3.3 million delegates. Most of the largest conventions in existence are held in Las Vegas, including the Consumer Electronics Show (100,000 delegates), the National Association of Broadcasters (90,000 delegates), the Specialty Equipment Marketing Association (60,000 delegates) and the huge computer industry show Comdex (225,000 delegates).

In addition to the convention centres detailed below, almost every hotel has some designated convention area for smaller-scale events, including local business meetings and corporate lunches.

Even with all those rooms, however, it is advisable to book early and to call around for the best rate. Some hotels offer discounts to convention delegates, but others raise their prices, to offset the perceived frugality of convention attendees. A popular local joke is that Comdex delegates arrive in town with a clean white shirt and a clean $20 bill, and never change either one.
For further information, consult **www.lasvegas24hours.com/calendar/index.html**

Cashman Field Center
850 Las Vegas Boulevard North, at Washington Avenue, North Las Vegas (386 7100). Bus 113.
Located just north of Downtown, Cashman Field is used only for smaller events.

Las Vegas Convention Center
3150 Paradise Road, opposite Convention Center Drive, East of Strip (892 0711). Bus 108.
The largest single-level convention and meeting facility in the US, and still growing every few years. After the most recent expansion, completed in 1998, the facility now comprises a total of 1.9 million sq ft (176,700sq m), more than one million of which are available for exhibitions. There are 91 meeting rooms, with seating capacities ranging from 200 to 2,000. The on-site business centre provides access to computers, fax machines, telephones and courier services. Parking is extremely limited, so walk if you're staying in the area, or use hotel shuttles. *Website: www.lasvegas24hours.com*

Sands Expo & Convention Center
210 Sands Avenue, at Koval Lane, East of Strip (733 5556). Bus 203.
Second in size to the Las Vegas Convention Center, this facility offers the same state-of-the-art amenities, with even worse parking frustrations.

Convention dates
Consumer Electronics Show
1-10 Jan 2001; 8-11 Jan 2002 (125,000 delegates).

Men's Apparel Guild in California
14-17 Feb 2000; 29-31 Aug 2000; 13-16 Feb 2001; 27-30 Aug 2001 (75,000).

National Association of Broadcasters
10-13 Apr 2000; 23-26 Apr 2001 (90,000).
A good time for star-gazing.

Specialty Equipment Market Association/APAA/ASIA/MEMA
31 Oct-3 Nov 2000 (65,000).
Automobile accessories and hundreds of flashy custom cars.

Comdex
13-17 Nov 2000; 12-16 Nov 2001 (225,000).

Couriers

The courier services listed below all offer worldwide delivery. Each service has drop-off points throughout the city. If you're attending a convention, there will probably be a drop-off box on site, and many of the big hotels have business centres with courier services.

Airborne Express
1-800 247 2676. **Open** 8am-5pm Mon-Fri; 8am-noon Sat. **No credit cards.**

Federal Express (FedEx)
1-800 463 3339. **Open** 9am-5.30pm Mon-Sat. **Credit** AmEx, DC, Disc, MC, V.

United Parcel Service (UPS)

1-800 742 5877. **Open** 8.30am-5.30pm Mon-Fri. **Credit** AmEx, MC, V.

Libraries

For a complete list of Las Vegas's libraries, *see page 199* **Culture**.

Lied Library

4505 S Maryland Parkway, between E Flamingo Road & Tropicana Avenue, University District (895 3531). Bus 109, 201, 202. **Open** 7am-midnight Mon-Thur; 7am-6pm Fri; 9am-9pm Sat; 10am-midnight Sun.
Scheduled to open in 2000, UNLV's $40-million Lied Library comprises the most expensive public-works building project in Nevada's history. The facility (which replaces the Dickinson Library) houses 1.8 million volumes, and is serviced by an automatic book retrieval system. It's the best library in Las Vegas, but call first to make sure it's open – hours vary with the university's class schedule.

Chances are you'll find everything you need here, except for a place to park: most of the spaces are reserved for students or faculty members. Look for the handful of spaces with parking meters and bring plenty of quarters. The next best library is Clark County, located five minutes west of the university at 1401 E Flamingo Road (733 7810). *Website: www.library.nevada.edu*

Office equipment & services

Kinko's

The Promenade, 4440 S Maryland Parkway, at Harmon Avenue, University District (1-800 800 8899/735 4402). Bus 109, 213. **Open** 24hrs daily. **Credit** AmEx, Disc, MC, V.
America's most prominent chain of copy shops, although half the self-service machines are usually out of order. There are six locations in Las Vegas, all open 24 hours – except the Fourth Street branch in Downtown (open 6am-11pm daily). Services include on-site use of computers, typesetting, printing, fax and

phone facilities, as well as courier service via FedEx.
Branches: 4750 W Sahara Avenue (870 7011); 830 S Fourth Street (383 7022); 2288 S Nellis Boulevard (431 5076); 7208 W Lake Mead Boulevard, Summerlin (255 7141); The Galleria at Sunset Mall, 671 Mall Ring Circle, Green Valley (436 7370).
Website: www.kinkos.com

Officemax

Sahara Pavilion South, 2640 S Decatur Boulevard, at Sahara Avenue, South-west Las Vegas (221 0471). Bus 103, 204. **Open** 7am-9pm Mon-Fri; 9am-9pm Sat; 10am-6pm Sun.
Credit AmEx, Disc, MC, V.
Phone 1-800 788 8080 to find your nearest of Officemax's seven Las Vegas locations. Each store carries a full line of office supplies, computers, furniture and business machines.
Website: www.office.com

Consulates

The only countries with a consulate in Las Vegas are Ecuador (735 8193), Germany (734 9700) and Italy (385 6843). Nationals of other countries will either have to call their Los Angeles consulate (listed below) or ask directory assistance for the number of the Washington office (directory assistance for Washington is 1-202 555 1212).
Canada *1-213 346 2700;* **Spain** *1-213 938 0158;* **Japan** *1-213 617 6700;* **United Kingdom** *1-310 477 3322/1-213 856 3755 24hr emergency number.*

Consumer

For gambling-specific complaints against casinos, call the Enforcement department of the **Gaming Control Board** on 486 2000.

Better Business Bureau

5595 Spring Mountain Road, Las Vegas, NV 89104 (320 4500).
This private agency can give you a report on the background of businesses and review written complaints.

Consumer Affairs Division

1805 E Sahara Avenue, Las Vegas, NV 89104 (486 7355).
The state division overseeing correct business practices.

Disabled & elderly

Las Vegas is a very disabled-friendly city: most of its buildings are relatively new, and the casinos have always relied on luring a sizeable elderly clientele. In addition, they complied swiftly with the Americans with Disabilities Act for fear of losing their gambling licences. Hence all Strip casino resorts are fully wheelchair-accessible, from their pools, spas and toilets through to their gambling and parking facilities (things are a little harder in the older properties Downtown). A handful, notably **Caesars Palace**, also offer games designed for sight- and hearing-impaired players. Disabled parking is ubiquitous and both buses and many taxis are adapted to take wheelchairs (ask when you book).

The New York-based **Society for the Advancement of Travel for the Handicapped** (1-212 447 7284/fax 1-212 725 8253) can offer advice for disabled people planning trips to all parts of the United States.

Southern Nevada Center for Independent Living

6200 W Oakey Boulevard, at Jones Avenue, South-west Las Vegas (870 7050 inc TDD). Bus 205. **Open** 8am-5pm Mon-Fri.
Services SNCIL offers that are relevant to visitors include advice, information, counselling, transport and equipment loan (including wheelchairs). It can also refer you to other disabled organisations and support groups.

Electricity & appliances

Rather than the 220-240V, 50-cycle AC used in Europe, Las Vegas and the United

States use a 110-120V, 60-cycle AC voltage. Except for dual-voltage, flat-pin plug shavers, most foreign visitors will need to run any small appliances brought with them via an adaptor, available at airport shops. Bear in mind that most US videos and TVs use a different frequency from those in Europe: you will not be able to play back camcorder footage during your trip. However, you can buy and use blank tapes.

Health & medical

Abortion, contraception & STDs

Planned Parenthood
3220 W Charleston Boulevard, between Rancho Drive & Valley View Boulevard, North-west Las Vegas (878 7776). Bus 206. **Open** *by appointment only* 9am-6pm Mon; 9am-5pm Tue; 10am-6pm Wed; 9am-4pm Thur, Fri; 9am-2pm Sat.
This non-profit organisation can supply contraception (including the morning-after pill), treat STDs, perform abortions and test for AIDS (results take a week). You'll need an appointment for everything except a pregnancy test.

Dentists

Southern Nevada Dental Society
733 8700
Referrals, including Medicaid and Medicare practitioners.

Hospitals

All hospitals listed below have 24-hour emergency rooms.

Desert Springs Hospital
2075 E Flamingo Road, at Burnham Street, East Las Vegas (733 8800). Bus 202.

Lake Mead Hospital Medical Center
1409 E Lake Mead Boulevard, between Las Vegas Boulevard, North & Eastern Avenues, North Las Vegas (649 7711). Bus 113, 210.

St Rose Dominican Hospital
102 E Lake Mead Drive, at Boulder Highway, Henderson (564 2622). Bus 107, 212.
A non-profit hospital that never turns patients away. No trauma unit.

Summerlin Hospital Medical Center
657 Town Center Drive, at Hulapai Way, North-west Las Vegas (233 7000). No bus.
Las Vegas's newest hospital, with excellent maternity care.

Sunrise Hospital & Medical Center
3186 S Maryland Parkway, between Sahara Avenue & Desert Inn Road, East Las Vegas (731 8000). Bus 109.
Nevada's largest hospital has a poison control centre and a children's hospital.

University Medical Center
1800 W Charleston Boulevard, at Shadow Lane (383 2000). Bus 206.
The only hospital in Las Vegas that by law must treat all applicants. It's a good one, too. The ER entrance is on the corner of Hasting and Rose Streets.

Valley Hospital Medical Center
620 Shadow Lane, off Charleston Boulevard, between Rancho Drive & Martin Luther King Boulevard (388 4000). Bus 206.

Pharmacies

All-night pharmacies are rife: they're listed in the Yellow Pages under 'Pharmacies'. All branches of **Sav-on** are open 24 hours daily; closest to the Strip are the branches at 2300 E Tropicana Avenue (736 4174) and 1360 E Flamingo Road (731 5373).

Walgreen Drug Store
1111 Las Vegas Boulevard South, at Charleston Boulevard (417 6844). **Open** 24hrs daily.

White Cross Drugs
1700 Las Vegas Boulevard South, at Oakey Boulevard (382 1733). Bus 301, 302. **Open** *store* 24hrs daily; *pharmacy* 7.30am-1am daily. **Credit** AmEx, Disc, MC, V.
Centrally located drugstore and pharmacy with a delivery service.

Helplines & agencies

Addiction

Alcoholics Anonymous
598 1888
Gamblers Anonymous
385 7732
Narcotics Anonymous
369 3362

AIDS/HIV

See also page 226 **Nightlife: Gay & lesbian**.

Aid for AIDS of Nevada
382 2326/hotline 474 2437
Clark County Health District
385 1291
Nevada AIDS Hotline
474 2437/1-800 842 2437

Legal

If you are arrested, use your phone call to call either your insurance company's emergency number, your consulate or the referral service listed below. If you do not have a lawyer, the court will appoint one for you.

State Bar of Nevada Lawyer Referral Service
382 0504. **Open** *telephone enquiries* 9am-4pm Mon-Fri.
For a fee of $45, you will be referred to an attorney who specialises in a specific field.

Immigration & customs

Though direct flights are plentiful from Tokyo and are scheduled to start from London in June 2000, few international flights arrive in Las Vegas. You will usually have to change at another US city, and will go through Immigration and Customs there. This means that you can't check your baggage straight through: you will have to reclaim it at the transfer airport, take it through Customs and then check it in again. The airlines try to make this a painless process by having a transfer check-in desk just outside Customs at most major transfer airports; however, you will have to make

Directory

your own way to the domestic departures terminal. Connection times do take account of this, and the fact that you may have to queue at Immigration, but we suggest you go through the transfer process and check in for your Las Vegas flight before you take any time to relax.

The flight attendant on your flight to the US should have given you two forms, one for Immigration, one for Customs. Make sure you've filled them in accurately, front and back, or you'll risk another long wait in line. Hand them in at the appropriate desk.

US customs regulations allow foreign visitors to import the following, duty-free: 200 cigarettes or 50 cigars (not Cuban; over-18s only) or 2kg of smoking tobacco; one litre (1.05 US quart) of wine or spirits (over-21s only); and up to $100 in gifts ($400 for returning Americans). You can take up to $10,000 in cash, travellers' cheques or endorsed bank drafts in or out of the country tax-free. Anything above that you must declare, or you risk forfeiting the lot. Depending on the state in which you land, you may also need to declare any foodstuffs or plants you have with you. Many food and plants are prohibited entirely, while canned or processed items are permitted with restriction. Check with US Customs (www.customs.gov/travel/travel.htm) to be sure.

UK Customs & Excise allows returning travellers to bring in £145 worth of gifts and goods and an unlimited amount of money, as long as you can prove it's yours.

Information lines

Chamber of Commerce
735 1616
Road conditions
486 3116
Weather forecast (Las Vegas)
248 4800

Weather forecast (national)
1-900 932 8437
The Weather Channel's 95¢-a-minute state-by-state forecast.

Insurance

Non-nationals should arrange baggage, trip-cancellation and medical insurance before they leave home. Medical centres will ask for details of your insurance company and your policy number if you require treatment; keep this information with you. For hospitals and emergency rooms, *see page 293* **Health & medical**.

Left luggage

There are two sizes of left-luggage locker inside terminal one at **McCarran International Airport**. Exact change in quarters is required.

Media
Newspapers

There are two daily newspapers in Las Vegas. The *Las Vegas Review-Journal* (50¢, $2.50 on Sunday) offers bland but service-able coverage of local and national stories. Recently, long-time political columnist Jon Ralston (and his column) was bought by the publishers of rival paper the *Las Vegas Sun*. The *R-J* responded by hiring Steve Sevelius away from free weekly *CityLife*. The Friday 'Neon' section is the *R-J*'s entertainment guide; there you'll find listings for movies, shows and restaurants. Entertainment critic Michael Pakevich's reviews are generally reliable – he's one of the few souls brave enough to pan Wayne Newton.

The *Las Vegas Sun* (50¢, Mon-Fri) used to offer a populist alternative to the conservative *R-J*, reflecting the shoot-from-the-hip style of its maverick founder and editor, Hank Greenspun. The newspaper has steadily declined since Hank's death in 1989, though most of his family is still on the payroll. The *R-J* outsells

the *Sun* more than five to one (though only about one-in-ten locals has a subscription to either paper), perhaps another reason why the paper took on Ralston's wacky political column. Both dailies have hired gossip columnists – a bad sign in any daily newspaper environment.

The *Los Angeles Times* (50¢) is widely available throughout the Valley and sells out quickly. Most large Strip hotels will carry the *LA Times*, *Wall Street Journal* (75¢) and *New York Times* ($1) in addition to the local papers. International newspapers and magazines can be trickier to find.

Free weeklies

CityLife has a huge restaurant guide, a calendar of workshops for organisations such as the Las Vegas Chess Club and all the sleazy classifieds that one expects from a free tabloid. It has also scooped the town's mainstream press on occasion. You'll find *CityLife* at most bookshops, cafés and bars.

Las Vegas Weekly, formerly known as the *Scope* until it was sold to and diluted by the publishers of the *Sun*, is the city's answer to the *Reader* publi-cations found in major US cities: counterculture journalism surrounded by ads for coffeehouses and tattoo parlours. The *Weekly*'s calendar is an excellent guide to Las Vegas's alternative music scene.

Numerous freebie mags – *The Vegas Visitor*, *Today in Las Vegas* and *What's On in Las Vegas* and others – are distributed at hotels and other tourist spots. The editorial is uncritical and not always comprehensive, depending on who's buying adverts that week, but each contains a cornucopia of handy tourist facts and phone numbers, plus coupons.

Magazines

Three city magazines constitute overkill for a town the size of Las Vegas. The bi-monthly *Las Vegas Magazine* ($3.95) emphasises upscale fashion and shopping, blended with chi-chi adverts and articles on everything from alien invasions to recipes from Spago chef Wolfgang Puck. The *Las Vegan* (monthly, $2.95) is a serviceable glossy, but can be hard to find. Better is *Las Vegas Life* (monthly, $2.95), which has higher editorial standards, some big-name writers and good public radio and TV listings.

Nevada Magazine (bi-monthly, $3.95) contains an events calendar for Las Vegas, Reno and the rural areas in between; most articles focus on Nevada's pioneer history. A new entry in the local magazine rack is the bi-monthly *Nevada Woman* ($3.95), which contains exactly the type of articles you'd expect.

Business news is covered by the *Nevada Business Journal* (monthly, $5) and the *Las Vegas Business Press* (weekly, $1.25), which provides coverage of Nevada's business scene with an emphasis on non-gaming industries. For gaming news, check out *Casino Journal* (monthly, $10) and *Gaming Today* (weekly, $1.95).

Television

The Las Vegas affiliates of the four major American networks are KVBC channel 3 (NBC), KVVU channel 5 (Fox), KLAS channel 8 (CBS) and KTNV channel 13 (ABC). The two new would-be networks UPN and WB are represented by channels 25 and 21. KLVX channel 10 is Las Vegas's public broadcasting affiliate, where you'll find 20-year-old British comedies and the Teletubbies. Every hotel TV will get these stations, and most will also carry some of the more popular cable networks, such as CNN (news), ESPN (sport) and HBO (movies). Cable channel 1 features Vegas-oriented progammes, including the hugely popular *Points of View*, aired weekdays at 5pm, 6pm and 9pm.

Daily TV listings can be found in the *Review-Journal*, *Showbiz*, *What's On* and the ever-popular *TV Guide* ($1.79).

In the TV news industry, Las Vegas is classified as a mid-market town, which means all

the good reporters and anchors are quickly promoted to bigger cities, while the merely adequate stay forever. If you're interested in what's happening in town, KTNV's 11pm news presents the top stories in just 11 minutes. Local public affairs shows are of value only as a cure for insomnia. But if you must and if you're up early enough, there's *Good Morning Las Vegas* (KTNV, weekdays at 5.30am).

Radio

With a rather limited local music scene to draw upon for inspiration, Las Vegas radio is relegated to the same spectrum of formats available in any American city. The medium is a magnet for advertisers trying to reach the thousands who drive into town on weekends; commercial breaks hype 'fabulous' shows, 'delicious' buffets and 'discount' hotel rates.

Both KMXB (94.1 FM) and KSTJ (105.5 FM) feature a solid mix of contemporary music and '80s hits. For light-pop, KMZQ (100.5 FM) will satisfy fans of Mariah, Celine and Elton, but beware the occasional Michael Bolton bombast. KLUC (98.5 FM) covers the Top 40 with an emphasis on dance tracks, while the slow grooves and urban contemporary mix on KCEP (88.1 FM) can be a tonic for unwinding in gridlocked traffic. Classic rock, heavy on Led Zeppelin, can be found on KKLZ (96.3 FM). KXTE (107.5 FM) programmes heavily with aggro-rock, while KOMP (92.3 FM) fulfills the mainstream rocker's needs.

KWNR (95.5 FM) delivers all the country and western 'hat' acts – Clint Black, Garth Brooks, Alan Jackson – and KFMS (102 FM) will sneak in the occasional Merle Haggard and Johnny Cash song with the current Nashville chart-toppers.

KJUL (104 FM) pulls the over-60 crowd with ballad after ballad by Johnny Mathis, Frank Sinatra and Barbra Streisand. Classical music devotees should tune to KNPR (89.5 FM), also the Las Vegas affiliate of National Public Radio, with its in-depth

(but at times intellectually snobbish) news shows *Morning Edition* (weekdays 7-9am) and *All Things Considered* (weekdays 4-6pm). KUNV (91.5 FM) emanates from UNLV. It's a National Public Radio affiliate like KNPR, but programmes jazz music round the clock.

In talk radio, Las Vegas presents no homegrown talent to speak of, but all the most popular national hosts are syndicated on one of the local stations. These include right-wing rabble-rouser Rush Limbaugh (KXNT, 840 AM, weekdays 9am-noon), the crude but often hilarious Howard Stern (KXTE, 107.5 FM, weekdays 7-10am) and veteran New York renegade Don Imus (KVBC, 105.5 FM, weekdays 7-10am). Sports talk enthusiasts will enjoy the humour and insight of Dan Patrick (KBAD, 920 AM, weekdays 10am-1pm).

Traffic reports are played every few minutes on many stations during morning and evening rush hours. Catch one before deciding whether to take the I-15 or a surface street.

Money & costs

Though Las Vegas has a reputation for being cheaper than most resort cities, recent changes mean that difference has been cut to about 20 per cent. Accommodation, car hire, shows and most restaurants remain good value and shop prices are reasonable. Petrol prices are far cheaper than in Europe, but among the most expensive in the US. There are some great deals around on everything from meals to show tickets. (*See chapter* **Las Vegas on the Cheap** for cost-cutting tips.) However, even here you get what you pay for: the top restaurants and shows aren't much cheaper than they would be in New York, for example.

The big difference, of course, is that you may spend a substantial amount of money on gambling – the average visitor's gambling budget is about $600. Whether you're

Websites

www.lasvegas24hours.com
The official and very useful website of the Las Vegas Convention & Visitors Authority. Has a section on how to play nearly every casino game, from bingo to Pai Gow poker.

www.vegas.com
All-encompassing Vegas portal site. Book hotels, get concert and event listings from a constantly updated calendar, search for local restaurants, and more. The *Las Vegas Sun* newspaper, the alternative *Las Vegas Weekly, Vegas Golfer* and other publications are hosted here.

www.lasvegas.com
Sponsored by the *Review-Journal*, this site focuses on local news, community events and resources. Hosts *CityLife*, an alternative Vegas weekly.

www.gayvegas.com
A directory of gay-friendly establishments, ranging from nightclubs to restaurants, plus a list of community resources and an events calendar.

www.lasvegastaxi.com/index.html
Who knows a city better than its cab drivers? See for yourself as these cabbies share everything from adult entertainment info to tips on avoiding getting ripped off by other cabbies.

www.well.com/user/nitewalk/guide/index.html
A former local journalist uncovers the other side of Vegas, from hip coffeehouses to gay bathhouses, and more. Lots of links to other websites.

http://hiddenvegas.com/
A trip through 'the Vegas no one knows'. Includes homepages for wild art-terrorists the LaserVida

arts collective, the UNLV Arboretum and local artist/ unofficial Vegas historian Anthony Bondi.

www.knpr.org/
Run by the local National Public Radio affiliate, KNPR (89.5 FM), this site has a great local programming archive that includes transcripts as well as Real Audio files of informative restaurant reviews, cultural calendars and essays about life in Las Vegas.

www.prairienet.org/~scruffy/homepage.html
From *Fear and Loathing* to *Bugsy*: if any part of it was filmed in Las Vegas, you'll find it on Scruffy's Las Vegas Movie List. The site also features a map of the historical Strip, pre-implosions.

www.lvlocalmusicscene.com
Every local band, live music venue and musician has a space in this locally produced, grassroots Vegas music site.

www.sincity.com
The official website for Vegas's unofficial emissaries and full-time madmen, Penn & Teller, is all you might expect from two guys whose idea of a good time is sawing each other in half.

www.stripclubreview.com/vegas.html
Constantly updated information by some guy who obviously spends too much time watching strippers do their thing.

www.crecon.com/vintagevegas/matches.htm
Nothing here but images of classic Vegas casino matchbooks, postcards and gambling chips, but isn't that enough?

---

playing slot machines or table games, your money doesn't last long in a casino. If you're here to gamble, it is essential that you set, and stick to, a budget.

Credit cards are almost a necessity. You won't be able to rent a car without one, for a start. They are accepted (with few exceptions) in hotels, restaurants and shops, but keep a bit of cash on hand just in case. Dollar travellers' cheques from the major companies are also widely accepted. Requests for picture ID when using credit cards or travellers' cheques are

increasing, especially at casino cages and bureaux de change, so be sure to carry one.

Sales tax is currently 7.25 per cent; food (groceries) purchased in stores is exempt. Accommodation tax is 9 per cent (11 per cent in Downtown, until the hotels there have paid off their investment in the Fremont Street Experience).

Cashing cheques

Money makes this town go round, and you will never have trouble getting hold of the green stuff, day or night. Casinos are

so keen for you to have a ready supply of cash that pretty much all of them have ATMs in every corner, though tacked-on fees can be high. Some have their own bank or bureau de change and all have a 24-hour, seven-days-a-week cashier's cage where you can cash most bank (US only) and travellers' cheques. If you're staying at a non-casino hotel, you should be able to cash travellers' cheques at the front desk.

Now that ATMs are rife, cashing standard cheques is seldom necessary (although at least it's easy now that most US banks are linked in national networks). If you do need to cash an out-of-state cheque from a non-affiliated bank, your best bet is the cashier's cage of the casino at which you're staying.

American Express
MGM Grand, 3799 Las Vegas Boulevard South, at E Tropicana Avenue (739 8474). Bus 201, 301, 302.

Travel agents across town, notably the many branches of **Prestige Travel** (see the phone book) and **Mickey Cole** in the Gold Coast (876 1410), act as AmEx agents, but this is the only specialist office in town. Opposite the registration desk on the main lobby, it offers the full range of cardholder and travel services, including cheque-cashing, poste restante, currency exchange and the buying and selling of travellers' cheques. If you lose your card (*see below* **Lost & stolen cards/travellers' cheques**) ask for the replacement to be issued here, as it will be faster.

Currency exchange
The cages at the big casinos will be able to exchange most major currencies on the spot, and the good news is that they don't usually charge commission, just the bank rate. Smaller casinos accept a smaller range of currencies. In our experience, the casinos offer better rates on currency than American Express desks. There's a **Travelex** exchange bureau at the airport.

ATMs
Automated Teller Machines are ubiquitous – we doubt that any city in the US has as many as Las Vegas. Casinos are full of them. They are undoubtedly the most convenient way for visitors to top up their funds, now that national/international networks such as **Cirrus** and **Plus** allow you to withdraw money from your usual account (using your usual PIN) from any machine that bears the appropriate symbol. Call 1-800 424 7787 to locate your nearest Cirrus machine, 1-800 843 7587 for the nearest Plus.

The only problem with ATMs is that they don't always tell you if and how much you'll be charged for the transaction, especially if it's international. If you're concerned, check with your bank at home before you leave. In our experience the fee is reasonable, comparing favourably with the interest incurred when using your credit card to withdraw cash at ATMs.

Follow the usual safety procedures when using an ATM. Don't let anyone see your PIN and stick to brightly lit locations with people around.

International networks
There are now more ways than ever before for international travellers to get at their bank account. The cash card networks explained above are also linked to **Maestro** (Cirrus) and **Delta** (Plus), which let the card function as a debit card for paying for goods and services (like Switch and Delta in the UK) and getting cash back in foreign countries. Debit cards, even those issued by a credit company, are not acceptable for car hire.

Banks
Given the casinos' willingness to supply you with your own money, you are unlikely ever to need to visit a bank (unless, perhaps, you forget your PIN and need to get cash on your credit card; casinos do this but charge more). If you do, it will not be hard to find one, though few are close to the Strip. In addition to the main branches, usually only open on weekdays, from 9am to 5pm, there are (full-service) in-store locations open more generous hours (up to 7pm or 8pm during the week, and a good chunk of Sunday). Wells Fargo has branches in Lucky, Bank of America in Vons and Nevada State Bank in Smiths Food & Drug. For branch locations and opening hours, call the numbers below.

Bank of America *1-800 388 2265;* **Nevada State Bank** *1-800 727 4743;* **US Bank** *1-800 872 2657;* **Wells Fargo** *1-800 869 3557.*

Lost & stolen cards/travellers' cheques

American Express cards
1-800 528 4800
American Express travellers' cheques
1-800 221 7282
Diners Club
1-800 234 6377
Discover
1-800 347 2683
JCB
1-800 366 4522
Mastercard
1-800 307 7309
Thomas Cook travellers' cheques
1-800 223 7373
Visa
1-800 336 8472

Financial crisis
You should never gamble more than you can afford to lose, but if you do find yourself broke, the best thing you can do is call **Western Union** on 1-800 325 6000 and arrange for someone to wire some money to you. There are lots of locations, including branches of Mail Boxes etc and some supermarkets, where you can pick up wired money.

Numerous pawnbrokers, especially in Downtown, can convert your goods to cash. **Superpawn** has 12 locations, the closest to the Strip at 1611 Las Vegas Boulevard North (642 1133) and 2300 E Charleston Boulevard (477 3040).

Opening times

Two extremes: the casinos, their cashier's cages, bars and at least one restaurant/coffeeshop are open all day, every day (other tourist attractions also keep long hours); supermarkets are often open 24 hours a day, seven days a week; and the chain stores and department stores open late and on Sundays.

On a more local level, Las Vegas still keeps to small-town hours: many restaurants take last orders before 10pm and may not open for lunch or on certain days (the same goes for

Directory

some casino restaurants); non-chain shops may shut at 6pm and won't open on Sundays. Standard and government office hours are 9am to 5pm, give or take half an hour, but public institutions such as libraries and museums are open slightly longer and at weekends.

Places of worship

There are over 500 places of worship in Las Vegas, serving 65 denominations. To find your nearest Lutheran church, call 456 2001, Episcopal 737 9190 and Methodist 369 7055. For others, see the phone book.

Congregation Ner Tamid

2761 Emerson Avenue, at Eastern Avenue & Desert Inn Road, East Las Vegas (733 6292). Bus 112. Jewish Reform.

First Baptist Church

300 Ninth Street, at Bridger Street, Downtown (382 6177). Bus 301.

First Presbyterian Church

1515 W Charleston Boulevard, just west of I-15, West of Strip (384 4554). Bus 206.

Latter-Day Saints Las Vegas Temple

827 N Temple View Drive, off Bonanza Drive, East Las Vegas (452 5011). Bus 208.
Only members of the Church of Jesus Christ of Latter-Day Saints (Mormons) can attend this lavish temple set in beautiful gardens. For other LDS locations, call 435 8545.

Guardian Angel Cathedral

336 Cathedral Way, next to E Desert Inn Road, at Las Vegas Boulevard South, East of Strip (735 5241). Bus 301, 302.
The cathedral church of the Catholic diocese of Reno-Las Vegas. Stained glass in the sanctuary depicts a pair of rolling dice at the foot of a cross.

St Joan of Arc

315 S Casino Center Boulevard, at Bridger Avenue, Downtown (382 9909). Bus 301.
The city's oldest church, with real bricks and mortar. Catholic.

Temple Beth Sholom

9700 Hillpointe Road, off Hills Center Drive, Summerlin (804 1333). Bus 211.
The city's oldest Jewish congregation in a new building. Morning services are held here, but call for details of Friday-night alternatives. Jewish Conservative.

Postal services

Stamps are on sale everywhere (from shops and machines that take a cut), which is fine if your mail is standard-sized and domestic. 'Contract stations' (there's one at **Allstate Ticketing** in the Forum Shops at Caesars Palace) can send international mail, but charge a supplement. If you need a full-service post office, you have to head away from the Strip. Most central is the Strip Station, behind the Stardust on Industrial Road; the main office, open longer hours, is near the airport. There are **Post Office Express** offices in several Lucky grocery stores, open for longer hours and on Sundays: 10.30am to 7.30pm Monday to Saturday; 11am to 7pm Sunday. For locations of these and other offices, call 1-800 275 8777 (you'll need to know the Las Vegas zip code of the area you're looking in).

US mailboxes are red, white and blue with the US Mail bald eagle logo on the front and side. Due to increases in terrorism, mailings exceeding a maximum weight must be taken directly to a counter employee. There is usually a schedule of pick-ups and a list of restrictions inside the lid. Make sure you don't put mail into FedEx or other couriers' boxes.

Downtown Station

301 Stewart Avenue, between Third & Fourth Streets, Downtown (1-800 275 8777). Bus 107, 403. **Open** 8.30am-5pm Mon-Fri.
This is where you can pick up general delivery mail. Ask

correspondents to send it to: General Delivery, Las Vegas, NV 89125. You will need to show picture ID when you pick it up.

Main Post Office

1001 E Sunset Road, between Paradise Road & Maryland Parkway, East Las Vegas (1-800 275 8777). Bus 212. **Open** 7.30am-9pm Mon-Fri; 8am-4pm Sat.

Strip Station

3100 S Industrial Road, at Stardust Way, West of Strip (1-800 275 8777). Bus 301, 302. **Open** 8.30am-5pm Mon-Fri; 10am-2pm Sat.

Relocation

The **Chamber of Commerce** (*see page 299*) and the **Post Office** (*see above*) offer useful leaflets for people moving to Las Vegas, and some of the major websites (lasvegas.com, in particular) can be especially helpful. The CoC can also send out a relocation package, including CD-Rom, for $20.

Security

Considering that Las Vegas contains so many wide-eyed tourists wandering around carrying large amounts of cash, crime is relatively low. But pickpocketing, theft and muggings do nevertheless happen, and more frequently than the tourist industry would like.

Only take out with you what you need for that trip: leave the bulk of your money and travellers' cheques either in your room safe (if you have one) or in a safety deposit box (ask at the front desk). Keep a separate note of the numbers and details of your passport, driving licence, travellers' cheque numbers, travel/health insurance policy and cards (credit, bank, phone etc), along with the phone numbers you'll need to report their loss. (*see above* **Lost & stolen cards/ travellers' cheques**) It's a good idea to leave the same list with somebody at home.

Take the usual precautions with your wallet or handbag, especially on buses; don't keep valuables in your pockets; and try not to let the excitement of gambling make you forget to keep tabs on them.

Casinos have such elaborate security systems that they're virtually police states, so few serious offences take place within their confines. But on the streets, especially outside the well-lit, busy tourist areas of the Strip and Fremont Street, Las Vegas has the same crime problems as any large town. If you are threatened with a weapon, give your assailants what they want, with no fuss. When they've gone, go to the nearest phone and call the police (911 toll-free).

Be careful in the seedier looking areas of Downtown, especially after dark. The Strip is generally safe all night. It's probably not a good idea to look too much like a tourist in the Naked City area behind the Stratosphere.

Telephones

There are two area codes for Nevada: **702** for Clark County (in which Las Vegas sits) and **775** for the rest of the state. Within the Las Vegas area, as far north as Mount Charleston and as far south as Boulder City, calls are local and there is no need to use the area code (just dial the seven-figure number). Outside this area, calls are long distance (and charged as such): you need to dial 1, then 775, then the number. To dial other US and Canada numbers, again, you dial 1 followed by the appropriate area code. Numbers prefaced by 1-800, 1-888 and 1-877 are toll-free.

Local calls are free, but most hotels nevertheless charge a flat fee of between 50¢ and $1 for them – which can quickly mount up. This charge also

applies to toll-free numbers, which makes using a phone card costly, too. You can get round this at some hotels by using a house phone and asking the operator to connect you to your number. Alternatively, you will usually find payphones in the lobby or near the restrooms (local calls cost 35¢).

If you want to make long-distance and international calls, you will often have to leave a credit card or cash deposit behind the desk. The rates will be high, however, so you are better off using a US phone card, whether tied to your domestic account or bought on a one-off basis. Supermarkets, drugstores and convenience stores sell them in various denominations, which you can 'charge up' with your credit card. Shop around for the longest talk-time for the lowest price.

AT&T (1-800 225 5288) allows you to make calls on a Visa credit card. Britons will find that it is cheaper to use this service to call home than to use their own domestic phone chargecard (eg BT chargecard).

For local enquiries, call 411; for national long-distance enquiries, dial 1 + [area code] + 555 1212 (if you don't know the area code, dial 0 for the operator). For international calls, dial 011 then the country code (UK 44; New Zealand 64; Australia 61; Germany 49; Japan 81 – see the phone book for others). For collect (reverse charge) calls, dial the operator on 0. For police, fire, or medical emergencies, dial 911.

To use a public phone, pick up the receiver, listen for a dialling tone and feed it change (35¢ for a local call); some phones ask you to dial first and then assess the cost. Operator, directory and emergency calls are free. If you need to use a payphone for long-distance or international calls – not advisable; you're better off with a phonecard – you will need

plenty of change (a quarter is the highest denomination a payphone will accept). A recorded voice will tell you how much you need to put in. Some payphones, notably at the airport and at the bigger casinos, accept credit cards.

If you encounter voicemail, note that the 'pound' key is the one marked # and the 'star' key *. On automated answering systems, 0 often gets you straight to an operator.

Time

Nevada operates on **Pacific Standard Time**, which is eight hours behind Greenwich Mean Time (London), one hour behind Mountain Time (Denver), two hours behind Central Time (Chicago) and three hours behind Eastern Standard Time (New York). Clocks go forward by an hour in late April, and back again in late October. Note that Arizona has no daylight saving time, and so in summer is one hour behind Nevada.

Tourist information

You will see many self-styled tourist offices on the Strip, but only those listed below are official. The others are primarily tour and booking agents. There are several free tourist magazines, widely available; see page 294 **Media**.

Cellet Travel Services
47 High Street, Henley-in-Arden, Warwickshire B95 5AA (brochure line 0990 238 832/fax 01564 795 333).
The British outpost of the Las Vegas Convention & Visitors Authority (*see below*) will send out its visitors' pack.

Las Vegas Chamber of Commerce
Hughes Center, 3720 Howard Hughes Parkway, between Sands Avenue & E Flamingo Road, East of Strip, Las Vegas, NV 89109 (735 1616). Bus 108, 203.
Open 8am-5pm Mon-Fri.

Advice, brochures, maps and a few coupons available in person; there's also a good phone info service on the number above, and you can write in advance for a visitor pack. The office is conveniently close to the airport.
Website: www.lvchamber.com

Las Vegas Convention & Visitors Authority
3150 Paradise Road, opposite Convention Center Drive, East of Strip, Las Vegas, NV 89109 (892 0711/fax 892 2824). Bus 108.
Open 8am-5pm Mon-Fri.
A comprehensive and helpful office. Write to the CVA for a visitor pack that includes lists of hotel and motel addresses and phone numbers, a brochure, a map and the regularly updated *Showguide*. Staff in the small office in the front of the Convention Center are friendly and can supply you with vast amounts of info and bumpf.
Website: www.lasvegas24hours.com

Visas

Under the Visa Waiver Program, citizens of the UK, Japan, Australia, New Zealand and all west European countries (except for Portugal, Greece and the Vatican City) do not need a visa for stays in the US of less than 90 days (business or pleasure) if they have a passport that is valid for the full 90-day period and a return ticket. An open standby ticket is acceptable.

Canadians and Mexicans do not need visas but must have legal proof of their residency. All other travellers must have visas. Full information and visa application forms can be obtained from your nearest US embassy or consulate. In general, send in your application at least three weeks before you plan to travel. Visas required more urgently should be applied for via the travel agent booking your ticket.

US Embassy Visa Information (UK only)
Recorded information 0891 200 290 (50p per minute)/advice &

appointments 0991 500 590 (£1.50 per minute)/fax 0171 495 5012.

When to go

Two factors should influence the timing of your trip (apart from travel costs): accommodation prices and the weather. Though there is no real off-season in Las Vegas, there are times when it's slightly quieter and hotel prices lower. These are between Thanksgiving (fourth Thursday in November) and Christmas, and during the extreme heat of July and August. Public holidays are always busy, especially the New Year, a major event in Las Vegas. If you're planning a short visit, try to avoid the weekend crowds (and higher accommodation prices).

Las Vegas's busy convention schedule has a major effect on visitor numbers: when over 125,000 delegates hit town at once, hotel and car prices and availability naturally suffer. For dates and numbers, *see page 291* **Convention dates**.

Las Vegas has blue skies and little rain, year round: the percentage of sunny daylight hours runs from 77 per cent in December and January to 92 per cent in June). Daytime temperatures vary from burning hot – afternoon temperatures reach 110°F (43°C) in July and August, remaining above 90°F (32°C) at midnight – to pretty chilly – they can approach freezing in December and January, though 50-60°F (10-15°C) is more usual during the day.

This being a desert, the heat is at least dry, but it can be intolerable if you're not used to it: don't plan on doing too much walking in summer, drink lots of water and take and use a hat, sunglasses and sunscreen, especially for children. Air-conditioning is ubiquitous and overused; ironically, the

cool clothes you'll need for the street may not keep you warm enough indoors. Note that hotel swimming pools close from roughly March to October – the same period that you may need to wear a sweater or jacket.

Women

Las Vegas presents an interesting contradiction in feminist politics. On the one hand, women are continually objectified in the adult industry, billboards and in short-skirted cocktail waitress outfits (ever seen a cocktail waiter?). On the other hand, they fare well in the job market, often occupy positions of power and are well represented in politics. There is no single women's centre or contact point, but the grass-roots movement is healthy.

Albeit for dubious reasons, most Las Vegas bars and clubs offer free or discounted admission to women.

UNLV Women's Studies Office
895 0837
The starting point for anyone researching women's issues.
National Organisation of Women (Southern Nevada)
382 7552
Shade Tree
385 4596
24-hour emergency-only shelter for homeless women (and their children). Qualified staff can counsel victims of domestic or street violence.

Working

The rules for foreigners seeking work here are no different from anywhere else in the US. A US company must sponsor you for an H-1 visa, which enables you to work in the US for five years. It will also have to convince the Immigration department that no American is qualified to do the job. Contact your American embassy for full details.

Further Reading

Non-fiction

Casino: Love and Honour in Las Vegas by *Nicholas Pileggi*
Book of the film: a cracking read.
Dino by *Nick Tosches*
Scorching biography of the Rat Pack principal.
Fabulous Las Vegas in the 50s by *Fred E Basten & Charles Phoenix, with Keely Smith*
A nostalgic full-colour collection of photographs, dinner menus, postcards and so on from the lost glory days of Vegas.
The First 100: Portraits of the Men and Women who shaped Las Vegas edited by *AD Hopkins & KJ Evans* (Huntington Press)
A thought-provoking, well-written, newly published history of the most important 100 pioneers that shaped Las Vegas.
Fly on the Wall by *Dick Odessky*
Amusing anecdotes and first-person insider accounts told by long-time Vegas reporter and publicity man Odessky.
Hiking Las Vegas by *Branch Whitney* (Huntington Press)
Subtitled '60 hikes within 60 minutes of the Strip'. Clear instructions, good detail. A follow-up volume, *Hiking Southern Nevada*, came out in spring 2000.
Howard Hughes in Las Vegas by *Lyle Stuart*
It's out of print, but if you can get hold of a copy, this history of Mr Las Vegas gets behind the privacy of the legendary recluse.
Into Nevada by *David Thompson*
Musings on Nevada – its mining, nuclear and gambling history – by an expat Brit-Californian.
No Limit – The Rise and Fall of Bob Stupak & Las Vegas' Stratosphere Tower and **Running Scared –The Life and Treacherous Times of Las Vegas Casino King Steve Wynn** both by *John L Smith*
Review-Journal columnist Smith, the only man to risk ruffling feathers in Corporate City, dishes the dirt on two of the major players in the casino business.
Las Vegas: The Great American Playground by *Robert D McCracken*
History, biting commentary and a great read.

Las Vegas: The Social Production of an All-American City by *Mark Gottdiener, Claudia C Collins & David R Dickens*
A fascinating look at the social phenomenon of Vegas, from how a city grows in the desert to what it means to live depending on the tourist dollar and a created image.
Literary Las Vegas edited by *Mike Tronnes*
An excellent anthology of journalism from 1952 to the present day, featuring Tom Wolfe, Hunter S Thompson, Noel Coward and Joan Didion.
The Newtonian Casino by *Thomas Bass*
Can the casinos be beaten? Yes, according to these Reservoir Dogs of computer geekery.
Rat Pack Confidential by *Shawn Levy*
A modern appraisal of the Rat Pack years and beyond, written in a very funky style.
The Real Las Vegas edited by *David Littlejohn*
A group of Berkeley grad students look down their noses at the Las Vegas underbelly.
The Success of Excess by *Frances Anderton & John Chase*
Gorgeous large-format photo book on Vegas's theme park architecture.
24/7: Living It Up and Doubling Down in the New Las Vegas by *Andrès Martinez*
Mexican attorney and journalist Martinez spends his $50,000 book advance in this first-person, modern-day *Fear and Loathing*.

Fiction

The Death of Frank Sinatra by *Michael Ventura*
Cracking private-eye story set among the implosions of the early 1990s.
Desert Rose by *Larry McMurtry*
The *Terms of Endearment* writer turns his attentions to a portrayal of a washed-up showgirl.
Fear and Loathing in Las Vegas by *Hunter S Thompson*
The drug-crazed classic is always worth re-reading, even if this ain't the '60s any more.
Last Call by *Tim Powers*
A fantasia on the Las Vegas myth, in which Bugsy Siegel is the

Fisher King and Tarot cards the deck of choice at the Flamingo's poker tables. Don't come here looking for facts.
Leaving Las Vegas by *John O'Brien*
Love, loneliness and alcoholism in the city of fun. Better than the film.
Fool's Die by *Mario Puzo*
The Godfather author with another 'sweeping epic' – lots of casino colour and semi-autobiographical detail.
Sin City by *Wendy Perriam*
Personal drama played out against an impersonal city.

Gambling

Gambling books are ubiquitous, but many are poorly researched and dangerously misleading. We recommend ordering material direct from **Huntington Press** (1-800 244 2224/www.huntingtonpress.com), or visiting one of the specialist bookshops in our **Shopping** chapter. The titles below are from Huntington Press.

Bob Dancer Presents WinPoker
Software tutor (PC only) on proper strategies for video poker. An absolute must for anyone who plays these machines.
Burning the Tables in Las Vegas by *Ian Anderson*
One of the world's most successful high-stakes blackjack players reveals how he gets away with it.
Comp City: A Guide to Free Gambling Vacations by *Max Rubin*
Classic text on the casino comps system. A hilarious read.
Knock-Out Blackjack: The Easiest Card-Counting System Ever Devised by *Olaf Vancura & Ken Fuchs*
Revolutionary 'unbalanced' count eliminates most of the mental gymnastics of all the other count systems. Not still easy, but doable.
Madam: Chronicles of a Nevada Cathouse by *Lora Shaner*
Deepest look inside a legal Nevada brothel ever published, by a full-time madam (brothel-greeter, hostess, shift boss, den mother).

Index

Youth Activity Center 108
Michael Flatley's Lord of the Dance 57, **217**
mining towns 262, 264-265
Mirage 12, 30, **54-55**, 61, 92
  buffet 160
  Danny Gans 54, **214-215**
  Dolphin Habitat & Secret Garden 54, **77-78**, 110
  hotel rooms & services **120**, 193
  Lagoon Saloon 54, **211**
  restaurants 55, 133, 141, 151
  Siegfried & Roy 54, 214, **215-216**
  volcano 81, **83**
  white tigers 54, **78**, 83
Mitchell Caverns 275
Mojave National Preserve 248, **274-276**
  Joshua trees 249
money 295-297
Money Plays **166**, 234
Money Wheel 24
monorails 288
Monte Carlo 12, **55-56**, 92
  hotel rooms & services 120-121
  Lance Burton 56, 110, **215**
  Pub & Brewery 56, **212**
  restaurants 56
  wedding chapel 37-38
Mormon Fort 5, **99**
Mormons 5, 14-15, 249, 283
  Temple 100, **298**
motels 32, 93, 94, 95, 129, 192
  out of town 256, 262, 267, 268, 272-273, 289
motor racing **238**, **243**
  Winston Cup Race **103**, 106
motorbikes 289
  Harley Davidsons 92, 155, 263
Motown Café 155
Moulin Rouge 99
Mount Charleston 239, **259-260**, 261
  hiking tours 250
Mountasia Family Fun Center 241
Movie & Magic Hall of Fame 81, *85*, **85-86**
museums **84-86**, 110, 180, **201-203**, 254, 262
  automobiles 84, 86, 264
  Indian culture 4, 258, 260, 269
  in Los Angeles 277, 278-279
  see also specific museums
music, live
  blues, country & folk 73, 74, 75, 166, **234**
  classical 197
  jazz & swing 235
  listings 294, 296
  rock, punk, hip hop, pop & rave 73, 104, 156, **232-234**
music festivals 104
Mystère 61, 110, 214, **217**

Narcotics Anonymous 293
NASCAR 103, 243
National Automobile Museum 263, **264**
National Park Service 250
Native Americans 4, 5, 6, 257, 258, 260
  festivals 102
  rock art 257, 258, 260
  sites & museums 4, 258, 260, 269, 270

see also Paiute Indians
Nellis Air Force Range 259, **267-268**
  see also Nevada Test Site
Neon Museum 95
neon signs 30, 32, **34**, *69*
Neonopolis 86-87
Nevada 248-268
  Commission of Tourism 250
  maps 246-247, 252-253
Nevada Ballet Theater 206
Nevada Department of Wildlife 237
Nevada Development Authority 291
Nevada Institute for Contemporary Arts Gallery 96, **206-207**
Nevada State Museum & Historical Society 202
Nevada State Parks 250
Nevada Test Site 10, **11**, 267
  tour **11**, 268
Nevada Theatre Company 205
New Frontier Hotel 62, 93, 149
New Year 102, 106
New York-New York 12, 30, *31*, 31-32, *56*, **56-57**, 92
  Hamilton's 57, 163, *211*, 211
  hotel rooms & services 121
  Lord of the Dance 57, **217**
  restaurants 57, 134, 152, 155
  rollercoaster 57, 81, **87-88**, 109
newspapers 294
  outlets 94, 173, 185
Newton, Wayne 101, 218
Nicholas J Horn Theater 197
Nipton 275, *276*, 276
North Las Vegas **100**, 156, 166
North-west Las Vegas **97-101**, 127, 156, 166, 169, 171, 172
Notre Dame de Paris 58, **217**
nuclear tests 10, **11**
Nutcracker Holiday Market 105

O (show) 46, 110, 214, **217**, *217*
Off-Broadway Theater 205
office services & supplies 292
Old Frontier Hotel 91
Olympic Garden 94, *220*, 220, **221**
opening hours 134, **297-298**
opticians 172, 178-179
Orleans 73-74, 97
  Bourbon Street Cabaret 73, **210**
  bowling alley 240
  cheap drinks 193
  childcare facilities 108
  cinema 73, **198**
  restaurants 73
O'Sheas 92, 193
  Movie & Magic Hall of Fame 81, *85*, **85-86**
Our Backs to the Wall Players 205
Overton 4, 255, 258

p

Pahrump 282
Pai Gow 25
Paiute Indians 4, 5, 6, 265
  Las Vegas Paiute Reserve 241
  Paiute Tribal Smoke Shop 189
  Walker River Reservation 262

Palace Station 74-75, 97, 193
  buffet 159
  Loading Dock Lounge 212
Paradise Park 242
Paris 12, 30, 32, **57-58**, 92, 107
  Eiffel Tower 57, **79**, 81
  hotel rooms & services 113, **121**
  Notre Dame de Paris 58, **217**
  restaurants 58, 133, 134, 139, 140
parking 289
  disabled 292
parks 110
  see also Sunset Park
pawnbrokers 297
Peppermill's Fireside Lounge 93, *163*, **163**, 167
pharmacies 293
photocopying 292
photographic services 173-174
piercing 94, 187
pizzas 151
Planet Hollywood 156
Planetarium 84
Plaza Hotel 6, 94, 95
poetry readings 203
Poison Control Center 290
poker **24-26**, 73
  commissions 16
  World Series 69, **104**, 106
police 95, **290**
Polo Towers 92, **131**
pool tables 242
population 15
postal services 95, **298**
Primm 109, 274
  Primadonna Casino Resorts 109
Professional Bull Riders Tour *103*, **105**, 106
prostitution 219, 282
Providence Mountains State Recreation Area 275
pubs & microbreweries 72, 97, 163, 164-165, 166, 167, 212, 235
Pyramid Lake 265

r

Race Rock **86**, 95, *95*
Rachel 267, 268
radio stations 295
rafting 238, 273
railways 6-7, 271-272
Rainbow Company Children's Theatre 205-206
Rainbow Library & Amphitheater 200
Rancho Circle 99
Rancho Road 99-100
Rancho Strip 72
rape helpline 290
Rat Pack 10, 98, 99, 208, *209*
Red Rock Canyon Conservation Area 98, 236, 238, **256-257**
  Cowboy Trail Rides 237
  tours 89, 250
Reed Whipple Cultural Center 196-197, 205-207
relocation 298
Reno 261, **263-266**
Residence Inn by Marriott 119, **129**
Resort at Summerlin 113, 114, *122*, **127**, 147, 191

Maps

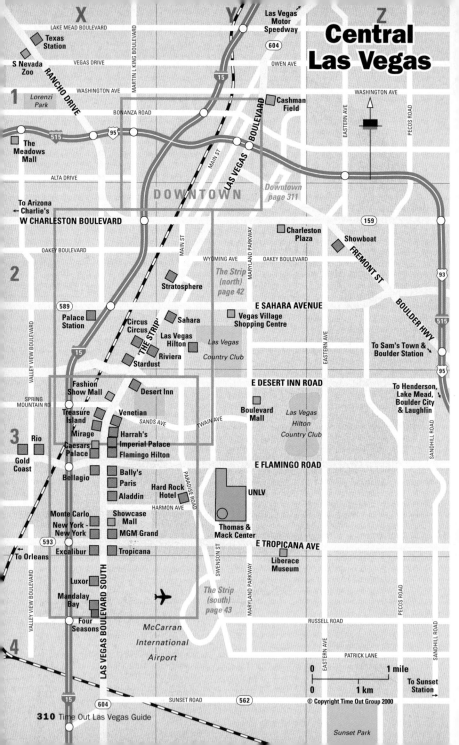

Central Las Vegas

X **Y** **Z**

LAKE MEAD BOULEVARD

Texas Station

S Nevada Zoo

VEGAS DRIVE

RANCHO DRIVE

MARTIN L KING BOULEVARD

Las Vegas Motor Speedway

604

OWEN AVE

1

Lorenzi Park

WASHINGTON AVE

BONANZA ROAD

15

Cashman Field

LAS VEGAS BOULEVARD

MAIN ST

WASHINGTON AVE

EASTERN AVE

PECOS ROAD

515

95

The Meadows Mall

ALTA DRIVE

DOWNTOWN

Downtown page 311

To Arizona ← Charlie's

W CHARLESTON BOULEVARD

MAIN ST

MARYLAND PARKWAY

Charleston Plaza

159

Showboat

FREMONT ST

93

OAKEY BOULEVARD

WYOMING AVE

OAKEY BOULEVARD

BOULDER HWY

515

2

The Strip (north) page 42

589

Palace Station

Stratosphere

Sahara

Circus Circus

THE STRIP

Las Vegas Hilton

Riviera

Stardust

E SAHARA AVENUE

Vegas Village Shopping Centre

Las Vegas Country Club

EASTERN AVE

To Sam's Town & Boulder Station

95

15

VALLEY VIEW BOULEVARD

SPRING MOUNTAIN RD

Fashion Show Mall

Desert Inn

E DESERT INN ROAD

To Henderson, Lake Mead, Boulder City & Laughlin

SANDHILL ROAD

Treasure Island

Venetian

SANDS AVE

TWAIN AVE

Boulevard Mall

Las Vegas Hilton Country Club

3

Rio

Gold Coast

Mirage

Caesars Palace

Bellagio

Harrah's

Imperial Palace

Flamingo Hilton

E FLAMINGO ROAD

Monte Carlo

New York - New York

Bally's

Paris

Aladdin

PARADISE ROAD

Hard Rock Hotel

HARMON AVE

UNLV

Thomas & Mack Center

Excalibur

593

To Orleans

Showcase Mall

MGM Grand

Tropicana

SWENSON ST

E TROPICANA AVE

Liberace Museum

MARYLAND PARKWAY

Luxor

LAS VEGAS BOULEVARD SOUTH

Mandalay Bay

Four Seasons

The Strip (south) page 43

McCarran International Airport

RUSSELL ROAD

EASTERN AVE

PECOS ROAD

SANDHILL ROAD

To Sunset Station

4

15

604

SUNSET ROAD

562

PATRICK LANE

0   1 mile

0   1 km

© Copyright Time Out Group 2000

Sunset Park

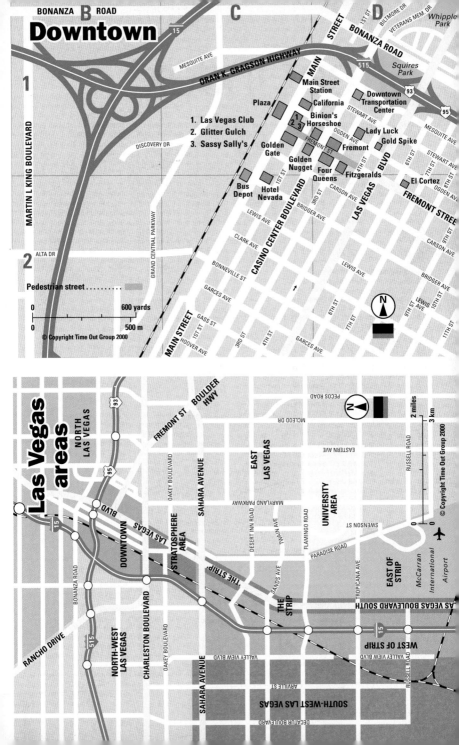

Downtown

BONANZA **B** **ROAD**

C

STREET

D

BILTMORE DR

VETERANS MEM DR

Whipple Park

MESQUITE AVE

ORAN K. GRAGSON HIGHWAY

MAIN

BONANZA ROAD

Squires Park

MARTIN L KING BOULEVARD

1

DISCOVERY DR

Plaza

Main Street Station

California

Downtown Transportation Center

STEWART AVE

1. Las Vegas Club
2. Glitter Gulch
3. Sassy Sally's

1
2. 3

Binion's Horseshoe

Lady Luck

Gold Spike

OGDEN AVE

Golden Gate

FREMONT ST.

Fremont

Golden Nugget

Four Queens

Fitzgeralds

LAS VEGAS BLVD

7TH ST

6TH ST

MESQUITE AVE

STEWART AVE

FREMONT STREE

Bus Depot

Hotel Nevada

CARSON AVE

El Cortez

OGDEN AVE

GRAND CENTRAL PARKWAY

CASINO CENTER BOULEVARD

3RD ST

BRIDGER AVE

LEWIS AVE

CARSON AVE

2

ALTA DR

CLARK AVE

BONNEVILLE ST

LEWIS AVE

BRIDGER AVE

Pedestrian street ....

GARCES AVE

600 yards

0

500 m

© Copyright Time Out Group 2000

MAIN STREET

GASS ST

1ST ST

2ND ST

3RD ST

4TH ST

HOOVER AVE

GARCES AVE

6TH ST

7TH ST

9TH ST AVE

11TH ST

N

Las Vegas areas

93

FREMONT ST

BOULDER HWY

PECOS ROAD

MCLEOD DR

NORTH LAS VEGAS

95

OAKEY BOULEVARD

SAHARA AVENUE

EAST LAS VEGAS

EASTERN AVE

N

2 miles

3 km

LAS VEGAS BLVD

DOWNTOWN

STRATOSPHERE AREA

DESERT INN ROAD

MARYLAND PARKWAY

TWAIN AVE

FLAMINGO ROAD

UNIVERSITY AREA

SWENSON ST

RUSSELL ROAD

© Copyright Time Out Group 2000

BONANZA ROAD

THE STRIP

SANDS AVE

PARADISE ROAD

McCarran International Airport

RANCHO DRIVE

515

CHARLESTON BOULEVARD

OAKEY BOULEVARD

THE STRIP

TROPICANA AVE

EAST OF STRIP

LAS VEGAS BOULEVARD SOUTH

15

WEST OF STRIP

NORTH-WEST LAS VEGAS

VALLEY VIEW BLVD

VALLEY VIEW BLVD

RUSSELL ROAD

SAHARA AVENUE

ARVILLE ST

SOUTH-WEST LAS VEGAS

DECATUR BOULEVARD

Street Index

CAT Bus Routes

101 NORTH/SOUTHBOUND
201 EAST/WESTBOUND
301 STRIP ROUTES
401 LIMITED/EXPRESS ROUTES

MAP NOT
TO SCALE